CARSON

Books by H. Montgomery Hyde

The Rise of Castlereagh
The Russian Journals of Martha and Catherine Wilmot (with the Marchioness of Londonderry)
More Letters from Martha Wilmot: Impressions of Vienna (with the Marchioness of Londonderry)
The Empress Catherine and Princess Dashkov
Air Defence and the Civil Population (with G. R. Falkiner Nuttall)
Londonderry House and its Pictures
Princess Lieven
Judge Jeffreys
Mexican Empire
A Victorian Historian: Letters of W. E. H. Lecky
Privacy and the Press
John Law
The Trials of Oscar Wilde
Mr and Mrs Beeton
Cases that Changed the Law
Carson
The Trial of Craig and Bentley
United in Crime
The Strange Death of Lord Castlereagh
The Trial of Sir Roger Casement
Sir Patrick Hastings: His Life and Cases
Recent Developments in Historical Method and Interpretation
Simla and the Simla Hill States Under British Protection
An International Case Book of Crime
The Quiet Canadian
Oscar Wilde: The Aftermath
A History of Pornography
Norman Birkett
Cynthia
The Story of Lamb House
Lord Reading
Henry James at Home
Strong for Service: The Life of Lord Nathan of Churt
The Other Love
Their Good Names
Stalin: The History of a Dictator
Baldwin: The Unexpected Prime Minister

EDWARD CARSON by J. G. Day

H. MONTGOMERY HYDE

CARSON

The Life of Sir Edward Carson,
Lord Carson of Duncairn

CONSTABLE LONDON

First published 1953 by William Heinemann
Reissued 1974 by Constable and Company Limited
10 Orange Street, London WC2H 7EG
Paperback edition 1987

ISBN 0 09 468190 2

Printed in Great Britain by
St Edmundsbury Press Limited
Bury St Edmunds, Suffolk

To the memory of
Ruby Lady Carson

CONTENTS

ILLUSTRATIONS

ACKNOWLEDGMENTS

TO THE following, who in various ways have helped me to write this book, particularly by putting documents and other material and information at my disposal, I wish to express a deep sense of obligation:

Lady Carson, the Hon. Edward Carson, M.P., the Hon. Mrs. Gerald Chesterman, the Hon. Mrs. Walter Carson, Miss Bella Carson, Lt.-Colonel Walter Lambert, the Marchioness Dowager of Londonderry, D.B.E., the Marquess of Londonderry, Cecile Viscountess Craigavon, Lord Beaverbrook, the Earl of Birkenhead, Viscount Simon, Lord Killanin, Lord Pakenham, Sir Thomas Comyn-Platt, the Rt. Hon. Winston Churchill, M.P., Sir Wilfrid and Lady Spender, the Rt. Hon. J. M. Andrews, M.P., the late Major Frederick Crawford, Sir Wilson Hungerford, the late Sir Patrick Hastings, the Rt. Hon. Sir Travers Humphreys, the Rt. Hon. L. S. Amery, Mr. Lionel Curtis, Mr. Thomas U. Sadleir, Mr. R. W. Blake, Mr. Frank Owen, Sir Douglas Savory, M.P., Canon H. O'Connor, Mrs. Anna Debenham, Mr. A. R. Rountree, Mr. J. C. Corsan, Mr. Andrew Stewart, formerly Controller of the B.B.C. Northern Ireland Region, Mr. William Douglas, O.B.E., Secretary of the Ulster Unionist Council, and the staffs of the British Museum, the London Library, the House of Lords Library, the House of Commons Library, the Library of New College, Oxford, the Library of the King's Inns, Dublin, the Library of the Historical Society, Trinity College, Dublin, and the Linenhall Library, Belfast.

I am also indebted to those who have kindly allowed me to reproduce pictures and documents in their possession. Particulars will be found beneath the illustrations in the text.

H. M. H.

INTRODUCTION TO NEW EDITION

This book was first published in 1953 and has long since been out of print. Meanwhile second-hand copies have been much in demand and when obtainable have been fetching high prices even by today's inflated costs of production. Its reprint now is particularly appropriate in the light of the changes which have been and are taking place in the constitutional development of Northern Ireland, whose close political links with Great Britain the subject of this biography devoted the greater part of his political career in an endeavour to preserve. That a lawyer born and bred in the Nationalist and separatist south of Ireland should have become the leader of the Unionist and "loyalist" north is one of those curiosities of politics which from time to time distinguish and enliven the British political scene.

Edward Carson was primarily a lawyer whom the Irish question made into a politician. The reason for this metamorphosis may be found in a succinct remark of the Liberal Prime Minister, Lord Rosebery in 1895. Writing soon after the rejection of Gladstone's second Home Rule Bill, Rosebery observed that the Irish question had "never passed into history, for it has never passed out of politics." Carson's great cases as an advocate and judge which I have described—Oscar Wilde, George Archer-Shee ("The Winslow Boy"), the Soap Trust, the Cadbury libel, the Marconi scandal, the Scott will, the Russell divorce, and many others—will always enshrine and illumine his legal reputation. But it is as a politician that he will be remembered above all in Ulster, the six north-eastern counties of which were excluded from the ambience of the Home Rule Act of 1914 largely as the result of his sustained efforts. He and his Ulster Unionist followers would have preferred the six counties which at present constitute Northern Ireland to remain completely integrated with Great Britain, but he accepted the compromise solution embodied in the Government of Ireland Act, 1920, which provided for the setting-up of a separate Parliament of Northern Ireland within the framework of the United Kingdom. "Ulster wants peace, and above all to be removed from the arena of party politics in the Imperial Parliament," he wrote when the measure was being debated at Westminster, "and we have therefore made up our minds that in the interests of Ireland, Great Britain, and the

Empire, the best and only solution of the question is to accept the present Bill and endeavour to work it loyally."

Shortly afterwards he relinquished his political leadership. In doing so he gave a statesmanlike piece of advice to the Ulster Unionists whom he correctly anticipated would have a majority in the new local legislature and would consequently form an administration.

> From the outset let us see that the Catholic minority have nothing to fear from the Protestant majority. Let us take care to win all that is best among those who have been opposed to us in the past. Whilst maintaining intact our own religion let us give the same rights to the religion of our neighbours.

The Northern Ireland Parliament lasted from June 1921, when it was opened in state by King George V, until March 1972 when it came to an ignominious end through the re-imposition of direct rule from Westminster. The period was one of unbroken Unionist rule at Stormont where Carson's larger than life-size statue continues to dominate the physical scene in characteristic pose, appropriately if somewhat ironically, with its back to the Parliament and Government buildings and with arms outstretched facing the south whence its subject came.

Unfortunately things did not work out in Northern Ireland as Carson had hoped. If the Catholics did not co-operate fully and at times boycotted the Stormont Parliament, the ruling Unionist Protestant clique lost little time in nailing its colours to the mast of the new political barque. Sir James Craig, later Lord Craigavon, the first Prime Minister of Northern Ireland, designated the assembly at Stormont as "a Protestant Parliament for a Protestant people." Sir Basil Brooke, later Lord Brookborough, who became Prime Minister in 1943, had been appointed Minister of Agriculture ten years previously by Craig. He signalised his joining the Craig Cabinet by dismissing 125 Catholic workers on his estate in County Fermanagh, in order to set an example to other landowners. "I have not a Roman Catholic about my own place," he said shortly afterwards. "I would appeal to Loyalists, wherever possible, to employ good Protestant lads and lassies."

According to the gospel of religious apartheid preached by Brooke and enthusiastically practised by his political supporters, Catholics were regarded as second-class citizens and were to be treated as such. In fact, they were flagrantly discriminated against in such matters as employment and housing. Any advantage which they might have gained through the voting system of proportional representation as provided by the 1920 Act was removed when PR was abolished in the early days of Stormont. "I can't stick PR," Craig confessed to Dr Thomas Jones, the Deputy Secretary of the English Cabinet. "Does not seem to be British. Too Continental." Proportional representation was not abolished in the south. But its disappearance in Northern Ireland in 1929 no doubt helped to prolong the now outmoded conception of Protestant Ascendancy there. So did the retention of property qualifications in local government elections which might give one man, almost invariably a Protestant, as many as twenty votes. Even where the Catholics were in a numerical majority, as in Londonderry, the wards were "gerrymandered" in such a manner that the Unionists controlled the corporation, which meant the best jobs and houses for Protestants to the detriment of the local Catholic majority. The inevitable outcome of this prolonged injustice was the birth and rapid growth of a civil rights movement. This in turn led to a tremendous political explosion in 1969 and the end of the old Stormont legislature amid a welter of terrorist shooting and bombing.

The resumption of direct rule from Westminster in 1972 was foreshadowed by the Report of Lord Cameron's Commission on the causes and course of the struggle for civil rights. The Report was a devastating condemnation of the policy of successive Unionist Governments at Stormont and must have made Carson turn in his grave. It examined, and found proved, all the Catholic grievances about discrimination in the matter of housing, as well as many specific allegations against the para-military Royal Ulster Constabulary. This was to lead in turn to the disbandment of the notorious Protestant "B" Specials, and the placing of a small armed police reserve under the British Army Commander in Northern Ireland for emergency security duties.

Northern Ireland now has a fresh constitution, a different legislative assembly elected by proportional representation, and and entirely novel power-sharing political executive, while responsibility for security continues to reside at Westminster, an experiment which I am convinced would have commanded Carson's approval had he been alive to see it in operation. A significant element in the new arrangements is the Council of Ireland which was provided for in the Act of 1920 and which Carson accepted at the time but which immediately became a dead letter through the refusal of the south, which had set up its own parliament in the Daíl, to implement the Act in so far as it nominally applied to the south.

If he accepted that measure, albeit with some reluctance, Carson was much less happy with the Anglo-Irish "Treaty" concluded in the following year, which heralded the withdrawal of British forces from southern Ireland and the grant of dominion status to the emerging Irish Free State. Apart from his view that this agreement was a betrayal of England's friends in the south who had trusted her and were now to be left to the tender mercies of the new establishment—a fate which incidentally did not turn out to be comparable in animosity as that in store for the religious minority in the north—Carson could not help feeling that Great Britain's remaining links with the south as provided for in the "Treaty" would be eroded and eventually destroyed notwithstanding their guarantee by President Cosgrave. His fears were confirmed by the passing of the Statute of Westminster in 1931 and the displacement of Cosgrave as President by Mr de Valera shortly afterwards.

During the debates on the Statute of Westminster a minority of Tory diehards in the House of Commons including Mr Winston Churchill supported an amendment incorporating a clause with the object of preventing the Irish Free State from repudiating the provisions of the "Treaty" which the unfettered sovereignty conferred by the Statute would otherwise enable the Free State to do. The amendment was defeated by a large majority as being offensive to southern Ireland and the other Dominions. Anyhow surely Mr Cosgrave could be trusted to abide by the terms of the "Treaty"? He could. But this did not go for his principal opponent, Mr De Valera, who displaced him in the following year. Carson's worst fears were gradually realised.

In November 1934, a few months before his death, Carson dictated a speech which he was too ill to deliver to a meeeting of southern Irish Unionists, but which his wife read for him. In it he had this to say:

> One would really think that in dealing with Ireland England had lost all sense of honour. They spend millions of money, and the

> time of her great men, in holding conferences to uphold their relations throughout the international world. Most of these conferences have, I regret to say, been futile. But can you wonder at the little respect felt for conferences and treaties when you see such a violation openly taking place of the Irish Treaty?
>
> Take for instance the abolition of the Oath of Allegiance, the abolition of the Right of Appeal to His Majesty in Council, the abrogation of the constitutional prerogatives of the Crown exercising through the Governor-General, and many other breaches equally serious, and yet apparently this country feels no obligation upon it to uphold their honour in taking care that such things cannot be allowed to the detriment of those who have ever been their true friends.

Carson characterised the Free State as "this humbug" and admitted to Balfour's niece Mrs Blanche Dugdale that there was "more decency" in a Republic. "In fact I'd rather see a Republic," he said. But he did not live to do so.

* * *

Although some of Carson's papers were destroyed when his London house was bombed during the second world war, an extensive archive has survived, amounting to about 3,000 documents. It includes the interesting MS diaries of Carson's second wife, Ruby Lady Carson, which she kept with a few breaks from the beginning of 1915 to the middle of 1929. Some years ago the whole collection, comprising (1) and (2) of the Carson Papers as described in my bibliography below—see page 498—was acquired by the Government of Northern Ireland and is now preserved in the Northern Ireland Public Record Office in Belfast. The reappearance of this book after more than twenty years serves as a convenient pretext for me to draw attention to the existence and location of this important and valuable collection, particularly for students of Anglo-Irish relations in the first quarter of this century. It is admirably housed in the new premises of the Record Office, where, I might add, the working conditions for students are considerably more comfortable and commodious than those of the Public Record Office in London. No study of the history of the Home Rule struggle down to the passing of the Government of Ireland Act, 1920, can be considered complete without consulting the relevant papers in this collection.

As might be expected in the case of a man like Carson, who wrote to many correspondents in his own hand and did not keep copies of his letters, the collection is considerably richer in letters to him than letters from him. His wide range of correspondents in the former category includes Balfour, Asquith, Mrs Asquith, Lloyd George, Bonar Law, Winston Churchill, Lord Halsbury, Lord Milner, Lord Northcliffe, Lord and Lady Londonderry, Admiral Jellicoe and Rudyard Kipling, to name only a few. Of the letters written by Carson there are not many, and consequently I have had to seek the majority which I have used in other collections such as those of Balfour, Londonderry, Craig and Bonar Law.

One correspondent to whom Carson revealed himself frankly and intimately from the time that he began to write to her until she died in 1919 was Theresa Marchioness of Londonderry, wife of the sixth Marquess and the leading Conservative and Unionist political hostess of the period. She exerted all her influence towards the advancement of Carson's career when he decided to leave the Irish Bar and settle in London. He could never forget her kindness and help, while she for her part appreciated that he had renounced the greatest prizes in his chosen profession, including the Woolsack, which might otherwise have been his. Carson's letters to Lady Londonderry, from which I have quoted at some length, are of particular interest. Incidentally I am glad to have been instrumental in enabling the Public Record Office in Belfast to acquire the originals of these important letters, together with Lady Londonderry's papers relating to the Home Rule struggle when she was President of the Ulster Women's Unionist Association.

"As you say," Carson wrote to her in his last letter a few weeks before she died, "I have made great sacrifices for Ulster—everything in fact so far as personal ambition is concerned. However, I had a cause in which I believed and the example of sincerity must do some good. Anyhow I am quite happy about it all which is something."

Such was the essential spirit of the man whose biography I am now glad to introduce to a new generation of readers.

Westwell House
Tenterden
Kent

H. MONTGOMERY HYDE

April 1974

CHAPTER ONE

Growing Up

I

EDWARD CARSON was a giant among men. Not only did he dominate them physically, standing out head and shoulders in the common throng of mankind, but he possessed in an exceptional degree qualities of character which set him apart from his fellows. Courage, perseverance and kindness of heart—these were the characteristics stamping his peculiar genius. Like his compatriot and contemporary, George Bernard Shaw, he was a valiant man. He was also a stayer. His experience in the affairs of life was that so few were able to finish the race, 'run the last hundred yards', as he put it. He could and did so. Kindly and understanding, Carson was the soul of honour in all his dealings. He hated injustice and disloyalty.

Carson divided his life between law and politics, and in each of these fields he was pre-eminent despite the chronic ill-health from which he suffered and of which he always made much. Yet politics, which played so large a part in his life, were never a primary consideration with Carson. Lloyd George once asked him whether the Irish Nationalist leader John Redmond, who had started with him on the same Bar Circuit, had much practice. "No," said Carson, "but it was because he became a politician. That I have never done. I have remained a lawyer first and a politician afterwards."

I remember once discussing his professional skill with the late Sir Patrick Hastings, who was Carson's junior in a number of cases and who largely modelled his own style of advocacy on that of his leader. "I never knew anyone at the Bar," said Sir Patrick, "who succeeded so well as Carson in convincing the Court of the merits of his case. He believed passionately in his client's cause and he made judge and jury believe in it too." He did not strive to be oratorical, but he was one of the most remarkable and powerful orators which the Bar has ever produced. Wrote Lord Reading, who as Rufus Isaacs was perhaps Carson's ablest as well as most frequent opponent in the Courts: "He had a shrewd and wise insight into human nature and was not a little assisted in his persuasive influence by the charm of his attractive personality."

It was the same with his championship of the Ulster Loyalists in their struggle against Home Rule, which has earned him an undying name in Northern Ireland. To serve Ulster, Carson declined the richest prizes, which were unquestionably within his grasp had he chosen to reach out for them. Although he had been a Law Officer in both Ireland and England, he twice refused the supreme legal office of Lord Chancellor, while as a politician he might well, if he had wished, have become his party's leader and eventually Prime Minister. "You are one of the least ambitious of all the public men I have met," said the newspaper owner Lord Riddell to him in 1918. "Yes," replied Carson, "I have no ambitions. What I like best is to read my briefs, conduct my cases and spend my leisure in my home." He cared nothing for money if it stood between him and what he conceived to be his duty. He did not spare himself. As he told his friend Lady Londonderry, "I have always walked up the hill with the collar hurting me." During the First World War he dropped his law practice to serve in both the Asquith and Lloyd George Coalition Governments. Yet he resigned from each on an issue of principle. He also played a part of great importance, though it was little known to the world at large, in the downfall of the first Coalition and the formation of the second. Nor is it generally known how much Great Britain, as well as Northern Ireland, is indebted to Carson for his work at the Admiralty and in the War Cabinet which followed.

Sometimes a biographer is handicapped in his writing by the fact that he was on terms of close friendship and intimacy with his subject. There are things he would like to write, but he feels that if he were to do so he might be betraying a confidence. Whatever the shortcomings of this book, I cannot plead any such personal knowledge. It was never my fortune to meet Edward Carson in the flesh. But I did see him on one unforgettable occasion. It was a few years before his death and, curiously enough, the place was the Cathedral Church of St. Anne in Belfast, which now enshrines his mortal remains. Though an old man and much broken by illness, he had come to attend divine service. I shall never forget the piercing eyes, the firm set of the mouth, and the jaw jutting out as he surveyed the scene in the Cathedral on that Sunday morning many years ago. His rugged features seemed to display the aura of greatness. He had reached the sunset of his life and there was little more left. But I felt the fighting spirit was still there. His impression remains in my memory more vividly than any artist can portray.

In Ulster Carson had long been regarded as a hero. While he was still alive, a statue of him larger than life was unveiled outside Ulster's Parliament Buildings. As a child I was brought up in the atmosphere and background of the Ulster Volunteers, where Carson was idolised. 'King Carson', his enemies used to sneer. Yet, though he was a Southern Irishman, he proved the ideal leader of the Northern Unionists. He became a legend, interwoven in the tumultuous history of his native country. Though they might sneer at him, his political opponents respected him, because they knew he could be trusted to keep his word. In Ulster he acquired almost divine attributes. Not only the men and women but the children too came near to worshipping him. "Can any of you tell me who is the Supreme Being?" asked a Belfast clergyman who was inspecting a local boys' school. A united shout of "Carson" was the reply. Only one lad timidly suggested a more orthodox hypothesis. "Ah, you Papist!" his schoolfellows yelled at him in derision for this apostasy.

To Englishmen it has always seemed strange that a Southern Irishman should have become the hero and chosen leader of the Ulster people, commanding the absolute confidence and passionate devotion of the self-willed Northerners as no man has commanded them before. But to his own countrymen the growth of Carson's influence and authority in Ulster seemed perfectly natural and intelligible. In religion he was a Dublin Protestant of the Church of Ireland and by political upbringing a Liberal, as many Southern Protestant families of the middle classes were in those days. When Mr. Gladstone announced his conversion to Home Rule, the Southern Protestants of all shades were inevitably drawn to their fellow Protestants in Ulster, the majority of whom were Presbyterians of Scottish ancestry. The prospect of an all-Ireland Parliament, sitting in Dublin and dominated by the Roman Catholic hierarchy, obliterated all distinction between Church of Ireland and Presbyterian, Conservative and Liberal, among the Protestants in all parts of the country, especially the North, who saw in the maintenance of the Union with Great Britain their only hope of survival. Thus Carson naturally turned towards the North as the potential spearhead of resistance to Home Rule. His achievement was to weld together the instruments of resistance with a masterly hand and an iron control. What in a weaker leader would have led to sporadic riots and street fighting became a coherent and disciplined movement under his direction, which won the support of the Conservative Party in England and ultimately secured for Ulster her present constitutional position as a political unit within the United Kingdom. Lord Craigavon, who as Sir James Craig was his close political friend and faithful lieutenant, later becoming the first Prime Minister of Northern Ireland, has summed up Carson's career in a sentence: "His birthplace was Ireland, his sphere of activities largely in England, his greatest triumph saving Ulster for the Empire."

Today a new generation has grown up in Ulster in an atmosphere of relative political security. To its members Carson is a great name, albeit a name, while the detail of his political achievement is shrouded in the haze of history. Of his successes in the Courts a few stories are remembered. That is all. Such is the lot of the advocate, whose triumphs must necessarily be fleeting. Nevertheless, as he told Sir James Craig when the Government of Northern Ireland came into being, "Ulster will always be my first love and my greatest memory." So it remained. It was fitting that when he was eventually created a peer he should have taken, as a compliment to his old constituency in Belfast, the title of Lord Carson of Duncairn, and that when he died his body should have been laid to rest in the heart of the Ulster capital city.

The tale of Carson's life is varied, and its span covered many changes, social as well as political. Here is the verdict of one who knew him as a boy in his father's house and who always admired his grand gifts and character, though the two men were for a long while separated by a deep political gulf—Mr. Winston Churchill. "He lived to see the ascendancy of many ideas to which he was inveterately opposed," said Mr. Churchill on his death. "But he lived, also, to see his beloved Ulster, to whose cause he had devoted himself, firmly anchored to the United Kingdom, safe and secure in the British Parliament and Empire. They have long memories in Ireland. No name will be cherished with greater affection in Ulster than his, and few will command wider respect among all classes of Irishmen, North or South, Protestant or Catholic, orange or green."

2

The Carsons were originally Scots and Presbyterians. In an early age they had been Covenanters, who supported Montrose and later fought against the Young Pretender. Edward's grandfather,

William Carson, crossed the Irish Sea from Dumfries about the year of Waterloo and settled in Dublin. It has been suggested, notably by Carson's first biographer Marjoribanks, that William Carson was of near Italian descent and that his name was really Carsoni. It is impossible to find any foundation in fact for this belief. On the contrary the name Carson had long been familiar in Dumfriesshire, and such variants were met with there as Carsane, Corsane and Kersane. If there was any Italian blood in his veins, it must have gone back a long way, certainly before the fourteenth century. As for the myth of immediate Italian ancestry, it has a simple explanation.

When William Carson arrived in Dublin, he established himself in business as a general merchant. The city directories of the period give his address as 12 Great Longford Street, where he kept a 'chip and straw warehouse'. Later on, in the thirties and forties he moved to 3 Cork Hill, near Dublin Castle, at that time a popular thoroughfare for the business community of the city. William Carson specialised in Leghorn and Tuscany hats, which were then much in fashion, particularly with children. It seems likely that the manufacturer in Italy from whom he imported this picturesque headgear addressed his communications to 'Signor Carsoni'. Hence in later years sprang up the story of Edward Carson's Italian forebears.

William Carson married and had three sons, who were all born in Dublin. William, the eldest, and James, the youngest, were educated at Trinity College, and became clergymen of the Episcopal Church of Ireland.* They were Edward Carson's uncles and remained bachelors. Uncle William, indeed, had a remarkable career. He first studied medicine, became a doctor, and went north to Ulster, where he built up a successful practice. Then one day he felt the call of the Church, gave up his practice to become curate of Ardmoyle, a poor parish in County Tipperary. Here his medical skill, which he made available alike to Catholics and Protestants without fee, made him a widely beloved and eventually a legendary figure. Outside his door every day, it is said, there would be a long line of horse-drawn carts, which brought the sick from all over the country to be cured at the hands of the Rev. Dr. Carson. He died in 1865, at the comparatively early age of forty-four.

The elder William Carson's second son, Edward Henry, father of Edward Carson, was born in 1821. He became an architect and civil

* They are described in the admission registers of Trinity College as 'sons of William Carson, Mercator': G. D. Burtchæl and T. U. Sadleir, *Alumni Dublinienses* (1935), at p. 139.

engineer, setting up in practice in Dublin at 28 South Frederick Street. We are told that in appearance he was of medium height, fair and good-looking and moreover had 'an excellent nose', a feature which he transmitted to his son. He made progress in his profession, eventually being elected Vice-President of the Royal Institute of Irish Architects. For some years too he sat on the Dublin Corporation, representing Fitzwilliam Ward as a 'Liberal-Conservative'. It was no doubt through this municipal association that he was employed as architect of the Pembroke Town Hall near the site of Dublin's famed 'Horse Show' at Ball's Bridge. Another of his architectural achievements was the remodelling of St. Peter's Parish Church in Aungier Street, a considerable undertaking which took several years to complete.

William Carson died suddenly in 1850 whilst on a visit to London, presumably on business. By this time his three sons were getting on in their careers. In May, 1851, Edward, the architect, married into a well-known county family in the West of Ireland. His bride, Isabella Lambert, was the daughter of Captain Peter Fitzwalter Lambert, squire of Castle Ellen, a sizeable estate, as yet unencumbered with debt, situated about seven miles from the town of Athenry in County Galway. The Lamberts were an Anglo-Irish family, members of the so-called Protestant Ascendancy in Ireland, and they had been settled in that part of the country since the end of the seventeenth century. They were descended from 'Honest John Lambert', a Yorkshireman, who became one of Cromwell's major-generals and took a leading part in the council of officers which offered Cromwell the post of Protector, when the Parliament at Westminster was broken up in 1653. It is interesting to note that General Lambert was Edward Carson's ancestor, since he was one of the most striking figures in the English Civil War, a man of great personal courage, who treated his opponents with a generosity unusual in those times. However, his descendant was not to share 'Honest John's' admiration for his master wholeheartedly, for when at the close of the century the House of Commons resolved to erect a statue of the Protector within the precincts of Westminster, Carson joined with the Nationalist Members in opposing the resolution. For, although he was by family tradition and political conviction a Unionist, Edward Carson 'never was un-Irish', as his opponent Tim Healy once put it.

Mrs. Isabella Carson has been described as 'a regular Lambert', with blue eyes, dark hair and a clear complexion, more like the native Irish than the English settlers whose blood was intermixed with theirs. On her mother's side she was connected with another Anglo-Irish family in the same county, for Mrs. Peter Lambert had been Eleanor Seymour of Ballymore Castle. This property, near Ballinasloe, had been granted by King William III to one of his officers named Thomas Seymour after the Revolution of 1688 and the Battle of the Boyne. Thus Edward Carson had a rooted family association with the sovereign of 'pious, glorious and immortal memory' and, though not an Ulsterman, it can be said that he was bred in the loyal Orange tradition.

When Edward Henry Carson and Isabella Lambert got married, in 1851, they went to live with his widowed mother in the Dublin suburb of Rathgar. Here their eldest son, William, was born. A year or so later they moved to Harcourt Street, nearer the centre of the town and close by picturesque St. Stephen's Green, which served as a convenient playground for the children. At this period the Irish capital was a pleasant enough city to live in for those of her citizens who could afford it. If Dublin no longer had her own Parliament, there was the Castle where the Lord Lieutenant entertained in viceregal splendour, there were balls and hunting in winter, sailing and swimming in summer, riding and racing all the year round. 'Dear and dirty' Dublin's 'fair city' may have been, but she enjoyed the benefits of the superb town-planning which had been executed in the eighteenth century, and the architectural beauties of that period had not yet fallen into mournful decay. Inside the houses there may have been stuffed birds and antimacassars, destined to survive somewhat pathetically to a later age in Dublin lodging-houses, but there were also thick Turkey carpets and solid mahogany furniture, warmed by cheerful coal fires and illumined by incandescent gas.

About two years after their marriage the Carsons moved to No. 4 Harcourt Street, a small three-storey Georgian house standing at the south end of the street, almost at the entrance to St. Stephen's Green. Here was born, on February 9, 1854, their second son, the future Lord Carson of Duncairn.* Five weeks later, on April 16, the baby was baptised by the Rev. James MacSorley in St. Peter's Parish Church in Aungier Street, the church with which the father was professionally associated. He received the paternal names of Edward Henry.

* The house is now an hotel.

3

It was a happy household in Harcourt Street. In it there were eventually six children, four boys and two girls. As the family increased in numbers and began to grow up, a move was made to a larger house up the street, No. 25.

Meanwhile the father had his offices at the back of the house, where he and the clerks and pupils worked together. Young Ned used often to be there, and he would amuse himself by working out a drawing in perspective. "You're doing this better than I did when I was older than you," said the paterfamilias and architect. "But you're not to go on with it." From an early age, it seems, the father's mind was made up that his second son was not to follow in his footsteps. "You're to be a barrister," he said to him. Thus, as Edward Carson himself expressed it later: "I was put to the Bar."

But this is to anticipate. First, he had to be educated to fit him for this profession. His first school was a small day school kept by a Church of Ireland clergyman, the Rev. James Rice, a few doors away from his home in Harcourt Street. Here he attended, accompanied by two of his brothers, William and Walter. Another pupil of this academy, whom he met for the first time, was Alexander Blood, a future colleague at the Irish Bar and a King's Counsel. Blood used to recall in later years how much Carson as a young boy was attracted by oratory, and how he kept his schoolfellows spellbound by reciting choice passages from the speeches of Burke, Sheridan and the younger Pitt.

Shortly after his twelfth birthday, Edward Carson, along with his two brothers, was removed to Arlington House, a boarding school in Portarlington, Queen's County. The school, which had been in existence for a quarter of a century, is said to have been patronised chiefly by the sons of Protestant professional gentlemen, of whom there were in those days a considerable number in Ireland. The headmaster, the Rev. F. H. Wall, LL.D., had recently taken over the management of the school from his father, who had founded it, and under his rule it had already become widely popular. It is interesting to note that Dr. Mahaffy, the famous Provost of Trinity College, Dublin, regarded it as being 'quite at the head of Irish schools' at this time. Pupils who were contemporaries of Carson included William Ridgeway, afterwards the well-known Professor of Classical Archæology at Cambridge, and Sterling Berry, later Bishop of

Killaloe. His closest friend at the school was a boy called James Shannon, a youngster of exceptional promise, who was to exercise a brief but profound influence on Carson's life.

At Arlington House, as later at the University, Carson did not shine in scholarship. He was, however, conspicuous in the school debating society. By dint of hard work he managed to reach the sixth form, where his bent was toward the classics. A weak heart prevented him from repeating his brothers' feats on the playing fields. Truth to tell, Ned Carson was an overgrown, ungainly schoolboy. 'Rawbones' was his nickname, abbreviated to 'Bones'. In fact he used for a while to sign his letters to his friends by this nickname or else by its Latin form of 'Ossa'. He was certainly not miserable at school, but he would jokingly head these letters 'Arlington Gaol'. Indeed the Rev. Dr. Wall took a strong fancy to him, and they spent two of the summer holidays together, one on a walking tour in Wales and the other in Switzerland. As a result they became friends for life.

The school was not devoid of bullying, particularly by some of the older boys. Carson seems to have been regarded by the youngsters as their champion, and in spite of his delicate physique he frequently resorted to his fists on their behalf. He was not afraid to take on boys bigger and stronger than himself, when he was convinced that wrong had been done. On one occasion, after a cricket match, a member of the opposing team was particularly objectionable to a small boy and Carson told him to put up his fists. The older boy immediately did so and soon the two were hard at it. Carson took a lot of punishment from this brute, older and heavier than himself. But his pluck and fierceness astonished everyone who witnessed this encounter. Soon the elder boy was glad to stop.

This spirit of combativeness, thus nurtured in his school days, was to run throughout Carson's legal and political career. It was not that he was by nature aggressive or cantankerous—he never picked a quarrel for its own sake—but he had a tremendous sense of justice and fair play ingrained from these early days. Once he was satisfied that a hardship or evil existed, he could not rest until it had been put right. One example of this trait at Arlington House must suffice. There had been some thefts of money and other articles in the school. One boy was suspected of the thefts and, as a result of continued pressure of the schoolboy variety, he made a half-hearted confession of guilt. Carson felt sure he was not the thief. A committee of investigation was appointed, consisting of sixth-form members, and Carson took charge of the inquiry. He noticed that the real culprit kept looking at his feet. "Take off your boots," said Carson sternly. Reluctantly the culprit did as he was told, and sure enough there the missing coins were found.

It had now been decided that Edward Carson should follow his uncle's example and go up to Trinity College, Dublin. In the summer of 1871 he took the entrance examination, at which he gained a fair place in classics. The headmaster of Arlington House was anxious that he should also sit for a scholarship, and it was arranged that he should do this at the next examination, which was due to take place shortly after the beginning of the college term in October.

4

Within its gracious compass Dublin's 300-years-old University embodied both academic distinction and architectural charm. Situated in the middle of the city, with the clatter of traffic at its gates, it was in some ways more in touch with contemporary happenings and influences than the older foundations of learning at Oxford and Cambridge. It was, of course, a largely Protestant society, although Catholics were never unwelcome within its walls. For long Trinity College had enjoyed a high reputation for classical scholarship, and this reputation was enhanced by the election this same year of Dr. John Pentland Mahaffy to the Chair of Ancient History. Mahaffy, who was only thirty-two at this time, was already an accomplished man of the world, whose encyclopædic knowledge extended from Greek poetry and Egyptian papyri to snipe-shooting and the cultivation of wines. Another versatile classicist was Robert Yelverton Tyrrell, who became University Professor of Latin in 1871 and whose lectures Carson was also to attend with profit to himself.

Edward Carson duly became a 'junior freshman', as the first-year students were called at Trinity. As arranged he sat for the scholarship examination, but he did not win a classical scholarship. Instead he was awarded an exhibition, which came at least as a financial help to him at this time. He decided to continue reading classics, but without either particular enthusiasm or particular distinction. His tutor was Dr. Arthur Palmer, a pleasant Canadian, who was greatly liked by his pupils. Under his instruction Carson applied himself with some industry to his studies, and in several of the subsequent half-yearly examinations secured second-class honours in classics. But he eventually emerged, after some five years' study, with an ordinary pass degree. So far as college studies went, he was a plodder. He showed few if any signs of future promise, unlike a number of brilliant contemporaries. Besides his old school friend James Shannon, there were John Ross, later Lord Chancellor of Ireland, Charles O'Connor, later Master of the Rolls, Richard Cherry, later Lord Chief Justice, and J. H. Campbell, later Lord Glenavy and first President of the Irish Free State Senate.

Most brilliant perhaps of all Carson's contemporaries at Trinity was a young man of the same age, for whom Fate had in store many years later a tragic encounter with his classmate in London's Central Criminal Court. The son of the leading eye surgeon in Dublin and his poetess wife, this student rejoiced in the high-sounding names of Oscar Fingall O'Flahertie Wills Wilde. Winning an entrance scholarship in the same examination for which Carson sat, he carried everything before him in the academic field. He was invariably placed in the first-class honours list, eventually departing in a blaze of academic glory to achieve further distinction at Oxford. But at Trinity, though they knew each other and were on speaking terms, Edward Carson and Oscar Wilde were never friends, contrary to general supposition. Carson disliked this long-haired student genius and distrusted his flippant approach to life. He liked Oscar's elder brother Willie little better.

Nevertheless there was considerable truth in Wilde's description of the majority of their classmates at Trinity. "They thought of nothing but cricket and football, running and jumping," said Oscar, "and they varied these intellectual exercises with bouts of fighting and drinking. If they had any souls they diverted them with coarse *amours* among barmaids and women of the streets. . . . Their highest idea of humour was an obscene story." As against this, Tyrrell and Mahaffy represented for Wilde whatever was good in Trinity. Prominent in the field of sexual promiscuity was Oscar's elder brother Willie, who shared this interest with his father. One morning Sir William Wilde accidentally opened a letter intended for this son, in which Willie was accused of having made a girl pregnant. "Here is a most disgraceful letter," fulminated Sir William. "Yes, sir," remarked Willie gravely when he had read it, assuming it was intended for his father. "What are you going to do about it?"

There were other sports in vogue at Trinity besides those

mentioned by Wilde, and in two of them at least Carson indulged himself, so far as his health allowed. He joined the University Boat Club and went on the river now and again; he used too to go swimming regularly at near-by Sandycove. He also played the old Irish game of hurling, which had lately been revived under its present name of 'hurley' after a long period of abeyance. This sport was not unlike hockey, of which indeed it was the native counterpart. It was played with a wooden ball covered with leather, the sticks in use often being cut by the players themselves and seasoned over a turf fire. He performed in several of the college teams, and on one occasion at least was mentioned by a local sporting journal, *The Irish Sportsman*, as having distinguished himself on the field. Otherwise his athletic prowess, like his scholastic achievements, was not particularly notable.

On the other hand, he was not by any means the perfect student. He shared the boisterous spirits of his companions in college, and on one occasion they got him into serious trouble with the authorities. The incident arose during the state entry into the capital of a new Lord Lieutenant, the Duke of Marlborough, which took place toward the end of the year 1876. Carson seated himself on the top of some high railings inside the college and proceeded to hurl squibs into the crowd watching the procession below.

"Come down," shouted Vice-Provost Jellett, "or you'll be rusticated."

This was no empty threat, for it meant that Carson might be forced to leave Trinity without a degree.

However, the culprit answered merrily: "I've only a dozen more," and he did not descend until he had despatched the remaining squibs in the direction of the most promising targets in College Green.

In due course he was summoned before a disciplinary committee of College Fellows. Fortunately the committee included the classical tutor, Dr. Palmer, who was greatly attracted to his refractory pupil and succeeded in getting the dread sentence of 'rustication' commuted to a severe reprimand.

But the culprit remained unrepentant to the end. "You really ought to say you're sorry," said Dr. Palmer in admonitory tones.

"D'you really think I ought to tell that lie?" was the characteristic reply.

Carson lodged at home with his parents and every morning would make the journey from Harcourt Street to the College on foot, through St. Stephen's Green and along Grafton Street to College Green. In the vacations he would often visit his mother's people at Castle Ellen in Galway. It was about this time that his Uncle Peter moved out of the old Castle into a fine modern house, which he had built in the grounds near-by. Behind the house were the stables, which were constructed on the most lavish scale at the same time and were said to be among the three finest in Ireland. Here Captain Peter Lambert kept a fine pack of hounds.

At Castle Ellen the young Trinity student met and lost his heart to his cousin, Katie Lambert. This girl, who was his Uncle Peter's only daughter, possessed considerable personal beauty and was very popular in the county. She was also a most accomplished horsewoman and regularly hunted her father's hounds. In this hunting household Edward Carson found political principles which combined staunch Conservatism with fidelity to the Union with Great Britain. With the latter belief Carson was in agreement, even at this early age, but otherwise, like many young men, he tended toward Liberalism, if not Radicalism.

It was during one of these visits that he decided he would like to marry the beautiful Katie Lambert.

5

Among the students with whom Carson made friends in college was John Ross, destined to become Lord Chancellor of Ireland and to be the last to hold that office. It is worth recording that both men in their old age shared the same thoughts about their Alma Mater. Ross looked back on his time at the University as the happiest period of his life. And shortly after his own eightieth birthday Carson wrote: "I have no more pleasant recollection in my life than my career in Trinity College, Dublin, and especially in the College Historical Society." Although he joined this Society early in his third year at the University, it was not until he had taken the degree of Bachelor of Arts three years later and was continuing his studies as a post-graduate student of law that Edward Carson became conspicuous in its deliberations.

The Historical Society, or more popularly 'the Hist', is the oldest known British university debating society in existence. Founded toward the middle of the eighteenth century by Edmund Burke, it speedily became the recognised nursery for orators in the country.

The earlier members included such patriots as Grattan, Yelverton, Wolfe Tone, Robert Emmet and Tom Moore. The tradition had been carried on in the succeeding century by men such as William Magee, subsequently Archbishop of York, W. E. H. Lecky, the historian, and Isaac Butt, later first Home Rule leader in Parliament. In the year that Carson was elected to membership, the office of Auditor, as the president was called, was filled by a remarkable student, whose name was Bram Stoker. This individual, who was also athletic champion of the university, managed to combine his student activities with writing novels and, nominally at least, discharging the duties of a clerk in the Chief Secretary's office in Dublin Castle. The sensational 'thriller' *Dracula* is said to have been written by him in his rooms in college at this time. If his subsequent career did not fully justify his early promise—most of his later life was spent in managing the Lyceum Theatre in London for Sir Henry Irving—Bram Stoker was unquestionably a person of many gifts and wide interests. The subject of his inaugural address was one which made a particular appeal to Carson, being entitled 'The Necessity of Political Honesty'.

Edward Carson was elected to the Historical Society in 1873, in the same session as Oscar Wilde. His proposer was his old school friend James Shannon; he was seconded by James Campbell, the future Lord Glenavy. During his student years, and for a time after his graduation, he took part in most of the debates and other exercises. In 1876 he was awarded the Silver Medal for Composition on a theme more suited to Oscar Wilde's pen than his own—'Early Excursions into the Realms of Art'—but by this date Oscar had migrated to Oxford, otherwise no doubt he would have carried off the trophy. This incidentally Carson presented to his sweetheart, Katie Lambert. A year later he received the Society's 'marked thanks' for oratory.

The Historical Society's minute books, which have been preserved, contain a record of the motions on which Carson spoke. They show too his Liberal, not to say Radical, sympathies at this time. For instance, he spoke in favour of women's rights, he advocated the abolition of capital punishment, he defended the dramatic tastes of the times, he espoused the disestablishment of the Church of Ireland, he denounced the memory of Cromwell and he argued that 'the French Revolution has been more beneficial than injurious in its results'. At the same time, in agreeing that 'Pitt's Irish policy was worthy of a wise and upright statesman', he declared himself to be an ardent Unionist. His friend and contemporary John Ross afterwards used to recall his ability in debate and remembered his speeches as being remarkable for their sincerity.

In due course Carson presented himself as a candidate for office in the Society. At the election of officers in 1876 he was chosen Librarian, receiving thirty votes against twenty-eight cast for the only other candidate, G. D. Burtchael, later well known as an Irish herald and genealogist. In this office it was his duty to keep and sign the minute books of the Society, and on the occasion of the debate on the motion 'that the dramatic tastes of the day show marked signs of degeneracy' which took place on December 20, 1876, and which incidentally he opposed, the newly-elected Librarian jokingly if a trifle prematurely signed himself 'Edward Carson, Esq., Q.C., Attorney-General'.

In the following session he entered a spirited contest for the Society's chief office of Auditor, being proposed by the outgoing Auditor, James Campbell, and seconded by John Ross. For this he was defeated by Charles O'Connor, another future judge, who stood as a 'Home Ruler' and headed the poll with twenty-eight votes. Carson came second as a 'Protestant Liberal' with twenty-one votes, while the remaining candidate, A. W. Samuels, later a Law Officer and judge, who was also to share the representation of the University with Carson in the House of Commons, secured twenty votes as a 'Protestant Episcopalian Conservative'. Had Carson come forward again next year, it is very likely that he would have been voted into the Society's chair, but he preferred to stand down in favour of his friend John Ross, whom he did not wish to oppose and who was consequently elected Auditor. He was content instead to serve on the General Committee. By this date he had grown a moustache, with which he appears in a group photograph of the officers and committee of the Historical Society taken during the year of Ross's presidency. Moustaches were evidently in vogue in Trinity at the time, as will be seen from the accompanying illustration, in which seven out of eleven of the young men in the group are wearing them.

It was customary to invite several distinguished men as guest-speakers to the opening meeting of each session, when the Auditor delivered his presidential address. In the year that Charles O'Connor defeated Carson for the auditorship, the visitors included two Members of Parliament, Edward Gibson, Attorney-General for Ireland, afterwards Lord Ashbourne, and Lord Randolph Churchill, whose father, the seventh Duke of Marlborough, had recently arrived in Dublin as Lord Lieutenant. Little did Carson think, when he made the acquaintance of these two M.P.s on this occasion, that they were destined to exercise a determining influence on his subsequent career, the one in law and the other in politics.

6

In those days Irish Bar students first took the arts course in college, graduating a year or so earlier than their English counterparts. They then proceeded to spend a year in the Trinity law school, while the remaining two years were devoted to instruction and study at the King's Inns, which corresponded to the Inns of Court in London. The King's Inns, though always referred to in the plural, were in fact one Inn and probably owed the form of their name to the fact that, when Inns were really resident colleges, the Dublin society consisted of several groups of chambers. But the King's Inns did not play the same part in the corporate life of the Irish Bar as the Inns of Court in London, since at this period there were no 'chambers' there for barristers to inhabit. Situated in Henrietta Street, on the north side of the city, the King's Inns possessed a fine Hall and library, but they were some distance from the Courts, which had their own library, and in consequence their use was almost entirely confined to students and the governing body of 'Benchers', who supervised the details of legal education and decided on admissions to the Bar.

As a condition of call to the Irish Bar students were also obliged to join one of the English Inns of Court and 'keep' a certain number of terms there by 'eating dinners'. Although this rule was regarded by some, in Carson's own words, as "one of the badges of servitude on the Irish nation", it really had an excellent effect. It brought the budding Irish barrister into contact with his English and Colonial brethren, and it gave him some first-hand knowledge of the English judiciary, whose decisions were at that time binding on the Irish Courts. Charles Russell, a fellow Irishman and future Lord Chief Justice of England, who ate his dinners some years previously at Lincoln's Inn, thus recorded his impressions at the time: "I enjoy this part of the business very much," he wrote; "you meet well bred and informed men—many of them distinguished as literary or professional men. At a table at the end of the magnificent dining hall sit the presiding powers . . . consisting of such of the Judges, Queen's Counsel and Serjeants as happen to be members of this Inn."

Gray's Inn was greatly favoured by Irish students at this time, but some also enrolled themselves in the Middle Temple, which could boast of such great names in Irish advocacy on its register as Grattan and Curran. It was this latter society which Edward Carson joined. However, when he sat down to dinner for the first time in the historic Middle Temple Hall, he had little thought that he would one day be the Treasurer—the senior figure in this august society with the reputation of being one of the greatest advocates of the English Bar. At that time his ambitions did not extend beyond a modest competence at his native Bar in Ireland, with possibly the position of Resident Magistrate or County Court Judge at the end of thirty years or so.

Regularly four times a year Carson would make the journey to London, sometimes by packet-boat to Holyhead and at other times by 'long sea' round Penzance and up the English Channel. This route was particularly popular with Carson's friends and other fellow students. They frequently sailed with the commander of the steamship line, who was a deeply religious man, and when the ship put into Falmouth on Sundays would make his passengers don top hats and accompany him to church. On one occasion he brought the young men into his cabin and exhorted them to live a religious life. Suddenly one of the ship's officers appeared and announced that something had gone wrong in the landing of part of the cargo. The Captain immediately rushed out and went on to the bridge, whence he poured out a string of violent oaths. Seeing the astonishment of Ross and the others, he thereupon hastened to explain that this was the only kind of language that seafaring men could understand and really meant nothing!

In April, 1877, Edward Carson took his final examination at the King's Inns. In preparing for this he received some help from Swift MacNeill, later a Nationalist M.P., who had come out top in the previous year and lent him his note-books. In the result Carson was seventh out of the ten candidates who passed and he duly received a certificate to this effect. He was now eligible for 'call' to the Bar, and for this process he was formally proposed by Richard Armstrong, Q.C., Serjeant-at-Law. Serjeant Armstrong, whose acquaintance young Ned Carson thus made, had been one of the most remarkable advocates of his day in Ireland, and though almost entirely forgotten now, he had been retained in many celebrated cases. At the height of his powers he became temporarily insane while travelling from Dublin to Holyhead one night in the mail boat. Some time afterwards he was restored to reason, only to suffer a relapse a year or two later from which he never recovered. It was during this lucid interval, when he resumed his not inconsiderable practice, that he proposed Carson as a junior barrister.

Unlike the English custom, whereby students were called to the Bar by the Treasurer of their Inn in Hall, Irish students were called by the Lord Chancellor in open Court. The newly admitted barristers would assemble in the Lord Chancellor's Court, where his Lordship would bow to each in turn, at the same time asking "Do you move?" Each would bow in reply with equal solemnity, after which they would all withdraw, as often as not to a long period of briefless waiting.

In this picturesque fashion Edward Carson was called to the Irish Bar by Lord Chancellor Ball in the ensuing Easter Term of the same year.

7

In those days the Irish Bar had much to recommend it as a profession. Its fees, it is true, were lower than those prevailing at the Bar in England, and the highest positions it had to offer were not so lucrative as their equivalent on the other side of the Irish Sea. On the other hand, as a profession it had an abundance of comradely fellowship and good cheer. Furthermore, it was open to men without means, who could carry on their profession untrammelled by the expenses attendant upon the English system of 'chambers'. Very few newly-called barristers in the Temple could hope to exist for the first year after their 'call' to the Bar without private means or some other form of income, out of which they had not only to subsist, but also to pay the rent of their chambers and the clerk's remuneration. Irish barristers had neither chambers nor clerk to worry about. Their financial responsibility was limited to an annual subscription of two guineas to the Bar Library and one guinea to the dressing-room. For the latter contribution the barrister's wig and gown were cared for and mended and, when necessary, despatched by parcel post to Sessions and Assizes.

The headquarters of the profession were in the Four Courts, a beautiful domed Georgian building on the north bank of the River Liffey, fated to be wantonly destroyed in the civil war of a later generation. This building, it may be noted here, derived its name from the fact that it contained the four civil Courts of Queen's Bench, Exchequer, Chancery and Common Pleas. It was only a year after Carson's call to the Bar that these four Courts, together with the landed estates, probate and matrimonial Courts, became fused under the Judicature Act into the High Court of Justice, although for administrative purposes they retained their identities in separate and distinct divisions of this single Court. There was also created, as in England, a Court of Appeal, which with the High Court went to make up the Supreme Court of Judicature.

Head of the Irish judiciary was the sixty-two-years-old Lord Chancellor, John Thomas Ball, a most scholarly and eloquent lawyer, as well as a learned historian and educationalist, who is particularly remembered for his drafting of the constitution of the Church of Ireland on its disestablishment. As we have seen, it was by this Lord Chancellor that Carson had been called to the Irish Bar. Other judges with whom the young barrister came into contact during his early years in practice included Sir Edward Sullivan, Master of the Rolls; Chief Justice Chichester May of the Queen's Bench; Sir Michael Morris, Chief Justice of the Common Pleas; and Christopher Palles, Chief Baron of the Exchequer. For Morris, later Lord Morris and Killanin, Carson never particularly cared: one cannot say why, since, though a Catholic, Morris was a strong Unionist and Conservative, as well as a caustic critic of Government shortcomings from the Bench. To Palles, a Catholic and a Liberal, on the other hand, Carson was devoted from the beginning, for as a judge he was both fearless and learned in the law, besides being full of kindliness. Known affectionately as 'the last of the barons', Palles had been appointed to the Bench at the age of forty-three by Gladstone on the platform of Paddington Railway Station as that statesman was on the way to Windsor to surrender the seals of office in 1874; he was destined to carry out his judicial duties for the unprecedented period of forty-four years.

It was the library in the Four Courts which gave the Irish Bar its peculiar corporate personality, for it was here that its members 'most did congregate'. The main section was a long rectangular chamber divided by pillars into bays with books round the sides and a desk with four seats to each bay. In the middle of the room there were larger desks and opposite the principal fireplace there was the 'Round

Table' which accommodated twelve individuals. In these somewhat cramped surroundings the barristers worked and gossiped when not in Court or otherwise engaged. Strictly speaking, no barrister was entitled to any particular seat, but he usually acquired a prescriptive right to the seat he customarily occupied, much in the same way as an M.P. does to his seat in the House of Commons. Adjacent there was a smaller room, to which solicitors and their clerks came to confer with counsel. Near the entrance sat an attendant known as 'the crier' who kept a record of the movements of every barrister. He was a tall ex-Guardsman named Bramley and, when any visitor appeared, he would shout out the barrister's name in tones which could be heard all over the library, as if he were on the parade ground. This individual would also bawl instructions to the 'boys' (one at least was over seventy) employed to fetch and carry the books. The noise was terrific and at first the newly-called barrister found it extremely difficult to concentrate on his work. Gradually, however, he became as a rule impervious to all sounds except that of his own name.

At this time the Bar Library was probably the best social club in Dublin. There was much less specialisation at the Irish Bar than in England—an Irish barrister was prepared to take any case on any subject—and the library system with its friendly atmosphere was invaluable in imparting knowledge to the beginner. In this way too the Catholics and Nationalists, who were then coming to the Bar in increasing numbers, were always on excellent professional terms with their Protestant fellow barristers, though deeply divided by politics. (Eight out of the sixteen judges who sat on the High Court Bench at this time were Catholics.) The library closed at five o'clock, but in the evenings work would be continued by the barristers in their own homes. Consultations between junior barristers and Queen's Counsel customarily took place in the house of the 'leader', often in the congenial and informal atmosphere provided by a bottle of claret or champagne. Every evening on the shutting of the library the barrister's books and papers would be conveyed in his brief-bag to his house, by women employed for the purpose. They were known as 'bag women', the best known in Carson's time being affectionately called 'Snuffy Maggie' from her addiction to snuff. The bags would be collected again in the morning and be waiting at the barrister's place in the library on his arrival at the Four Courts. This was the system in vogue at the time of Carson's call, but not long afterwards the 'bag women' disappeared and their place was taken by a horse-drawn van, which made the round of the barristers' dwellings and from its leisurely mode of progress was jocularly alluded to as the 'Legal Express'.

In England a newly 'called' barrister intending to practise usually served a period as a 'pupil' of an experienced member of the profession, not a Queen's Counsel, but a 'junior' in a good way of business. This practice was followed in Ireland, though not to the same extent. By no means all young Irish barristers could afford to pay the fifty guineas demanded for this privilege, and they consequently preferred to pick up their experience as they went along, in the library or in the Courts as spectators. But those who could scrape up the premium did so. They followed their 'master' round from Court to Court and attended his conferences in the library or at his home. Carson apprenticed himself in this way to a Chancery practitioner named George Price, whose work mostly consisted of conveyancing. Price was an accomplished draughtsman and a sound lawyer, but was quite tongue-tied whenever he had to get up on his feet in Court. He had, too, a delightful sense of humour and was most painstaking with his pupils, who also included Carson's Trinity classmates Charles O'Connor and John Ross. From him Carson learned the all-important lesson for every junior barrister, how to 'settle pleadings', that is, to prepare the formal arguments put forward in writing by each side in every civil suit. These 'pleadings', which are signed by the junior barrister, are known respectively as the 'Statement of Claim' and the 'Defence'. Many an action has been spoiled by a vital omission from them, for when the case comes into Court neither side can go outside their contentions except by special leave of the judge.

Carson did not immediately begin to practise when he had completed his pupillage. His father had never disguised the fact that he could not afford to maintain his sons out of his own pocket and that they must set about earning their own living without delay as soon as they could. Consequently, in order to make ends meet, Carson agreed to the suggestion of a recently qualified solicitor of his acquaintance named David Dunne that they should go into partnership as law tutors, or 'grinders', for the college law examinations. But the two men did not have much success and after about a year the partnership was dissolved.

At this time the principal law 'grinder' in Dublin was a man named John Falkiner, who had the reputation of being decidedly rough with his pupils. The story is told that one of them, unable to stand this treatment any longer, informed Falkiner that he was leaving his establishment.

"Oh," said Falkiner, "I suppose you are going to that man Carson." Carson was reputed to be very polite to his pupils.

The pupil reluctantly admitted that such was his intention.

"Well, if that's where you're bound for," continued the 'grinder', "you will be sure to fail!"

8

When Carson eventually began to practise, about a year after his 'call' to the Bar in Dublin, he found that briefs were few and far between. His first one came after a period of waiting. It was a difficult and technical case which arose out of the absence from Ireland of one of the parties to a lawsuit. Carson had to argue that the mode of 'substituted service', by which notice of the proceedings was served on the opposing party abroad, was good in law. The case gave the budding barrister little opportunity of displaying his powers of advocacy, but nevertheless he appears to have acquitted himself well and was complimented by the judge on his performance.

One of his early cases which deserves mention led to a curious result, of which the outward and visible sign can still be seen. A certain Low Church clergyman, the Rev. M. Bradshaw, for whom Carson appeared, sought to prohibit one of his High Church brethren, who was rector of the fashionable Dublin church of St. Bartholomew, from placing a cross on the altar or Communion table. The canons of the Church of Ireland are quite clear on this point and forbid the erection of such a cross on the altar. Carson accordingly won his case and the rector was ordered to remove the offending emblem. He did so, but in such a way that the cross was merely raised a few inches above the altar and suspended by a long wire from the roof. And in this ingenious position it remains to this day.

The first case of any substance which he argued came to him as the result of his father's influence. It concerned a sum of money due under a building contract in which his father had been engaged as architect, and young Edward Carson appeared for the defendant against whom the builder had brought suit. Although he had never been allowed to see the contract by the plaintiff's solicitors, Carson cleverly pleaded that a condition precedent to payment was the grant of the architect's certificate. Eventually Chief Baron Palles, the judge trying the case, ordered the production of the contract in Court. The clause which defence counsel had pleaded was found to be included in it, and judgment was given for the defendant. The architect, who incidentally had the unusual experience of being examined in Court by his own son, was delighted. The successful barrister was also pleased. The trial had lasted for several days, so that in addition to his brief fee, which was a good one, Carson received by the custom of the profession additional daily 'refreshers'. He subsequently confessed, "I lived off that case for a long time."

The young barrister also attended regularly at the Criminal Courts in Green Street, which was Dublin's Old Bailey. On one of his first appearances in this grim old Court House he was engaged to defend a number of Trinity College students on a charge arising out of an incident at the Dublin Regatta. The students, all personal friends of his, had put money on the winning crew with a bookmaker who had 'welshed'. The students thereupon gave chase and, having caught him and relieved him of his ready cash, were about to throw him in the river when the police suddenly came upon the scene and rescued him. In the result the students were summoned for assault.

"How did you know they were going to drown you?" asked Carson.

"And how did I know? Shore, I knew right enough. Didn't they howld me by the leg over the say wall!"

"Which leg?" asked Carson sternly. "Was it your *black* leg?"

Afterwards the prosecutor admitted that Carson had been too much for him. "Ye may say what ye like," he declared, "but that Carson's a champion. He'd puzzle and fluster the very Divil himself."

This impression was confirmed in the mind of another onlooker who happened to drop in to the Green Street Court on one occasion in these early days. His Uncle Lambert, who was a solicitor, arrived as the tall young barrister was addressing the jury. Carson mentioned a particularly far-fetched story on the part of one of the witnesses. "Gentlemen of the jury," he went on in the rich brogue which he had cultivated, "I'm sure your throats are not large enough to swallow that." The solicitor left the Court convinced that his eloquent nephew would make his way in the profession.

Like most of his fellow barristers who hoped to pick up work outside the Four Courts and Green Street, Carson joined one of the six Circuits into which the country was divided at that period. He chose the Leinster Circuit, largely because his friend James Shannon had begun to practise there. Its membership was small, consisting of forty barristers, nicknamed the 'forty thieves' because, by the recent alteration of the order of towns visited on Assize, they acquired much of the work which had previously been remitted from Dublin to the Home Circuit. The Circuit Bar Mess, which had its own 'steward', formed a cheerful and convivial company, dining and debating together at the end of each day's work in Court. Here the corporate personality of the Bar was at its best. The Assize towns included Kildare, Wicklow, Wexford, Carlow and Tipperary.

Carson had first to make his way at Quarter Sessions and in the County Courts of the Circuit where he had elected to practise. These institutions, unlike their counterparts in England, were closely and sometimes indistinguishably associated, since the local County Court Judge was *ex officio* Chairman of Quarter Sessions as well, and, although the criminal business which came before him only formed a small proportion of his total work, the name of Quarter Sessions came to be applied to his whole sitting. Owing to the extremely low cost of bringing suits—counsel's fee in any action up to £10 was only half a guinea—the County Courts were always fairly busy. The Irish County Court Judges were popular officers and on the whole possessed the full confidence of the people, although many of them were of a rare old age. The Irish have always been more prone to litigation than the English. The Irish litigant of those days preferred flowery and ingenious methods of advocacy and even when he lost he was always content if his 'counsellor' had given the Court a good run for his money. If not so successful at first as some of his contemporaries, Carson's methods in the end, as we shall see, proved more effective.

Carson got on well with the judges in spite of their antiquity, which did not make appearing before them any easier. One day, for instance, Carson happened to meet Judge Wall, who, though stone-deaf, presided over the Tipperary County Court.

"Well, Judge," said Carson, who had been engaged elsewhere, "had you an interesting case in Court today?"

"Eh?" he said, holding his hand to his ear. Carson shouted the question again.

"Oh yes," he replied, "a very interesting case. I'm not certain what it was about, but I think it was a choral society complaining about an instrument. I suppose it was a harmonium."

Next morning, to his astonishment, Carson discovered that the action really concerned the price and quality of a Singer's sewing machine!

Carson found Quarter Sessions and the County Courts an excellent training in the art of cross-examination and of handling witnesses. For the Irish witness is quite different from his English fellow. In England most witnesses go into Court unwillingly and apprehensively, sometimes indeed in a state of nerves bordering on fright. In Ireland, as the late Maurice Healy, K.C., once put it, the majority go to give their evidence as a cricketer walks to his wicket. "Each is confident he will not be bowled until he has knocked up a good score; each is very disappointed if the bowler limits his efforts to preventing the score from rising and does not attack his wicket." They usually had their story carefully rehearsed beforehand and committed to memory, and if it had some claim to literal veracity, it did not matter to them how wide of the facts it really was. This disregard for the spirit of the truth is well brought out by an incident in a case heard in an English Court by Mr. Justice Darling. One of the witnesses was an Irishman, who gave his evidence as if he had been in his own County Court at home. "Tell me," said the judge to him sternly, "what happens in your country to a witness who does not tell the truth?" "Begor, me Lord," replied Paddy with characteristic candour, "I think his side usually wins!"

The 'I-suggest-that-you-are-wrong?' type of cross-examination, which goes down so well in England, was quite out of place on the other side of the Irish Sea. Such an approach merely produced a deluge of irrelevant matter from an indignant witness, while he was thinking up a plausible answer. In Ireland subtler methods had to be employed, and there it was necessary for everyone concerned in Court to know exactly how much to believe and how much to discount in a witness's story. Carson realised this at a very early stage in his professional career, and he got to know his fellow countrymen well. But his objective was crystal-clear. "What am I to say?" one of his own witnesses would ask him. "You must tell the truth," was his invariable reply. But this precept, admirable as it was in principle, was often far from easy to carry out in practice.

The foundation of Carson's subsequent skill as a cross-examiner was laid in one of his very early cases. It was an action brought by a 'fancy lady' to recover certain presents which she had received from a man who had refused to marry her, as he had promised. In cross-examining this defendant Carson, for want of a better question, asked him: "Why don't you give the lady back her presents?"

The witness began to bite his hat and appeared embarrassed. Then he pulled himself together and looked Carson straight in the face. "I think, yer honour," he said, "that's a very leading question." By this, of course, he did not mean a question suggestive of a particular answer, as the expression is understood among lawyers, but rather a question leading direct to the root of the matter at issue. In fact he was caught by this simple question and he knew it. Carson never forgot this incident. It caused him to reflect and eventually brought him to the conclusion that for a successful cross-examination it is best to ask a 'very leading question'. Thus he developed his technique, for which he later became famous, when cross-examining witnesses, of asking a few but extremely pertinent questions and then sitting down. It was a brilliant technique, but so unlike the usual style in vogue in Ireland that at first it tended to have a perplexing and puzzling effect. Indeed it was not until he went to England fifteen years later that the technique was to be appreciated to the full. As Lord Darling said of him then, he was so very relevant, so unlike all the other Irishmen he had seen: "He simply would not talk balderdash."

In Dublin, as he stood on the threshold of his career, his forensic gifts remained concealed. As yet he made no stir in the Courts, while contemporaries such as James Campbell and Charles O'Connor were rated far above Edward Carson. "We used to say of him at the Bar that he improved every year," his friend John Ross later recalled, "and probably the highest type of mind is one that is always growing." But if he was outstripped in the professional field by his more brilliant contemporaries, his innate personal characteristics did not go unnoticed. "The one thing about him that impressed us all," noted Ross, "was his transparent integrity and courage."

Throughout his student days, and also during his first years at the Bar, Carson had continued to be warmly attached to his beautiful cousin, Katie Lambert. Unfortunately any thoughts they may have had about getting married were dashed by her father, who would not hear of Katie marrying a penniless barrister. Thus the romance faded away. A year or so later Katie Lambert married a young army officer and shortly afterwards died in childbirth. By that time Edward Carson had found a wife elsewhere.

CHAPTER TWO

Marriage and the Irish Bar

I

IN the summer, after the Courts had risen for the day, Carson used often to go out to one of the seaside resorts near Dublin, such as Kingstown or Sandycove, and hire a boat for a couple of hours' sailing. He was coming ashore one evening with his friend James Shannon, who had been his companion on this occasion, when his attention was suddenly caught by the figure of a slim fair-haired girl among the onlookers watching the boats from the land. Carson noticed how smart she looked and how well she wore her clothes. He immediately asked his friend if he knew who she was. It so happened that Shannon did know. He told Carson that she was a Miss Annette Kirwan and lived at Kingstown with her father, a retired County Inspector in the Royal Irish Constabulary.

Carson begged to be introduced, but for some reason Shannon appeared reluctant to oblige him. Carson argued and Shannon made various excuses. At last Carson said he would go up to her and introduce himself, and in the face of this threat Shannon gave way. And so, toward midsummer of the year 1879, Edward Carson and Annette Kirwan made acquaintance with each other. For Carson it was a case of love at first sight. Further meetings followed swiftly, and in a very short time the couple were engaged to be married.

The young barrister had only lately passed his twenty-fifth birthday. He had been practising his chosen profession for little more than a year and during this period he had been living at home with his parents and making barely enough to keep him in pocket money. His fiancée was as poor as he was; nor could she bring any dowry with her on their marriage. Thus it was small wonder that Edward's father received the news with singularly little enthusiasm when it was broken to him. "Who is she?" he asked. "I have never heard of her." "That is quite likely," his tall son replied and proceeded to relate what he knew of Annette and her family.

Sarah Annette Foster Kirwan, to give the lady her full names, was a year younger than Edward Carson. Like the Lamberts, her father, Henry Persse Kirwan, ex-County Inspector, R.I.C., came from County Galway, but his people were by no means as well-to-do as the Castle Ellen family. The Kirwans had a house called Tristan Lodge and a little land near Ballinasloe, for which they paid rent to the Earl of Clancarty. Henry Kirwan made his career as an officer in the Constabulary, the Irish police force with a fine tradition of service which had been founded by Sir Robert Peel. He served in various parts of the country, for the rule of the force was that members of it must be prepared to do duty in any district except their own native county. At the time of his retirement, in 1875, he was County Inspector at Trim, County Meath.

Mrs. Ann Kirwan, Annette's mother, whose maiden name was Foster, had died some years previously. By reason of his duties, which kept him away from home for considerable periods, it was difficult for Henry Kirwan to bring up his daughter as he would have liked. Consequently an arrangement was arrived at by which she was adopted by a Kirwan relative, John Joseph Andrew Kirwan, who had been a Resident Magistrate at Castlecomer in County Kilkenny. Annette always referred to him as her uncle, but it seems that she used the term loosely as the custom is in Ireland to describe any elderly family connexion. At all events, after he had retired from his post of Resident Magistrate in Kilkenny he came to live at Duleek in the same county as his kinsman Henry was stationed. She remained with his family until her father retired and returned to end his days, as so many like him have done, on the stretch of coast between Kingstown and Dalkey.

Carson had about £50 saved up in the bank, and with this modest capital he made up his mind to get married. The decision was taken quickly as soon as the Courts rose for Christmas, and there was no time to put up the banns. The marriage was celebrated by licence according to the rites of the Church of Ireland, on December 19, 1879, in Monkstown Parish Church, near Kingstown. The officiating clergyman was Carson's former schoolmaster the Rev. Frank Wall, LL.D. while his close friend and colleague at the Bar, James Shannon, acted as best man. The bride, who looked extremely smart in her wedding dress, was given away by her father. There was only a handful of friends at the church on that winter morning, for the ceremony took place soon after eight o'clock, so that when it was over the bridal couple could catch the mail boat to Holyhead on the first stage of their honeymoon. Among those present was Edward's younger sister Bella, who incidentally was to live to describe the scene for the benefit of the present writer over seventy years later.

The honeymoon, which included Christmas, was spent in London, and the newly-married couple were deliriously happy together. But the expedition exhausted most of the husband's accumulated savings, so that when he returned to Dublin with his wife for the beginning of the Law term in January, there was little money left. Indeed his ready cash is said to have amounted to no more than sixpence. Prospects looked bleak, but three days later the situation was saved when Carson received a brief marked three guineas. It was a small case, but he won it. He celebrated the victory by a day in the country with Annette. They made plans together for similar expeditions when his work should increase.

Meanwhile Annette's 'uncle', John Kirwan, the retired Resident Magistrate by whom she had been adopted, had offered the young pair a home until they should find their feet. They accordingly moved into his house in Herbert Place and there began their married life with its accompanying struggles. Briefs were still few and far between, but when one came Carson would sit up working on it until the small hours, his wife helping and encouraging him with her presence. It was not long before she had a significant piece of news for her husband. She was going to have a baby. Husband and wife now wanted a home of their own and Edward decided to take a chance. It happened that the small house at No. 9 Herbert Place was to let. The young Carsons decided to leave old Mr. Kirwan's hospitable roof and set up on their own. They accordingly installed themselves in the vacant house. Here, to their great joy, on October 2, 1880, Annette was safely delivered of a son. He was given the names of William Henry Lambert.

It would be idle to deny that Carson's parents were far from pleased with the marriage. His father in particular had tried to prevent it and actually had had a stormy interview with Annette's father when 'words' are said to have 'passed between them'. However, he gradually became reconciled to the alliance, and it was a source of great satisfaction to Edward's mother to know that he should have lived to see his first grandchild. A few months later, early in 1881, Edward Carson, senior, was suddenly taken ill and died, leaving his widow none too well provided for. Thus the young barrister was conscious of a new domestic responsibility as he followed his father's remains to their last resting place in Dublin's Mount Jerome Cemetery.

But Carson was not the man to shirk responsibility. Annette was expecting another baby, who in due course appeared in the form of a girl and was called Aileen Seymour.* With her two infant children and her toiling husband the young mother was extremely contented, although times were not always easy. A barrister's fees seldom accompany the briefs on delivery and he often has to wait many weeks or months for them. Consequently Annette often enough in these early days found it a problem to meet the household bills, with the incessant demands of a growing family. But money went a lot further in those days than it does now, and somehow they managed to scrape along. Edward was by nature most generous and open-handed with money, particularly where his family were concerned: indeed it is doubtful whether he ever really understood its value. Luckily for him Annette was a good housekeeper and she ran the house well. If then she had any troubles, particularly of a financial kind, she was inclined to keep them from her husband. Edward's sister Bella remonstrated with her about this habit on one occasion. "Surely they are Ned's troubles as well," she said.

Edward Carson was deeply in love with his wife at this time and she returned his feeling with an unfailing devotion. She watched tenderly over his precarious health, and twice during the early years of their marriage she nursed him through dangerous and painful illnesses. The first was when he succumbed to an attack of typhoid fever, which he caught, it seems, from his great friend James Shannon.

It was largely on his friend's account that Carson had joined the Leinster Circuit, where Shannon was already in a fair way of practice. By this time, indeed, Shannon had considerably outstripped Carson both in ambition and achievement. In addition he was not handicapped by the poor health which was to dog Carson's footsteps throughout his life. It was thus all the more remarkable that Shannon, a man seemingly in full vigour and on the threshold of what promised to be a brilliant career, should have been fatally stricken down by this disease. Shannon's young wife begged Carson not to visit her husband, but Carson insisted on going to see him on his death-bed. In fact Shannon almost died in his arms. "Give up the world, Ned," were the dying man's last words to his friend, "and meet me in Heaven." A few days later Mrs. Shannon, distraught by

* November 13, 1881.

MRS. ISABELLA CARSON

Mother of Edward Carson.

From a photograph in the possession of Lady Carson.

COMMITTEE OF THE HISTORICAL SOCIETY, TRINITY COLLEGE, DUBLIN, IN 1877

Carson is standing in the back row with his hand in his pocket, directly behind the Auditor, John Ross.

From a photograph in the possession of the Historical Society, Trinity College, Dublin.

her loss and with no wish to live, contracted the fever and followed her husband to the grave. But Carson, a much weaker man physically, survived the fever, nursed as he was by Annette, who in his opinion saved his life.

Carson's second illness at this period was caused by an acute attack of gallstones. About the same time a fellow barrister, T. L. O'Shaughnessy, later a judge, was suffering from the same complaint. They discussed possible remedies. O'Shaughnessy was against anything drastic, preferring a course of medical treatment. But Carson, who had any amount of pluck, was in favour of surgery, although an operation of this kind was then considered both hazardous and unpleasant. The upshot was that Carson submitted to the operation, which was successful. After a comparatively short period of convalescence, during which he was tenderly cared for by his devoted Annette, he was able to get up and go about his work. His colleague O'Shaughnessy, on the other hand, was laid up for several months swallowing reducing agents before he could be pronounced cured.

Edward Carson's partnership with Annette was destined to last for more than thirty years. Throughout this period he was never to forget what a great helpmate she had been to him, though the domestic scene was not to remain by any means unclouded, particularly after the family had migrated across the Irish Sea and later when the children had grown up. Eventually, as her own health began to fail, he realised fully what a wonderful wife she had been to him and in her final illness he was to repay the devotion she had shown him in the past. Then, when she had gone, was he to experience what he called "the miseries of a very lonely man" in an acute form. "I suppose it is because I never lived alone and have always been made so comfy by my poor wife that I feel it all the more," he confessed at the time. "I don't think that is any exaggeration of what she did for me."

2

For Anglo-Irish relations the nineteenth century had hitherto been largely one of lost opportunities. In a celebrated speech, which Disraeli delivered in the House of Commons a few years before Carson's birth, the future Conservative Prime Minister truthfully described Ireland as possessing "a starving population, an absentee aristocracy, and an alien Church, and in addition the weakest executive in the world." The Act of Union, passed in 1800 to create a United Kingdom with a common Parliament, had left intact institutions like the Established Church and the land system which many of the Irish people regarded as unjust and oppressive. Furthermore the Roman Catholics had accepted the Union on the understanding that this legislative act was to be followed at once by full political emancipation. Unfortunately the English Government's proposal foundered on the rock of King George III's conscience and the question was temporarily shelved. When eventually, in 1828, the measure did receive the Royal Assent under another monarch, after it had been wrung from a reluctant Tory Government as the result of formidable agitation led by Daniel O'Connell, it came too late to serve as a means of reconciliation. But if it had failed in this respect, it had taught O'Connell and his followers that they could play successfully upon British fears. Thus the movement for emancipation quickly developed into one for the total repeal of the Union.

In other words, the aim of Wolfe Tone and his Society of United Irishmen, formulated at the close of the preceding century "to break the connection with England and . . . to unite the whole people of Ireland" received fresh driving force. This found expression in political rebellion. The torch of liberty, kindled by romantic Robert Emmet in 1803, had burned again at the hands of Smith O'Brien and John Mitchel in 1848, and during the period of Carson's boyhood had once more been grasped by the Fenians, the brotherhood started in the United States after the Civil War and dedicated to securing the independence of Ireland by physical force. The Fenians employed bombs, daggers and pistols to reinforce their political arguments, not without effect upon Her Majesty's Ministers. The first points of this policy had appeared in 1869, when a Liberal Government headed by Mr. Gladstone carried through Parliament the Act disestablishing the Irish Church, thereby removing the strongest bulwark of 'Protestant ascendancy' in the country. Meanwhile at Westminster Irish nationalist aims were being advanced by the lawyer Isaac Butt, who in 1870 had founded the Home Rule Association, designed to secure by constitutional means within the parliamentary framework what the Fenians were seeking to achieve outside it at the point of the gun.

Resistance to British rule in Ireland had so far proved a failure, whether in the form of a concerted rising or isolated acts of physical violence. Something more was needed than the abstract ideal of political liberty to stir the rank-and-file of the Irish people into action and hold their imagination. The man who supplied it was a Protestant landed gentleman from County Wicklow. His name was Parnell, and he was soon to displace Butt in the leadership of the Home Rule Party at Westminster. Charles Stewart Parnell was the first leader in his country to realise that Irish nationalism could only find effective expression in practice when the aim of political independence was joined with that of agrarian reform. The first and essential step towards the undermining of British authority in Ireland, he declared, was to destroy the landlords. Only thus might Ireland become independent. "Let us not forget that this is the ultimate goal at which all Irishmen aim," he told an American audience in 1880. "None of us, whether we be in America, or Ireland, or wherever we may be, will be satisfied until we have destroyed the last link which keeps Ireland bound to England."

Ireland's population, largely agricultural, had undergone a remarkable increase during the earlier part of the century, rising from less than three millions in 1785 to over eight millions in 1845. This process, which involved the rapid multiplication of small holdings, had been dictated partly by the sudden demand for cereals during the Napoleonic Wars, which necessitated a change-over from pasture to tillage, and partly by the enfranchisement of the Catholic peasantry, which prompted the landowners to create additional vote-carrying tenancies, thereby increasing their own political influence with those who paid them rent. Unfortunately the increase in population was not accompanied by any increase in national resources for maintaining it. The peasants, whose standard of living was always much lower than that of the English tenant farmer and even the English agricultural labourer, thus tended to press more and more upon the country's means of subsistence. Nor had they any fixity of tenure in their holdings. Except in the North-East, where they were protected by the celebrated 'Ulster tenant right', they could be evicted at will without receiving a halfpenny by way of compensation for any improvements made by them during the term of their tenancies. For evicted tenants the only refuge was the workhouse, but even there the test was severe. No person in possession of more than a quarter of an acre of land could be deemed to be destitute.

With the fall in the price of corn after Waterloo and the consequent swing back from tillage to pasture, the Irish landlords had tended more and more to clear their estates of their poorer tenants and concentrate their holdings into farms of a size which sound economy demanded. Evictions were carried out wholesale, particularly by the absentee landlords' agents and with an utter disregard for the sufferings of the unfortunate peasants. On the whole the wealthier resident landlords behaved well to their tenantry, but others, when estates had become encumbered with debt, often due to their extravagance and ostentation in the matter of building, necessarily had recourse to harsh methods in order to satisfy their creditors. This process reached its tragic climax in the terrible famine of 1846, caused by the failure of the potato crop for two consecutive seasons, when half a million died of starvation and pestilence. Carts with sliding bottoms were used to convey the corpses from the workhouse or wayside to the burial pits, where they were interred in a mass. The story is told how one of the carters, who was short of a corpse for his load, actually ordered the dying inmate of a workhouse to come with him, saying "You'll be dead before you're down." Meanwhile a steady stream of emigrants left the country for Boston and Philadelphia. Lord Macaulay, who visited Ireland shortly afterwards, found "hundreds of dwellings in ruins, abandoned by the late inmates who fled to America—the labouring people dressed literally, not rhetorically, worse than the scarecrows of England, the children of whole villages turning out to beg of every coach and car that goes by."

Thereafter the population of Ireland began to fall steadily. In the year of Carson's birth it was less than six and a half millions, that is, a drop of nearly two millions in ten years. Meanwhile the agrarian grievance continued unabated. It was not until 1870, following the Fenian agitation and the disestablishment of the Irish Church, that Gladstone, who appreciated the difference between the English and Irish land systems, introduced his first Irish Land Act. This gave to the Ulster tenant right to the force of law throughout the country in the matter of compensation for disturbance and unexhausted improvements. But it only touched the fringe of the problem. It afforded the tenant no protection against raised rents nor did it give him security of tenure. These matters were brought to the fore a few years later with the formation of the Land League, an organisation founded by Michael Davitt in 1879 to fight the landlords and warmly supported by Parnell. Evictions were now answered by the 'boycott', a device named after one of its early victims, and the weapon of terror was brought into play against both the landlords and their agents. The reign of 'Captain Moonlight' was beginning.

Gladstone's reaction was to give the Irish donkey a dose of both the stick and the carrot. A Coercion Act entitled the authorities to imprison anyone they liked without trial. Another Land Act was designed to remedy the outstanding agrarian grievance. This revolutionary Act, which was passed in 1881, aimed at securing to the Irish tenants what came to be popularly known as 'the three Fs'—fair rents to be settled by a judicial tribunal, fixity of tenure for all who paid their rents, and free sale so that the tenants could dispose of their interest without hindrance. The immediate outcome of this important legislation was to bring an enormous amount of work to the Irish Bar. There was a great rush of litigants both to the County Courts and the newly-established Land Commission in Dublin, where incidentally much amusement was produced at its first sitting when the Court registrar, by an unfortunate slip of the tongue, declared in a loud voice that "the Court of the Land League is now open." Something like half a million lawsuits resulted, and however the Irish Land Act of 1881 ultimately benefited the general community there is no doubt that it brought substantial rewards in its train to all those lawyers who practised in the Irish Courts.

'Counsellor' Carson was among the barristers who secured a large share of these 'fair rent' cases, particularly on the Leinster Circuit. At first he appeared exclusively for the tenants, but it was not long before the landlords recognised his talents and their solicitors also began to instruct him.

Immense interest was taken throughout the country in these cases, and the result of each one was hailed with jubilation or despondency, according to the interest of the parties. As the Nationalist M.P. Tim Healy, later first Governor-General of the Irish Free State, put it in his memoirs, to the landlords every defeat seemed a Waterloo, and to the tenants every victory an Austerlitz.

In one of the cases, where Carson represented the tenant, the landlord had gone to the expense of calling three valuers, or 'valuators' as they were known in Ireland, to testify as to the high value of the field rented by Carson's client. Carson asked the County Court Judge who was hearing the case that each valuator should give his expert testimony out of earshot of the other two. This was done. After the first valuator had come in and described the field in detail, he gave its fair annual rent in his opinion as £10 15s. 2d. The second man gave precisely the same assessment, and so did the third. Carson now felt it was time for him to intervene. He began to cross-examine this third witness.

"Ye said ye went over the field carefully by yourself?"

"Yes."

"What sort of field did ye find it?"

"It had a wall round it. I noticed everything about it."

Carson gave the witness a beaming smile as he put his next question.

"Did ye notice any coincidence about the field?"

"Yes, indeed," replied the witness confidently. "I didn't rightly recall it at first, but now ye come to remind me, there was a little heap of them lying up in a corner of the field by themselves."

Many of Carson's successful appearances on behalf of the tenants were in the Waterford County Court, where he was often instructed by Tim Healy's solicitor brother Maurice. The tall young 'counsellor' threw himself with such zeal into these cases on his clients' behalf that the local Nationalists actually approached him to stand for Parliament and contest Waterford as a 'No Rent' candidate, where he would have the support of the Land League. Much to their surprise Carson declined their offer, informing the members of the deputation who waited upon him that, though he was something of a Radical, he was also a firm believer in the Union between England and Ireland which the Land League was seeking to break. In any event, he went on, he had no time for politics. He had his living to make.

3

In the career of every successful barrister there is usually one spectacular case which brings him to the public notice and, what is more important for him, to the notice of a wide circle of solicitors who as a result begin to entrust him with their work. With Carson the *cause célèbre* was provided by a Miss Anthony, who became known afterwards as the 'lady litigant' from the number of actions in which she appeared as a party.

Miss Anthony was a person of somewhat eccentric character, who lived in the town of Tallow in County Waterford. On the occasion which gave rise to her introduction to the Courts she was travelling on the railway, as it happened without a ticket. When the train arrived at Dungarvan, she was ejected on to the station platform by a porter, receiving injuries in the process. She determined to bring an action against the railway company at the next Assizes.

The question of legal advice, however, she delayed to the last moment, when she heard there was a 'counsellor' putting up at the local inn.

Carson happened to be in bed at the time. To his intense surprise a middle-aged and wild-eyed lady burst into his bedroom and tried to brief him then and there. Having heard what she had to say, the astonished barrister referred her to a solicitor, who in due course instructed him to appear for her. His advocacy on his client's behalf impressed the jury and they awarded heavy damages against the railway company. The company appealed and Carson appeared for the respondent in long drawn-out litigation in which the whole law of negligence was discussed. Again she won. But, alas, her triumph gave the eccentric Miss Anthony an unfortunate taste for litigation. Far from being grateful to her 'counsellor' she dispensed with his services, and henceforth conducted her cases in person. In several of these cases Carson was instructed to appear against her, which provoked her to extreme indignation. On one of these occasions she vehemently attacked his personal character, ending up with this taunt: "And your mother is no better than she should be." Carson was more amazed than annoyed at this strange conduct. "My poor saintly mother," he murmured in an aside to his solicitors.

As a litigant in person Miss Anthony enjoyed a remarkable success. First of all, she pledged a ring with a tradesman in Tallow in order to obtain a supply of bacon. Wanting her ring back she issued a writ against the tradesman for illegally taking pledges, and so recovered her property. Then she proceeded against her parish priest for slandering her reputation by passing her over at the altar rails when she presented herself for Holy Communion. The priest, who feared for his own reputation, naturally compromised the action, as a result of which she received a substantial sum in settlement. She next sued the local rates collector for 'excess' in his collection. This time she lost, and to save her goods from seizure in execution of the judgment she persuaded the Christian Brothers in Tallow to take her sheep into their field. Having done this, she proceeded to borrow money from these unsuspecting brethren, whom she subsequently sued for the return of the animals, so as to avoid repayment of the debt. The Christian Brothers were frightened of going into Court and sent back her sheep.

She now turned her attention to the legal profession itself. She served a writ for slander on a Dublin solicitor for some imaginary defamation. The solicitor, who had never heard of Miss Anthony, threw the writ into the waste-paper basket. Naturally he was not present in Court when the case came on for hearing. The result was that he had £1,000 damages awarded against him 'in default of appearance'! He subsequently moved to have this judgment set aside, and though his motion succeeded, Miss Anthony was granted costs.

The lady litigant was now treated as a privileged person wherever she went. She was allowed to travel free on the railway, as the companies preferred her to do this than have the inconvenience of defending her suits. Tradesmen too were afraid to sue her for their unpaid bills, and so she was accorded unlimited credit. Eventually, however, she went mad, and the jurisdiction of the Lord Chancellor's Lunacy Commissioner was invoked, as a result of which she became an inmate of Cork County Asylum. There she hanged herself, but no newspaper of the time dared mention her suicide in their columns, lest she might have circulated an unfounded rumour in order to start a libel action!

Although Edward Carson took no part in the proceedings which resulted in the certification of his old client, he could not help remembering with gratitude that it was Miss Anthony's initial appearance in Court which brought him as well as herself into the public eye. In fact Miss Anthony really launched him on his professional career.

If Carson's reputation at the Irish Bar was made by this litigation, it was considerably enhanced by a sensational case of homicide in which he figured at this time. It was a political crime of the kind countenanced if not encouraged by the Land League and indicative of the mounting wave of lawlessness which culminated in the assassination in broad daylight of the Irish Chief Secretary, Lord Frederick Cavendish, and the Under-Secretary, Mr. Edward Burke, in Dublin's Phœnix Park. Known as the Dorset Street tragedy, it occurred a few weeks before the shocking affair in Phœnix Park.

About midday on March 28, 1882, a young worker in the printing trade named Joseph MacMahon entered a public-house in Dorset Street, not far from the King's Inns, where he was accompanied by two friends of the same class, John Brennan and Thomas Martin. There was a crowd in the bar at the time, and they asked for a private room. They were shown into a 'snuggery' or 'snug' (as it is usually known today), that is, a part of the bar separated from the main saloon by wooden partitions which do not reach to the ceiling. Five minutes later the report of a shot rang out and smoke was seen rising above the partition. Then the door of the 'snug' opened and Brennan emerged, forcing his way through the astonished crowd, and took to his heels. He was pursued and eventually pulled off a jaunting-car by one of the crowd. Meanwhile Martin remained beside the prostrate and, as it turned out, lifeless body of young MacMahon. Two revolvers were found lying on the floor; one was fully loaded, the other, with one cartridge fired, was pointing towards the dead man. Five other bullets were found under a seat. Brennan and Martin were arrested and charged with the murder of Joseph MacMahon.

The trial took place before Chief Baron Palles in Green Street, the prisoners being defended by Carson. His task was far from easy, conducted as it was in an atmosphere highly charged with popular alarm at current outbreaks of violent crime. Nor was it reassuring to know that quite an arsenal had been discovered by the police in MacMahon's house. "What brought these young men here with these deadly weapons?" asked the Crown Prosecutor. "There is at present an alarming state of affairs prevailing in this city. We cannot tell to what secret obligations these young men are bound or what they may have been planning to do that day."

Carson put the view to the jury that the whole affair was an accident. He called the driver of the jaunting-car to prove that Brennan had told him to drive back to the public-house to succour a dying man. Other witnesses, as might be expected, came forward to testify to the good character of the accused. Carson begged the jury not to convict on a capital charge because of the disturbed state of the city. "You must put out of your minds any speculation as to what may have been the object of these young men going into the snuggery. You have here a charge of murder without evidence of any motive whatsoever. Have you ever in the course of your experience heard of a murder perpetrated thus? In the midst of a crowded shop, in broad daylight, with two policemen in the street outside? Is it likely, I ask you, if a murder was intended, the murderer would use a weapon which must bring upon him immediate detection? I do not ask for mercy; I demand justice."

After a long retirement the jury were unable to agree upon a verdict and were discharged. The prisoners were brought up at the next commission, when their counsel prudently offered a plea of manslaughter. This plea the Crown accepted and the two men were sentenced to terms of imprisonment. There can be little doubt that they were rightly convicted of the lesser charge, and that the firing of the revolver had been accidental. As Carson pointed out also, no motive had been shown, and until the last the three men had been associated in terms of closest friendship.

The Phœnix Park murders followed a few weeks later. Shortly afterwards Mrs. Brennan, the mother of one of the prisoners in the Dorset Street case, came to see Carson and thank him for what he had done for her son. It throws a sinister sidelight on the times that she should have expressed her gratitude to her son's defence counsel, not for his conduct of the case, but for having advised the young man to plead guilty to the lesser charge of manslaughter. This meant that he was in prison at the time of the affair in Phœnix Park. Otherwise, she pointed out, he would have been compelled by his oath to have taken part in this conspiracy.

Mr. Justice Lawson, who presided at the second trial, took a serious view of the deplorable state of society which the case had revealed. He found it most disquieting that three decent men of the artisan class should be in possession of formidable weapons, especially when there was a proclamation out against them. He found it even more disquieting that not even a verdict of manslaughter could be had from the jury in the first trial.

Lawson, whose firm conduct on the Bench made him obnoxious to the lawbreakers, was himself the victim of an attack by one of the Phœnix Park murderers, as he was walking along the street on his way to the Kildare Street Club. Thereafter he always sat in Court with a loaded revolver on the Bench. He was a scholarly as well as a courageous judge, but he was occasionally inclined to be a little intolerant of junior counsel arguing before him. This led to an angry brush with Carson in open Court, but neither bore the other any ill-will. Shortly afterwards as the judge was preparing to set out on the Leinster Circuit, he happened to meet Carson.

"Did you know I was coming on the Leinster?" he asked, "and will you promise not to be setting upon me in every town?"

"My Lord, I will," answered Carson with sincerity, "if you'll promise me that if you'll be strong, you'll be merciful."

The judge gave his word. But it was not easy to temper justice with mercy in the lawless Ireland of those days.

4

Parnell and his principal supporters, including Tim Healy, had been arrested under the powers of the Coercion Act in the autumn of 1881. They were lodged in Kilmainham Gaol in Dublin, where they spent the next six months. The Government thereupon issued a proclamation suppressing the Land League, to which Parnell replied with a 'No Rent' Manifesto.

Asked in gaol how the No Rent campaign was progressing, Parnell replied: "All I know about it is that my own tenants are acting strictly up to it." However, in spite of the behaviour of the leader's own tenantry, the campaign did not catch on. Many tenants were seriously in arrears with their rents owing to a succession of bad harvests. Yet they shrank from repudiating their debts, since to do so was regarded by the priests as sinful. Nevertheless the arrears question was grave, and its burden tended to nullify much of the good of the Land Act.

Eventually, as the result of secretly conducted negotiations, Mr. Gladstone, the Prime Minister, agreed to release Parnell and the others on condition that he undertook to use his influence to put down crime. On its side the Government promised to put the arrears question on a more satisfactory basis. The intermediary in these negotiations, the so-called 'Kilmainham Treaty', was Captain William Henry O'Shea, M.P., whose wife was Parnell's mistress.

At the time of his arrest Parnell had foretold that while he was in prison his place as Home Rule leader would be taken by 'Captain Moonlight'. His prophecy was amply fulfilled by the series of shocking murders which were committed during this period. They were reflected in the Dorset Street tragedy and exemplified by another terrible crime, in which Carson was also professionally concerned.

In April, 1882, Mrs. Henry Smythe left Dublin to spend Easter with her brother-in-law Mr. Barlow Smythe at his beautiful country home, Barbavilla House, near Collinstown, in County Westmeath. She was accompanied by her two daughters, who had recently 'come out' in Dublin society. Her host and kinsman was a man of seventy-one, the senior Deputy-Lieutenant of the county and a former High Sheriff. He was a good landlord and had lived all his life at Barbavilla, which he had inherited as a boy. He had recently offered all his tenants free registration of reduced rents before the new Land

Commission, this offer being contained in a circular letter which began, "My friends". He naturally had every reason to believe that these tenants were happy and contented. Indeed, until shortly before his sister-in-law's visit, he had not evicted a single one for fifty years. However, he had lately been obliged to get rid of a farmer named Riggs, who had leased a large farm and refused to pay rent. This tenant had refused to pay even a nominal rent, and, as he had belonged to the old Fenian body, it was thought that his attitude was dictated by some similar organisation. But nobody believed that the other tenants would take any offensive action on his account against such a generous landlord as the master of Barbavilla House.

The day after Mrs. Henry Smythe's arrival was Palm Sunday. In the morning the family went to church with guests who included Lady Harriet Monck, a relative of Mr. Barlow Smythe and a close friend of Queen Victoria. The church was a mile or so distant at Collinstown. After morning service, Mrs. Henry Smythe's two daughters and two young officers, also in the house-party, left to walk back to the house, while the others stayed for Holy Communion. As the young ladies and their escorts walked through the woods towards Barbavilla, one of them thought he heard a low whistle and a rustling of the leaves in the trees, but no one paid any particular attention to this at the time. Meanwhile, after the Communion Service was over, Mr. Barlow Smythe, his sister-in-law and Lady Harriet Monck drove back by carriage. Mrs. Smythe sat in one of the seats with her back to the horses. This was a seat which normally would have been occupied by a gentleman, but since her brother-in-law was an old man, Mrs. Smythe preferred to leave the two seats facing the horses to him and Lady Harriet.

The carriage was approaching Barbavilla House along the winding and thickly-crowded drive when two loud explosions were heard. Mr. Barlow Smythe thought at first it was thunder. Actually it was gunfire. For the next few moments the coachman was kept busy controlling the horses, who had taken fright. Nevertheless he saw the figure of a man in a stooping position to the left and partly hidden by a tree. Then came a third report which shattered the carriage glass, the windows being splashed with what Mr. Smythe took to be mud. "Good God, we are under fire!" he exclaimed, as the horses galloped towards the mansion. It was only when they reached the front door as the coachman pulled up the horses that Mrs. Smythe was seen to be dead. She had suffered the most frightful wounds. What her brother-in-law had thought to be mud on the carriage window was really a mixture of her blood and brains.

The news of this crime, in which the victim was a woman, despatched a wave of horror through the civilised world. The Queen sent a message of condolence, and Mr. Gladstone, who was to lose his nephew Lord Frederick Cavendish by the assassin's knife a few weeks later in Phœnix Park, expressed deep and heartfelt sympathy. Meanwhile Mr. Smythe sent another circular letter to his tenants. "I do not go through the former farce of calling you friends," he wrote. "Few of you are so. Most of you by your silence assent to the deed of blood, and many of you only regret that one who has passed his life and spent his income among you was not the victim." Mr. Smythe was right. There was no doubt that he, and not his sister-in-law, was the intended victim. Indeed for long afterwards the affair was spoken of in the neighbourhood as 'the accident'.

In the weeks that followed, not one person dared to come forward and identify the murderer or murderers, despite a large reward of £2,000 offered by the Government for information leading to their conviction. The only clue the police had was an empty whisky bottle which was picked up near the scene of the crime. However, they felt they had to take some action, and the evicted tenant Riggs and his family were arrested. It was soon evident that they were not the culprits. It was not until over a year later that an informer appeared. He was a peasant named Patrick McKeon and he lived near Barbavilla House. His information together with that of his son, who bore the same name, led to a number of arrests. An inquiry was opened by the local Resident Magistrate under the Crimes Act, and the suspects were examined by him over a considerable period.

The elder McKeon stated that the plot to murder Barlow Smythe had been hatched in the near-by cottage of a Mrs. Fagan, 'the widow Fagan', mother of Michael Fagan, one of the Phœnix Park murderers, who for his part in that crime had already paid the penalty with his life. A murder society had been formed there at a dance, when Michael Fagan and his fellow conspirator, Francis Cowley, also executed for his part in the Phœnix Park murders, had sworn in a number of young men in the neighbourhood. McKeon forbade his son to take the oath and stood aside with him when it was being administered to the others. The conspirators pledged themselves to assassinate Barlow Smythe and other local landlords. The younger McKeon identified the actual murderer as a youth named Robert Elliott, who worked with him in a blacksmith's forge. Young McKeon said he saw Elliott carrying a sawn-off shot-gun on the day of the crime and later searching for a bottle of whisky which he concluded he had left behind him in Barbavilla Wood.

Elliott and three other prisoners were eventually charged with the crime. Another of the suspects, Pat Hanlon, had turned King's Evidence at the preliminary inquiry by the Resident Magistrate. His story was that he was collecting branches in Barbavilla Wood when he saw four of the prisoners enter the wood—after which he heard six shots fired in rapid succession—and then emerge, scattering in different directions.

The Grand Jury found a 'true bill' against Elliott for murder, but would only return a similar bill against the others for conspiracy. The Crown decided to proceed against all four on the latter charge. They were tried at Green Street before Lord Chief Justice Morris, their defending counsel being Dr. Walter Boyd, Q.C., later Mr. Justice Boyd, and Edward Carson. The MacDermot, Q.C.,* an able advocate and one of the few members of aristocratic families who made a success at the Bar, Peter O'Brien, Q.C., whose nickname was 'Peter the Packer', from his skill in 'packing juries',† and Constantine Molloy, Q.C., reckoned the greatest authority of the time in Ireland on criminal law, led for the prosecution.

The Crown Counsel did not call Hanlon; their principal witness was the elder McKeon, and he did not turn out to be a very satisfactory one. He had been worried, and in order to avoid supporting his wife he had joined the Army, swearing a false declaration that he was not married. He excused this lie on the ingenuous ground that he had not 'kissed the book'. He further admitted that if he had taken the oath at the Widow Fagan's he would have willingly committed murder if instructed to do so. As a witness his testimony was thus considerably discredited.

The defence was what was known as a 'Tipperary alibi', that is, that it was sought to establish not only the absence of the prisoners from the scene of the crime, but also the similar absence of the chief Crown witness. For instance, evidence was called to show that Robert Elliott was in another part of the county on the fatal Sunday,

* Hugh Hyacinth O'Rorke MacDermot (1834–1904), styled The MacDermot, hereditary Prince of Coolavin. He later served in successive Liberal Governments as Solicitor-General and Attorney-General for Ireland.

† Peter O'Brien (1842–1914), later Lord O'Brien of Kilfenora and Lord Chief Justice of Ireland.

that Pat McKeon was also elsewhere, and that there was no meeting at the Widow Fagan's on the evening alleged.

Afraid that this testimony, much of which was undoubtedly perjured, might result in an acquittal, Peter O'Brien began to press the Crown case with more than his customary vigour. This brought him into collision with Dr. Boyd, whom he somewhat unwisely, if in the heat of the moment, called "a damned coward". This led to a violent altercation between the two opposing counsel and produced a stern rebuke from the judge. O'Brien withdrew the expression, but he refused to apologise.

In view of this undignified scene Dr. Boyd seems to have thought it might serve his clients' interests better if he left his junior to make the closing speech for the defence. At all events Carson was given the chance of addressing the jury, and he took full advantage of it. "At what time in the history of this country," he asked the twelve men in the box, "has it ever been more requisite that jurors should be careful to act only on the strictest and clearest proof? No matter what abhorrence you feel for the crime, you must act on the evidence alone." He then went on to accuse the Crown of having withheld evidence which would have conclusively shown that the McKeons were liars. He made strong play with the prosecution's failure to call Hanlon:

> Where is Hanlon the informer, the man who, to save his life, gave evidence with regard to Mrs. Smythe's assassination, the man who made a deposition in the present case, the man who was alleged by the McKeons to have been present at the meeting of the 24th, and who, it was alleged, went down to the demesne gate on the occasion of the murder? . . . The Crown dare not produce him, because Hanlon would have given the lie to the McKeons.
>
> This, gentlemen, is not the way to get at justice. This thirst by the Crown to secure a conviction is not the way to secure an honest conviction.

This speech created a great impression, not only in the closely-packed and stuffy court-room, but throughout the country, and even further, for it was reported all over the world. It may be said to have made Carson's name as a junior in Ireland.

Thirty years later history repeated itself in England. Carson, who was leading counsel for the defence in a sensational libel action brought by Robert Sievier, the racehorse owner and gambler, against Richard Wootton, the trainer, received an urgent summons to Ulster during the trial. Consequently he was obliged to leave the conduct of the case to his junior. The name of this junior was Patrick Hastings. Such is the luck of the Bar. "When Carson went to Ulster," said Hastings in looking back on his own career, "he brought me fortune." Much the same thing happened to Carson when Dr. Boyd left the closing speech to him.

Had the trial run its normal course, it might have ended with an acquittal. For the sake of justice perhaps it was as well that it did not. As the Lord Chief Justice was about to sum up, one member of the jury complained that another juror was incapable of considering their verdict. To give the jury a rest the judge adjourned until the following morning. Next day the ailing juror, who had had a mental breakdown—he later went mad—was absent, and the judge decided that the trial could not continue with only eleven jurors. The prisoners were accordingly committed for retrial at the next Assizes. They duly came up again before the same judge, but Carson took no part in the second trial. This time the jury disagreed and the prisoners were once more remanded. Their final trial took place before Chief Baron Palles in April, 1889, when they were all convicted and received sentences of ten years' penal servitude.

Two months later six more of the suspects were arraigned for their part in the same crime. The trial took place at Green Street before Mr. Justice Lawson. Peter O'Brien had now been promoted to the rank of Serjeant-at-law, so that he led for the Crown with The MacDermot and Constantine Molloy. Carson appeared for a prisoner named John Magrath, being led by Dr. Webb, Q.C.* The proceedings largely followed the lines of the earlier trials and ended in another disagreement. Thereupon Peter O'Brien managed to empanel a special jury at the same Assize—it was said to be one of his best efforts at jury-packing—and convictions eventually resulted. The prisoners got seven years' penal servitude with the exception of Carson's client, who was sentenced to one year's imprisonment. "We will come out as innocent as we went in," said one of the prisoners as he left the dock. "We have been found guilty by a packed jury."

Peter O'Brien took a view which was somewhat different and, it

* Thomas Ebenezer Webb, LL.D. (1827–1903), a native of Cornwall, who was sent to Dublin University, where he had a remarkable academic career, becoming a Fellow and later a Professor of Moral Philosophy and also of laws. His learning was encyclopædic, his publications including works on metaphysics, Shakespeare, a verse translation of Goethe's *Faust* and a series of essays on the Irish Land Question. He became County Court Judge of Donegal in 1887. Marjoribanks, apparently unaware that he was an Englishman, describes his appeal on behalf of Magrath at this trial as 'typically Irish': *Life of Lord Carson*, at p. 66.

must be admitted, considerably nearer the truth. "Justice, slow and sometimes baffled, but ever sure, has triumphed in the end," he said.

5

Carson's speech to the jury in the first of the Smythe murder trials was widely reported and much talked about at the time in Dublin. It was indeed an amazing performance for a young man who had not yet passed his thirtieth birthday. It brought him a fresh access of work from solicitors and he now found himself well abreast of his old college classmates like Campbell, Ross and O'Connor in their profession. It also commended him particularly to Peter O'Brien, who had led for the Crown in these trials. O'Brien was then well on his way to becoming a Law Officer and leader of the Irish Bar, and the determination, which he formed at that time, to make use of Carson's services was destined to exercise a profound influence on the junior's career.

A Roman Catholic in his early forties, Peter O'Brien was a big man physically; he had a strong sense of humour coupled with an intimate knowledge of his fellow countrymen and their foibles. He was a genial host and sportsman, never so happy as out in the hunting field, but he was also a courageous and tireless advocate. His famous soubriquet of 'Peter the Packer' he acquired during the early days of the Land League, when it was impossible in many parts of Ireland to obtain convictions. He used to say that he should really have been called 'The Great Unpacker', as his object was to eliminate from the jury box those jurors whose minds he suspected were prejudiced, 'Landleaguers' and others who might be too timid to convict. To this end he usually challenged every juror appearing in Court without a collar. There was, of course, nothing arbitrary or illegal in this procedure. The right of challenge was a statutory one, conferred under an Irish Juries Act. A similar right existed in England, as it still does, but there it has rarely been found necessary to invoke it. Also, the prisoner had his right of challenge as well, so that hours and even days were often spent, particularly in a murder trial with a political or agrarian background, before a satisfactory jury could be empanelled.

The point of this proceeding, which is a common feature in American trials, was neatly illustrated by Carson in a conversation he had with an English lawyer during this period. They were discussing the difference between the English and Irish Courts in the matter of criminal practice and procedure.

Carson asked at what stage a trial in England began.

"Oh, when the jury is sworn," replied the Englishman.

"That's curious," remarked Carson. "With us it's all finished when that business is over."

The Juries Act, which had been passed in 1871, lowered the previous standard of qualification for jurors and admitted men who were often illiterate and generally unsuited for the functions of a jury. Unwashed and malodorous, they received the nickname of 'the Wild Flowers of Tullaghoge', from a popular perfume of that name. The story has often been told of twelve of these new jurors who, on being directed by the Clerk of Assize to take their usual places in Court, made a wild and undignified scramble for the dock.

Carson made a careful study of O'Brien's tactics with jurors. No doubt it was facilitated by the friendship which sprang up between the two men at this time, fostered by the strong spirit of comradeship which prevailed at the Irish Bar. They had previously met outside the Courts, for both were Liberals in politics and kept in touch with the politicians who successively occupied the position of Chief Secretary to the Lord Lieutenant during this period in Dublin Castle. In fact they were present on an occasion when a plot to assassinate one of these Ministers miscarried on the eve of the Phœnix Park murders.

The intended victim was the unfortunate Lord Frederick Cavendish's immediate predecessor, Mr. W. E. Forster, to whose lot as Chief Secretary it had fallen to introduce in the House of Commons a drastic Coercion Act. It was under this agitation that Parnell and his principal associates as well as nearly a thousand of 'the Wild Flowers of Tullaghoge', so aptly described by Forster as 'village ruffians', had been imprisoned without trial. Several attempts were made on his life, from which his escape was little short of miraculous, and he became popularly known as 'Buckshot Forster'. He resigned in the spring of 1882 because he disagreed with the policy of the 'Kilmainham Treaty', by which Parnell and the other imprisoned Home Rulers were released. It was announced that he would leave Dublin on April 19 by the mail train which connected at Kingstown with the steamer for Holyhead.

O'Brien and Carson went along together to Westland Row Station to say good-bye to the departing Chief Secretary. Unknown to them at the time, fifteen members of the murder gang known as the Invincibles, an offshoot of the Fenian organisation, were waiting on the platform to stab the Minister to death as he appeared. However, Forster had got through his work at the Castle that day rather sooner than he anticipated and, at his private secretary's suggestion, he had already left by an earlier train for Kingstown, so as to be able to dine there comfortably before going on board the steamer. Carson learned this news from Mrs. Forster, whom he saw in one of the carriages with her daughter, though he did not realise until the trial of the Phœnix Park murders a year later how he and O'Brien had narrowly missed being spectators of a similar tragedy. "If the Chief Secretary had been there," admitted the informer Carey at that trial, "he would not have been alive today." As it was, Forster's health had been seriously undermined by his gruelling experiences in Ireland, and he had not long to live.

Two other contemporaries of Carson must be mentioned as making headway in their profession at this time, since, not only were they frequently Carson's opponents in the Courts, but they were also soon to be ranged against him in the wider political arena. Like O'Brien they were Catholics, but unlike him they were also Nationalist Members of Parliament and fervent supporters of Parnell. Their names were Healy and Redmond.

Timothy Michael Healy, destined to be the first occupant of Dublin's Viceregal Lodge on the creation of the Irish Free State, was a most remarkable product of his country. A year younger than Carson, he came of peasant stock in County Cork, and he began to earn his living at the age of thirteen, with only the advantages of a primary school education. But he was gifted with an astonishing memory—he could recite most of Shakespeare by heart and once during a spell in prison he memorised the whole of the Bible. He became a railway clerk in Newcastle-on-Tyne, and also worked in a London floor-cloth factory. While in London he contributed a weekly parliamentary letter to the Nationalist *Nation*. This brought him to the attention of Parnell, who was also impressed by the fact that he was an expert shorthand writer, and the Home Rule leader made him his private secretary. A seat in Parliament followed—he was returned unopposed for the borough of Wexford in 1880—and he was then called to the Irish Bar, where his gifts of memory and quick-wittedness soon brought him into good practice.

For instance, he was once opposing a motion for an adjournment which had been frequently made on behalf of the defendant in the action. Healy asserted that the defendant would never be ready to go into Court. "I declare when the last trump sounds on the day of judgment," he added, "the defendant's solicitor will get up and apply for a postponement of the whole proceedings on the ground that he was taken by surprise."

From the beginning of their acquaintance, Healy and Carson were warm friends, though their political sympathies were sharply divided. Indeed throughout his life Healy had a tremendous admiration for Carson's sterling character. "He was a man whose word you could rely on," said Healy on one occasion when Carson was being attacked as a turncoat. "When he said 'Yes' it was 'Yes'; if it was 'No' with him, it meant 'No'. He said 'No' all his life to a United Ireland, more's the pity. But I would trust my soul to Carson."

Several stories are told of their friendly association at this period. After a hard-fought battle on Circuit, they were enjoying a bottle of claret together over a meal in the local inn.

"You know really, Tim," said Carson, "you're quite a decent fellow when you're in good company. Will you tell me why you're such an awful blackguard over there in Westminster?"

"Really, Ned, will you tell me this," replied Healy in as rich a brogue as his companion. "Do you think honestly that any other role would suit me?"

On another occasion, they were on opposing sides in a case concerning the upbringing of a child, one of whose parents was Protestant and the other a Catholic. Each of the Churches claimed the child for its education. Healy won for the Catholic on technical grounds, but when it came to the question of costs Carson spoke so eloquently that no order as to their payment was made.

"That was a wonderful speech you made, Ned," said Healy as they were leaving the Court. "You must have had a grand breakfast to have done it. What did ye have?"

"A bottle of medicine," answered Carson, who was bathed in perspiration.

By contrast with Healy, John Edward Redmond came of an old landed Catholic family, which had been established for many generations in County Wexford. His father had been M.P. for the borough of Wexford. On his death in 1880 the son would have succeeded him but for Parnell's particular desire to bring in Healy, as the Nationalist leader said, "rebuking, restraining, and setting by the prior right of my friend Jack Redmond." However, Parnell did not forget him, and when a vacancy occurred at New Ross in the following year he was elected. A little later he joined the Irish Bar, where he quickly proved himself a born orator, his speeches being masterpieces of diction and beautifully delivered. Though he was eventually to leave the Courts to devote himself entirely to a political career, he made a great reputation for himself during the few years that he was in practice. Though he lacked Carson's powers of insinuating cross-examination and, to some extent, also Carson's acute knowledge of the Irish character, John Redmond was a great advocate and a fine gentleman incapable of any mean or base action. Of all the opponents Carson had to face either in the Courts or in politics, he was perhaps the worthiest and most high-principled.

One story of their early relations is worth repeating, since it illustrated Carson's peculiar gift of writing light verse on the spur of the moment. It concerns a murder trial in which Carson prosecuted and Redmond appeared for the defence. Two youths had gone into a tobacconist's shop in a country district, kept by a poor old woman. Soon afterwards she was found dead. Some tobacco and a few coppers which were stolen from the shop were subsequently found in a loft where the two youths were proved to have slept. Among the coppers was a halfpenny with a hole in it. A witness called by the prosecution stated he had bought a small quantity of tobacco from the old woman not long before her death. Among the coins he had tendered in payment was a holed halfpenny. Redmond put up a most skilful and eloquent defence. When he sat down, he was surprised to receive a piece of paper on which Carson had neatly summarised the opposing arguments in rhyme:

> If a halfpenny is evidence, I think on the whole
> I find in your case a terrible hole,
> If tobacco is evidence, so Redmond spoke,
> I think your case must all end in smoke.

Carson's argument prevailed in the face of Redmond's eloquent efforts, and the jury convicted both of the accused.

It is significant that neither in his early days as a barrister, when he had occasional prosecutions, nor later when he became Crown Prosecutor did Carson ever attempt to secure a conviction by suggesting to the jury that the disturbed state of the country warranted it. He despised such arguments. "You must act on the evidence alone," he would tell the jurors. "You must not speculate, or attempt to find by speculation, a case against the prisoners at the bar."

6

Besides the Courts such as Assizes, in which practice was confined to members of a particular Circuit, there were other Courts like the County Courts which were open to the entire Bar. During his first half-dozen years or so in practice Carson picked up a good deal of work in the open Courts throughout the south-west, in the area covered by the Munster Circuit. This factor eventually led him to consider leaving the Leinster Circuit in favour of the Munster.

Now there is an inflexible Circuit rule, which is the same in Ireland as in England, that unless there is a very special reason a man must stick to his first choice. The fact that he would do better on another Circuit is no grounds for granting his application for transfer. Consequently when Carson applied to join the Munster, he was 'blackballed', although his candidature had been strongly supported by Peter O'Brien, who himself belonged to the Munster. This cast no slur on Carson's character—indeed it was considered a considerable compliment when it became known in Dublin, since it showed that the Munster barristers were plainly afraid of his competition. Nor did this mean that he was altogether debarred from appearing in the Munster's close preserves. By the custom of the profession he could do so if he had a brief marked 'special'; in other words, he must receive, in addition to the normal fee, a special fee of fifty guineas.

As might be expected, relatively few clients could afford the luxury of retaining counsel outside their own Circuits in this way, and such 'special fees' were exceptional. Curiously enough one of the first which Carson received was for a case not on the Munster Circuit, but on the North-East. The case, known as the 'Croagh Orphanage Case', was tried at Belfast Assizes, and it signalled Carson's first visit to the Ulster capital city, with which he was later to become so intimately and prominently associated.

The trial in Belfast was the second trial, following disagreement by the jury at Kildare Assizes on Carson's Circuit, when the venue was changed at the instance of the prosecution. The prisoner, whom Carson defended on each occasion, was an elderly Episcopalian clergyman, the Rev. Mr. Cotton, who had resigned his living in order to take up philanthropic work. He ran an orphanage for Protestant children in the village of Croagh in County Kildare, and the institution was maintained entirely by voluntary subscriptions. Indeed the reverend gentleman spent the greater part of his time travelling around the United Kingdom in search of funds. Unfortunately no accounts were ever published, and, what was worse, the orphanage became overcrowded, most of the children suffered from starvation and neglect, and some of them died as a result of maltreatment. At length this sorry state of affairs came to the attention of the local constabulary, and the prosecution of Mr. Cotton resulted.

Much of what took place in the orphanage was no doubt without Mr. Cotton's knowledge, but of course that did not relieve him of responsibility. Nevertheless an emotional Kildare jury could not bring themselves to convict this venerable and benign-looking old man who came into Court with an ear trumpet and pretended not to hear any awkward questions. The more practical Ulster jury were not so easily taken in. They had little difficulty in finding Mr. Cotton guilty.

The judge at Belfast was the great Chief Baron Palles. As soon as the verdict had been announced Carson rose and addressed the Bench. To the general surprise, he submitted that His Lordship had no jurisdiction to try the case at all on the ground that the indictment presented to the Belfast jury was not identical with that drawn for the Kildare jury. It appeared that in its passage through the Attorney-General's office in Dublin Castle several fresh charges of cruelty or neglect had been added to it. This fact, argued Carson, rendered the Belfast trial of no account.

Most of the onlookers in Court thought the judge would quickly brush aside this objection. But the Chief Baron was a profound lawyer, and his immediate reaction was that there might well be some substance in Carson's submission. "Upon my word, Mr. Carson," he said, "I believe you're right." Having complimented Carson on his learning, the judge went on to say he would reserve sentence until the next Assizes. Meanwhile the question of his jurisdiction would be referred for decision to the Court of Crown Cases Reserved, which was the old appeal tribunal on points of law in criminal cases.

Carson again rose to his feet, to put forward a plea in mitigation of sentence. Never easy at any time, this plea is particularly difficult for an advocate when his client has originally pleaded not guilty. Carson's performance on this occasion is said to have drawn tears from the eyes of several listeners. It was talked about for long afterwards on the North-East Circuit, and it helped to set the seal on his career as a junior at the Irish Bar:

I beseech your Lordship to consider the position of this old man. At the time of disestablishment he, even then advanced in life, sacrificed his own interests in order to promote the interests of the religious body to which he belonged. In all the long period of his ministry there never was a whisper that he was selfish, or avaricious, or careless of the suffering of others. Is it according to our experience of human nature that vicious qualities should suddenly display themselves in a man within the verge of old age? He started the orphanage. Who, entering upon such a course, could reasonably look forward to ease or opulence, and, in heaven's name, who could think that any personal ends could be served by systematic neglect of the orphans?

My client, in engaging in such work, was very ill-advised, especially as he proceeded on the absurd principle—respectable enough in itself, but impossible to be carried out—that, as far as possible, no orphan that applied for admission should be turned away from the orphanage. . . . The number of applicants was very soon so great that even he had to draw the line. . . . There simply was no more room. But worse: happy would it have been for him if the orphanage had been only full—full to overflowing—of reasonably healthy children. But, in carrying out his absurd, if charitable, notion, he received many children that were hopelessly diseased, the offspring of dissolute, debilitated and diseased parents. These beings, wretchedly nourished, even scrofulous, these proved the ruin of the place: for the orphanage funds were not sufficient to provide them with proper food, never to speak of medical attendance, and many were deposited at the orphanage often by selfish relatives who wanted to get rid of them when they should have been sent to a hospital.

Meantime, to obtain funds, this old man was compelled to be as constantly on the road as if he had been a commercial traveller. The orphanage saw very little of him, and, while he toiled to collect funds, the working of the place devolved very much on others. . . . Legally of course my client is guilty . . . but the prerogation of mercy lies with your Lordship.

Pray reflect on the enforced, yet fruitless, hopeless conditions of this old man who in an evil hour for himself and others undertook duties which he very soon found he could neither discharge nor escape from. He went from town to town virtually a beggar, and all the money he obtained he threw into the apparently bottomless pit of the orphanage, only to hear, as he often did, that the expenses incurred in connection with the treatment of scrofulous children alone swallowed up the greater part of this or that considerable remittance. My client was very foolish, hoping always for some turn in his luck; but I find it hard to consider him as a mere vulgar criminal.

I trust implicitly in your Lordship's sense of fair play, your feelings of human sympathy, and perhaps I might venture to add of equity, when you come to pass sentence on this broken old man.

The Court of Crown Cases Reserved affirmed the judge's competence to try the case, although, remarkably enough, the Chief Baron, who was himself a member of this appellate tribunal, delivered a dissenting opinion, thus supporting the arguments advanced by Carson to him at the trial. At the next Assizes the Rev. Mr. Cotton was sentenced to two years' imprisonment, a comparatively light punishment for those severe times. To his disgrace he was again prosecuted for the same offence some time after his release and he was again convicted.

At the time of this first visit to Belfast, Carson naturally had no thought that he would one day lead the proud and uncompromising Ulster people in their heroic struggle to remain within the United Kingdom. Indeed his first impressions were by no means wholly favourable, for he found them blunt, outspoken and obstinate to the point of ill-manners. This feeling was reinforced by an amusing misunderstanding which happened at the time. Carson had been invited to dinner with the judges at the Assize and to reach their lodgings he hired a cab, which proceeded at a leisurely pace. Carson begged the driver to go faster as he was late. "Can't get up the hill," said the cabby in gruff Belfast tones. Carson thought he was telling him to get to Hell instead of expressing his inability to get up the hill which led to their destination.

While he was thus establishing his position as a successful junior barrister, Edward Carson was also adding to his domestic responsibilities. Toward the end of 1885 Annette presented him with another daughter.* This latest addition to the household in Herbert Place received the names of Gladys Isabel, and the event determined Carson on a step which he had been considering for some time. He needed a larger house, and his practice justified moving to a more fashionable part of Dublin.

Accordingly, when the next quarter day had come round, Edward and Annette Carson with their three children and domestic staff migrated to No. 80 Merrion Square, a fine house set in that spacious quadrangle of Georgian buildings which was inhabited by the leading professional men of the city.

* October 20, 1885.

CHAPTER THREE

Crown Prosecutor

I

IN a celebrated speech which he made at Liverpool in 1881, Mr. Gladstone, then Prime Minister for the second time, had denounced Parnell and his associates as "marching through rapine to the disintegration and dismemberment of the Empire". These indeed were their methods and object. Up to this time Royalty visiting Ireland could depend on demonstrations of loyalty throughout most of the country, even from the masses. Her Majesty's health was drunk at every public dinner or banquet. Daniel O'Connell, in spite of his rantings against England, had always been at heart faithful to the British throne. "They may talk of the Queen against O'Connell," he had said at the time of his own prosecution, "but let no man say O'Connell against the Queen."

But this feeling had been changed by Parnell, the Land League and 'Captain Moonlight', with the added stimulus of Irish-American money. At the Lord Mayor's Banquet in Dublin on New Year's Day, 1885, the toast of the Queen was hissed and that of the Lord Lieutenant omitted. A majority of the Dublin Corporation declined to present the Prince of Wales with an address of welcome when he visited the country shortly afterwards, while a flag was officially hoisted over the Mansion House on which the Irish harp appeared without the crown. Meanwhile the Prince met with a rough reception during his tour—something like a riot broke out in Cork, and there were hostile demonstrations along other parts of the royal route. 'God Save the Queen' came to be regarded as a party tune, to which the Nationalist counterpart was 'God Save Ireland'.

Gladstone had long been considering the grant of a measure of local self-government to Ireland. At first he did not wish to see the authority of the Imperial Parliament weakened or compromised in any way. His abandonment of this view and his conversion to Home Rule was unquestionably encouraged by the peculiar condition of the parties at Westminster. By the middle of 1885 Parnell and his Nationalist supporters had come to hold the balance of power between the parties in the House of Commons and were in a position to make and unmake Governments. In June of that year they joined with the Conservatives to defeat the Liberals on the Budget proposals. Mr. Gladstone resigned and was succeeded by the fifty-year-old Marquess of Salisbury, who agreed to head a minority Conservative Administration—a 'Ministry of Caretakers', as it was called—until the General Election, which was due to be held in November.

It was now the turn of the Conservatives to carry on a flirtation with Parnell and his party. The new Government did not renew the Crimes Act, which expired in August, and they brought forward a measure of land purchase which was acceptable to the Nationalist leader. Lord Carnarvon, a nobleman known to have Home Rule sympathies, was appointed Lord Lieutenant, and during the summer he had conversations with Parnell in circumstances which lent them a considerable air of mystery. The negotiations, as it turned out, broke down, since Parnell, who appreciated the position, put up his price, and the Conservatives were unwilling to go the whole length of a separate Irish Parliament. The fact remains, however, that they were prepared to conclude a bargain with Parnell in return for his party's support, which would ensure them a working majority at Westminster.

In Dublin there were more than a few Liberals who believed in the political union of the two countries and were afterwards deeply shocked at what they felt to be an ignominious surrender on Gladstone's part. They included Edward Carson among their number. As the General Election approached they made emphatic protests against any such policy. On November 25, 1885, Carson attended a Liberal meeting, held in the Harbour Division of the city, to support the Conservative candidate, Sir Rowland Blennerhassett. At this meeting, which was addressed by several leading Liberals, a resolution was unanimously passed calling upon all "loyal men irrespective of creed and party" to vote for the Conservative candidate, "being of opinion that the maintenance of the existing Union between Great Britain and Ireland is essential to the well-being of our party."

Carson, who also spoke at this meeting, made his own position quite clear. He said:

I crave your sympathy as a Liberal voter in the St. Stephen's Green Division, who is going to support the Conservative candidate, and who comes here now asking you as a Liberal to vote for the Constitutional candidate. If I am asked why I am here, I would say that the resolution that has been proposed and seconded furnished the answer—it is the necessity of maintaining the Union between England and Ireland . . .

Notwithstanding, however, the taunts of our opponents, I believe we will win, for we have on our side the leading merchants, the leading Liberals, and the leading Conservatives. We are now, thank God, able to meet together on one platform for one common cause.

In Ireland, where the electorate had increased from 200,000 to 700,000 as the result of recent legislation, the Nationalists triumphed at the Election, securing no less than eighty-five out of a total of 103 seats. Elsewhere in the United Kingdom the outcome was disappointing for the Conservatives. The Liberals lost only twenty seats, which put them in a minority of four when faced with the combined strength of Tories and Nationalists.

For the moment Lord Salisbury and his Cabinet continued in office, but with an important qualification of their Irish policy. They decided to oppose Home Rule, and with this end in view the party's fidelity to the Union, previously enunciated by Disraeli, was affirmed in the Queen's Speech, with the customary reading of which the new Parliament was opened in January, 1886. Consequently the Nationalists voted with the Liberals to defeat the Government during the debate on the Address, and by the end of the month the 'Grand Old Man' Gladstone was Prime Minister for the third time. Although he persuaded Mr. Joseph Chamberlain, a convinced Unionist, to join his Ministry, the new Premier had already made up his mind on the dominant question in British politics. He even hoped to win over Chamberlain to his way of thinking.

There were others in the Liberal Party who thought as Chamberlain did. The man who was quickest to realise how these dissident elements in the ranks of the Liberals could be joined with the Conservatives in support of the Union was the brilliant thirty-six-year-old Lord Randolph Churchill, who had been a member of the Salisbury Cabinet which had taken the decision to oppose Home Rule. So much for Great Britain. In Ireland there was another card to play, which was indicated in a letter which Lord Randolph sent to a friend within a few weeks of Gladstone's return to Downing Street. "I decided some time ago that if the G.O.M. went for

Home Rule," he wrote, "the Orange card would be the one to play. Please God, it may turn out the ace of trumps and not the two."*

Lord Randolph lost no time in carrying out his intention. Indeed he had already made arrangements to visit Ulster and address a mass meeting in Belfast. On February 22, 1886, he landed at Larne harbour in County Antrim, where he received a tumultuous greeting from several thousands who were waiting for him at the quayside. At Carrickfergus, through which ancient town his train passed, he spoke to an equally enthusiastic crowd assembled on the station platform. The climax was reached in Belfast's historic Ulster Hall, when he harangued an immense crowd for an hour and a half in a speech which Lord Salisbury publicly alluded to as a brilliantly successful effort and which his son Winston later described as one of the most memorable triumphs of his life. While stirring the Orangemen to the depths of their emotion, he avoided the language of bigotry or intolerance, while at the same time he appealed to the Catholics in the country to stand firm by the Union.

"Her Majesty's Government hesitates," he declared. "Like Macbeth before the murder of Duncan, Mr. Gladstone asks for time. Before he plunges the knife into the heart of the British Empire he reflects, he hesitates. . . . The Loyalists in Ulster should wait and watch—organise and prepare. Diligence and vigilance ought to be your watchword; so that the blow, if it does come, may not come upon you as a thief in the night and may not find you unready and taken by surprise. . . . If it should turn out that the Parliament of the United Kingdom was so recreant from all its high duties, and that the British nation was so apostate to tradition of honour and courage, as to hand over the Loyalists of Ireland to the domination of an Assembly in Dublin which must be to them a foreign and an alien assembly. . . . I do not hesitate to tell you most truly, that in that dark hour there will not be wanting to you those of position and influence in England who would be willing to cast in their lot with you and who, whatever the result, will share your fortunes and your fates."

In his famous peroration he quoted a verse from the poet Thomas Campbell which, by altering a single word, he adapted with great skill and effect to the occasion.

* Winston S. Churchill. *Lord Randolph Churchill*, II, 59. The passage is unfortunately misquoted by Marjoribanks in his *Life of Lord Carson*, at p. 87.

The combat deepens, on, ye brave
Who rush to glory or the grave.
Wave, Ulster—all thy banners wave,
And charge with all thy chivalry.

A few weeks later Lord Randolph Churchill reiterated his views in a letter to a Liberal M.P. which received considerable publicity, containing, as it did, a phrase destined long to be remembered. "If political parties and political leaders," he wrote, "should be so utterly lost to every feeling and dictate of honour and courage as to hand over coldly the lives and liberties of the Loyalists of Ireland to their hereditary and most bitter foes, make no doubt on this point—Ulster will not be a consenting party. Ulster at the proper moment will resort to the supreme arbitrament of force; *Ulster will fight, Ulster will be right*; Ulster will emerge from the struggle victorious, because all that Ulster represents to us Britons will command the sympathy and support of an enormous section of our British community, and also, I feel certain, will attract the admiration and approval of free and civilised nations."

These memorable words, as well as the rest of their author's historic speech in Belfast, produced a deep impression in all quarters of the United Kingdom. In Ulster they sowed the seeds of a local defence movement. However, this militant organisation was to grow slowly. The Ulster people were as yet unorganised and they lacked a leader. The leader was not to emerge until another quarter of a century had gone by, but when he did appear, in the person of a barrister who at the time of Lord Randolph Churchill's Belfast speech was largely unknown in the North except to the local Bar, he was to formulate his own arguments on the pattern so spectacularly fashioned by the Conservative statesman. For the moment Carson pondered deeply on these historic utterances. He applauded Lord Randolph's subsequent appeal for a coalition against Home Rule and he supported his plea that all opponents of the contemplated measure should adopt the generic name of 'Unionists' to show that they belonged to 'the party of the Union'. Here too he was at one with Joseph Chamberlain.

Meanwhile Gladstone was pushing ahead with his scheme for the 'better Government of Ireland'. On April 8 the Home Rule Bill was given its first reading in the House of Commons. It provided for a Parliament in Dublin with jurisdiction in purely local affairs and an Irish Executive responsible to it. Taxation, defence, foreign relations, coinage and the postal service were reserved to the

Imperial Parliament. In respect of these reserved services Ireland was to make a contribution to the Imperial exchequer of over £3 millions annually. And she was to have no representation at Westminster. These arrangements were approved in principle by Parnell and the Nationalist Party.

In reality the Liberals were hopelessly split on the Home Rule issue. From his home in Birmingham, Joseph Chamberlain launched the Liberal-Unionist Association to combat the Bill. In the division on the Bill's second reading on June 7, Chamberlain led ninety-three of his 'Liberal-Unionist' sympathisers, including John Bright, into the Opposition lobby. In the result the second reading was defeated by thirty votes. The Home Rule Bill was wrecked. Dissolution and another General Election quickly followed.

An incident occurred at this time in Carson's life for which he was later to be bitterly assailed. For some time past his name had been before the committee of the National Liberal Club in London for election as a country member to that once celebrated institution. He was duly elected on June 2, 1886, that is to say, two months after the introduction of the Home Rule Bill and five days before its defeat on the second reading. His political opponents, notably the Nationalist, Joseph Devlin, were later to allege that he was in reality 'an ardent Home Ruler' at this time and only embraced the Unionist cause for the sake of office under a Conservative Administration 'when the forces of honour and justice were beaten'.

Carson's language was not too strong when he branded this charge as 'an infamous lie'. Indeed his sympathies had always been for the maintenance of the Union. We have seen how, in the election campaign of the previous November, he had joined with the Dublin Liberals in supporting a local Conservative candidate on this issue. Then, when Joseph Chamberlain formed the Liberal-Unionist Association, he gave the new organisation his full support. He became a founder-member of the Dublin branch, and also a founder-member of the Liberal-Unionist Club in London. As for his membership of the National Liberal Club, this was quite consistent in any Liberal holding Unionist views. He was proposed by Mr. Cecil Roche, a well-known Resident Magistrate and one of the most vigorous opponents of Home Rule in Southern Ireland. Later on, of course, Home Rule did become a fundamental plank in the Liberal platform, when Chamberlain's Liberal-Unionist followers gradually became merged in the Conservative ranks. At the time, however, candidates for election to the National Liberal Club were not required to sign anything in the nature of a declaration pledging support to the Home Rule policy, which Mr. Devlin was later erroneously to assert. Besides Devlin, two Liberal M.P.s, Mr. J. M. Roberts and Mr. Hamar Greenwood (afterwards Lord Greenwood), were to attack Carson on the point during the Home Rule crisis in 1912, and Greenwood was to initiate a correspondence in *The Times*, to which Carson was to reply with some acerbity. Indeed Greenwood made considerable play with the statement that, having joined the National Liberal Club, Carson only became an opponent of Home Rule after he had made up his mind 'that Home Rule was no go' and had accepted an appointment as Crown Prosecutor in Ireland. This suggestion was "as contemptible as it is untrue", protested Carson; "the Club at that time was just as strongly Liberal-Unionist as Liberal", he wrote in the course of this correspondence, "and every effort was being made to retain Liberal-Unionists in the Club".*

Meanwhile Carson again openly declared his Unionist views. In the Election, which took place in July, 1886, he spoke in support of Sir Edward Sullivan, later Lord Chancellor of Ireland, who stood as a Liberal-Unionist for the St. Stephen's Green Division, where Carson was a voter, and he also campaigned in South Dublin for Mr. Jonathan Pim, one of the city's leading Liberals, who had joined Mr. Chamberlain's colours. This time it was a Tory landslide. With their Liberal-Unionist allies, of whom seventy-eight were returned, the Conservatives secured a majority of 218 over the combined strength of the Liberals and Irish Nationalists. Lord Salisbury went back to Downing Street. The remedy he now proposed for Ireland was twenty years of resolute government. Curiously enough, with one short break, twenty years was the period the Unionists were to remain in office.

2

The first task confronting the new Government in Ireland was to maintain the law impartially as between northern Orangemen and southern Nationalists. It was no easy task. During the Home Rule debates feeling between the rival factions in Belfast, encouraged by Lord Randolph Churchill's rhetoric, rose to fever pitch. Explosions

* Carson resigned on October 21, 1887. Further details will be found in the letters of Greenwood and Carson, published in *The Times*, Jan. 29, Feb. 15, 1912.

ANNETTE CARSON.
Carson's first wife.

From a portrait by an unknown artist in the possession of the Hon. Mrs. Walter Carson.

A. J. BALFOUR.

From the portrait by L. Alma-Tadema in the National Portrait Gallery.

followed in the form of serious rioting, which continued intermittently throughout the summer. The trouble began on the day following the rejection of the Home Rule Bill, when the inhabitants of the strongly Protestant working-class district of Shankill lit bonfires in the streets to celebrate the event. The police proceeded to stamp them out. This action naturally infuriated the crowd, who attacked the police with paving stones which they ripped up and any other missiles they could lay hands on. The police fired back and there were many casualties. A coroner's jury brought in a verdict of wilful murder against the R.I.C.—'Morley's murderers', as they were popularly called from the fact that the Liberal John Morley was Chief Secretary at the time. The Catholics of the equally strong Nationalist Falls Road area joined in the fray. The city was in a state of siege, and many of the dead were secretly buried in back yards.

These riots, tragic and terrible as they were, did not lack their lighter side. The story is told of one rioter who caught a policeman and, holding his head down, proceeded to batter him. Presently a second rioter appeared on the scene.

"What have you there, mate?"

"A policeman."

"Hold on," said the second rioter, "and let me have a thump at him."

"Get along out o' that," shouted the first between the thumps, "and find a policeman for yerself."

It was unfortunate that the Ulster Unionists at that time had no leader round whom they could rally and who could exercise a restraining influence upon their more exuberant elements. Carson, on whose mind these events made a deep impression, realised that the Unionist movement in Ulster, if it was to succeed in its object, must be disciplined and orderly. Meanwhile, with the appointment of a new Lord Lieutenant and a new Chief Secretary, the Belfast riots subsided and the city resumed its normal peaceful existence.

For the Viceregal Lodge Lord Salisbury chose the thirty-three-year-old Marquess of Londonderry, a popular nobleman who had previously sat in the House of Commons and who possessed strong Ulster family and territorial connections. Unlike Lord Carnarvon, Lord Londonderry was a convinced Unionist. Indeed he claimed kinship with that Lord Castlereagh to whom more than any other statesman of his time is due the credit for having placed the original Act of Union on the statute book, a factor which the Conservative Prime Minister seems to have had in mind when he made the selection. He was accompanied to Dublin by his young wife Theresa, a daughter of the Earl of Shrewsbury, a woman of striking beauty and forceful personality, who did much to advance her husband's interests and the interests of her friends. Their love of horses and patronage of racing endeared them to the masses, while their hospitable entertaining at the Castle and 'the Viceregal' made them generally liked in the higher ranks of society. Among those to whom they sent out invitations were Edward Carson and his wife. For him the occasion was the beginning of a friendship which was to last throughout the remainder of their lives.

The new Chief Secretary was Sir Michael Hicks-Beach, an experienced and assiduous Conservative politician of middle age who had held the same post twelve years previously under Disraeli; known familiarly as 'Black Michael', he had the reputation of being somewhat dour and bad-tempered. He was also suspected of unduly favouring the Nationalists at the expense of the landlords. That there was some truth in this latter belief appeared when he attempted to withhold from the landlords the protection of military or police in carrying out evictions. This brought him into conflict with the Lord Lieutenant, himself a considerable landlord, as well as with Chief Baron Palles, who plainly hinted that he would find himself in gaol if he persisted in this course. Perhaps it was fortunate for him that at this moment Hicks-Beach developed acute eye trouble, which led him to send in his resignation to Lord Salisbury and quit the Chief Secretary's Office.

This office had now come to be generally regarded as the grave of political reputations, and in the two days which followed Hicks-Beach's resignation there was considerable speculation as to whom Salisbury would next choose for this invidious post. Many could hardly believe their ears when they heard that he was to be the Prime Minister's nephew, Arthur Balfour, a comparatively young man hitherto more interested in philosophical abstractions than practical politics, whose delicate appearance had earned him the nickname of the 'Tiger Lily'. The Irish Nationalists at Westminster expressed delight, convinced they would make short work of the newcomer. "We have killed Forster and blinded Beach," they said. "What shall we do to Balfour?"

The Irish Members were to get the surprise of their lives. If the new Chief Secretary's talents were a secret to the outside world, it is reasonable to assume that his uncle in Downing Street was well aware of them. At the time of his appointment Arthur James

Balfour was thirty-eight years old, and was the author of several works on philosophy. He had been in Parliament for the past thirteen years, had held various minor offices and had recently as Secretary for Scotland been promoted to Cabinet work. For a time he had associated himself with Lord Randolph Churchill and his 'Fourth Party', but had eventually found that political meteor's views too Radical for his liking. In office he had served conscientiously but without any particular distinction, giving the impression that he preferred philosophy to the House of Commons. With a certain air of languorous grace about him, he appealed essentially to the few rather than the many—indeed he was not strong in what is known as 'the common touch'.

Now was his great political opportunity and he grasped it with both hands. Passed as fit by his doctor, he immediately caught the mail train to Holyhead, crossed to Dublin and was sworn in by Lord Londonderry, the Lord Lieutenant, whom he described in a fragment of autobiography as "long my friend and once my fag at Eton". He then returned to Westminster to introduce the most drastic and comprehensive Crimes Bill which ever reached the statute book.

The latest development in the Irish scene which necessitated this legislation was the notorious 'Plan of Campaign', invented by the Nationalist propagandist M.P., William O'Brien, and launched towards the end of 1886. Under this scheme the tenants on each estate would put aside a sum which they thought a reasonable rent, offer it in bulk to the landlord, declining to pay him anything at all if he refused it. Such moneys were then used to assist any tenant who might be evicted. The 'Plan' was immediately put into operation on forty estates, and any reluctance on the part of the tenants to co-operate was overcome by the old and tried methods of boycotting and intimidation applied by the Land League.

These methods were exemplified in a murder trial which opened at Wicklow Assizes on March 28, 1887. The evidence revealed by its proceedings afforded ample proof of the need of the new Irish Crimes Bill, which by a noteworthy coincidence was introduced by Arthur Balfour in the House of Commons on the same day. Peter O'Brien, recently appointed Solicitor-General for Ireland, led for the Crown in this trial; he had Edward Carson with him as junior counsel.

Two young men, Daniel Hayes and Daniel Moriarty, were accused of murdering a farmer named James Fitzmaurice early one morning, about three months previously, outside the village of Lixnaw, near Tralee, in County Kerry. The murdered man had been 'boycotted' at the instance of his thriftless brother Edmund, who had appealed to the Land League. It appeared that the two brothers had farmed the land together as joint tenants and had both been evicted owing to Edmund's falling into arrears with his rent. James, however, managed to redeem the arrears and took possession of the whole property, although he offered to give his brother a third share of it and stock it for him, an offer which Edmund contemptuously refused. Edmund then persuaded the local secretary of the Land League, whose name was James Dowling, to get a resolution passed calling on the public to treat the unfortunate James as 'a landgrabber of the most infamous kind'. As a result James was given police protection, but unfortunately for himself he saw fit to dispense with it on the night of his murder. The crime took place on the road as he was driving to market. At the time he was accompanied by his daughter, Norah, who subsequently identified the accused as the murderers to the police authorities. At the trial she proved an unsatisfactory and even reluctant witness, her identification of the prisoner was unconvincing, and she seemed in a state bordering on panic.

By the law then in force the prisoners could not give evidence on their own behalf. Their defence was an alibi, and it was supported by the parish priest, who swore that he had talked with Norah Fitzmaurice on the morning after the murder and she had admitted to him that she did not know the murderers. However, according to the priest, she had described their appearance, stating that one was like a neighbour named Cavell, who happened to be in Court and was totally unlike either of the accused.

O'Brien left the cross-examination of this witness to his junior, and in the process Carson succeeded in throwing a different light on the priest's previous testimony. The priest admitted that he had cautioned the girl on several occasions and it soon appeared that Norah's reluctance was explained by her pastor's repeated admonitions.

Hoping to save his neck, Moriarty now offered to turn Queen's Evidence and inculpate his companion. At the time this offer was made both prisoners had been taken back to their cells for the night. Carson was also in bed and he was wakened by the Crown solicitor, who required his advice, as Moriarty had made a written and signed confession. Carson was of the opinion that the jury would convict both prisoners and he disliked the idea of one of them escaping the gallows in this manner. O'Brien, when consulted, was not disposed to agree, but finally came over to his junior's way of thinking. As soon as his offer had been refused Moriarty attempted to commit suicide by cutting his throat with glass he had obtained from breaking his cell window. A warder had heard the sound of broken glass, rushed to the cell and prevented him from achieving his purpose in the nick of time.

As events turned out, Carson was right in his judgment. The jury brought in a verdict of guilty against the two prisoners and they both went to the scaffold, Moriarty withdrawing his confession before the execution. Afterwards Dowling, the local Secretary of the Land League, organised a 'boycott' of Norah Fitzmaurice, for which he was subsequently prosecuted under the Crimes Act and awarded a sentence of six months' imprisonment.

The new Crimes Act became law in July, 1887. It gave power to the Lord Lieutenant to 'proclaim' any association as 'dangerous' and suppress it; the Executive could also 'proclaim' any district, with the result that criminal trials which would ordinarily have taken place there could be removed to another part of the country and be placed before a 'special jury' with a property qualification in preference to the more usual 'common' jury. In addition, the Act made certain offences such as conspiracy, intimidation, unlawful assembly and obstructing officers of the law punishable on summary conviction before the Resident Magistrate. This meant that these serious offences could henceforth be tried without a jury. Furthermore, witnesses could be compelled to give evidence in such a Court, even though such evidence might tend to incriminate them.

If this Act was to be administered effectively, it was clear to the legal department in Dublin Castle that a resolute Crown Prosecutor should be selected to undertake the Court work which it involved. Peter O'Brien had been greatly impressed by Carson's previous appearances for the Crown, and he strongly recommended his brother Law Officer, John Gibson, the Attorney-General, to select Carson. Accordingly, a few days after the Crimes Act received the Royal Assent in Parliament, Edward Carson was appointed Counsel to the Attorney-General for Ireland or, in the current legal jargon, 'Attorney's Devil'.

Thus at the age of thirty-three Edward Carson found himself cast in what was to prove a most difficult and dangerous role as well as an extremely responsible one. Its discharge in dramatic and often sensational circumstances during the next four years was to make him known throughout the length and breadth of Ireland as 'Coercion Carson'.

3

The first prosecution under the new Crimes Act, which it fell to Edward Carson to conduct, took place at Mitchelstown in County Cork. The neighbourhood had previously been 'proclaimed' following on an attempt of William O'Brien, M.P., to put the 'Plan of Campaign' into operation on the estate of the Countess of Kingston. The Attorney-General with Balfour's approval decided to proceed against O'Brien and a fellow M.P. named John Mandeville on a charge of conspiracy. The two Nationalists, who were out on bail, were duly summoned to appear before the Resident Magistrate's Court at Mitchelstown on September 9, 1887. They decided to hold a mass meeting in the town with the object of inciting Lady Kingston's tenants to further resistance. The meeting was held and developed into a serious riot. The police fired on the crowd, several lives were lost and the incident was magnified into a ghastly massacre. Gladstone's memorable phrase, 'Remember Mitchelstown', was taken up eagerly and became a Home Rule battle-cry. Indeed Mitchelstown was destined to be 'remembered' vividly, but alas it was not by any means 'remembered' either calmly or accurately.

Carson had slept the previous night in Fermoy, since local feeling was such that it had been impossible for the Crown counsel to obtain accommodation at any inn in Mitchelstown. He drove over early in the morning, accompanied by the Crown solicitor for the county, from whom he received his professional instructions. On approaching the town he saw the roads and lanes were dense with people on their way to the mass meeting. Many of them were on horseback and all were armed with heavy sticks. Carson put the numbers at 4,000, though according to other sources they were more. At all events their size and demeanour were such as to alarm the car driver when he saw them.

"This is a dangerous business, yer honour," said the man to Carson. "Do you mind if I throw up my cap and say 'Three cheers for William O'Brien'?"

"Not in the least," replied Carson nonchalantly, as the driver made haste to suit his action to his words.

Arrived at the Court House, Carson looked round and saw no sign of the prisoners, who did not appear, to surrender to their bail. In fact they were haranguing the crowd some little distance away in the town square. Carson then applied to the Bench for warrants for their arrest. "What about a warrant for an M.P. when the House is sitting?" asked one of the magistrates nervously. Carson explained that this made no difference. The warrants were issued and the Court adjourned. The Crown Prosecutor was urged by the police to leave by a side door, as they refused to be responsible for his safety once the news of the issue of the warrants got about. Carson refused. "The King's highway was made for all, and by that I will go or not at all," he replied and promptly stepped out of the building into the main street.

An immense crowd, sullen and hostile, thronged the street. Several people asked him if the warrant for William O'Brien's arrest had been issued and he replied that it had. But impressed by his bold and courageous bearing, the crowd made no attempt to interfere with him. They did not even jeer or demonstrate as Carson walked slowly through their ranks in the direction of the entrance to the Kingston estate, Mitchelstown Castle, at the upper end of the town. Then he heard sounds of cheering and bands in the distance, which turned out to be the procession which had gone to meet the two M.P.s outside the town and was now returning. As they passed the Castle gates where Carson was standing, they indulged in loud booing and shook their fists and sticks in his direction. Carson then walked into the temporary police barracks near-by, where he was joined by Captain Seagrave, one of the Resident Magistrates. While they were talking a police constable came running up to say that the County Inspector wanted the R.M. in the town, where trouble had started. As Captain Seagrave turned to go, several shots were fired in the distance.

As he approached the square, Carson met people running away in every direction, a good many with signs of having been severely handled by the police. In the square itself he found that the mob had been dispersed, and that about forty police were drawn up there, while others were standing near the main barracks. The police presented a very battered appearance. Most of them were bleeding, many of them seemed to have been knocked down, as their backs were covered with mud. Carson also noticed that the windows of the priest's house were broken, but this turned out to be from stones hurled at some of the police who had taken refuge there. Among those who remained in the square was John Dillon, the Nationalist M.P., who had been addressing the meeting. In the account of the affair which Carson wrote the next day he noted that this individual "appeared very much cowed and looked more wretched than usual". In fact he came up to Carson and asked whether he was the R.M. On learning that he was not, Dillon then complained that there was no officer in charge. This, however, was untrue. Both the County Inspectors of the R.I.C. were present and within view near the barracks, not to mention two head constables as well as the R.M.

Outside the barracks, where the police were likewise drawn up, Carson saw a man lying dead within a few feet of the battered door and broken windows. He asked some of the bystanders to remove the body to the nearest public-house, but they refused, while the publican, who had been asked, declined to admit the corpse. Meanwhile the police remained quite calm, and there was no attempt on the part of the crowd to congregate again. Indeed within a few minutes of the shots having been fired they were running away in all directions. As for the prisoners whose intended trial had been a contributory cause of the rioting, their conduct at this stage was described by Carson as 'very bad': they kept walking up to any police they saw engaged with the rioters, asking their names and ranks and 'attempting to interfere'.

From the carman who had driven him into Mitchelstown that morning as well as several others with whom he spoke, Carson was able to piece together the full story of what had happened.

The meeting was held in the square. As the crowd was being addressed by Dillon from a wagonette, an official Government reporter appeared on the scene to take a note of what was said. The crowd then proceeded to stone the police who were somewhat rashly endeavouring to escort the reporter to within earshot of the speaker. As further reinforcements of police arrived, the mounted peasantry rode them down and trampled them underfoot. In their retreat to their barracks the police then fired the volley which caused two fatal casualties. But it also had the effect of dispersing the crowd and restoring order. "It struck me that there was the utmost consternation inspired by the firing of the police," noted Carson at the time, "and I am inclined to think that they will be slow again to molest them in this district."

On his return to Dublin, Carson wrote an account of the day's happenings. Although he did this in a 'great hurry', as he subsequently admitted, at Lord Chancellor Ashbourne's suggestion, the report was forwarded to John Gibson, the Attorney-General, who was with the Chief Secretary in London. "I think so far as the people are concerned," wrote Carson in his covering letter to Gibson, "the firing will have a satisfactory result." The Attorney-General passed on the document to Balfour, who had it before him when he was called upon to defend the action of the police in the House of Commons a few days later.*

Looking back on this episode in his old age more than forty years later, Carson told Balfour's niece, Mrs. Dugdale, that he felt the affair had been badly muddled. There were insufficient police and no preparations to cope with the mass meeting. "On top of that," he added, "the few police there were tried to push the Government reporter through the crowd. It was lunacy." At the same time he expressed his admiration for the way in which the affair and its aftermath were handled by the Chief Secretary, who was henceforth to be known by Nationalists and Liberals alike as 'Bloody Balfour', while he himself began to be called 'Coercion Carson'. Balfour, according to Carson, "never boggled about anything. He simply backed his own people up. After that there wasn't an official in Ireland who didn't worship the ground he walked on." Consequently he paid no attention to the verdict of wilful murder which, after an inquest lasting seventeen days, the local coroner's jury found against the County Inspector and five of his constabulary.

In short, said Carson afterwards, "It was Mitchelstown that made us certain we had a man at last."

4

No time was lost in executing the warrants and the two M.P.s were lodged in Cork Jail. O'Brien's journey to Mitchelstown to stand his trial a fortnight later took on something in the nature of a triumphal procession. Huge cheering crowds lined the roadside, all the pretty girls in the neighbourhood presented him with bouquets of flowers, and the people came out from their cottages waving green boughs as the prisoners passed by, strongly escorted by a troop of dragoons. Arrived at the Court House, which was also strongly guarded, O'Brien presented a striking spectacle, as he was covered with dust from head to foot. Here he was met by many sym-

* *See* B. E. C. Dugdale, *Arthur James Balfour*, I, 141–143. The original is among the Balfour Papers in the British Museum.

pathisers, including John Dillon, M.P., and his counsel Tim Harrington, who was also a Nationalist M.P. as well as Secretary of the National League.* Soon the small court-room was packed to suffocation. "Who's that?" asked the prisoner as the Crown Prosecutor came in. "That's Carson," replied Harrington. O'Brien gazed hard at the tall figure before him. "He looks very young," he commented. It was the first time O'Brien had set eyes on this "liverish young man" as Carson also appeared to him, "with the complexion of one fed on vinegar and with features as inexpressive as a jagged hatchet." They were destined to encounter each other in many an eventful hour to come.

Barely thirty-five years old at this time, William O'Brien possessed one of the most remarkable personalities in the Nationalist Party. Exceptionally gifted as a speaker, a political organiser and a writer, he easily ranked next to Parnell as the leader of the patriotic movement. As a mob orator he was unrivalled, the 'Plan of Campaign' had been the offspring of his fertile genius, and in editing *United Ireland* he had made this weekly the most militant political journal ever published in Ireland. Its cartoons were extremely pungent and spared nobody, from the police and bailiffs who had to carry out the evictions to the Lord Lieutenant's Chief Secretary, who "lusted for slaughter with a eunuchized imagination". Founded six years previously, this journal had already achieved great notoriety through its exposure during Lord Spencer's viceroyalty in 1883 of the celebrated 'Dublin Castle scandals', in which Mr. Gustavus C. Cornwall, Secretary of the Post Office, Detective-Inspector James Ellis French, and others prominent in Government circles at the time were denounced by O'Brien as operating a club of homosexuals in the capital. After O'Brien had successfully defended a libel action brought against him by Cornwall and sundry prosecutions had followed, a correspondent wrote a letter to *United Ireland*, which the editor published, suggesting that Earl Spencer, the Lord Lieutenant, should be raised a step in the peerage, "with the appropriate title of the Duke of Sodom and Gomorrah".

At the sitting of the Court Harrington submitted that his client could not be tried for two speeches on a single information. The Court ruled against him, and Carson proceeded to deal with both speeches in his opening. Harrington was continually on his feet

* Timothy Charles Harrington (1851–1910) was described at this time by an English visitor, Wilfrid Scawen Blunt, as 'very amusing with astonishing go and impudence'. He later became Lord Mayor of Dublin.

protesting, "This is an effort to prejudice the case of my client." Carson was not in the least put out by this interruption. "That is the usual blather," he said, and went on with his speech. Soon opposing counsel were at each other hammer and tongs.

"I denounce this," shouted Harrington, "as an outrage on the liberty of my friend."

"I will submit to any ruling the Bench make," replied Carson, "but the remarks about outrage on liberty I treat with contempt."

"I would advise you not to indulge in language of that kind, as I am a capital hand at it myself."

"That is only the emanation of an excited mind, and I don't heed it."

The principal Crown witnesses were the police officers who had taken a note of O'Brien's speeches. Harrington raised every kind of objection, and the proceedings rapidly tended to become farcical.

"Oh, go on," said Carson under his breath, "this is proper humbug."

"It is not a proper humbug," declared Harrington, who had overheard the remark. "You are a humbug to use such language."

"Don't address me, please," retorted Carson sharply.

"I have not the slightest ambition to have a lifelong acquaintance with you," hissed Harrington.

Carson smiled grimly. "It looks as if you did."

At this point the witness, who was in the box, observed that he had left the meeting "when it began to stir".

HARRINGTON: "That's an Irish answer anyway."

CARSON: "It's none the worse for that."

HARRINGTON: "I'm very glad you're so good an Irishman."

CARSON: "As good as you."

A little later O'Brien's counsel attacked the Crown Prosecutor as being low, mean, contemptible, venal and corrupt. "You think by this display," Harrington taunted, "you will get some position from the Tory Government, for whom you are doing this job."

This sally provoked such loud applause among the spectators in the public gallery that the Resident Magistrates ordered the Court to be cleared. This was accordingly done and the trial proceeded.

In the course of the evidence of one of the police officers it transpired that another report of O'Brien's speech, which was in the possession of the authorities, had been marked 'Not to be used'. This fact, which was elicited by Harrington in cross-examination, was originally made known to him by a Nationalist sympathiser who worked in Dublin Castle. There was no sinister significance in the withholding of this second report: it was probably not as full as the one which was put in evidence. But Harrington made a great issue of it, claiming that it was deliberately suppressed by the Crown. "I am saying that it is the prosecution who are doing it," he declared with an air of injured innocence. "I say it was deliberately suppressed for the purpose of making it more easy to imprison my friend."

Carson was on his feet in a moment.

"That is a pure fabrication."

"That is a lie, sir," Harrington shouted back.

At this point the Bench threatened to have Harrington removed from Court. But the ebullient defence counsel, who had carefully prepared this scene beforehand so as to give his client an opportunity of addressing the Court, thereupon announced that he would remove himself and take no further part in such farcical proceedings. He flung down his papers in a melodramatic gesture and solemnly stalked out of the court-room, followed by his solicitor. The Court then adjourned and the prisoner was taken back to gaol. As he himself was leaving to the accompaniment of the boos and hisses of the crowd outside, Carson could barely conceal an expression of annoyance at the action of some of the troops on guard in hoisting their shakos on to the tops of their rifles and giving O'Brien a hearty cheer on his way.

However, a threat of violence to his own person left him unmoved. Another Nationalist M.P. who was present, fiery little Dr. Tanner, rushed up to Carson and shook his fist in his face. "You are a mean ruffianly coward," he spat at him, "and I'll take care that before you leave Mitchelstown your head and both your legs will be smashed."

Back in his cell O'Brien spent the evening singing patriotic songs with his fellow prisoners, so loudly indeed that the gaoler was obliged to come in and administer a peculiarly Irish caution. "Gentlemen," he told them, "I don't wish to interfere with your diversions, but I would remark that there is an echo in this place and I'm afraid you'll be heard by them bloody Bobbies outside."

Next morning O'Brien had the limelight to himself, when he conducted his own defence in vigorous but largely irrelevant language. He had two tones in his voice, one low, soft and appealing, the other strident and declamatory. He used both to great effect. But his oratory availed him nothing. He was convicted on the clearest evidence and, along with his fellow prisoner, sentenced to three months' imprisonment. Both men immediately gave notice of appeal and they were then released on bail.

The appeal was heard soon afterwards at Midleton Quarter Sessions. Here the proceedings opened with an amusing incident. A telegram in the official Government cypher was handed to the Crown solicitor. It purported to come from Peter O'Brien in Dublin Castle, instructing Carson, for reasons that would later be communicated to him, to have the appeal adjourned to the next Sessions. This would have meant a further respite of three months for the prisoners. Carson, who felt that the telegram could not possibly have been sent by the Solicitor-General, decided to disregard it. "It's not genuine," he whispered to the Crown Solicitor, "it's forgery." He was soon proved right. One of O'Brien's friends in the Dublin Post Office had got hold of the cypher key and had concocted the message as a joke.

Various versions of the telegram were subsequently published in the Nationalist *Freeman's Journal* and alleged to have been sent to Carson, so that both Peter O'Brien and Carson had to write to that newspaper pointing out that they had not been in touch with each other at any time during Carson's absence from Dublin. As soon as he got home Carson sent the following letter to the editor:

80 *Merrion Square,*
3rd October, 1887.

SIR,

With reference to the telegram alleged in today's issue of your newspaper to have been sent to me by the Solicitor-General, I beg to state that I never received any such telegram, or any to a like effect. I had no communication by telegram or letter or otherwise, direct or indirect, from the Solicitor-General from the time I left Dublin to conduct the Mitchelstown prosecutions until my return.

The whole story is absolutely false.

Your obedient servant,
EDWARD CARSON.

Eventually after more appeals and delays, designed, as O'Brien subsequently admitted, to gain time so that he could continue the conduct of the Plan of Campaign, the convictions were upheld and the two prisoners had to serve their sentence. Unfortunately Mandeville died in prison, though his death was in no way related to the treatment he received there. O'Brien, on the other hand, carried on the battle from his cell and lent a touch of comedy to his confinement by refusing to wear the prison trousers provided for him.

His own trousers were consequently removed, and for some time he lay semi-nude on his plank bed until a pair of Marney tweed breeches were smuggled in by a warder, and these he was allowed to keep after the matter had been referred to the Chief Secretary.

By men like Tim Harrington and Dr. Tanner, and even occasionally O'Brien himself, all these proceedings were treated in a lighthearted manner, compared with serious-minded Nationalists like John Dillon. "However tragic the Irish struggle may be to Dillon," noted an English visitor of Nationalist sympathies at the time, "to them it is an excellent farce, in which they play their parts admirably to an ever laughing and delighted audience."*

5

Soon after Mitchelstown, when Carson had returned to Dublin, the new Chief Secretary asked Lord Chancellor Ashbourne to give a dinner so that he could meet the members of the Irish Bar. The dinner duly took place. Balfour was taken round and introduced to each guest by the Attorney-General, John Gibson, who was a brother of the Chancellor. On reaching Carson the Chief Secretary paused and looked hard at the tall spare young man before him with the determined expression and deep blue eyes who was but a few years his junior. "So you're Edward Carson," he said, "I am very glad to meet you. There's a great deal I should like to say to you."

Later they met and talked together. From the beginning of their acquaintance, which was destined to ripen into a lifelong friendship, the barrister was strongly drawn to the politician. He was captivated by the charm of Balfour's manner and the knowledge of the world and affairs which his cultured mind expressed, so different from the talk he was accustomed to hearing on the Leinster Circuit or round the library fire in the Four Courts. Looking back on this meeting many years later, Carson told a friend: "I wish I could give you any notion of the impression he made on me the first time he came over, at any rate the first time I met him. I was only a provincial lawyer, and, till I saw A.J.B., as he was then, I had never guessed that such an animal could exist. I had never seen anybody like him—nobody in Dublin had." Well might Carson wonder, for rarely have such elegance of manner and the social graces been combined with such determination and strength of character in a single personality.

* W. S. Blunt *The Land War in Ireland* (1912), at p. 324.

Though he did not as a rule care much for lawyers, Balfour on his side took a strong liking for the new Crown Prosecutor. He immediately decided to make the fullest use of his services in the difficult and dangerous work of pacifying the country. The outcome of their association at this time was thus described by Balfour to his niece many years afterwards. "I made Carson in a way. I made Carson and he made me," he said. "I've told you how no one had courage. Everybody right up to the top was trembling. Some of the R.M.s were splendid, but on the whole it was an impossible state of affairs. Carson had nerve, however. I sent him all over the place, prosecuting, getting convictions. We worked together."

No one was spared, no matter how highly placed. As one Nationalist put it, if a man made a speech to which Dublin Castle took exception and was prosecuted by Carson, he might just as well make arrangements for six months in Kilmainham Gaol before he went into Court. One of the most spectacular of such prosecutions was that of Dublin's Lord Mayor, the Right Honourable T. D. Sullivan, which occurred not long after the Mitchelstown affair, on October 6, 1887. The Lord Mayor was well known as a poet and propagandist in the Nationalist cause: he had written the celebrated patriot song 'God Save Ireland', and he edited the notorious *Nation*, in which he had published reports of meetings of the suppressed National League. The city council decided to attend the Court in state, which they did in a carriage procession which included the Lord Mayor in his robes, attended by his civic officer bearing the sword and mace. The city fathers together with the sword-bearer attempted to take up their place in front of the dock, but this was not allowed by the Bench and they were reluctantly compelled to withdraw to the gallery.

The Mayor, cleverly defended by Tim Healy, was acquitted on a legal technicality. The policeman who deposed to the holding of the meeting at which Sullivan had spoken was unable to give any account of the speeches delivered, since he had not heard them. Healy argued that this was fatal to the prosecution and the magistrate dismissed the case. No evidence had been adduced, Healy said, to show that the meeting had any connexion with the National League. For all that appeared to the contrary it might have assembled to make arrangements for the building of a spire to the local parish church. *Punch* described the scene between the two opposing counsel in an amusing ballad which contained this stanza:

Then up stood Mr. Carson, just as quiet as any
parson,
And read out his indictment with a settled stone-
like face.
Till Tim Healy quick replying rose then and
there denying
That the Counsel for the Crown had the shadow
of a case.

The Mayor's return to the Mansion House was consequently triumphal and he addressed a cheering crowd of spectators from the mayoral balcony. But his triumph was short-lived. The assiduous Carson took the matter to the High Court, with the result that a new trial was ordered. This time Lord Mayor Sullivan was convicted and had to go to prison after all.

Another interesting prosecution which it fell to Carson to conduct at this time was that of Wilfrid Scawen Blunt, an Englishman in his late forties who had espoused the Home Rule cause with peculiar zest. He was a man of means, as well as of considerable intellectual gifts, but he was also eccentric and somewhat of a crank. He had spent much of his life in the Middle East, where he had formerly been in the diplomatic service. Here he became known as a breeder of Arab horses. He frequently adopted the Oriental custom of squatting on a carpet instead of sitting on a chair, and though he belonged to an old Catholic family—he had a country house in Sussex and moved in the same social set as Balfour—he was according to himself half Mohammedan in religion. He thought the British Empire was synonymous with exploitation, and he had denounced British rule in India and British occupation of Egypt. Recently he had turned his attention to Ireland and, after two unsuccessful attempts to enter Parliament as a Home Ruler, had crossed the Irish Sea to lend his support to the Plan of Campaign. He was accompanied by his wife, a granddaughter of the poet Lord Byron, who shared his enthusiasms: indeed it was not long before both of them became more Irish than the Irish themselves.

At the invitation of William O'Brien, this political Don Quixote consented to address a meeting at Woodford in County Galway on a certain Sunday in October, 1887. The purpose of the meeting was to exhort the tenants of the local landlord, the Marquess of Clanricarde, to resist eviction, and to promote the Plan of Campaign generally. Lord Clanricarde, it may be noted here, was the most notorious and reactionary of all the Irish landlords at this period. The absentee owner of 56,000 acres in County Galway—he preferred to live in the Albany, Piccadilly—he devoted his life to the preservation of what he conceived to be his natural rights. Utterly careless of public opinion, he clung with characteristic obstinacy to the old idea that a landlord could exercise arbitrary power over his tenants. When they disobeyed him, the weapon with which he fought them was eviction. The process was carried out wholesale and ruthlessly on his estates, which were consequently marked with much agrarian crime. "Do they think they will intimidate me by shooting my bailiffs?" he is supposed to have asked when one of his agents had been treated in this manner.

The meeting, which had been advertised in advance, was proclaimed by the Lord Lieutenant, and all persons were warned to abstain from taking part in it under penalty of being 'proceeded against according to law'. Notwithstanding this proclamation, however, the meeting was held as planned in the presence of about 300 people. Blunt was pulled off the platform by the police as he was attempting to speak, and arrested along with a companion named Roche, a local poor law guardian. Both men were offered bail on condition they would not hold the meeting that night. They refused and were sent to Loughrea Prison. Next day Blunt was tried before two magistrates and sentenced to two weeks' imprisonment. He availed himself of the liberty to appeal to Portumna Quarter Sessions and was released on bail.

The appeal was heard before His Honour Judge Henn in the County Court at Portumna, within sight of the Clanricarde demesne, where by a twist of fate the prisoner in earlier and happier days had been an honoured guest of the owner. The case was considered one of supreme importance by the Law Officers, as they were anxious that it should demonstrate once and for all the illegality of the Plan of Campaign. For this reason they decided that a barrister with a silk gown should be briefed along with Carson for the Crown. It thus came about that John Atkinson, Q.C., later Lord Atkinson, at this time the leading 'silk' in Crown practice apart from the two Law Officers, was sent down to lead Carson in this important prosecution.* The prisoner was defended by The MacDermot, Q.C., and Tim Harrington.

* In his recollections of the trial Blunt wrote: 'The case against me was conducted by Atkinson and Carson, two of the Castle bloodhounds, who for high pay did the evil agrarian work in those days for the Government by hunting down the unfortunate peasantry when, in connexion with the eviction campaigns, they came within reach of the law. It was a gloomy role they played, especially Carson's, and I used to feel almost pity for the man when I saw him, as I several times did, thus engaged in the West of Ireland Courts': W. S. Blunt, *The Land War in Ireland*, at p. 365.

The prisoner, in an excess of Nationalist exuberance, later denounced his trial as a travesty of justice. It is unnecessary to describe the proceedings in any detail. They lasted for five days and ended in the judge dismissing the appeal and confirming the sentence. The lesson it conveyed was a salutary one. "I was delighted to see you had run Wilfrid Blunt in", wrote Lord Salisbury to Balfour at the time of his first arrest. After the trial the Prime Minister added: "I think as to Blunt the impression among the new electors is good. The great heart of the people always chuckles when a gentleman gets into the clutches of the law."

In January, 1888, a number of fresh legal appointments was made in Ireland. The Attorney-General, John Gibson, became a High Court Judge: his place as a Law Officer was taken by the Solicitor-General Peter O'Brien, while O'Brien was succeeded by Serjeant D. H. Madden, Q.C., well known as an authority on Shakespeare as well as on the law. Carson's appointment as Crown Prosecutor or 'Attorney's Devil', being personal to the Attorney-General, was subsequently confirmed by the new leader of the Irish Bar. Normally Carson would have been succeeded by another man, but O'Brien considered '*bon diable*', as he used familiarly to refer to him, indispensable in the work of administering the Crimes Act. In any case they were already firm friends and accustomed to working together. As for Carson, he welcomed the change in Law Officers, as he regarded Gibson as 'rather a rabbit', to use his own expression. "It was a great relief when Peter the Packer took his place," he said, looking back afterwards on these days.

Carson, whose health had never been strong, was now beginning to feel the strain of his constant journeyings all over the country in difficult and dangerous circumstances. He had always looked forward to ending his days on the Irish Bench, preferably in some subordinate appointment. Consequently, when a County Court judgeship became vacant at this time, Carson applied for it to Peter O'Brien.

The good-natured Attorney-General would certainly have bestowed the appointment on someone of lesser attainments than his 'devil', but in Carson's case he had no hesitation in refusing the request point blank. He begged Carson to think carefully.

"Here you are, Ned Carson, thirty-four years old," he said to him. "If I do what you ask, in ten years you'll be a County Court Judge; in twenty years you'll be a County Court Judge; and maybe in fifty years you'll be a County Court Judge; and the Almighty meant you for bigger things than that."

The younger man reluctantly agreed. Thus did the celebrated 'Peter the Packer' save Edward Carson, at a critical stage in his career, from a subsequent lifetime of obscurity.

6

As might be expected, the Crown Prosecutor's work in Ireland at this time was carried on literally at the risk of his life. Day and night 'Coercion Carson' was shadowed by police officers, although he had no wish for this form of protection. When he put on his coat to leave home in the morning, Annette never knew whether he would return to Merrion Square alive. Sometimes the police would go on ahead of him, when he was driving along country roads, and beat out the hedges on either side in search of possible assassins. Threatening letters reached him frequently; he received postcards adorned with a skull and crossbones, and other emblems of mortality such as model coffins were sent to him. All these threats left him unmoved, and he carried on oblivious of all danger. Humble folk who were seen speaking to him incurred the dreaded penalty of being 'boycotted', while his name as that of an ogre would even be used by peasant women to frighten their children when they were naughty. Once he was stoned in the streets: his assailants were caught and received six months in prison for their behaviour. It was a nasty feeling, as he subsequently admitted, to feel the stones flying through the air so near him.

On another occasion, on his way to conduct an important prosecution he was being seen off at the railway station in Dublin by the Attorney-General Peter O'Brien. A sinister-looking man, who had been following them through the streets, boarded the same train. He was later observed by Carson stealthily creeping along the corridor. Carson, who invariably carried a revolver with him on his travels, immediately drew his weapon and pointed it at the man, who disappeared and contrived to get away undetected, although the whole train was subsequently searched. There is no doubt that he planned to murder the Crown Prosecutor. At a later date Carson was asked had he not been afraid for his life at this period. "No," he replied characteristically, "but I was in constant dread that my depositions would be stolen."

Then there was the excitement of the trials themselves, well described by a Home Rule sympathiser, the late Sir James O'Connor:

"The saturnine face of Edward Carson, a moustached promising junior, the awe-inspiring choler of the bibulous stipendiary, the majestic frames of the Royal Irish Constabulary, the noble countenances of the Nationalist M.P.s, who came either as accused or as counsel or as sympathisers for the accused, here were all the elements of a great drama, in which the powers of goodness and light battled with those of evil and darkness. The chance of surreptitious applause under the noses of the police in a packed Court House was a delicious, if terrific gamble. The penalty was instant expulsion and possibly a clout on the lug, if the peeler could identify the foot that tapped the floor. Involving more terrible risks and still more thrilling was a chance of a conflict between the police and the people."*

As we have seen, the gallant R.I.C. worked under equally difficult and dangerous conditions. When they discovered anything in favour of a prisoner, they never hesitated to bring it out. On the other hand, they were constantly harried by the Nationalists, subject to systematic persecution, frequently assaulted and sometimes murdered. Meanwhile the prisoners were just as fairly treated by the Bench. Lord Chief Baron Palles in particular was always severe on Crown prosecutions. "He would admit no excuse for a slip or error", wrote Carson's contemporary John Ross, who himself appeared for the Crown in many of these trials. "If he could find any technical flaw in the proceedings, the conviction was quashed and the prisoners went home rejoicing." The most subtle and difficult points in the criminal law were raised by defending counsel, and Peter O'Brien and Carson had to be ready to argue them at short notice, since it was a question of the liberty of the subject. In Ross's words, "The Attorney-General and Carson were towers of strength before me. No matter what surprise was sprung on us, they sat there unmoved."

In the middle of 1889 Carson ceased to be the Attorney-General's 'devil', though he continued to be briefed for the Crown in important prosecutions. O'Brien, who had successfully dissuaded his 'devil' from applying for a County Court judgeship in the previous year, now advised him to make the customary application to the Lord Chancellor which every barrister must make if he wishes to exchange the junior's stuff gown for the silk of a Q.C. Again Carson took the hint. Lord Chancellor Ashbourne granted his application and on June 24, 1889, he was appointed one of the 'Queen's Counsel

* Sir James O'Connor, *History of Ireland*, Vol. II, at p. 134.

in Ireland learned in the law'. He thus became at thirty-five the youngest Q.C. in the country.

Carson now took his place in the front row of benches, in the Four Courts, reserved for senior counsel. At Green Street and in the other criminal Courts he now sat beside the Attorney-General, instead of behind him. In O'Brien's case, however, the association was only to last a few months, since before the year was out 'Peter the Packer' had been promoted to the Bench. One of the last and politically most significant prosecutions on which they were engaged together was the Gweedore tragedy.

This tragedy arose out of the activities of Father McFadden, the parish priest of Gweedore, a wild and barren district in the north-western part of the County Donegal. The priest, an arrogant, vain man, had been active in inciting his flock to participation in the Plan of Campaign. He had recently served a term of six months' imprisonment for his activities and on his release had immediately resumed his illegal conduct. The authorities decided to rearrest him and a warrant was issued for this purpose. Unfortunately the police chose to execute the warrant at the moment Father McFadden, attired in full canonicals, was leaving his church after saying Mass on the following Sunday morning. The congregation did not disperse after the service but remained standing about in threatening groups. District-Inspector Martin, accompanied by seven men who remained at some distance from him, stepped up to the priest and informed him that he was under arrest. Father McFadden asked to see the warrant, and as the Inspector called to his sergeant to bring it the priest tried to push his way past towards his house. The congregation then made a mad rush at the sergeant and his men, whom they knocked down, and a few minutes later set on Inspector Martin, who had by this time drawn his sword, and battered in his skull. Shortly afterwards a strong reinforcement of police arrived and picked up the Inspector in a dying condition. They drove away the people and took Father McFadden into custody.

Eventually twenty-three persons were arrested; ten were charged with murder and thirteen with conspiracy. Their trial took place before Mr. Justice Gibson, the former Attorney-General, at Maryborough, the Assize town of Queen's County, to which the venue had been transferred from Donegal, so as to secure a fair trial. Peter O'Brien led for the Crown with Carson, John Ross and other counsel. The prisoners were defended by The MacDermot and Tim Healy.

The first prisoner was convicted of manslaughter—he had been the first to strike Inspector Martin—and was sentenced to ten years' penal servitude. But when the turn of the second prisoner came, the jury disagreed; they were much impressed by Healy's argument that a man who drew his sword in such circumstances as the Inspector did would be considered by the Donegal peasantry as about to commit sacrilege or treason to their religion. A compromise was thereupon reached between the Crown and defending counsel by which it was agreed that the majority of the remainder of the prisoners should plead guilty to lesser charges, with one or two exceptions against whom the Crown offered no evidence. This was done. Father McFadden pleaded guilty to the charge of obstructing the police and was bound over. The others who pleaded received comparatively light sentences. However, the trials aroused great interest in England, where they were to become the subject of bitter party controversy in Parliament.

7

Soon after these trials various legal changes in Ireland were announced. Sir Michael Morris, the Lord Chief Justice, went to the House of Lords as a Lord of Appeal in Ordinary with the title of Lord Morris and Killanin. Peter O'Brien followed Morris to the Bench in Dublin's Four Courts, while Serjeant Madden became the senior Irish Law Officer. Balfour would have liked to see Carson take Madden's place as Solicitor-General, but the claims of John Atkinson, Q.C., were too strong to be passed over and he was appointed. At the same time the Chief Secretary was anxious that Carson should know how highly his services as Crown Prosecutor were regarded. Balfour accordingly wrote to him in terms which could not have failed to give Carson great pleasure when he read the letter:*

Confidential *Chief Secretary's Office,*
Dublin Castle.
28th December, 1889.

. . . You have never been in any direct communication with the Chief Secretary's Office, but still I am well aware that some of the most difficult and responsible work connected with the administration

* Hitherto unpublished. This text is taken from a copy preserved with the Balfour Papers in the British Museum.

of the Crimes Act has devolved upon you, and that you have shown sometimes under very trying circumstances the greatest ability, discretion and courage in conducting work entrusted to you by the late Attorney-General.* Any substantial recognition of these services it has not been in my power to give, as the only legal vacancy in the gift of the Irish Government was due to the high standing and distinguished abilities of the present Solicitor-General,† but I take this opportunity of saying that, in my judgment, should a vacancy occur among the Law Officers of the Crown, no man at the Irish Bar has claims to it comparable to your own.

I am aware that in putting such an expression upon record I am violating a very sound general rule of official procedure, and I am also aware that no expression of opinion from me can bind my successors in office whether they belong to the same or to different political parties. This, of course, you will readily understand, and will take this letter to be no more than what it professes to be, *i.e.* a very distinct expression of my personal opinion as to the character of the services you have rendered to the Government and as to the proper method by which these services should be recognised. . . .

By this date Balfour's determined policy, which Carson did so much to implement in the Courts, had taken considerable effect, and, although Balfour was to remain in occupation of the Chief Secretary's lodge for two further years, lawlessness had in great measure been curbed throughout the country and order restored. There were, of course, other factors which contributed to this change, particularly the Vatican's condemnation of the Plan of Campaign. The Pope in a rescript had declared that it was unlawful to break voluntary contracts, that the Law Courts were available, and that the funds for the Plan were collected by intimidation; he also denounced 'boycotting' as being contrary to justice and charity, and an instrument of persecution. The edict was far from popular among the ranks of the faithful, though it could not be disregarded by the bishops and priests. Indeed it provoked one witty Ulsterman to make a celebrated jest to a Catholic acquaintance. "Say, Paddy, have ye heard the news?" he quipped. "The Pope's turned Protestant."

The public was also beginning to tire of the antics of William O'Brien and his more ebullient friends, and became reluctant to condone the repeated breaches of the peace which their conduct provoked. O'Brien himself sensed the way the wind was blowing, and while out on bail he suddenly decamped to France and thence to America, where he remained until the Nationalist Party was split by

* Peter O'Brien, later Lord O'Brien.
† John Atkinson, later Lord Atkinson.

the scandal of Captain O'Shea's divorce suit which so deeply implicated Parnell. Carson's last encounter with O'Brien took place in Tipperary in 1890 after a riot had broken out during his trial for conspiracy. At the subsequent trial of the rioters O'Brien gave evidence and also John Morley, the Liberal ex-Chief Secretary, whom O'Brien had invited to be a witness at his own trial and who had seen the collision between the crowd and the police.

Morley's version was that a small crowd trying to enter the Court peaceably were attacked by the police. He thought that the whole affair could have been dealt with by two English village policemen. But then he was unable to disguise his sympathies. "I cannot drop my politics at Tipperary railway station," he declared from the witness-box. Carson, in a good-humoured cross-examination which incidentally gained him Morley's friendship, made great play with the 'two village constables', asking him if he would have used them had he been on the spot at the time of the Belfast riots in 1886.

> MORLEY: No. I should have allowed the crowd to go on till it reached the point of disorder which called for police intervention.
>
> CARSON: At what particular point would you intervene?
>
> MORLEY: When there was a breach of the public peace.
>
> CARSON: Unless a policeman were wounded, you would not say there was very serious disorder?
>
> MORLEY: Oh, I would not say that.

This trial ended with two remarkable incidents. While the judge was addressing the jury, a heavy piece of wood fell from the roof of the Court on to Carson's head. "I think, my Lord, it was accidental," said Carson. But the judge was not so sure. A few moments later there was a cry of "Fire". At first the judge thought it was only a chimney smoking, but soon the building began to blaze. The court-room emptied and outside a delighted crowd watched the hated emblem of British Justice burn to the ground. They were particularly pleased when the flames reached the Union Jack on a flag-pole surmounting the Court House and came toppling down in flames. It was an ominous portent.

The Court adjourned and met next day in another building. Two of the prisoners were acquitted and the jury disagreed about the other three. It appears that eleven jurymen were for a conviction but one, an inveterate 'Land Leaguer', held out for acquittal. "We had not challenged him," said Carson afterwards. "He looked so eminently respectable."

This case provided a demonstrable justification of 'coercion', if any was needed. In a country where jurors obstinately refused to convict in the face of the clearest evidence, 'coercion' was necessary if justice was to be done. But if it did arrive at the truth and punish the criminal, it unfortunately could not enlist the mass of the people on the side of the Government.

But coercion was not the sole plank in Balfour's programme. The stick was accompanied by the carrot—'the kicks and halfpence policy', as Carson called it. "The halfpence were very well done too," said Carson afterwards. "Look at the fund he raised and the arrangements he made when the potato crop failed." The Chief Secretary also built light railways and launched other schemes of public utility which, besides providing employment in the poorer districts, were of undoubted permanent benefit to the country. Carson once recalled how an old peasant woman had said at the time: "Thanks be to Mary and all the saints, and to Bloody Balfour, ould Ireland will be saved yet!" He added: "And she was right."

We have already seen how strongly Balfour and Carson were drawn to each other and how successfully they worked together. We have seen too how Balfour placed on record his high opinion of the younger man's abilities. On Carson's side his admiration for the Chief Secretary soon grew into steadfast devotion. On his desk stood a drawing of 'A.J.B.' by Lady Granby, and it was to remain there throughout his life, while his pocket-book contained the Chief Secretary's photograph. Carson always looked back on these days of their first association with the happiest feelings.

"You can't think what fun we had," Carson said to Balfour's niece long afterwards. "You can't think how quick he was at seeing points. I suppose I'm prejudiced about this as I am about other things—but I don't think he ever rose to quite such heights as he did in Ireland."*

* Mrs. Blanche Dugdale, Balfour's niece and biographer, recalled this conversation at the time of Carson's death, when she described her experience of 'seeing the light of battle kindle in his eye as he spoke of his devotion to the Chief Secretary whose courage was equal to his own': *The Times*, Oct. 24, 1935.

CHAPTER FOUR

Parliament and the English Bar

I

THE end of 1891 saw Carson thoroughly established in his profession and in a fair way of prosperity. An Irish barrister's fees were not comparable with those earned at the English Bar in those days, but living was cheap in Ireland and money went a great deal further than it does today. Besides the big house in Merrion Square, Carson had a smaller house overlooking the sea at Dalkey, where Annette and the children spent the summer months and he would join them at week-ends and in the Long Vacation. Harry, the eldest boy, was already at school; the two girls, Aileen and Gladys, were also growing up; while in the nursery there was another baby, Walter Seymour, who had been born in 1890. Though she saw less of her husband than in the early days of their marriage, Annette was quite happy looking after her home and the children.

Except for becoming a Law Officer or a judge, there was no higher position within Carson's reach at the Irish Bar. He was a Queen's Counsel, a Bencher of King's Inns and Senior Crown Prosecutor for the City and County of Dublin. This meant that he was in charge of all Crown work at the Green Street Court House, a position equivalent in England to that of Senior Treasury Counsel at the Old Bailey. Still troubled by delicate health, Carson looked forward in a few years' time to a place on the Bench, where the judicial duties would be light and he might enjoy a well-earned ease.

One man who viewed this prospect with alarm was A. J. Balfour. As he had indicated at the time of Peter O'Brien's promotion to be Lord Chief Justice, the Chief Secretary was most anxious that his able lieutenant should become a Law Officer when the next vacancy arose, with a seat in Parliament. In the summer of 1890 it looked as if this might happen. There was considerable talk at the time that the Attorney-General, Serjeant Madden, who was also one of the two M.P.s returned to Westminster by Trinity College, would accept a judicial appointment. The leading electors in the University took steps to select another candidate. In the past they had invariably been represented by Tory Members. In agreeing to let his name go forward as a Liberal-Unionist, Carson was thus conscious that he was breaking new ground and would probably encounter stiff opposition.

He embarked on this new venture with a significant letter from the Chief Secretary.

Private *Irish Office,*
Great Queen St., S.W.
12 *May*, 1890.

DEAR MR. CARSON,

I do not know that I have any right or title to interfere directly or indirectly in the question now pending with regard to the representation of Trinity College in the event of there being a vacancy, but if my opinion in the matter be desired I see no reason why you should not state that you have my good wishes for your success and that I regard your presence in the House of Commons in the event of the Attorney-General leaving it as not merely a matter of convenience to the Government but one little short of absolute necessity.

There is no objection to your showing this to Dr. Stubbs or any other leading member in the constituency should you think it advisable, but I feel so strongly that I have no title to express an opinion on the choice by the Constituency of their representative in Parliament that I should hesitate to publish it in any form or shape lest I should give rise to misconception.

Yours very truly,
ARTHUR JAMES BALFOUR.

To another graduate, the Rev. James Rountree, who had considerable influence with those electors who were resident in England, Balfour sent a similar letter. "I very earnestly hope that Mr. Carson will be elected to fill the vacancy in the representation of Trinity College which would occur if the Attorney-General were promoted to the Bench," he wrote. "It is not merely a matter of convenience but a matter of vital necessity to the Irish Government that it should have one Law Officer at least in the House of Commons, and if through any cause this should be found impossible, I do not see how Parliamentary work could be effectively carried on. For these reasons, and because I believe Mr. Carson to be a most able and excellent man of whom any constituency might be proud, I trust that the electors of Trinity College will find it consistent with their views to elect him."

Unfortunately there was trouble with the college dons who disliked Carson with his Radical past: they had not forgotten his record in the Historical Society. In consequence they looked round for a candidate with a thoroughly Tory background, and they found one in the person of Colonel J. C. Lowry, a steady-going Conservative of no particular merits, but withal a gallant soldier who had fought in the Crimea and led the Royal Horse Artillery to victory in India. A by-election now seemed imminent, and Carson established committee rooms in No. 6 Building in College. "The fight is a tough one," he told the Rev. James Rountree, "but we will win." However, it was eventually decided that Madden should wait until the General Election before retiring, and so the matter was shelved for the time being.

Meanwhile remarkable changes had taken place in the political scene, which had seriously affected the fortunes of the Nationalist Parliamentary Party. Through the sensational scandal of their leader's private life the Parnellites were divided into two bitterly opposing factions. Never had there been a personal catastrophe like it in British public life. In 1889 Parnell's reputation was at its highest. There had been a great wave of feeling in his favour following the exposure as forgeries of a series of letters published by *The Times*, which sought to implicate him in the Phœnix Park murders and the policy of violent crime in Ireland. A large sum of money, over £40,000, was raised for him by public subscription, he received the freedom of Edinburgh and Gladstone invited him to stay as an honoured guest at Hawarden. Then like a thunderbolt came the news that Captain O'Shea, M.P., had filed a petition for divorce and had cited Parnell as co-respondent. At first the Irish people refused to believe it: surely this must be another dirty trick to discredit their beloved leader! Only did they come to accept it as true when the somewhat unromantic details of Parnell's intrigue with his parliamentary colleague's wife trickled out in the Courts, and Captain O'Shea obtained his decree.

It had been an ill-fated moment for the Nationalist leader when Mrs. O'Shea was first brought to the House of Commons by a friend, and Parnell had stooped to pick up a rose which had fallen from her dress. After a while he began to absent himself from Westminster and, though he was naturally of an uncommunicative disposition, his principal supporters soon discovered that he was not in Ireland. In fact, he was at Mrs. O'Shea's house at Eltham, where the liaison was carried on while the husband was in his constituency or elsewhere. On one occasion, at least, the gallant Captain returned home unexpectedly, and Parnell was obliged to make a hurried departure. In his uncontrolled desire for a woman the uncrowned king of the Irish people staked and lost all.

Leaders of Church and State alike combined to hound Parnell out of public life. Gladstone, with the bulk of English Liberal and Nonconformist opinion behind him, let it be known that Parnell's continuance in the Irish Party leadership "would not only place many hearty and effective friends of the Irish cause in a position of great embarrassment, but would render my retention of the leadership of the Liberal Party, based as it has been mainly upon the presentation of the Irish cause, almost a nullity." The Catholic bishops likewise condemned Parnell's conduct, while the Nationalist M.P.s had a long series of meetings in Committee Room No. 15 in the House of Commons to decide who would now be the master of the party, or, as Tim Healy put it with unaccustomed venom, who would be 'the mistress' of the party.

Though he was strongly opposed to Parnell's political aims and policies, Carson could not help feeling sorry for the man and the way he was treated by so many of those who had formerly fawned upon him. One day, when he was in the Courts, he happened to encounter John Redmond, the Nationalist Member, in counsels' robing room.

"Well, John Redmond," said Carson, "are you too going to desert your leader in his hour of need?"

"No," Redmond replied. "Would I be leaving him because of the love of his life?"

"I'm glad to hear it," said Carson.

This answer gained for Carson Redmond's lasting respect and friendship, and Redmond was as good as his word. On that fateful winter's evening when the final 'split' occurred in Committee Room No. 15, Redmond remained behind in the gas-lit room with twenty-eight colleagues, while forty-four others, including O'Brien, Healy and Dillon, walked out. Thus Parnell was left, in his own phrase, to the "English wolves now howling for my destruction".

Parnell married Mrs. O'Shea immediately the divorce decree was pronounced absolute and he was free to do so. But their wedded happiness did not last long. In a hopeless attempt to regain the political ascendancy that had once been his, the fallen leader wore himself out, speaking in the open air and travelling in all weathers, while a sick man. Less than four months after his marriage he was dead. But even this tragedy did not heal the breach among his former followers, who were to assail each other most bitterly for years to come.

2

By midsummer of 1892 it was known that the long-expected General Election would take place in July. This enabled Salisbury and Balfour to make the fresh legal appointments in Ireland which they had in mind. Madden, the Attorney-General, was promoted to the Bench; Atkinson, the Solicitor-General, moved up to Madden's place; and Carson was appointed to succeed Atkinson as the junior Law Officer. On July 1, 1892, Carson was sworn in to his new office in Dublin Castle.

Three days later the Rev. Dr. George Salmon, Provost of Trinity College, sat in the Examination Hall as Presiding Officer to receive nominations for the election of two M.P.s for Dublin University. Three candidates appeared. Two were Conservatives, David Plunkett, Q.C., the sitting member, and Colonel Lowry. Carson came forward as a Liberal-Unionist. Although only graduates were entitled to vote, the contest aroused great excitement among the student body, who clustered round the door and made a deafening din. As the sitting member, Plunkett was certain of election; while the dons and clerical graduates favoured Lowry, the lawyers and younger graduates were for Carson. The Vice-Provost, who was also called Carson, was so disturbed at the prospect of the University becoming 'tainted with Liberalism' that he wrote to the newspapers expressing the hope that no one would be induced to vote for Mr. Edward Carson under the false impression that this candidate was related to himself. The candidate duly replied that he was glad the Vice-Provost had taken this course, as otherwise he would have been obliged to write a similar letter pointing out in the public interests that he was no kinsman of Vice-Provost Joseph Carson.

As soon as the election writ had been read, the Provost called on the proposers and seconders of the three candidates and then upon the candidates themselves, who were all garbed in academic dress. All the speakers were shouted down by the undergraduates in the Hall, who treated the occasion as a glorious 'rag'. Carson's nomination was proposed by the Rev. Dr. Stubbs, Senior Fellow of the College, and seconded by Richard Falkiner, Q.C., Recorder of Dublin. Dr. Stubbs persisted in reading his speech to the end, though scarcely a word was audible, gesticulating earnestly but vainly for a hearing. "What about the bicycle case?" screamed the students at Falkiner, referring to a recent decision of the learned Recorder in banning these machines from the Dublin streets.

In such of his remarks as could be heard above the general din Plunkett came out strongly on Carson's side, saying Carson would certainly have his vote, since in view of Carson's special qualifications he "could not but desire to give effect to Mr. Balfour's wish that his Law Officer should be returned to Parliament". Lowry, on the other hand, in proclaiming himself a lifelong Conservative referred to the work he had done for the Conservative cause in his native County Tyrone: he then went on to impeach Carson's right to represent Dublin University as a Liberal-Unionist and insisted on the necessity of an independent representative "who would look after the interests of the professions and protect the Irish landlords". The fact that Colonel Lowry, who had not taken a degree, had to appear in an undergraduate's gown, while the other two candidates were robed resplendently as Masters of Arts was not lost upon the audience, who alternately roared their approval and derision.

Carson, who was received with loud cheers, said his Conservatism was approved by Lord Londonderry and Mr. Balfour and so he did not care whether it was commendable to Colonel Lowry or his backers who trumpeted forth that he was unfit to represent the University. "Some sixteen years ago," he continued, "I left the University to engage in the great struggle of life in the noble profession which I adopted, and I have come back after that comparatively long period, having now the confidence of Mr. Balfour and Her Majesty, and having had bestowed upon me the high honour of Solicitor-General for Ireland (*Applause*). I come here to ask you to elect me to Parliament (*A Voice*: 'We will') not because I want promotion but because I have got it" (*Loud applause*).

After pointing out that the highest honour which could be conferred on any citizen was to represent his university in Parliament, Carson neatly demolished Colonel Lowry's claims. Colonel Lowry had asked why Carson did not go elsewhere to look for a seat. "I will tell him," said Carson. "Because I prefer and am determined to represent my University in Parliament (*Renewed applause*). And now, would you allow me, as I have answered that question, to ask Colonel Lowry why *he* does not stay at home and seek representation there?"

Colonel Lowry made no attempt to answer this question. The Presiding Officer then proceeded to call for a vote by a show of hands. As the hands went up, it was clear that Lowry was in a decided minority. However, the gallant Colonel's proposer insisted on demanding a poll and, since he was legally entitled to it, the Provost had no alternative but to appoint the following day for this purpose. Thereupon the meeting dispersed, while Carson was 'chaired' by his student supporters round the quadrangle and deposited on the steps of his committee rooms, where he was forced to deliver another speech.

The poll remained open for five days. Eventually, on July 9, the result was announced as follows:

Rt. Hon. D. R. Plunkett, Q.C., (Conservative)	2,188
E. H. Carson, Q.C., (Unionist)	1,609
Colonel J. C. Lowry (Conservative)	897

Plunkett and Carson were accordingly declared elected as the University burgesses in the House of Commons.

As soon as the result of the poll was announced, Carson had to make another speech to the crowd of cheering undergraduates who thronged the college quadrangles. "It is not for me in the infancy of my parliamentary career to make any boastful promises," he said. "I feel indeed a great pride in being elected as the colleague of your representative (Mr. Plunkett), who has more than attained his majority. . . All I can say is that I earnestly hope that when I have served for twenty-three years as he has done, and come back to ask you for a renewal of your confidence after that period, I shall, as he is today, be proudly returned at the top of the poll, showing the renewed confidence in which you hold him after that length of time (*Applause*). The present Parliament will probably be an historic Parliament. . . . It may be that we will be upon the Opposition benches, or it may be that we will be upon the Government benches, but wherever we be we will have the one and the same duty to perform—the duty of preserving intact the Union between Great Britain and Ireland (*Loud cheers*). For that we stand pledged (*Cheers*). To that you stand pledged" (*Cheers*).

To a friend who came up and asked him about his plans for the future, Carson replied: "Well, thank God, that's all over. I'll be staying in Parliament for two or three years, then I'll go on the Bench at the Four Courts and lead a quiet life."

Not for one moment did Carson think that close on thirty years of vigorous parliamentary life awaited him at Westminster, before he would be free to seek the comparative quiet of the judicial Bench for which he longed.

3

Although the Unionists gained slightly in Ireland at this General Election of 1892, through the continuance of the Parnellite split, the rest of the country reversed the decision it had made seven years previously on the Home Rule issue. The Conservatives lost forty-eight seats and their Liberal-Unionist allies dropped thirty-one, which gave the combined forces of Gladstonian Liberals and Nationalists a majority of forty in the new House of Commons. This meant that the days of Lord Salisbury's Government were numbered and that incidentally Edward Carson's tenure of the office of Solicitor-General for Ireland would be of short duration.

Carson travelled over to Westminster on the mail-boat from Kingstown. Also on board were a number of his parliamentary colleagues. They included his Trinity classmate and fellow barrister, John Ross, who had scored a resounding victory in the historic city of Londonderry, where he had ejected the sitting Nationalist Member, Mr. Justin McCarthy. These two passengers not unnaturally fell to discussing their future plans as the boat steamed towards Holyhead. It was clear that the Conservative Government would be defeated in the debate on the Address, the debate which traditionally takes place after Parliament has been opened with the reading of the Speech from the Throne. And it was obvious that Gladstone would once more become Prime Minister and in accordance with his election pledges would introduce another Home Rule Bill for Ireland. Carson would consequently have to be in constant attendance at Westminster so as to advise Arthur Balfour, who as Leader of the Opposition would be in charge of the campaign against the measure in the Commons.

"I think I shall give up the Irish Bar and try to find some work in England," Carson told his travelling companion. "I advise you to do the same." But Ross demurred. Like Carson he had built up a fine practice, but unlike him he was unwilling to sacrifice it. He said that he had not the courage to take such a plunge.

Carson admitted that he was taking a decided risk, but with his parliamentary obligations he saw no alternative. His proposed course was also an innovation. No Irish barrister he knew of had ever abandoned his practice at home to come to the English Bar, though Irish counsel made occasional appearances before the supreme appellate tribunal of the House of Lords. There, it must be admitted, they had not created a particularly good impression. Their advocacy was regarded as too flowery, they were inclined to bluster, and they were suspected, not without good reason in some instances, of bullying witnesses in cross-examination. Furthermore, Carson was totally unfamiliar with the mode of life in the Temple, which was quite different from the daily round in the Four Courts, where counsel made their headquarters in the library.

Carson's ignorance was illustrated by a noteworthy experience which he had immediately after his arrival in London.

One of the first things he did on reaching London was to visit the Carlton Club, to which famous institution, then situated in Pall Mall, he had recently been elected. Here he was introduced to a fellow member who turned out to be Mr. Charles Darling, Q.C., M.P., later the well-known judge. Darling, who was Carson's senior by five years, had followed the younger man's career with some attention, although they had never met before.

"I suppose you've come over here to take the bread out of our mouths," said Darling.

"No," replied Carson, "but I dare say I'll have a desk in the library."

Darling was momentarily puzzled by this allusion which he did not understand. On being enlightened by Carson on the mode of practice at the Irish Bar, which has been described in an earlier chapter of this book, he remarked that in England barristers only went into the library to consult authorities or reports which were not available in their chambers. Darling then proceeded to explain how the chambers system worked. Several barristers would join together in the same chambers, sharing the services of a clerk, whose duty it was to arrange all matters concerning fees with instructing solicitors and to keep their masters' fee books. Carson was interested but not encouraged. He wondered how on earth an English barrister ever got a brief.

"It'll be no use my taking chambers here," he said, gloomily. "I'll be no one, and nobody'll know me."

Darling did not agree. As a matter of fact, Carson's name was already widely known in England through his work as Irish Crown Prosecutor.

"You mustn't think we haven't heard a lot about you over here," he told him. "And Arthur Balfour here thinks the world of you."

This was true, for the prosecutions which Carson had conducted under the Crimes Act in Ireland had been extensively reported in the English Press.

Darling felt strongly drawn to the tall Irishman with the piercing blue eyes and the delightful brogue.

"Look here, Carson," he went on, "I tell you what. You let me paint your name up outside my chambers, and you'll have five times my practice inside a year."

"I know I won't," answered Carson with a smile, "but I'll bet you a shilling."

"Done," said Darling.

Although Carson had been admitted to the Middle Temple as a student seventeen years previously, since membership of an English Inn of Court was a condition required of all Irish barristers, he had not been called to the English Bar. The matter was therefore left between the two men that, when this formality had been completed, Carson would join Darling in his chambers at No. 3 Dr. Johnson's Buildings in the Temple.

The new Parliament met on August 4 for the swearing-in of Members. There was the usual queue of those who came down to the House in the early hours of the morning so as to secure good seats. Before the doors were unlocked at eight o'clock, several of the Irish Nationalist M.P.s had arrived, and something very like a free fight broke out between them and their Unionist opponents. The swearing-in process was lengthy and tedious, since in those days there were 670 members. However, as Edward Carson stood at the table in the historic Commons Chamber to take the oath and sign the roll, he experienced the thrill which every newly-elected M.P. senses on becoming a fully-fledged member of that assembly for the first time. He saw, too, his old adversaries in the Courts, such as O'Brien, Healy and Redmond, who sat with the Nationalists below the gangway on the Opposition side of the House, not to mention a number of others whom he had prosecuted in Ireland. No doubt these men looked forward to the opportunity of paying off old scores.

His office of Solicitor-General for Ireland entitled Carson to take his seat with other members of the Government on the Front Bench, an experience which falls to the lot of comparatively few M.P.s on their first election. But he was not to make his maiden speech from this bench, since Balfour considered it advisable for him to wait for a while as there were plenty of speakers already available on the Government side for the debate on the Address. However, he answered two questions from the Front Bench on Irish affairs, and though he remained silent during the general discussion, he had the advantage of seeing and hearing most of the great parliamentary figures of the time. Outstanding among them, of course, was the aged Mr. Gladstone, to whom before his conversion to Home Rule Carson as a Radical had once borne allegiance. With flowing white hair and expressive intellectual features, the Grand Old Man sat proudly on the Opposition Front Bench, his amazing faculties and powers of speech little dimmed by the passing of time.

The Queen's Speech was a colourless affair of a few lines—believed to be the shortest on record—since the Government, with the knowledge of impending defeat, had prepared no legislative programme for the session. The resultant debate was more lively, ranging as it did almost exclusively round the controversial issue of Home Rule for Ireland. As usual the Nationalist Members had their full say on Ireland's wrongs. Yet the most significant contribution to the debate, and that which impressed Carson more than any other, did not come from their benches or from any English Member. It came from another Irishman, Colonel Edward Saunderson, M.P. for North Armagh, the humorous and hard-hitting leader of the small compact group of Conservatives and Unionists who sat for Ulster constituencies. Saunderson was endowed with an imposing presence, a fine voice and considerable fluency of speech; he employed all these qualities to advantage on this occasion. He spoke about the new Home Rule Bill which Gladstone clearly intended to introduce as soon as he returned to Downing Street, and how the measure would be regarded in that part of Ireland with which he and his friends were connected.

He pointed a menacing finger in the direction of the Opposition benches. "No man who comes over to Belfast will laugh at the Ulster Loyalists," he declared. "I say that whether the House of Lords rejects this Bill or does not, *we* reject it; and that, although you may occupy the House of Commons in years to come with academic debates on the values of this Home Rule Bill, when all is said, and even if you pass this Bill, I say in the name of my people, we will reject it."

A scornful voice broke in from the Opposition side of the House. "Who are you?"

Colonel Saunderson bridled. "No man has a better right to say that than I," he answered in an historic peroration. "I say in their name that we will reject it, and if you ever try to erect it in Ireland we will crumble it into dust."

These harsh and uncompromising words were dismissed by Redmond in a subsequent speech as an absurd boast. Nevertheless, they had the ring of ominous prophecy about them. Carson for one was to remember them frequently in the years to come.

Meanwhile the debate continued. The Opposition amendment of censure had been moved for the Liberals in the most polished English by a scholarly barrister, Mr. H. H. Asquith, whose star was rapidly rising both in the House and the Law Courts. In a classical Latin phrase Mr. Asquith had pronounced the Government's demise: "*Roma locuta est. Causa finita est.*"*

Carson's newly-found friend, Charles Darling, tried to turn this allusion by suggesting that though Rome had undoubtedly spoken, it was the Church of Rome which decreed the result of every Southern Irish election. "The Archbishops and Bishops of Ireland have spoken," he said, "the priests have acted, and the case is finished."

But this sally could not save the Government. In the division lobbies the Opposition amendment was carried by forty votes, and Lord Salisbury resigned. Mr. Gladstone became Prime Minister, for the fourth time, at the age of eighty-three. In the new administration H. H. Asquith, who was barely two years older than Carson, became Home Secretary, while John Morley returned, after an absence of twelve years, to the Chief Secretary's Lodge in Dublin.

The House of Commons thereupon adjourned until the following February, and Carson went back to wind up his practice in Ireland.

4

Morley's first act on reaching his old room in Dublin Castle was to repeal the provisions of the Crimes Act which permitted special inquiries by Resident Magistrates, and thus put an end to the work, to which Carson had conducted with such conspicuous success as Crown Prosecutor. The Chief Secretary also ordered the unconditional release of those who had been convicted for their part in the killing of Inspector Martin at Gweedore and were still in prison. The prisoners, who were all serving terms of penal servitude, were accordingly released. These acts of clemency or, as some thought, weakness on the part of the Executive were immediately answered by another outrage, which occurred under the very walls of the Castle.

* 'Rome has spoken. The case is finished'.

A stick of dynamite, detonated there, caused a violent explosion and blew the constable on duty to pieces.

Morley's next move was to set up a special Commission to consider the claims of tenants who had been evicted by their landlords for participation in the Plan of Campaign. Were they to get back their old tenancies? And, if so, what was to happen to the new tenants, most of whom were generally regarded as traitors and outcasts and already enjoyed police protection? To resolve these questions the Chief Secretary appointed Mr. Justice Mathew as President of the newly-constituted Evicted Tenants Commission. The selection of this Roman Catholic judge from Cork was most unfortunate. Though he had proved on the whole a success on the High Court Bench in England, Sir James Mathew was a convinced Home Ruler and the father-in-law of John Dillon, the Nationalist M.P. From the outset he made no secret of the fact that his sympathies lay in the direction of restoring the old tenants, which he conceived to be the proper policy of the Government. Furthermore, he refused to be bound by any of the rules of judicial procedure.

Carson had received a brief to appear for a number of landlords, including Lord Clanricarde, whose acquaintance as the best hated landlord of his times in Ireland has already been made in this book. It was not a brief that Carson by any means relished, but he felt bound to accept it as sent to him in the ordinary course of practice. He felt too that this notorious landlord's harshness toward his tenants had been somewhat exaggerated.

The Commission sat in a private house in Merrion Square, not far from Carson's own. Early in the opening day—November 7, 1892—Carson found himself at loggerheads with the President on the subject of his client. Lord Clanricarde was not present in Court. If his Lordship refused to attend, observed the President, he must be prepared for the inference that is properly drawn when evidence is deliberately withheld.

"I appear for him," Carson broke in, "and I don't see why these observations should be made."

The President went on to say that he might have to exclude the Press on the grounds that both tenants and landlords wished the inquiry to be conducted in private. Carson interjected to point out that, so far as the landlords were concerned, this was not so. "I hope you will pardon me," he added. "I speak in order that there may be no misapprehension."

Trouble then arose on the question of cross-examination. The first witness was Mr. John Roche, Nationalist M.P. for East Galway and the organiser of the Plan of Campaign on the Clanricarde estates. He made a long rambling statement, almost entirely hearsay, about the iniquities of the landlords and the wrongs of the tenants. Carson asked leave to cross-examine. The President demurred. Carson repeated his request. The President said he might do so after lunch if he was ready. But when the afternoon sitting began, the President had changed his mind and said he might prepare written questions which if they were relevant might then be put to the witness by one of the Commissioners. Carson protested vigorously. Thereupon the President ordered him to leave the room.

Carson was furious. "I insist upon my rights until every Commissioner orders me to withdraw," he said. "I will stand up here and now for justice to be done to Lord Clanricarde as well as to anyone else."

The President quickly interposed that the Commissioners had consulted and had come to the unanimous conclusion that they would not hear him.

"My Lord," Carson spoke slowly and deliberately, "if I am not at liberty to cross-examine, I say the whole thing is a farce and a sham. I willingly withdraw from it. I will not prostitute my position by remaining any longer as an advocate before an English judge."

"I am not sitting as a judge," remarked Mr. Justice Mathew.

"Any fool could see that," muttered Carson under his breath, but loud enough to be heard by nearly everyone in the room.

The President glowered with rage. "Your observations are disgraceful," he said.

Shortly before this, Mr. William O'Brien, the Nationalist M.P. and founder of the Plan of Campaign, had come in and sat down. He now added his voice to the altercation. "You are not in a Coercion Court now," he shouted at Carson, no doubt with the recollection of Mitchelstown sharply implanted in his mind.

Mr. William Kenny, Q.C., who appeared for another landlord, joined in on Carson's side, only to be rebuked in equally heated language by the President. "I entirely concur in the observations made by Mr. Carson," said this counsel. "I say that is equally impertinent and disgraceful," remarked Mr. Justice Mathew. Finally Carson threw down his papers on the table in front of them and walked out of the Court followed by the other counsel.

The incident caused a considerable sensation on both sides of the

Irish Sea, and Carson was alternately praised and attacked for the line he had taken. In particular he was accused of improperly interrupting the President. To refute this charge he sent a letter of explanation to *The Times*. "When the President proceeded to threaten Lord Clanricarde," he wrote, "I interrupted by stating I appeared for him, and by protesting against his condemnation before enquiry. I again interrupted when the President stated, contrary to the fact, that the landlords required the enquiry to be conducted in private. The above were my only interruptions, and if I erred it was because I am accustomed to practise in Courts where parties are heard before they are condemned, and where judges never complain if they are in a respectful manner corrected as to a misapprehension of a matter of fact." Public as well as professional opinion, however, was largely with Carson, and supported the view of *The Times* that his words, strong as they were, were not too strong in the circumstances. Certainly the Commission fell greatly in the general esteem and, though it continued to take evidence and reported in due course, two of the Commissioners resigned and the landlords as a body likewise refused to take any further part in its proceedings.

This was Carson's last professional appearance in Ireland. Shortly after New Year's Day, 1893, he left Dublin, his mind made up to seek anew his fortune at the English Bar. The Four Courts and the Green Street Court House were thus to know him no more. Annette and the children he left behind in Merrion Square, saying he would send for them when he had found somewhere to live in London.

5

The meeting of Parliament had been fixed for January 31. Ten days previously Balfour as Leader of the Opposition sent a personal letter to every Conservative and Liberal-Unionist. "It is certain that business of the greatest importance will be at once brought forward," he wrote, "and I trust that you may find it convenient to be in your place on that day." The business here alluded to was, of course, the Home Rule Bill for Ireland which the Gladstone Government was pledged to introduce at the earliest opportunity and which was thus to form the principal feature of the Queen's Speech at the opening of the new session.

At the same time Balfour wrote Carson a private note on the

subject of the debate on the Address, which customarily follows the reading of the Gracious Speech from the Throne in the House of Lords. "I think undoubtedly something should be said about the Gweedore prisoners," he wrote, "and I shall be most grateful if you will come to my house to give me any points likely to prove useful. . . . A little conversation on the Irish situation will be most valuable to me."

The interview took place at Balfour's town house, No. 4 Carlton Gardens, and here Carson was able to brief the Opposition Leader in the sense he asked, particularly as regards the suspension of the Crimes Act provisions and the activities of the Evicted Tenants Commission, as well as the Gweedore prisoners. They also discussed the question of a contribution to the debate from Carson himself. Balfour explained that it was the parliamentary practice for the Leader of the Opposition to follow the mover and seconder of the Address and to make a sort of general survey of the situation. It was not supposed to be the right thing to do, he went on, to couch the opening attack in very controversial language—that was left to the later stages of the debate. So far as the Irish situation was concerned, Balfour's plan was to put up Carson with his first-hand knowledge to give a detailed answer to Chief Secretary Morley, who was expected to speak toward the end of the debate.

When the doors of the Commons Chamber were opened in the morning of January 31, there was the usual scuffle for seats. The Nationalists tried to keep the Irish Unionists out of their usual places. Little Dr. Tanner, the pugnacious Member for Mid-Cork, not content with placing several hats on the Unionists' places, took off his coat and waistcoat and also, it is said, his trousers, and laid these clothes on the benches. When the Irish Unionists arrived they put their hats in their usual places, whereupon Dr. Tanner threatened to sit on them, but he eventually desisted when one of the Unionists, Colonel Tom Waring, M.P. for North Down, threatened to call a policeman. Fortunately the crisis had subsided by the time the equally pugnacious Colonel Saunderson arrived. Carson, however, was not troubled by these antics, since he exercised his right as an ex-Law Officer of the Crown to sit on the Opposition Front Bench.

Balfour led off for the Conservatives and Unionists in a lengthy and polished survey of events at home and abroad, in which incidentally he showed that he had profited from Carson's coaching. He condemned in studied terms the composition of the Evicted Tenants Commission as unfair. As for its President, this is how he described his conduct: "He appeared to riot and revel in his sudden freedom from the trammels which bind an English judge, and he could not refrain from indulging in the unwonted luxury of delivering the verdict before he had heard the evidence." On the subject of John Morley and the Gweedore prisoners Balfour was equally convincing, choosing his words with great care: "the Minister who shows his contempt for the safety of the police by arbitrarily diminishing the just punishment of these malefactors in using the prerogative of mercy not as it was intended to be used—namely, as an instrument of justice—but that political ends may be furthered."

On the third day the debate was opened by Colonel Saunderson in a characteristically fighting speech. What right, he asked, had the Government to turn adrift in Ireland the atrocious ruffians who brutally and savagely murdered Inspector Martin at Gweedore? He went on to speak of "this ruffian McFadden", but his reference produced loud interruptions and shouts of "Withdraw" from the Nationalist benches.

"I will amend what I said," the Colonel proceeded, "and say this murderous ruffian McFadden."

There were further shouts of "Order" and "Withdraw". One Nationalist Member interjected: "I say the expression of the honourable gentleman is a ruffianly expression."* Something approaching pandemonium then broke loose, the Speaker refusing to interfere and Colonel Saunderson refusing to withdraw. After some minutes of Babel, during which he made no attempt to continue his speech, the Colonel endeavoured to end matters by moving the adjournment of the House.

The Prime Minister thereupon rose in his place and earnestly appealed to Saunderson to abate the expression he had used and continue his speech in a more moderate tone. In this he was supported by the Opposition Leader, who expressed the hope at the same time that both parties would endeavour not unduly to irritate their opponents. At this Colonel Saunderson consented to substitute the words 'excited politician' for those which had been objected to, and so the House calmed down and the debate continued.

It was not until shortly after ten o'clock that John Morley was called by the Speaker. In those days the debate went on until midnight, so that Carson expected to have ample time for his reply. Unfortunately, Morley, who was frequently interrupted in the course of his speech, did not resume his seat until close on 11.30 p.m.

* Charles Diamond, M.P. for North Monaghan.

As this gave Carson barely half an hour, which he felt to be quite insufficient for the purpose of answering the Chief Secretary's arguments, he leant across to Balfour and suggested that it would be preferable to adjourn until the following day, rather than make his speech in two parts. Balfour agreed, and at his request the motion for the adjournment was made from one of the benches behind by Mr. Charles Darling, who hoped thereby to render his new friend a useful service. But Darling's motion was opposed on behalf of the Government by Sir William Harcourt, the Chancellor of the Exchequer. After some further discussion, in which Tim Healy joined, the motion was put to a division and defeated. This occupied an additional twenty minutes, so that when at last Carson's name was called and he got on his feet, the hands of the clock above the Speaker's Chair pointed to a quarter-to-twelve.

No one who has not experienced it himself can fully appreciate the terrifying ordeal of addressing the House of Commons for the first time. Little wonder was it that Carson felt nervous, though he did his best to conceal his feelings. He remembered that the Irish Members had shouted down Disraeli, when the future Conservative leader had attempted to make his maiden speech. Judging by the howls and groans of derision from the Nationalist benches which now greeted the tall frock-coated figure of the Member for Dublin University, he could not hope to escape similar treatment, although the convention had now come to be fairly generally accepted in the House that a maiden speaker should be heard without interruption. However, Carson had one advantage over Disraeli and other back-bencher speakers in his plight. Unlike them he was able to speak from the Front Bench, from which he had the assistance of the dispatch box and table on which to place his notes. In this respect indeed he established an interesting precedent. While various Members have on occasion spoken for the first time from the Treasury Bench on joining the Government, Carson is believed to be the only one who has ever delivered a maiden speech from the Front Bench on the Opposition side of the House.

When the jeers had died down below the gangway, Carson began quietly and modestly asking in his distinctive brogue for the indulgence of the House before, as he put it, "I have succeeded, at all events to my own satisfaction, in mastering the details of its procedure." He referred to his suggestion that it might have been more convenient to adjourn the debate until next day as appearing to him "a fair and reasonable proposition," but as the House had not acceded to it, he would proceed to analyse the past six months of Morley's Irish administration. He began by describing his repeal of the Crimes Act provisions as "the first heroic act" of the right honourable gentleman in Ireland. Morley had boasted that there had been a diminution in crime and had quoted statistics to prove it. But what about agrarian crime, asked Carson, and how many agrarian criminals had been brought to justice since Morley's regime began? Carson then went on to show the existence of many agrarian criminals who had recently committed outrages of a terrible character. Yet, as a result of the repeal of the Crimes Act, there had not been a single conviction of those charged at the last Assizes.

Fidgeting and whispering had now ceased on all the benches, and the House was listening attentively to the speaker. Here, Members were thinking, was someone who clearly knew what he was talking about.

Carson, who turned round towards Balfour every now and again, as if for encouragement, went on to examine Morley's next boast—"further evidence of the great success of his administration"—that rents were being better paid than ever before. Yet it was admittedly a period of agricultural depression. "It is certainly a curious coincidence," he continued, "that in the year in which there is this great agricultural depression we should find the Chief Secretary for Ireland boasting that the rents are particularly well paid in Ireland."

As Carson uttered these words, the chimes of Big Ben in the Parliament Clock Tower struck the hour of midnight. "Order. Order," called the Speaker, and the debate stood automatically adjourned.

Carson went off to bed in pessimistic mood. He had in truth succeeded in gaining the ear of the House, but he did not realise his success. A friend who called to see him next morning found him still in bed, complaining that he felt ill and convinced he had failed miserably. In the circumstances it seemed to him that the only thing to do was to hurry through the remainder of his speech as best he could.

He went down to the House early, but found he had to wait for some time, since after questions had been taken writs were moved for a number of new elections in constituencies—mostly Irish, where election petitions had been presented and the returns had been declared void on grounds of corruption—and this led to considerable discussion. It had already grown dark and the gas-lamps had been lit when Carson again got up in front of the dispatch box.

Continuing his theme from where he had left off the night before, Carson declared that payment of rent in Ireland was not dependent on the condition of the tenant farmers but whether men like John Dillon and other Nationalist leaders told them to pay. He then passed to the Evicted Tenants Commission, which he described as a "monstrous pretence" from its inception to the time it left Dublin. As for the President's opening statement, it was not only scandalous but incompetent as well. He proceeded to explain why. He (Carson) had appeared for Lord Clanricarde, whose case the President had segregated from those of the other landlords. "Yes," he said amid cheers, "I am not one of those counsel who selects his clients when they are on their trial. I am always quite willing to appear, to see that justice is done to any man." The learned judge ("if I may call him a judge") had stated that Lord Clanricarde had been invited to attend and had refused in an insulting manner. That was not true. His Lordship had not been invited to attend and had not refused. "On the contrary," said Carson, "he instructed me to attend for him and to examine him when he came before the Commission to see he got fair play."

Then there was the President's refusal to allow cross-examination. Carson was not even allowed to tell the Court why he particularly wished to cross-examine Mr. John Roche, M.P., the first witness. But he told the House of Commons, explaining that he had been present at a trial in Dublin when matters of the gravest responsibility had been proved against Roche in relation to the Clanricarde estate, but he had stolidly refused to give evidence. In fact, Roche had made a speech inciting the tenants to attack Lord Clanricarde's land agent, as a result of which the unfortunate man's body was shortly afterwards found riddled with bullets. According to his information, Roche had also stated that he was among those present at an eviction who helped to resist the Sheriff.

At this moment the Member in question, who had been sent for outside by one of his friends, hurried into the chamber. He broke into Carson's speech, defying him to find out when he said he was there for the purpose of resisting. "I said I was present at the eviction," he added, "and I was proud to be present."

"Exactly," said Carson. "I make no charge against the honourable Member. I am not accusing him of resisting the eviction, but having regard to the fact that he was there and proud of it, I suggest that at least I was entitled to put one question in cross-examination."

There was audible laughter on the surrounding benches as

Carson made this comment, and went on to refer to another speech of Mr. Roche in which he exhorted the tenantry of a certain landlord named Lewis to throttle him "until the glass eye fell out of his head."

Roche was again indignantly on his feet. "I did not tell the tenantry to throttle him," he said, "but I admit that in the heat and excitement of the moment—I was led away to an extent—I did make use of the expression that by adhering loyally to their pledges they would throttle him, and I hoped that they would not loose their grasp until the glass eye fell out of his head."

"Well," remarked Carson amid general laughter, "I really will leave it to the House whether that was a matter upon which one might have been allowed to put a question to the witness." There were no further interruptions from Mr. Roche.

Carson, who had by this time lost all traces of nervousness, went on to deal at length with the Gweedore prisoners, reinforcing the arguments which he had provided for Balfour. While not favouring such strong language as that used by Colonel Saunderson about Father McFadden, he showed, through quotations from the priest's speeches, that Father McFadden had publicly expressed the hope that vengeance would fall on the police "in this world as well as the next." Yet a Liberal M.P. in the same debate had admitted his regard and friendship for the reverend father. "The honourable gentleman is quite entitled to make his own friends," Carson commented acidly. "It is purely a matter of taste."

Carson had now been speaking for over an hour, and although it was past the usual time for dining, the House remained full and listened to him eagerly. He brought his speech to an end by saying that, after all the useful measures that had been set on foot in Ireland by Balfour, the only hope held out by his successor in office was "this miserable Home Rule Bill". Yet after six years of coercion the Irish Unionist representation in the House had actually increased by five at the recent General Election. "I do ask the right honourable gentleman, in all honesty and sincerity, in the interests of Ireland, if this policy is to be adhered to," he wound up, "not to keep the matter open one day longer than is necessary, and to take the verdict of the country upon the net issue." As he sat down he thanked the House, under a deep sense of obligation, "for the manner in which it has received me."

The cheering which followed this remarkable performance lasted for several minutes. Balfour patted him on the back, and Members poured round him with their congratulations in the lobby. From the Government Front Bench Asquith nodded approvingly. Morley called it an effort of signal ability and Mr. Gladstone said it was the best maiden speech he remembered.

Perhaps the most glowing tribute came from Joseph Chamberlain. As he drove away from the House that night, he said to his son Austen: "A new force has arisen in politics." And when he got home, the Liberal-Unionist leader sent Carson a warm note of congratulation. "It was the best debating speech I have heard for a long while in the House of Commons," he wrote, "and for a maiden speech I think it was unprecedented."

6

It would be an exaggeration to say that Carson woke up on the morning of February 4, 1893, to find himself famous. What he did find, however, and what everyone else found who read that morning's newspapers, was that overnight he had succeeded, at the age of thirty-eight, in establishing a brilliant parliamentary reputation. *The Times* devoted a leading article to his speech. "Mr. Carson made his points with convincing conciseness and lucidity," it wrote. Other journals, including the Liberal ones, were equally enthusiastic in their praise. "In Mr. Carson the Opposition have secured a redoubtable ally," wrote the *Pall Mall Gazette*. "On all sides," wrote the *Sheffield Telegraph*, "the opinion is ungrudgingly conceded that a rich acquisition has been made to the debating power of the House, and that the Unionists have added to their Front Bench an orator of the first rank." Even a men's fashion paper admired the way he had been dressed for the occasion, noting with approval that the revers of his frock-coat were "nicely covered with silk" while "in length the frock reached almost to the knees."

In expectation of a strenuous session Carson took a set of furnished rooms at No. 19 Bury Street, off St. James's Street, which he found convenient for the House and the Carlton Club. He hoped too that he might be able to get some law work, but discovered that he had to apply for readmission to the Middle Temple, and that he could not consequently be called to the English Bar until after Easter. Having gone through this ceremony, he went to see Charles Darling, who, in fulfilment of the promise he had made the previous summer, had Carson's name painted on the door of his chambers in Dr. Johnson's Buildings.*

* Carson was called to the English Bar at the Middle Temple on April 26, 1893.

The newly-called barrister contemplated his prospects in the Temple with the gloomiest forebodings. Life was expensive in the English capital. He had Annette and the children to maintain in Dublin, and his savings were fast becoming exhausted. But, as events turned out, he did not have long to wait. His first brief was delivered in a curious way—not, as usually happens, through the intervention of a friend or the clerk in his chambers. An English solicitor went along to the House of Commons and sent in a visitor's 'green card' addressed to him. Carson came out to the central lobby and, somewhat to his surprise, was asked by the visitor if he would be willing to undertake a Chancery case. There was a particular reason for his request. A dispute had arisen over the precise meaning of a deed which on examination turned out to have been drawn by Carson when he was a pupil of George Price, the equity draughtsman, in Dublin over fifteen years before. Carson accepted the case, and in due course appeared before Mr. Justice Chitty in the Chancery Division of the High Court, where his unique knowledge of the subject matter enabled him to justify his client's interpretation of the deed.

This case proved to be one of the few occasions on which Carson was briefed in Chancery. Briefs began to trickle into No. 3 Dr. Johnson's Buildings, but they were largely on the Queen's Bench side, though some of them involved visits to the Old Bailey. Despite the fact that he was an Irish Q.C., Carson was rated as a junior at the English Bar.* Cases came to him, however, in which he was instructed as a leader, and this meant that on account of his very recent call to the Bar virtually every 'junior' briefed to appear with him in these cases was senior to him in standing. By the etiquette of the Bar, they were obliged to leave the Court when Carson began to examine or cross-examine a witness. "Who the dickens is Carson?" one of these juniors asked the instructing solicitor on such an occasion. The junior, in age four years younger than his 'leader', was soon to be enlightened. His name was Edward Marshall-Hall, and while a great career as an advocate lay before him, the only opponent in the Courts he was to fear was Edward Carson.

Carson's first big case in England occurred within three months of his call to the Bar there. It was a libel action brought by a Liberal M.P. and trade union leader against the *Evening News*. The plaintiff,

* Marjoribanks makes a curious mistake in his life of Carson when he gives this as the reason for Darling's action in having Carson's name painted on the door of his chambers without the initials 'Q.C.' (*Life of Lord Carson*, at p. 137). No English 'silk' in fact ever has these initials appearing after his name on the door.

Mr. Joseph Havelock Wilson, who sat for Middlesbrough in the House of Commons, was the founder and general secretary of the National Amalgamated Sailors' and Firemen's Union, afterwards known as the National Union of Seamen. His financial administration of the union's affairs had been violently attacked by the *Evening News*, which described "the prodigality with which the pence of the sailors are spent by the general secretary and executive of the union," asserting that the accounts were so jumbled together that it was difficult to arrive at the gross costs of administration, and denounced as "a scandalous state of things" the relatively large sum (£10,000) which found its way into the pockets of the general secretary and his staff by way of salaries. "If J. H. Wilson, M.P., thinks the incompetency which he has displayed in the management of the affairs of the Sailors' Union is to be tolerated for ever, he is very short-sighted." The newspaper also alleged that Wilson had deliberately promoted a strike in the previous year in order to burke enquiry into the financial affairs of the union and suggested that the seamen were paying their pence into a hopelessly insolvent concern.

The action came on at Guildford Assizes before Mr. Justice Grantham on July 24, 1893. Carson appeared for the *Evening News*, leading Mr. H. C. Richards and Mr. W. M. Thompson, two practitioners on the South-Eastern Circuit. As a defence he pleaded that the words complained of were "fair comment on a matter of public interest." The plaintiff was represented by the Hon. Bernard Coleridge, Q.C., Mr. Corrie Grant and another junior. The other junior counsel for the plaintiff was the brilliant thirty-two-year-old Rufus Isaacs, who had once been a stockbroker and been 'hammered' on the Exchange, and was only just beginning to make his way at the English Bar. It was the first time Isaacs had met Carson, and the first of many occasions on which they were to be pitted against each other in the Courts. On this particular summer day the Assize Court was crowded with interested onlookers, who included Mr. Keir Hardie, M.P., Mr. Tom Mann and other pioneers of the trade union movement.

In opening the plaintiff's case, Mr. Coleridge told the jury that his client claimed £7,000 from the *Evening News* for the very grossest libel, which the defendant newspaper did not attempt to justify in a manly way. Although it had virtually charged Mr. Wilson with bribery and corruption, the paper nevertheless preferred to rely on the defence of 'fair comment'. Said counsel: "The paper must now prove its charge or pay damages." But Carson refused to be drawn by this invitation to amend his defence, which, if he had accepted it, might well have led him into a trap.

Wilson went into the box with a jaunty air. He answered his counsel's questions with marked confidence.

Then Carson rose to cross-examine. He began very quietly. Had the witness himself founded the union? Yes, in 1887. The sailors paid only sixpence a week. Wilson's salary was only £250 a year. He had very little to do with the funds of the union. He was concerned with policy. Local secretaries collected the money and, after deducting branch expenses, sent the rest to headquarters.

So far Mr. Wilson was on good ground. Then came the first delicate question. Had there been any defalcations by the local secretaries? Yes, possibly to the amount of £2,000 since the union was formed.

Carson then went on to ask Wilson about his various election expenses. The witness said he had spent £201 at Deptford and £506 at Bristol.

Carson held up a paper in his hand.

"You say in your declaration, your sworn declaration, that at Bristol the expenses of your election had been £900 odd?"

"Yes."

Carson picked out another document from the pile beside him.

"Yet in this balance sheet there is £500 donated by the union for the expenses of that very contest?"

"Yes." Wilson looked uncomfortable, as he added, "I cannot explain that."

Carson continued with a stream of embarrassing questions.

"You also say that no club or association paid anything for you. You say that in your sworn declaration. How do you explain that?"

Wilson began to mop his brow.

"I did not think there was anything illegal in that at the time," he said.

Wilson was then asked about the allegation that the union executive had called a strike 'to burke enquiry into the finances'.

"Was there a strike?"

"Yes."

"Did you say at that meeting that if there were not a strike you would be ruined?"

"No, I do not think so."

"Did you say you were liable to £600 on bills?"

The witness now looked plainly unhappy. He replied haltingly:

"I do not know. I said I had received money from various friends, which I had paid away on behalf of the union, and that I was liable for these."

Next day Wilson was asked about the union rules. It appeared that there was no power to alter the rule governing the date of the annual meeting, yet the general secretary had done so. "We did not act upon the rule," he said.

The rules had been further violated by the payment of strike money to other unions. Large sums had been given for this purpose on Wilson's own initiative, without the authority of the executive committee. The Glasgow dock labourers, for example, got £400 and the Sausage-Skin Manufacturers' Union £50.

"What have sausage-skin dressers to do with seamen?" asked Carson with an affected air of bewilderment.

This question provoked loud laughter in Court. Then Carson found another paper, which he glanced at as if searching for something, and continued: "Ah, was not this union in Deptford, where you were a candidate?"

"I cannot say."

And so it went on. Carson's remorseless cross-examination elicited a pathetic story of financial recklessness and incompetence. The climax came at the end of the second day when Wilson was asked about the Parliamentary Labour Commission which sat to enquire into working conditions.

"What is this item of £44 given as payment to witnesses at the Labour Commission? Doesn't the Government pay witnesses?"

"Yes."

"Why do you pay yours as well?"

Wilson did not answer. Carson repeated the question. At last the witness spoke. He was clearly on the verge of breaking down.

"These men told me they had been employed by the Shipping Board to ruin the union and me, and I asked them to go before the Commission to say so. £30 was given them against a possible boycott by the shipowners, and to enable them to start in business."

Carson looked round the Court.

"Why was one of these witnesses here today?"

The Member for Middlesbrough could stand this inquisition no longer. He burst into tears and was led away from the courtroom sobbing pitifully.

Next morning Wilson returned to the box a broken man. Luckily his ordeal was almost over. He was asked now about the union's 'legal expenses'. Had £600 of these been used to launch a prosecution for criminal libel against a fellow member of the union for calling the general secretary "a thief, a villain and a rascal"? Yes —and the prosecution had been dismissed!

Carson had won his case by this cross-examination. Thus when he opened his defence, he took the unusual course of calling no witnesses and merely addressing the jury in a short speech.

After retiring for a short time the jury brought in a verdict for Carson's clients, except in respect of one minor statement for which they awarded Wilson the handsome sum of one farthing damages.

The case aroused the greatest interest, and was discussed up and down the country, serving as it did to focus public attention on the trade union movement.

For his performance in it the Press were as generous to Carson as they had been about his maiden speech. "Rarely has there been such a fiasco in a law Court," wrote *The Times* in a leading article in which it paid a warm tribute to "Mr. Carson's most thorough and searching cross-examination."

At this time the acknowledged leaders, of the English Bar were Sir Charles Russell and Sir Edward Clarke. Patrick Murphy, Q.C., an old hand at the game, who sat through the whole of Carson's cross-examination of Havelock Wilson at Guildford, gave it as his considered opinion that Carson was better than either of these distinguished advocates.

Carson appreciated these compliments. But what touched him most was a telegram of congratulation he received from the Four Courts in Dublin. It was signed by a representative committee of the Irish Bar. His old friends and colleagues in the library had not forgotten him.

7

While building up a new practice in the English Courts, Carson could not afford to neglect his parliamentary duties. He had to justify the reputation which he had established with his maiden speech. He did so a few weeks afterwards when the question of the cost of the Evicted Tenants Commission, before which tribunal he had himself appeared in dramatic circumstances in Dublin, came before the House on a vote. The Liberal Attorney-General, Sir Charles Russell, intervened in the debate to defend the course which had been adopted by the Commission's President in the matter of cross-examining witnesses, asserting that no commission analagous to this one had ever allowed the right of cross-examination in the sense in which it had been claimed by the junior Member for Dublin University.

This brought Carson quickly to his feet. He explained to the House that he did not claim as an absolute right the privilege of cross-examination, but he submitted that in this particular case, if someone did not undertake the process of sifting the truth by cross-examination, the proceedings would be 'a farce and a sham'. He then proceeded to brand the Commission's recommendations in its Report as 'audacious' and 'fraudulent devices' to fulfil political promises. "I venture to suggest that this Report is so absolutely useless for any purpose that can be suggested," he added, "that we as custodians of the public purse have no right to spend a penny on the Commission."

Carson's speech was full of vigour and fight, and, though it did not dissuade the House from accepting the Report and agreeing to the cost, which it did by thirty-seven votes, the speech greatly heartened the Opposition and pleased Balfour. But it was in the prolonged debates on Gladstone's second Home Rule Bill, which continued throughout the session, that Carson really consolidated his parliamentary reputation.

This measure was introduced by the Prime Minister in a speech of two-and-a-quarter hours, an amazing feat for a man of eighty-four, even if it lacked something of the fire which had marked his previous performance in 1886. The Bill differed from the earlier measure in several important particulars. Most important was the retention of eighty Irish Members at Westminster. In the original draft Bill these Members were only to vote on Imperial and Irish affairs, but this limitation was subsequently dropped and they were to have representation for all purposes. Defence, foreign relations, postal services, coinage and Customs were to be reserved to the Imperial Parliament, and for three years also the vexed land question; Customs and Excise levied in Ireland were to be regarded as the country's contribution for the Imperial services which she enjoyed.

While Salisbury and Balfour harangued excited crowds in Ulster against the Bill, the House of Commons sat throughout the hot summer of that year, discussing the measure at seemingly interminable length long into each night. 1,400 speeches were delivered by the nation's rulers on this contentious piece of legislation in proceedings which occupied altogether more than 200 hours of parliamentary time. Yet everyone knew that this Home Rule Bill was bound to be rejected by the Lords, while the Nationalist Party held mixed views as to its merits. John Redmond, who likened it to a "toad, ugly and venomous, yet wearing a precious jewel in its head," gave it but grudging support. "No man in his senses," he said when it finally emerged from Committee, "can any longer regard it as either a full or final or a satisfactory settlement of the Irish question."

Night after night Carson came down to the House to spend many weary hours on the Opposition Front Bench, watching the Bill at every stage. He proved indefatigable in moving amendments and new clauses, arguing about lines here and lines there, phrases and single words. It was an invaluable if gruelling experience for him, for he emerged a thoroughly experienced parliamentary hand at the end of the session. Those he came up against in the process included such tried House of Commons men as Harcourt, Russell, Asquith, Morley and Gladstone himself, not to mention O'Brien, Healy, Redmond, Dillon and the other leading Nationalists. Yet, effective as he was, Carson could not shake off the manner which he had acquired as Crown Prosecutor in Ireland. Among those who watched his performance from the Press Gallery and noted this trait was the correspondent Henry Lucy, who as 'Toby, M.P.' reported proceedings in Parliament for *Punch*. "When he is discussing the speech or action of an hon. or right hon. gentleman opposite," wrote Lucy of Carson at this time, "he always treats him as if he had found him in the dock, and as if his brief hinted at unutterable crimes brought home by the inquiry and testimony of members of the Irish Constabulary. The manner is so natural and ingrained that there is doubt whether it will ever be overcome or even modified. This is a pity, for it is simply professional. Nevertheless—indeed, therefore—it will never do in the House of Commons." This criticism has often been applied to lawyers generally in Parliament, and in Carson's case it had undoubted substance. However, as the years passed it must be admitted that he did succeed in modifying this peculiar characteristic, although he never entirely lost it.

The most exciting as well as the most remarkable incident in the Home Rule debates of this session occurred at the conclusion of the Committee stage. In fact it must have been one of the most extraordinary scenes ever witnessed in the House of Commons. It was the night of July 27, 1893, when the debate was due to end at ten o'clock; since the closure would be moved at that hour, all the clauses in the measure would be put to the vote one by one from the Chair. The Unionist leader, Joseph Chamberlain, was speaking in a crowded and excited House, describing the Liberal Party's blind obedience to their Prime Minister. "Never since the time of Herod has there been such slavish adulation," he said. This allusion proved too much for one Nationalist Member, T. P. O'Connor, founder of the successful London evening newspaper the *Star*, who sat for the Scotland division of Liverpool. "Judas, Judas," O'Connor shouted at the man whose action he considered had betrayed the Home Rule cause seven years before. A few moments later, in the midst of loud cheering and counter-cheering, Big Ben struck ten and the Chairman proceeded to put the question. A Conservative Member, Mr. Vicary Gibbs, was seen to be 'seated and covered' according to the parliamentary tradition which requires any Member wishing to raise a point of order during a division to do so remaining seated with his hat on his head. He accordingly moved that Mr. O'Connor's words should be 'taken down', with a view to the Member either withdrawing them or apologising. Above the uproar which had now developed, the Chairman was heard declaring that the expression had not reached his ears. "It reached mine," shouted the indomitable Vicary Gibbs. "I move that it be taken down."

Mr. Gibbs persisted in trying to raise his point of order, but he was shouted down. Eventually the Chairman put the question again, and Members began to file into the division lobbies. But many of the Opposition thought that their Member should be heard, and they remained in their places. Others clustered angrily round the door, also refusing to enter their division lobby until the Chairman took action.

In those days, when a division took place, Members from both sides of the House, instead of leaving the chamber by opposite doors as they do at present, passed into the lobbies through the door behind the Speaker's Chair, where the two moving streams met and commingled. On this occasion the entrance became blocked, since there were further shouts from the Opposition Front Bench which caused Members to linger by the door to see what further disturbance was afoot. Some Liberal Members were standing in the centre of the Chamber, and this provoked Carson and some of his friends to shout "Bar! Bar!", meaning that they should retire below the Bar. At this Mr. J. W. Logan, Liberal M.P. for Market Harborough, crossed over to the Opposition Front Bench and addressed its occupants in strikingly unparliamentary language. "Hold your bloody row," he said. To this unexpected salutation Carson replied in equally spirited terms: "Get out, you gagger." This was the description customarily applied by those wishing for the continuance of the debate to those who sought to terminate it by the 'gag' or closure.

Logan, who appeared flushed and excited, thereupon seated himself in a threatening attitude beside Carson on the Front Bench. But any offensive action which Logan contemplated taking was promptly anticipated by another Member, normally a most quiet and respectable individual, named Hayes Fisher, afterwards Lord Downham. He sat immediately behind Carson and now leaned forward, seizing Logan under the chin and pulling his head back over the bench. Logan then struck out at Carson, but was overpowered by several of Carson's colleagues who interfered. The Irish Nationalists thereupon joined in with a yell, hitting out right, left and centre, the principal object of their attentions being the redoubtable Colonel Saunderson. That stalwart Unionist was soon in his element, distributing blows on all sides against his attackers. When little Dr. Tanner approached him from behind and struck him on his bald head, Saunderson turned round and sent him flying with a sweep of his long arm. The fracas now became general, and soon fights were seen to be going on in every corner of the Chamber. At least forty Members—what is known in quieter times as a quorum—were inextricably mingled below the gangway. One Member was knocked down and dragged out of the scuffle by his heels. John Ross, who was watching the scene from the Bar, ran forward to assist an elderly gentleman who had been felled to the ground with a particularly severe blow. He was forcibly restrained by a fellow Member who was convinced he was intent on further revenge. "No, you don't! No, you don't!" murmured the restraining Member as he held Ross fast.

The scrimmage lasted for nearly twenty minutes, hats being blocked, coats torn and faces bruised. Thick clouds of dust arose throughout the Chamber as the fighting became fiercer. A rail on one of the benches became dislodged in the turmoil and suddenly stood upright—a strange omen, as Tim Healy noted, like a dead arm thrusting itself from a corpse in *rigor mortis*. Meanwhile, the Serjeant-at-Arms strode about doing his best to induce Members to enter the division lobbies, but his efforts were unheeded. The onlookers in the galleries, shocked at the spectacle of elderly frock-coated M.P.s belabouring each other, began to hiss, and their admonition had some effect on the disorderly groups below. Suddenly the uproar ended, as swiftly as it had begun.

Mr. Speaker Peel, who had been sent for, was observed standing beside the Chair, surveying the extraordinary scene with an Olympian frown. The noise died down. In a few moments everything was quiet. "Will some Member tell me what has occurred?" The Speaker spoke in the sternest tones.

For a moment or two there was silence as honourable Members eyed each other uncomfortably. Then Mr. Gladstone rose in his place, like the head-boy of a class who had failed to keep order in the teacher's absence. He looked embarrassed as he gave his explanation. His embarrassment was increased by an old Member from the Opposition side who kept interrupting, "All your fault! All your fault!" Suddenly everyone began to laugh. The Grand Old Man sat down, obviously discomfited, while T. P. O'Connor, the original cause of all the trouble, got up to apologise. Honour was satisfied.

The incident ended on a note of humorous anti-climax. The Clerk of the House proceeded to the next business on the Order Paper, solemnly announcing the title of the legislation concerned and the name of the honourable Member introducing it.

"Order! Order! Plumbers Registration Bill. Second Reading, the Marquess of Carmarthen."

Carson joined in the general merriment, as the future Duke of Leeds rose to move formally that this important measure be read a second time.

As for the Home Rule Bill, it passed its third reading in the Commons by thirty-four votes, a small enough majority for a measure embodying such constitutional changes. Then it went to the Lords, where its fate was a foregone conclusion. Their Lordships, most of whom rarely visited Westminster, turned out in unprecedented strength to vote against the obnoxious measure. It was said that a number of them, who had been kept under restraint as mental cases, were specially 'enlarged' for the occasion, and walked through the 'Not Content' division lobby to record their votes under the eyes of their 'keepers'.

At all events, the Lords rejected the Bill by 378. It was a cruel disappointment for Gladstone, who had hoped to see a measure of Home Rule for Ireland on the statute book before he retired. Yet another generation was to have grown up before that object was to be achieved in the most momentous days of Carson's life.

It was during this arduous session that Carson found himself at some non-party gathering beside the Liberal Chancellor of the Exchequer, Sir William Harcourt, who was shortly to become Leader of the House of Commons. "You're a young man, full of enthusiasm for your cause, are you not?" Harcourt addressed him. "Yes," said Carson. "And you put absolute trust in your party," continued Harcourt, "I can see that." "Yes," said Carson.

"Well, sir," said Harcourt, "sooner or later there is going to be a terrible disillusion for you. The Conservatives, mark my word, never yet took up a cause without betraying it in the end, and I don't think you'll betray it with them."

When the final settlement with Ireland came nearly thirty years later, Carson had occasion ruefully to remember this prophecy.

CHAPTER FIVE

Queen's Counsel

I

IN the 'nineties, and indeed for long afterwards, when newsprint was abundant, proceedings both parliamentary and legal were reported at much greater length than they are today. While Carson's exertions during the Home Rule debates were thus widely noticed, the word began to go round the Temple that here was a new man from Ireland who charged less than the English fees but gave clients as good if not better value for their money. After his success in the Havelock Wilson case the flow of briefs to Dr. Johnson's Buildings took on a steady spurt, and Carson would rise at five o'clock in the morning to work on them by candlelight.

In November, 1893, he received the coveted distinction of a cartoon in the fashionable weekly magazine *Vanity Fair*. This was entitled 'Dublin University' and depicted him in a characteristic attitude speaking in front of the dispatch box in the House of Commons. The cartoon was accompanied by a character sketch in which the writer, who veiled his identity behind the signature 'Jehu Junior', employed as bold and vigorous strokes as the artist. "Having more knowledge of Ireland than most Members of Parliament," so read this miniature biography, "he contrives, though he has not yet made a great name as a statesman, to say even more distasteful things about the oppressed Nationalists than the most brutal of Saxons. He is a bold and sinuous person, who pays no heed at all to the persuasions of the Nationalists who so prettily chide him for his want of patriotism. He seems to like the disgrace of being stigmatised as Mr. Balfour's Crown Prosecutor; nor is he put out when he is openly said to be as big a blackguard as ever was Peter the Packer . . . yet he is not without virtue. He has not much of a practice in England; but he has appeared in a case which arose out of a modern Labour trouble, and it is possible that he will get more clients. For he is a hard-working, painstaking, lynx-eyed practitioner who can speak strongly. He is a lean, pale-faced Irishman, who has as much wit and as much ability as Irishmen often have. He has not fattened even on robust Unionism."

The anonymous author of this contribution to *Vanity Fair* did not realise how rapidly Carson's practice was growing. By the following spring Carson had been practising for a year at the English Bar, and Darling reminded him of their bet. "I told you that if you allowed me to paint your name over my door," said Darling, "you'd have five times my practice within a year, and you bet me a shilling you wouldn't." Darling was right. His clerk had been going through Carson's fee book, and he did owe Darling this sum. Carson smilingly paid up—in kind. A few days later he brought with him to chambers a stout Irish blackthorn walking-stick which had cost exactly a shilling. It bore a silver band with the inscription, 'C.D. from E.C. 1894'. Carson told his colleague that it had once belonged to a fearless Irish Resident Magistrate named Cecil Roche, and had done good service on the heads of some of his fellow countrymen. "It has a sword grip," said Carson, "and it won't turn in your hand, as it grew between two stones." Darling accepted the stick, and it remained one of his treasured possessions until his death: he always liked telling the story of how he acquired it.

Among the judges before whom Carson appeared at this time, particularly at the Old Bailey, was Sir Henry Hawkins, later Lord Brampton, the greatest criminal judge of his time and himself a master of the art of cross-examination. They became friends and the judge used to invite Carson to his room in the Courts, as he enjoyed a good Irish story. One day, early in the year 1894, Hawkins remarked that Carson should be made a Queen's Counsel, and he suggested that he should send in his application to the Lord Chancellor for a silk gown. Carson did so, but he was not included in the next batch of 'silks', whose names for that year were announced according to custom at Easter. Lord Herschell, the Liberal Lord Chancellor, replied that there was no precedent for the creation of a Q.C. of scarcely a year's standing at the English Bar, even if he was an Irish Q.C., and that he would have to undergo the necessary period of qualification, which was nine years. Carson was furious at this rebuff. That an Irish 'silk' and former Solicitor-General for Ireland, in good and increasing practice in the English Courts, must continue to wear the stuff gown of a junior barrister he considered not merely an affront to himself but to the whole Irish Bar. It seemed absurd too that in the House of Lords and Privy Council, the highest Courts of appeal in the land, he could don the silk gown of an Irish Queen's Counsel. The *Evening News*, grateful for his defence of their interests in the Havelock Wilson case, described the refusal as "a piece of flagrant injustice", though it might appear quite consistent to Lord Herschell. "This is not due to Queen Victoria," wrote that newspaper, "but the Lord Chancellor Herschell, the Keeper of the Queen's Conscience, has refused to allow him to wear his silk gown in the ordinary Courts of law." The truth was that Carson was far from popular in Liberal circles, where his attack on Mr. Justice Mathew as President of the Evicted Tenants Commission had been greatly resented.

In view of what had happened, Carson determined never to renew his application so long as Lord Herschell remained on the Woolsack. But another took up the cudgels on his behalf. Mr. Justice Hawkins, who had prompted the original application, wrote to the Lord Chancellor saying that it was a scandal that Carson was not made an English Q.C. The result of this letter, aided no doubt by the protests in the Press, was that Lord Herschell relented and agreed to the creation of an additional Queen's Counsel if Carson would accept this honour at his hands. Carson agreed to do so when he was approached, as he had no wish to suffer through his own obstinacy. Accordingly, he went down alone to receive his patent from the Lord Chancellor. Each was dressed, as the occasion demanded, in full-bottomed wigs, knee-breeches and buckled shoes. Not a word was exchanged between them, as Lord Herschell solemnly handed over the patent. Carson withdrew without even a congratulatory handshake and made his way back to the Strand, where he was called 'within the Bar' by the presiding judge in each Court. Usually, of course, all the Q.C.s appointed every spring participate in this picturesque scene together. Carson made his progress from Court to Court unaccompanied by any of his fellows, bowing to the judge and counsel as he took his place in the front row of the barristers' benches. The last Court which he visited was that of Mr. Justice Kekewich, a Chancery judge, whom he discovered had finished his work and risen for the day.

Curiously enough the very first brief Carson had as an English Q.C. was in this very Court next morning. As Carson opened his case, the judge, who liked all the forms to be strictly observed, kept interrupting: "I can't hear you, Mr. Carson." Carson raised his voice, which eventually reached a shout. He said it had never been his experience in the past that his voice was not audible to the Bench.

"Mr. Carson, you don't take my point," interposed the judge. "You have not been called within the Bar of my Court. But I don't propose to send you home to put on your knee-breeches, as perhaps I should."

"I should hope *not*," said Carson.

The judge sat up. "What's that? What's that you say?" he asked petulantly. "I warn you I shall tolerate no impertinence."

Carson smiled. "I thought your Lordship could not hear me," he remarked pleasantly. There was a general outburst of laughter at this, in which even Mr. Justice Kekewich joined, and the case proceeded.

The new Q.C. received many congratulations, both public and private. The newspapers on both sides of the Irish channel noted his promotion with interest as well as approval, since there were two striking precedents involved. No silk gown had ever previously been given to a barrister within such a short time of being called to the Bar. Also, it was the first time that an Irish Q.C. had ever 'taken silk' in England. In the seventeenth and eighteenth centuries an English barrister had occasionally sat on the Irish Bench, resuming his practice as a 'junior' in England on the termination of his appointment. But no one had ever previously attained the rank of senior counsel at both the English and the Irish Bars. To Mrs. Darling, the wife of his colleague in the Temple and at Westminster, who sent him her best wishes, Carson replied: "I feel somewhat like what I should think a man getting married for the second time feels—as if I was quite accustomed to the ceremony."

Two other friends who expressed their unfeigned pleasure at Carson's success were Lord and Lady Londonderry. They extended to him in London the same generous hospitality as they had done when they occupied the Viceregal Lodge in Dublin. "A great friendship developed between us," Carson recalled long afterwards. "Anything like Lord Londonderry's kindness to me in those days I've never known. When I came over here, if he had been my own brother he could not have been kinder." His beautiful and gifted wife, who had a passion for politics, was equally kind. She would always refer to him familiarly as 'the Solicitor', in allusion to his first office. Londonderry House, the splendid mansion in Park Lane where the host and hostess entertained on a magnificent scale, became a second home for Edward Carson. It was the same at their country places, Mount Stewart, their lovely County Down home on the shores of Strangford Lough, and Wynyard Park, with its beautiful gardens and terraces, in County Durham. Here Carson was a frequent and welcome guest, and there was no political house-party at either of these places to which he was not invited. "I am sure," he once wrote to Lady Londonderry, "the most interesting chapter in my biography will be the one headed *Visits to Wynyard and Mount Stewart*—but how will the biographer ever really understand how delightful these visits have been and why you and his Lordship have always been so kind to me? . . . No one is ever more helpful than yourself and you have indeed been a kind and affectionate friend."

Lady Londonderry often attended debates in the House of Commons, seated behind the grille high up above the Press Gallery, the only place from which ladies were permitted to view the proceedings in those days. Here she watched 'the Solicitor's' parliamentary progress with interest and satisfaction. The session of 1894 had opened with the retirement of Gladstone from the Treasury Bench and his replacement as Prime Minister by that spoiled child of fortune, Lord Rosebery, while Sir William Harcourt became Leader of the Commons. The new Premier wished to curb the power of the House of Lords by abolishing the veto, a policy which provoked that Chamber to reject many of the Bills which had previously passed through the Commons. He also created consternation in his own party as well as exasperating the Nationalists by announcing that "before Irish Home Rule is concluded by the Imperial Parliament, England as the predominant member of the partnership . . . will have to be convinced of its justice and equity." This was interpreted as meaning that Home Rule could only be passed with the aid of purely English votes.

During this session Carson scored a notable triumph with a speech on the Evicted Tenants Bill, which aimed at restoring tenants in Ireland who had been evicted as long as fifteen years previously for non-payment of rent, regardless of whether the property was in occupation of new tenants. These evicted tenants had, of course, deliberately refused to pay their rents, as part of the Plan of Campaign. "You are putting a premium on illegality," said Carson, pointing an accusing finger at Chief Secretary Morley, who had introduced the measure; "the purpose of the Bill is to restore, not tenants who could not pay, but those who could but would not for political reasons. . . . It is equivalent to telling people that, if they will only commit a sufficient number of outrages, they will bring the question they desire to raise within the sphere of practical politics."

Though Carson's arguments did not prevent the Bill being passed by the Commons—it was later rejected by the Lords—his speech won praise from his political opponents. R. B. Haldane, M.P., a future Liberal Lord Chancellor, referred to it as "a brilliant speech worthy of his great reputation," while the Liberal *Daily News* described it as "by far the best thing he has done in Parliament." The same newspaper described Mr. Balfour as being "in raptures over it".

One night, while such a discussion as this was in progress, Lord Randolph Churchill, who had returned to the Opposition Front Bench with the shadow of a fatal illness heavy upon him, invited Carson home to dinner. His young son Winston had been listening to the debate from the gallery, and they all drove back together to Lord Randolph's house in Grosvenor Square.

"What do you think of it all?" Carson asked the young man.

"I see you've been remarkably busy this session," replied the eighteen-year-old Winston solemnly. "The worst of it is you are likely to continue so, as the ship of State will be in very stormy waters so long as the Government steers its present course."

2

In the same month as Carson 'took silk' at the English Bar, its leader, the Liberal Attorney-General Sir Charles Russell, went to the House of Lords as a Lord of Appeal, with the title of Lord Russell of Killowen. A few weeks later he succeeded Lord Coleridge as Lord Chief Justice of England. Russell was the ablest all-round advocate of his day, and the only one whom Carson really feared. His elevation was thus of particular significance to the younger man. As a contemporary newspaper put it in remarkably prophetic language, "Exit one Irishman; enter another—Sir Charles Russell will no longer plead a cause, and his place looks like being taken by Mr. Carson." By a strange stroke of fate it was through Russell's solicitor son, a partner in the firm of Russell and Day, that Carson jumped into the first rank of English advocates in one of the most tragic criminal cases ever heard at the Old Bailey. Indeed it was at the suggestion of the Lord Chief Justice, whom the son consulted, that the leading brief was delivered to Carson. When he opened it, Carson found to his surprise that it was to defend Lord Queensberry on a charge of criminal libel. The libelled person who had instituted the pro-

40, Prince's Gardens. S.W.

Friday night

Dear Mr Carson

You must allow me to congratulate you warmly on your splendid speech. It was the best debating speech I have heard for a long while in the House of Commons, & for a maiden effort I think it was unprecedented.

Yours very truly

J. Chamberlain

LETTER FROM JOSEPH CHAMBERLAIN TO EDWARD CARSON CONGRATULATING HIM ON HIS MAIDEN SPEECH IN THE HOUSE OF COMMONS.

From the original in the possession of Lady Carson.

GLADSTONE INTRODUCING THE SECOND HOME RULE BILL IN THE HOUSE OF COMMONS, FEBRUARY 13, 1893

Carson can be seen leaning back in the middle of the Opposition Front Bench.

From an engraving of the painting by Sir William Ponsonby Staples, Bt.

secution was no other than Carson's old college contemporary, Oscar Wilde, now at the height of his success as a playwright.*

Apart from this *cause célèbre*, the eccentric eighth Marquess of Queensberry is best remembered as the author of the rules of boxing which bear his name. Otherwise his career bears little credit. He was a professed atheist, who as a representative peer of Scotland refused to take the oath in the House of Lords, as he objected to such 'Christian tomfoolery'. Arrogant and ill-tempered, he bullied his family unmercifully: indeed for a long time past he had not been on speaking terms with any of them. In 1891 his third son, Lord Alfred Douglas, then a handsome youth of twenty-two, who was an undergraduate at Oxford, had been introduced to Wilde. The two men immediately became warm friends. Douglas found in the elder man a most entertaining companion, and it flattered his vanity to be seen in the company of such an acknowledged wit as Wilde. Wilde, on the other hand, was attracted by the undergraduate's marked good looks as well as by his undoubted poetic gifts, and he was also influenced by the fact—for, like many Irishmen, he had a strong vein of snobbery in his make-up—that his young friend was a lord. On Wilde's side, at least, the friendship rapidly developed into infatuation, and he made no secret of his feelings, flattering the younger man and writing him ecstatic letters and sonnets. Unfortunately for Wilde, two of these letters, which were accidentally left in the pocket of an old suit of clothes given by Douglas to an unemployed clerk named Wood whom he had befriended while still up at Oxford, and which were subsequently used in an unsuccessful attempt to blackmail Wilde, later found their way into Queensberry's possession. "It is a marvel that those red rose-leaf lips of yours should have been made no less for music of song than for madness of kisses," Wilde had written in the first of these letters. "Your slim gilt soul walks between passion and poetry. I know Hyacinthus, whom Apollo loved so madly, was you in Greek days."

The boxing Marquess was determined to break up this association, which he considered most harmful to his son. He warned the managers of the various restaurants frequented by Wilde and his son that he would thrash them both if he discovered them together on the premises. He called at Wilde's house in Tite Street, accom-

* The account given here is necessarily condensed. For a more detailed narrative, together with a full transcript of the proceedings in Court, the reader is referred to *The Trials of Oscar Wilde*, edited by the present writer, with a Foreword by Sir Travers Humphreys (Notable British Trials Series), 1948.

panied by an ex-prize-fighter, and repeated his threat. He attempted to create a scene on the first night of *The Importance of Being Earnest*, when he turned up at the theatre with a bouquet of vegetables, but failed to secure admission. Finally he resorted to the characteristic and offensive action which was calculated to bring the matter to a head. He called at the Albemarle Club, to which Wilde and his wife both belonged, and left a visiting card with the hall porter which he asked should be given to Wilde. On the back of this card the irate caller had written: "To Oscar Wilde posing as a somdomite", the latter word being thus misspelled in his fury. The porter, who looked at the card without understanding the meaning of the inscription, put it in an envelope on the afternoon of February 28, 1895. On his next visit to the club ten days later, the envelope was handed to Wilde. He immediately consulted his solicitor, with the result that Queensberry was arrested next morning and later the same day brought before the magistrate in Great Marlborough Street Court.

After hearing formal evidence, the magistrate adjourned the case for a week and released Queensberry on bail. His solicitor was Sir George Lewis, head of the well-known firm of Lewis and Lewis and a shrewd lawyer, who had a reputation for clever handling of awkward society cases. But, while he appeared for his client at this hearing, he told him immediately afterwards that he could no longer act for him. Apparently this was because Lewis knew Wilde socially and was unwilling to appear in a sensational case involving a man at whose house he had been a guest. At all events Lewis returned his instructions and Queensberry had to obtain the services of another solicitor. The day happened to be a Saturday, and the only offices which he was able to find open were those of Russell and Day in Norfolk Street. It was as the result of this accident of being in his office on a Saturday afternoon that Charles Russell Junior was entrusted with the conduct of this remarkable case, in which, after consulting with his father, he decided to brief Edward Carson.

Carson disliked the idea of appearing against a fellow classmate, although he had never been friendly with Wilde at Trinity, and in fact since their college days they had not set eyes on each other until a chance meeting a few months before Lord Queensberry left his notorious visiting card in the Albemarle Club. One day he happened to be crossing the Strand, having just left his chambers for the Law Courts, when a fine carriage drawn by two spanking horses drove past him, splashing him with mud and nearly knocking him down.

The carriage stopped and out of it stepped the slightly over-dressed person of Oscar Wilde. He seemed prosperous, but had put on a lot of weight, and his features bore unmistakeable signs of self-indulgence and good living. He wore a white flower in his button-hole. So did his coachman. "Hullo, Ned Carson, how are you?" said Oscar, holding out his hand, which Carson took. He went on in a tone of friendly and good-humoured banter: "Fancy you being a Tory and Arthur Balfour's right-hand man! You're coming along, Ned." The conversation ended with Wilde inviting Carson to his house in Chelsea. "Come and dine with me one day in Tite Street," he said, getting back into his carriage and driving off.

Like most invitations extended at chance meetings, this one was not intended to be taken seriously by either party, neither of whom in this instance had much in common with the other. Carson was as little attracted to his fellow Irishman as he had been in their college days, while Wilde's political sympathies were with Carson's Nationalist opponents in the House of Commons. Yet if Carson had somehow been induced to go to Tite Street, Wilde's eventual fate might have been different, since the advocate made it a strict rule never to appear against anyone whose hospitality he had received. As it was, Carson did return the brief, telling Russell that in the circumstances he felt he could not undertake such a case.

Russell was now in a quandary. To establish a successful defence to a charge of criminal libel, his client had to prove to the jury's satisfaction that the words he had written were true and that they were 'published' for the public benefit. The law required that the substance of this defence should be embodied in a written plea of justification, a copy of which had to be delivered to the prosecutor before the trial. Russell realised that on the evidence available it would be far from easy for Queensberry to justify the libel. So far this consisted of the two letters to Lord Alfred Douglas and Wilde's published writings, so that the achievement of proving immoral tendencies would indeed be formidable. It is true that there were ugly rumours going round London about the prosecutor's private life and for some time past Queensberry had been employing a private detective in an attempt to discover evidence of practices which would show that Wilde had gone far beyond mere 'posing'. These inquiries had led the detectives to the rooms of a young man of good education named Alfred Taylor, which it appeared were the centre of an extensive homosexual circle. It had transpired that Wilde had been in the habit of visiting these rooms, but as yet there was no evidence linking him criminally with any of the young men, mostly in the humbler walks of life, who were also known to frequent them. Nevertheless, Russell considered that if only one of the youths whose names were found there could be induced to come forward, evidence incriminating Wilde was bound to be forthcoming. At all events he felt that this development justified his asking Carson to reconsider his decision, and accordingly he went round to Dr. Johnson's Buildings again.

Carson listened to what the solicitor had to say, but he still hesitated before finally accepting the brief. In fact it was not until he had consulted Lord Halsbury, a former Lord Chancellor, that he did so. "The great thing is to arrive at justice," that eminent jurist told him, "and it is you, I believe, who can best do it."

The adjourned hearing at Great Marlborough Street Police Court was due to come on in a day or two, so that there was no time to be lost. Immediately before it took place a consultation was appointed in Carson's chambers which was attended by the solicitor and his lay client, as well as by Mr. Charles Gill, later a close friend of Carson's, who had been instructed as junior counsel. Even at this late hour Carson was inclined to advise Queensberry to plead guilty. He only altered his opinion at the last moment, on being informed that Russell had discovered the whereabouts of a youth named Charles Parker, with whom there was little doubt that Wilde had committed indecencies in the Savoy Hotel, and that the solicitor hoped to obtain a statement from him. Parker, a former valet, had been introduced to Wilde by Taylor when out of employment. After being caught during a police raid on a notorious house in Marylebone some time later, he had dropped his former associates and enlisted as a gunner in the Royal Artillery. He was serving with this regiment when Russell succeeded in tracking him down.

The launching of such a libel prosecution as this by a successful dramatist against a well-known peer and sporting character was bound to attract widespread public interest. It was therefore in a Court densely packed with spectators that Queensberry again appeared before the Great Marlborough Street magistrates on the morning of March 9. After further formal evidence had been taken and the hearing of some legal argument, the magistrate asked the defendant whether he had anything to say in answer to the charge.

"I have, simply, your Worship, to say this," replied Queensberry, who appeared a diminutive figure as he stood up beside his tall counsel. "I wrote that card simply with the intention of bringing matters to a head, having been unable to meet Mr. Wilde otherwise, and to save my son, and I abide by what I wrote."

"Then," said the magistrate, "you are committed for trial and the same bail will be allowed you as before."

3

The trial of the Marquess of Queensberry for criminal libel on the prosecution of Oscar Wilde opened at the Old Bailey on April 3, 1895. Presiding on the Bench was Mr. Justice Henn Collins, later Lord Collins of Kensington, an excellent criminal judge and, like Wilde and Carson, an Irishman and graduate of Dublin University. In the barristers' seats a distinguished array of counsel had been instructed. For the prosecution there appeared Sir Edward Clarke, Q.C., M.P., Mr. Charles Willie Mathews, and Mr. Travers Humphreys, while as junior counsel for the defence Carson had with him Mr. Charles Frederick Gill and Mr. Arthur Gill. Mr. Edward Besley, Q.C., and Mr. J. L. Monckton held watching briefs for Lord Alfred Douglas and for Lord Queensberry's eldest son, Lord Douglas of Hawick, whose name was also to be mentioned in the proceedings.

These proceedings were conducted in the gloomy old building, pulled down some years later to make room for the present Central Criminal Court; if, unlike the present building, it was dingy and depressing, it certainly accommodated more spectators.

The Court began to fill up long before the judge was due to take his seat on the Bench. Someone made a joke about "the importance of being early," which raised a laugh. Soon there was not a seat or corner to be had, while the gangways and gallery were crowded with curious spectators. It was observed, however, that no ladies were present. First of the parties to arrive was Lord Queensberry. He came in alone and stood beside the dock, an unaristocratic-looking figure with a drooping lower lip and red whiskers, set off by the Cambridge blue hunting stock which he wore instead of the more usual collar and necktie. He was followed some time later by the prosecutor, who immediately sat down in front of his counsel and began to talk to them in animated tones. Wilde was smartly dressed in a frock-coat and a flower decorated his buttonhole. He is said to have smiled at Carson, who looked coldly past him. Actually Queensberry's leading counsel, who was suffering from an extremely bad cold, was feeling far from well that morning. In the seats reserved for the defendant's solicitors Mr. Charles Russell was seen to be in conversation with Inspector Littlechild, the private detective who had been instrumental in procuring the evidence on which the defendant was relying to complete his plea of justification. Meanwhile, in another room in the building, carefully guarded from further contamination by the outside world, a wretched band of youths was waiting to substantiate the evidence, laughing together and smoking cigarettes.

The judge was a little late but, when he arrived, no time was wasted in preliminaries. First, the jury took their place in the box and were sworn. Then, in answer to the usual question put to him by the Clerk of Arraigns, the defendant, speaking in a clear voice, pleaded not guilty, and that the words complained of were true and 'published' for the public benefit. As he did so, he cast a glance of undisguised contempt in the direction of the prosecutor.

By the time the hands of the clock in the court-room pointed to eleven o'clock, Sir Edward Clarke had begun his opening speech for the prosecution. A former Conservative Solicitor-General, Sir Edward enjoyed a huge practice and was the outstanding advocate of his day at the English Bar. Short, stout and bewhiskered, he looked more like an old-fashioned parson than a successful Queen's Counsel. On this occasion he was at his best, although in its studied moderation his speech did not commend itself to Lord Alfred Douglas, who had been hoping for an all-out attack on his father. "I never heard anything to equal it in all my life," said Carson afterwards to a friend in the House of Commons. "Both matter and manner were superb."

At the outset Sir Edward Clarke emphasised that the words of the libel were not directly an accusation of the gravest offence, but that the person of whom they were written had 'posed' as a person guilty of or inclined to the commission of the gravest offence. He then went on to point out that in Lord Queensberry's written plea of justification, which had been considerably expanded beyond its original form, the names of various persons were mentioned, it being alleged that Wilde had solicited them to commit the gravest offence with him and that he had been guilty with each and all of them of indecent practices. Having outlined Wilde's career and described the course of his association with Lord Alfred Douglas, Sir Edward related the story of the unsuccessful attempts to blackmail Wilde on account of his letters to Douglas, quoting the first of these letters, already mentioned above. The text of that letter, he told the jury to the amusement of the spectators in Court, might "appear extravagant to those in the habit of writing commercial correspondence," but Mr. Wilde was a poet, the letter was considered by him as a 'prose sonnet' and he was not ashamed to produce it anywhere as the expression of true poetic feeling, and with no relation to the hateful and repulsive suggestion put upon it by Lord Queensberry.

Finally, he dealt with the literary part of the case. The defendant had alleged that *The Picture of Dorian Gray* as well as Wilde's 'Phrases and Philosophies for the Use of the Young', which appeared as an introduction to this work but were originally published separately as a contribution to an undergraduate magazine called *The Chameleon*, were calculated to subvert morality and encourage unnatural vice. As for the epigrammatical 'Phrases and Philosophies', Wilde's counsel remarked that they gave brilliancy and effect to dialogue and even supplied wisdom in a witty form. As for *Dorian Gray*, Sir Edward went on, "I shall be surprised if my learned friend can pitch on any passage in that book which does more than describe, as novelists and dramatists may—nay, must—describe, the passions and fashions of life."

After the Albemarle Club porter had formally proved 'publication' of the libel, the prosecutor himself went into the box. Wilde answered his counsel's questions with an easy assurance, and was in fact an excellent witness, being quite clear and definite in his evidence. However, the statement that his age was thirty-nine caused Carson to sit up suddenly and make a note. When the witness was on the subject of his first meeting with Lord Alfred Douglas, Queensberry asked for writing materials and from his place in the dock proceeded to scribble furiously, the result ultimately being handed down to Carson by one of the ushers.

Sir Edward Clarke sat down shortly before the luncheon adjournment, and his opponent rose to face his former classmate. When Wilde had first learned, through his junior counsel Travers Humphreys, that Carson was to cross-examine him at this trial, he had said: "Then I am sure he will do so with all the added bitterness of an old friend." As we have seen, Carson and Wilde were never friends at any time, even at college, otherwise Carson would never have consented to appear against him. On the other hand, there seems little doubt that Wilde seriously underestimated Carson's skill as a cross-examiner, which in fact was revealed by the very first question he put to him. Carson always attached prime importance to the opening question, but when he went into Court on that April morning in this case he had no idea what it would be. Wilde's statement about his age gave him his cue.

"You stated that your age was thirty-nine. I think you are over forty? You were born on the 16th October, 1854?" Carson emphasised the point of the question by holding up a copy of Wilde's birth certificate.

Wilde appeared unconcerned. "I have no wish to pose as being young," he said. A titter ran round the Court. "I am thirty-nine or forty. You have my certificate and that settles the matter."

"But being born in 1854 makes you more than forty?" Wilde paused for a moment, as if to congratulate Carson on a remarkable feat of mathematics. He then gave a long-drawn-out: "Ah! Very well."

It was a small point, but at the very outset Wilde had been detected in a stupid lie. The effect of this was not lost upon the jury, particularly when Carson followed it up by contrasting Wilde's true age with that of the twenty-four-year-old Lord Alfred Douglas, with whom the witness admitted to have stayed at many places both in England and on the Continent. The damaging effect of these admissions, however, was to some extent offset by Wilde's sparkling answers to the questions put to him about *Dorian Gray* and other of his writings. Here Wilde scored off Carson heavily, and soon had the whole Court in fits of laughter.

Carson mentioned a highly improper story called 'The Priest and the Acolyte', which had appeared in the same issue of *The Chameleon* as Wilde's 'Phrases and Philosophies for the Use of the Young'.

"You are of opinion, I believe, that there is no such thing as an immoral book?"

"Yes."

"May I take it that you think 'The Priest and the Acolyte' was not immoral?"

"It was worse. It was badly written."

Questioning Wilde about a sentence in *Dorian Gray*, 'I quite admit that I adored you madly', Carson asked: "What do you say to that? Have you ever adored a young man madly?"

"No, not madly," Wilde replied. "I prefer love—that is a higher form."

"Never mind about that. Let us keep down to the level we are at now."

"I have never given adoration to anybody except myself." Carson felt nettled by the mirth which this answer caused. "I suppose you think that a very smart thing?" "Not at all," replied Wilde blandly.

Carson quoted another passage from *Dorian Gray*—'I have adored you extravagantly'—which he put to the witness.

"Do you mean financially?" countered Wilde.

"Oh, yes, financially," remarked Carson in tones of deepest sarcasm. "Do you think we are talking about finance?"

"I don't know what you are talking about," answered Wilde.

For a moment Carson fixed the witness with a steely stare. He looked grim. "Don't you?" he said. "Well, I hope I shall make myself very plain before I have done."

He then passed to the 'prose sonnet' letter.

"Suppose a man who was not an artist had written this letter, would you say it was a proper letter?"

"A man who was not an artist could not have written that letter."

"Why?"

"Because nobody but an artist could write it."

Carson read the letter, picking on the phrase, 'Your slim gilt soul walks between passion and poetry'. He repeated it in a tone of voice which made it abundantly clear to the jury what he thought of it.

"Is that a beautiful phrase?" he asked Wilde.

"Not as you read it, Mr. Carson," came the answer. "You read it very badly."

Carson was now near to losing his temper with this unusual witness. "I do not profess to be an artist," he said hotly, "and when I hear you give evidence, I am glad I am not."

At this point Sir Edward Clarke interrupted with a sharp rebuke. "I don't think my friend should talk like that." But he also gave his client a rap over the knuckles. "Pray do not criticise my friend's reading again," he said to the witness.

"Is that not an exceptional letter?" Carson went on.

"It is unique, I should say," retorted Wilde.

"Have you often written letters in the same style as this?"

"I don't repeat myself in style."

Carson picked up the second letter which Wilde had written to Douglas from the Savoy Hotel. "Will you read it?" he asked the witness. "No, I decline," said Wilde. "I don't see why I should." "Then I will," said Carson grimly.

> . . . Bosie, you must not make scenes with me. They kill me, they wreck the loveliness of life. I cannot see you, so Greek and gracious, distorted with passion. I cannot listen to your curved lips saying hideous things to me . . . I must see you soon. You are the divine thing I want, the thing of grace and beauty . . . Why are you not here, my dear wonderful boy?

"Is that an ordinary letter?" continued Carson.

Wilde affected a look of surprise. "Everything I write is extraordinary. I do not pose as being ordinary. Great heavens, ask me any question you like about it."

But Carson only asked him one question.

"Is it the kind of letter a man writes to another?"

"It was a tender expression of my great admiration for Lord Alfred Douglas. It was not, like the other, a prose poem."

Carson then passed on to the names of several of the young men mentioned in the plea of justification. The mention of Alfred Taylor and his rooms in Little College Street, followed by the names of two acknowledged blackmailers, introduced an ominous note into the proceedings. Then there was a young man named Shelley, employed by Wilde's publishers, whom Wilde had invited to hotels and restaurants and to whom he had given money and books. Carson's last question before the Court rose for the day concerned a lad named Alphonse Conway at Worthing, with whom Wilde and Douglas used to go out sailing. Did he not sell newspapers at the kiosk on the pier? "No," said Wilde, "it is the first I have heard of his connexion with literature."

Wilde was at his best in this kind of sparring, and the Court rocked with laughter. Carson, with a look of dogged determination, put more questions about this youth.

"What was he?"

"He led a happy, idle life."

"He was a loafer in fact?"

"He seemed to me to be just enjoying life."

"Was his conversation literary?"

"On the contrary, quite simple and easily understood. He had been to school, where naturally he had not learned much."

This was all very amusing, and the witness seemed to be enjoying it as much as the spectators, but the jurymen did not appear to be so amused. One or two of them seemed slightly shocked at the account they heard of Wilde's association with these youths. Then, had not Wilde given them presents? Yes, he had. Suddenly, to the general astonishment, Carson produced a signed photograph of Wilde, a cigarette case and a silver-mounted walking-stick, which Master Conway had accepted from him.

"Did you take the lad to Brighton?"

"Yes."

"And provide him with a suit of blue serge?"

"Yes."

"And a straw hat with a band of red and blue?"

"That, I think, was his unfortunate selection."

"You dressed this newsboy up to take him to Brighton?"

"I did not want him to be ashamed of his shabby clothes."

"In order that he might look more like an equal?"

"Oh, no, he could not look like that."

What had they done in Brighton? They had dined at a restaurant and stayed the night at the Albany Hotel, where Wilde had taken a sitting-room and two bedrooms.

Wilde looked rather less sure of himself now. So did the jury. Nevertheless he was still confident that he could explain all these matters to their satisfaction.

4

Next morning Wilde again took his place in the witness box. But his air was not so jaunty: indeed, he appeared considerably more subdued than on the first day. However, his repartee was still in characteristic vein.

Carson questioned him further about Alfred Taylor, about the youths he had met in Taylor's rooms, and about the mode of Taylor's life.

"Did he use to do his own cooking?"

"I don't know. I don't think he did anything wrong."

"I have not suggested that he did."

"Well, cooking is an art."

"Another art?" queried Carson. This time the laughter was against the witness.

It appeared that Taylor's rooms were exotically furnished and artificially lighted, the curtains drawn tight across the windows, through which the daylight seldom if ever penetrated. The faces of the middle-class jury looked solemn, as they listened to Wilde's description of an establishment so different from their own homes.

And what about these youths, whose names rolled so uncompromisingly from Carson's lips? Wood, Mavor, Atkins, Parker. . . . Did Taylor introduce him to Charles Parker? Yes. And did they become friends? Yes. Was Wilde aware that Taylor and Parker had both been arrested in a police raid in a house in Fitzroy Square? Yes.

"Did you know that Parker was a gentleman's servant out of employment?"

"No."

"But if he were, you would still have become friendly with him?"

"Yes. I could become friendly with any human being I liked."

"How old was he?"

"Really, I do not keep a census."

"Never mind about a census," said Carson sharply. "Tell me how old he was."

"I should say he was about twenty," replied Wilde with an air of bored resignation. "He was young and that was one of his attractions."

"Was he a literary character?"

"Oh, no."

To further questions as to whether Parker was intellectual and an educated man, Wilde was forced to admit that "culture was not his strong point". Nor was he an artist. But then, Wilde explained, education depends on what one's standard is.

Had Wilde also been introduced to Parker's brother? Yes. Did he become friendly with him too? Yes. In fact, he became friendly with him at their first meeting, when he had invited them to a birthday dinner he gave at Kettner's for Taylor.

"Did you know that one Parker was a gentleman's valet and the other a groom?"

"I did not know it, but if I had I should not have cared. I didn't care twopence what they were. I liked them. I have a passion to civilise the community."

"What enjoyment was it to you to entertain grooms and coachmen?"

"The pleasure to me was being with those who are young, bright, happy, careless and free. I do not like the sensible and I do not like the old."

Carson asked about the dinner, which was in a private room. Was it a good dinner? "Kettner's is not so gorgeous as some restaurants," was Wilde's answer, "but it was Kettner at his best."

"Was there plenty of champagne?"

"Well, I did not press wine upon them."

"You did not stint them?" went on Carson.

"What gentleman would stint his guests?" Wilde asked the advocate.

Carson looked at Wilde contemptuously. "What gentleman would stint the valet and the groom?"

Both Wilde and his counsel protested at this remark. Carson took no notice, but went on with his cross-examination.

"Do you drink champagne yourself?" he asked.

"Yes," replied Wilde. "Iced champagne is a favourite drink of mine—strongly against my doctor's orders."

"Never mind your doctor's orders, sir," said Carson sternly.

"I never do," said Wilde, as the Court laughed loudly.

The Court laughed once more with the witness. It was when he was asked whether Parker's rooms were about ten minutes' walk from Tite Street. "I don't know," said Wilde. "I never walk." "I suppose when you pay visits you always take a cab?" "Always." "And if you visited, you would leave the cab outside?" "Yes, if it were a good cab."

Carson had led Wilde on to very dangerous ground. The questions now had a particularity about them which made Sir Edward Clarke distinctly uneasy. Parker, Atkins, Scarfe. . . . Introduced to Wilde like others by the obliging Taylor, these youths were either grooms or valets or else out of employment. What could a man like Wilde have in common with them? Yet he admitted that he had given them all money or presents, having received nothing in return except the pleasure of their company. The witness, now obviously nettled, reiterated his delight in the society of people much younger than himself, those who might be called idle or careless. "I recognise no social distinctions of any kind," he added by way of explanation, "and to me youth, the mere fact of youth, is so wonderful that I would sooner talk to a young man for half an hour than——" here Wilde paused for a moment and then ended with a smile—"than be cross-examined in Court."

It was the last time Wilde scored in this remarkable cross-examination. A few minutes later everyone sat up in Court when Carson asked Wilde about a letter he had received from Charles Parker. It was merely a note asking whether he might have the pleasure of dining with him one evening, but it led to a significant piece of information on Carson's part. Carson had the letter in his hand. "I should like to see the handwriting," said Sir Edward Clarke. Carson looked grimmer than ever. "We will see all about that," he said. "Parker himself will be here, which is better."

No wonder everyone looked surprised, since it seemed incredible that an accomplice, on whom no immunity had been conferred, since he was not technically a Crown witness, was willing to come forward and supply testimony which would almost certainly incriminate himself. But there it was. Carson had the evidence after all to substantiate his line of cross-examination.

The climax to this sensational cross-examination came shortly afterwards, when Wilde was asked about a boy named Grainger, who was a servant in Lord Alfred Douglas's rooms in Oxford.

"Did you kiss him?" asked Carson.

For a moment, a fatal moment, Wilde was off his guard. "Oh, dear no," he replied unthinkingly. "He was a peculiarly plain boy. He was, unfortunately, extremely ugly. I pitied him for it."

Quick as lightning Carson pressed home his advantage. Was that the reason Wilde had never kissed him? "Oh, Mr. Carson, you are pertinently insolent." Why had he mentioned his ugliness? "I do not know why I mentioned he was ugly," said Wilde, now on the verge of breaking down, "except that I was stung by the insolent question you put to me and the way you have insulted me throughout this hearing."

But Carson continued remorselessly in a sharp staccato repetition: "Why? Why? Why did you add that?" Wilde began several answers almost inarticulately. At last he managed to stammer out: "You sting me and insult me and try to unnerve me, and at times one says things flippantly when one ought to speak more seriously. I admit it."

A few more questions, on minor matters, and Carson gathered up his papers and sat down, to the witness's intense relief. Sir Edward Clarke then began his re-examination, first of all putting to his client a number of letters written by Lord Queensberry to his son, containing statements about Wilde, which the witness swore were quite unfounded. Clarke also sought to show that Wilde's association with Taylor and the various youths, whose names had been mentioned was perfectly innocent. But it was too late. The damage had been done, and the foolish slip about the boy Grainger which caused it could not be covered up.

When the Court reassembled after the luncheon adjournment, Wilde was not in his place in the witness box. Clarke's introduction of fresh evidence in his re-examination gave his opponent the right to cross-examine upon it, and the rumour quickly went round the Old Bailey that Wilde had thrown up the case and was fleeing abroad rather than face Carson again. But the rumour turned out to be false, for about fifteen minutes later Wilde hurriedly appeared and apologised to the Bench for being late, explaining that the clock in the restaurant where he had been lunching was slow.

As soon as Wilde's re-examination was concluded, his counsel declared that the case against Lord Queensberry was closed. Carson did not ask to cross-examine further, but proceeded to his opening speech on behalf of his client. This he did in his most effective manner. He made it clear that the defendant adhered to all the charges he had put forward against the prosecutor, and he called upon the jury as fathers to say whether Lord Queensberry was not justified in endeavouring by every means in his power to rescue his son from Mr. Wilde's baneful domination. He then went on to say that he was proposing to put into the witness box the various young men with whom Wilde had been criminally associated and most of whom had been introduced to him by Taylor. And where was Taylor? Why had he not given evidence? Because he was "a most notorious character," who "occupied rooms which were nothing more or less than a shameful den." Then there was the blackmailer Wood. No wonder Wilde was so anxious to ship him off to America, where no doubt he hoped he would remain for good. "But as a matter of fact," announced Carson, "Wood is here and will be examined before the jury." A gasp of amazement went round the Court at these words.

Next morning, the third day of the trial, Carson continued his remorseless haranguing. Charles Parker would also go into the witness box, albeit reluctantly. "Parker will tell you that when he went to the Savoy with Mr. Wilde," said Carson to the jury, "he had whiskies and sodas and iced champagne—that iced champagne in which Mr. Wilde indulged contrary to his doctor's orders. Parker will furthermore tell you of the shocking acts he was led by Mr. Wilde to perpetrate on that occasion." He would also call the hotel masseur and other servants to prove the character of Mr. Wilde's relations with his visitors. Was there any wonder that reports of scandal should have reached Lord Queensberry, whose son was living a portion of the time at this hotel? "The wonder is not that the gossip reached Lord Queensberry," Carson went on, "but that, after it was known, this man Wilde should have been tolerated in society in London for the length of time he has."

Carson next proceeded to deal with the lad Conway, who, he observed, had not been procured by Taylor but by Wilde himself. Had there ever been confessed in a Court of Justice a more audacious story than that confessed to by Wilde in relation to this lad? Wilde had got the boy a suit of clothes to dress him up like a gentleman's son, put some public school colours on his hat, and generally let him look like a lad fit and proper to associate with Mr. Wilde. The whole thing in its audacity was almost past belief. Why did Wilde dress him up? "If Mr. Wilde were really anxious to assist Conway, the very worst thing he could have done was to take the lad out of his proper sphere, to begin by giving him champagne luncheons, taking him to his hotel, and treating him in a manner in which the boy could never in the future expect to live."

At this point Sir Edward Clarke, who had previously left the Court for a short time with his junior Willie Mathews, was seen to return and pluck Carson by the gown. He whispered into Carson's ear that he had been in consultation with his client and his instructions were now to withdraw from the prosecution. After a few moments Carson resumed his seat and Clarke addressed the judge. He spoke under the obvious strain of great emotion.

"I think," said Clarke, "it must have been present to your Lordship's mind that those who represent Mr. Wilde in this case have before them a very terrible anxiety." He and his colleagues, he went on to explain, felt that what had already been admitted "might not improbably induce the jury to say that Lord Queensberry in using the word 'posing' was using a word for which there was sufficient justification" to entitle him to take the action he had. Consequently, if the case were to continue, as he could not expect a verdict for his client, "we should be going through, day after day, investigation of matters of the most appalling character." In these circumstances he was prepared to accept a verdict of not guilty—not guilty having reference to the word 'posing'. "I trust," he concluded, "that this may make an end of the case."

"I can only say, as far as Lord Queensberry is concerned," observed Carson, "that if there is a plea of not guilty, a plea that he has succeeded in his plea of justification, I am quite satisfied." With this remark the judge agreed. Accordingly the jury found Lord Queensberry not guilty, that it was true in substance and in fact that the prosecutor had 'posed' in the sense of Lord Queensberry's words, and that the words had been 'published' for the public benefit. Lord Queensberry thereupon stepped out of the dock a free man. A few hours later Wilde was arrested in the Cadogan Hotel in Sloane Street.

Thus ended what was perhaps the most sensational trial of the 'nineties. Its repercussions were to be felt for long afterwards. For Queensberry it resulted in a triumphant acquittal, while the unfortunate Wilde was soon to take his place in the dock, thence to Reading Gaol and finally to disgrace and exile. For Carson too it was a triumph, but one not untinged with regrets, since he disliked intensely the role which he was fated to play in this tragic case. Had it been fought out to the end, his task would have been even more unpleasant. As it was, his conduct of the case earned him striking praise from many quarters, including an enthusiastic note from the judge. "I never heard a more powerful speech, or a more searching cross-exam," wrote Mr. Justice Collins from his room in the Law Courts after it was all over. "I congratulate you on having escaped most of the filth."

In the subsequent criminal proceedings against Wilde Carson declined to take any part, although he might have had the leading brief. On the contrary, after the jury had disagreed, and it was proposed to bring Wilde up again at the next sessions, Carson went to Sir Frank Lockwood, the Solicitor-General, who intended to prosecute in the next trial. "Cannot you let up on the fellow now?" he asked. "He has suffered a great deal."

"I would, but we cannot," replied Lockwood. "We dare not. It would at once be said, both in England and abroad, that owing to the names mentioned in Queensberry's letters we were forced to abandon it."

Wilde's second trial, in which Lockwood led for the Crown, resulted in his conviction and the maximum sentence of two years' imprisonment. On his release from Reading he went to live on the Continent, dying three years later in Paris. There is a story that, shortly before his death, Carson, who was on a visit to the French capital, accidentally knocked a man into the gutter while crossing the street and looking down 'recognised the haggard, painted features of Oscar Wilde.'

If it were true, this story would be a remarkable example of dramatic irony, especially when read in the light of Carson's previous meeting with Wilde in his prosperous days, when the successful dramatist's carriage had nearly run him down in the Strand. But, as it happens, it is entirely a tale of imagination, which has no basis of fact whatever.*

5

Midsummer's Night, 1895, saw the defeat of the Rosebery Government in the House of Commons. It was a snap division on a vote relating to the supply of cordite to the Army, so that the motion was not one of confidence. Consequently the Government need not have resigned. But Lord Rosebery was tired of 'ploughing the sands', and he asked the Queen to dissolve Parliament. This step was immediately followed by a General Election, at which the Conservatives were returned with a majority of 133. Lord Salisbury became Prime Minister for the third time, with A. J. Balfour as First Lord of the Treasury and Leader of the House of Commons.

For some time past Carson had been tipped by the newspapers as 'a good outsider for a law office in the next Tory Administration.' Indeed he seemed to stand an excellent chance, particularly since Sir Edward Clarke, who had been Solicitor-General in the previous Conservative Government, refused to hold the office again, as under a new ruling he would have been obliged to relinquish the whole of his private practice at the Bar, which he was unwilling to do. Carson was passed over in favour of Sir Richard Webster and Sir Robert Finlay, two sound English practitioners, whose claims were felt to be superior to his. Of course, he could, if he had wished, have been appointed to his old office of Solicitor-General for Ireland, but this would have involved abandoning his already considerable practice in the English Courts. As events turned out, the breathing space which the next five years afforded him as a back-bencher was invaluable, since he was able to expand and consolidate his practice in a way which he could not have done had he been in office.

But one honour, which he appreciated, did come his way at this time. David Plunkett, his colleague in the representation of Dublin University, was raised to the peerage as Lord Rathmore and went to the House of Lords. Carson thus became the senior Member for Trinity College, his place as junior Member, though considerably

* This story was originally related by Marjoribanks in his *Life of Carson*, at p. 231. It has been conclusively disproved by Vincent O'Sullivan in his *Aspects of Wilde* (1938), at p. 154. Incidentally Wilde never painted his face.

senior to him in years, being taken by the historian, W. E. H. Lecky, whom incidentally he had the agreeable task of introducing when he took his seat in the Commons. The senior Member for the University was traditionally a member of the Privy Council in Ireland. Hence Carson found himself in due course sworn of that body by Her Majesty's Lord Lieutenant, Earl Cadogan, in Dublin Castle, with the right to style himself 'Right Honourable'.*

Before this ceremony was carried out, he received the following letter from Lord Cadogan, who was also a member of the Cabinet.

The Castle,
Dublin.
February 26, 1896.

My dear Carson,

I have received the sanction of Her Majesty for your appointment as a Member of H.M.'s Privy Council in Ireland, and as I am aware that you are willing to accept the honour, I am now taking the necessary steps to complete the appointment. You will receive the usual official intimation in due course, but I cannot deny myself the pleasure of being the first to congratulate you on a promotion which so fittingly expresses the sense which we all entertain for the admirable services which you have rendered to the Unionist Party and the maintenance of the United Kingdom.

Believe me,
Yours very truly,
Cadogan.

As an ex-Minister and now a Privy Councillor, Carson was entitled to a seat on the Treasury Bench in the House of Commons, but he did not claim it. He preferred the greater independence of the back benches. Early in this Parliament a serious difference occurred between him and the party leaders over their Irish policy. This led him to take up his position in the corner seat on the third bench below the gangway, the place traditionally reserved for former Ministers who have resigned or 'revolted'; it had been previously occupied for seven years by the Liberal-Unionist leader Joseph Chamberlain. Carson's trouble arose over the Irish Land Bill, which was introduced by Arthur Balfour's brother Gerald, who had been appointed Chief Secretary for Ireland in the new Administration.

Balfour's Bill was designed to extend the scope of the Act of 1881 by admitting classes of tenant excluded by the earlier Act and generally expediting the process of land purchase. It was the very

* Carson was sworn of the Privy Council in Ireland on April 5, 1896.

core of the policy aptly described at the time as 'killing Home Rule by kindness'; its purpose was to remove the principal grievance of the Nationalists. But Carson thought it went too far at the expense of the landlord. Its terms were based on the recommendations of an all-party Committee presided over by the late Liberal Chief Secretary John Morley. Carson had been the leading Opposition representative on this Committee, and because he considered that his proposals were not receiving fair consideration he had withdrawn from the Committee, followed by most of the other Conservatives and Unionists. At that time his action commanded the full approval of the Conservative leaders. Now it seemed to him that he had merely been made use of in Opposition as a move in the party tactical game, and he felt justifiably hurt. He also felt that the interests of the Irish landlords were being betrayed, that small and faithful garrison of Unionists who had remained steadfast in every adversity to the British connexion. "Each successive Government," he told the House of Commons, "has thought it necessary from time to time to bring in a Bill dealing with the Irish land policy, and, no matter how the law might have been settled, to take a small slice of what remains to the landlord. It is part of the everlasting attempt to make peace in Ireland by giving sops to one party at the expense of the other."

Carson found himself in a similar position to that in which he had been when serving on the Morley Committee. One after another of his amendments, which he moved during the Committee stage, was resisted by Gerald Balfour, while amendments moved by the Liberals or Nationalists were accepted. This led to several harsh exchanges between him and the Government Front Bench, whom he accused of going back on their word. "I do not know," he said, "why the Chief Secretary has given the go-by to what he said a year ago, except that one's ideas of property alter according as one finds oneself on one side of the House or the other." Arthur Balfour reproached him for thus attacking his brother: "I cannot help regretting the line which my right honourable friend is taking. I cannot understand him taking the view he has taken, and expressing it with the trenchant hostility which has characterised his remarks."

But Carson pursued his way undaunted by this rebuke and continued to lead forty or fifty Unionists, including his Trinity colleague Lecky as well as Colonel Saunderson and the bulk of the Ulster Members, into the division lobbies to vote for his amendments against the Government. "Carson is a great help to us all," wrote Lecky at the time. "He is so quick and subtle in catching points." He had, of course, a tower of strength in the redoubtable Colonel, with whom, while the debates were in progress, he managed to find time to visit a photographer's studio, where these two Unionist stalwarts were photographed together. Unfortunately the product of the camera on this occasion has not been discovered.

Incidentally Saunderson made an impassioned speech on the Bill's second reading. As he sat down, he asked Carson, who was seated beside him, how it was. "Excellent," said Carson, "but you might have said something about the Bill." "How could I?" retorted the gallant Colonel. "I never read it."

Eventually the patience of the Balfour brothers was exhausted. Carson's amendments were treated with scant courtesy or no courtesy at all. Then, one evening when the Chairman called on him to move his next amendment, Carson retaliated by adopting the tactics which he had followed at Arthur Balfour's instigation on the Morley Committee. "I do not intend to move the next or any other amendment," he said. "It is quite apparent that no amendments of any importance of mine will be accepted, and that if they are accepted, the Government will go back on them." With these words Carson stalked slowly out of the chamber, followed by Colonel Saunderson, Lecky and a handful of his other friends, while the Nationalists cheered him ironically.

Henry Lucy, the well-known parliamentary reporter for *Punch*, writing in the pages of that journal, described Carson's withdrawal from the scene in this manner as 'pettishly melodramatic'. That there was an element of melodrama in Carson's action cannot be denied, but there was nothing pettish about it. He made this clear by showing that his refusal to move any more of his own amendments to the measure would not prevent him from speaking on the amendments moved by others. Indeed one of his interventions provoked the sharpest clash which ever occurred between him and his party leader. The amendment sought to relieve the landlord of any obligation to compensate a tenant, where improvements had taken place as a result of 'the inherent capabilities of the soil'. The Bill left this question open.

"I do not rise to advise my friends to persist in this amendment," said Carson bitterly. "I only rise to say that it occurs to me that it is an extraordinary thing that in one year all our views are changed because we are removed from one side of the House to the other. When a similar Bill was brought in last year, I opposed it, and I am glad to say that I had no greater supporter than the Leader of the House. But we move rapidly in these matters. In 1870, Mr. Isaac Butt said that no one would think of alleging that the inherent capabilities of the soil were the property of the tenant. How are we to account for these transitions?"

"What transitions?" asked Arthur Balfour.

"I call it a transition," declared Carson, amid the cheers of his friends, "when a right honourable Member at one time professes certain principles as those which ought to be embodied in an Act of Parliament, and when he is on the other side of the House says that it is not necessary that they should be put into the Bill of his own Government."

Balfour looked profoundly unhappy, and his discomfort was increased when John Morley, the Liberal ex-Chief Secretary for Ireland, accused him of betraying his old principles and adopting the Liberal Bill which had been rejected in the previous year. This was too much even for Balfour's philosophical outlook. He disliked the idea of a breach between him and his former lieutenant, and when it came to his time to reply, he made a strong appeal for a reconciliation.

"My right honourable and learned friend and I have been political colleagues," he declared. "We have fought side by side in times of stress; I have regarded him in times past with feelings of absolute confidence; I have felt that on his judgment I could rely. But when he turns round and, on the subject of this Bill, makes an attack upon one who is certainly an old colleague, and whom I hope he will consider an old friend, I admit I cannot allow his observations to pass without some remark. He accuses me and the Government of which I form a part of having changed our opinions in the last year, and of having, as he would generously imply, for the sweets of office given up opinions which we once held and since defended from this side of the House." So far as the question of "the inherent capabilities of the soil" went, Balfour felt that it should not be decided one way or the other if the present Bill was to have any chance of passing into law. That was the doctrine he stood by, and which he described as a straightforward and honourable doctrine. "It is consistent with everything I have said or done," he added, "and I trust that every follower of the Government will support the Government in this clause in the course they are going to pursue."

Any other man than Carson would have made some public response to this gesture. Being what he was, Carson ignored the shouts for him to speak, and sat on in his place, pale, grim and silent, with his hat tilted over his eyes, while the House sat throughout the night to complete the Committee stage of the Bill. One phrase of Balfour's had caused him particular pain, however—the accusation that his criticism bore any suggestion of his leader's opinions personally being affected by the 'sweets of office'—and when he got home he wrote Balfour a note to this effect. "Knowing well your views of office and at what sacrifice you remain our only possible and most trusted leader, so mean a thought never crossed my mind."

Carson then proceeded to offer Balfour the real explanation of his conduct. "When I was your Solicitor-General," he told him, "I gave a pledge in my election address to my constituents that I would resist to the best of my abilities any further interference with the landlords' property in Ireland. If I have gone too far in carrying out this pledge, it will no doubt justify a change in your opinion of my judgment and wisdom, but I hope it will not lead you to think I am the less grateful or devoted to the leader to whom I owe so much and whom alone I would ever consent to follow."

To this communication Balfour immediately sent a graceful and characteristic reply, written in his own hand:

House of Commons,
Friday, 24th July, '96.

MY DEAR CARSON,—Your note, just received, has given me great pleasure. I have ever felt confident that a friendship like ours, tried as it has been both by adversity and prosperity, was not destined to vanish and become as if it had never been. We have too often had to rely on each other in circumstances of difficulty and perplexity to permit our mutual confidence to be easily disturbed.

I have watched your brilliant career at the English Bar with the satisfaction of an old friend and the pride of an old colleague—but in my eyes it has been somewhat dearly purchased at the cost of the severance of our old official relations. However, I cannot expect you to take this view, and, though I do not get accustomed to seeing you off the front bench, I am delighted at the success to which that absence is due.

Yours ever,
ARTHUR JAMES BALFOUR.

Balfour expressed himself with similar generosity of feeling in the daily account of proceedings in the House which it was his duty as Leader to send the Queen. "Mr. Carson has always taken a very exaggerated view of the possible injuries to Irish landlords which the Irish [Land] Bill may possibly produce," he informed Her Majesty;

"he is a man of great ability, and has a somewhat bitter tongue. He made a speech to which Mr. Balfour thought it necessary to make a strong reply. But no permanent breach has, or will, result; which is a source of great gratification to Mr. Balfour, as he has a great admiration and regard for Mr. Carson, who served under him as Solicitor-General for Ireland through many difficult times."

Fortunately Balfour's prophecy to Queen Victoria proved correct. Yet for a time there was a breach in his public relations with Carson. This was reflected in Carson's action—always a courageous thing for any M.P. to do, and often a risky one—in going to the Conservative Chief Whip and telling him that he would no longer have the party Whip, or daily notice to attend, which as a Unionist supporter of the Government he had been in the habit of receiving regularly. "Henceforward," he said, "I am resolved to take whatever course is best for Ireland."

Yet, uncompromising as he was on what he considered to be a matter of principle, Carson had too fine a sense of political understanding to allow him to bear any malice or not to give credit where credit was due. "I am perfectly sure," he said when Gerald Balfour moved the third reading of his controversial Irish Land Bill, "that all we have differed upon was as to the best method of promoting what we both have seriously at heart—the interests of Ireland, and the maintenance of the Union."

6

As a profession the Bar has one striking characteristic. It rarely provides the barrister with an even flow of work. As a rule he either has too little or too much. With Carson at this period the problem was how to deal with the ever-increasing flood of briefs which poured into Dr. Johnson's Buildings, piling up on the table, the mantelpiece and even the floor. For Carson, although he had necessarily to farm out some of the preparatory work in his cases to 'devils', would never accept two briefs in cases which came on for hearing at the same time. He would always return one of the briefs, instead of getting a 'devil' to 'hold' it for him. Carson believed that when a lay client had had him instructed, his duty, come what may, was to appear personally for the client in Court. His clerk accordingly told disappointed clients that it was no good: Mr. Carson would only do one case at a time.

Encouraged by the rival success of Rufus Isaacs, against whom Carson found himself more and more frequently appearing at this time, Carson's clerk began to increase his master's brief fees so as to keep pace with those charged by Mr. Isaacs. The clerk, whose name was Herepath, whenever Carson was instructed in a case against Isaacs, would confer with the rival's clerk and arrange to charge the same fees. These eventually went up to 500 guineas, a record figure for those days. In the first case in which this sum was marked on the brief, Carson's instructing solicitor protested and insisted, contrary to the usual practice, on seeing Carson himself to discuss the matter. With some reluctance the clerk showed him into Carson's room. It was dusk on a winter's afternoon and the blinds were drawn.

The solicitor eyed the great man apprehensively.

"The fee you ask is a very large sum," he began.

"My clerk says I mustn't talk to you about it," said Carson, adding with a smile, "I don't know whether he's right, I'm sure."

"But it's a very big fee, Mr. Carson."

"You're quite right," answered Carson, "I think it's a most exorbitant fee."

The solicitor looked relieved. "I'm glad you take my view," he said eagerly.

For a moment or two Carson said nothing. Then he got up from his chair, and taking the solicitor by the arm led him to the window. He pulled up the blind to reveal a sight familiar to every inhabitant of the Temple. There were scores of other barristers' chambers, each one with its lighted windows, through which could be seen men poring over their books and papers, holding conferences or consultations with their clients, or just idly talking and waiting for work to come in. These were the gentlemen of the Bar, making their fortunes or with their fortunes to make.

"D'ye see all those rooms?" said Carson. "In every one of those rooms there's a light, isn't there?" The solicitor nodded. "In all of them," Carson went on, "you may assume there's one man, probably two or three, who'll do the case as well as I'll do it myself, and most of them will charge a far more reasonable fee."

"Oh, no," answered the solicitor, "that's not my point. I wouldn't dream of letting anyone but you do it, with Mr. Isaacs on the other side."

"Well, if you're such a fool as that, after all I've shown you," rejoined Carson, "you'll just have to pay what my clerk asks you to pay."

The fee was paid, and, incidentally, Carson won the case.

There is another story about the clerk Herepath which throws an amusing sidelight on his master's immense volume of work in these years. One afternoon, about four o'clock, a caller knocked at the door of No. 3 Dr. Johnson's Buildings. Could he see Mr. Carson? He spoke with a strong Irish brogue. "What name, sir?" asked the clerk. "O'Brien," said the caller. Herepath eyed him suspiciously. He had unpleasant visions of some ruffian sent to jail by his master in the Crimes Act days now come to take his revenge in the Temple. Herepath, who nearly slammed the door in the visitor's face, told him brusquely that Mr. Carson was in Court, and he could not say when he would return. Then the visitor produced his card. Herepath took it and, to his astonishment, read the legend: 'Lord O'Brien of Kilfenora, Kildare Street Club, Dublin'. Sure, it was none other than 'Peter the Packer', now Lord Chief Justice of Ireland. Herepath immediately showed the distinguished visitor into Carson's room. As he sat down to wait for an affectionate reunion with his old friend and former 'devil', his Lordship could not help noticing the piles of briefs lying about, all tied up neatly in pink tape.

"I see," said Lord O'Brien, "that Mr. Carson has a great many briefs in the Queen's Bench."

"Yes, my Lord," replied the imperturbable Herepath. "But I can assure your Lordship that we are equally good in Chancery."

Only a very few of the cases in which Carson was engaged at this time are described here: they have been selected for reasons of particular interest attaching to them, like the Queensberry-Wilde drama and the Jameson Raid adventure. This latter episode deserves some notice, although in the resulting trial Carson played a relatively minor part.

For some years past trouble had been brewing in the Transvaal. This Boer Republic, which was governed by the autocratic old President Kruger, was completely independent in regard to its internal affairs, although in its foreign relations it acknowledged the sovereignty of Queen Victoria. In addition to the original Dutch settlers and their descendants, it had a considerable population, much of it British, attracted from outside by the profitable gold and diamond mines. These people, known as 'Uitlanders', contributed much of the country's revenue, but they were without political rights of any kind and President Kruger steadfastly refused to concede them any such rights. The moderate request for the franchise after five years' residence was turned down. Not unnaturally the discontented Uitlanders cast about for help to alleviate their position, which was rapidly becoming unbearable. From Capetown Cecil Rhodes, the Prime Minister of the Cape, whose aim was to secure a federation or union of all the South African States in the British Empire, sent money and messages of encouragement. Plans for a rising were concerted to take place at the end of 1895. Across the border to the north in Matabeleland and Mashonaland, Rhodes's coadjutor Dr. Leander Starr Jameson was engaged in establishing the embryo colony of Rhodesia, and 'Doctor Jim' undertook to come to the assistance of the insurgents with a mounted force which he had raised for the purpose.

Dr. Jameson was convinced that he must give a lead, and he believed that once he marched into the Transvaal the Uitlanders would rise. Despite messages from Rhodes to hold his horses, he eventually crossed the border at the head of 500 men. Their fate is well known. The 'Raid' was a terrible disaster. Counsels were divided among the insurgents, most of whom now hung back. Boer commandos quickly gathered on Jameson's way, and after twenty-six hours' sharp fighting, in which they suffered some casualties, Dr. Jameson and the remains of his gallant band surrendered a few miles from Johannesburg.

Taken captive to Pretoria, Dr. Jameson and his principal officers were handed over to the British authorities and sent to England to stand their trial on charges of contravening the Foreign Enlistment Act. This Act, which was passed during the Franco-Prussian War to check the enlistment of British subjects as combatants in foreign armies, made it an offence to fit out a warlike expedition from British territory against a State with which Great Britain was on friendly terms. For the defence of Jameson and his companions Sir Edward Clarke was retained as leader, with Carson, Sir Frank Lockwood, Charles Gill and other counsel. The prosecution was conducted by the two Law Officers of the Crown. The trial itself took place 'at Bar', that is, before a specially constituted Court of three judges and a special jury. In this instance the Lord Chief Justice, Lord Russell of Killowen, presided, with the assistance of Baron Pollock and Mr. Justice Hawkins.

The case aroused great public interest, and the prisoners attracted much sympathy. The Government was obliged to take action, but most of its members shared in the public sympathy, increased by a brazen telegram of congratulation to President Kruger from the

Kaiser. Unfortunately Clarke's instructions were that he was not to pursue any line of defence which might embarrass the Government. Consequently he determined to rely on technicalities; Carson, on the other hand, wished to put up a bold defence, arguing that this was no military expedition in the generally accepted sense, but rather a public duty imposed on Dr. Jameson to interfere on behalf of many thousands of his fellow countrymen, who were being oppressed by a Government which had abdicated its proper functions. But Carson's advice on this occasion was not followed, and Clarke preferred to follow his own line.

A number of witnesses came forward on behalf of the Transvaal Government, and under skilful cross-examination the whole disgraceful story of Boer oppression of the Uitlander population might have been elicited in all its detail. Time and again Carson would pluck Clarke by the gown, suggesting some profitable line of questions. "You must pursue that," he would say. But Clarke, who preferred to rely on the effect of his marvellous oratory, would brush these suggestions on one side. "I'll deal with it in my speech," was his invariable answer. Although the prisoners were unable by the law, as it then was, to give evidence, on the facts, of course, their guilt was clear. But, even so, the jury was most reluctant to convict. The Lord Chief Justice put a number of questions to them, such as whether the prisoners had in fact been engaged in the preparation of a military expedition with the intention of proceeding against a friendly State. The jurors answered all the questions in the affirmative, yet declined to bring in a verdict of guilty until sternly reminded of their duty by the presiding judge. "These questions, answered as they are, amount to a verdict of guilty, and to nothing else," said Lord Russell. "They are capable of no other construction, and therefore I direct you . . . that you ought all to return, in accordance with the terms of these findings, a verdict of guilty."

The jury finally obeyed their judicial direction and found all the prisoners guilty. Dr. Jameson, along with his companion Sir John Willoughby, was sentenced to fifteen months' imprisonment without hard labour, and the others to lesser terms. They were already national heroes; now they became popular martyrs. Before they left the dock, the public crowded round them in sympathy and admiration. Privately this feeling was shared by most if not all the members of the Government, including Joseph Chamberlain, the Colonial Secretary. Although in public they did not attempt 'to excuse the inexcusable', Balfour, for example, admitted to his sister that if he had been living in South Africa at the time he would probably have joined Jameson himself. At an evening reception shortly after the trial, the Prime Minister, Lord Salisbury, came up to Carson. "I wish you'd brought Dr. Jim with you," he said.

As for the raid, its author said afterwards: "I know perfectly well that, as I have not succeeded, the natural thing has happened, but I also know that if I had succeeded I should have been forgiven." It only remains to add that, emerging from gaol largely broken in health as a result of his prison experiences, Dr. Jameson made a wonderful recovery, politically as well as physically. Indeed he lived to become a baronet, a Privy Councillor, Prime Minister of Cape Colony and incontestably the foremost figure in South African politics.

7

Reports of only a fraction of the cases in which Carson appeared at this time are available. Accounts of the more important or sensational cases will be found in the Law Reports of the period and in contemporary files of *The Times* and other newspapers. As the *Westminster Gazette* put it: "Mr. Carson is no longer a dark horse; the cause list and his fee book proclaim the high rank he has immediately taken." The same journal noted "with sorrow" that "already his brogue shows signs of corruption", but added, "we trust this is only a passing failing".*

His earnings in 1899, according to his fee book, reached the sum of £20,000, an enormous figure for those days, when living was cheap and income tax eightpence in the pound. It is said that in the same year he refused briefs of which the fees amounted to an additional £30,000.

This phenomenal success brought its meed of social invitations, and he found himself in ever-increasing demand by society hostesses for their dinner tables and house-parties. Pressure of work obliged him to decline many of these invitations, including Lady Londonderry's, although he enjoyed her gatherings more than any others. One invitation, however, he could not refuse, since it was in the nature of a command. This was for the Royal Garden Party held at Windsor as part of Queen Victoria's Diamond Jubilee celebrations.

* *Westminster Gazette*, March 3, 1896.

The thought of meeting the small majestic old lady filled him with emotion and, before being formally presented to the Queen in her wheeled chair, he retired behind one of the large trees in the Castle grounds and wept. He said to himself: 'This was the girl to whom Melbourne and Wellington knelt, the woman of whom Palmerston was afraid to speak, to whom Disraeli made love. And now she is going to speak with me.' The meeting was one of the memorable experiences in his life which he could never forget.

Such a career of success, as might be expected, involved some changes in Carson's mode of living, although it left his character entirely unspoiled. The furnished rooms in Bury Street which had been Carson's first London home were now a thing of the past, as were the lodgings in Granville Place, near the Marble Arch, into which he had moved with Annette and the family when they finally left Dublin and the house in Merrion Square was given up. For a time, too, they had lived in a top-floor flat in the Cromwell Road. In its place he now took a fine mansion in Rutland Gate. He also acquired a large Victorian seaside house in the charming village of Rottingdean, Northgate House, on the edge of the Sussex Downs. Here he would go for week-ends and vacations. For exercise he would ride over the Downs on an old hunter called 'The Cob', which he had bought from 'Peter the Packer'; this animal would also carry him on many a morning from Rutland Gate to the Law Courts. At Rottingdean he made the acquaintance of several other well-known people who had come to live there, notably the artist, Sir Edward Burne-Jones, and his son Philip, who was later to paint his portrait, also the poet and writer, Rudyard Kipling. He also made friends with the family of a future Prime Minister and his wife, Mr. and Mrs. Stanley Baldwin; he liked to play games with their children, by whom he was affectionately known as 'The Black Man'.

Carson had always been devoted to children, and he was never happier than when he was with them, playing games or telling them stories. Except for the eldest boy, Harry, his own children were at school and he consequently only saw them during the holidays. Harry, now a lad of eighteen, was something of a problem. His father had pinned great hopes on him, but he showed no inclination to follow in his footsteps in any way. After several costly experiments at home Carson eventually paid his fare out to South Africa to try his hand at farming. Through Cecil Rhodes he secured a farm for him in Southern Rhodesia. Harry Carson was there when the South African War broke out in 1899. He promptly enlisted in

Rhodes's famous cavalry. He later joined the 1st Battalion of the South Staffordshire Regiment and served throughout the campaign. This action gladdened Carson's heart for a time, but in other ways, owing to his extravagance and restlessness, the boy proved a sore trial to his father.

But this was not the only domestic anxiety. Now that Harry was in Rhodesia and the other children were away for long periods at school, Annette had more time on her hands. She missed the happy-go-lucky atmosphere of Dublin; she did not find life in the English capital by any means as congenial, where the people seemed so reserved and even superior compared with Irish standards. That she subsequently grew somewhat apart from her husband, whose time was now so fully occupied with law and politics, cannot be denied. She certainly tried hard to understand her husband's work and interests and to appreciate his success in his new sphere of activity. It was not altogether her fault that to some extent she failed to do so.

In the political field Carson still ploughed a solitary furrow. He seldom now intervened in debates, except to speak on purely Irish questions. On one of these at least he even became estranged from his former Unionist allies and was supported by the Nationalists. This was the project for the establishment of a Catholic National University, which was eventually achieved under the Liberal Government of Sir Henry Campbell-Bannerman. "It would be better and safer to give the Roman Catholics the necessary money and charter," so he wrote to Balfour, "and allow them to work out their own scheme on purely denominational lines." Trinity College had thrown open its gates to Catholic students, but the experiment had been a failure. As Carson told the House of Commons, "I often think that Members of this House, who meet habitually in England, do not thoroughly understand that the Irish Catholics are a people passionately devoted to their religion. They are a people who will not accept any institution in relation to the education of their children which is in conflict with their views; and, this being the fact, and all other expedients having been tried, what can be the use of believing that the aim of university education should be the aim of secularism, when the great bulk of the Catholic people in Ireland will not accept and could not accept that solution? . . . The truth is that honourable Members in their heart of hearts are afraid of something or other connected with the Catholic religion, which they will not suggest and which they will not explain. I ask, what is this fear of a Catholic University? That you lose the chance of a mixed education in the sense of the denominations coming together. But, sir, that system has been tried, and it has failed. Do you think that the Catholics of Ireland will be worse off with the enlightenment of a university education than they are now when they are deprived of it? That is the reality of the situation. I can only say that, speaking for myself, I have no fears of a Catholic University."

Surely this was not the voice of a bigoted Protestant, but rather that of the wise statesman who said that if the union between the two countries was to be perpetuated, all causes of religious discord must be removed. Balfour himself sympathised with Carson's views, but he realised that he had no chance of getting such a project through that Parliament; it was not destined to be achieved until the advent of a Liberal Government to power nearly ten years later.

Carson still refused the Government Whip, and one day the Leader, who believed in Carson's sincerity and the honesty of his political opinion, sent for him to ask him if he would not consider taking office again under the Crown. Carson said he saw no reason why the Conservatives should offer him anything.

"There are other questions besides Ireland," said Balfour.

"I know," replied Carson, looking at him steadily. "But it's only for Ireland that I'm in politics."

"DUBLIN UNIVERSITY."

Cartoon by "Lib" in *Vanity Fair*, November 3, 1893.

Central Criminal Court.
City of London. E.C.

5th April 1895

Dear Carson

I never heard a more powerful speech or a more searching cross xam.

I congratulate you on having escaped the most of the filth.

Yrs ever
R. Henn Collins

LETTER FROM MR. JUSTICE COLLINS TO EDWARD CARSON AT THE CONCLUSION OF THE WILDE–QUEENSBERRY TRIAL.

From the original in the possession of Lady Carson.

CHAPTER SIX

Solicitor-General

I

SHORTLY after Easter, 1900, Balfour again sent for Carson. The Leader of the House of Commons told his wayward follower that the Attorney-General, Sir Richard Webster, was accepting a judgeship and would become Master of the Rolls. This meant that the Solicitor-General, Sir Robert Finlay, would be promoted to Attorney, and that Finlay's present office would almost immediately be vacant. Would Carson accept it? The Prime Minister, said Balfour, was anxious that he should do so.

Carson asked for a short time to consider the offer. The salary attached to the office of Solicitor-General was £6,000 a year, and its holder usually received about an equivalent sum in addition as fees marked on Crown briefs. Nevertheless, as Carson realised, it would mean a considerable financial sacrifice for him. It also involved a good deal of detailed and not very exciting work over revenue and tax cases in which the Solicitor-General usually represents the Treasury. His fellow countryman, Mr. Justice Henn Collins, before whom he had appeared in the Queensberry-Wilde trial and many other cases, begged him not to take the office. "Stay at the Bar and be the greatest and richest advocate of our time," said the Irish judge. "That is your real bent." Lord Salisbury, however, was most pressing, and wrote to him in his own hand: "Your acceptance would strengthen the Administration. I trust you will see your way to do so."

The Prime Minister's view eventually prevailed. Carson accepted the offer, and wrote to Balfour as follows:

39 *Rutland Gate*,
S.W.
May 2, 1900.

DEAR MR. BALFOUR,

I felt so perturbed yesterday at our interview by all kinds of mixed feelings that I feel I really came away without conveying to you my very sincere appreciation of all your generous friendship has done for me. I can assure you that my appointment as Solicitor-General for Ireland, and now as Solicitor-General, are trivial rewards to me as compared with the knowledge that in difficult times I had won your confidence.

I know that in my new office, for a time at least, I will require some consideration from my colleagues, as many matters will be new to me, but I am certain you may rely on my best efforts faithfully to serve the Government and the country.

With many thanks, I remain,

Sincerely yours,
EDWARD CARSON.

When the name of the new Solicitor-General was announced, it caused general surprise. Favourite for the vacant office had been Mr. Charles Alfred Cripps, Q.C., M.P., later Lord Parmoor, whose appointment was favoured by the Conservative Whips. Mr. Cripps was Attorney-General to the Prince of Wales and was an authority on ecclesiastical law. He had also been a most loyal and dutiful party member, always voting as the Whips directed, whereas Carson had been a 'rebel', who caused them a lot of trouble and had actually declined to receive their instructions for a time. Yet it was the recalcitrant Carson who was now rewarded with a job which has always been regarded as a sure stepping-stone to the judicial bench. Many people scratched their heads, and confessed themselves unable to understand it.

Another party 'rebel', who had opposed the Irish Land Bill and other Government measures in the Upper House, was Carson's friend, Lord Londonderry. His services were similarly recognised, and he entered the Government as Postmaster-General. Henry Lucy ('Toby, M.P.') wrote in *Punch*: "Lord Salisbury has by his double selection for Ministerial office strengthened a dangerous tendency. He has confirmed an impression always existent in the House of Commons, that it is no use being good and docile. Sandford and Merton have no chance at Westminster. The history of the Idle and Industrious Apprentice is reversed. In an ordinary way, following the thread of Hogarth's story, we should expect that at the end of the chapter Mr. Carson would stand in the dock while Mr. Cripps, Q.C., raised to the judicial bench, would hide his face behind his hands as, in voice broken with emotion, he sentenced his early companion to a felon's doom. Of course there is no expectation that these *roles* will literally be reversed. All the same, it is not the Industrious Apprentice who in this case is first in the running for a seat on the judicial bench. The preference given to Mr. Carson over Mr. Cripps confirms the dangerous doctrine that the surest and shortest way to promotion in political life is, not to be good, rather to be naughty."

The Liberal *Westminster Gazette* came out with an amusing cartoon by F. C. Gould, which depicted Lord Salisbury as a head-master of a school giving the term's prize to the 'Naughty Big Boy', while the 'Good Little Boy' looked on distinctly mortified.* In fact the 'Good Little Boy' afterwards went to Carson and told him that if the appointment had been given to anyone else, it would have left him with a sense of grievance. "Nonsense," said Carson, who was undeceived by his approach. "You know very well that you've a sense of grievance now."

There had been cases of Irishmen becoming English Law Officers in the past, such as Lord Russell of Killowen. Indeed Russell had made history by being the first Roman Catholic to be appointed Attorney-General since the Reformation. But Carson was the first and, as it happens, also the only Solicitor-General for Ireland in history subsequently to become Solicitor-General for England. He was fêted by his colleagues, both at the Bar and in the House of Commons, and at one of the dinners given in his honour the chair was taken by the veteran Conservative Lord Chancellor, Lord Halsbury.

The acceptance of any Government office by an M.P. in those days involved the office-bearer in a by-election. Trinity College honoured its senior member by giving him an unopposed return. The Middle Temple, at which Inn of Court he had been called to the English Bar only seven years previously, now elected him a Bencher. Finally, he received the honour which is traditionally conferred upon every English Law Officer of the Crown. He was knighted, being one of the first upon whom the accolade was bestowed by the Prince of Wales. And all this at the age of forty-six.

In October of that year there was a General Election—the so-called 'khaki election', for British troops were fighting the Boers in South Africa—and Dublin University again returned Carson unopposed.

Meanwhile the new Law Officer had thrown himself into his official duties with such vigour that by the close of the year the work had taken heavy toll of his health. On January 22, 1901, the long and glorious reign of Queen Victoria came to an end at Osborne

* The artist, later Sir Frederick Gould, presented Carson with the original drawing. It is now in the possession of Lady Carson.

House, in the Isle of Wight. The House of Commons, which was in recess, was immediately recalled to pay honour to the dead Queen's memory and swear allegiance to her successor. Though feeling extremely unwell and in considerable pain, Carson insisted on being in his place on the Treasury Bench throughout these impressive proceedings. He was glad afterwards that he had made the effort, as he would otherwise have missed Balfour's graceful tribute to Her late Majesty. "She passed away with her children and her children's children to the third generation around her, beloved by all," said the Leader of the House. "She passed away without, I well believe, a single enemy in the world. Even those who loved not England loved her. She passed away not only knowing that she was, I had almost said, worshipped and reverenced by all her subjects, but that their feelings toward her had grown in depth and intensity with every year she was spared to rule over us."

The same day Carson saw his doctor, and as soon as he got home he wrote to Balfour:

39 *Rutland Gate,*
S.W.
Jan. 25, '01.

MY DEAR MR. BALFOUR,

I am sorry to have to write to you and say that I have been advised by my Dr. to lie up for a few weeks and do absolutely nothing.

I feel very much leaving my work for even a short time, but, as I have been for some time afflicted with a neuralgic pain in my side, I fear there is no other way of trying to get rid of it. I am assured I will be quite well again and indeed at times I feel better than I ever did.

I do not think my absence for a short time will cause any serious inconvenience, as I know the A[ttorney] G[eneral] will willingly do all he can, which is a great deal. But, should there be any such inconvenience or should I be unable to return as soon as I expect, you will, of course, consider that you have in your hand my resignation.

May I once more express my many obligations to you for your kindness and consideration, and I feel glad that, before I went to my incarceration, I had the pleasure of hearing your dignified and eloquent panegyric on our late beloved Queen.

Please don't mind answering this, I know how busy you are, and I feel certain you will be sympathetic.

Yours sincerely,
EDWARD CARSON.

To this letter, Balfour, who promptly dismissed the suggestion of resignation from his mind, sent the following characteristic reply:

10 Downing Street,
Whitehall, S.W.
Jan. 26th, 1901.

MY DEAR CARSON,

I am truly distressed at what you tell me about your health. You have absolutely *no* alternative but to take your Doctor's advice, and, though we shall miss you in the House during the early part of the Session, we shall at all events have the consolation of knowing that you are laying up a store of strength for future work. I have felt for some time past that you were perhaps overdoing yourself, and it would really be criminal folly not to take every precaution while there is yet time. I hope soon to welcome you back completely restored.

Ever yours,
ARTHUR JAMES BALFOUR.

One of the first tasks which awaited Carson on his recovery was to advise on a curious discovery which had been made in connection with parliamentary procedure on the demise of the Crown. Indeed it appeared at first sight that the discovery might also prove an embarrassing one. Prior to 1867, Parliament had to be dissolved within six months of demise, fresh writs being issued under the seal of the new Sovereign. The Reform Act of 1867 seemingly made the duration of Parliament independent of the death of the Sovereign and the succession to the Throne. However, someone on examining the statute discovered that by some strange confusion its provisions apparently did not apply either to Scotland or to Ireland. It therefore looked as if fresh General Elections must take place in those parts of the United Kingdom inside the ensuing half-year. The matter was duly referred to the Law Officers for their opinion. In the result Finlay and Carson both advised that the obvious intention of the Act was that a dissolution should not necessarily follow on the demise of the Crown in any part of the Kingdom and consequently that there was no necessity for fresh elections.

2

Not long afterwards Carson had to appear in a remarkable State trial which, though his part in it was necessarily little more than formal, deserves some notice, since it was the last but one of its kind to take place in this country. The case was the trial of the thirty-six-year-old Earl Russell for bigamy before the House of Lords in July, 1901.*

Lord Russell, a man of considerable ability, who was a grandson of the Victorian Prime Minister, Lord John Russell, had married as his first wife an attractive girl, Mabel Edith Scott, in 1890. Unfortunately Mabel Edith's figure of striking beauty concealed a cunning and bitter heart. The truth was that the youthful Earl had been ensnared into the marriage by his wife's mother, Lady Scott, who was in reality a common adventuress. Three months later Mabel Edith left her husband, and much litigation followed between them. Despite several applications to the Divorce Court, they remained tied to each other. At the same time the titular Lady Russell and her mother began to circulate the most abominable stories about the Earl's morals, which resulted in their prosecution and conviction for criminal libel at the Old Bailey, followed by a term of imprisonment.

Meanwhile Lord Russell had become attached to a lady named Mrs. Mollie Somerville, whom he had met while contesting a seat on the London County Council. Wishing to marry her, and, seeing no chance of being able to do so under English law in England, he determined to go to America and marry her there after acquiring a technical domicile in that country. Against the advice of his solicitor, he carried out this plan, obtaining a divorce in Nevada and going through a ceremony of marriage with Mrs. Somerville next day before a local judge, whose name was Curler. This was in April, 1900, and Lord Russell made no secret of the matter, sending home particulars for insertion in *The Times*. But, however it may have been good according to the laws of the State of Nevada, the ceremony before Judge Curler was certainly not valid under English law, which requires very strict evidence of change of domicile. Mabel Edith Lady Russell promptly filed a petition on the ground of her husband's bigamous adultery, and obtained a decree dissolving the marriage. Immediately afterwards Lord Russell was arrested and charged with bigamy.

The law, as it then stood, required a peer of the realm charged with any felony, as distinct from misdemeanour, to be tried by his fellow peers, although the difference between the two classes of crime had become largely nominal. By the Offences Against the

* The last case of a peer being tried before the House of Lords was that of Lord De Clifford for manslaughter in 1935, after which the cumbersome and expensive procedure was abolished.

Person Act, 1867, Section 57, 'whosoever being married shall marry any other person during the life of the former husband or wife, whether the second marriage shall have taken place in England or Ireland or elsewhere, shall be guilty of felony.' Consequently Lord Russell was brought up before the House of Lords and charged under this section. As Parliament was sitting at the time, the trial took place in the Royal Gallery, the magnificent long chamber adorned with Maclise's great mural paintings through which the Sovereign customarily passes on the way to open Parliament. The Lord Chancellor, Lord Halsbury, presided as Lord High Steward, in the presence of 160 peers in their robes, and eleven judges of the High Court similarly attired. The Attorney-General and Solicitor-General appeared for the Crown, while Lord Russell was defended by Mr. W. S. Robson, K.C., M.P. (later Lord Robson), and Mr. Horace Avory, K.C. (later the well-known judge). The walls were lined with tier upon tier of smartly-dressed ladies, who had come to see this amazing spectacle.

When the Lord High Steward had taken his place on the Woolsack and the King's Commission summoning the peers had been read, the defendant was asked whether he pleaded guilty or not guilty. Before Lord Russell could reply, his leading counsel Mr. Robson had risen to argue that the indictment was bad. The argument briefly was to the effect that the section defining the offence, quoted above, did not in express terms apply to any offence committed beyond the King's dominions—that the word 'elsewhere' must be read with a limitation, *i.e.* that it meant 'elsewhere within the King's dominions'. Had it been intended to apply to places beyond the King's dominions, Mr. Robson submitted, words would have been added to that effect. Mr. Robson went on talking for several hours and was 'followed' by Mr. Avory.

But Lord Halsbury brushed aside this ingenious plea. "My Lords," he said, "we have the advantage of having His Majesty's Judges here. I have been myself of opinion for some time that the matter which has been discussed at such inordinate length is really too plain for argument. . . . The statute is plain in its ordinary signification."

On being asked again to plead to the indictment, Lord Russell declared that, on the advice of his counsel, he pleaded guilty. He was then asked whether he had anything to say in mitigation of sentence. "My Lords," he replied, "I thought I had acquired a proper domicile in Nevada—a sufficient domicile. I believed in the goodness of that decree in Nevada, and in the righteousness of my marriage there." He went on to say that he had spent eight months in Nevada for the purpose of obtaining that decree and would not have done so if he had not supposed it legalised his new 'marriage' with Mrs. Somerville. He spoke of his 'unfortunate union' with Mabel Edith and the series of misfortunes in which this marriage had involved him. "I did not know," he continued, "and I venture to think that ninety-nine laymen out of one hundred would not know, that under any circumstances a second marriage in a foreign State could be punishable as bigamy in this country. Still less, my Lords, did I think that a second marriage which was valid and which is at this day undisputed in the State of Nevada could be the subject of prosecution for bigamy here."

The peers then retired to consider the measurement of punishment, returning after a short interval to inform the defendant, through the mouth of the Lord High Steward, that "allowing for the provocation you have received and the extreme torture you have suffered during a long period of your life," the sentence was three months' imprisonment in the first division. The Court was thereupon dissolved, after the Lord High Steward, in accordance with traditional custom, had broken his white staff of office across his knee.

Lord Russell duly served his sentence in Holloway Gaol. A year or two later Mabel Edith died of consumption and the Earl got married to Mrs. Somerville under English law. But the conviction for felony rankled with him for long afterwards. Eventually, in 1911, he went to Mr. Asquith, who was then Prime Minister, and asked for a free pardon.

"Why do you say you should have a pardon?" asked the Premier.

"Well," said Lord Russell, "the official reason is that I have been a good citizen for ten years since the offence, and that my conduct is free from any reproach. But if you ask me for the real reason, I should say because the conviction was a piece of hypocritical tosh."

Whether Mr. Asquith took that view or not Lord Russell never discovered, but he was instrumental in obtaining the royal pardon for him under the Great Seal.

It only remains to add that Lord Russell lived to become a much respected member of the House of Lords and, like the unfortunate Dr. Jameson, and also Dr. Krause, whose case is next considered, subsequently rose to high office in the State.

3

The case of Dr. Krause arose directly from the South African War. This individual was tried at the Old Bailey on January 17 and 18, 1902, before the Lord Chief Justice, Lord Alverstone, on a charge of incitement to murder. Carson led for the prosecution as Solicitor-General, while the prisoner's leading defence counsel was Mr. Rufus Isaacs, K.C. Particular interest attached to this trial by reason of the fact that the prisoner, his proposed victim, his leading counsel and the Solicitor-General were all members of the Middle Temple.

Dr. Frederick Krause was a young South African from the Transvaal who had made his mark as an advocate in his native country. He had studied law in Amsterdam and London, and had been called to the Bar at the Middle Temple. On his return to South Africa he had rapidly established himself in practice, and in 1898 had been appointed First Public Prosecutor in Johannesburg. Soon afterwards he was appointed acting Attorney-General for Witwatersrand, the district in which Johannesburg is situated, and, after the outbreak of the Boer War, Military Governor of the town. It was he who entered into the negotiations with Lord Roberts which led to the surrender of the town in May, 1900, and his conduct on this occasion earned the praise of the British commander. "Thanks to your energy and vigilance," Lord Roberts had written to him, "order and tranquillity have been preserved, and I congratulate you heartily on the result of your labours."

The occupying authorities now decided to withdraw the right of following the profession of advocate from all those who were not British subjects or who refused to take the oath of allegiance. Krause, who had given a written parole that he would not leave Johannesburg without permission and would not render any assistance to the Republican forces while hostilities continued, applied for and obtained leave to go to Europe. He reached London about April, 1901, and remained in England until the time of his arrest. During his stay in London Krause dispatched a number of letters in Dutch to a Boer named Cornelis Broeksma, who had been his colleague in the Public Prosecutor's office in Johannesburg, and it was these letters which led to his undoing.

While in Johannesburg Krause had come into contact with an English barrister practising there named John Douglas Forster.

He had conceived a violent dislike for this colleague, subsequently amounting to hatred. This was due to political reasons, since Forster had been a strong pro-Uitlander and, as President of the South African League, strongly advocated the maintenance of British supremacy in South Africa. After the outbreak of war Forster departed for Capetown, where he was eventually attached to Lord Roberts's staff. In this capacity he had been one of those who had conducted the negotiations on behalf of Lord Roberts for the surrender of Johannesburg. Forster subsequently became legal adviser to the British Military Governor, and as such had been responsible for the decision to withdraw the right to practise from Krause and others who refused to take the oath of allegiance. Since June, 1901, he had been special correspondent in Johannesburg of the London *Pall Mall Gazette*, in which he wrote with great bitterness about the Boers, urging that those still in the field ought to be treated not as belligerents but as rebels without any claim to be accorded the courtesies and conventions of war.

Forster's conduct continued to rankle with Krause, and the more he thought about it the more he became obsessed with it. He first sought to discredit Forster by approaching an impetuous Liberal M.P., Mr. Arthur Markham, whom he persuaded to write a letter to *The Times* describing Forster as 'a man of very doubtful character'. Forster promptly issued a writ for libel against the M.P. and the publishers of that newspaper. *The Times* immediately apologised and withdrew from the action, but Mr. Markham commenced steps to defend the action, taking the singular course of having Dr. Krause retained as his counsel in the case. Meanwhile Krause wrote to Broeksma, asking him to hunt up discreditable details about Forster's private life. "From about 1883 to 1888," wrote Krause, "F. deserted his wife and treated her in a shameful way, and openly lived in adultery with a certain Madame Piermain. He travelled about with her in a theatrical company under the name of Adolphus Ellis. . . . Will you be good enough to obtain definite information (with dates and places) for me with regard to his relations with this woman, and whether this all took place openly? . . . the woman subsequently (*i.e.* 1895, 1896, etc.) became practically a whore, and died at Johannesburg. Get the date and cause of death—I believe she died of drink."

Broeksma sent a good deal of information about Forster, but Krause was not satisfied. He changed his tactics, his wish now being to remove Forster altogether from the scene of his activities. "This man must be got out of the way, cost what it may," he wrote on August 6. "His influence is very damaging." And again on the same date: "The lies which are published here with design is (*sic*) unbelievable, and the person F. of whom I wrote, is greatly the cause of this, and therefore I also wrote to you the previous week that our people should be made aware of this, so that he can be shot dead in some lawful way, or otherwise put out of the way. This is absolutely necessary, and the sooner the better for our cause. . . . You must write to me immediately . . . what has happened to F."

These letters never reached their intended recipient. Before they could do so, Broeksma was arrested on a charge of high treason, tried by court-martial and shot. The letters were intercepted by the censorship in Johannesburg, and later sent to England. "The case for the Crown rests on these letters," said Carson in his opening speech to the jury. "Public order in this country could not be secure if such incitements to crime were left without notice by the authorities. The prisoner, too, as a lawyer was well able to appreciate the character and tendency of his actions." At the same time Carson was manifestly fair to the prisoner in his remarks. "Dr. Krause is a prisoner of war on parole," he reminded the jury, "but it is not necessary to impress upon you that there is no difference between even alien enemies and our own citizens in the case of a crime. All alike are entitled to absolute justice, and this country has never failed in the most complete and chivalrous fairness to all, friends or strangers, charged with offences."

Except for Forster, the Crown witnesses were largely formal in their evidence, since, as Carson had said, the prosecution's case really rested on the two letters, the authorship of which was not denied by their writer. In opening his defence Rufus Isaacs argued a point of law with great skill. He submitted that, as there was no evidence that Broeksma had ever received the letters, there could be no offence, since it was necessary for the mind of the person solicited to be reached. From this view Carson dissented. "Suppose I ask a man in Court to shoot somebody and the man proved to be stone-deaf," he said, "would there be no solicitation? Or suppose a man received a letter, but did not read it, or if a letter was in a foreign language which the recipient did not know, could it be said there was no attempt or endeavour to reach his mind?" The real question for the jury, he added, was whether the prisoner had written this letter, whether it incited to murder and the prisoner intended its delivery to the person addressed.

Isaacs rejoined with the submission that mere intention was no offence under the law, and that intention plus an act were not sufficient to convict when the person to be affected was not reached. After a night's reflection, the Lord Chief Justice upheld this view, which is undoubtedly the correct one, with the result that Carson was obliged to drop this part of the indictment and concentrate on the lesser charge of attempting to solicit a person to commit murder.

The jury took only ten minutes to return a verdict of guilty on this count, and Krause received the maximum sentence of two years' imprisonment. "This is to me a most painful case, and no ordinary case," said the judge to the prisoner in passing sentence. "You are a barrister of the Middle Temple, a member of my own profession, and, I doubt not, a very able and energetic young man. You have been most ably defended. Nothing that could be said in your favour has been omitted, and nothing has been pressed against you . . . I entirely agree with what was said by the learned Solicitor-General —and I wish to repeat it—that, although in the interests of justice I ruled in your favour regarding the statutory offence, the moral offence was as great as though the statutory offence had been completed, and I do not hesitate to say that I regard this case as proving that you were willing that the weapon of the murderer should be used against a political opponent."

Happily this was not the end of Dr. Krause's career. At the expiry of his sentence he returned to South Africa, where, like Dr. Jameson, he lived to render useful and distinguished service to his country.

Meanwhile the case of *Rex* v. *Krause* remains the authority for the important proposition in law that, where an accused is charged with soliciting a person to murder another and the incitement is by letter, evidence of receipt of the letter must be given if the charge is to stand.

4

Another State trial, and one of the most significant in which Carson appeared as Solicitor-General, was the prosecution for high treason of the Irishman and M.P.-elect known as Colonel Lynch. Like the Krause case it too was the outcome of the South African War, but it also served to establish a precedent which was to be quoted in two subsequent treason trials of similar constitutional importance—that of Sir Roger Casement in the First World War, and that of William Joyce in the Second.

Arthur Alfred Lynch, who was forty-one years of age at this date, was born in Australia of a Southern Irish father and a Scottish mother. He had been well educated and had travelled widely. After graduating as a civil engineer in Melbourne University, he came to Europe, where he studied physics and psychology in Berlin and medicine in Paris. He then became a journalist, and was thus engaged in London for six years, in the course of which he stood unsuccessfully as a Parnellite candidate against an anti-Parnellite in Galway city in 1892. He was later Paris correspondent of the *Daily Mail* and went to Pretoria as correspondent of a Paris newspaper. He immediately joined the Boer side, being granted a certificate of naturalisation, and was appointed Colonel in the 2nd Irish Brigade, a composite body of seventy men who had been recruited from every country in Europe except Turkey. For a time he commanded the brigade, swearing an oath of allegiance to the Government of the Transvaal and issuing an address to the local Irish to 'rally to the green flag' and join the Boers. After six months' active campaigning he returned to Paris by way of New York, when the republics had been overrun, to find that his exploits had gained him considerable notoriety.

In November, 1901, a vacancy occurred in the parliamentary representation of Galway city, which he had previously contested without success. The original intention of the Nationalist Party was the seemingly fantastic one of putting up Paul Kruger, the deposed President of the Transvaal Republic, who was then an exile in Europe, and running him as their candidate. The objection that 'Oom Paul', as he was popularly known, being a foreigner and not naturalised, was incapable of sitting in the House of Commons was met by the ingenious argument that, the Transvaal having been formally annexed to the Crown, the ex-President forthwith became a British subject. However, when it was pointed out in the constituency that a former Parnellite candidate who had borne arms against the Queen would be equally objectionable to the Saxon, 'Colonel' Lynch was invited to stand as an Independent Nationalist. He sent the secretary of the local association a letter of acceptance, and in due course issued an election address, but neither of these documents referred to the war in South Africa or to his connection with it. In spite of the fact that he did not visit the electors, who had by this time discovered that he was Colonel Lynch of the Irish

Brigade, he was returned at the head of the poll, easily defeating the Unionist candidate, Mr. Horace Plunkett, in spite of the latter's brilliant reputation as the official exponent of the policy of agricultural co-operation in Ireland.

For some months he made no attempt to claim his seat, but eventually in June, 1902, he wrote to the Speaker of the House of Commons, announcing his intention of coming to England for the purpose of doing so and setting out the motives which prompted his actions in South Africa. He regarded himself as an Australian, and since the Australians were not fighting the Boers he felt he was entitled to fight with them in defence of their country. In fact, he stated that he "was not consciously actuated by any antagonistic feelings to England" in the course which he pursued, concluding with an appeal to his fellow M.P.s in the words of Themistocles: "Do not beat me, but hear me."

A few days later the Colonel arrived on the cross-channel steamer at Newhaven, an action in which he showed undoubted courage, since he might have remained quite safely in Paris. He was immediately arrested and charged under the Statute of Treason, an old Act passed in 1371 in the reign of Edward III, which enacts that the crime of treason is committed 'if a man do levy war against our Lord the King in his realm, or be adherent to the King's enemies in his realm, giving to them aid and comfort, in the realm or elsewhere'. After fairly lengthy proceedings in the magistrate's Court, in which Carson led for the Crown, 'Colonel' Lynch was committed for trial.

The trial, which like that of Dr. Jameson took place 'at Bar', opened in the Lord Chief Justice's Court in the Law Courts on January 21, 1903, before Lord Alverstone, Lord Chief Justice, Mr. Justice Wills and Mr. Justice Channell. Sir Robert Finlay, the Attorney-General, and Sir Edward Carson, the Solicitor-General, appeared for the prosecution, with four junior counsel. The prisoner was defended by Mr. Henry Shee, K.C., who had a great reputation on the Northern Circuit as a defender of prisoners, Mr. Horace Avory, K.C., later Mr. Justice Avory, who was engaged to argue the legal aspects of the case, and Mr. H. C. Biron, later Sir Chartres Biron, the Metropolitan Magistrate. A tremendous crowd besieged the Law Courts, waiting to catch a glimpse of the prisoner, and when Carson appeared in his wig and gown he had to appeal to the policeman on duty for assistance in getting through. "I'm the Solicitor-General," he said. But it took some time to convince the policeman of Carson's identity. "That's what they're all saying," the policeman remarked, shaking his head.

Before the prisoner pleaded to the indictment, Mr. Avory moved to quash it on the ground that it did not disclose any offence under the statute of 1371, arguing with great skill, then and later in the trial when he moved in arrest of judgment, that the words in the section already quoted must either mean that the accused must be within the realm or the enemy must be within the realm. Asked by Lord Alverstone what the words 'or elsewhere' meant, Avory said that if the accused person was in the realm he might be giving aid or comfort to the King's enemies outside the realm, *e.g.* sending information from the realm to an enemy abroad. In other words, the words 'or elsewhere' must be read with the rest of the sentence and were qualified by the words 'in the realm', which immediately preceded them. To come under the statute, Avory submitted, the prisoner must have been 'in the realm', which in the present case he was not at any time. On the Crown side the Attorney-General pointed out that the effect of Mr. Avory's suggestion was that a British subject might engage with a foreign power and war with this country so long as he remained abroad, and went on to show that the authorities were all against this proposition. The Bench upheld the Attorney-General and dismissed a similar argument that the certificate of naturalisation which Lynch had obtained afforded him any protection. Otherwise, observed Mr. Justice Wills, whole regiments and divisions of an army might get letters of naturalisation and desert to the enemy in the hour of battle and yet not be subject to the penalties of high treason. "That seems to me so extravagant a conclusion," said the judge, "that I think the foundation of an argument of which it is the logical result cannot possibly be sound."

The prisoner pleaded not guilty, but since the essential facts were really not in dispute, he declined to go into the witness box and give evidence on his own behalf, which, since the passing of the Criminal Evidence Act in 1898, he had the right to do. For the prosecution various witnesses came forward to identify Lynch as the commander of the Irish Brigade. A telegraph operator named George Kidney, who had also become a naturalised Boer, swore that he was present during a commando skirmish at a place called Sundays River Bridge and that he saw the prisoner giving orders to fire on the British forces. A burgher of the Orange Free State named Kiljoen remembered seeing Lynch appeal to the Irish to join the Boers and he recognised his signature to the document. Finally, an

American named Gregg, who lived near Johannesburg, then testified to an interview which he and two companions had with the prisoner at Vereeniging, when the Boers were in occupation of that town and they were arrested at the railway station on their way back to Johannesburg for alleged espionage. Lynch, who examined the three of them in the presence of the local commandant and several Boers, was dressed in khaki and carried a revolver. "I want to show you that these men are British spies and ought to be shot," Lynch was supposed to have said to the commandant. "Those words," added Gregg amid laughter, "made an impression on my mind."

It appeared that in his evidence at the police court Mr. Gregg had said that Lynch's words were "I want to show you that these men are really spies," and before he was examined there, he had given a signed proof of his evidence to the Treasury Solicitor.

"What did you say in that as to this matter?" asked Carson.

On Mr. Shee's objecting to the admission as evidence of what the witness had stated in his written proof, Carson said that if there was any real objection to it, he would not press the matter.

Another Crown witness named Louis Handley, whose evidence had been taken on commission, deposed to an interview with the prisoner at a farm where the Irish Brigade encamped and did some damage during the retreat from Ladysmith. To Handley's statement that he (Handley) was in charge of the property, Lynch was alleged to have said that it did not belong to him but to the Boers, that he (Lynch) was a British subject as well as Handley and knew the law as well as he did. "If you are a British subject," asked Handley, "why are you fighting for the Boers?" "For fun," Lynch is supposed to have replied. However, it is only fair to add that the defence had no opportunity of cross-examining this witness, since he had put in written evidence, and that the accuracy of his account of the meeting was subsequently denied by the prisoner.

When the turn of the defence came, Lynch's counsel made no attempt to deny that he did take up arms on the Boer side. His witnesses were little more than evidence as to character, being designed to show that he was a reputable journalist and that his action in joining the Boers was really in furtherance of his work as a war correspondent. "The prisoner need not have come back to this country," Mr. Shee told the jury. "In Paris English law is powerless, and he came over in the full belief of his own innocence. . . . He honestly believed he was a Boer and had the fullest right to fight in the Boer armies."

For the Crown the Solicitor-General then addressed the jury, whom he brought back to the realities of the case. "What is the issue?" Carson asked them. "Mr. Shee has made it appear that it is whether a journalist can be convicted of treason or whether he can be convicted unless he believed he was guilty. That is not so. The law is that adherence to the King's enemies is treason. Thus the only question is a question of fact, not of belief—did the prisoner adhere to the King's enemies? Why, there is no denial that the prisoner did take up arms. There is nothing else in the case to try . . . Admitting that he was a British subject, he voluntarily and without pressure elected to take up arms against this country—aye, this Empire, his own fellow colonists in Australia. Could there be a clearer adherence to the King's enemies than to desire to put off allegiance and to transfer it to a country at the moment engaged in war with a man's native country? If there is no treason in that, treason is a thing of the past. . . . Mr. Shee has said that this gentleman was under the impression that the law of England allowed him to become a burgher. But here you are dealing with an educated man. Does any intelligent man with the smallest trace of patriotism imagine that under such a flimsy pretext a man may throw off his allegiance on the ground of having received so-called letters of naturalisation?"

Carson then proceeded to deal with the admitted facts. "The prisoner became a member of the so-called Irish Brigade, which did not observe its name, for it was a composite and not really an Irish body. Was that adherence to the King's enemies? Certainly it was." Then came his oath of allegiance to the Transvaal Government and his appeal to attract recruits to fight against the British forces. Was not that adherence to the King's enemies? There followed his instructions to his men, his directions to attack the British troops, his allusion to Gregg and the others as spies. Were not all these things adherence? "The case is abundantly clear," Carson concluded. "It is for you, gentlemen of the jury, not to discuss the character, the goodness or badness of the law, but, the law being as it stands, to find whether the acts proved to have been committed by such a man, a man of trained intellect, do or do not constitute the crime of high treason. With that simple issue before you, and with these admitted facts, your duty is as clear as clear can be—to weigh these matters and take these simple issues and decide them. Whatever may be the consequences, with that you have nothing to do. Those consequences are entrusted to others to consider. You will have discharged your duty and satisfied your consciences by deciding the simple issue involved and leaving to others the task of seeing that no injustice or illegality is perpetrated."

The Lord Chief Justice summed up strongly against the prisoner. On the legal aspect of Lynch's acts, he held—and here he was supported by his two judicial brethren—that the law does not permit a British subject to become naturalised in an enemy State in time of war, and that the act of becoming naturalised in such circumstances is in itself an act of treason.

The jury retired and, after an absence of twenty-six minutes, brought in a verdict of guilty. The judges assumed their black caps while the death sentence was pronounced by Mr. Justice Wills, as the senior puisne judge, speaking on the verge of tears. Read in the cold print of half a century ago, it was a remarkable allocution, occupying over fifteen minutes in delivery and showing the deep feeling of affection felt by all classes for Queen Victoria at the close of her reign. "Against what a Sovereign and what a country did you lift your hand!" said Mr. Justice Wills to the man in the dock. "A Sovereign the best beloved and most deeply honoured of all the long line of English Kings and Queens, and whose lamented death was called back to my remembrance only yesterday as a fresh sorrow to many an English household. Against a country which has been the home of progress and freedom, and under whose beneficent sway, whenever you have chosen to stay within her dominions, you have enjoyed a liberty of person, a freedom of speech and action, such as you can have in no other country in Europe and, it is not too much to say, in no other country in the world."

The Government was criticised in some quarters for instituting what was felt to be a shabby prosecution, particularly since peace had been concluded with the Boers, and there was a feeling that it would not have taken place but for the prisoner's having been elected a Member of Parliament. But once Lynch had voluntarily put himself within reach of the law, the authorities had no alternative but to take the course they did. As for the conduct of the prosecution itself, Lynch admitted that "their presentation of the case was on the whole scrupulously fair and even judicial." And this applies to the subsequent action of the Government in the matter. The death sentence was immediately afterwards commuted to one of penal servitude for life, and after he had served only a few months in prison Lynch was released. It is said that he owed his release to the intervention with King Edward VII of Sir Thomas Lipton, the Irish millionaire and close friend of the King, who felt that this action would create a favourable impression in Ireland, which the King was about to visit.

The subsequent career of this remarkable man is worthy of note. In 1907 he received a free pardon, and this further example of royal clemency was fully justified. Two years later Lynch was elected, by six votes, Nationalist M.P. for West Clare, for which he sat until 1918. During the First World War he strongly advocated a more vigorous prosecution of hostilities against Germany, and one of his speeches on this subject in the House of Commons earned warm praise from Carson, to whom incidentally he had never borne any ill-will. "He had done his part in condemning me to death," wrote Lynch in his autobiography, "but these are not the things that induce bad blood among men of understanding." Lynch actually received the King's commission for the purpose of conducting a recruiting campaign in Ireland. Thus the former 'Colonel' in the Irish Brigade, who had been condemned to death for high treason, lived to purge his offence by becoming a Colonel in the British Army against which he had once fought on the side of the Boers in South Africa.

5

Two months after the condemnation of Arthur Lynch, Carson led for the Crown in another trial where the accused was charged with a capital offence. This time it was murder, indeed the only murder case in which Carson ever appeared as a Law Officer in the English Courts. The Solicitor-General does not normally prosecute in murder trials, but in cases of murder by poisoning, as this one was, it is settled practice for one of the Law Officers to do so. The reason for this was indicated by Carson in his opening address to the jury. "These cases of poison, although rarer, are perhaps more important than other cases of murder which more frequently come before the Courts," he said, "because of the difficulty in tracing them out. If a distinction can be made in degrees of murder, I submit that no murder can be more determined and more malicious than that by poison such as the one we are now inquiring into."

The accused was a thirty-six-year-old publican, a Pole by birth, who went under the alias of 'George Chapman', but whose real name was Severin Klosowski. He was charged with murdering a young woman called Maud Marsh, whom he had employed as a barmaid and with whom he had been living as his wife. His trial opened at the Old Bailey on March 16, 1903, before Mr. Justice Grantham, and lasted for four days. He was defended by two experienced criminal practitioners, Mr. George Elliott, K.C., and Mr. Arthur Hutton, while the Solicitor-General had with him appearing for the Crown two Treasury Counsel, Mr. Willie Mathews and Mr. Archibald Bodkin, each of whom subsequently became Director of Public Prosecutions.*

The facts of this remarkable case, as unfolded by Carson to the jury, were as follows:

The accused, who was brought up in a Polish village where his father was a carpenter, for a time followed the profession of *Feldscher*, or barber-surgeon, in his native country. This calling has long since died out in England, although the pole outside most barbers' shops serves as a reminder of the days when hairdressing and surgery were combined and customers for a haircut were also bled or cupped. When he was about twenty-four years of age he migrated to London, where he found work as a hairdresser's assistant in Whitechapel. Soon after his arrival he married a Polish woman named Lucy Baderski, and together they went to America, where they stayed for several years. Here they separated, owing to the husband's fondness for other women, and she returned to England alone. He followed a little later, turning up again in the East End. Here he began living with a young woman named Annie Chapman, thenceforth adopting the surname and calling himself George Chapman, by which name he was afterwards generally known. Fortunately for herself she too left him when they had been together for only a short period. Both these women subsequently gave evidence in the case.

Chapman now took up with a woman named Mrs. Mary Spink, the wife of a porter on the Great Eastern Railway, who had left her on account of her intemperate habits. They posed as man and wife, and, as Mrs. Spink had a little money of her own, Chapman gave up his job as a hairdresser's assistant and with her financial help opened a barber's shop in Hastings. An unusual feature of this establishment was a 'musical shave', Mrs. Spink playing the piano while her 'husband' attended to the customer's beard. Among the customers was a chemist named Davidson, from whom he bought an ounce of

* For a fuller account of this interesting case the reader is referred to *The Trial of George Chapman*, edited by H. L. Adam for the Notable British Trials Series (1930). This volume was dedicated to Carson by the editor 'with his cordial agreement'.

tartar emetic. This purchase was entered by the chemist in his poisons book, as required by law, and he obtained Chapman's signature to it. The main ingredient of this poison is antimony, a substance almost tasteless to the palate and colourless to the eye. Two grains have been known to be fatal to the human body: Chapman's purchase contained about 150.

In 1897 Chapman and his supposed wife returned to London, where he became the lessee of a public-house in Finsbury. Hitherto a healthy woman, in spite of her frequent drinking bouts, Mrs. Spink now became ill; she was confined to bed suffering from severe vomiting attacks and distressing abdominal pains. She slowly became weaker and eventually died in acute agony on Christmas Day. The doctor who had been called in, Dr. Rogers, made no difficulty in granting a death certificate, believing from the emaciated condition of her body that she was a victim of consumption. She was buried in a common grave at Leytonstone. Chapman appeared much affected by her end and received considerable sympathy from the neighbours.

Not long afterwards Chapman advertised for a barmaid, and there were numerous applicants for the position. Eventually his choice fell on a strong, healthy young woman named Bessie Taylor, a farmer's daughter. She was engaged and, like the late Mrs. Spink, soon became known as Mrs. Chapman. By this time Chapman had moved to the Monument Tavern, in the Borough, on the south side of the Thames. In due course she became ill, displaying similar symptoms to those of her predecessor, gradually becoming thinner and eventually on February 13, 1901, dying in great pain. Dr. Stoker, the medical practitioner who attended her during her illness, was puzzled by her case. On the death certificate which he wrote out he ascribed her passing to 'exhaustion from vomiting and diarrhœa'. She was buried near her native village in Cheshire.

Six months later Chapman chanced to see an advertisement in which another young woman sought a position as barmaid. The name of this advertiser was Maud Marsh, and it was by reason of her death that Chapman was ultimately arrested and brought to justice. Chapman answered the advertisement and she was engaged. To satisfy her parents, who were naturally interested in their daughter's future, he told them that he was a widower and that there was a family living in the house. Neither of these statements was true, but in the faith of them Maud Marsh went to live in the Monument

Tavern with her employer. Shortly afterwards it was given out that they had got married. Early in 1902 they removed to the Crown Tavern in the Borough, the Monument having been burned down. In fact Chapman almost certainly set fire to the place himself in order to get the insurance money, but the insurance company refused to pay and cancelled his policy. In June of that year Chapman made the acquaintance of a girl named Rayner and asked her to go to America with him. She refused, saying, "You have got a wife downstairs," to which he replied, "Oh I could give her *that* (snapping his fingers) and she would be no more Mrs. Chapman!" It was at this time that Maud Marsh was taken ill, with the familiar symptoms which had marked the cases of Mrs. Spink and Bessie Taylor.

The unfortunate Maud became so ill that she was removed to hospital. Here the doctors were at a loss to know what was the matter with her, but, as she was away from her supposed husband's attentions, she gradually recovered and was sent home. Almost immediately there was a return of the mysterious illness. Stoker was called in and once more professed himself completely baffled. The services of a nurse were engaged, while the patient's mother, who was very worried, also arrived to help. Meanwhile Chapman insisted on preparing the patient's food and drink, and it was noticed that whenever she took any, her condition became worse. When Mrs. Marsh and the nurse refreshed themselves with a brandy and soda which had been prepared for the sick woman, they were both immediately seized with painful attacks of vomiting and diarrhœa. Mrs. Marsh then summoned the assistance of her own doctor, a Dr. Grapel of Croydon, and on examining the patient he came to the conclusion that she was being poisoned. He telegraphed Dr. Stoker to this effect, telling him to look out for arsenic. But it was too late. Chapman, having evidently taken fright at Dr. Grapel's visit, administered a stronger dose than usual, which brought about the sudden end of the patient. This happened on October 22, 1902.

Because of Dr. Grapel's message, Dr. Stoker refused to give a death certificate. At this Chapman was very much annoyed and asked the doctor why. "I cannot find what is the cause of death," replied Dr. Stoker. "It was exhaustion," said Chapman, "caused by inflammation of the bowels." "What caused the inflammation?" asked the doctor. "Continual vomiting and diarrhœa," answered Chapman. "What caused the vomiting and diarrhœa?" the doctor persisted. To this last question Chapman made no reply.

A post-mortem examination of the body took place, as a result of which over twenty grains of antimony were discovered. In Carson's words, "the body of the deceased woman was literally saturated with antimony." At the coroner's inquest the chemist Davidson, who read of the case in the newspapers, remembered selling the tartar emetic to Chapman in 1897 and dutifully came forward to assist the authorities. A week or so later Chapman was arrested and charged with the murder of Maud Marsh. He decided to plead not guilty, though among the articles found by the police in his possession were various medical books treating of poisons, and strangely enough a book written by Berry, the executioner, giving details of his career as a hangman.

One extraordinary effect of antimony, as Carson told the jury in this case—and it was a novel discovery then—is that, if it is administered in the lifetime of the person, it preserves the body in a remarkable degree, so that even several years after death the body of the deceased person is easily recognisable. This was confirmed by Dr. Stevenson, the Home Office pathologist, under whose supervision the remains of Mrs. Spink and Bessie Taylor were exhumed. From the witness box he described what he saw when the lid of Mrs. Spink's coffin was removed by the grave in the cemetery at Leytonstone. "The body was altogether remarkable," deposed Dr. Stevenson. "The face and head were those of a woman who might have been coffined that day from the appearance. Even the eyes were unruptured, a very unusual circumstance. There was not the least difficulty in recognising her." The body of Bessie Taylor was similarly well preserved, and was easily identifiable. Both corpses were quite free from putrefaction or odour, unlike those in the adjacent coffins.

"We have awakened these poor women from their long sleep," said Carson, "to give unassailable evidence against the prisoner. But I am sure, if they could have spoken, they would not have asked you to avenge them but to do justice." On this point Mr. Elliott, for the defence, submitted that the prosecution was bound by the facts connected with the indictment in respect of Maud Marsh only, and could not introduce other facts for the purpose of prejudicing the case. This is indeed the general rule of criminal procedure, but there is an exception when evidence of similar acts is allowed to be given to rebut a defence of innocent intent or accident. So Carson argued and the judge ruled. "The matter is really too clear for argument," said Mr. Justice Grantham, holding it admissible to refer to previous instances to disprove any suggestion of mistake as the result of any action on the part of the prisoner in the particular case which was charged against him.

In the face of this admitted evidence, the task of the defence was truly hopeless. Mr. Elliott did not attempt to put his client into the witness box and he called no other evidence. In his speech to the jury he contented himself with stressing the absence of any motive for the murder, suggesting that Maud Marsh had committed suicide because Chapman refused to give her any children, and finally begging the jurymen not to let themselves be carried away by prejudice on account of the prisoner's alien nationality. Carson dealt with this last point as he had in the case of Dr. Krause. "In this Court we know no difference between the alien and the stranger and a citizen of this country," he said. "It is our proud boast that here, at all events, whatever it may be in other countries, it matters not to us who is the person on his trial, as all are entitled to the same law and the same justice." As for the question of motive, Carson went on, "in this instance there was the most ample motive, for the prisoner's was a history of unbridled, heartless and cruel lust."

The judge summed up strongly against the prisoner and, after an absence of only eleven minutes, the jury returned a verdict of guilty. He received the death sentence, with which the Home Secretary refused to interfere, and he was duly hanged. There is no doubt that he was a sadistic maniac, who met his just deserts. "I have never seen such a villain," said Carson afterwards, recalling the details of the trial. "He looked like some evil wild beast. I almost expected him to leap over the dock and attack me." It was later discovered that, before he came to England, he had married a woman in Poland and had beheaded her. Yet he died protesting his innocence to the last. When asked if he wished to see any of his friends, he replied bitterly: "I have none."

The trial of Severin Klosowski, alias George Chapman, is of unique interest for three reasons. First, because of the discovery which enabled the Home Office pathologist to show the peculiar power of antimony and how it preserves the human body after death. Secondly, it was the first trial in which it was found possible, as well as legal, to bring forward evidence of two other persons who had died by the poison administered to them by the accused. Thirdly, the trial led the police authorities to believe that the Borough poisoner was the same person as one of the most notorious figures in the annals of modern crime. That is to say, they sought to identify him with the mysterious murderer of Whitechapel, who is popularly known as 'Jack the Ripper'. While it is true that the mystery of the 'Ripper' murders has never been officially solved, the grounds for supposing that this sadistic Pole was the author of them are very strong.

These murders took place in Whitechapel during the years 1888 and 1889. The victim was invariably a prostitute, who was killed at night with a sharp knife, her throat being cut and the lower part of her body horribly mutilated. The reasons for supposing that Chapman and Jack the Ripper were one and the same person are as follows. The murders all took place in Whitechapel when Chapman was living there or within easy reach. It was thought that the Ripper had medical knowledge: Chapman had certainly been a student of medicine. According to his wife, Lucy Baderski, Chapman was often out until three or four o'clock in the morning at the time the murders were committed. The description of Jack the Ripper as to height, complexion and curled moustache might be exactly applied to Chapman. Again, there were American expressions in the callous messages which the Ripper sent the police: Chapman liked to pass himself off as an American and was in the habit of indulging in grim pleasantries of language. Finally, the murders ceased in 1890, but between that year and 1892 similar murders occurred in the locality of Jersey City, during the period that Chapman was living there. The Jersey City murders ceased at the time Chapman left to return to England.

Chief Inspector Abberline of Scotland Yard, who had charge of the investigation into the Whitechapel murders, was quite convinced that Chapman and Jack the Ripper were identical. His theory was that when Chapman returned from America he came to the conclusion that the 'Ripper' type of murder was too dangerous, and he consequently turned to poisoning as a safer mode of killing. When Chapman was eventually arrested, the Chief Inspector said to his colleague in the force who had carried out this duty: "You've got Jack the Ripper at last!"

If Chief Inspector Abberline's theory is correct—and there is much to be said in its support—society owes Carson an additional debt for having been instrumental in bringing this multiple murderer to justice.

6

In the summer of 1902 the aloof old Marquess of Salisbury resigned the Premiership on account of failing health and withdrew into private life. He had never struck the popular fancy as did Gladstone and Disraeli. From time to time he made his appearance on the public platform, usually in connection with some function of the Primrose League. Otherwise, save for those who were familiar with the political cartoons of the day, his Lordship's plump bearded figure passed unrecognised by the masses. By many it was thought that the King would now send for Mr. Chamberlain as his successor, for the vigorous and outspoken Colonial Secretary was, above all, the man the masses knew. But the royal summons was despatched not to 'Joe' but to Arthur Balfour, the Leader of the House of Commons, and thus 'A.J.B.' became Prime Minister at the age of fifty-four.

The change of Premiers left Carson's position as Solicitor-General unaffected, but it did involve certain changes in the Government. While 'Joe' Chamberlain remained at the Colonial Office with a seat in the Cabinet, his son Austen entered it for the first time in the office of Postmaster-General, which was vacated by Lord Londonderry, who likewise received promotion as first President of the Board of Education. Another entrant to the Cabinet was Balfour's scholarly protégé, George Wyndham, who already held the post of Chief Secretary for Ireland. Finally, Sir Michael Hicks-Beach quitted the Treasury, his place as Chancellor of the Exchequer being taken by Mr. Charles Ritchie, who had previously been Home Secretary. Ritchie, who conducted a successful jute business in Dundee, was an uncompromising Free Trader. Given to heavy and affected pleasantries, he was also sadly lacking in *savoir-faire*: on one occasion, when Queen Victoria received him standing, he is said to have offered her a chair. The fact that his fiscal views were completely at variance with those of Joseph Chamberlian did not augur well for the Government's future.

Meanwhile in the House of Commons the Irish Nationalists continued their customary tactics, which increased the strain of attendance upon M.P.s. For one, at least, this strain proved too much. This was Carson's fellow representative for Dublin University, the historian Lecky, who retired at the end of the year, his place as junior member for Trinity being taken by Carson's former colleague in college and at the Irish Bar, J. H. Campbell, K.C., who now occupied Carson's old office of Solicitor-General for Ireland.

Another M.P. who disappeared from the parliamentary scene was the turbulent Member for Mid-Cork, Dr. Tanner, who had been one of Carson's most vitriolic opponents. Indeed the little doctor's parliamentary practices had grown too strenuous for even his

Nationalist friends, to whom his death came as a matter of relief. And on them he played one last trick. It was given out that his mortal remains were to arrive at Paddington Station on a certain train, and a deputation of mourning parliamentary colleagues turned up on the platform to pay their last respects to the memory of the departed Member. But all that was mortal of Dr. Tanner had been brought to town by an earlier train, and while the deputation was anxiously searching the luggage van for the coffin it was at that moment being lowered into the grave in distant Kensal Green cemetery. What the mourning Nationalists said to each other when they made this discovery was discreetly withheld from newspaper reports of the incident.

While the familiar figures of Dr. Tanner and W. E. H. Lecky were no longer seen in the lobbies at Westminster, others made their appearance. Most striking of the newcomers was undoubtedly the twenty-eight-year-old Conservative M.P. for Oldham, Mr. Winston Churchill, who was destined to cross swords with Carson on many occasions in the future. For the moment, however, he sat on the Government benches behind Carson, learning the elements of the political game.

Conditions in the House at this time were well described by Lecky, in one of the last letters which he wrote before his retirement:

> We are having a most dreary session of persistent Irish obstruction—skilfully carried out—involving divisions on nearly every item, and bringing with it very late nights and a general dislocation of the Parliamentary machine. It is curious how through the influence of all this our House of Commons is losing its old character—how the private member is being turned into a mere voting machine—how the power of the Cabinet is growing, and how, through the excessive prolongation of debates, real and moderate criticism of supply is becoming more and more difficult.

The strain of parliamentary life, in addition to that of his heavy work in the Courts, was also beginning to tell on Carson. It will be remembered that he had been laid up for some weeks at the beginning of 1901 and, though he had completely recovered, his doctor recommended regular treatment at a foreign spa. Thus Carson about this time came to pay his first visit to Homburg, the picturesque Rhineland watering-place near Frankfort which had recently become popular with English visitors through the patronage of King Edward VII. Besides a tennis club and casino—its gaming rooms were the first of their kind in Europe, antedating their more famous counterpart at Monte Carlo—Homburg boasted remarkable sparkling chalybeate and saline springs, which attracted patients with stomach trouble. Apart from the waters Carson found the company he met there congenial, and he made up his mind to return in the following season. Indeed his visits were to become an annual affair.

Chartres Biron, who had been one of the defence counsel in the Lynch treason trial, used to tell a good story about Carson on one of these visits. They met one morning at the springs, where the Solicitor-General was walking about with a letter in his hand and a most serious expression on his face. Biron asked him if anything was wrong.

"I have had a very disagreeable letter from Joe Chamberlain," said Carson. Chamberlain was still Colonial Secretary.

"What is in it?" Biron ventured to enquire.

"Well," replied Carson, "some time ago a man wrote to me and asked for a recommendation as he was applying to be made Chief Justice of some remote island in the tropics. I did not know the man, but I saw he had a good Irish name and thought he must be good enough for the tropics; so I wrote one. Chamberlain now writes, *My dear Carson, who is this fellow you recommended as a Chief Justice? He landed in the colony three weeks ago drunk, and he is not sober yet.*"

Carson paused for a moment, fixing Biron with his sombre gaze. Then he added: "That is a disagreeable letter to write to a man." And so indeed it was.

The tendency to overwork probably accounted for habits of absentmindedness which Carson had always shown to some extent but which became much more pronounced in these years. On one occasion, for instance, he found he had accepted three invitations to dinner with three different hostesses on the same evening. Rather than favour one at the expense of the other two, who would certainly be bound to learn of his action, he told his secretary to telephone all three and say he was ill. He then retired to bed for the night.

On another occasion when he and his wife were spending Christmas at the Hotel Metropole in Monte Carlo, then much patronised by the English legal profession, he thought he had lost some money. There was another barrister named Abinger also staying in the hotel, and Carson went to his room one morning, asking if he would do him a favour. "I had £250 in banknotes which I left on the mantelpiece of my dressing-room when I went to my bath," he said. "When I came back, they had gone. I want you, like a good fellow, to go and stop the numbers at the Casino, at the railway station and at Smith's, the bankers."

The obliging Abinger did as he was asked. Later in the day he found Carson at Ciro's and was about to broach the subject of the £250 when Lady Carson, who was lunching there with her husband, held up a warning finger. Abinger said nothing, but after lunch he got hold of Annette and asked her why she had stopped his speaking about the lost banknotes. "Well," she said, "Ned found them afterwards in the pocket of his pyjamas."

In the House of Commons Carson did not let the fact that he was a member of Balfour's Government interfere with the championship of the rights of the University he represented, when he considered those rights were in jeopardy, or with what he thought was for the good of Ireland generally. On one occasion, at least, he caused the Party Whips grave concern by taking his seat, not on the Government Front Bench, but in his old place below the gangway. That was when he spoke again in favour of the establishment of a Catholic University in his native country, though Balfour and the bulk of the Conservatives were opposed to it. "I prefer Roman Catholicism highly educated to Roman Catholicism in ignorance," he said on that occasion, "and the only way in which that result can be brought about is by the establishment of a generous system of higher education."

Similarly he accorded but a modified support to the extensive measure of land purchase embodied in Wyndham's great Irish Land Act, which was introduced in the session of 1903. He did not oppose it, as he had done Gerald Balfour's Bill a few years before, because, unlike the earlier measure, it did not seek to solve the Irish land question at the expense of the Irish landlord. Its object was to transfer by voluntary action, and in such a way as to satisfy the legitimate claims of all parties concerned, the ownership of Irish land in full from the landlord to the tenant. But Carson had grave doubts that it would afford the permanent solution in the sense that it was acclaimed by the Conservatives, and he did not hesitate to say so in a speech at Oxford, which was much resented at the time by the rank and file of the party, and which, because it was misrepresented, caused Balfour some uneasiness of mind. "They call this the last Irish Land Bill," he said, "they talk of a permanent solution. I have been hearing of a last Irish Land Bill, and of a permanent solution, all my life, and I have no doubt that I shall hear of them again." As a result of his speech Carson was obliged to send the Prime Minister a letter of explanation.

House of Commons,
4th May, '03.

I am very anxious to make it clear that, in what I said at Oxford with reference to the Irish Land Bill, I never intended in the least to be disloyal to you or the Government. It is quite true that, when I stated I would give the Bill the 'minimum of support which my official position required' I had in my mind the dislike of my constituency to the policy of land purchase (and which I share) and its probable effect in the university, but I thought that in adding that I gave it this support 'because I had no alternative', it would be clear my view was that, however disagreeable this policy was, it was my view that it was the only one. I see it has been represented that I said I had no alternative but to support it, which was not in the least what was intended and which would be ridiculous.

. . . I need hardly add that, so long as I have the honour of serving under you, I never could intentionally do a disloyal act.

During the debate on the second reading of Wyndham's Bill the lobby correspondent of the *Westminster Gazette* noted that the Solicitor-General, far from being in his accustomed seat on the Government Front Bench, was 'lounging in a very detached attitude' in his old place below the gangway. This immediately gave rise to the rumour that Carson had already tendered his resignation and as he emerged into the Members' lobby, the journalists crowded round him hoping for this sensational news. But Carson had not resigned, nor did he do so. On the contrary, he was kept busier than ever both in the House and in the Courts.

7

Carson felt very much the strain of this long and arduous session of 1903, and as it approached its end he found himself on the verge of complete mental and bodily exhaustion. The final straw came when he was asked to appear for the British Government in an important and complicated dispute with the United States of America over the boundary of Alaska. He had to take on the case with little more than a month to prepare it owing to the sudden illness of the counsel who had previously been instructed. "Such was the state of fatigue in which I was at the end of the session," he recalled afterwards, "that I went home and cried like a child." And well he might despair, for the immense pile of documents in the case almost completely filled the library of his new house in Eaton Place, into which he had recently moved from Rutland Gate.

Who could help him in this colossal task? He wondered and racked his brains. From time to time he had sent out work to be 'devilled' by other men at the Bar, and he remembered some notes by one of these 'devils' on an international case had impressed him at the time by their exceptional learning and accuracy. He asked his clerk who this 'devil' was. "He must be a man of great experience," he said. To his surprise he was told that the man in question was a young barrister named John Simon, recently down from Oxford, and that he had only been at the Bar for a few years. Nevertheless Carson decided to appeal to him for assistance, and on the last day of the summer term he sent for him to come and see him in his chambers. Thus it happened that young Mr. Simon, who was one day to become Lord Chancellor, went round to No. 3, Dr. Johnson's Buildings. He was shown into a gloomy room which he found 'not too well-equipped with law books.' The Solicitor-General, who was seated at a table, appeared near to collapse. He told the young man that he was tired out by his work in Parliament and the Courts and now he had this tremendous case about the Alaskan boundary. Would Simon help him with it? He explained that the case would be heard before an international arbitration tribunal in London during the last month of the Long Vacation, and he invited Simon to come down to the country and work with him on it in a furnished house which he had taken for the remainder of the summer at Exbury. Simon at once consented, as Carson subsequently put it, "with that readiness which always characterises him, and with that love of work which is the great feature of his success." Indeed he was glad to do so, since, besides the honour of thus being singled out by the Solicitor-General, he had recently suffered a grievous personal loss in the death of his young wife after barely four years of married life, and he welcomed the distraction provided by such a task as Carson suggested. Indeed, Carson, who had heard of the young man's loss and sympathised deeply, advised him with truth that the best relief he could find was in the preoccupation of unceasing work.

Lepe House, which Carson had taken at Exbury, was near the mouth of the Beaulieu River and looked across the Solent towards Cowes and the Isle of Wight. In such pleasant surroundings as these the two lawyers worked hard for the next five weeks, devoting the mornings and evenings to the case and the afternoons to sport and exercise. Simon later recalled how he was made a most welcome member of the household by Lady Carson. Walter, the youngest of the Carson children, was now a boy of thirteen at home for the holidays, and the young barrister spent many happy hours playing games with him, which included a cricket match on Saturdays. On other occasions Simon would join Carson and his family in a launch, exploring the upper reaches of the river or cruising up Southampton Water. As for Carson, he enjoyed nothing more than this pastime. "I will miss the launch," he wrote to Lady Londonderry when he was leaving Lepe House. "As you know, I love the sea."

The facts of the boundary dispute were briefly as follows: Alaska had been first discovered by Russian explorers in the eighteenth century and subsequently incorporated in the Russian empire. In 1821 the Czar promulgated a decree designed to exclude navigators from the Bering Sea and the Pacific coast of his possessions within a distance of 100 miles. This led to immediate protests from the United States and Great Britain, as a result of which treaties were concluded for the purpose of determining the extent of the Czar's jurisdiction. The Anglo-Russian Treaty, which was signed in 1825, described the boundary as following 'the summit of the mountains running parallel to the coast' from the Portland Canal in the south to the 141st meridian in the north (*i.e.* to Mt. St. Elias), provided that if the line of mountains should anywhere exceed 'ten marine leagues' (34½ miles) from 'the ocean', the boundary should be formed 'by a line parallel to the sinuosities of the coast and which shall never exceed the distance of the marine leagues therefrom.' In 1867 Russia sold the whole Alaskan territory to the United States for just over seven million dollars, it being agreed that the purchasers were to assume all the rights and obligations under the treaty of 1825. Thus Canada, who had acquired dominion status in the same year, suddenly found herself cut off from development from the north-west.

For the next thirty years very little was heard of the American purchase. Indeed it was generally regarded as something of a white elephant, being popularly known as 'Seward's Ice Chest' from the Secretary of State who had negotiated the purchase. In fact it was regarded as a remote land of grinding ice floes and glaciers. World attention was suddenly concentrated on it through the discovery of gold in the Canadian Yukon in 1896 and the resulting 'gold rushes' to Klondyke in the two following years, when £100 millions of gold

EDWARD CARSON, Q.C., M.P.

From the portrait by Julia Folkard in the possession of Lady Carson.

CARSON OR CRIPPS?

LORD SALISBURY (Head Master): "*Shall I give the prize to the good little boy Cripps, or the big bad boy Carson?*"

Cartoon by Sir F. C. Gould in the *Westminster Gazette*, May 9, 1900.

were produced. Alaska now became of prime importance, since the Yukon could best be reached from the coast to the south up the rocky inlets and across the mountain passes which formed the boundary between the two territories. In the process of prospecting the Americans pushed a considerable distance inland from the coast, establishing settlements as far inland as Lake Bennet in British Columbia. In short, they claimed the mountain passes into the gold country as well as the heads of all the inlets, including the 100-mile-long canal of vital importance to navigation, thus cutting off Canada from all access by sea to the Klondyke region. This was justified by their interpretation of the word 'coast' in the treaty of 1825 as meaning literally the rugged edges of the mainland, including those of the deep channels and inlets.

The British and Canadian Governments on the other hand believed the word 'coast' to mean the general trend of the mainland coast, and not the edges of the tidal inlets, like the Lyon Canal which ran far inland. They naturally protested and eventually, at the instance of the American President Theodore Roosevelt, the British Foreign Secretary, Lord Lansdowne, agreed to refer the matter to arbitration. The proposed tribunal was to consist of a Commission of 'six impartial jurists of repute', three to be appointed by each of the two Governments. When the names of the American jurists were announced, it was seen that they could hardly lay claim to the title of 'impartial'. Instead of nominating three judges of the Supreme Court as had been confidently expected, three prominent politicians were appointed, much to the surprise of the British and the indignation of the Canadian Governments. They were Mr. Elihu Root, President Roosevelt's Secretary of War, who with the President's concurrence had dispatched American troops into the disputed territory, and two Senators, Henry C. Lodge of Massachusetts and George Turner of Washington, who were known to be strongly in favour of the American claim. To put it bluntly, President Roosevelt accepted arbitration but only on condition that the award was favourable to him. Otherwise he was prepared to resort to force. However, instead of Lord Lansdowne breaking off negotiations at once as urged by the indignant Canadians, the British Government selected Lord Alverstone, the Lord Chief Justice, as the principal British Commissioner, who agreed to preside, in company with two distinguished Canadian lawyers, Mr. A. B. Aylesworth, K.C., of Toronto, and Sir Louis Jetté, a former Governor of Quebec. No wonder Carson was unfavourably impressed by the way the matter had been handled at the Foreign Office. "I have no confidence in Lord Lansdowne," he told Lady Londonderry at this time, "as I am thoroughly sick of the way the Alaska negotiations were carried out, and I fear very bad results."

As we shall see, Carson's fears were to be confirmed. However, he had been instructed in the arbitration and he had to make the best of it he could. For hours each day he and Simon would pore over old maps and charts, accounts of bygone travels and explorations, treaty texts, and conversations between statesmen and diplomats. Many of the documents were in French and some were in Russian, all of which Carson found very baffling. But his young junior was a mine of information and erudition. "I can assure you I am really speaking what I absolutely feel," Carson subsequently told an audience of Simon's constituents, "when I say that I could never have brought my part of that great trial to a satisfactory result but for the assistance I received from him." What is more, Carson showed his gratitude in tangible form. When the preliminary work was finished and Simon was saying good-bye, Carson asked him: "Where are you going from here?" Thinking that the Solicitor-General wished to send him a friendly letter of appreciation for his industry, Simon wrote down his address: he was going north, to Scotland. "Have you a frock-coat?" Carson then asked. With a puzzled look Simon replied that he had. Nothing further was said and the two men parted. It was not until he reached Scotland and found a telegram waiting for him that Simon discovered the purport of these questions. The telegram was from the Treasury Solicitor. It informed him that he had been briefed as junior counsel in the Alaska arbitration case, which was due to open a few days later, and summoned him back to London at once.

It was a wonderful opportunity for a twenty-nine-year-old barrister to figure in a case of such international importance and the young junior made the most of it. Some years later Simon publicly thanked his benefactor at a gathering at which they were both present. "We know Sir Edward Carson as a powerful advocate and a terrible cross-examiner," said Simon on that occasion, "but I know him best as one who has always been far too kind to me. . . . Sir Edward Carson has referred to the fact that I was the envied among the most enviable of the junior Bar in having a great brief with a great fee marked upon it in a great arbitration for a great colony. It was he who got that brief for me. There is a strict rule in the profession to which both he and I belong, that there must be no touting, and I do not accuse him of breaking that good and salutary rule; but at the same time I strongly suspect that on another occasion than the present he exercised that priceless Irish quality of blarney."

The arbitration tribunal sat to hear arguments for nineteen days in the Foreign Office in Downing Street, under the presidency of Lord Chief Justice Alverstone, between September 3 and October 8, 1903. The British side of the case was presented by the two Law Officers, together with four K.C.s of the Canadian Bar, and two junior counsel of the English Bar, Mr. Sidney Rowlatt (later Mr. Justice Rowlatt) and Mr. John Simon. The inclusion of Simon in the British team was seen to be justified from the outset. At one of the conferences which took place before the sitting of the Court at which the juniors were present, Mr. Sefton, the Canadian Minister of the Interior, drew Carson aside and said: "Who's that young man, Sir Edward? He seems to know so much more about the case than anyone else." "That's young Simon," replied the British Solicitor-General. Time and again during the protracted hearing Simon reminded his leader of points which he had overlooked.

The American team was led by the Hon. Judge Jacob M. Dickinson. His case depended on being able to introduce maps, correspondence, notes of conversations between diplomatists, claims to sovereignty and other events prior to the conclusion of the 1825 treaty, together with general principles of international law, the cumulative effect of which, in his submission, was to modify the treaty. The British case, on the other hand, was that everything was properly expressed in the treaty itself and that, in accordance with the accepted principle of English law, extraneous matters could not be introduced to vary or supplement it, provided that its meaning was clear and unambiguous. "I ask the tribunal to keep to the treaty itself," Carson urged, "until we arrive at some difficulty which requires external assistance." In this context the Americans relied upon a conversation which took place between Mr. Stratford Canning, the British Ambassador at St. Petersburg in 1825, and Mr. Middleton, the American representative, just before the signing of the treaty. But this was not good enough for Carson. "In the account Mr. Middleton gives in his interview with Mr. Canning," observed Carson, "he says that Mr. Canning explained to him that the treaty said that from the top of the Portland Canal they were to go east. Well, all I can say is that if we are to act in this way in construing a treaty, that somebody goes to somebody else and tells him what the treaty did, and that somebody else reports his view and recollection of what took place at that interview, I think it would be much better to have no treaties at all."

Carson's speech, which lasted for nearly two days, was the closing one for the British side. With his clear logical mind and innate common sense he reduced all the complicated and detailed questions to a single issue—the meaning of the word 'coast' in the treaty. "You have to go to the language of the treaty, the language in its plain ordinary sense, and you have to try to see what is meant here by 'coast' . . . not from the definition of writers or international law. I say here that the coast is the edge of the ocean, and I say that no other possible construction can be given to the treaty." The 'ten marine leagues' were to be measured from the ocean, "the water which separates great continents one from another," and not the minor waters whether they be called seas, inlets or canals. "I say that the 'ocean' means something which does not run up the inlets, and I prove that by the treaty itself, because it says you are to draw a line parallel to the coast, which is the edge of the ocean. But if you are to take it as being the edge of the salt water you have only to look at any of the maps to see that it is absolutely impossible ever to have expected that the mountains should run parallel to these various inlets." Nor was it in any degree possible to draw a line parallel to these 'sinuosities'. "Why," said Carson, pointing in the direction of the Thames, "if the ocean is to be taken as everywhere we can find salt water, this enquiry is perhaps being conducted on the edge of the ocean."

When Carson sat down after his long argument, the President congratulated him with a touch of sardonic humour, but in words which were intended as a great tribute to his powers. "Mr. Solicitor," said Lord Alverstone, "having conquered Ireland and annexed England, you now proceed to bring one of the principal colonies of His Majesty under your influence." A tribute was also paid to the Solicitor-General by the principal American advocate, but of a different kind. Mr. Dickinson, in appealing to the tribunal not to decide the matter on the narrow construction of the meaning of words, argued that Carson's definition of the word 'coast' would give Great Britain every safe harbour and anchorage and every point useful for defence or protection of trade. He said that the maps of 1825 showed that it was not to the mountains bordering the sea, but to the mountains passing round the heads of the inlets, that the negotiators referred, and there was no such continuous range of mountains. "It becomes necessary for Great Britain to select a set of peaks," he argued. "There is nothing in the treaty to justify the selection of peaks nearest to the sea. The Solicitor-General skips from peak to peak like Ariel."

A fortnight later, on October 20, the tribunal issued its award. It was signed by the British President and the three United States Commissioners, but the two Canadian Commissioners refused to subscribe their names to a document the effect of which they considered manifestly unfair to their country. In construing the word 'coast' in accordance with the American view, the written judgment deduced a mountain frontier unfavourable to Canada; in other words, the mountains were not those nearest to the coast but a series of peaks further back along a line behind and roughly parallel to the deep inlets, such as the Lyon Canal. In brief, the effect of the award was thus to exclude the Canadians from all the inlets as far south as the Portland Channel, thus cutting them off from the water approaches to the Yukon and other gold-fields. In respect of the Portland Channel the decision was largely, though not entirely, favourable to the British claims. Canada got the two larger and inner islands, but the two smaller and outer ones went to the United States for no very clear reason, the result being further to irritate the Canadians, who alleged that strategically the two smaller islands would neutralise the value to them of the larger ones.

The Canadians were not unnaturally resentful at what they considered to be not a judicial decision at all but a compromise based on political expediency, and the award intensified the demand in the Dominion for treaty-making powers. However, the hard feelings engendered by the award gradually died down, a process helped forward by the conciliatory and loyal speech made by one of the Canadian Commissioners, Mr. Aylesworth, on his return home. "The ties that bind Canada to the Motherland," he said, "will stand the strain of many Alaska awards." On the whole, the object, described by Carson in his closing speech before the tribunal, was achieved, if not in quite the happiest manner that he would have liked to see—namely, "the removal of one of the causes of difference between two great and friendly nations."

8

The next case of public interest in which Carson appeared occurred in the following year, a few weeks after he had passed his fiftieth birthday. It was the further hearing of a divorce petition on the initiative of the King's Proctor, the official who is charged with intervening in divorce suits where there is occasion to believe that the evidence for the decree has been fabricated or some other irregularity has taken place. This particular case was considered of such importance as to justify the Solicitor-General being briefed on behalf of the King's Proctor. It was also a sensational case, and it led to an equally sensational prosecution at the Old Bailey, in which Carson was also instructed.

The facts were briefly these. In November, 1902, a petition filed by Mrs. Kate Pollard against her husband Thomas Pollard came on for hearing before Mr. Justice Gorell Barnes (later Lord Gorell) in the Divorce Division. The suit was undefended, and the evidence on which the petitioner relied seemed to be of the usual sordid kind in such cases, although the solicitor had thought it worth while to instruct an eminent K.C., Mr. Bargrave Deane, to appear for her. It transpired that the petitioner, a good-looking woman, was employed as a waitress in a café. Her husband, whom she had married in 1891, was much older than herself: he had been in the tea trade and had later worked as an insurance broker, in neither of which jobs he had been at all successful. In addition, according to her evidence, he had been drinking heavily for years and had treated her badly. They had eventually separated, and at his wife's request he had gone to live with his parents in Plymouth. While he was residing there, it was alleged that he had committed misconduct with a woman named Maud Goodman. Miss Goodman, a woman of easy virtue, gave evidence of this and identified the husband from a photograph. The hearing of the case, which was not reported in the newspapers, only occupied a few minutes, and the judge thereupon granted Mrs. Pollard a decree *nisi*.

Mrs. Pollard expected to secure her freedom at the end of six months, when in the ordinary course of events she would have applied to have the decree made absolute. But events did not turn out as she had hoped. First of all, Mr. Thomas Pollard wrote to the King's Proctor stating that the evidence against him was fabricated and that, if he had not been without means, he would have defended the suit. On the strength of this uncorroborated letter the King's Proctor decided he could take no action. Shortly afterwards, however, he received another communication, which prompted him immediately to intervene.

The evidence against the husband had been collected by a

notorious firm of private detectives named Slater's Detective Agency, which boasted that it had never had a failure in the Divorce Court during the past seventeen years. In actual fact £3,000 had been spent on this petition. Although Miss Goodman had only been paid a modest sum to cover her expenses, the solicitor who prepared the case had received £677 and the rest had gone in other ways on the costly business of investigation. These unsavoury details came to light when one of Slater's clerks, a man named Cartwright, was dismissed. He joined a rival agency named Simmond's, composed of some other ex-employees of Slater's, and he brought with him the contents of his desk at Slater's. These included some papers relating to the Pollard divorce, and as they suggested that a false case had been presented to the Court, Cartwright sent them to the King's Proctor. Hence the present proceedings, in which the original case was reopened.

The proceedings took place before the President of the Divorce Division, Sir Francis Jeune (later Lord St. Helier), and a special jury, commencing on March 16, 1904, and lasting for eleven days. Carson appeared for the King's Proctor, along with Mr. Willie Mathews and Mr. Guy Stephenson. Mrs. Pollard had an equally powerful team of advocates representing her, consisting of two 'silks', Sir Edward Clarke, K.C., and Mr. Bargrave Deane, K.C., and two 'juniors', Mr. W. T. Barnard, who had also represented Mrs. Pollard in the previous trial, and Mr. J. P. Valetta.

In his opening speech Carson explained how so much money had come to be spent on the original case. A certain Mr. Hugh Charles Knowles, a wealthy man, had come to take a romantic but otherwise quite innocent interest in Mrs. Pollard's welfare. He wished to help her to get free of the miserable life she was living with her husband and, having heard that Slater's had a reputation for working wonders in cases like this, went off one day in September, 1901, to call at their offices. He saw the manager, a gentleman known as 'Slater Junior', whose real name was Mr. George Henry, and explained his business to him. The obliging Mr. Henry pointed out that inquiries by private detectives were apt to prove expensive, but it appeared that with Mr. Knowles money was no object. Mr. Henry then rang up a firm of solicitors, Messrs. Osborn and Osborn. Now it so happened that the two firms had had a good deal to do with each other in previous divorce matters, and their premises were connected by a private telephone line. For some weeks the unfortunate husband was watched, without result. He kept very much to himself, and did not seem to care for the society of women. Mr. Henry then suggested to Mr. Albert Osborn, the solicitor, that a detective should make the acquaintance of Mr. Pollard and try to make him commit an act of adultery upon which a petition might be based. "If that is true," said Carson, "it will be a matter of great public importance, for such an act would be an interference with public justice."

Acquaintance with Pollard was in due course struck up in a public-house in Plymouth by one of Slater's agents. Pollard was then introduced to various girls, but at first nothing came of these meetings. Then another agent, whose name was Davies, took Pollard away on a trip to Jersey, paying all expenses. Here the evidence was so scandalous that the solicitor thought it too dangerous to use. Eventually, at Henry's suggestion, the solicitor went down to Plymouth, where, after visiting several brothels, he induced Pollard to come to a meeting place when Maud Goodman was also present, unknown to Pollard, for the purpose of identification. After several subsequent interviews with Osborn, Miss Goodman signed a statement identifying Pollard as a man with whom she had committed misconduct. Subsequently considerable difficulty was experienced in persuading her to come to London to substantiate her statement in the witness box. She insisted on a woman friend accompanying her, and the friend insisted on another woman coming along too. "And so," said Carson to the astonished jury, "this interesting party left Plymouth for the precincts of the Divorce Court, composed of three women and two detectives as a bodyguard, and, in order that there might be no illegality, there too, in full force, was Mr. Osborn, the solicitor, all coming to London so that Maud Goodman should prove one single act of misconduct on the part of the respondent."

Numerous witnesses were called by each side, and there were some amusing passages in Court. The core of the case centred in Maud Goodman, who swore she had been frightened into giving evidence at the previous trial by the solicitor. To her denial that she had ever committed adultery with Mr. Pollard, Sir Edward Clarke objected on the ground that the questions put to her in her examination-in-chief, which was conducted by Mr. Willie Mathews, should be limited to the evidence given at the trial. This objection brought Carson to his feet.

"My learned friend is mistaken as to the issue here," he said. "We are not here to re-try the issue raised at the trial in November, 1902. That we cannot do. The issue we have before us today is whether the whole case is one which has been concocted against the respondent."

In this view the President supported the Solicitor-General. "The real question before the Court, and it is no use mincing matters," declared the judge, "is whether or not Mr. Osborn concocted this case. It has come to this—did Maud Goodman speak substantially the truth, or did the solicitor induce her to state what was entirely false?"

The solicitor, it must be admitted, cut a sorry figure in the witness box, particularly when questioned on the subject of his costs.

"Will you pledge your oath," Carson asked him, "that all these costs which go to make up £677 were legitimate costs?"

"They were the costs that I have received," answered Osborn.

Carson looked from the rows of figures on the sheet of paper in front of him to the two counsel on the other side, whom the solicitor had instructed in the original petition.

"I am sorry to see," said Carson, with a wry smile, "that with all this money you did not give my friends Mr. Deane and Mr. Barnard very much."

Here the President intervened. "There are disproportions in this world," he observed sagely, as the spectators laughed.

In the course of his testimony Osborn admitted he had given one woman witness £1.

"What, buy her evidence?" asked Carson in horrified tones.

The witness was nettled by this question. "I am entitled to pay," he said, "if a witness says she won't come to Court."

"You had better not act on those principles in future," the President told him sternly.

Mrs. Pollard then went into the witness box, where she made a much more favourable impression than her solicitor had done. Again and again she said: "I wanted to be free and to end this miserable life."

That she was sincere to the point of naïveté appeared from her cross-examination by Carson, of which this is an example:

The Solicitor-General: Do you approve of your husband's photograph being taken into brothels?

Sir Edward Clarke: I object to that question. It has no relevance to the case at all.

The President: I think it has.

The Solicitor-General: Do you approve?

Witness: Yes, if that is the way these things are worked.

Among the other witnesses whom Sir Edward Clarke put into the box was the proprietor of Slater's Agency, a well-preserved elderly man of military appearance, who had changed his name several times, and now called himself 'Captain Scott'. His real name was Tinsley. For some time past he had taken little part in the management of the business, which he left to 'Slater Junior' and, fortunately for himself as it turned out, had been abroad at the time of the Pollard divorce. He had formerly been a pawnbroker's assistant before becoming a private detective, and he had no right to the military title he assumed. Carson quizzed him humorously on his repeated changes of nomenclature.

> THE SOLICITOR-GENERAL: Why Scott?
> WITNESS: I had no reason.
> THE SOLICITOR-GENERAL: And why Captain?
> WITNESS: At the office I was called the boss, the Captain, the Governor and eventually I took the title of Captain.
> THE SOLICITOR-GENERAL: I see. It meant Captain of the Detective Corps. But why Scott? Was it because it reminded you of Great Scott?

When 'the Captain' did not reply, Carson put to him an article which had been published calling him by his true name and describing him as an 'exposed creature still practising as Slater's bogus agency.'

Mr. Bargrave Deane objected to this. "I am rather surprised that a public officer——" he began.

Carson interrupted him. "A public officer will do his duty regardless of your sneers." Mr. Bargrave Deane said no more on this point.

Carson's sense of public duty was illustrated by another incident which occurred during his cross-examination of this witness. He asked him for his bank pass-book; but, when he was told that it contained many thousands of names, some of them of persons well known in society and public life, he did not insist on its production, as he had no wish to see the scandal of the case being spread abroad unnecessarily.

Another noteworthy passage occurred in his cross-examination of George Henry, the manager of Slater's.

> THE SOLICITOR-GENERAL: I ask you, sir, in these circumstances do you represent that this was a legitimate business you were carrying on?

WITNESS: Yes.

THE SOLICITOR-GENERAL: And a respectable one?

WITNESS: Yes. I have never been attacked like this before.

THE SOLICITOR-GENERAL: You may never have been found out before.

WITNESS: There has been nothing to find out.

Unfortunately for those concerned there was a great deal to find out, and this case revealed much of it. In his final speech Sir Edward Clarke argued with his customary eloquence that the case was the result of a conspiracy on the part of Simmond's Agency to ruin their rivals in business. Carson brought the jury back to the realities of the matter. "This is a case which raises questions far beyond our sympathies and feelings," he said. "This is a case which goes to the root of the administration of justice in this country. If it is true that Slater's exists as an agency for procuring the registration of dishonest evidence as a decree of a Court of Justice, if it is true that the solicitor in the case—an officer of the Court—has presented a false case to this Court in consideration of a large sum of money, we are confronted with a grave danger to the administration of justice in this country, and we must put aside all feelings against Mr. Pollard and in favour of Mrs. Pollard. Sir Edward has said that documents have been stolen, but the question is not whether they were stolen, but whether they were genuine. The question is not how they were obtained, but whether they are true, and whether Slater's is an illegitimate business, to procure evidence, rightly or wrongly, to earn these enormous sums."

As for the solicitor Osborn, Carson went on: "It does seem a serious matter for him to go round the brothels of Plymouth and interview these wretched women, who were only there to sell their souls and their bodies for five shillings or ten shillings, these outcasts from society, who did not care whether their shame was known or not, for, after all, their shame was their daily employment. His conduct was but a trick to get one prostitute to obtain a statement from another, and this becomes evidence in a Court of Law! And yet, gentlemen, you are discharging a great and valuable public service in hearing this case. As far as the King's Proctor is concerned, he has only faithfully and honestly performed his duty in bringing this matter to your attention. For, above all, in the interests of justice itself, you should take care that no one shall be allowed to tamper with the truth and see that the justice which is administered in these Courts is absolutely pure and undefiled."

Not for the first time was a speech of Carson's greeted with warm applause in Court as he sat down. After the President's summing up the jury retired. It only took them five minutes to find that the King's Proctor's intervention was justified, since the agent Davies, acting under Henry's instructions and with the knowledge of Osborn, had induced Pollard to commit adultery, and that consequently a false case had been presented to the Court. The divorce decree was accordingly rescinded, but on her counsel's application the President granted Mrs. Pollard a judicial separation.

Once more the Solicitor-General rose in his place. "I ask that all the documents in this case be impounded," he said. The President agreed. This meant that the papers would be sent to the Director of Public Prosecutions.

The result was the trial at the Old Bailey, which opened six months later, on October 25, 1904, before Mr. Justice Darling, as Carson's old friend and benefactor had now become. In the dock were Albert Osborn, the solicitor in the Pollard case, 'Captain' Scott, the proprietor of Slater's Agency, George Henry, the manager, John Davies and three other agents of Slater's, all charged with conspiring together 'to pervert and defeat the due course of law and justice.' Carson led for the Crown, along with Willie Mathews, Archibald Bodkin and other counsel. Osborn was defended by Mr. Charles Gill, K.C., and Mr. J. P. Valetta, Scott by Mr. Rufus Isaacs, K.C., and Mr. R. D. Muir, and the other defendants were also professionally represented.

The trial occupied eleven days, of which the first two days were devoted to Carson's opening speech. Most of the evidence in the divorce proceedings was repeated, but none of the prisoners went into the witness box to give evidence on his own behalf, as he was entitled to do, not wishing to undergo this ordeal a second time.

The case was enlivened by some sharp exchanges between Gill and Carson, who despite their wrangling in Court were on most friendly terms outside it. In cross-examining Maud Goodman, Gill said he was attempting to get at the real facts by questions and not by speeches. "I do not know how many thousand speeches you have made," observed Carson. "At any rate," Gill retorted, "I have not made one of eight hours' duration."

Later Gill asked Miss Goodman whether a statement she had given the King's Proctor was not taken from a house of ill-fame in Plymouth, which he described as "turning a brothel into a solicitor's office." At this the judge addressed the witness. "That is not an attack upon you," said Mr. Justice Darling. "It was a thrust at the Solicitor-General." "Or thought to be," remarked Carson, amid the general laughter.

At another stage in the case, when Carson was addressing the jury, Gill rose and protested against "these outbursts of eloquence against the men in the dock."

"The main part of the objection seems to be that the Solicitor-General was eloquent," Mr. Justice Darling observed smilingly. "I cannot interfere in the exercise by the Solicitor-General of a natural gift."

"No wonder juries disagree in Ireland," said Gill, who himself hailed from Ulster.

"You know as much about Ireland as I do," replied Carson, amid more laughter.

One other passage in this trial is worth noting. Rufus Isaacs was cross-examining the clerk Cartwright, who, it will be remembered, had left Slater's Agency for Simmond's, taking the incriminating Pollard papers with him. "Don't you think," Isaacs asked him, "that if they could ruin Slater's it would be a fine thing for Simmond's?" Cartwright did not reply.

"Come," said Mr. Justice Darling to him, "don't you think that if anyone turned the Solicitor-General out of office it would be a very fine thing for the person who turned him out?"

Carson joined in the mirth which this question produced. "I am not quite sure about that," he commented, thinking of his opponent's enormous private practice. "I can only say I do not mind being turned out. I should be glad to exchange with Mr. Isaacs."

Curiously enough this is what happened, when in the ensuing Liberal Government Rufus Isaacs did eventually step into the post which Carson had vacated.

The result of the trial was that all the prisoners were convicted, except the solicitor, as to whose guilt the jury could not hold out any prospect of agreement, and 'Captain' Scott, whom the judge had discharged, since he was abroad at this time of the matters in issue and had no knowledge of them. Henry was sentenced to twelve months' imprisonment, and the others to lesser terms. Osborn was ordered to be re-tried at the next sessions, but eventually it was decided not to prosecute him again and, on Carson's advice, the further proceedings against him were dropped.

To the Solicitor-General's resolute advocacy in these two trials the community was thus indebted for the exposure of a growing scandal in the administration of justice in England. Henceforward private detective agencies were to conduct their business with due respect for the law.

9

The same year that saw Carson engaged in the Pollard divorce case and its Old Bailey sequel also found him extremely busy on the Government Front Bench in the House of Commons. He was put in charge of a legislative measure of some consequence, a Licensing Bill, which meant that he was responsible for seeing it successfully through all its stages in the House. The Bill originated in this way. At that time the number of public-houses in the country was generally considered to be excessive and to constitute a social evil. But the justices, before whom applications for renewal of publicans' licences came up at the annual 'brewsters sessions', as a whole had shown themselves reluctant to refuse such applications, since this would have meant depriving publicans of their livelihood. The matter was brought to a head by some members of the Chamberlain family, who sat on the magisterial bench in Birmingham, suddenly refusing to renew licences. This provoked an outcry on the part of the licensed trade, which eventually led the Government to introduce a Bill designed to remedy this situation. It simply conferred power on the magistrates to give compensation in cases where publicans had failed to secure a renewal of their licences. The decision to regard licences as a species of property, which the Bill embodied, provoked considerable controversy in the country and brought all the forces of the temperance movement into play.

This was the only measure which Carson was destined to pilot through the House of Commons. During the Committee stage he made over ninety speeches on it, coming down to the House night after night. In the end his conduct won a warm tribute from the Front Opposition Bench, where Mr. Asquith referred to the Solicitor-General's "uniform courtesy, unfailing lucidity," and, he felt impelled to add, "inexhaustible resource." Seated beside Mr. Asquith, leading the attack for the Liberals, was forty-two-year-old David Lloyd George, who argued that a publican's licence had never been in the nature of property and he drew attention to an abundance of legislation on the statute book since the reign of Henry VII which aimed at suppressing 'common ale houses' as a public mischief.

"What a pity," said Balfour to Carson one day after the brilliant Welshman had been speaking. "There's a first-rate man, so very clever, but there's always something in every speech that spoils it. I suppose it was engrained in him as a country solicitor."

"Then I'm a good match for him," said Carson, "for I was only a country lawyer when you first knew me."

That was seventeen years ago when Carson was only thirty-three. Now, at fifty, he was an established figure both in the Courts and the House of Commons. We have seen how he had made a considerable financial sacrifice by relinquishing his private practice when he became Solicitor-General. But during this period the amount of Crown work with which he was entrusted in his capacity of Law Officer had increased to such an extent that he was now earning over £7,000 a year in fees in addition to his salary.

Only a few of the many cases in which Carson was professionally engaged at this time have been described, on account of their public interest, in these pages. One of them, which deserves brief mention, was the prosecution for fraud of the financier, Ernest Terah Hooley, and an inventor named H. J. Lawson toward the end of 1904. Hooley, who was charged with obtaining a large sum of money from a shareholder in one of the companies in which he was interested, was defended by Rufus Isaacs. Lawson, who has been credited with the invention of the 'safety' bicycle, was similarly charged, being also indicted for issuing a false company prospectus; he conducted his own defence. It is worthy of note that whereas the inventor was convicted, the financier was acquitted, which may perhaps be an example of the advantage which a defendant represented by counsel has over one who conducts his own defence.

The Solicitor-General was sitting in his chambers at the commencement of the new Law Term in 1905, when a letter was brought to him. He opened it and, to his surprise and gratification, found it was from the Lord Chancellor, Lord Halsbury, offering him a judgeship in the High Court. Sir Francis Jeune, the President of the Probate, Divorce and Admiralty Division, was retiring, and the Lord Chancellor, who had been greatly impressed by Carson's appearance for the King's Proctor in the Pollard case, now considered him to be the best possible successor to the retiring President of that Court. "I hope you will accept," wrote Lord Halsbury, "as I think it would be good for you as releasing you from the choice of

Parliament and the profession, and I am sure it would be very good for His Majesty's lieges."

Darling, already a judge, happened to be in his old chambers when the letter came, and the two men discussed it together. Carson's immediate reaction was to refuse the offer straight away. He was impelled to do this by the feeling that the Balfour Government's days were numbered and that in all probability he would be in private practice again before the year was out; neither did he wish to sever his connexion with the House of Commons, which acceptance of a seat on the judicial Bench would have obliged him to do. "I don't want the appointment," he said, "I love my work at the Bar."

Darling begged him to give the offer a little consideration before turning it down, which Carson agreed to do. He immediately wrote a letter to Balfour, asking the Prime Minister if acceptance would meet with his approval. "You have been so much to me," he added, "and so good a friend during my career that I should feel sorry indeed if you thought I placed my personal feelings of advancement before what you would consider right and best under all the circumstances. I am quite willing to go into Opposition if I am of any real use to you and the party, and my only anxiety is that in any course I take I should meet with your approval. I feel bitter pangs at the idea of severing my connection with politics and, above all, at leaving your service."

Balfour, who was visiting his constituency in Manchester, telegraphed in reply that the offer had been made with his approval, and that he would approve of whatever course Carson took. "Your loss will be deeply felt," he said, "but I think you should do what suits your own view." At the same time the Prime Minister told his private secretary, J. S. Sandars, that he was confident Carson meant to accept the offer. He was thus all the more surprised to learn from Sandars of Carson's eventual decision. On January 25, 1905, Carson wrote to Sandars after a long conversation with him on the previous day: "After a good deal of hesitation I have declined the offer of the L[ord] C[hancellor]. Whether I have been wise or unwise matters little, as I have acted upon my own instincts and my own wishes in the matter."

At this news, after he had told Balfour, Sandars expressed evident relief. "Just before leaving for Manchester to join the Chief," he wrote to Carson a day or two later from Downing Street, "let me tell you that I had a word of thanksgiving from him on hearing from me that you had declined judicial office, and that you had accordingly elected to stay by his side in our future strenuous fight in Opposition. So don't think him ungrateful, for grateful he is."

In his letter to the Lord Chancellor declining his offer, Carson stated that it had come upon him as a surprise, since he had no such expectations or aspirations. By return he received the following reply from Lord Halsbury:

> 4 *Ennismore Gardens,*
> *S.W.*
> 25.1.1905.
>
> MY DEAR SOLICITOR,
>
> I am very sorry for the sake of the public and the profession that you have come to the conclusion which your letter announces, but I fully recognise that every man is the best judge himself as to what makes for his own happiness and usefulness.
>
> As a member of the Government I ought to rejoice that we are not to lose your services, though for the reasons I have given I regret it. At all events I think our friendship will still continue, and in the meantime,
>
> Believe me, always very truly yours,
>
> HALSBURY.

Thus did Carson, who sixteen years previously had applied for an Irish County Court judgeship, refuse one of the principal judicial offices in England on the eve of his fifty-first birthday.* For one part of the United Kingdom it was fortunate that he did so: had he become President of the Divorce Court, Ulster would have been deprived of the leadership which she was to enjoy in what was the most dramatic and perhaps also the greatest phase in his career a few years later. Many more great cases, too, lay ahead of him in the Courts, including one concerning a young naval cadet which was to command his interest and attention possibly more than any other in his remarkable legal armoury. One other feature of the rejected appointment is worth mentioning. If Carson had accepted it, special enabling legislation would have had to be introduced into the House of Commons, since the law recognised that the office must be held by a barrister of not less than fifteen years standing at the English Bar. Carson, having been 'called' in 1894, did not therefore fulfil this qualification.

Less than two months afterwards Carson refused another

*Commenting on the incident some years later, Carson remarked: "Of course he [Lord Halsbury] would not believe what I said, but I was quite sincere." *Lord Riddell's War Diary*, 138.

appointment, this time a political one—that of Chief Secretary for Ireland. Indeed he held the post for a day, but this fact was not published at the time, nor was it generally known. It came about in the following way.

After he had introduced his comprehensive Land Purchase Act in 1903, George Wyndham, the Irish Secretary, had begun to suffer from ill-health. Overwork brought him to the verge of a nervous breakdown, and during the summer of the following year he had gone abroad to recuperate. While he was absent, the Permanent Under-Secretary in Dublin Castle, Sir Anthony MacDonnell, wrote him two letters, full of administrative matters, in which he casually mentioned that he was engaged with Lord Dunraven, a peer of Home Rule sympathies, in framing a scheme of 'devolution' of local legislation and decentralisation of financial arrangements, thus transferring a measure of control from Westminster to Dublin. Unfortunately Wyndham did not appreciate the significance of the 'devolution' scheme. MacDonnell was an ex-Indian civil servant with the reputation of being a capable administrator, but he was also a Roman Catholic and, though a civil servant, he did not disguise his own Home Rule sympathies. In fact he lent willing counsel and assistance to the Dunraven scheme, and the draft of the scheme was actually written on Dublin Castle notepaper in his office. This caused an outcry, when the scheme was published, from the Irish Unionists, who regarded it as an attempt to introduce Home Rule by the back door. The Ulster Members at Westminster were immediately up in arms, notably Colonel Saunderson, now nearing the end of his life, John Atkinson and H. O. Arnold-Forster, Balfour's War Minister, who, though an Englishman, sat for a Belfast constituency which possessed a strong Catholic and Nationalist minority. They were supported by Carson, who considered it intolerable that a civil servant, who was supposed to profess no party politics in his official capacity, should have behaved like this. "The grievance of Ulster Unionists," he said, "is, rightly or wrongly, that the scheme originated with a permanent official retained under a Unionist Government in Dublin Castle."

Carson thereupon threatened to resign his own post in the Government if the Chief Secretary was committed to such a scheme, which might put Ulster under a Catholic majority in the matters concerned. He was supported in his resolve by Arnold-Forster and John Atkinson in the Commons, and Londonderry and Ashbourne, the Irish Lord Chancellor, in the Lords, who likewise threatened to resign their offices if the obnoxious scheme was carried into effect. "You know," Carson told Balfour, "it is only for the sake of the Union that I am in politics at all, and this idea is a particularly insidious attack upon the Union."

"I know it is, and I think George has been very indiscreet," replied the Prime Minister. He then put his arm affectionately round his Solicitor-General's shoulders. "Now, do help me," he added. "I am in a great difficulty. Besides, I can make a very good logical defence of George."

Carson laughed. "What would be the use," he asked Balfour, "of my saying to one of my juries: 'My client comes before you, gentlemen, with a very good logical defence'? What I must know is whether you have a *real* defence for him. What are the realities of the matter?"

The realities of the matter, as we have seen, were that Wyndham was a sick man, and he had not properly appreciated what was in the wind in Dublin Castle when his Under-Secretary wrote to him. When he realised its significance, he repudiated the scheme, and sent in his own resignation to Downing Street. To everyone's surprise, Sir Anthony MacDonnell, though severely censured by the Cabinet, remained in his post.*

Balfour promptly offered the Chief Secretaryship to Carson. After some discussion Carson accepted it on condition that, if MacDonnell carried on, all official communications should come direct to the Chief Secretary without first passing through the Under-Secretary's office. A further difficulty then arose. The most important Castle official, after the Under-Secretary, subordinate to the Chief Secretary, was the Irish Attorney-General. This post was still held by John Atkinson, under whom Carson had served as Solicitor-General in 1892. On reflection Carson thought that his tenancy of the Chief Secretary's Lodge in Dublin's Phœnix Park might possibly embarrass his old colleague, who was unquestionably the ablest man at the Irish Bar as well as its leader. This consideration accordingly led him to ask the Prime Minister to relieve him of an office which he had held for barely twenty-four hours and which had not yet been gazetted. Balfour agreed, and the appointment eventually went to Walter Long (later Viscount Long of Wraxall), a genial and courageous West-country gentleman, who represented South Bristol

* For a full account of this affair, including his correspondence with Wyndham which Balfour refused to publish at the time, see the article 'The Wyndham-MacDonnell Imbroglio' by Mrs. Blanche Dugdale in the *Quarterly Review*, January, 1932; also *George Wyndham*, by John Biggs-Davison (1951).

in the House of Commons, and who was to make himself so popular in Ireland that he was shortly afterwards adopted for a Dublin constituency.

The Conservatives were now hopelessly divided among themselves on the question of Tariff Reform, on which Joseph Chamberlain, as the principal exponent of Imperial Preference, had resigned from the Government two years previously, in order to put his views before the country. There were unmistakeable signs too that the Balfour Government had lost the confidence of the electorate. Carson hoped for a dissolution and General Election before Whitsuntide, as appears from a letter which he wrote to Balfour's private secretary, Sandars, at this time:

> *Carlton Club. 30 March*, 1905. . . . The present situation is an intolerable one and I sincerely hope the P.M. is going immediately to end it.
>
> For myself, I feel acutely the position in which the P.M. is placed after all his splendid work, but it seems hopeless for even his most devoted followers to do anything.

But Balfour clung to office with a persistence which caused widespread surprise. One reason was that the negotiations for the Anglo-Japanese Treaty, which had been proceeding for some time, were not complete. However, the treaty was signed in August, and with the prorogation of Parliament in the same month there was now no reason why Balfour should meet the Commons again before an election. "I suppose the days of the Ministry are numbered," remarked Balfour to Carson at this time. "The avidity of the lawyers for position is usually a sure sign!"

On December 4, 1905, A. J. Balfour resigned office as Prime Minister, and all the members of his Administration likewise sent in their resignations. At this time Carson might have had almost any judicial office he pleased, but, as we have seen, he had made up his mind to stay on in Parliament and throw in his fortunes with those of his chief. One distinction he did, however, agree to receive. For the past twelve years he had been a Privy Councillor of Ireland but not of England. Accordingly, Sir Edward Carson was sworn a member of His Majesty's Most Honourable Privy Council in England in the week following Balfour's departure from Downing Street.

CHAPTER SEVEN

Opposition Advocate

I

ON Balfour's resignation as Prime Minister, the King sent for Sir Henry Campbell-Bannerman, who had succeeded Harcourt as Leader of the Liberal Opposition in the House of Commons, to form a Government. 'C.B.', as he was popularly known, was then in his seventieth year and in failing health, but he set about the task with a will and, in spite of internal difficulties with some of his own party who wished to 'kick him upstairs' to the Lords, he succeeded in completing his Administration within a week. The result was a somewhat mixed bag. It included, among the moderates, Asquith as Chancellor of the Exchequer, Sir Edward Grey at the Foreign Office, Haldane as War Minister, and, among the extremists, John Burns as President of the Local Government Board and Lloyd George as President of the Board of Trade. Mr. Winston Churchill, who had crossed the floor of the House two years previously, was given a junior post, Under-Secretary for the Colonies. But some of the other appointments were not so impressive. Sir John Lawson Walton became Attorney-General, and Sir William Robson Solicitor-General. In Ireland the Earl of Aberdeen went to the Viceregal Lodge, while James Bryce, the historian and diplomatist, was appointed Chief Secretary. On these latter appointments the opinion of that veteran Tory, Sir Michael Hicks-Beach, is worth quoting. "The Law Officers are inferior to Finlay and Carson, who were exceptionally good," he wrote at the time. "The Irish Government (Aberdeen, his wife and Bryce) will all, I feel sure, take the Irish too seriously: there is no greater mistake, yet it is one which most Englishmen commit."

Carson's opinion is also of interest. "I am very glad the resignation is over," he wrote to Lady Londonderry on December 12. "I feel sure it is right and sets us free to turn the flank of the enemy. As for myself, I have already received a number of retainers and I was offered yesterday 500 guineas to go to Liverpool on Thursday, so I hope to have plenty of work. . . . I take very little interest in the new appointments to the Government. I think in any event they will be a rotten lot, and the real head of the Government will be Redmond. Poor Ireland! But it is long since hopeless, and greatly through Unionist weakness. W. Long, I know, is sorry to have to abandon his good work, but he has shown himself true and faithful and a man."

The formation of a Liberal Government was a prelude to the General Election, which was to come early in the New Year. For Carson, of course, the contest involved no anxiety and very little expense, since he was always assured of an unopposed return in Dublin. But during the next four weeks he was kept extremely busy speaking for his old colleagues, many of whom faced difficult contests and indeed the loss of their seats. He also spoke on behalf of one aspiring newcomer to Westminster, Viscount Castlereagh, the twenty-seven-year-old son and heir of his friends, the Londonderrys, who had recently resigned his commission in the Army to fight Maidstone, one of the marginal seats in Kent. "I do not recollect in my lifetime when the name of England stood as high abroad," Carson told the electors of Maidstone in launching this young nobleman's candidature. "The Unionist Government have laid down their office when they may well be proud of their achievement. Never has England been counted as a friend and an ally as she is at the present time. Yet when the Unionist Government came into power, England was scoffed at for her betrayal of Gordon, and despised for the surrender of Majuba Hill."

On returning to London Carson wrote to Lady Londonderry:

5 Eaton Place, S.W.
17.12.'05.

MY DEAR LADY LONDONDERRY,

Our meeting at Maidstone was a great success—it was very full and many could not get in. Castlereagh was very well received and made a sensible short speech, not touching on fiscals and leaving the bulk of the evening for me. I was quite delighted with the way he met the people, and he was affable and jolly with them. I hope it may have been of some use, tho' I wish I had been in better form, but I was tired. I have been speaking so much lately and I get stale.

The more I go about, the more I see that Chamberlain has got hold of the bulk of our people. I don't mean so much our leading men as those of the working classes who follow us. I greatly fear the outcome as, if the majority of Conservatives and Unionists who are returned are Chamberlainites, I don't see how A.J.B. is to go on with the leadership. This idea distresses me as I feel the matter will take an acute form when Chamberlain makes his first move on an amendment to the Address. I really do think A.J.B. will have to declare how his policy is to be carried out, and I can meet no one who understands it—or at least who agrees with it.

I was very sorry not to see you when in town but I have been a good deal hustled in the change of my office. I am not going abroad this Xmas as it would not be worth while owing to the General Election.

I hope you are very well.

Yours sincerely,
EDWARD CARSON.

This is an interesting letter, since it shows how deep-rooted was Carson's sense of loyalty to his party leader. When Chamberlain first enunciated his views on Tariff Reform, he had found a ready supporter in the Solicitor-General, who advocated tariffs as a guarantee of the British wage-earner's standard of living. "How can we compete with countries where the factory laws are different," he asked, "where wages are different, and whose exports are subsidised by grants from the State?" For a solution he looked toward the ideal of a united economic Empire. "It cannot be beyond the wit of man," he had said at that time, "to find a method whereby the mother country can treat the colonies, and the colonies treat her, in a manner which will give them both some advantage over those who are strangers in blood and strangers in language." In an attempt to keep his divided party together Balfour had declined to commit himself one way or the other on Chamberlain's proposals, and out of loyalty to Balfour Carson had more recently steered clear of them in his speeches and made no reference to them during the election campaign. However, the fact that he had previously supported them caused him to be classified by the Press as a Chamberlainite. This caused him further anxiety and led him to write the following letter to his chief, who was then in Scotland:

To A. J. Balfour

5 *Eaton Place, S.W.* 30.1.'06. You have observed statements in the Press, e.g. *Morning Post* of today, classifying the party into your followers and those of Mr. Chamberlain. As I am classed among the latter, Sir E. Clarke suggested to me I should write to the Press contradicting this statement. That course does not commend itself to me on many grounds; and I do not see that a newspaper should be in a position to require notice being taken of what they are pleased to insert for their own purposes. However, as Clarke thought the

matter of some importance, in order that the City might know the classification was incorrect, I thought I might mention the matter to you.

Of course, I have never even mentioned C[hamberlain]'s policy in any of the many speeches I made nor in my [Election] Address.

If you agree with me, please do not mind answering this. I am very distressed over the whole situation, and it will be a great help to me when you come back.

In his election speeches Carson concentrated on the old question of Home Rule for Ireland, although this question, which had been the primary issue at the three preceding elections, was now relegated to the background. The electors were much more interested in the fiscal issue, which really dominated this election, and in such questions as the employment of Chinese 'slave' labour in the Transvaal mines, and the judgment in the celebrated Taff Vale case, which had made trade unions legally responsible for the acts of their agents. But Carson hammered away at the Home Rule bogey, which he knew was far from having been laid. He challenged the Government to state whether they had abandoned the idea of setting up a separate Parliament for Ireland, with a separate Executive accountable to it. He felt that recent Conservative legislation, extending local government in Ireland and providing £120 millions to enable Irish tenants to purchase their land, should be "allowed to work itself out and bring about, as we desire, beneficent results," without further dismemberment of the Empire. He feared that to achieve Home Rule Campbell-Bannerman had entered into a compact, real or implied, with John Redmond, who had succeeded in healing the Parnellite split and uniting the Irish Nationalists under his leadership in the House of Commons. "It should never be forgotten that we are a Unionist Party and it is our first duty to maintain the Union," said Carson in one of his speeches at this time. "There are forces gathering which may necessitate our girding ourselves once more to go forth to do battle for the good cause."

But if the writing on the wall was plainly visible to Carson, the majority who voted at this election were blind to it. It is improbable that alarm at Home Rule lost the Liberals many votes in the tremendous electoral landslide which followed. It was indeed a crushing defeat for the Conservatives and Unionists, the most severe the party had ever suffered at the polls. In the final result the Liberals gained 377 seats, which gave them an absolute majority of eighty-four over both opponents and allies. The latter included eighty-three Nationalists and fifty-three Labour candidates, Labour emerging for the first time as a cohesive parliamentary party. With their combined support the Liberals could thus count on 513 out of a total House of 670. This left the Conservatives and Unionists with 157, of whom rather more than 100 were Tariff Reformers in Mr. Chamberlain's sense.

Many old and familiar faces consequently disappeared from Westminster, to be replaced by a horde of newcomers who crowded the Government benches to overflowing. Balfour was among the many who lost their seats; he was defeated in North-West Manchester and, although another seat was soon found for him, he was necessarily absent when the new Parliament assembled on February 13, 1906, his place as Leader of the Opposition being taken by Joseph Chamberlain. Among the many newcomers on the Government side was Carson's former 'devil' and junior in the Alaska boundary arbitration, Mr. John Simon. The newcomers who took their places on the Opposition benches were relatively few, but they included three young men with whom Carson was to be closely associated in the future. They were Lord Castlereagh, who had been returned by a narrow majority for Maidstone; a brilliant barrister on the Northern Circuit, Mr. F. E. Smith, who won a Liverpool seat and who was shortly to electrify the House and inspire his party with a maiden speech even more thrilling than Carson's had been; and Captain James Craig, the new Unionist M.P. for East Down. Craig, the eldest of the trio, was thirty-five, and, like Castlereagh, a soldier turned politician; he was an Ulsterman too with all the Ulster characteristic sterling qualities. Captain Craig was destined soon to supersede the dying Colonel Saunderson as the principal spokesman of the Ulster Unionist Group at Westminster and eventually to become Carson's lieutenant in the coming struggle against Home Rule which Carson had envisaged.

There was no intention on the part of the new Government of shelving the Home Rule issue, and the King's Speech made a direct reference to it. "My Ministers," so ran the relevant paragraph in the Speech, "have under consideration plans for improving and effecting economies in the system of Government in Ireland, and for introducing into it means for associating the people with the conduct of Irish affairs." To Chamberlain, who opened the debate on the Address for the Opposition, this paragraph appeared somewhat enigmatical. "Are they not associated now?" he asked. This question was answered by loud shouts of "No" from the Irish Nationalists below the gangway, and when Redmond rose to speak he declared emphatically that the Irish question would never be satisfactorily settled except by the concession of Home Rule. For the rest, Chamberlain's speech evoked no controversy, nor did it in any way justify the fears which Carson had expressed in his letter to Lady Londonderry. He simply assured the House that the country had not heard the last of Tariff Reform. "We believe that Tariff Reform is closely connected with the great question of the condition of the people," he said. "Do what you like, and say what you may, it will be continually cropping up in one form or another . . . and when at length you have failed to satisfy the expectations you have created, when the issues change, when the people once more desire a change of Government, then you will find that we have lost none of our activity, none of the conscientious belief in the necessity and justice of our cause." These words were singularly prophetic. Nearly twenty years were to elapse before the Conservatives, under the Premiership of Carson's neighbour at Rottingdean, Mr. Stanley Baldwin, were to implement a substantial measure of Chamberlain's policy.

Among the Bills promised in the King's Speech was one dealing with the law of trade unions and trade disputes. This had been done in fulfilment of a Liberal pledge to remedy the effects of the judgment in the celebrated Taff Vale case, to the effect that trade unions could be sued for the acts of their agents, whether authorised or not, and their funds made liable to meet the claims of successful plaintiffs in civil actions which might be brought against them for damages—a judgment which, incidentally, had cost the Taff Railway Company's strikers £50,000 in 1902 and was largely responsible for the unions entering politics. In its original form the Trade Disputes Bill, which was introduced by Lawson Walton, the Attorney-General, in March and aimed at securing the unions against such damages, contained a clause excepting from immunity those tortious acts which could be proved to have been committed with the authority of responsible union officials. The Bill also legalised 'peaceful picketing' and otherwise relaxed the law of conspiracy in relation to trade disputes.

This did not go far enough for the Labour Members, one of whom now proceeded to bring in a Bill of his own based on the doctrine of complete immunity, while strongly opposing the Government measure. Not wishing to alienate his Labour supporters, Campbell-Bannerman gave way to this pressure, and Lawson Walton was obliged to execute a *volte face* and redraft the clause on similar lines to that in the Private Member's Bill which it was designed to supersede.

Carson led the attack on the Government for this surrender to the trade unionists and denounced the unfortunate Lawson Walton for "the words . . . which he has now ignominiously eaten." He protested that this piece of legislation would put the unions in a privileged position. "There is no precedent for this in all the laws of this country," he thundered. "What the Attorney-General ought to have said to make the thing quite complete was . . . 'The King can do no wrong: neither can a trade union . . .' I regret the ignominious surrender which the Government has made. . . . It is most unfortunate that the Government has not shown itself able to resist the 'powerful persuasion' which has been addressed to it, and the intimidation which has resulted in an utter change of front." But this protest was of no avail. The Bill was passed and became law. Among those who supported it in its revised form from the Liberal benches was young Mr. John Simon; he chose the occasion to make his maiden speech, contesting Carson's view, as he put it, "with all respect to a much greater lawyer than myself."

But events were to prove Carson right in his misgivings. It encouraged the Socialists to promote strikes with political aims on an ever-increasing scale, until Nemesis overtook the country in the disastrous General Strike which occurred just twenty years after the passing of the ill-fated Trade Disputes Act.

2

Carson's relinquishment of office freed him to resume private practice. But he had first to finish up his official work. At the time of Balfour's resignation he was engaged as Solicitor-General in arguing a revenue dispute relating to income tax for the Crown. Against him there appeared Mr. H. A. Asquith, K.C., who had just been appointed Chancellor of the Exchequer. As the case was part heard at the time of the change of Government, it was agreed that the same counsel should complete it. Asquith represented the aggrieved taxpayer in the dispute, and Carson was accordingly able to indulge in some good-humoured sarcasms at his anomalous position, as Asquith later recalled, "in asking the Court to cut down my own prospective revenue." Not only was it the last case in which Asquith found himself associated with Carson, but it was also the last in which the Liberal politician ever appeared at the Bar. "I forget which way the case, not of much importance, was decided," wrote Asquith many years later in his *Memories and Reflections*, "nor was it one which called for any special exercise of forensic skill, but I always regarded Carson as an exceptionally dangerous antagonist. . . . After the elevation of another Irishman, Charles Russell, to the Bench, he was in my opinion unsurpassed as an advocate in the handling of witnesses and in the presentation of a case to a jury. I must add that though at the Bar, as in politics, we were almost invariably on opposite sides, I always found him not only a most honourable antagonist but charming and considerate in every personal relation."

Within a few days of the fall of the Balfour Government, he received a 500-guinea brief, as we have seen, and many more followed, some of them marked even more highly. His principal antagonist in the majority of these cases was Rufus Isaacs. For the next four years, until Isaacs himself became a Law Officer, they were to be pitted against each other in a long series of forensic duels. The incomes made by these men during this period were phenomenal, and it is improbable that such large sums will ever again be earned at the English Bar.

One of the cases constituted a record. It was the action entitled *Wyler and the Ibo and Nyassa Corporation* v. *Lewis and others*, in which damages for conspiracy were claimed in connexion with the affairs of the corporation in Portuguese Nyasaland. Isaacs was for the plaintiffs and Carson for the defendants, and each leader had a fee of 1,000 guineas marked on his brief, together with a daily 'refresher' of 250 guineas. The trial, which came on in the spring of 1908 before Mr. Justice (later Lord) Phillimore and a jury in the King's Bench Division, lasted for thirty-three days, and another eighteen days in the Court of Appeal, so that the two leaders received over £12,000 apiece for that one case. Yet it was a matter of little public interest. The dispute was purely a commercial one between two groups of financiers over certain concessions in Portuguese East Africa. Largely owing to Isaacs's financial knowledge the jury awarded the plaintiffs the enormous sum of £64,472. But Carson took the case to the Court of Appeal, where the findings of the lower Court were reversed, in spite of a speech by Isaacs lasting nine days, probably the longest which has ever been delivered before that tribunal. The decision of the Court of Appeal was later confirmed by the House of Lords.

These two outstanding leaders of their time had certain qualities of advocacy in common, but they differed greatly in method and technique. Each was eloquent and each could be devastating in cross-examination, but while Isaacs was suave and coaxing with witnesses, Carson was dominating and masterful. It was not merely the difference between the rapier and the bludgeon, for Carson had a ready wit which Isaacs never attempted to rival. Isaacs, on the other hand, had an amazing facility for mastering intricate details, particularly figures, and a discretion and tact in handling judges and juries in which he could and did outshine Carson. There was, of course, much of the actor in Carson, and though he never stooped to melodrama, he could be intensely dramatic, and he had a truly wonderful gift in convincing juries of the soundness of his client's case. There were also differences in physique and temperament. Isaacs was medium-sized and always appeared composed, his wig and gown in place. Carson was tall and lantern-jawed, his manner frequently alternated between depression and excitement. He always wore his wig, which incidentally always looked old and small—no doubt it was a relic of his early days at the Bar in Ireland—resolutely pushed to the back of his head. Isaacs was usually cheerful and physically fit; Carson was a prey to hypochondria and ill-health. Many a time Carson came into Court looking the picture of woe. "My dear Rufus," he would say, "I don't know how I shall get through the day. I ought to be in bed." But when the moment came for him to go into action, he would suddenly forget all about his aches and pains and would sail through the case with little sign of sickness or fatigue. Yet these encounters exhausted his nervous energy and he would often be seen dripping with perspiration at the end of the day.

Both men were offered very substantial fees to go out to Jamaica in the Long Vacation of 1907 and assist in the examination of witnesses, whose evidence had to be taken on the spot, in connexion with insurance claims arising out of the terrible earthquake which had laid much of the island in ruins at the beginning of that year. Both men refused, but for different reasons. Isaacs had arranged a holiday which he did not wish to forgo. Carson, on the other hand, was at first attracted by the idea of a visit to the West Indies, but turned it down when he heard about the tropical climate. "I have made up my mind not to go to Jamaica," he told Lady Londonderry. "My clerk was very emphatic in his views about it, and I am told it is a damp heat never under eighty-five in the shade and I could not stand it. For many reasons I should have liked to have gone—some you can guess—for I am in some respects upset and I am not sure I see or think clearly, which is a great source of bother."

Though they were such vigorous antagonists in the Courts and, to some extent too, in Parliament, Carson and Isaacs were always good friends and were to remain so to the end of their lives. Indeed, as we shall see, his professional appearance on behalf of Isaacs in a libel action, which arose out of the unfortunate Marconi scandal in 1913 subjected him to harsh criticism at the hands of his own political friends and associates. The two men were to die within a few weeks of each other and in their last illnesses each would send sympathetic messages to the other. "In all the cases in which Rufus and I were against each other, we only once had a serious row," Carson once recalled, "but that lasted a long time. For it took place in Court about twelve-thirty, and when I went down to my lunch, there was he already eating his without having ordered anything for me!"

One immortal incident in Court at this period has sometimes been attributed to Rufus Isaacs, but it actually occurred in a case in which Simon was Carson's junior. The issue concerned a right of way in the country, and the other side produced a long stream of country witnesses who repeated the same evidence with monotonous regularity. One of the witnesses was a gentleman with a very florid countenance. As he stepped into the box, Carson whispered to his junior: "Anything known about this fellow?" "Nothing," Simon whispered back. Presently Carson rose to cross-examine, purposely exaggerating his natural Irish brogue.

"Are ye a teetotaller?"

"No, I'm not," replied the rubicund-faced one, looking slightly hurt.

"Are ye a modtherate dhrinker?"

This time there was no answer.

"Should I be roight if I called ye a heavy dhrinker?"

The witness now looked definitely injured. "That's my business," he replied tartly.

"Have ye any *other* business?" asked Carson in his smoothest tones, as the Court dissolved in laughter.

Carson's theory, as we have seen, was that every case depended upon one fundamental point. He would seize on this and hammer away at it, regardless of all other points, no matter how attractive they might seem. Only a very strong advocate could have pursued such a policy with success, since it meant sacrificing much promising material. It also meant that his aim at the issue on which he had chosen to concentrate must be unerringly accurate. That it almost invariably was may be gauged from the character of his many successes.

One illustration of this method is worth describing. Carson appeared with Mr. Travers Humphreys, later the well-known judge, for the Gas, Light and Coke Company, which was being sued for malicious prosecution by a discharged collector, represented by C. F. Gill. This man had devised a complicated system by which he misappropriated the moneys which he collected, but it was so complicated that it completely bemused the Grand Jury at the Old Bailey, who returned 'no bill' and the man was released. This encouraged him to bring a civil action for damages against the company which had employed him.

When he went into the witness box, the man, who had a bluff, hearty personality, gave the impression of outraged innocence, and the jury were plainly impressed by the story he told in answer to his counsel's questions. When it came to Carson's turn to cross-examine, he disregarded many items in the man's accounts which might or might not have inculpated him. He simply seized on one damning entry.

SIR EDWARD CARSON: In January, 1894, you had collected £94?
WITNESS: Yes.
SIR EDWARD CARSON: In March, 1894, you had accounted for £24?
WITNESS (*after some hesitation*): Yes.
SIR EDWARD CARSON (*leaning forward and sticking out his chin*): What became of the seventy pounds?

The witness did not reply. Carson repeated the question. No answer.

SIR EDWARD CARSON: "Did ye put it in yer pohkut?"

This question was also repeated several times, Carson slapping his own pocket each time. Finally, the plaintiff answered with a feeble protestation. "Yes, I suppose so," he said, "but I want you to understand that I meant to repay it."

SIR EDWARD CARSON: I do not dispute that. Is there anything else you want to say?
WITNESS: No. I think not.
SIR EDWARD CARSON: I ask you no more questions.

Carson had taken in the situation at a glance. By this time the jury had begun to look down their noses in a way juries have when a witness who is being cross-examined before them is found out. Carson sat down, and the case was won. He called no evidence for the defence, since, as the judge observed in his summing up, "no one could say there was not reasonable and probable cause for believing a trusted servant to be acting dishonestly when he admits he has taken and put into his own pocket money belonging to his masters."

Many counsel, perhaps the majority, would have thought it safer to call the defendant company's witnesses, but Carson, as he told his junior, Travers Humphreys, in discussing the case with him later, was afraid of the effect a long rambling argument on some small items might have. "We could have made certain of the judge," he said, "but we might have lost the jury."

More difficult, of course, than the art of cross-examination is that of re-examination, but here Carson pursued the same tactics with equal success. One example of this, though it belongs to a somewhat later period, may conveniently be given here. Carson appeared for the plaintiff in a libel action, to which the defendants had pleaded justification, the plaintiff being a married man who, it was alleged in the libel, was an adventurer, living entirely on his wife's fortune. Carson's fundamental point was that there is every difference in the world between the man who exploits his rich wife and the man who, having married a rich wife, allows her to help him. Both the plaintiff and his wife were severely handled in cross-examination. "When did your husband last do a day's work?" the wife was asked. She did not know. "Your husband is wearing a very handsome astrakhan coat. Where did he get it?" "I gave it to him." "Who paid for the Rolls-Royce you arrived in this morning?" "I did." "How much money did he put up toward the purchase of your mansion in the country?" "Nothing." There were many similar questions on the expenses of this unfortunate married couple, at the end of which the cross-examining counsel sat down with a very satisfied expression on his face.

Carson slowly rose to re-examine the wife, smoothing his gown and pushing his worn and tattered wig well back on his head with a familiar gesture.

"Mrs. X," he asked in melancholy tones, pausing for a moment to let his rich musical voice sink in—"Mrs. X, were you in love with your husband?"

There was only one answer possible. "I was," she replied faintly.

THERESA MARCHIONESS OF LONDONDERRY.

From the portrait by John Sargent in the possession of the Marquess of Londonderry.

Villa Hermitage
Homburg v der Höhe

Aug 7th 10

Dear Mrs. Archer Shee.

Very many thanks
for your letter. You are quite
right as to my belief
in George. Will you please
tell him I hope he
will always look
upon me as a friend &
I sincerely hope the whole
incident may in the
long run turn out to
his advantage. He will
I am sure do well
at whatever profession
he adopts & he has the
good wishes of everyone.
I have come here for
a change being very
tired after all the
work in the Courts.
With best wishes
Believe me
Sincerely yrs
Edward Carson

LETTER FROM SIR EDWARD CARSON TO MRS. ARCHER-SHEE.

From the original in the possession of Mrs. Anna Debenham.

"Is there any one of those things about which my friend has asked you, which you regret?"

"No."

"Mrs. X, if the opportunity arose again today, would you be proud and happy to do it all again?"

"I would," replied the lady, seemingly elated.

"Thank ye, Mrs. X," said Carson and sat down.

The jury returned a verdict for the plaintiff, Carson's client, and awarded him £5,000 damages. But it was those three questions which really gained the verdict.*

3

One of the most interesting cases in which Isaacs and Carson appeared at this time was that of *Bryce* v. *Bryce and Pape*, popularly known as 'The Gaiety Girl Divorce Case'. Its interest lies in the fact that it is one of the very few cases in which the two famous advocates worked together, appearing as they did for the respondent and co-respondent respectively in this defended divorce suit, and it brings out very clearly their fundamental differences of method in Court.

The petitioner, Francis Bryce, a young Devon man of good family, had met his beautiful wife, then Mabel Duncan of the Gaiety company, while working at an army coaching establishment. In spite of strenuous family opposition, he had married her in Paddington Registry Office in 1898, resigning his commission in the Army and going on the Stock Exchange. This persistence had its reward, since the engaging ex-musical comedy actress was eventually received into her husband's family and 'accepted' in the county. Unfortunately for her the story of young love did not end there. She was an attractive and popular woman, fond of social gaiety, racing and other amusements, and her husband had on her account to devote more of his time to those pursuits than he really cared for. Among the social functions which they attended in the summer of 1905 was Commemoration Week at Oxford; there they met a rich young undergraduate and Old Etonian from Christ Church named Harold Pape. As not infrequently happens when a young man meets an attractive married woman rather older than himself, Pape soon found himself in love with Mrs. Bryce and determined to see more of her.

* The last question was really a leading one, and therefore inadmissible, but it was justified in the circumstances, since it was already clear to everyone in Court that this was what the witness wished to say.

Consequently the Bryces came to stay with Pape and his father in Scotland, Monte Carlo and elsewhere. Harold Pape was an accomplished amateur rider, and while Bryce was at work in the City he and Mabel would attend race meetings together, although Mabel told her husband she was accompanied by a woman friend on these occasions. In January, 1906, they all went to the County Ball at Exeter, where Pape danced for most of the evening with Mabel, while Francis Bryce was very attentive to a young lady who was to shelter in the subsequent action beneath the anonymity of Miss 'A'. Some months later Bryce saw his mother, who told him that people were 'talking' of a liaison between Mabel and Harold Pape, and she advised her son to see a solicitor. Bryce accordingly consulted Mr. (later Sir) George Lewis of the well-known firm of Lewis and Lewis, and detectives were then employed to watch the suspected pair.

In July, when the husband was away, Mabel went down to Windsor to stay with her friends Dr. and Mrs. Ellison. Another guest called Miss Kindersley had been invited, and, as the Ellisons' accommodation was rather limited, they decided to put up at the White Hart Hotel near-by. It now turned out that Harold Pape had engaged the next room for himself, but on seeing Mabel he gallantly surrendered it to her, taking a smaller room for himself. In August Mabel again went to stay with the Ellisons—this time at Bembridge, where they were on holiday—and Harold again stayed in a neighbouring hotel. Again they were shadowed by detectives, who reported, amongst other things, that one afternoon Harold Pape had been in the house with Mabel Bryce when she was changing her dress, at a time when the Ellisons were out. Finally, Bryce discovered amongst his wife's things a bundle of love letters from Pape, and he decided to institute divorce proceedings. He shut up the house, turned her and her things out, refusing to see her or hear a word of explanation. He did, however, subsequently consent to a meeting, which took place at his solicitor's office, but it made no difference to the course of action he resolved to take.

However, Mabel had no desire for her marriage to be dissolved, and on his side Pape wished to remain a bachelor. Consequently she proceeded to contest the petition, both of them denying they had ever committed adultery. The co-respondent further pleaded that, if there was any adultery, the petitioner had condoned and connived at it, but this allegation was subsequently withdrawn. The trial, which lasted for fifteen days, began before Mr. Justice Bargrave Deane and a special jury on May 4, 1907. Mr. Henry Duke, K.C. (afterwards

Lord Merrivale), and Mr. Barnard, K.C., were for the petitioner. Rufus Isaacs led for the respondent and Carson for the co-respondent.

Mr. Duke, who opened the case for the petitioner, painted an unflattering picture of the co-respondent as the worst type of idle and dissolute man-about-town, who, "having been educated at Eton and Oxford, had acquired a certain social vogue and had contrived to obtain admission to the best class of English society." To establish his case the petitioner largely relied on four matters—the night at the hotel in Windsor, the episode at Bembridge, the evidence of a former chauffeur of the Bryces, who had seen Mabel and Pape "kissing and cuddling like lovers," and finally Pape's love letters. The letters certainly showed affection and Duke endeavoured to show that adultery might be inferred from a careful reading of them. Incidentally, many of them were couched in an elementary and somewhat childish code, which consisted of inserting the letters 'ap' into certain words. Thus 'yapou sapaid yapou caparaped fapor mape; dapou yapou rapeallapy?' meant 'you said you cared for me; do you really?'

Isaacs directed his cross-examination of Bryce to his relations with Miss 'A', from whom he had received letters, with a view to proving that it was her husband's familiarity with Miss 'A' that caused the trouble between Mabel and himself, which led him to throw his wife into Pape's company. At one stage the judge intervened to ask whether Isaacs was not really covering Carson's case, since his own was a mere denial of adultery.

"I do not wish the same ground to be gone over twice," said Mr. Justice Bargrave Deane.

Isaacs replied that the incidents in question did come into his case and he could not disregard them. "I say at once," he added, "that any ground I cover my learned friend will, I know, leave untouched."

Here Carson interposed. "I would be very glad to be relieved of it all," he said, to the amusement of the Court.

Cross-examined by Carson, Bryce said that on the occasion of visits to the theatre he had suggested to his wife that Miss 'A' should accompany her in a hanson and that Pape should go with him, but Mabel had replied that "that was absurd, as there would be no one to help her out of the cab or pay the cabman." Carson asked why they could not all have gone in a four-wheeler.

This suggestion shocked Bryce's sense of social conduct. "No one ever goes in a four-wheeler to the theatre!" he said stiffly.

"Well," commented Carson to the accompaniment of more laughter, "I am perhaps out of date myself!"

There had been more 'pairing off' when they had gone on the river at Sonning. Bryce admitted to having left his wife with Pape for over nine hours, during which period he was in a punt with Miss 'A'. He said he punted up towards Reading.

> SIR EDWARD CARSON: How far?
>
> WITNESS: About a mile.
>
> SIR EDWARD CARSON: What, in nine hours! What else did you do?
>
> WITNESS: I sat and read, smoked and lunched—the usual things everybody does on the river (*Laughter*).
>
> SIR EDWARD CARSON: Nine hours is a long time, and you knew that all the time your wife was with the co-respondent. I take it that was what usually occurred on these river trips?
>
> WITNESS: Yes, it was the ordinary way—it was natural.
>
> SIR EDWARD CARSON: The natural way to treat your wife?
>
> WITNESS: I treated the co-respondent as a friend. I was not using him as a convenience.
>
> SIR EDWARD CARSON: Could you not have obtained a boat that held four people?
>
> WITNESS: From the point of view of comfort it was impossible to go four in a punt.
>
> SIR EDWARD CARSON: Then it was for comfort and not for convenience that you occupied separate punts? (*Laughter*).

Bryce's favourite phrase seems to have been 'in the ordinary way', as he kept repeating it in his evidence. He said he loved his wife at this period, not so much as in the first year of their married life, but 'in the ordinary way'.

"Everything you do seems to be in the ordinary way," said Carson.

"Yes, because all these incidents are all very ordinary ones," replied Bryce. "I followed my mother's advice and went to a solicitor in July."

"You are thirty years of age," observed Carson, "and she advised you to go to Mr. George Lewis—in the ordinary way—and you went—in the ordinary way?" This short summary was greeted with loud laughter.

"That was on July 26?" Carson went on.

Here Bryce's counsel intervened—he was annoyed at the treatment his client was receiving. "August," corrected Duke. Then, looking at his brief, he added: "No, I see you are right."

"I am glad I am right for once," said Carson sarcastically.

"It is a phenomenon, no doubt," rejoined Duke in the same tone.

Miss 'A' was the next to give evidence. She was a pretty girl of nineteen and, as the publicity of such a case would have been extremely harmful to her if her name had been published, all parties agreed that her identity should remain anonymous. She was treated gently in the witness box, where at the outset of her evidence she provoked a humorous exchange between the three leading counsel. She stated that she had written to Mabel Bryce, saying she had been to a tea party.

"I think she described it as a 'ghastly tea party'," said Isaacs.

"They generally are, I fancy," commented Duke.

"I do not know that," Carson broke in, "I never go to any."

When it came to Carson's turn to question her, this witness was 'unable to remember' many incidents.

"Come now, can't you remember?" he asked her. "Are you clever?"

"No, I have a bad memory," she replied.

"Then you mustn't be offended," said Carson, "if I venture to say I do not agree with you."

The following dialogue took place when she was questioned about the time she had spent in the punt with Bryce.

SIR EDWARD CARSON: Did you see Mrs. Bryce, your chaperone, during all these hours?

WITNESS: No.

SIR EDWARD CARSON: Is it the usual way to treat a chaperone?

WITNESS: She told me to go and I went.

SIR EDWARD CARSON: Oh, I see. She said to you 'Go with my husband and amuse him for six or seven hours, and be a good girl,' and so you, like a good girl, obeyed?

WITNESS: I was told to go and I went.

SIR EDWARD CARSON: I am not blaming you. I only want to know what occurred.

The next witness was the chauffeur, whose name was William Amos. He said he had seen Mrs. Bryce and Mr. Pape "cuddling and kissing like lovers" on the road when they were staying with Mr. Pape senior in Scotland. He added that he was not shocked, as he had often seen such things before.

"Where?" asked Carson.

"Everywhere," replied this much-travelled young man. "In England, Ireland, Scotland and Wales."

"Oh, please leave Ireland out, Mr. Chauffeur," said Carson, as everyone in Court laughed.

The cross-examination continued amid renewed laughter with this question: "Is cuddling and kissing, in your experience, an epidemic all over the United Kingdom?"

In answer to further questions the chauffeur said he could not fix the exact date of this alleged incident, but he remembered that it was when he had gone out to look for some white heather to send away.

"To a lady?" enquired Carson with mock solicitude. "Did you get any?"

As the witness seemed to hesitate, Carson went on: "Come now, that's an awkward question?"

But Amos, who thought he was doing very well in the witness box, now turned saucy.

"What business is it of yours?" he answered insolently.

A moment later he regretted his answer. Carson fixed him with that formidable stare which had caused many another witness to tremble.

"Will you say that again just in the same tone?"

The chauffeur looked sheepish. He did not repeat it. All he said was, in a forced attempt at jocularity: "I did find some and sent it away too."

This cross-examination affords a striking example of the difference between Carson's methods and those of Isaacs. The latter never treated witnesses in a spirit of banter and, lacking Carson's native wit, he was seldom tempted to make jokes at their expense. He would never, for instance, have addressed a witness as 'Mr. Chauffeur'. On the other hand, he assuredly had a suavity of manner which Carson lacked, and he was never brought into sharp conflict with his fellow counsel as had happened in this case between Carson and Duke.

The rest of the story may be shortly told. Mabel Bryce proved a good witness and made a favourable impression on the jury. She fainted three times during the proceedings, when juries were of exclusively male composition. There was too an almost artful simplicity about some of her answers, particularly when questioned about Pape's letters.

"When Mr. Pape wrote: 'I want you tonight awfully, awfully,' what did you understand?" she was asked by her counsel.

"I thought he wished me to be with him."

"But did you not understand by that something improper?" interposed Mr. Justice Bargrave Deane.

"No, my Lord; he so often put into his letters: 'I wish you were here'."

"But 'tonight'," said the judge testily. "You are a married woman and understand these things."

"I looked upon the words as a figure of speech," she replied simply.

The co-respondent in the circumstances also acquitted himself well in the witness box. He did not deny he had been in love, but strenuously denied adultery. He was helped to some extent by the famous surgeon, Sir Alfred Fripp, who stated that he had performed an operation on him for hæmorrhoids at the end of July, 1906, which necessitated the wearing of bandages for a month. This made it highly improbable, though not impossible, that he could have committed adultery in Bembridge on the occasion so strongly stressed by the petitioner.

Carson wisely made no attempt to defend Pape's conduct in the matter of his letters to Mabel Bryce, letters, he said, which his client "bitterly regrets". But he reminded the jury that all sentiment and decency do not die because a young man of twenty-four has the misfortune to fall in love with a young and pretty married woman. "Accord him censure for his acts," he said, "but do not let these letters weigh in the scales of justice against a woman who was only the recipient of them, and against whom there is not one act or gesture in evidence to show that she has been other than the faithful wife to him who is now trying to get rid of her."

This is in fact what the jury did. They found that no adultery had been committed, but added that "the conduct of the co-respondent, as disclosed in this case, is deserving of the severest censure." The petition was accordingly dismissed.

This case, which cost the parties to it over £15,000 as well as much unpleasant publicity, should never have been brought at all. From the point of view of Carson's story, however, it has much interest, throwing interesting light on his methods in Court and forming an instinctive contrast with Isaacs, with whom on this occasion he was in alliance.

An example of the humorous side of this alliance may be quoted in conclusion. A discussion arose in Court as to the legibility of the respondent's handwriting in the hotel register at Windsor.

"I hope our moral characters are not to be judged by the badness of our handwriting," Isaacs remarked.

"If they are," said Carson, who was never loath to make a joke against himself, "then I come out top."

4

Two months after the 'Gaiety Girl Divorce Case' Carson figured conspicuously with Isaacs in another trial which caused the greatest public interest. It was an action for libel brought by a well-known soap manufacturer against a popular newspaper, and the particular interest of this so-called 'Soap Trust Case' lies in the fact that it resulted in the largest sum by way of damages hitherto awarded in an action of this kind.

Mr. William Lever, M.P. (later Lord Leverhulme) had built up a gigantic soap business from very small beginnings at Port Sunlight, where 3,000 tons of soap were turned out weekly and 3,500 workers were employed in the process. The capital of Lever Brothers amounted to many millions of pounds and vast sums were spent each year by the firm in advertising their product. In the previous year the price of the raw material for soap rose owing to the discovery of new uses in the manufacture of margarine and other foodstuffs. The firm dealt only with retailers and not directly with the public. Rather than increase the price of his product, Lever decided to reduce the weight of the 1-lb. tablet of Sunlight soap, which he did by notice attached to each carton delivered to the retailers. As the scarcity of raw material continued, Lever entered into negotiation with other soap manufacturers with a view to eliminating expensive competition through lavish advertising. These proceedings attracted the unfavourable attention of Lord Northcliffe, previously known then as Sir Alfred Harmsworth, who in ten years had built up the *Daily Mail* to be the most successful popular newspaper in the country. The *Daily Mail* proceeded to attack Mr. Lever and his proposed soap trust as a conspiracy against the public interest, alleging that the trust was being formed not to reduce costs, but to exploit the consumer by 'cornering' the raw materials market and raising the price of the finished article all round. This newspaper also argued that, although the retailers might have had notice of the alteration in weight, the information had never reached the consuming public. It was further alleged that Levers had dismissed large numbers of their employees owing to the formation of the combine, that they had attempted to bribe the Press and moreover had used certain unsavoury fish oils in the manufacture of certain of their products.

This attack, which was carefully planned and carried out over a period, had a disastrous effect upon the Port Sunlight business. Sales declined sharply, the shares in Levers fell by as much as 30s. a share, heavy trading losses were incurred, and Levers were eventually forced to revert to the 16-oz. tablet in order to preserve their goodwill. At the same time it was clear that, if their business was to survive, they must rebut these grave accusations in as public a manner as possible. Mr. Lever decided first to take counsel's opinion, and he consulted a well-known K.C., who delivered a long-winded document in which the counsel endeavoured to dissuade his lay client from taking any action through the Courts. But Mr. Lever was not satisfied. He went to another solicitor. This solicitor suggested that the papers should be laid before young Mr. F. E. Smith, who had recently left the Liverpool Bar for London on his election as an M.P. Smith happened to be spending the week-end in Oxford, when a telegram reached him asking him to come back to town immediately on the most urgent legal business. On arriving at his chambers he found a stack of newspapers and other documents nearly four feet high waiting for him. He was told that an opinion was required by nine o'clock next morning. The story goes that he ordered a bottle of champagne and two dozen oysters and spent the night working on the papers. At eight-thirty next morning he scribbled the following opinion:

> There is no answer to this action for libel and the damages must be enormous.
>
> F. E. Smith.

In accordance with his opinion Mr. Lever instructed his solicitor to go ahead and issue a writ for libel. The action duly came on for hearing at Liverpool Assizes on July 15, 1907, before Mr. Justice Lawrence and a special jury. For the plaintiff firm there appeared Sir Edward Carson, K.C., Mr. T. G. Horridge, K.C. (later Mr. Justice Horridge), Mr. F. E. Smith (later Lord Birkenhead), and Mr. E. G. Hemmerde (later Recorder of Liverpool). The defendants were represented by an equally formidable array of counsel led by Mr. Rufus Isaacs, K.C., which included Mr. H. E. Duke, K.C. (later Lord Merrivale), Mr. Norman Craig and Mr. G. A. H. Branson (later Mr. Justice Branson). Carson and the others with him stayed in Mr. Lever's luxurious house as his guests throughout the case.

The case was anticipated to last for a fortnight, but Carson determined, after his opening, to put Lever in the box and expose the futility of the defendant's case on the facts at his disposal. This is what he did. "Gentlemen," he told the jury on the opening day, "this libel is of a very exceptional and serious character, deliberately carried on for several weeks, and was made with the object of smashing up Lever Brothers. It is a libel which has been persisted in up till the present moment. . . . If you find that Messrs. Lever Brothers are not robbers and swindlers, fraudulent traders and all the rest of it, and if you find that all the other charges are untrue, what are the damages to be given to them? The damage is incalculable. . . . No money can wipe out the sufferings of weeks and months during which the charges were hurled against the business of Lever Brothers. You must, without shirking, try to assess something that will be compensation for what has been done. For the rest, up to the time of the issue of the writ, the plaintiff's trading losses have been £40,000. Those losses have continued. The *Daily Mail* have not only admitted but gloated over these losses that have been caused by them. But that is a small part of the total loss. The whole company has been shaken from top to bottom. Two million preference shares have been reduced in value £1 apiece, with a loss to those who held the shares of £200,000. On the ordinary shares it is impossible to say what the loss has been. The whole concern has been shaken up as if by an earthquake. Then you have to ask yourselves how the goodwill of the company is to be restored, and at what price. It has to be rebuilt to some extent and that can only be done by a verdict of the jury."

Carson then called Mr. Lever and, as his client walked to the witness box, the advocate turned again to the jury with a characteristic touch. "I have put my first witness, my client, Mr. Lever, into the box," he said. "Let my learned friend, Mr. Rufus Isaacs, cross-examine him to his heart's content, and, when his time comes, I hope he will be able to follow my example and do the same, and call as his first witness his own client, Lord Northcliffe. I hope he'll be able to play cricket with us."

Lever proved as convincing a witness as he was a popular employer, and Isaacs could get very little out of him to help his own client. Indeed Lever managed to score several times off his opponent's leading counsel. He said that, when he took an ounce off the 1-lb. carton, he considered it his duty to tell the consumer the weight because it was less than the consumer expected.

Isaacs: Then why simply alter the wording slightly on the inner flap of the carton, instead of putting it outside?

Witness: For several reasons, one being in regard to printing.

Isaacs: Why not have it put in a more prominent place?

Witness: I am perfectly sure, wherever we had put it, it would not have pleased you, Mr. Isaacs (*Laughter*).

Next morning, as Carson and his client motored to the Court from Mr. Lever's house, refreshed after an excellent dinner and a good night's rest, Carson expressed the opinion that Isaacs had probably spent a disturbed night, not knowing what to do. "I'll wager he's been on the telephone with Harmsworth," he said, "and he'll be on the steps of the Court waiting to make me an offer."

There, sure enough, when they drove up to the Court House was 'poor Rufus', as Carson called him, looking tired and worried. His client was not with him. "Well, Rufus," said Carson, smiling broadly. "Where's Harmsworth? Are you going to make us an offer?"

By this time Isaacs had realised that the prospect of gaining a verdict for his client was hopeless. On the contrary, he felt that if the case continued and went against him, as it inevitably must, not only would the damages be colossal, but the reputation of his client's newspaper would suffer. There was nothing for it but surrender, and he advised Northcliffe accordingly.

"We'll give you £10,000," said Isaacs.

Carson and Lever treated this offer with contempt, and they all went into the Court. As the case was about to be resumed, Isaacs was seen whispering to Carson. "You can't stop me withdrawing my defence and going to the jury on an assessment of damages alone." Carson shook his head.

Isaacs then rose and with a great display of magnanimity announced that, in view of Mr. Lever's evidence and the impression made by it upon himself and his friends, it was impossible for his clients to continue their defence; he would therefore withdraw it without any reservations, leaving the jury only the question of the amount of the damages.

Carson now pretended to be surprised by this move, although, as we have seen, he had been in reality expecting it. "The course adopted by my learned friend has taken me completely by surprise," he declared, addressing the Bench. "I ask for time to bring witnesses on the question of damages to the Court."

To this proposal the judge agreed. Then there followed an

amazing scene, in which Isaacs in audible tones made repeated offers for settlement, each being rejected.

"Look here, Ned, you can have £15,000."

Carson communicated this offer to Lever. "I won't have his £15,000," said the plaintiff.

The offer was increased by instalments to £40,000, and finally to £50,000.

"What do you say to that, Mr. Lever?" asked Carson.

"That's a substantial offer," said Lever. "I'll take it."

Actions against the *Evening News* and other Northcliffe newspapers were settled on similar lines; the total amount of damages and costs which this Press magnate's organisation, The Associated Press, had to find amounted to nearly £220,000. "It is satisfactory to us that the defendants should pay the sum formulated by Mr. Lever," said Carson at the conclusion of the first case in Court. "The defendants have accepted our own measure of our loss." Yet Northcliffe, in spite of the staggering blow, proved a generous loser. He subsequently bore no ill-will toward either Carson or F. E. Smith. To the latter he was to give a good deal of legal work in connexion with his newspapers, and to the former assistance in the anti-Home Rule campaign.

Once, discussing the Soap Trust case with Carson, Northcliffe said to him: "Carson, you're the biggest enemy I ever had."

"Why didn't you employ me, then?" answered Carson. "I dare say you'd have won!"

But no barrister is invariably on the winning side. More often than not, it is true, that was the side Carson was on, but he had his losses too like every other barrister, and sometimes the losing side was also the unpopular one. Such a case was the trial of Robert Sievier, the racehorse owner and journalist, for blackmail at the Old Bailey in July, 1908. Once again Carson and Isaacs were in opposition, Carson being for the prosecution with Charles Gill, now a K.C., and Archibald Bodkin, and Isaacs for the defence with Montague Shearman, K.C., and R. D. Muir.

Though it aroused immense public interest, the Sievier trial was far from edifying, either in its subject matter or in its result. 'Bob' Sievier was an adventurer, who amongst other activities edited a sporting weekly called *The Winning Post*. He ran a series of articles to this journal entitled 'Celebrities in Glass Houses', in which he satirised prominent public individuals. One of these subjects was another racehorse owner, Mr. J. B. Joel, who was attacked in successive issues. Finally, Sievier, who was known to be in financial difficulties at the time, proposed to publish a photograph taken at the time Joel had fallen foul of the law in South Africa in the 'eighties for illicit diamond-buying and circulated by the police, showing Joel between two murderers. This came to the ears of Joel, and after some complicated negotiations conducted through two intermediaries, one of whom was a professional backer named Mills, Joel agreed to pay Sievier £5,000, if he would refrain from publishing the libellous photograph. Unfortunately for Sievier the police learned of the transaction and in the result Sievier was indicted on a charge of attempting to extort money by threats.

The case called forth all the resources of advocacy on both sides. Indeed, in spite of its unattractive nature, Isaacs's son and biographer regarded it as his most spectacular success in the long series of his battles against Carson. There had been no direct dealings between Joel and Sievier, but the facts seemed to show that the first approaches had been made by Joel through the intermediaries. At all events, this was the view taken by the jury.

One incident of the trial is worth noting. After Isaacs had put his client in the box and concluded his case, an argument developed between him and Carson as to who had the right to the last word with the jury. Although Isaacs had called no witness of fact except the prisoner, he had put in certain documentary evidence, and it was a question whether or not this documentary evidence was sufficient to deprive him of his right. Finally Carson gave way. "If there is the smallest doubt about it," he said, "I think the prisoner ought to have the benefit, and I waive my right."

"Thank you very much, Sir Edward," said the prisoner from the dock.

"I don't want any thanks from you," grunted Carson.

Sievier's acquittal was greeted by amazing scenes outside the Court, where a crowd of several thousand had gathered to hear the result of the trial. Sievier and his leading counsel got an immense ovation from the cheering crowds, who were wild with enthusiasm over the verdict, incidentally causing a severe rebuke from *The Times* for their conduct. Carson had seen nothing like it since the acquittal of Lord Queensberry after the case brought against him by Oscar Wilde.

Three other cases in which Carson and Isaacs figured at this time, may be briefly mentioned. The first, known as *Cole* v. *Ellis*, was the only one in which Carson ever led Isaacs on the same side.

The plaintiffs, for whom they appeared, were the executors of the late C. J. Dickins, of the well-known West-End store of Dickins and Jones. After his retirement from active business Dickins had taken to collecting old china, in the course of which he had employed a Bond Street dealer trading as Joseph Philpot, whose real name was Arthur Ellis, to buy Dresden china for him on a fifteen per cent commission basis. But Ellis had cheated him. One piece, for instance, purchased by Ellis for £75 and resold to Dickins for £1,200 was detected as a fake when subsequently put up for sale with the rest of the collection at Sotheby's. At the trial the jury returned a verdict of over £10,000, and the judge ordered the papers to be sent to the Public Prosecutor. In the result Ellis was convicted of fraud, although the Court of Criminal Appeal subsequently quashed the conviction.

The second case was an action for libel brought by Mr. Lloyd George, who had by this time become Chancellor of the Exchequer, against the owners of *The People* newspaper for the repetition of a gross libel on his private reputation. In the summer of 1908 *The Bystander* magazine had hinted that, in addition to his political difficulties, the Chancellor of the Exchequer was in trouble over a woman. This magazine had subsequently admitted that there was no foundation for this statement, which it unreservedly withdrew, at the same time making a public apology and paying 300 guineas at Mr. Lloyd George's request to the Cærnarvon Infirmary. Unfortunately the rumours persisted, being embellished in London clubs and drawing-rooms until they found expression in several articles which appeared in *The People* in January, 1909. The articles did not mention Lloyd George by name, but they left no doubt in the reader's mind that the Chancellor was the person referred to. In short, the articles alleged that he was about to figure as co-respondent in a divorce suit, that it had been ascertained that there was no doubt as to his guilt, that he had committed misconduct with a married lady, that the resultant Court proceedings must inevitably involve him in social and political ruin and degradation, that his friends were making extreme efforts to avert the catastrophe, but the injured husband persisted in going on. Later another article appeared headed 'The Price of Peace' which stated that Lloyd George's friends had succeeded in their efforts, that the suit would be conspicuous by its absence from the list of causes for trial in the Divorce Court, and that the price the Chancellor had to pay to secure this result was £20,000.

The action came before Mr. Justice Lawrence in the King's Bench Division on March 12, 1909. Rufus Isaacs, K.C., with F. E. Smith, K.C., and Mr. Raymond Asquith, appeared for Lloyd George. Carson led Henry Duke, K.C., and Mr. E. F. Spence for the proprietors of *The People*, of whom the principal was Sir George Armstrong.

After Isaacs had set out the circumstances of the libel, Carson told the Court that the articles had appeared without his clients' knowledge. "The defendants had no desire that their paper should be the means of circulating such a scandalous libel," he said, "and the more so having regard to the position of importance and dignity held by Mr. Lloyd George." He added that as soon as they had heard about it and he had himself been retained by them, they had done everything possible to mitigate the mischief caused by the articles. He consequently offered a complete apology on their behalf and admitted that the statements in the articles were unfounded and absolutely without justification. Mr. Lloyd George then went into the witness box, where in reply to his leading counsel he described the offending paragraphs as "absolute invention—every line of them." In addition to the defendants' apology, Lloyd George also accepted £1,000 by way of damages, which he likewise handed over to charity.

The third case, *Baker* v. *Mayo and Others*, in which Carson appeared for the first-named defendant, Lord Mayo, was a claim for damages by an investor against the promoter and directors of a company formed to convert peat into a product of at least equal calorific value to coal. The trial, which lasted for sixteen days, terminated in favour of all the defendants except one, who, perhaps rashly for himself, had decided to conduct his case in person. One of the other defendants was represented by Mr. John Simon, who had just become a K.C.

Carson was delighted that his old 'devil' had 'taken silk', which Simon had done at the same time as F. E. Smith, the two men at thirty-five years of age thus becoming the youngest K.C.s in the country. At a dinner given by Simon's constituents at the Great Eastern Hotel in London on March 6, 1908, to celebrate the event, it gave Carson great pleasure to propose the health of the guest of the evening. In the speech which he made on this occasion, with characteristic charm of manner, the older man was at his best.

"I don't know if you fully understand the extent of my generosity," he told the audience, with a touch of prophetic insight, "because the honour conferred upon my friend will, in the long run, materially affect my own pocket. One result of Mr. Simon's being called within the Bar is that my own business will diminish. But, after all, he and I belong to a profession which is a generous profession, and I hope we have no petty jealousies. When we see a good man, we appreciate him. I have posed in many capacities, but seldom as a prophet; still, I will tell you that, if Mr. Simon is spared health and length of life, he will go far in his profession. Indeed there's no honour which he may not most worthily take."

5

At the beginning of the Michaelmas Law Term in 1908, Carson wrote to Lady Londonderry: "I have been very hard at work all the week in the Courts and it distresses me to find how difficult it is to get time for politics. The law cases are so long and require so much attention that I am quite exhausted when the day is over." Yet, in spite of this great pressure of work as well as recurrent attacks of neuralgia, he did manage to put in a great deal of time in the House of Commons, also speaking in the country at this period. With Balfour's personal influence waning he seemed clearly marked out as a future leader of the Opposition and even Prime Minister. But he had no wish to supplant Balfour, although he was not blind to the increasing weakness of Balfour's position as leader. As for becoming Prime Minister, when his friend Thomas Comyn-Platt put the proposal to him, Carson modestly brushed it on one side. "How would I be Prime Minister?" he asked. "What would I ever know of foreign affairs?"

Although he spoke on many general subjects, his efforts were largely directed toward compelling the Government either to enforce the law in Ireland, or else declare openly for Home Rule and let the electors decide the issue. The Crimes Act had been repealed, an action which was immediately followed by widespread agrarian outrages and other crimes of violence including murder. Cattle-driving, that is taking an unpopular person's cattle and driving them twenty miles away and then leaving them bruised and starving on the roadside, was generally practised, being instigated by a Radical M.P. named Ginnell, a land communist who advocated a 'Gaelic State'. Mr. Augustine Birrell, a cultured and witty Chancery barrister, who had succeeded Bryce as Chief Secretary, proved himself quite incapable of dealing with the situation, describing Carson and his Unionist friends in the House of Commons as "carrion crows, whose sole object is to malign and misrepresent their native country." He refused to reintroduce the Crimes Act even when two of Carson's own relatives were murdered.

"Only three or four weeks ago," said Carson in a speech at Macclesfield on December 8, 1907, "my own kinsmen were shot as they were leaving their place of worship on Sunday in the presence of a jeering and cheering crowd. This is a disgrace to civilisation under the British flag. I warn the Government and Mr. Birrell that no man ever made a greater mistake than to play with crime in Ireland. I speak vehemently as an Irishman to English people, and say that if you are not prepared to govern Ireland according to the ordinary elementary conditions of civilisation that prevail in every country, then go out of Ireland and leave us to govern ourselves. . . . I was born and bred loyal to your Sovereign, who is my Sovereign. I was taught at my mother's knee that no nation, either in history or at the present day, was so keen and anxious for justice and liberty as the English nation. I believed it. I am beginning to doubt it when I see people in this country standing up and giving consideration and welcome to those who they know have only one object, and that is to sever your country from mine."

That Carson had been absent from his place in the House of Commons for some weeks, owing to illness at this time, was noted by another of Lady Londonderry's correspondents, brilliant Mr. F. E. Smith, who was busily engaged in scaling the twin ladders of parliamentary and forensic fame. "When is the Solicitor coming back?" he wrote to her on December 22, 1907. "He ought to be in the thick of it. I know he is ill, but so am I, horribly, and so are most of us." However, he was back at the beginning of the new session in 1908, when he crossed swords with Mr. Birrell, whose year's record as Chief Secretary he had severely analysed in an article which he had written for the *Quarterly Review*.* "Will Radical Governments ever learn that submission to lawlessness, so far from appeasing only whets the appetite in Ireland?" he had written in this article. "Time will tell. But whatever may be concealed in the womb of the future, those who have watched the operation of the Irish Government during the past year, with the terrible consequences to law-

* 'Mr. Birrell's Record in Ireland': *Quarterly Review*, col. ccviii, 283 (Jan., 1908). This article appeared anonymously.

abiding citizens, will feel that Mr. Birrell has not in the words of Mr. Bryce 'seized the precious opportunity'."

Carson reinforced these arguments in a powerful speech during the debate on the Address, which drew praise from many quarters, including the Chief Secretary himself. "I thought, if I may say so, you spoke with great force last night," wrote Birrell to him next day, "and you will, I am sure, heartily believe that I am not blind to the dangers of the situation. But your argument really amounted *almost* to this, that, when there are half a dozen really bad cases of tyranny and oppression which the ordinary law is powerless to protect, the ordinary law should be superseded and justice done, at any cost and at whatever risk. I can't go as far as that. I may have been wrong in not putting Ginnell on his trial. He would, of course, have got off."

Some of Carson's activities and views on political affairs may be gathered from his correspondence with Lady Londonderry at this period.

> *Northgate House, Rottingdean. December* 23, 1907. . . . I am supposed to be writing an article on Ireland for the *Quarterly* [*Review*], but I make no progress. I never could write, as you know, so I expect my effort will be humiliating.
>
> I had hoped to go to Monte Carlo, but a business engagement at Chester on Monday next prevented me, so I will ride about here and do my best to restore my decrepit frame before the session commences.
>
> We ought to have a good time but what we really suffer from is want of first class men. Look at the autumn—only 3 or 4 men altogether did anything and A.J.B. made *two* speeches! Excellent they were, but Gladstone would have had a campaign and there was lots of material for one.
>
> I have all my family down here, including my grandson who seemed to recognise me at once. . . .

Early on Sunday morning, April 5, 1908, a courier arrived at Biarritz, where King Edward VII was staying, bearing Sir Henry Campbell-Bannerman's resignation on account of ill-health. The King immediately sent for Mr. Asquith and requested him to form a ministry. It had been understood for some time that Asquith would succeed Campbell-Bannerman in Downing Street, and that several changes would be made in the Government, including the promotion of Mr. Lloyd George to the Chancellorship of the Exchequer and of Mr. Winston Churchill to Cabinet office. Next day the announcement of Asquith's succession to the Premiership was made in Parliament.

> *Carlton Club, Pall Mall, S.W. April* 6, 1908. . . Well, things here moved quickly and, although perhaps not unexpectedly, still suddenly . . .
>
> There are many rumours about changes. . . . Harcourt I hear wants to go to the Admiralty and the Admiralty want Lloyd George. It is said Morley won't serve under Lloyd George as Chancellor of the Exchequer and that he will go to the Lords, and it is also said we are to have several by-elections . . .

> *Rottingdean. April* 10. It is generally thought that the new P.M. will not be very long before appealing to the country, but I suppose it depends on circumstances. He probably would be wise not to stay too long, if it was found that there was a real change in the feelings of the electors. I imagine he will strengthen the moderate element and I am sure the vast bulk of the people are for moderate reform . . .

In the Government reshuffle which followed, Mr. Lloyd George went to the Exchequer and Mr. Reginald McKenna to the Admiralty, while Morley took a peerage, retaining his post as Chancellor of the Duchy of Lancaster. At the same time Mr. Churchill succeeded Lloyd George as President of the Board of Trade and was given a seat in the Cabinet. This involved Mr. Churchill in a by-election in North-West Manchester, where he found himself opposed on the Unionist platform by Mr. Joynson-Hicks, the future Lord Brentford, as well as by a Socialist candidate. In spite of support from the Irish Catholics in the division, Mr. Churchill lost this triangular contest to Mr. Joynson-Hicks by over 500 votes, a defeat which the new President of the Board of Trade described as a heavy blow to the cause of Liberalism and Free Trade. However, his wounded feelings were immediately solaced by the offer of another seat at Dundee, which he eventually secured.

Carson's dislike of Mr. Churchill as a politician, which he shared with Lady Londonderry, was largely attributable to the fact that the son of the great Unionist champion, Lord Randolph Churchill, should have been converted to the Home Rule cause. His remarks on Mr. Churchill's defeat in Manchester are interesting, especially in the light of subsequent history.

> *Rottingdean. Sunday* [*April* 26] . . . I have been trying to picture your feelings at Winston's defeat. I am bound to say I felt almost a savage satisfaction, and I think the effect on the Government must be

serious. I think W. Churchill really degrades public life more than anyone of any position in politics, and I doubt if he will ever mature into the kind of serious and reliable politician the majority of people have confidence in . . .

Two other references to Mr. Churchill in this correspondence may be conveniently inserted here.

Rottingdean. September 13, 1908 . . . I suppose you did not come to town for Winston's wedding. I never saw anything so much advertised—nearly as much as 'Eno's Fruit Salts!' . . .

The Temple, January 26, 1909. . . . I dined with Lord St. Aldwyn on Thursday. Winston and his wife were there and he laid down the law on every subject. I took a back seat and sneered—it was all I could do.

The House of Commons reassembled after the Easter recess on April 27, 1908. After paying tributes to the memory of Sir Henry Campbell-Bannerman, who had died the previous week, they proceeded to debate the second reading of the Licensing Bill. This measure was designed to effect a much more rapid reduction of licences than that produced by the Conservative Act of 1904, which had been at the rate of 1,200 a year. It proposed to allot licences according to density of population, and it also proposed to limit compensation to dispossessed licensees to a period of fourteen years, a time limit vigorously denounced from the Conservative benches as a step toward Socialism. On the fourth day of the debate Carson wound up for the Opposition, following Mr. Lloyd George, who depicted the evils of drink in the most lurid language.

It was late at night when he rose to speak and, since he had been obliged to remain in his place for most of the debate, he had not had time to have any dinner. He had, however, managed to slip out for a few minutes and fortify himself with a half bottle of the best Burgundy which the House of Commons could produce. How far this libation was responsible for the standard of Carson's oratory on this occasion it is impossible to say, but the fact remains that he was at his best, although necessarily traversing familiar ground. "The right honourable gentleman, although he differs from me in politics, I hope does not imagine for a moment that he abhors the evils of intemperance any more than I do," he said, pointing at Lloyd George. "On the question of intemperance I can assure him I agree with every word he said. . . . But he forgot to show us, and he could not explain to us, what was the connexion between the number of licences and the amount of intemperance which he was so vividly depicting to the House." He then dealt with the objectionable time limit, pointing out that the precedent might be applied to other large-scale undertakings like the railways. "Members should be careful in establishing precedents of this kind," he declared, "for a time limit as to compensation for recognised interests may be applied to every species of property which derives its sanction from the House of Commons. . . . I believe that altogether above and beyond the opposition to this Bill the fear of the country is that you are by this measure creating a precedent as regards other property, and, as far as I am concerned, I will with all my heart oppose it."

He received a tremendous ovation as he sat down. Amongst those who heard the speech in the Peers' Gallery was Lord Londonderry, who immediately called for pencil and paper and sent him down a note of congratulation. "It was *magnificent*," he wrote, "you simply pulverised the other side. It took all my time to prevent myself applauding you from the Peer's Gallery. *Well done*, you." Next day Lady Londonderry sent him a telegram in similar terms from Wynyard, where he had recently been staying, and incidentally had attributed the fact that his wife thought he looked so fit to "all the port his Lordship insists on my drinking."

> *3 Dr. Johnson's Buildings, The Temple* [*May* 6, 1908]. So good of you to wire. The London papers (except *Times*) gave me a good report. *Times* only has room for Government speeches, but considering Lloyd George's speech, I think they might have put a little more of mine in. However it makes no matter as the *Daily Mail* is the real operator, I suppose, amongst the masses. . . .

The subsequent history of this measure is of some constitutional importance, since the struggle which it provoked formed part of the larger struggle ranging round the powers of the House of Lords, which the Liberals wished to curtail.

> *Rottingdean. Sunday* [*October* 18, 1908]. . . . As far as I can diagnose the situation, the Government are far more unhappy than even we think and some of them make no secret of it. I do not myself see how, if the Lords wreck the Licensing Bill, they can go on with any prestige and I am sure Asquith will feel that.
>
> I am told the Cabinet is divided, as Winston, Lloyd George and your friend 'Lulu' [Harcourt] are for passing very Socialistic measures, and I was told that Haldane and Grey said it was unlikely they (H. and G.) would ever 'be in the Government again'! I hope things will not progress too rapidly as time is on our side.

As for Asquith, Carson's opinion of him was that "he is not as strong as he looks, for the nation (like women) love a strong man."

> 5 *Eaton Place, S.W. October* 29. . . . I have Aileen staying with me but I never get home owing to this tragic Licensing Bill. It is being knocked about a lot in Committee, and I believe there is a growing feeling, even amongst Liberals, that it is unfair and has gone too far . . .
>
> I am very nervous that the Lords may be induced by faddists or funks to read the Bill a 2nd time—it will be the greatest mistake in my opinion they have ever made. I saw Lord Cadogan yesterday and I can easily see there is a wavering section, so there you have a field to exercise all your powers of persuasion upon . . .

Carson's fears turned out to be groundless. On November 27 the Lords rejected the Licensing Bill, on its second reading, by 272 to 96. "I am sure the Lords did the right thing," wrote Carson to Lady Londonderry. Naturally the result was bitterly resented by the Liberals. "The House of Lords is now a purely Tory organisation," said Mr. Augustine Birrell, "a Second Chamber that has abdicated its functions." However, the Liberals, particularly the temperance advocates, comforted themselves with the reflection that the liquor interests might be dealt with in the next Budget by drastic taxation, which the Lords could not touch except by rejecting the whole Budget. Thus was the stage set for the fateful struggle between the two Houses, or 'peers against people', as it was popularly called.

A campaign against the Lords was now launched by the leading Liberal politicians, particularly Mr. Lloyd George and Mr. Winston Churchill, whom Carson denounced as a pair of buffoons. "All this palaver of theirs about the House of Lords is a kind of Christmas pantomime," he said.

> *Carlton Club, Pall Mall, S.W. December* 20. . . . I cannot see how the Government are to go on. Everyone is laughing at them and the campaign against the Lords is simply jeered at. Why should they bring in a Budget which will do no one any good? It is not like having a surplus to divide and bribe with. No one cares about taxing others unless it puts something into his own pocket and so the Budget must injure them.

The early months of 1909 made it clear that the Government's policy was far from being in the nature of a pantomime. On April 29, 1909, Mr. Lloyd George, in a record speech of eight hours, introduced his famous Budget, which contained revolutionary taxation proposals and was deliberately designed to bring the issue with the Upper House to a head. Besides the novel land taxes and heavy increases in liquor and other duties, the Budget contained considerable increases in direct taxation on the well-to-do classes, including the imposition for the first time of a 'super-tax' of 6d. in the £ on all incomes over £5,000. These proposals were in due course embodied in a Finance Bill which was published during the Whitsuntide recess.

Rottingdean. Sunday [*June* 6, 1909]. . . . I have had a dull and gloomy time here reading the Finance Bill—its scheme of plunder is not very delightful—and I feel bitter, oh! so bitter. I would almost welcome a German invasion to put a sudden end [to] rather than have a gradual decay of our body politic . . .

I go back to work tomorrow to try and earn more 'super-tax' for the Government and, when the work has killed me, to leave them more death duties . . .

While the Finance Bill was in Committee, Carson was conspicuous in the Opposition attack on the measure, sitting up night after night in the House supporting a long series of amendments designed to modify or abate the new taxes.* As a result the Bill went to the Lords shorn of some of its more objectionable features, although he was discouraged considerably by Mr. Lloyd George's utterances outside the House which seemed at variance with his conduct inside it.

It was during this period, on July 30, that the Chancellor of the Exchequer made his celebrated speech at Limehouse in which he defended his Budget before an audience of 4,000 in language which reeked of class warfare. "Without you we can do nothing," he said, "with you we can brush the Lords aside like chaff before the wind." Next day Carson wrote as follows to *The Times*:

House of Commons, July 31, 1909.

May I suggest that the speech made yesterday by the Chancellor of the Exchequer, or rather by Mr. Lloyd George, opens a new page in political controversy?

In the House of Commons the Chancellor has been posing as a Minister anxious to meet objections to the Finance Bill, and as a

* 'Your Solicitor is very sorry for himself; he has stuck to it splendidly, but I think he should have allowed himself a month's holiday': Mr. F. E. Smith to the Marchioness of Londonderry, October 2, 1909.

responsible trustee for the public welfare and peace. In his speech at Limehouse, Mr. Lloyd George has taken off the mask and has preached openly a war of the classes, the satiation of greed, and the excitement of all the passions which render possible the momentary triumph of the unscrupulous demagogue.

Now, under these circumstances, is it not worth consideration as to how far it is worth while or indeed politic to ask for or receive amendments of the Finance Bill? Any such concessions are, in my opinion, only calculated to delude the public and mislead the taxpayer. We now know from Mr. Lloyd George that the Budget means the beginning of the end of all rights in property, and the shallow pretence of discussing finance is given up; the result therefore appears inevitable,—*viz:* that, before such a policy can prevail (if it is to prevail) it must at least be endorsed by the people; and the sooner that opportunity is given the better for the nation.

All necessity for discussing constitutional precedents or principles is now at an end, when the Minister of the Crown responsible for the finances of the country proclaims that he is about to legislate, not for a Budget, but for a revolution.

The fate of the Bill in the Lords was to make constitutional history. "Let us reject the Budget and damn the consequences," said the Unionist Viscount Milner. That is exactly what their Lordships did a few days later. On November 30 the Lords threw out the Finance Bill in its entirety by an overwhelming majority—350 to 75.

The action of the House of Lords determined Mr. Asquith to seek an immediate dissolution of Parliament and appeal to the country.

6

On the day before the 'People's Budget' was rejected by the House of Lords a remarkable libel action, in which Carson was briefed as leading counsel for the defendants, opened on the Midland Circuit. Involving as it did a group of Conservative newspapers and a well-known firm of chocolate manufacturers, which professed extensive philanthropic interests as well as associations with the leading Liberal organ of the day, the case thus had wide social and political as well as legal implications. Its public interest was further heightened, as the action proceeded, by the imminence of a General Election. Incidentally, too, it was the last case in which Carson and Isaacs appeared against each other as private practitioners.

The plaintiffs, whom Rufus Isaacs and John Simon represented in this action, were Messrs. Cadbury, the cocoa and chocolate manufacturers, Quakers, temperance reformers and Radicals, who combined their famous business in the garden city of Bournville with control of the Liberal *Daily News*. The defendants were Standard Newspapers Ltd., which controlled the three Conservative journals, the *Standard*, the *Evening Standard* and the *St. James's Gazette*. During the 1906 election campaign the Conservatives had suffered heavily through charges of Chinese indented 'slave' labour employed in the South African mines, which the *Daily News* had been assiduous in bringing to the notice of the electors. Now, at the very moment this newspaper, in which the Cadbury family was so deeply interested, was thundering against conditions in the diamond mines, it appeared that much of the raw material used by Cadbury's in their business was itself the product of slave labour, infinitely worse than anything known in the Rand. This was the discovery which the *Standard* group made and which they proceeded to publicise.

Cadbury's had a small well-managed plantation in Trinidad, but this was quite insufficient to meet their commercial needs. For a number of years most of their raw material had come from two Portuguese islands off the coast of West Africa, San Thomé and Principe. In 1901 information reached the Cadbury brothers that a system of compulsory labour was in force there, barely distinguishable from the worst forms of slavery. Eventually they joined with the other leading cocoa manufacturers in the country in sending out a special commissioner, Mr. J. Burtt, to investigate conditions on the spot. His report confirmed their worst fears. Mr. William Cadbury then took the report to the Foreign Office, where he asked the Foreign Secretary, Sir Edward Grey, whether he would advise the report to be published and also whether the firm should cease buying their raw material from this questionable source. But Sir Edward was against publication, or at least immediate publication of the report. He felt this was a case for diplomatic intervention with the Portuguese Government, and it seems to have been his view that the report should be withheld from the public and that Cadbury's should continue to do business with the island, at any rate while diplomatic negotiations were in progress. Meanwhile an English journalist, Mr. H. W. Nevinson, had been commissioned by an American magazine to conduct a similar investigation, and his findings were subsequently published. They were equally horrifying. Some time after this Mr. Cadbury decided to visit the islands on a 'Quaker filibustering', in the words of the *Standard*. "We congratulate Mr. Cadbury upon his journey, which does not come too soon," wrote the same journal on September 26, 1908. "One might have supposed that Messrs. Cadbury would themselves have long ago ascertained the conditions and circumstances of these labourers on the West Coast of Africa and the islands adjacent who provide them with raw material. That precaution does not seem to have been taken." The newspaper in its article then went on to refer to Mr. Nevinson's book;

> It is a book of great power, transparent sincerity and most painful interest. No Englishman can read it without a certain sense of shame, for it shows that the negro slavery, which it is one of the glories of our history to have assailed, still flourishes in its wickedness and its cruelty in these Portuguese colonies. It is not called slavery—"contract labour" they name it now—but in most of its essentials it is that monstrous trade in human flesh and blood against which the Quaker and Radical ancestors of Mr. Cadbury thundered in the better days of England . . .
>
> The so-called contract is a farce. . . . About one of these free and independent labourers in every five dies in the first year, and worst of all this slavery and slave-driving and slave-dealing is brought about by the necessity of providing a sufficient number of hands to grow and pick cocoa on the islands of Principe and San Thomé, the islands which feed the mills and presses of Bournville!
>
> Such is the terrible indictment made, as we have said, by a writer of high character and reputation on the evidence of his own eyesight. There is only one thing more amazing than his statements and that is the strange tranquillity with which they are received by these virtuous people in England whom they intimately concern.

It was not until January, 1909, that diplomatic intervention was judged to have failed, and Messrs. Cadbury stopped buying raw cocoa from the islands. Meanwhile, they could not ignore the article in the *Standard*, and they accordingly issued a write for libel against the proprietors. The defendants pleaded justification (*i.e.* that what they wrote was true) in so far as the article consisted of statements of fact, and in so far as it consisted of opinion that it was fair comment on a matter of public interest. To some extent, however, they aggravated the libel by their written defence, which was prepared by the junior counsel in the case, since this alleged that the Cadburys' steps to remedy conditions in the colonies had been taken merely in an attempt to anticipate attack, while the numerous references contained in the defence to the campaign against 'Chinese slavery' in the Transvaal conducted by the *Daily News* clearly suggested that the Cadburys were not sincere in their actions. This added considerably to the difficulties of Carson's task as leading defence counsel.

The action, which began on November 29, 1909, at Birmingham Assizes, was heard before Mr. Justice Pickford, later Lord Sterndale, and a special jury. For the plaintiffs it was appropriate that, in a case of such political implications, two Liberal Members of Parliament should be briefed, Mr. Rufus Isaacs, K.C., and Mr. John Simon, K.C. They were supported by Mr. Norman Craig, K.C., and Mr. H. H. Joy. For the defendants it was equally appropriate that a leading member of the Conservative Opposition in the House of Commons should appear. Sir Edward Carson, K.C., M.P., had with him Mr. Eldon Bankes, K.C., later Lord Justice Bankes, Mr. H. A. McCardie, later Mr. Justice McCardie (the 'bachelor judge'), Mr. A. Profumo and Mr. H. St. John Field, later a County Court Judge. The case lasted for a week and aroused intense interest throughout the country, throwing into relief the great political issue of Free Trade in its ethical side, on which amongst others the electors would shortly be invited to express their opinion at the polls.

Rufus Isaacs opened the case for the plaintiffs in a skilful speech in which he contrasted the high integrity of his clients with the base attack made upon them by the *Standard*. There were their efforts to improve conditions in the islands, the visit of Mr. Burtt's commission financed by Messrs. Cadbury at a cost of £3,000, of which of course the defendants had been unaware at the time, and the opinion of the Foreign Office, which was to be supported by Sir Edward Grey himself. "The issue in this case," thus Isaacs put it, "is whether it is true to say that, when once the knowledge was brought home to my clients, they did nothing. . . . The defence is, in essence, that the plaintiffs are a lot of canting hypocrites." On the contrary, Messrs. Cadbury had done their best in circumstances of great difficulty and on the most competent advice. Mr. W. A. Cadbury had given up a large part of his time to the question for nearly eight years and had done everything in his power to produce an improvement. Ultimately, on the occasion of his third visit to Angola, he was told by the Portuguese Governor-General that the situation had scarcely altered, and his firm then took the step of ceasing to purchase cocoa from such tainted sources. The *Standard*, on the other hand, had contended that Messrs. Cadbury had procrastinated inexcusably and had deliberately concealed the truth from the public.

The plaintiffs' principal witness was Mr. W. A. Cadbury, who was examined by Mr. John Simon, but before he had been long in the box his examination-in-chief was interrupted by the arrival of Sir Edward Grey, whose evidence was interposed. The Foreign Secretary confirmed the plaintiff's contention as to the attitude of his department. "My recollection is quite clear on the point," he said, "that a certain situation had arisen, and that the information which Messrs. Cadbury had should not be made public use of at the time. My opinion was that the information should be dealt with first by negotiation with the Portuguese Government before any public step was taken." Mr. Cadbury then continued the story of his efforts on behalf of the unfortunate 'contract labourers'. He had told the Foreign Secretary that he was quite willing to cease buying cocoa from the islands if Sir Edward Grey thought this course desirable or expedient. That Mr. Cadbury was an honourable man, with a genuine horror of these conditions, was clear, and indeed it appeared that he had exerted considerable efforts to ameliorate them, emphasising that the steps he had taken were solely directed toward this end and not for preventing attacks on his character as a philanthropist.

"In your judgment, then and now," asked Mr. Simon, "were the steps you took the best steps to take if you were going to have any influence at all?"

"Yes," replied Mr. Cadbury, "and looking back over the past I honestly cannot see any other steps we could have taken."

This answer ended Mr. Cadbury's examination-in-chief, and Mr. Simon resumed his seat. Sir Edward Carson then rose to cross-examine. So far Mr. Cadbury had proved a convincing witness, who gave an impression of deep sincerity, despite his somewhat pompous and self-righteous manner. Faced by any other advocate than Carson, his seemingly unshakeable evidence would probably have won the case for the plaintiffs hands down, particularly with a Birmingham jury whose members were familiar with his reputation as an employer and philanthropist. But Carson was no ordinary advocate, and he now threw the whole weight of his tremendous personality into the conduct of this cross-examination. Discussing the case more than forty years afterwards, Lord Simon, as the plaintiffs' second leading counsel had then become, told me that the first ten minutes of Carson's cross-examination of Cadbury was "the most devastating thing he had ever heard." Its blistering effectiveness could certainly never be forgotten by anyone who was in Court at the time.

What Carson set himself to show was that Cadbury was aware of all the horrors mentioned in the *Standard* article. He began quietly. The witness answered the first few questions without embarrassment. Cadbury Brothers Limited was a private company. It was a family concern. In 1903 the capital was £2 millions. Several of the directors, including the witness, had long been subscribers to the Aborigines Society for the improvement of native conditions generally. Carson then turned to the conditions which were the subject of the libel.

SIR EDWARD CARSON: Isn't it a fact that San Thomé cocoa has been slave-grown for eight years?

WITNESS: As far as the report from Angola and the island of San Thomé is concerned, I am quite satisfied that slave-grown cocoa described the conditions, generally speaking.

SIR EDWARD CARSON: Was it slavery of a very atrocious character?

WITNESS: In Angola itself the reports that have come to my knowledge give me every reason to suppose that in many cases, at least, it was exceedingly bad.

SIR EDWARD CARSON: Would you say it was slavery of an atrocious character?

WITNESS: Generally speaking, as far as the collecting of labour in Angola goes, that is true.

SIR EDWARD CARSON: The cocoa you were buying was procured by atrocious methods of slavery?

WITNESS: Yes.

SIR EDWARD CARSON: Men, women and children taken forcibly away from their homes against their will?

WITNESS: Yes.

SIR EDWARD CARSON: Were they marched on the road like cattle?

WITNESS: I cannot answer that question. They were marched in forced marches down to the coast.

SIR EDWARD CARSON: Were they labelled when they went on board ship?

WITNESS: Yes.

SIR EDWARD CARSON: How far had they to march?

WITNESS: Various distances. Some came from more than a thousand miles, some from quite near to the coast.

SIR EDWARD CARSON: Never to return again?

WITNESS: Never to return.

SIR EDWARD CARSON: From the information which you procured, did they go down in shackles?

WITNESS: It is the usual custom, I believe, to shackle them at night on the march.

SIR EDWARD CARSON: Those who could not keep up with the march were murdered?

WITNESS: I have seen statements to that effect.

SIR EDWARD CARSON: You do not doubt it?

WITNESS: I do not doubt that it has been so in some cases.

SIR EDWARD CARSON: The men, women, and children are freely bought and sold?

WITNESS: I do not believe, as far as I know, that there has been anything that corresponded to the open slave markets of fifty years ago. It is done now more by subtle trickery and arrangements of that kind.

SIR EDWARD CARSON: You do not suggest it is better because it is done by subtle trickery?

WITNESS: I have every reason to believe that various subterfuges are resorted to in order to get hold of labour by the dealers. They are brought to the coast by various agencies, and they have contracts with the San Thomé planters to supply so many people.

SIR EDWARD CARSON: The children born to the women who are taken out as slaves become the property of the owners of the slaves?

WITNESS: I believe that the children born on the estate do. I have never been able to find any regulation that gives a child any freedom. I have been told a child is free, but I cannot substantiate it and I do not believe that he is.

SIR EDWARD CARSON: Was it not the most cruel and atrocious form of slavery that ever existed?

WITNESS: I am not justified in distinguishing between slavery and slavery. All slavery must necessarily be atrocious.

SIR EDWARD CARSON: Knowing it was atrocious, you took the main portion of your supply of cocoa for the profit of your business from the islands conducted under this system?

WITNESS: Yes, for a period of some years.

SIR EDWARD CARSON: You do not look on that as anything immoral?

WITNESS: Not under the circumstances.

To get the full effect of this masterly cross-examination, one must see the tall, lean figure with the drooping lower jaw and hear the rich Irish brogue, as question succeeded question, from slavery to cruelty, from cruelty to atrocity, and from atrocity to large-scale murder. "The wretched creatures were whipped if they tried to escape. *Ye knew that?*" "Yes, but——" "Never mind the buts. They never did escape. *Ye knew that?*"

By way of contrast Carson read from an advertisement in which the Cadburys' factory at Bournville was described as 'the girl workers' paradise.' Mr. Cadbury, by now thoroughly unhappy, said he had objected to the use of the word 'paradise' and that it had probably slipped in inadvertently.

This rigorous cross-examination ended with a question which

considerably upset Mr. Cadbury, whom the jury had now come to regard with feelings akin to distaste.

"Have you formed any estimate of the number of slaves who lost their lives in preparing your cocoa during those eight years?"

Mr. Cadbury threw up his hands in horror. "No, no." he said, looking most unhappy.

The witness's brother, Mr. George Cadbury, the head of the firm and a director of the *Daily News*, fared little better at Carson's hands. He said he looked with an eye of abhorrence on slavery.

> SIR EDWARD CARSON: And anybody trying to make a profit out of slavery? What do you think of that?
>
> WITNESS: Sentiment told me that the slavery ought to be stopped, but common sense told me I should do no good by stopping buying at that time.
>
> SIR EDWARD CARSON: And common sense was against your sentiment?
>
> WITNESS: I knew we could only approach the subject of altering the conditions in the Portuguese colonies through the Portuguese Government. It was a question of common sense.

When Carson came to open his defence, he caused general surprise by deciding to call no witnesses, not even Mr. Nevinson, the author of the book quoted by the *Standard*, who had been sitting in Court all week. The advocate preferred to rely instead on the effect of his cross-examinations of the plaintiffs' witnesses and his own concluding speech. It was a dangerous course to take, since the written particulars of defence contained many allegations against the plaintiffs which other counsel would certainly have sought to substantiate by calling oral evidence. But Carson had a wonderful way with juries, and, as events turned out, he thought it wiser to take advantage of the changed atmosphere which had been brought about by his cross-examination of the Cadbury brothers.

The *Standard*, he told the jury, was a newspaper of high reputation, which believed that it was its duty to call attention to this slavery, which was slavery of the vilest type. "Let there be no mistake. There is no crawling down in this matter. We stand by our colours." He referred to the Cadburys as people who put themselves forward as champions of morality and good labour conditions and who subscribed to societies for suppressing slavery—but they had paid £1,300,000 for slave-grown cocoa! They should have refused to buy anything from those islands as soon as they heard of the conditions prevailing there, but instead they had gone on buying, with the explanation that it was in the ultimate interests of the slaves that they should do so, because some day they could refuse to buy any more unless conditions were improved. In point of fact Cadbury's had been spinning the matter out for eight years and continuing to buy cocoa on the grounds that it was a useful lever in negotiation. "Is it necessary to keep that lever in position for eight years?" Carson asked scornfully. "Gentlemen, if the thing was wrong, the duty of the plaintiffs was to get rid of it at once. That was exactly what they did not do. I submit that, if they had had the real interest of the people at heart, they would never have allowed all the long years to go by in which the bartering of men, women and children was the foundation of the products which were being sent for the making up at Birmingham." He concluded with an appeal which raised the case almost to the level of a national issue. "I ask you, gentlemen," he said, "to look upon this as being a matter of public interest on which the defendants have the right to comment, as raising a public question which is of importance as regards the whole character of our dealings with force in commerce."

Rufus Isaacs objected to this last statement in point of law—and he was a more profound lawyer than Carson—submitting that his opponent was not entitled to claim that the *Standard* article was 'fair comment', because the newspaper had pleaded in its written defence that its statements were true and it must stick to the defence without introducing others. The judge upheld this submission, referring to it again in his summing up, which was strongly in favour of Cadbury's. The only question for the jury to decide was—"Had the *Standard* proved its words to be true?"

After nearly an hour's absence the jury filed in and the foreman announced their verdict. It was for the plaintiffs. There were loud murmurs of approval, increasing in volume from the defendants' sympathisers when the foreman went on to announce the amount of the damages which the jury had found—one farthing. Carson immediately jumped to his feet and asked that the costs of the action should be given to his clients. But Mr. Justice Pickford said he would "leave the costs where they were by law."

Although Standard Newspapers were thus saddled with the costs of this expensive action, the contemptuous damages awarded against them in the shape of the smallest coin of the realm proclaimed to the world that they had at least won a moral victory. That this moral victory was due in great measure to Carson's marvellous advocacy on this occasion was also abundantly clear.

"I had only a few minutes to catch the train when the verdict was given," he wrote to Lady Londonderry when he was back in his chambers in the Temple, "and so I could not wire you the result which I think was a great triumph. I am very tired after it all. . . . It was a very big case and everyone seemed delighted. Of course the judge took, and was probably bound to take, a legal technical view, but the jury were disgusted with the plaintiffs for dealing so long in slave-made cocoa."

CHAPTER EIGHT

Unionist Leader

I

AS soon as the Cadbury case was over, Carson, who felt quite exhausted by his exertions in Birmingham, booked a passage for himself and Annette to Madeira. He planned to be back in time to spend Christmas at Rottingdean, before plunging into the election campaign, but an unexpected delay postponed their return till New Year's Day.

To Lady Londonderry

Reid's Palace Hotel, Funchal, Madeira. 23.12.09. I feel so like a prisoner here on the island! We were to have started homewards on Tuesday, but there was such a storm we could not get on to the boat and so I am stuck here for another week—no letters papers or anything, and the worst of weather except that it is hot.

I am wondering what is going on in England and how the campaign is going on. I am sorry I came away as it is difficult to realise the loneliness of isolation.

The gardens and flowers here are simply exquisite and you would revel in them, but there is nothing to do. I play roulette all the afternoon to pass the time—not very intellectual! Is it? . . .

Rottingdean. January 2, 1910. We got home last evening after a most enjoyable passage of 5 days, calling at Lisbon, Vigo and Cherbourg. The sea set me up, and I am off to Burnley tomorrow to commence speaking. I feel quite stupefied at all the engagements which have been made for me and I doubt if I will have the strength for all. . . . The candidates who have written to me all seem cheery. I have had innumerable requests to speak but of course I can only do a certain amount . . .

The campaign centred round the future of the House of Lords, the Budget and Tariff Reform. Little was said about the Irish problem, although Carson and some other Unionists took care to bring home to their audiences that every vote for a Liberal must be a vote for Home Rule.

To Lady Londonderry

Carlton Club, Pall Mall, S.W. January 18, 1910. . . . I went to Retford on Friday [January 14] and we had a splendid meeting, packed as could be. I said a good many insulting things about Winston and generally ridiculed the impossible position of the Government in their shouts against the House of Lords.

I had to come back Saturday and was sorry as the Duchess of Portland kindly asked me to Welbeck and I should have liked very much to see it. I hear the Duke is becoming a Radical by degrees and has a Radical agent! . . .

Rottingdean, Saturday [*January* 22] . . . Well it is all over now and the future is in the lap of the gods and it is difficult to forecast anything.

We dined with the Farquhars on Thursday. I sat next to Mrs. George Keppel and rubbed in the constitutional arguments. She said one of the Cabinet had told her they would not be long in office, but I don't take that view as I think it will be to the interest of Ireland's Nationalist M.P.s to play up as the House of Lords question is being fought, *i.e.* if it is going to be fought seriously. . . .

I am very full of work having neglected it so long. I think the Bar is better than office, but you don't agree.

I am so pleased that Sussex is Unionist—it makes me like the place . . .

The result of the election, though it greatly disappointed Carson, was a serious loss of strength to the Government. The commanding majority of 1906 over all parties in the House of Commons disappeared, the Liberals coming back only 275 strong as against 273 Conservatives and Unionists. In addition Labour won forty seats and the Irish Nationalists eighty-two. Thus the Nationalists once again held the balance of power at Westminster and were thus in a good position to enforce their leader John Redmond's threat to make Asquith 'toe the line'. That they would in turn be forced to do likewise once they had got what they wanted went without saying. "Of course," as Carson told Lady Londonderry, "the Irish will simply do as they are told and will act solidly with the Government, so they will have a big majority."

Walter Long, the Chairman of the Irish Unionist Parliamentary Party, who had previously represented South Dublin, was returned at this election for a London constituency. It therefore became necessary to find another Chairman, since this position had always been occupied by a Member holding an Irish seat. After careful discussion and looking round, the Party's Honorary Secretary, Mr. J. B. Lonsdale (later Lord Armaghdale), M.P. for Mid-Armagh, was requested to convey the Members' unanimous invitation to Carson to fill the vacant place. The invitation reached him in his chambers in the Temple, and there he pondered carefully over it. Acceptance, he knew, must inevitably cut him off from all promotion, whether political or legal, and it would also involve him in substantial sacrifices of income, leisure and probably health as well. On the other hand, as he had so often pointed out to Balfour and others, it was only for the sake of the Union that he was in politics at all, and with the Union in danger now, as it undoubtedly was, he came to the conclusion that it would be shirking the cause of duty if he were to refuse the offer in Lonsdale's hand. Plainly the position was something more than being head of a parliamentary group. He saw that it meant the leadership of the Unionists in Ireland, and particularly of those in the North, where they were in the majority, but where, nevertheless, they needed guidance in the crisis that must arise if another Home Rule Bill reached the statute book.

Carson eventually told Lonsdale that he had made up his mind and would accept the offer. Thus it came about that on February 21, 1910, the day the new Parliament assembled to hear the King's Speech, Sir Edward Carson met the other members of the Irish Unionist Parliamentary Party in the House of Commons and was formally elected their Chairman. "I dedicate myself to your service, whatever may happen," he told them.

To Lady Londonderry

House of Commons. Thursday evening [*February* 24] . . . Everything here is very upsetting, as no one has the least idea what is going to happen. I think you will say that at all events the present House contrasts very favourably with the last and our younger men seem full of 'go'.

I like being Chairman of Irish Unionists and they are a very good lot.

The Speech from the Throne was brief. As Balfour observed in opening the debate on the Address, whatever else could be said of the King's Speech, there was very little in it. The only legislative project foreshadowed was that "to define the relations between the Houses of Parliament, so as to secure the undivided authority of the House of Commons over Finance, and its predominance in Legislation," and on this subject the Speech was highly ambiguous. Meanwhile, pending the introduction of another Budget, revenue to meet expenditure authorised by the last Parliament was being raised by temporary borrowing. This led to a dispute between the Government and the Nationalists as to whether priority was to be given to passing the Budget rejected in the previous session or to the Parliament Bill which was to deprive the House of Lords of its constitutional power to reject legislation passed by the Commons. Redmond, the Nationalist leader, regarded the Upper House as 'the last obstacle to Home Rule' and was determined to do all he could to remove the obstacle. He now expressed his displeasure in debate that what he called 'guarantees' had not been obtained from the King. In other words, he was dissatisfied that Asquith had not yet extorted a promise from the Sovereign that he would be prepared to create a sufficient number of peers to secure the acceptance of the Parliament Bill, or the Veto Bill, as it was alternatively called, by the Lords. The financial crisis, he argued, was a great weapon, which the Irish would not throw away. Let the Government give reasonable assurances that they would carry their Veto Bill the same year, and the Nationalists would vote for the Budget. But they would not pay the price for nothing. "With us the question of the Veto is the supreme issue," he said. "With us it means Home Rule for Ireland."

The Veto Resolutions appeared on the Order Paper of the House of Commons for the first time on March 21. The first of these disabled the House of Lords from rejecting or amending Money Bills; the second resolution limited the power of the Lords respecting other Bills, so that any such Bill which had passed the Commons in three successive sessions and had been rejected each time by the Lords should automatically become law, provided two years had elapsed from the date of the Bill's introduction; the third resolution reduced the duration of Parliament from seven to five years.

In order to clarify the purpose of these resolutions, Mr. James Chambers, an Irish barrister and a Unionist, who was the Member for South Belfast, tabled an amendment to exclude from their scope such Bills as gave administrative or legislative powers to subordinate Parliaments within the United Kingdom. This action was, of course, designed to bring the Home Rule issue into the open.

Redmond, meanwhile, was known to be conducting some close bargaining with Asquith, and on April 14, the same day as Chambers's amendment was due to be discussed, he had had an interview with the Prime Minister in his room in the House of Commons. Consequently the chamber was full, and a feeling of tense expectation prevailed when Chambers rose to move the amendment which stood in his name.

The Government spokesman put up to reply was Mr. Winston Churchill, who had become Home Secretary in the Cabinet reshuffle following the General Election. He stated quite bluntly that a Home Rule Bill passed under the safeguards proposed in the resolution would embody the settled will and convictions of the majority of the electorate, and that the Unionists could pass one under the existing system. Compared with the grant of a Constitution to South Africa, with which fortunately the Opposition had no power to interfere, a Home Rule Bill was less important and less grave. Great changes had taken place in Ireland since 1886, he said, and "the new generation that has grown up in our country is not going to be frightened out of its wits by the nightmares and bugbears of a vanished past." Home Rule, in the opinion of the Government, "would conduce enormously to the strength, unity and prosperity of the Empire."

While they naturally pleased the Nationalists, these remarks greatly annoyed the Irish Unionists, coming as they did from the son of a man whose memorable visit to Ulster in 1886 was ever fresh in their minds. All eyes were therefore turned towards Carson as their newly-elected leader. As it happened, Carson had come into the House not intending to intervene at all in the debate. However, as soon as Mr. Churchill sat down, he was on his feet in a moment, and proceeded to deliver an impromptu speech of devastating brilliance.

"I do not think anybody in this Committee," he began, "supposes for a moment that the Home Secretary will ever be frightened out of *his* existence by the nightmares and bugbears of *his* vanished past." Had not Mr. Churchill suggested that the Conservatives and Unionists might themselves bring in a measure of Home Rule? "I have no doubt if the right honourable gentleman had remained a member of the Conservative Party," he continued, "and had seen any political advantage to be gained from the introduction of Home Rule, or from opposition to Home Rule, he would have been equally willing to adopt the particular view that suited his particular interests for the moment. Does the right honourable gentleman not see that . . . if the Unionist Party were as corrupt as he seems to think they are—and nobody abuses their former friends as much as those who have fallen out with them—by a mere promise of Home Rule we could defeat his Resolutions, his Budget and everything else?"

Carson went on to taunt the Nationalists with the profligate bargain which, as he rightly guessed, they had concluded with the

Government, since at heart they disliked the Budget and were only prepared to support it as a stepping-stone to Home Rule. He then turned on the Government. "The whole object of bringing up this matter as a preliminary to getting their Budget," he said, "has been at the dictation of the Irish Nationalist Members, and solely with a view to improving their position in regard to the great national question of the dismemberment of the Empire." The term Home Rule covered all sorts of alternatives and unsolved difficulties and he ridiculed the idea that it was a small thing in comparison to the grant of a Constitution to South Africa. "You would not dare tomorrow to put Home Rule as a new issue before the country—and the only issue," he declared, pointing at the Government Front Bench. "No, you tried it twice, and you were twice defeated. Once through the action of this House and once through the action of the other House; but in each case it was emphatically decided by the people that they would have nothing of it."

> You have had it twice rejected, and now, by your bargaining with the Irish Nationalists, for the sake of your Budget, for the sake of remaining in office, you want to sneak this Bill through, breaking up the United Kingdom, without the people having an opportunity of expressing an opinion upon it, which they have expressed so emphatically upon former occasions.

Mr. Asquith thereupon rose to explain the intentions of the Government in the event of a defeat of the Veto Resolutions in the House of Lords. "I do think it right to say that if the House of Lords fail in regard to this or any other resolutions . . ." This was as far as he got before being interrupted by Balfour, who protested on a point of order that such a controversial statement could not be made when it could not be debated. The Chairman upheld the Opposition Leader, as pandemonium broke loose, the Liberals demanding that the Prime Minister should be heard and the Unionists shouting "Redmond" and "Dollar Dictator". Eventually the closure was moved, the amendment was defeated by 351 to 245 votes, and the resolution was subsequently carried. Afterwards, on the motion for the adjournment, Asquith made a somewhat equivocal statement, in the course of which he announced that if the Lords rejected or declined to consider the Government policy, Ministers would at once "feel bound to advise the Crown as to the steps necessary if that policy was to receive statutory effect in this Parliament." It would not be right to state at that moment the precise terms of that advice, Asquith declared, but if the Government were not in a position to ensure that statutory effect should be given to that policy in the existing Parliament, they would either resign or recommend a dissolution, but would not recommend a dissolution except "under such conditions as will secure in the new Parliament that the judgment of the people as expressed in the election will be carried into law."

Balfour denounced this anticipation of the prospective advice to the Crown—which was nothing short of suggesting the destruction of the Constitution—as going beyond the idea of duty of any previous Prime Minister. "He has bought the Irish vote for his Budget and has bought it successfully," said Balfour. "The price he has paid is the price of the dignity of his office, and of all the great traditions which he, of all men, ought to uphold."

Carson wrote in similar terms.

To Lady Londonderry

Carlton Club, Pall Mall, S.W. April 17, 1910. It *was* nice of you to send me a wire about my speech. I had no intention of speaking until Winston spoke and I had not the least idea that I was leading up to a row. However I think it came in useful and our men seem very pleased.

I feel boiling with rage and I hope there will be violence—it is a justifiable occasion if ever there was one. To disclose advice you give to H[is] M[ajesty] on a hypothesis and before, or *even after*, the occasion arises, is a public outrage, and it only shows how all decency has been lost in public life. Oh! How I wish I was in good health and had some youth left! I would not mind hanging for the occasion!

Ten days later Parliament adjourned for the spring recess under the shadow of an impending constitutional crisis. But to some extent the situation was altered by the sudden death of King Edward VII, which occurred in Buckingham Palace on May 6. The Law Courts having also risen, Carson took advantage of the lull in affairs to pay a short visit to Paris. He returned in time for the funeral on May 20, but preferred to attend the memorial service in the little parish church at Rottingdean rather than witness the solemn obsequies in Westminster Hall and at Windsor.

To Lady Londonderry

Rottingdean [May 21]. I only remained in Paris 4 or 5 days. It was very hot there, but the gardens were beautiful, and it was a change after a strenuous term. There was evident grief at the death of our King and nearly as much mourning as in London. I came back here by Newhaven and we had a very nice service on the day of the funeral.

Everyone in the village, Nonconformists and all, came to the church, which was fuller than it has ever been before, and it was quite as much as my temperament could bear. I do not care about great shows—they afflict me unnecessarily and in an inordinate degree. But I quite admit what you say that people ought not to shirk, and if I had been of the least importance I would have remained in town.

Everyone in London is asking the one question, 'What is going to happen now?' For my own part I think the situation is very little changed, tho' I dare say there may be some postponement of a crisis . . . it looks like a kind of political paralysis . . .

Carson's prognostication proved correct. The view had already been expressed in certain organs of the Press that the policy of attempting to coerce the Crown should be abandoned and that efforts should be made toward the settlement of the constitutional dispute by compromise. It was felt too that the new King ought not to be confronted immediately on his accession with the most serious political crisis with which the Crown had been faced since the Reform Bill struggle in 1832. These views were eventually accepted by both Government and Opposition, and on June 8, the day fixed for the reassembling of Parliament, it was announced that Ministers were ready to meet the Unionist leaders in conference. Thus, as the Prime Minister described it, "the nation witnessed an incident unparalleled in the annals of party warfare . . . the two combatant forces, already in battle array, piled their arms, while the leaders on both sides retired for private conference."*

2

We must now consider a case on which Carson had been working indefatigably for the past eighteen months in the face of many formidable obstacles. It was the case of a young naval cadet who was accused of stealing a five-shilling postal order. Carson's part in the trial of this issue, which took place, after long and aggravating delays, in July, 1910, may be regarded as the crowning forensic achievement of his career; his ultimate vindication of the boy's character in open Court was perhaps the happiest moment of his life at the Bar.

* Four were nominated from each side. The Liberals were Asquith, Lloyd George, Augustine Birrell and Lord Crewe. The Conservatives were Balfour, Austen Chamberlain, Lord Lansdowne and Lord Cawdor.

The story begins in 1908. In October of that year, Mr. Martin Archer-Shee, who was a banker, received a most distressing letter from the Admiralty about his thirteen-year-old son, George, a cadet at the Royal Naval College at Osborne, Isle of Wight. It appeared that the Commanding Officer had reported the theft of a postal order at the college, which was afterwards cashed at the local post office. "Investigation of the circumstances of the case," so the letter ran, "leaves no other conclusion possible than that the postal order was taken by your son, Cadet George Archer-Shee." Mr. Archer-Shee was accordingly requested to withdraw his son from the college. Although he was quite convinced of the boy's innocence, the authorities were adamant and he had no alternative but to comply with their request.

The admitted facts were briefly as follows. At breakfast on October 7, a cadet named Terence Back, who slept next to George Archer-Shee in the same dormitory, received a postal order for five shillings in a letter from home. He put the postal order in his writing-case, which in turn he placed in his locker. After lunch he went out to take part in a running race, returning to the college about three-forty-five. On going to his locker he found the postal order was missing. He immediately reported the loss to the chief petty officer. He also told his room-mate George Archer-Shee. Only two cadets had been given leave to go to the post office that afternoon, of whom Archer-Shee was one. The other was a boy named Arbuthnot. The chief petty officer then went along to see the postmistress, who said that Arbuthnot had bought a postal order shortly after two o'clock. About an hour later, she said, another cadet had come in and asked her to cash a postal order for five shillings which was endorsed 'Terence H. Back'. She had done so, and immediately afterwards, according to her account, the same cadet had asked her for a postal order for fifteen-and-sixpence, which he received. It was not disputed that George Archer-Shee had gone to the post office that afternoon to obtain a postal order for this amount, since he had made no secret of the fact that he had set his heart on a model steam engine priced at this figure in a London catalogue. Several cadets were paraded before the postmistress, but she failed to identify either Archer-Shee or Arbuthnot. The Commanding Officer then sent for Archer-Shee and asked him to write down Cadet Back's name on a piece of paper. George wrote 'Terence H. Back', which was this cadet's usual form of signature. This piece of paper together with the postal order were sent to Mr. Gurrin, the handwriting expert, and he pronounced the writing to be that of the same hand. On this evidence the Admiralty took the action already described, despite young Archer-Shee's repeated protestations of innocence. "All I can say is I never did it," he declared again and again.

Mr. Archer-Shee had an elder son by a previous marriage, Major Martin Archer-Shee, M.P., who had originally been in the Navy and had later served in the South African War, subsequently entering the House of Commons. He had regularly corresponded with his young half-brother at Osborne and was also convinced that the signature on the postal order was not his writing. Mr. Archer-Shee asked his elder son what they should do. "There is only one man who can help us," he told his father, "and that's Edward Carson." The advocate at once consented to see them, and on a bleak November afternoon Major Martin Archer-Shee, M.P., brought his father, together with young George, to Carson's chambers in Dr. Johnson's Buildings. Carson was naturally interested in hearing what they had to say, since his own son Walter had also gone to Osborne as a cadet and had only recently left. For three hours he subjected the boy to a thorough cross-examination on every aspect of his story, which must have been a severe test for the lad, in addition to what he had already suffered. But he came through with flying colours, and Carson was completely satisfied as to his veracity. "I saw nothing in his answer or demeanour when undergoing a very unpleasant ordeal," said Carson afterwards, "to lead me to the suspicion that he was otherwise than an honest and truthful boy."

When his visitors had left the Temple, Carson sat down at his table and wrote an opinion on the matter on which he had been consulted.* The case against the boy appeared to him to rest on two pieces of evidence—first, the allegation that the signature to the stolen postal order was stated by an expert to be in his handwriting; and, second, the assertion of the postmistress that the same cadet who obtained an order for fifteen-and-sixpence changed the postal order for five shillings. As regards the first, he attached little importance to it. "It is a class of evidence which in a case of this kind I think no Court would consider reliable, and it is especially to be discounted, having regard to the evident intention of the forger to imitate the writing in the body of the postal order." As for the second piece of evidence, Carson considered that, although it came from a lady against whom no suggestion of want of veracity had

* For the text of this opinion, and other information concerning the case, I am indebted to Mrs. Anna Debenham, sister of George Archer-Shee.

been made, the postmistress had admittedly failed to identify the cadet either by his appearance or his voice and she might easily have been mistaken in supposing that the same cadet changed the postal order and bought the other.

"I desire to point out," Carson continued, "that the charge is brought against a boy of thirteen years of age who had hitherto borne an irreproachable character at school and at home, who had won the confidence of his teachers, his comrades and his parents." Indeed, such had been his reputation at Stonyhurst, the Roman Catholic School where he had been before coming to Osborne, that the rector, on learning the news of his removal from the Naval College, wrote to his father asking to have him back. "We will receive him with open arms," said the rector. Nevertheless, Carson argued, even with such a boy there might have been a sudden impulse to yield to temptation, if it could be shown that he was in want of money at the time or that he had employed the money procured by the forgery in paying for the postal order for fifteen-and-sixpence or in any other way for his benefit. But it could not. At the time of the theft young Archer-Shee had £1 7s. 0d. in the hands of the paymaster, and £4 3s. 11d. in the Post Office Savings Bank. Also, he drew from the paymaster sixteen shillings to procure the postal order he required, and the postmistress had admitted that the two half-crowns paid out by her were not used for the purpose of paying for the postal order of fifteen-and-sixpence. "This is to my mind a matter of the highest importance," observed Carson, "as, if Archer-Shee was the thief, it is natural to suppose that he would have been anxious as soon as possible to get rid of the two half-crowns in order that they should not be found on him when the theft of the postal order was ascertained, as it necessarily would be, within a brief space of time. There is no suggestion that Archer-Shee used any half-crowns on or after October 7."

Then there was Archer-Shee's conduct on the day of the theft. Here was a boy, who was alleged to be going to commit a theft, not only asking leave to go to the post office, but even asking another boy to accompany him and making no secret of the fact that he had been at the post office. In Carson's view no weight could be attached to the fact that only two cadets were given leave to go to the post office, which was only 450 yards from the College, and only 250 yards of that were out of bounds. "I think it much more likely," he wrote, "that the person who committed the theft would go stealthily to the post office rather than ask leave to do so." Furthermore, it appeared that when he was handed the postal order for fifteen-and-sixpence by the postmistress, Archer-Shee filled it in incorrectly, writing his own name as that of the payee. If he was the thief of the five-shilling order, how could he have been in any such state of ignorance? Of course, he might have been play-acting, *i.e.* making evidence of his own ignorance. "That is to my mind a very far-fetched suggestion against a boy of thirteen of the character I have mentioned," remarked Carson, "but if he was so cleverly wicked, how did he come to sign his name unnecessarily, and in fact erroneously, as payee of the order for fifteen-and-sixpence, by doing which he would at once identify himself with the boy who changed the postal order in question?

Finally, there was the possibility of the postmistress having been mistaken, though she may honestly have thought she was not. "It is clear she is often called away when attending to customers, that people came in and out that she cannot remember, and that when first asked as to the forged postal order she was uncertain until she went to the drawer to look. The fact that a short time previously Arbuthnot, a cadet, had both changed and bought postal orders may lead her to imagine that the same thing happened in the case of the postal order in question." When one added to this the statement of a telegraph boy on duty at the post office that two cadets came in at a few moments interval at or about two-thirty—which was at variance with the time stated by the postmistress—could it not reasonably be concluded that she was mistaken?

"When I have arrived at the conclusion that the postmistress *may have* been mistaken", Carson added, "I am led to the conclusion that at least there is a reasonable doubt in the case, and I am of the opinion any legal tribunal would come to the same conclusion. Under the circumstances how is it possible, with any justice, to brand as a thief and a forger a boy of thirteen, of the antecedents and character I have already described? It means disaster to him at the threshold of his life."

On the strength of this masterly opinion, the family now thought that the case was strong enough to demand a judicial inquiry under the auspices of the Admiralty. As a result Mr. George Elliott, K.C., was sent down and also Mr. R. D. Acland, K.C., the Judge Advocate of the Fleet, but at neither of the investigations conducted by these gentlemen was the alleged culprit allowed to be legally represented, and there was consequently no opportunity for cross-examining any of the witnesses produced against him. In these circumstances it was scarcely surprising that the Admiralty should have refused to alter their decision and reinstate the boy.

Carson now considered various possible methods of having the matter adjudicated upon in Court. Of course, had young Archer-Shee been a fully-fledged naval officer, there would have been no difficulty; he would have had the right, enjoyed by every member of His Majesty's forces, of being tried by court-martial. Unfortunately this procedure could not be invoked in the case of a cadet. Endeavours were made to persuade the Director of Public Prosecutions to take criminal proceedings, and the possibility of a private prosecution being instituted through the collusive action of a friend was also examined. But both these solutions proved impracticable. Eventually Carson decided to proceed by what is known as Petition of Right. At that time, by reason of the operation of the maxim 'The King can do no wrong', the Crown could not be sued by a subject, but when the Crown had entered into contractual relations with a subject and breach of their agreement was alleged, the subject was allowed as a matter of grace to bring his action in the Courts, the writ of claim being endorsed by the Attorney-General on behalf of the Crown with the time-honoured words 'Let right be done'. The question in this case was whether a contract could be established between the Crown and the parents of a boy who was sent to be educated at a Royal Naval College. Carson, whose own son, it will be remembered, had been at Osborne, thought that there was, inasmuch as it could be argued that in consideration of the parent sending his child to undergo a prescribed course of training with a view to entering His Majesty's service, the King guarantees to furnish this training. Anyhow it was upon this basis that at long last the matter came before the Courts.

The claim brought by George Archer-Shee's father on a petition of right against the Crown came before Mr. Justice Ridley in the King's Bench Division of the High Court on July 12, 1910. Sir Edward Carson, assisted by Mr. Leslie Scott, K.C. (later Lord Justice Scott), and Mr. Eric Hoffgaard, appeared for the plaintiff. Sir Rufus Isaacs, who was now Solicitor-General, appeared for the Crown, along with Mr. Horace Avory, K.C. (later Mr. Justice Avory), and Mr. B. A. Cohen.

The Solicitor-General took the preliminary point of law that a petition of right would not lie, relying on the immunity of the Crown from legal proceedings and the absolute right which he claimed the Crown had to dismiss anyone who had entered its service. In reply

Carson contended that his point should have been taken before the trial and decided in one way or the other. "The plaintiff has gone to great expense in getting up the case on the facts," he added, "and I am surprised that the Crown should have taken this very unusual course."

"The plaintiff might himself have applied to have the point argued first," intervened the judge.

"Why should we?" retorted Carson. "We want to have the facts tried here."

Mr. Justice Ridley said that, though it might perhaps seem a hardship on the plaintiff in the face of the expense to which he had been put, he felt that the Crown had to have the point of law decided first.

"The Crown is shirking the issue of fact," Carson protested. "It is a public scandal. The Crown can, I suppose, be high-handed out of Court, but in open Court it is not to be tolerated."

The Solicitor-General thereupon submitted that he was entitled to judgment, and, after some further argument, the judge ruled in his favour.

Carson was furious at what he felt to be the most palpable injustice. "This is a case of the grossest oppression without remedy that I have known since I have been at the Bar," he said, looking disdainfully at the Crown counsel in the row beside him.

"All I can say is there have been various inquiries," said Rufus Isaacs.

"Only a hole-in-the-corner inquiry in which the boy was not represented," answered Carson.

"That is not so," Isaacs protested. "Mr. George Elliott, K.C., went down."

"Yes," said Carson, with a touch of bitterness in his voice. "*That* was our inquiry."

"Assisted by the Admiralty," observed Isaacs.

Carson turned towards his opponent. "It's a gross outrage by the Admiralty," he said indignantly.

"I do not think you should say that," the judge reproved Carson. "I know nothing of the facts. I have merely decided the point of law."

At this Carson picked up his papers and stalked angrily out of Court.

He immediately set about lodging an appeal, and through his unrelaxing efforts the matter came before the Court of Appeal in less than a week. On the Bench were Lords Justices Vaughan-Williams, Fletcher Moulton and Buckley, and Carson exerted all his powers of argument and persuasion to obtain a reversal of Mr. Justice Ridley's decision, skilfully introducing the all-important but as yet untried question of fact into his speech. "Your Lordships may be interested to know that the charge against the boy is that he stole a postal order and forged the payee's name," he said. "The charge is totally devoid of foundation. It is admitted that the boy's conduct was entirely satisfactory until the date of the letter calling on the plaintiff to withdraw his son from the college. The trumping up of such a charge cannot render his conduct unsatisfactory. It raises a serious question of fact which ought to be tried."

"Yes. Yes, where are the facts?" asked old Lord Justice Vaughan-Williams, whose sympathy had been aroused. "We want the facts."

The Solicitor-General repeated his previous objections, but the Court decided against him. The Lords Justices unanimously sent the case back for rehearing, with the instructions that the facts should be tried by a judge and jury before the legal objections were argued at all. Carson appeared personally before the Lord Chief Justice to apply for a speedy trial, and as a result of his efforts the case came on nine days later before Mr. Justice Phillimore and a special jury. It was an example of rapid action which is unhappily rare in our Courts of Law.

Carson fought the final round of his struggle on young Archer-Shee's behalf under severe handicaps. For one thing, he had numerous private worries on his mind. His wife's health had begun to cause profound anxiety, and he had other domestic troubles, which are described later in this chapter. Then there were the heavy responsibilities which he had recently taken on as Leader of the Irish Unionists, and he was constantly consulted by them on their affairs while the case was proceeding. Furthermore, as Carson opened the case, the judge began to lean heavily on the side of the Crown, and several unpleasant clashes occurred between the Bench and the advocate. The atmosphere was not improved by the weather. London was experiencing a tremendous heat wave, and the stifling conditions in Court were most trying.

The first witness was the plaintiff, Mr. Martin Archer-Shee, who was suing on behalf of his son. Until the previous year he had been agent of the Bank of England in Bristol, and had retired on reaching the age limit in the Bank's service. In the witness box he appeared the old-fashioned type of English banker, dignified and honourable.

"I have never at any time had reason to suspect my son's honesty," he declared in answer to Carson's questions. "His character is conspicuously open and straightforward. There is nothing secret about him." He then told the Solicitor-General, who cross-examined him, that as a banker he had had occasion to study many signatures. "I know nothing about the signature on the postal order," he said, "but whoever forged this signature used a feigned hand, and that person was not my son."

George Archer-Shee followed his father into the witness box. His answers to Carson's questions, as the advocate took him through the story, conveyed the impression that he had done nothing to be ashamed of. "Is there any truth in the charge made against you?" Carson asked him finally. "No, certainly not," replied the boy.

For nearly two days the lad submitted to a gruelling cross-examination by Rufus Isaacs, but he stood up splendidly to this ordeal. Only once did the Solicitor-General make a point which seemed to tell against him. When he was first questioned at Osborne, Archer-Shee had said he had visited the post office between 3.0 and 4.0 p.m. This corroborated the account of the postmistress, and the cadet admitted it frankly. "But I corrected myself at once," he added, stoutly rebutting the suggestion that it was only when his father's solicitors came upon the scene that he had alleged the time to be two-thirty.

This account was supported by Archer-Shee's fellow cadet and close friend, Patrick Scholes, who swore that he distinctly remembered Archer-Shee asking him to accompany him to the post office to get a postal order. The time was two-fifteen and, as he told Isaacs in cross-examination, he remembered it well as he was expecting some friends and kept looking at the clock. "Did you say at one time that Archer-Shee said that he was going to *cash* an order?" "I have never said that Archer-Shee was going to cash an order," replied this witness. Carson then proceeded to ask Scholes two telling questions in re-examination.

CARSON: Was any suggestion ever made to you until yesterday that you had said 'cash' and not 'get'?

WITNESS: No.

CARSON: Was it made to you yesterday by the Treasury Solicitor?

WITNESS: Yes.

SOLICITOR-GENERAL: The inquiry was made to settle a doubt in my mind.

CARSON: I do not suggest anything improper on the part of the Treasury Solicitor.

Carson looked at the jury. Although he had exonerated the Treasury Solicitor of any improper motive, it was clear from the expression on the faces of the jurymen that they did not like the fact that the Treasury Solicitor had made his inquiry from one of the plaintiff's witnesses for the first time in this manner.

Next came Cadet Arbuthnot, the other cadet who had been given leave to go to the post office on the day in question. He said he had gone there about two o'clock. This was confirmed by the telegraph boy, who stated that one cadet had come in about two, adding in support of Archer-Shee's story that another came in a few minutes afterwards, leaving about two-thirty.

In opening the case for the Crown, Rufus Isaacs reduced the matter to a single issue. Was the boy who bought the fifteen-and-six order the same boy who cashed the five-shilling order? If the jury believed he was, then the plaintiff's son was necessarily guilty. "What you have to determine," he told the jury, "is whether the boy or the postmistress is telling the truth."

The postmistress then went into the witness box, where she was examined by Mr. Horace Avory. "Are you sure that it was the same cadet who cashed the five-shilling order as bought the one for fifteen-and-six?" he asked her. "Perfectly," she replied.

A task of immense difficulty and delicacy faced Carson as he rose to cross-examine this key witness for the defendants. It was clear that she was an honest woman and had given her evidence to the best of her recollection. What Carson had to do was to show, in accordance with his written opinion previously quoted, that she may have been mistaken, and indeed probably was. The substance of his remarkable cross-examination was as follows:

CARSON: Is there anything in your books to show the order in which the postal orders are dealt with, or the time?

WITNESS: No.

CARSON: So that, on the point whether the same person cashed the five-shilling postal order as bought the one for fifteen-and-six, we must rely on your memory?

WITNESS: Yes.

CARSON: Are not all these cadets very much alike?

WITNESS: Yes.

CARSON: All smart, good-looking boys about the same age?

WITNESS: Yes.

CARSON: When did you first know anything was wrong?

WITNESS: The petty officer came up that night and asked me if a cadet had cashed a postal order who had no right to it.

CARSON: It was he who first suggested to you it was a cadet?

WITNESS: Yes.

CARSON: Did he say he had given leave only to two cadets?

WITNESS: Yes.

CARSON: Was he in a very excited condition?

WITNESS: I thought so, but I have never seen him before. I have said that he was almost raving.

CARSON: Did you say a word that evening about it being the same boy who bought the fifteen-and-six order who had cashed the five-shilling order?

WITNESS: I did not say it to the petty officer.

CARSON: Did you ever say it was a cadet who cashed the order before you saw Commander Colton the next day?

WITNESS: If I said 'I did not' to Mr. Elliott, K.C., it must be correct.

CARSON: Can you remember anyone else at all having a transaction or conversation with you that day?

WITNESS: No.

CARSON: Do you remember the appearance of anyone?

WITNESS: No.

CARSON: Do you remember if any of the cadets' servants came?

WITNESS: No.

CARSON: Were you ever asked about the cadets' servants by anyone?

WITNESS: No, I do not remember being asked as to anybody else.

CARSON: So you paid no attention to anyone else that day?

WITNESS: No.

CARSON: No one has attempted to test your memory on that point until now?

WITNESS: No.

Carson sat down. It was an amazing feat of cross-examination. Employing all his tact and characteristic charm, he had completely obliterated the damaging effect of her examination-in-chief, but he had not antagonised the jury by attempting to exhibit her as a deliberately untruthful witness. Her honesty was not in the least impugned; it was simply her recollection of events that was shown to have possibly been at fault.

The case, added to other responsibilities, was beginning to tell on Carson. When he came into Court for the opening of the third day of the trial, he told the judge that he was determined to finish the case himself, but that he might have to ask for an adjournment, as he was very unwell, owing to the heat of the Court on the previous day and the other work he had to do after the Court had risen. "Perhaps, however," he said, "I may get better as the case proceeds."

The witnesses who went into the box on the third day included

Cadet Back, the boy whose postal order had been stolen, the chief petty officer who had reported the matter, and Mr. R. D. Acland, K.C., the Judge Advocate of the Fleet, who had conducted the subsequent enquiry. The cadet said that Archer-Shee was not at his table at the time the postal order had come and he had not to his knowledge seen it at all. The chief petty officer's evidence conflicted with the postmistress's in certain important particulars—for instance, according to his account, their first conversation when she told him the culprit was a cadet did not take place in the post office at all but on the telephone the night before. He added that there had been a number of other thefts both before and after Archer-Shee's departure, and that the culprits had not been found. Carson objected to Mr. Acland's evidence since his enquiry had not been held in the boy's presence, but the judge overruled the objection. Carson thereupon only asked one question of this witness, who besides his duties as Judge Advocate of the Fleet sat as a Recorder. "When you try a prisoner as Recorder, you hear both sides, I suppose?" "Yes."

The climax came early on the fourth day. The Solicitor-General, after a hurried consultation with Carson, rose to make a statement, which took everyone in Court by surprise. The Admiralty had given in. "As to the issues of fact, the Court and the jury will not be further troubled," said Isaacs. "I say now, on behalf of the Admiralty, as a result of the investigation which has taken place, that I accept the declaration of George Archer-Shee that he did not write the name on the postal order; that he did not take it, and that he did not cash it; and that consequently he was innocent of the charge which has been brought against him. I make that statement without any reservation of any description, intending it to be a complete acceptance of the boy's statements." He added that, on the other hand, Carson accepted the statements of the Admiralty that all those responsible for what had happened had acted in good faith.

There were tears in Carson's eyes when he rose to speak. "The complete vindication of his son, George Archer-Shee, was the object of the plaintiff in bringing this action," he proudly declared. "That object has been entirely achieved. This is the first issue of fact. With regard to the other issues, I agree that those responsible acted *bona fide* under a reasonable belief in the statements put before them."

Jurors and spectators in Court crowded round Carson and his client to congratulate them. But the central figure of the drama, young George Archer-Shee, was absent. He had been to the theatre the night before and had overslept. Later in the morning he came to see Carson in his chambers to thank him.

"What a strange boy you are," said Carson, when he heard his explanation of why he was not in Court. "Didn't you feel too nervous to go out to the theatre?"

"Nervous, sir?" replied George. "I never had the slightest nervousness. When I got into a Court of Law I knew I'd be all right. Why, I never did the thing."

"Well," said Carson, approvingly, "after all, that's a very good way of looking at it."

As usual, Lady Londonderry sent the advocate a telegram of congratulation. "You know how I appreciate it," he told her. "It has been a great victory and I feel quite tearful over it. I was always convinced of the boy's innocence, and I know it all arose from the blundering suggestion of the officers-in-charge. You should have seen the boy when he came to thank me. He was so frank and honest. My regret is that the Navy will have lost so promising a boy."

To the boy's mother, who shared his conviction, he expressed himself in similar terms. "You are quite right as to my belief in George," he wrote. "Will you please tell him I hope he will always look upon me as a friend, and I sincerely hope the whole incident will in the long run turn out to his advantage. He will, I am sure, do well at whatever profession he adopts, and he has the good wishes of everyone."

No offer came from the Admiralty to reinstate George, nor from the Treasury to compensate George's father for the considerable expense he had been put to in connexion with the litigation. It was not until the matter was raised in the House of Commons that Mr. Reginald McKenna, the First Lord of the Admiralty, agreed to leave it to a tribunal composed of Lord Mersey, the great Admiralty lawyer, Isaacs and Carson. This body eventually awarded Mr. Martin Archer-Shee £7,120 by way of compensation, including costs.

Unfortunately young George Archer-Shee was not destined to enjoy a long life. Some months before the outbreak of war four years later he joined the Army and was commissioned in the South Staffordshire Regiment. He was wounded and posted as missing in the first battle of Ypres in 1914, and it is known that he died of the wounds he received in that action. His name is inscribed on the Menin Gate.

Since that date the story of his case and the vindication of his character by Carson has become widely known to succeeding generations. Just thirty-one years after his death and eleven years after Carson's, the story became the basis of a play by Terence Rattigan called *The Winslow Boy*, which had its première in London in 1946 and was subsequently filmed.

3

As always after a long and exhausting case, Carson sought relaxation in a complete change of surroundings. This time he went off to Homburg, which was then at the height of its season. "You were very kind to me last week as you always are," he wrote to Lady Londonderry on the day of his departure. "But you don't know what a strain these big cases are, and it is so restful to have an appreciative friend throughout."

Unfortunately the strain was not confined to the Law Courts. At this time Annette's health was beginning to fail, and he had difficulties with his children, all of whom, with the exception of his eldest daughter Aileen, already married, were problems in one way or another. Harry had come back from South Africa, with a wife whom he had married there, and had found it impossible to settle down to any regular work. Eventually he had enlisted in a yeomanry regiment, but his career there, because of his extravagant habits, was proving far from satisfactory. Then there was Walter, or Wally, the younger boy, who had joined the Navy and at this time was serving as a midshipman in H.M.S. *Albemarle* with the Atlantic Fleet. ("He is very fond of navigation and hopes to specialise in it. What a good time he can have if he only plays the game.") When he came home on leave, Carson confessed he found him difficult to make out. "I hope he may get some sense in time," was his comment. Finally, there was Gladys, now a young woman of twenty-four, and regarded by her father as the most intelligent of his children, "my dear little Gladys", as he called her. Unfortunately, she was extremely delicate and showed signs of tuberculosis. She was consequently packed off to a sanatorium at Glion, above Lake Geneva, where she promptly fell in love with an American. ("I have written her to be very circumspect as I do not relish foreign relations.") When he eventually met him, Carson was most unfavourably impressed. "Gladys's 'young man' is a terror," he told Lady Londonderry. "I think she must be quite topsy turvy to think of him, and I will have a lot of new troubles in this matter owing to her illness and the difficulty of dealing with her. My children are a rum lot."

To Lady Londonderry

Grosvenor Hotel, London, S.W. August 29, 1910. Got back yesterday from Homburg and go tomorrow to Rottingdean. I had such nice weather abroad, but find it miserable here and London like a city of the dead . . .

Politics seem to be dead, but of course you cannot fight while the Generals are in friendly conference.

Rottingdean. August 31 . . . I wish the Conference was over or the King would fall in love or Arthur Balfour get into the Divorce Court, or even Charlie Beresford become a 'Fisherite'!*

It is a good time for filling in Government forms and exercising one's ingenuity in giving as much trouble as possible.

Rottingdean. September 5. . . . I imagine the land forms are causing a good deal of dissatisfaction . . . they are really monstrous. I have had about 25, although I have no property! . . .

Have you heard anything of A.J.B. since his return? I hope the Gastein waters have done him good, but I don't suppose they will give him a tinge of vulgarity that would be very useful just now.

Rottingdean. October 3. . . . All my colleagues have been promoted to the Bench, and I feel very lonely as they were the men I met most in the arena. And now I see Simon is likely to be Solicitor-General. His has been a rapid rise.† The only pity is they get so conceited (I never did—did I?)

F. E. S[mith] is very wicked in taking up payment of Members.‡ I loathe the idea myself and would never support it, but I am getting out of date with the methods of advertisement and self-glorification.

I expect shortly to be examined before the Divorce Commission and will go in for no new-fangled theories of legislating for restless domestic ne'er-do-wells, who can settle down to nothing but unhealthy excitement and so-called liberation.§

The Conference of party leaders dragged on throughout the summer and autumn without any measure of agreement being reached. There is some doubt as to whether the Liberal Prime Minister ever really desired a compromise and whether he was not

* Admiral Lord Charles Beresford, former Commander-in-Chief of the Channel Fleet, had long been at variance with Lord Fisher, the First Sea Lord, on the policy of the Board of Admiralty and its organisation of the fleets.

† Simon's appointment to this office was announced a few days later. He succeeded Sir Rufus Isaacs, who became Attorney-General.

‡ Payment of M.P.s, at the rate of £400 a year, was introduced in 1911.

§ The Royal Commission on Divorce was appointed in 1909.

simply playing for time. Lloyd George and Winston Churchill, however, were certainly anxious for a settlement. They felt dependence on the Redmond faction to be irksome and humiliating, and they began to favour the idea of a Liberal-Conservative coalition which would render this reliance on the Irish Nationalist vote unnecessary. The first Conservative to be taken into their confidence was F. E. Smith, and he was employed as intermediary in the highly secret negotiations which were now opened with Balfour. The 'common programme of a Ministry' proposed included an increase in the Navy to meet the growing menace of German rivalry, a settlement of the constitutional issue and a measure of Home Rule for Ireland on a federal basis. The only members of his own party besides F. E. Smith whom Balfour is believed to have consulted were his three colleagues in the Conference, Austen Chamberlain and Lords Lansdowne and Cawdor, and outside the conference, his brother Gerald, Aretas Akers-Douglas (later Lord Chilston), who had been his Home Secretary, and Andrew Bonar Law, a Canadian of Ulster ancestry, who was a leading Tariff Reformer.

In spite of the secrecy in which these negotiations were conducted, rumours of what was afoot reached Carson's ears and naturally caused him grave disquiet. This was heightened by the publication of a series of letters signed 'Pacificus', which began in *The Times* on October 20 and was continued in subsequent issues. The anonymous author of these letters, at first wrongly identified with the King's Archivist, Lord Esher, was the brilliant publicist, F. S. Oliver, known as an active Unionist and Tariff Reformer. "Unionists cannot champion Home Rule," he wrote, "but they might nevertheless submit to it without loss of dignity or self-respect." The scheme of Federal Home Rule, or 'Home Rule All Round', which he outlined consisted of an Imperial Parliament at Westminster with separate Parliaments for England, Wales, Scotland and Ireland, these bodies being subject to it in the same way as the Canadian provincial legislatures were to the Dominion Parliament in Ottawa. This scheme found considerable support in the Press, particularly from Mr. J. L. Garvin in *The Observer*.

Meanwhile Carson was being pressed by the Irish Unionists to deny these rumours and at the same time was asked by the Irish Unionist Alliance, which represented Unionist opinion throughout Ireland, to move a resolution at the forthcoming Conservative Party Conference in Nottingham declaring its unalterable opposition to Home Rule.

To A. J. Balfour

5 *Eaton Place, S.W. October* 25, 1910. I am being pressed as Chairman of the Irish Unionist Party to state publicly my disapproval and opposition to the rumoured proposals for a settlement on the Home Rule question. This I had proposed to do in answer to a letter from the Irish Unionist Alliance and saying that I did not for a moment believe the rumours. However I sent a copy of my proposed letter to Sandars and he very kindly advised me not to publish it without communicating with you.*

Of course I know it is quite impossible for you to state anything about the conference, but I feel I must publish that I should oppose the setting up of a Parliament in Dublin with an executive responsible to it, and I do not like to take any course without informing you.

It is now proposed that I should move a resolution in Nottingham against Home Rule in any shape or form, and this, too, I think I ought to tell you of.

I hope you will understand I am not writing this letter under any feeling of apprehension but out of absolute loyalty and appreciation.

A few days later he wrote to a friend with considerable less restraint.

To Lady Londonderry

5 *Eaton Place, S.W.* [*October* 29] . . . I am sick to death of this Home Rule tragedy. It is weakening the position every day and from what I can gather there is truth in it. But what I hate most is the number of our people who are apparently quite ready to fall in with the idea. I have written to A.J.B. saying I was pressed as Chairman of the Irish Party to say something very definite from my point of view —but I have had no letter so far. I will wait till Monday, and then take my own course.

It will split the Party to pieces and, should it turn out to be true, I earnestly hope the Conservatives will never again be in office during my life. How can anyone suppose that those of us who have fought all our lives to prevent a separate Parliament and executive in Ireland now turn round and allow so base a surrender! We are all drifting and where to I don't know. I hate the whole situation . . .

'F.E.' is very full of himself and seems to approve of the Home Rule proposals! What next!

What Carson wrote about F. E. Smith was only too true. Within the past ten days 'F.E.' had written two letters to Austen Chamberlain advocating a coalition, with the common programme already mentioned, letters which he asked Chamberlain to destroy but which

* On the same day Sandars had written to Carson: 'It would be well that you should send your proposed letter to A. J. B. for his observations. You see you are writing about him, and there is a kind of tradition which favours the person quoted. And, of course, as a very old and devoted friend, you have every right to go to him thus.'

that politician neglected to do. Home Rule he described as "a dead quarrel for which neither the country nor the party cares a damn outside of Ulster and Liverpool." As for the scheme as a whole, "we cannot carry it through without losing some friends, but I think we should lose very few and those temporarily. . . . We should still be a united party with the exception of our Orangemen: and they can't stay out long. What allies can they find?"

On October 27 the Opposition Leader had sent Austen Chamberlain a "pair of Irish Unionist letters", possibly Carson's which he had just received, describing them as "the first drops in the storm which will assuredly break over us if any new departure be admitted." A day or two later Balfour, who had been at his home in Scotland, returned to London and breakfasted with Lloyd George at the latter's invitation. The Liberal Chancellor suggested that in the proposed coalition Balfour should lead the Commons and Asquith should go to the Lords, presumably remaining Prime Minister. The remaining offices, great and small, should be divided exactly between the two parties. And there was to be "a reasonable federal solution of the Irish difficulty." Back in his house in Carlton Gardens, Balfour told his friend and secretary, Jack Sandars, that he could not deny the scheme had some attractions, but considering the line he had taken in resisting Home Rule in the past, he could not be a party to the proposed arrangements, though, to quote Austen Chamberlain, "younger men less involved in the controversies of 'eighty-six and 'ninety-three might be free to contemplate what he could not accept." He subsequently informed Lloyd George to this effect. "I cannot become another Robert Peel in my Party," he said.

Although Carson had not yet seen Balfour, he rightly guessed that this was the course Balfour would follow as regards Home Rule.

To Lady Londonderry

Rottingdean. Sunday [*November* 6]. I did not go to see A.J.B. as I did not want to appear to be fishing for information, and it is very difficult to discuss without letting something fall which would enable one to draw an inference. However, I will see him this week I know . . . my own belief is that there is no fear of A.J.B. being likely to concede anything on Home Rule . . .

I think Socialism is spreading very fast and even in this little village it is going ahead with some very respectable people. My hope is that many Liberals may begin to appreciate the danger.

I saw Charlie Beresford today—he motored from Brighton to Rottingdean. He is very full of the defence question and I dare say he is right, but I doubt if 'the people' care. It is too sad . . .

> I imagine the Conference will be finished before the House meets. I think it is best that it should be so and let us get to work on whatever the situation may be . . .

On November 8 matters came to a head in the Conference. Balfour had previously proposed that if a Home Rule Bill was twice rejected by Parliament, it should go to a plebiscite. The Liberals could not agree to this, but suggested as a compromise that on the next occasion a Home Rule Bill passed the Commons and was rejected by the Lords, there should be a General Election—but only on that occasion. Home Rule Bills, if not introduced afterwards, should be treated like ordinary Bills. Balfour was inclined to disagree and suggested that he would sound the opinion of his followers.

He immediately summoned a meeting of about twenty prominent members of the party, including Carson, in Lansdowne House, where he outlined the proceedings of the Conference and asked whether he and his colleagues were to continue or break off. By a majority it was agreed that they should break off the negotiations. Carson, who was with the majority, was strongly opposed to the suggested Home Rule compromise on the ground that only one attempt to put the measure on the Statute Book would be safeguarded by a General Election and that it would consequently be open to any Government to get Home Rule passed without consulting the people, for such subsequent Bills would be treated as ordinary legislation.

On November 10 the Conference held its twenty-first and final session. The Prime Minister then made a public announcement that it had broken up without reaching any agreement. He also stated that he would ask the King to dissolve Parliament and that a General Election would take place in the following month.

Next day Carson, supported by Walter Long, J. H. Campbell and others, published a manifesto condemning the Federal Home Rule scheme, canvassed by certain newspapers, as "opposed to the most vital interests of the Kingdom and the Empire" and stating their conviction that "this country must remain a Union governed by one Parliament." A week later, at the Conservative Party Conference in Nottingham, he moved a resolution exhorting "all Unionists throughout the Kingdom to maintain unimpaired their unalterable opposition to the policy of Home Rule" and not to adopt a vacillating attitude over any legislation—he had in mind the Veto Bill—which would weaken the Union between Great Britain and

Ireland. The resolution was passed with enthusiasm and Carson's speech was loudly cheered, particularly that part of it which referred to the recent secret negotiations.

"Let us make an end of these announcements that a section of the Unionist Party is flirting and coquetting with Home Rule," he declared. "For my part I would rather for the rest of my life stay in the honest division lobby of the Opposition than surrender one particle of my principles to obtain the highest office in the land."

4

The General Election, which took place in December, 1910, left things very much as they were. Asquith studiously avoided the Home Rule issue until pressed by a heckler in his own constituency, when he repeated his previous pledge. This led Redmond to say that "we shall have Home Rule before we know where we are," a statement which Carson described in a letter to *The Times* as a complete confession of the "treacherous bargain" his party had made with the Liberals. "Even at this late hour," he wrote on December 9, "I now challenge Mr. Asquith to meet me on any platform he may choose and unfold and discuss his Home Rule proposals. Let us have a fight in the open and some fair play." But the Prime Minister did not accept the challenge.

The last polling figures were declared on December 20. The aggregate results showed the Liberals with 272 seats, and the Conservatives and Unionists with 271; the Nationalists had eighty-four and Labour forty-two. Once more the Liberals were at the mercy of Redmond and the Nationalists in carrying on the Government, and from the point of view of their obtaining an absolute majority the election was fought in vain. The result was no more satisfactory for the Unionists, as Carson realised.

To Lady Londonderry

Rottingdean, December 23, 1910 . . . I have been very seedy and depressed since the elections and I hate reactions more than pain! I am sure we have made many mistakes and it all comes of hastily pronouncing with a view to the moment and having nothing definitely laid down after full consideration and discussion. Now I believe there are the usual disagreements and no one knows where we stand or what we are going to do. No doubt this will all be fully considered after the Veto is abolished!

I fear the truth is there is no leader on either side. Everything is just to try and catch a few stray votes, whereas a policy with principle and a fight for everything we believe in would not only command respect, and in time power, but would certainly get us better terms in the long run . . .

On Boxing Day Carson left for a short holiday at Monte Carlo with his fellow barrister and friend Charles Gill.

5 *Eaton Place, S.W. January* 13, 1911 . . . I had a nice time at M[onte] C[arlo] as the weather, tho' cold, was bright and cheery and, as I like Gill who was with me, I enjoyed the trip. The great benefit of going away is to forget politics, which I thoroughly did even tho' Lloyd George and several others of the obnoxious ones were at M[onte] C[arlo]. But who cares for them there, as one reflects that there is a land of sunshine where pessimism can be banished and old age warmed up at a moderate cost? However, for the present I am back and so full of work I don't know what to do with it all.

I wish I could be in Ulster . . . to know whether men are desperately in earnest and prepared to make great sacrifices. I have a lot of plans as to what ought to be done . . .

I earnestly hope that all the liberated hate of the innate savagery of the human being will be brought to play on those who are prepared to adopt the role of vandals. I never felt more savage. I only wish I was younger and stronger for the fight! I hear no news except I am told the Government expect the Lords to give way, especially under petticoat influence! As if life was worth preserving when the 'causa vivendi' is gone.

I am very glad A.J.B. is gone to the Riviera—it may make him fit for the session. Personally I don't like his referendum. I believe it to be impracticable and dishonest, but I swore by it at the elections and will continue to do so. I think anyone who raises a discordant note just now is a traitor . . .

Asquith had been prompted by the breakdown of the Conference and the ensuing elections to contemplate what he called "reverting to a state of war". Carson had taken him up on this phrase during the campaign, and in doing so had issued a timely warning. "Perhaps, if the Prime Minister does not look out," he had said at Liverpool, "there is more real war in it than figurative war. It is my wish, and the wish of those with whom I act, to be law-abiding citizens. But, by heaven, I tell you this—*from what I know of the men of the North of Ireland, they will not yield their birthright, not one inch, without a struggle.*"

This feeling was reinforced in Carson's mind when he went over to Belfast at the end of January to preside at an important meeting of the Ulster Unionist Council. This organisation, which had come into being in 1905 largely through the efforts of Mr. William Moore, a vigorous barrister, who had succeeded Colonel Saunderson as M.P. for North Armagh,* formed a union of all local Unionist Associations, Unionist Clubs and Orange Lodges in Ulster. Its delegates, which were appointed by every polling district and drawn from all classes of the population, were thoroughly representative of the Ulster people, and by the democratic method of their election thus provided a permanent electoral machinery in the constituencies. The Duke of Abercorn was President and Chairman of the Standing Committee, which also included Lord Londonderry, James Craig and two eminent Liberal-Unionists, Mr. Thomas Sinclair and Mr. Thomas Andrews, who were also, like Carson, members of the Irish Privy Council. Under its rules, as Chairman of the Irish Unionist Party, he became Vice-President of the Ulster Unionist Council. "Sir Edward Carson needs no introduction to Ulstermen," so read the relevant paragraph in the Council's annual report for the year 1910, adopted at their meeting. "Ulster Unionists feel confident that they can place implicit faith in his guidance in the present crisis."

Meanwhile, unknown to the Opposition leaders in the House of Commons, Asquith had obtained a promise from the King to create sufficient peers, if necessary, to secure the passage through the Upper House of the Parliament Bill, as the measure was called which embodied the Veto Resolutions. With this assurance the Government pressed on with the Bill. Aided by a vigorous use of the closure, it passed its third reading on May 15, and it was then sent up to the Lords. Rumours of what had passed between the King and the Prime Minister now began to circulate and had the effect of stiffening Conservative resistance. "Let them make their peers," said the ex-Viceroy of India, Lord Curzon. "We will die in the last ditch before we give in." Hence, when the issue came to be joined in the House of Lords, those who were for resistance were known as 'ditchers' and those for giving way were called 'hedgers'.

At this point Carson, whose health had been troubling him, was obliged to undergo a course of treatment at Baden-Baden, and was consequently out of England when the Parliament Bill was being debated in the Lords.

* Later Sir William Moore, Lord Chief Justice of Northern Ireland.

To Lady Londonderry

Sanatorium Dr. Frey-Dengler, Baden-Baden. June 3, 1911. Baden is a very beautiful place but of course I am bored to death. I was so sorry to have to come here but Bruce-Porter* was very insistent about it and so I hope it may be of use.

I feel very despondent about the Home Rule campaign. No one seems serious about it or anything else. I imagine *The Times* and all Harmsworth's papers are going against us. I sent a letter to *The Times* just before I left, but they did not insert it—the first they ever refused that I wrote to them—so I will send them no more. After all they are not very important now.

I hope the Lords will stand firm and let the Radicals make their filthy Peers and then become ridiculous. I daresay there are many who will welcome even these blackguards amongst the aristocracy! People are too well off and fond of pleasure to care about anything except amusing themselves . . .

How I am to live through 3 weeks or a month here I don't know but I must try. The Tecks were here and went away yesterday. I am sorry as they were very agreeable . . .

How is Lord L? I know he would prescribe Port for me, but I am past that stage.

Baden-Baden. June 14 . . . This is a pretty place—most exquisite gardens and woods. One only wants the right person in person to make it perfect . . . I wander about all alone through the woods and I even wish sometimes I could discourse with a German Fraulein! . . .

Baden-Baden. Thursday [*June* 25] . . . The surroundings here are exquisitely beautiful. I never saw such foliage and trees and the views are wonderful, but of course to me it is miserably lonely and I am not able to walk much.

I quite despair of getting fit. I have done too much work and am suffering for it in consequence.

I am very depressed about the Home Rule question. It seems to me as if everything was helping it on. The fact that the Colonial Premiers dined with the Irish Party is of course a great help to the latter, and they will pose I presume as the real Imperialists.

I am also very concerned as to whether we can raise sufficient money for a really big effort, and I also do not see much sign of younger men taking up the work . . .

There is nothing to write about from this place. It is 'treatment' all day long, but whether it is of any use remains to be seen . . .

He returned to England at the beginning of July in a very depressed state of mind and doubtful whether he had benefited much from his visit to Baden-Baden. He did not stop long in London, but went to Lincoln, where he was engaged in a big case at the Assizes.

* His doctor.

To Lady Londonderry

White Hart Hotel, Lincoln. July 5, 1911. Here I am stuck in an awful hole and will probably be here for some weeks. It is the last [case] I will do in the country . . .

I am not sorry to get away from Baden, tho' it is a lovely place, but I fear it has not been of much use to me. However it is [too] soon to despair . . .

I am very depressed about everything. If I only was younger, I would take a very decided course.

I believe Lord L. is going over to Ulster for 12 July. I fear there is no chance of my getting there—I wish I could.

I so much want to have a talk. I feel so outside of everything!

The annual Orange celebration on July 12 of King William III's victory over King James II at the Battle of the Boyne was kept with more than usual fervour that year. Londonderry, who addressed an immense concourse of Belfast Lodges at Finaghy, just outside the city, declared that it was the first time a former Irish Viceroy had attended such a gathering, but that he had deliberately created the precedent owing to his sense of danger threatening the 'Loyalist' cause.

On his return to Westminster Carson had several long conversations with his Ulster Unionist colleague James Craig on future plans. Mr. Winston Churchill, in Craig's words, had "let the cat wholly out of the bag" by stating that Home Rule was to be forced through the present Parliament under the Veto Bill. It was therefore urgently necessary to prepare some kind of resistance in Ulster, and he suggested that Carson should come over and set the scheme in motion as soon as possible. Carson readily fell in with this suggestion, leaving the details of the arrangements to Craig, who had a genius for organisation. "He says I may fix up the whole programme," Craig reported to his wife, "and he will carry it out." At the same time Carson hoped that they meant business in Ulster. "We cannot, I think, depend even on the Lords throwing out a [Home Rule] Bill," he told Lady Londonderry, "and if anything is to be done, the Ulstermen must do it for themselves."

To James Craig

Rottingdean. July 29 [1911]. What I am very anxious about is to satisfy myself that the people over there really mean to resist. I am not for a mere game of bluff, and, unless men are prepared to make great sacrifices which they clearly understand, the talk of resistance is no use. We will, you will find, be confronted by many weaklings in our own camp, who talk very loud and mean nothing and will be the first to criticise us when the moment of action comes. For this we must be prepared, and as far as possible we ought to make sure of the Press, which unfortunately is not unimportant.

Personally I would be prepared to make any sacrifice, my time, business, money, or even my liberty, if I felt assured we would not in the end be abandoned. I am glad to have so good and true a friend as you to work with, and, if we get sufficient help, we ought to be able to call a halt.

I think the action of the leaders in the present crisis is lamentable—it will damp enthusiasm for a long time—and the open way in which the official party is joining hands with the Government is a positive calamity.

The reference in the final paragraph of this significant letter was to the disposition which had now manifested itself on the part of many prominent Unionists to offer no further resistance to the passage of the Parliament Bill in the face of the Liberal threat to swamp the House of Lords. This view, endorsed by Balfour, Bonar Law and Walter Long in the Commons, was taken in the Upper House by the Opposition Leader Lord Lansdowne, and he was supported among others by Lord Curzon, who had originally counselled resistance, and also by Lord Londonderry, whose action temporarily clouded his popularity in Ulster and caused Carson some concern. In the Lords resistance crystallised round the venerable figure of the ex-Lord Chancellor, Lord Halsbury, while in the Commons the 'die-hard' revolt was led by Carson, F. E. Smith and Lord Hugh Cecil,* and supported by George Wyndham and Austen Chamberlain. On July 23, when the Prime Minister rose to announce the Government's refusal to accept the Lords' amendments to the Bill, he was shouted down, and after several noisy scenes the Speaker was obliged to suspend the sitting.

Three nights later the 'die-hards' or 'ditchers' gave a dinner in honour of Lord Halsbury at the Hotel Cecil, at which Carson and others spoke and which was the occasion of an appeal for recruits to defeat the obnoxious measure in the Upper House. "We are told that, though we run away today, we will fight hereafter," said Carson in ringing tones. "My Lords, I prefer to fight today and tomorrow and hereafter. Courage is what we want."

The decisive vote in the Lords was due to be taken on the night of August 10. Lord Lansdowne advised the Unionist peers to abstain, though he declined to discourage those who wished to vote in favour of the Bill from doing so. Meanwhile, Balfour publicly

* Later Lord Quickswood.

rebuked the 'die-hards' and hinted that their course of action was tantamount to disloyalty. "It would, in my opinion, be a misfortune if the present crisis left the House of Lords weaker than the Parliament Bill by itself will make it," he said, "but it would be an irreparable tragedy if it left us a divided party."

Nevertheless, the issue remained in doubt until the last moment. The Opposition Whips in the Lords worked like Trojans, but their efforts eventually proved in vain. By a narrow margin of seventeen votes the Lords decided not to insist on their amendments, and the Bill became law. The majority of Conservative and Unionist peers abstained, but a number of them did vote with the Government. Carson was present at the final scene.

To Lady Londonderry

5 *Eaton Place, S.W. August* 11, 1911 . . . I feel very bitter at over 20 of our Unionist Peers voting with the Government last evening—it will do a deep and lasting injury to the Party.

I have no feelings whatever towards Lansdowne's adherents. They were just as much entitled as I was to their opinions and no more. But as for the Judas Peers, I hope they will be posted in every Unionist Club in the country until their names are a byeword.

I am sorry you were not at the finish; it was very interesting. Granard asked me "What is the betting?" I replied, "Do you think this is a joke, and cannot you realize my feelings?" He did squirm!

Galway was booed when going out of the Club, and afterwards we had speeches and cheering till a very late hour at the 1900 Club. And so ends the House of Lords!

5

Meanwhile James Craig was going ahead with preparations for the monster meeting which he planned to stage in the grounds of Craigavon, his house on the south shore of Belfast Lough, and which he designed as a means of bringing the Ulster people face to face with their new leader. A women's organisation had also recently been formed under the presidency of the Duchess of Abercorn, and in this body Carson's friend Lady Londonderry was the moving spirit. But it was by no means confined to titled ladies, since in the first few months of its existence over 40,000 members were enrolled, many of them mill workers and shop girls. "We will stand by our husbands, our brothers and our sons," they resolved, "in whatever steps they may be forced to take in defending our liberties against the tyrannies of Home Rule." Indeed it cannot be too strongly emphasised that the Ulster Protestant community's resistance to Home Rule and adherence to the Union had their roots firmly implanted in the Ulster working class.

To Lady Londonderry

Rottingdean, August 29, 1911. I got back here last Sunday after a very pleasant week's yachting and unfortunately was laid up for some days with some sort of fever which has left me seedy, and so I go tomorrow for a few days to Homburg, then to Scotland and Ireland for the meetings there.

I do not know anything about the Women's Meeting as J. Craig is arranging everything, but I think the bigger show we have all round the better.

I am much overwhelmed at all that lies before us, but I will make a big effort (my last in politics) to stir up some life over this Home Rule fight. You cannot conceive what dissatisfaction there is everywhere at the want of life and effort in the party. I get hundreds of letters from men only longing for strong action, so I hope we may be allowed to do something without cold douches every morning . . . I feel very doubtful about the way our leaders intend to fight Home Rule, but in any event I will lead for myself this time.

The whole country is in a shocking state—everyone is demoralised and weak, and still the country is calling out for a strong man . . .

Park House, Drumoak, Aberdeenshire, N.B. September 16. . . . I came back from Homburg on Tuesday and came on here to be near Gladys, whom I had not seen for 4 months. Her lung has healed up, I am thankful to say, but she is in a very nervous neurotic condition and I will have to take her to London to see Bruce-Porter and some nerve specialist—so I am upset naturally . . .

I am so glad you are coming to Belfast [for the meeting] . . . I am so nervous about it all and how it will come off . . . I quite agree that riots in Belfast are to be deprecated and anything that is done must be organized and orderly.

I do not know why you ask me if I want another split in the party? If you mean, do I want the party to be more active and show more life and fight, I certainly do. I am sure the whole party in the country is crying out for something more than 'the gentlemanly party'. I do not think you know the depth of despair and dissatisfaction that exists. I would rather be out of it altogether, if we are to dribble along on the old lines. However it will be very nice to see you and talk it all over and agree or disagree at Belfast . . .

The great gathering at Craigavon took place on Saturday afternoon, September 23, 1911. Annette accompanied her husband to Belfast on this occasion—it was destined to be her only visit—

and they spent the week-end together as the guests of the Craigs. "It was all magnificent and Craig managed everything splendidly," wrote Carson to Lady Londonderry next day. "The morning was very wet and I was in despair, but it cleared up and the sun came out at the right moment." The lawn in the front of the house, with its fine view of Belfast Lough and the distant Antrim coast, sloped steeply to the shore road and formed a sort of natural amphitheatre, ideal for a large open-air meeting. The platform was erected near the crest of the hill, so that the audience were spread out in a semi-circle on the lower levels and everyone had a view of the platform party, though naturally—since there were no loudspeakers in those days—the more distant spectators could not hear anything of what was being said. It was estimated that upwards of 100,000 were present, of whom the greater part arrived in procession. They marched in columns of four from the centre of Belfast, two miles away, taking over two hours to pass a given point. All the Belfast Orange Lodges, the County Grand Lodges, the Unionist Clubs and the Women's Association were represented. Yet absolute silence was maintained throughout the speeches, and no disturbance of any sort occurred during the day.

The Earl of Erne, who presided over this immense concourse in the unavoidable absence of the Duke of Abercorn, sounded a significant note at the outset, when he quoted from a letter written by his ancestor Gustavus Hamilton, Governor of Enniskillen, to "divers of the nobility and gentry in the north-east part of Ulster," whom he exhorted to resist the forces of King James II in 1689: "We stand upon our guard, and do resolve by the blessing of God to meet our danger rather than to await it." Mr. Thomas Andrews, the veteran Liberal-Unionist, then moved a resolution welcoming Carson as their leader. "We will never never bow the knee to the disloyal factions led by Mr. John Redmond," he assured him. "We will never submit to be governed by rebels who acknowledge no law but the laws of the Land League and illegal societies."

There followed the presentation of a great number of Addresses to Sir Edward Carson from various representative organisations, expressing determination to resist the jurisdiction of a Dublin Parliament. Then the cheering and singing and general enthusiasm gave way to an awed silence as Carson rose in his place on the platform. He knew that the time had now come for action, and from the beginning his hearers were deeply moved by his utterance. He went straight to the heart of the matter.

I know full well what the Resolution you have just passed means. I know what all these Addresses mean. I know the responsibility you are putting on me today. In your presence I cheerfully accept it, grave as it is, and *I now enter into a compact with you, and every one of you, and with the help of God you and I joined together—I giving you the best I can, and you giving me all your strength behind me—we will yet defeat the most nefarious conspiracy that has ever been hatched against a free people.*

But I know full well that this Resolution has a wider meaning. It shows me that you realise the gravity of the situation that is before us, and it shows me that you are here to express your determination to see this fight out to a finish.

So much for this common resolve. But how were they to give effect to it, now they no longer had any hope of salvation through the influence of public opinion in Great Britain? Carson provided the answer, which all were waiting to hear, in a few pregnant sentences.

Mr. Asquith, the Prime Minister, says that we are not to be allowed to put our case before the British electorate. Very well. By that determination he drives you in the ultimate result to rely upon your own strength, and we must follow all that out to its logical conclusion . . . That involves something more than that we do not accept Home Rule.

We must be prepared, in the event of a Home Rule Bill passing, with such measures as will carry on for ourselves the government of those districts of which we have control. We must be prepared—and time is precious in these things—*the morning Home Rule passes, ourselves to become responsible for the government of the Protestant Province of Ulster.*

We ask your leave at the meeting of the Ulster Unionist Council, to be held on Monday, there to discuss the matter, and to set to work, to take care, so that at no time and at no intervening space shall we lack a Government in Ulster, which shall be a Government either by the Imperial Parliament or by ourselves."

Assent was willingly given to this proposal, and, two days later, 400 delegates to the Ulster Unionist Council, assembled under the chairmanship of Lord Londonderry in the Rosemary Hall, Belfast. They promised their "unwavering support" in any danger their leaders might be called upon to face in resisting the establishment of Home Rule in Ireland, and went on to appoint a Commission of five leading local men "to take immediate steps, in consultation with Sir Edward Carson, to frame and submit a Constitution for a Provisional Government of Ulster, having regard to the interests of the Loyalists in other parts of Ireland: the powers and duration of such

Provisional Government to come into operation on the day of the passage of any Home Rule Bill, to remain in force until Ulster shall again resume unimpaired her citizenship in the United Kingdom." The Commission consisted of two Ulster Members of Parliament, Captain James Craig and Colonel Sharman Crawford; Mr. Thomas Andrews, the Liberal-Unionist; Colonel R. H. Wallace, a prominent member of the Orange Institution; and Mr. Edward Sclater, Secretary of the Unionist Clubs.

After the business of this meeting was concluded Lord Londonderry entertained the delegates to a luncheon, at which there were more speeches and Carson proposed his health. This Carson was very glad to do as it emphasised the mutual confidence between them, which had not been interrupted by their divergence of opinion over the Parliament Bill.

Next day Carson travelled through various parts of Ulster, receiving on his way addresses of confidence in his Craigavon declaration. That night he spoke at a large meeting in Portrush, where he dealt with an important question which had arisen out of what he had said at Craigavon. Would Ulster fight against the forces of the Crown? "No," he replied. "We are not going to fight the Army and the Navy, but if the Army and the Navy under a British Government come up to displace us, they will displace us at their peril. It is not that we mean to fight them. God forbid that any loyal Irishman should ever shoot or think of shooting the British soldier or sailor. But, believe you me, any Government will ponder long before it dares to shoot a loyal Ulster Protestant, devoted to his country and loyal to his King."

On his return to London Carson met a number of his parliamentary colleagues who had been present at the dinner given to Lord Halsbury when the struggle over the Parliament Bill was at its height in July. Those from the Lords included Selborne, Milner and Willoughby de Broke; and from the Commons there were F. E. Smith, Leopold Amery, George Wyndham and other 'die-hards'. Early in October they formed themselves into what shortly afterwards became known as the Halsbury Club.

To Lady Londonderry

Rottingdean. October 7, 1911 . . . Shortly we have resolved to keep our forces together. I hope to gain others with a view to active work and pressing forward a better fighting spirit and to co-operate in supporting each other in the House, on the platform and in the press. . . . We are of course working within the party, and there is no idea of any hostile attitude but we will go ahead as best we can . . .

There seems to be a good deal of activity everywhere including headquarters. But everyone is looking for a lead, and I feel quite nervous as to what A.J.B. will say. Milk and water won't satisfy the thirst of the party . . .

They were joined a few days later by Austen Chamberlain, when he had satisfied himself that the new organisation was not being directed against Balfour. On the other hand, the Halsbury Club did not lack critics, appearing as it did at a time when Mr. Leopold Amery was advocating with characteristic vigour in the pages of his *National Review* that 'Balfour must go.'

To Lady Londonderry

5 *Eaton Place, S.W. October* 18 . . . All this criticism comes to this—that everything should be let run on in the old miserable non-fighting groove. The 'do nothing' attitude but be gentlemen is what many of our followers would like.

Halsbury had a petition signed by a thousand or more individuals and associations asking him to be President of a new association within the party, and many emphasized the fact that they would have nothing to do with the old regime.

Even now we are on the eve of the session and none of us know what is going to be done on the Insurance Bill—nor are we likely to, as apparently there will be no conference before Parliament meets. It is really hopeless and the moment one tries to force the pace and get something done, we are called intriguers! I am very sick of it.

A man in Dublin said he had a letter from A.J.B. disapproving of my action in Ulster! I don't know whether that is true, but it may be.

Carlton Club, Pall Mall, S.W. October 23 . . . Everything is quiet here and no one knows as usual what we are going to do about anything.

I am working away in Court and have a very bad cold. I think next year I must give up the Courts if I am to properly work politics . . .

Four days later the recipient of these letters came to London and dined with Carson. She told him that she thought Balfour must soon retire. They discussed the question of the party leadership. Lady Londonderry said she thought Walter Long, who represented the purely Tory section of the party, wanted it and would probably get it, but that Austen Chamberlain and his Liberal-Unionist friends would do all they could to prevent this happening. She then suggested that to avoid a split in the party Carson himself would be "a very suitable leader", particularly in view of the importance of the Home Rule issue. "He did not appear to dislike the prospect," she noted afterwards, "but talked much about his health and the Ulster Party."

Unknown to both of them Balfour had already made up his mind to resign. The public announcement was made at a hastily summoned meeting of his constituents on November 8. The step was dictated solely by health considerations; the activities of the Halsbury Club had nothing to do with it. Carson was ill in bed when he heard the news, and, as soon as he got up, he sent his old chief the following letter.

3 Dr. Johnson's Buildings,
The Temple.
November 10, 1911.

DEAR MR. BALFOUR,

I hardly trust myself to write and express my feelings at your ceasing to lead the party. I have never had any other leader either inside or outside the House and I have the strongest feelings against serving under anyone else.

What I owe you in my career and life I cannot express. The only criticism I have ever felt during the temporary disagreement of last summer was one made by some newspapers of ingratitude towards you. However, as I knew it was untrue, I put it aside without comment, as I knew you would not for a moment believe it.

I earnestly hope you will be long spared to the country and the party. Please believe me that no one feels more than I do the great loss we have sustained in your retirement from the leadership.

Yours very sincerely,
EDWARD CARSON.

To this letter Balfour responded with equal sincerity. "We have been in many a critical engagement together, inside and outside the House of Commons," he wrote, "and I need not tell you how much I have always valued your friendship, and how greatly I have admired your courage."

6

On the morning after Balfour had announced his resignation from the Conservative Party Leadership, Lord Balcarres, the Conservative Chief Whip, called on Austen Chamberlain to tell him that the Irish Unionists had said that they must propose Carson to succeed him, but it was "as a demonstration" and "they did not expect to carry him". Later that day J. H. Campbell, Carson's colleague in the representation of Dublin University, went to see Carson, who was in bed in his house in Eaton Place. He told him that there was another candidate in the field, Bonar Law, but that Bonar Law had authorised him to say that he would not put his name forward if Carson wished to do so. Carson said he would not enter the field, and messages in this sense were accordingly sent to Chamberlain and Bonar Law. It now appeared that the two principal contestants for the position would run each other very close in the ballot, although on the second count, when Bonar Law's votes would have been distributed, it is probable that Chamberlain would have been elected. However, in view of Bonar Law's determination to press forward with his own candidature, and since he did not wish to divide the party, Chamberlain agreed to withdraw his name, if Long would do likewise, so as to enable Bonar Law to be elected without opposition. Long did so, with the result that Bonar Law, the 'compromise' candidate, eventually became the party's unanimous selection.

"I believe that many people think the best man (owing to the two sections) has been chosen," wrote Lady Londonderry at the time, "and I understand that he is a very good platform speaker and an excellent debater. Hitherto he has only been known as a great Tariff Reformer. He is of Scotch and North of Ireland ancestry, and I understand was born in Canada. Some of the Press have held this up as an inducement to vote for him, but I should have thought England and the Tory Party might have produced an Englishman to lead the latter. However, there is no more to be said than that he is a brilliant speaker and undoubtedly knows his own mind. Carson (whose opinion I value very much) thinks he will be a great success. Carson, the two Charlies* and I lunched together yesterday, and the first-named seemed quite pleased at having the Home Rule question to fight for without the Leadership." She continued:

> Although Mr. Bonar Law may be the best man, I am of the opinion that, had Sir Edward Carson been properly approached at the beginning of the crisis, he would undoubtedly have led the Party; but, as far as I can make out, Mr. Campbell went to see him on the Thursday morning [November 9], and told him Bonar Law would not stand if he (Sir Edward) wanted to. He was ill in bed; and we know people of emotional temperament and feeling change their

* Her son, Lord Castlereagh, and Lord Helmsley, who were both Conservative M.P.s.

minds; but the idea being new, he sent a message back to say he would not stand. He did not feel at that moment that he wished to be Leader, and I must say has said so consistently since.

Bonar Law was formally elected at a meeting which took place in the Carlton Club on the following Monday, November 13. He arrived with his friend and confidant, Sir Max Aitken, M.P., the future Lord Beaverbrook, who for some time past had been working quietly in the Press in support of the 'compromise candidate'.

"Don't run yourself down. Don't try to keep yourself in the background," Aitken kept urging his friend as they made their way to the meeting together. "Remember you are a great man now."

Bonar Law looked despondent. "If I am a great man," he replied, "then a good many of the great men of history are frauds."

As the senior Privy Councillor, Walter Long moved the election, and it was seconded by Austen Chamberlain. While this was being done, Carson left the room and returned with the Leader-elect, "like a bride on the arm of her father".

Carson, who had not shaken off the effects of his illness, again retired to bed, whence he wrote to Bonar Law, suggesting that they should dine together at Lady Londonderry's invitation to discuss the situation in Ulster. The fact that the new Leader's father came from County Antrim and that he himself was a son of the manse, who had been brought up among the Presbyterians in Glasgow, seemed to indicate that he had much in common with the Ulster people.

At this time Andrew Bonar Law was fifty-three years old and had only been in Parliament since 1900. His character and background were essentially middle class and in them he bore a striking resemblance to Joseph Chamberlain, whose political mantle as a Liberal-Unionist he may be said to have inherited. Both men were iron merchants, who had been successful in business before they entered politics; they were both effective speakers; they were both ardent believers in Tariff Reform and Imperial Preference, and neither belonged to the Established Church. In addition, Bonar Law was destined to be the first person of colonial birth to become Prime Minister of Great Britain. As Lloyd George said at the time of his election to the party leadership, "The fools have stumbled on their best man by accident."

If he was a man of great courage, Bonar Law was also a born pessimist. "There is lots of trouble ahead!" was a favourite phrase of his in ending an interview. Also he was extremely cautious and diffident—"meekly ambitious", Asquith called him—and there is no doubt that he owed much to the devoted support that he received from his friendship with Lord Beaverbrook, which resulted in his being pushed forward vigorously into the political limelight. Painstaking and industrious, he lived for his public work and had few interests outside it. To Lloyd George, whom he had recently met on holiday in the South of France, he confessed that neither scenery, music nor pretty women attracted him. "What is it that you do like?" asked the Liberal Chancellor of the Exchequer. "I like bridge," was the reply. He was an inveterate pipe smoker. As for his food, he had small regard for meals, and hated long ones, because they delayed the moment when he could pull out his pipe and light up. According to Lord Beaverbrook, he liked little food and plain—one course for preference—and simply swallowed it. This may explain his comment to Carson on Lady Londonderry's dinner invitation.

To Lady Londonderry

5 *Eaton Place, S.W. Wednesday.* [*November* 15] . . . I sent a note to B[onar] L[aw] and he has written to say that he will dine on Sunday 'but not with pleasure'. However it is very important he should get in touch with all concerned. I will go to dinner 'with pleasure', but Lady C[arson] cannot come. I think everything goes smoothly so far and everyone is prepared to be loyal.

I don't know but I am in bed again, suffering a good deal and so weak. I think I'm worn out—so little knocks me up . . . If you saw me, you would thank Heaven I was not the Leader.

Although Lady Londonderry and Bonar Law had not a great deal in common ("I feel that Mr. Bonar Law is not as interested in the various principles of the Tory Party as I should have liked, such as Church, Education and Home Rule"), nevertheless the dinner seems to have been useful. Bonar Law expressed sympathy with the movement which had been launched in Belfast. He promised to visit Ulster, and accepted an invitation from Lady Londonderry to stay at Mount Stewart when he did so.

Meanwhile the Prime Minister and his Cabinet colleagues, as well as the Nationalists, were pouring scorn on the activities of the Ulster Unionists. Mr. Churchill, in particular, who was smarting from the effects of Carson's recent public reference to him, scoffed at "the squall which Sir Edward Carson was trying to raise in Ulster—or rather in that half of Ulster of which he has been elected Commander-in-Chief." While condemning the Unionist Leader for attempting to set up "a rebel Government in defiance of laws which will have received the assent of Parliament and the Crown," the Home Secretary airily dismissed the attempt as an empty threat. "We must not attach too much importance to the frothings of Sir Edward Carson," he declared. "I daresay when the worst comes to the worst we shall find that civil war evaporates in uncivil words." Mr. Churchill proposed, rather rashly as it subsequently turned out, to put the matter to the test by visiting Ulster himself at the invitation of the Ulster Liberal Association and speaking in support of Home Rule on the same platform as John Redmond, the Nationalist Leader, and Joseph Devlin, the Nationalist M.P. for West Belfast.

If Mr. Churchill thought that the Ulster Unionists were bluffing, he was soon to be disillusioned. In fact, the Ulstermen had already begun to drill and were undergoing training in the use of arms. The example had been given by a contingent of Orangemen from County Tyrone, who had attended the demonstration at Craigavon and had attracted general attention by their smart appearance and the orderly precision of their marching. It was learnt that of their own accord they were being instructed in military drill. The example quickly spread to other Orange Lodges and to the Unionist Clubs, many of whom did not belong to the Orange Order. Responsibility for the organisation of this training was assumed by Colonel Wallace, a prominent Orangeman who had commanded a battalion of the Royal Irish Rifles in the South African War. So as to comply with the law Colonel Wallace, after consultation with Carson and Campbell, obtained for his men the necessary authority from the Belfast Justices, which they were empowered to give on certain conditions, namely, that "such authority is sought and will be used by them only to make them more efficient citizens for the purpose of maintaining the constitution of the United Kingdom as now established and protecting their rights and liberties thereunder." This was the origin of the Ulster Volunteer Force, to which local units throughout the province contributed under Wallace's energetic direction to make a single coherent organisation on a territorial basis.

The Belfast magistrates granted the application for leave to drill and practise 'military exercises, movements and evolutions', early in January, 1912. At the same time Carson was in the city for the purpose of raising funds for the new movement.

To Lady Londonderry

5 *Eaton Place, S.W. January* 13, 1912. . . . My visit to Belfast was very encouraging, as I have had a considerable promise of funds which are very requisite. I met many of the merchants and big men

> and they are all inclined to be very generous which shows me more than anything else that they are in earnest. I think James Craig is a bulwark of strength.
>
> I don't know what will happen when Winston Churchill goes over. There appears to be great indignation about it, but whatever is done should be after the fullest consideration and with complete control . . .

The Ulster Liberals, a small minority of the population led by Lord Pirrie, the ship-builder, had booked the Ulster Hall in Belfast for Mr. Churchill to speak on the night of February 8. This historic hall, which was the property of the Belfast Corporation, had been the scene of Lord Randolph's famous speech almost exactly thirty-four years previously when, it will be remembered, he had warned the Ulster Loyalists to "organise and prepare", so that the Home Rule blow, if it did come, should not descend upon them "as a thief in the night" and find them "unready and taken by surprise". The news that the First Lord of the Admiralty, as Mr. Churchill had now become, was to make a speech commending the policy of Home Rule in the very building where his father had so roundly condemned it was naturally very disturbing to the Ulster Unionists. They quickly formed the determination that the meeting should not be held in the Ulster Hall, though of course they had no objection to Mr. Churchill speaking in any other building in the city.

The Standing Committee of the Ulster Unionist Council met under the chairmanship of Lord Londonderry on January 16 to consider whether and how best this could be achieved. While they were thus deliberating, Colonel Wallace came into the room and told the Committee that the people outside were expecting the Council to discuss means for stopping the Ulster Hall meeting; that they were quite resolved to take matters into their own hands if the Council remained passive; and that, in his judgment, "the result in that event would probably be very serious disorder and bloodshed, and the loss of all control over the Unionist rank and file by their leaders."

This information confirmed the wisdom of the decision which had, in fact, already been taken by the Committee before Wallace arrived. This decision was embodied in a resolution moved by Captain James Craig and unanimously adopted: "That the Standing Committee of the Ulster Unionist Council observes with astonishment the deliberate challenge thrown down by Mr. Winston Churchill, Mr. John Redmond, Mr. Joseph Devlin and Lord Pirrie in announcing their intention to hold a Home Rule meeting in the centre of the loyal city of Belfast, and resolves to take steps to prevent its being held."

The publication of the terms of this Resolution caused a considerable sensation in England. The Liberal newspapers denounced what they considered to be an unwarrantable interference with the right of free speech, and special correspondents flocked over to Belfast, where they busied themselves in interviewing the local notabilities on each side and speculating how the Resolution was likely to be put into effect. Even in Conservative circles in London the Unionist movement was viewed with feelings of apprehension, as Carson discovered when he went into the Carlton Club.

To Lady Londonderry

Carlton Club, Pall Mall, S.W. Friday [January 19] . . . Everyone here is very much exercised about the Council's action with reference to Winston's meeting, but of course they are only beginning to realise the real gravity of the situation in Ulster. It is nearly time.

I do not know what are the tactics of the Council, but I have written to say F. E. Smith and I are prepared to hold a meeting the night before in [the] Ulster Hall and the night of W[inston Churchill]'s meeting in West Belfast. Certainly if the things goes on, I will go over, as I could not have it said I stayed comfortably in London.

So glad Lord L[ondonderry] was Chairman of the Council. I have impressed upon our friends that the resolution was with a view to keeping order.

I go to Liverpool for two mass meetings on Monday and one in [the] Free Trade Hall at Manchester on Tuesday. We may have a row! . . .

By the time he reached Liverpool to be greeted by F. E. Smith, Carson had made up his mind to go to Belfast, where, as he put it, "I ought to be and intend to be." He crossed on the following night after fulfilling his engagement in Manchester, where he addressed 5,000 people in the Free Trade Hall, and in the course of which he described the First Lord of the Admiralty as the "most provocative speaker in the whole party going under the most provocative circumstances to a place where the words of his own father are still ringing in the ears."

7

On arriving in Belfast Carson met the Ulster Unionist Council in a private meeting, which endorsed the action taken by its Standing Committee. He then went on to Mount Stewart, where he was to stay with the Londonderrys. Next day he wrote to the new Conservative Leader:

To Bonar Law

Mount Stewart, Newtownards, Co.Down. Thursday [January 25]. Everything here in Belfast is in a very serious condition and it is difficult to see a way out.

I believe the authorities in Dublin fully understand and at all events have the fullest information on the situation from the Police and, as far as I can learn, the Police have reported that they cannot be responsible without the interference of the Military. On the other hand, to hold the meeting under the protection of the troops is what the Government want to avoid.

I fear each day makes it more difficult to control the situation. From what I now know I feel certain the action of the Ulster Council was forced upon them, although the wording of the resolution might have been different.

I will stay here at all events for a few days to see if I can be of any use.

On the afternoon of the same day as this letter was written, an anxious meeting took place in the Liberal Whip's office in London, attended by Mr. Churchill; Sir Rufus Isaacs, the Attorney-General; the Master of Elibank, the Chief Whip; Lord Pirrie and two other members of the Belfast Liberal Association. Although the Ulster Unionist Council had not disclosed the steps it intended to take to prevent the Ulster Hall meeting from taking place, it was now known that the Council had engaged the hall for the preceding night and that members of the Ulster Volunteer Force were prepared to move in and occupy the premises against all comers for the next thirty-six hours. It would obviously be extremely difficult to eject them by legal process in time for the Liberal meeting. In view of these circumstances it was decided to seek alternative accommodation in Belfast for the meeting.

It was after 6 p.m. when Mr. Churchill left the Whip's office and returned to his room at the Admiralty. There he sat down and addressed the following letter to Lord Londonderry:

The Admiralty, S.W
25th January, 1912.

My Lord,

The very grave and direct personal responsibility which will fall upon you if serious rioting occurs in Belfast on the occasion of my visit makes me sure that you will not lightly seek to widen the grounds of the quarrel. For my own part, I only care about one essential thing. It is my duty to keep my promise to the Ulster

Liberal Association and to assert our right of free speech and public meeting.

If, as I now gather from the newspapers, the main objections of yourself and your friends are directed against our holding our meeting in the Ulster Hall, then, although such claims are neither just nor reasonable, I will ask the Ulster Liberal Association to accede to your wish. There will thus be no necessity for your friends to endure the hardships of a vigil or sustain the anxieties of a siege. Neither will it be necessary for you to break the law in an attempt to deprive us forcibly of the use of property to which we are lawfully entitled.

It is not a point of any importance to me where I speak in Belfast. On the contrary, I desire to choose whatever hall or place is least likely to cause ill-feeling to the Orange party. It has, however, become of importance to the public liberties that the meeting should take place in Belfast on the 8th of February, and I intend to hold it there in lawful exercise of the elementary rights of citizenship.

Yours faithfully,
WINSTON S. CHURCHILL.

Since the text of this letter was released to the Press the same evening, the first Lord Londonderry knew of it was when he opened his newspaper next morning at Mount Stewart. After consulting with Carson he made a dignified rejoinder, in which he began by expressing satisfaction that the idea of holding the meeting in the Ulster Hall had been abandoned. He continued:

By selecting the Ulster Hall, with its historic traditions and the memories connected with your late father's visit in 1886, and the advice he then gave to the people of Ulster, I have no doubt you intended directly to challenge the genuineness of the oft-expressed determination of those who have made up their minds never under any circumstances to allow themselves to be degraded from their present position under the Imperial Parliament, and, so far as you could by a choice of the locality, to falsely represent that those who are unalterably opposed to you were adherents of the policy you come to advocate. Against such an attempt, which was only the culmination of many acts of insult and arrogance towards the Loyalists of Ulster, the Ulster Unionist Council felt bound in the most emphatic manner to protest, with a full knowledge that peace and order could not be preserved if a meeting under such circumstances took place.

So far as the Council is concerned its major objection in the interests of law and order is removed if you determine to hold your meeting outside the districts which passionately resent your action, and if you do so, it would certainly be no party to, and would strongly deprecate, any attempt to interfere with your meeting. At the same time, having regard to the intense state of feeling that has been created by your proposed action, the Ulster Unionist Council cannot accept any responsibility with reference to your visit to Belfast, and they do not desire to give any assurance that they might be unable to fulfil.

Lord Londonderry concluded his reply by describing Mr. Churchill's references to the right of free speech as "almost cynical, having regard to the action of Your Government in repressing it in the House of Commons."

Next day the Ulster Unionist Council's Standing Committee had a further meeting, at which they approved the terms of Lord Londonderry's letter. At the same time Mr. Churchill was penning a rejoinder in which, to do him justice, he made it clear that the Ulster Hall had not been selected by him but by the Belfast Liberal Association because it happened to be free on the date in question. "One word more," he wrote. "Your letter forces me to refer to a personal matter. Your Lordship has a claim, to which I bow, to remind me of the memory of Lord Randolph Churchill. You were his friend, through evil as well as good days. The Unionist Party, who within a few months of the very speech which is now on their lips pursued him with harsh ingratitude, have no such right."

Meanwhile the Belfast Liberals, with the assistance of the Government Patronage Secretary, were busy scouring the city for a suitable hall in which to hold their much publicised meeting. In the course of the search Mr. F. W. Warden, the manager of the Grand Opera House, was offered a knighthood and a large sum of money for the use of his theatre, but he indignantly refused. The Nationalists offered them their largest building, St. Mary's Hall, but this the Liberals in turn declined, not wishing to be under such an open debt to the Redmondites. Eventually it was decided to hold the meeting on a football ground in the Nationalist quarter of the city, and a huge marquee was imported from Scotland for this purpose.

To Bonar Law

Mount Stewart, January 28 . . . There is no new development here. Tomorrow I will try and have a resolution passed deprecating any interference with W[inston] C[hurchill]'s meeting, but I must say there is a very difficult feeling here to control and I know the Government know it. There is now talk of a very large military force being sent, but I hope it may be unnecessary.

I will go to London on Tuesday and hope I may have an opportunity of seeing you. I have had a very difficult and anxious time.

Carson returned to London as he had planned, conscious that he had won the first round in the contest. A few days later he was the principal guest speaker at a dinner of the Junior Imperial League, at which Lord Castlereagh was in the chair. He told his audience he was glad to be able to attend "through the somewhat belated and reluctant consent of Mr. Winston Churchill." He went on to say that he hoped Mr. Churchill's visit to Belfast would prove peaceful, and his earnest wish was, "now Mr. Churchill had seen it was best to pursue Nationalist aspirations in Nationalist quarters he would meet with that respectful admiration from his Nationalist friends of which no one would in the least wish to deprive him."

To Lady Londonderry

3 Dr. Johnson's Buildings, The Temple. [*February* 5] I have been in bed with a bad cold the last two days but am much better. I should not have gone to the Junior Imperial League dinner, but I did not like to disappoint them. Castlereagh was an excellent chairman and we had a very enthusiastic dinner. I think the Juniors enjoyed themselves.

I have not seen many people since I came over, but any I have seen highly approve all the Ulster Council did and the letter in reply to C[hurchill].

I hope the Council will pass the resolution today and that our friends will try and have all disturbance avoided.

I do not suppose I will be required in Belfast at present. I have taken some work here, but of course if necessary I must return it . . .

I did enjoy my visit to Mt. Stewart, tho' I felt anxious all the time . . .

On the same day as this letter was written, the Standing Committee of the Ulster Unionist Council passed a resolution, moved by Colonel Wallace, the most influential of the local Orangemen, which strongly urged all Unionists, in view of the Ulster Hall victory, "to abstain from any interference with the meeting at the Celtic football ground, and to do everything in their power to avoid any action that might lead to any disturbance." The Resolution was circulated to all Orange Lodges and Unionist Clubs in Belfast and the neighbouring districts, with urgent injunctions to the officers to bring it to the notice of all members; it was also prominently displayed on hoardings in the city. It was expected that many thousands of people might come into Belfast from outside. This was to be a crucial test of discipline. Many people still remembered the terrible Belfast riots of 1886, and the Unionist leaders were not yet so influential with the rank-and-file of the movement as they afterwards became. Indeed the Orange Lodges were the only elements subject to any real discipline, and although seven-eighths, at least, of the volunteers belonged to them, they represented a smaller section of the population than was generally supposed in England, where all Ulster Protestants tended to be lumped together indiscriminately as Orangemen. The best guarantee of order, however, lay in the decision of Carson and the other leaders to be at hand while the meeting was taking place. Carson, therefore, returned his briefs and crossed to Belfast, where, joined by Londonderry, Craig and others, he remained throughout the day.

Meanwhile the Government, determined on taking no chances, had drafted strong military reinforcements to the area. Five infantry regiments, a cavalry squadron and a detachment of Royal Engineers were already in the city, through which they had marched to their barracks watched by curious but not unfriendly crowds. Fortunately the troops had nothing serious to do on the day of the Churchill meeting.

The First Lord of the Admiralty was accompanied to Belfast by his wife, secretary, and two Liberal M.P.s, including Mr. Hamar Greenwood, for whom fate had in store a much closer acquaintance with Irish disloyalty than was possible on the occasion of this fleeting visit. The party disembarked at Larne, as the First Lord's father had done a quarter of a century before, but instead of being welcomed like a king, Lord Randolph's son was greeted by a vociferous crowd shouting for Carson and singing the National Anthem. Hostile onlookers hissing and booing lined the route as he drove from the Midland Railway Station in Belfast to the Grand Central Hotel, but they made no attempt to interfere with his progress. But on his leaving the hotel in the early afternoon for the Celtic football ground a more ominous incident occurred. Royal Avenue, through which he had to drive, was now densely packed with people. As the car moved slowly along, men thrust their heads in, shaking their fists and muttering fearful imprecations. At one moment, two of the car's wheels left the ground, but whether this arose from a deliberate attempt to overturn the vehicle or merely from the involuntary pressure of the throng against its side is not clear. There is no doubt, however, that it was the most critical moment of his critical visit. It was said afterwards by many who witnessed the scene that, had it not been for the fact that Mrs. Churchill was also a passenger, the car might have been smashed and the Minister seriously if not fatally injured, before the police and military could have got through to his assistance. As things turned out, Mr. Churchill, who has never been lacking in courage, did not flinch, and no harm befell him.

The moment he entered the Nationalist quarter of the city, the atmosphere completely changed. Grotesque effigies of himself and Redmond were replaced by equally unflattering representations of Carson and Londonderry, while groans gave way to cheers, and the people crowded round to shake him by the hand. Arrived at the Celtic football ground, he duly held his meeting and addressed an audience of several thousand Nationalists, many of whom had come by special train from Dublin, in a speech which Carson described a few days later as "full of eloquent platitudes" and which certainly did little to satisfy the demand for information about the Home Rule Bill which the Government planned to introduce in the coming session of Parliament. He spoke in heavy rain, some of which found its way into the tent. At the conclusion of the meeting he did not return by the way he had come, since the police considered it safer for him to proceed to the railway station by a devious route through back streets. Nor did he wait there for the boat train by which he had arranged to travel, but was hastily despatched to Larne by a 'special' before it was generally known that he had passed the city boundaries. However, his departure, though somewhat resembling that of 'the thief in the night' of whom his father had bidden the Ulster people beware, did not pass entirely unnoticed. Some Unionist dockers and others who were hanging about the quayside at Larne seized the opportunity provided by his appearance on the gangway to hurl some rotten fish at him as he boarded the vessel which was to carry him away from such unfriendly and inhospitable shores.

Later the same evening Carson appeared on the balcony of the Ulster Club in Belfast, in response to the long continued cheering of the crowds outside when they discovered that he was within, and congratulated the assembled citizens on the magnificent self-restraint which they had shown during the day. He then advised them all to go home quietly, and the crowds thereupon dispersed. Before leaving the club Carson sat down and wrote to the Secretary of the Ulster Unionist Council, congratulating him and "all our friends" on the "very satisfactory and peaceful termination" of the day's proceedings. "In the difficult times that are ahead," he wrote, "it is essential that any action which may be necessary from time to time shall be fully organized and disciplined, and that under no circumstances shall peace and order be thoughtlessly and wantonly disturbed. We have a splendid cause to fight for, and our friends may feel certain that we will shrink from no organized action which may at any time be necessary."

CHAPTER NINE

The Ulster Crisis

I

A FEW days after Mr. Churchill's meeting in Belfast a new session of Parliament was opened. There was a ferment of speculation as to the terms of the new Home Rule Bill for Ireland, but no details were forthcoming on the part of the Government. "Wait and see," said Mr. Asquith in a characteristic phrase. As it was thought that the measure would be introduced before Easter, Carson and his Irish Unionist colleagues arranged for a monster demonstration to take place in Belfast during the recess. This would serve as a counter-blast to the Churchill fiasco and at the same time as a welcome to Bonar Law, who had consented to come over.

Meanwhile Carson on his doctor's advice paid another visit to Baden-Baden.

To Lady Londonderry

Dr. Dengler's Sanatorium, Baden-Baden [*February–March*, 1912]. I felt so sad coming away yesterday as you know I hate leaving *everything*, and it is so miserable here. However I want to be fit for '*the*' *Fight* and mean to do it with all my heart if I can . . .

I do not remember any time when politics were so interesting and it is a ray of consolation that (I think) English common sense is again asserting itself. It is impossible to believe that everything great and tending to greatness is going to be wiped out in an old valiant country like England. I should not wonder if there is a great re-action even amongst the poorer people and that they would realize that a body politic is or ought and must be a harmonious whole or it will cease to exist. How I *long* to see Home Rule defeated—it is, I think, a passion with me as I hate the degradation of Ireland being turned into a province, and our own splendid folk being put under in the race for progress . . .

I hope everyone will be very bitter this session. I cannot bear the hypocrisy of so called political toleration. I would make it as hot as h—— on every occasion, socially or politically, for the demagogues. Let them have the gallery and let us have our own friends!

I do not know how I will get through the time here, but I daresay that is part of the cure . . .

To help him to while away the time in this enforced idleness, Lady Londonderry sent him the biography of the Duke of Wellington by Sir Herbert Maxwell, which had just been published.

Baden-Baden. Friday [*March* 8]. Thank you so much for the book; it arrived last evening and I spent the evening reading it. The Duke was a rare instance of a man insisting on his own opinions without any dramatic attempt to force them on the mob. I imagine he thought too little of his own judgment to wish to enforce it on others, but I wish he was in full vigour today.

Today is beautiful here, sunny and crisp. I had a short walk at 8 o'clock this morning in the woods. I hope I will be able to stay some time as it is so quiet and restful and the doctor here is so good for anything dyspeptic or nervous. He says I am better when I was last here and have gained in weight. So perhaps I will get all right . . .

Baden-Baden. March 12. I hope your interview with B[onar] L[aw] was satisfactory. I think there is much power of development in him and my test of his ability is that I never heard him make a bad speech. He certainly has great difficulties ahead if we are to come into power, and to guide the evolution of events at present in the interests of the body politic will take a really great man . . .

Every day I feel greater contempt for Asquith. He has so many chances of showing himself great, just as he had at the time of the naval scare, and he will not do so. What a backing he would have of all reasonable men! I imagine he suffers from indolence and also from his consciousness of his lack of means should he have to retire.

It is in this respect that the modern development makes men weak. I suppose there is no one in the Cabinet to whom his loss of salary is not a question of importance. Although I should be sorry to suggest that they are all consciously affected by this consideration, still it does I fear subconsciously influence men's judgment.

To my mind it is extraordinary how men imagine that being in high office makes them great unless they show themselves such. It is the same from a king downwards, and I am sure the higher the office the greater the object of contempt in the holder unless he can shew himself a man.

Well, it is very lonely here. I have not spoken to a soul except the doctor, but the walks are beautiful in the woods and the weather fine. I go out every morning for a little at 8 o'clock and I certainly feel better. Still I think my energy is less than it was and, if Home Rule was killed, I should be glad to take it easy. I have always walked up the hill with the collar hurting me. How I wish I had done or could have done more! That you will understand . . .

Baden-Baden. Friday [*March* 22] . . . I don't know what happened yesterday in the House, but I was glad our party determined to oppose the 2nd Reading of the Wage Bill, even though it may be misunderstood by some people, and also that A.J.B. moved the rejection.* As far as I can see, there will soon be no protection for property in England at all, and it would be far better to invest money in America where they have a steady constitution and a strong executive.

I think Winston was unnecessarily offensive and provocative to Germany, and that is the feeling in Germany. But they have lots of troubles here too and socialism, I gather, is stronger here than in England.

I will be so glad to get home again and hope all this rotten time will have been of some use . . .

Everything seems quite advanced for the Belfast meeting. I do pray we may have a fine day and that the railways may be able to carry the people.

I wonder how the Government really stand in the country. The election, unless we got in by a large majority, would be fatal and put us back further than ever from real power. But it would be a real pleasure to see this Government of feebleness and funk sent about their business—but the question is what then?

Nothing interesting here to tell you. The great question is the minimum weight, not the minimum wage. How I get through the day I really don't know . . .

A week later Carson returned to London, only to develop a sore throat and cough, which, he complained, kept him awake at night and made him "a miserable being" during the day. He was also concerned to see that Annette had greatly failed in health during his absence.

To Lady Londonderry

5 *Eaton Place, S.W. March* 27 . . . I do my best to 'buck up', but I have many trials and I am not of a temperament which can easily discard them.

My wife suddenly asked me on Saturday, "How is Lady L?" I said you were in Ireland, and she said, "You ought to go there for a change." I thought her better but in the evening she lapsed away and has since not been so well and indeed sometimes almost comatose . . .

I dine tonight with Craig to meet Lord Roberts and I hope something may come of it. This is very private. I have made up my mind to recommend very drastic action in Ulster during this year

* The Coal Mines (Minimum Wage) Bill, which provided for minimum wages for coal miners to be fixed by district boards, was the immediate result of a coal strike, which had affected other industries and had involved two millions of workers being idle. It was opposed by Balfour and the Conservatives on the ground that it was an emergency measure and had been dictated by the use of a weapon of power which, 'if allowed unlimited sway, would absolutely destroy society, and from which the poor and unemployed remote from the scene of the struggle would suffer most'. The 2nd reading was carried by 348 to 225.

and also in the House when the H[ome] R[ule] Bill is on. There is a growing feeling that we do not mean business. I certainly think this is the critical year and am prepared for any risks.

I saw B[onar] L[aw] yesterday. He is torn asunder between extremes on both sides. I am bound to say I think anyone who breaks away from the agreement [to support him] is putting the party in grave peril.

I think the British League to help Ulster is a good move and will be a great success. Perhaps H.M. will pay some attention to them if he does not to us. I am told he is saturated with the idea of 'constitutionalism' which he translates into doing everything his P.M. tells him. What a good King!

The mass meeting which at Carson's instigation had been organised by Craig for the purpose of introducing Bonar Law to the Ulster people took place on April 9, 1912, in the Show Grounds of the Royal Agricultural Society at Balmoral, a suburb of Belfast. It was a truly formidable demonstration, outdoing in splendour and magnitude that held at Craigavon in the previous September. Over 100,000 people were present. Bonar Law, who was accompanied by about seventy Members of Parliament representing English and Scottish constituencies, was amazed at the enthusiasm and the warmth with which he was greeted. "If this is how you treat your friends," he said, "I am glad I am not your enemy." It took the procession of Ulster Volunteers three hours, marching four abreast, to pass the saluting base, where Bonar Law, Carson, Lord Londonderry and Walter Long stood to take the salute, before proceeding to the stand which held the principal platform for the delivery of the speeches. There the chair was taken by Carson, in the absence through illness of the Duke of Abercorn.

Bonar Law warned his audience that the Ministerial majority in the House of Commons, "now cemented by £400 a year", could not be broken up, and that it would have its own way with the Home Rule Bill. "You must trust in yourselves," he told his listeners, calling to mind the historic siege of Londonderry. "Once again you hold the pass, the pass for the Empire. You are a besieged city. The timid have left you; your Lundys have betrayed you; but you have closed your gates. The Government have erected by their Parliament Act a boom against you to shut you off from the help of the British people. You will burst that boom. That help will come, and when the crisis is over men will say to you in words not unlike those used by Pitt—you have saved yourselves by your exertions and you will save the Empire by your example."

In the centre of the ground was a signalling tower with a flagstaff ninety feet high, on which a Union Jack, measuring forty-eight feet by twenty-five and said to be the largest ever woven, was broken at the moment when the Resolution against Home Rule was put to the meeting. Another dramatic moment occurred when the Leader of the Irish Unionists and the Leader of the whole Unionist Party each grasped the other's hand in view of the assembled multitude, thus publicly ratifying the compact which they had made on the eve of battle.

Within forty-eight hours of the Balmoral demonstration the Liberal Prime Minister moved for leave to bring in the third Home Rule Bill. It provided the same safeguards and reservations as had been contained in the previous Bills. It proposed to set up an Irish Parliament of two houses, with an Executive responsible to it. Taxation powers, broadly speaking, were to remain at Westminster as before, although the Lower House in Dublin was permitted to levy ten per cent on or off existing duties. Carson immediately stated the case for Ulster in a powerful speech which made it clear that, while the whole Bill would be opposed clause by clause by him and his supporters, it was the setting up of a Parliament in Dublin with an Executive responsible to it that would be most strenuously opposed. He was in considerable pain when speaking in the House and had to go home immediately afterwards.

To Lady Londonderry

5 *Eaton Place, S.W. Sunday* [*April* 14] . . . I have had a bad time with this painful neuralgia and have been in bed almost ever since I came back.

The whole proceedings at Balmoral seem like a dream—it was the most thrilling experience I ever had or will have. But it has a demoralising effect in making me think of the criminal folly of decadent England in tampering with such a splendid people for the sake of throwing a sop to her implacable foes. B[onar] L[aw] was astounded at the magnitude of the Demonstration and it surpassed all he had imagined or expected. He is really very modest, and I don't think the evanescent nature of popular applause exhilarates him, but he is very real and genuine and has plenty of courage.

I am pleased you liked my speech on Thursday [on the Home Rule Bill], though if I had been well and able to work at it on Wednesday, I think I could have done better—at all events more to my own satisfaction. I was glad Castlereagh got in so early, but sorry I was not there as I had to go to bed with the pain.

The Bill seems to me to create no enthusiasm nor on the other hand any great excitement. There seemed to be some unreality in the situation which I don't fathom, but I imagine no one thinks the Bill can become law without being submitted to the electors.

I wish we could get an opportunity, a real and genuine one, of challenging the Government in Ulster—I mean by definite action. Nothing else will definitely bring home the feeling to them.

The opportunity for which Carson longed was to come, but not for many months yet. Meanwhile, there were many dangers to be countered, difficulties to be overcome, and preparations to be made for the vital struggle which clearly lay ahead.

2

Under the influence of Mr. Redmond's oratory the Nationalist Convention in Dublin, which met on April 23, accepted the new Home Rule measure with enthusiasm, in spite of some latent dissatisfaction with its financial clauses. On May 19 the second reading was carried by 101 combined Liberal, Labour and Nationalist votes. Just over three weeks later, on June 11, the Committee stage opened. On that date an amendment was down for debate in the name of a Liberal back-bencher, the Hon. T. G. R. Agar-Robartes, who sat for the St. Austell Division of Cornwall. This amendment proposed to exclude four of the nine Ulster counties—Antrim, Armagh, Londonderry and Down—from the jurisdiction of the Dublin Parliament, on the grounds of the fundamental division between the Protestants and Catholics in the island. "Orange bitters and Irish whisky will not mix," said Mr. Agar-Robartes.

This amendment was one which obviously required very careful consideration on the part of the Ulster Members, and they accordingly met at Londonderry House before the opening of the debate in the Commons. If they supported it, their enemies would undoubtedly represent their action as a desertion of all the Irish Loyalists outside the four counties named in the amendment. On the other hand, the Ulster Unionist policy, as laid down at Craigavon, was, in the event of Home Rule being carried, to take over the Government 'of those districts which they could control.' Consequently if the Ulster Members opposed the amendment and after the passing of the Bill incorporating the amendment an attempt was made to set up an Ulster Provisional Government, the Ulster Unionists would be accused of fighting for something which they had previously been offered by legislation. For this reason Carson and the Ulster Members decided to support the amendment, believing as they did that, if it came to the worst, they could be of more use to the Southern Unionists outside a Dublin Parliament than as members of it when they would be in a hopeless minority.

That this view was shared by the Southern Unionists was apparent from the ensuing debate. As one of them, Mr. Walter Guinness, later Lord Moyne, put it, "For Ulster to refuse this salvation could not be to help her friends, but would merely be taking up an attitude of mock heroics . . . It would merely be a dog-in-the-manger policy for us who live outside Ulster to grudge relief to our co-religionists because we could not share it. Such self-denial on their part would in no way help our compatriots in the North. We know perfectly well that Ulster fully shares our detestation of the Bill from a wider point of view than her own interests."

The Government spokesmen, who had no intention of accepting the amendment any more than the Redmondites, did their best to drive a wedge between the two sections of Irish Unionists. Even Sir John Simon, the Solicitor-General, taunted his old master with the charge of desertion. "Is it desertion? I do not agree," replied Carson. "Let me say for myself, and in no egotistical way, that as a Dublin man—the Solicitor-General was very anxious to know my pedigree—I should be the very last, with all my relatives living in the south and west of Ireland, and in various places, who would for one moment consent to what I believe would be in the slightest degree a desertion of any part of Ireland."

After a three-day debate Mr. Agar-Robartes's amendment was defeated, but only by sixty-nine, which indicated a certain falling away in Government support. Carson and his friends were not dissatisfied with this result. They had avoided what was an obvious snare, and they could now go forward with their plans to challenge the Government in the knowledge that they had offered to accept a settlement.

At the same time Carson regarded the Government's action over the amendment as a declaration of war against Ulster, their solution being to drive the Ulster people out of a community with which they were satisfied into a community which they detested. "We will accept the declaration of war," he said in the Albert Hall on June 14. "We are not altogether unprepared. I think it is time we should take a step forward in our campaign, and I will recommend that to be done."

Perhaps the most impressive moment at the Balmoral demonstration had been when the assembled masses repeated after Carson the words in which their Leader had abjured the detested measure—"We will not have Home Rule." This suggested to some of the leading Ulster Unionists a further demonstration or series of demonstrations in which the people might bind themselves to resist Home Rule under a solemn oath. Carson was attracted by the idea and asked James Craig to devise a suitable form of words.

Craig got his cue when sitting one day in the library of the Constitutional Club in London. He was joined by Mr. B. W. D. Montgomery, the secretary of the Ulster Club in Belfast, who asked him what he was doing. "Trying to draft an oath for our people at home," replied Craig, "and it's no easy matter to get at what will suit." "You couldn't do better than take the old Scottish Covenant," said Montgomery. "It's a fine old document full of grand phrases, and thoroughly characteristic of the Ulster tone of mind at this day." Together the two men took down from the library shelves a History of Scotland, which contained the text of the celebrated Solemn League and Covenant that by a strange coincidence, had been drawn up in 1581 by a certain John Craig. This declaration consequently served as a model and inspiration for the document which Craig drafted, with the assistance of various friends, and which was eventually adopted by the Ulster Unionist Council.

Meanwhile, Carson began a vigorous speaking campaign in the country, later crossing over to Belfast, where he enlisted the support of the Protestant working men in the shipyards and other industries. The eventual outcome was the formation of the Ulster Unionist-Labour Association, "the only true democracy in Ireland", Carson called it. In its inception this organisation owed much to the foresight and energy of Mr. Thomas Andrews's son, Mr. John Miller Andrews, a local industrialist, who was one day to succeed Craig as Prime Minister of Northern Ireland. On this occasion Carson stayed with Craig and his wife. "How kind you have been to me at Craigavon I cannot express," he wrote to Mrs. Craig after he had returned to England. "I can only feel it. I really enjoyed myself immensely. As for James, I don't know what 'the cause' would do without him and I certainly could not go on. But he hates being praised and thinks too deeply, as I do, to mind any trouble."

In spite of an encouraging speech from Bonar Law at Blenheim, the seat of the Duke of Marlborough, on July 29, in which the Conservative Leader said he imagined that there was no length of resistance to which Ulster would go which he and the overwhelming majority of the British people would not be ready to support, Carson was far from satisfied with the atmosphere he found on his return from Belfast. He was also perturbed about Annette's health. She now had two nurses with her in the house at Rottingdean.

To Lady Londonderry

Carlton Club. August 13 [1912]. I am going away to Homburg tonight for a change. I hate going but I suppose one cannot always stick at home.

The Ulster campaign was all I could desire, but it was a great effort to make so many speeches.

It is certainly a strange contrast to come back to the air of apathy and unreality in England, leaving behind those who are devoting all their time to preparedness, and coming into the world where selfishness and amusement are the only prevailing features. No one cares here and everyone does there—that is the whole difference. But the next few months will bring us all into the open and we will see where sacrifice is really intended.

. . . Articles like that in *The Spectator* as to the King are very sickening. Apparently if the King was asked to sign a bill for the abolition of the Monarchy he must as a constitutional sovereign obey! If he did the obvious bold thing, he would not let the matter come to exercise of veto at all but call on his P.M. to relieve him of an impossible situation. Now his name will be dragged down (whatever happens about the veto) into the political mire. I grow daily more and more bitter and what I have seen in Ulster adds to it.

My first engagement will be at Durham on my return from the continent and so that will give me the pleasure of seeing you. But really what the use of speaking is I don't know. Only it is the traditional method of doing nothing and is quite out of date for the present crisis . . .

I went to Rottingdean for the week end, but the tragedy of always dining and lunching with nurses is too great a strain!

Villa Henriette, Bad Homburg. August 16. . . . I have been reading Winston's fulminations and it makes me angry to know how little Englishmen appreciate the real feelings of the North of Ireland. When the abandonment of a nation is compared with a dock strike, all sense of proportion seems to have vanished. We will have a stormy time in front of us and the weak kneed must fall out of the ranks—that is all! . . .

I try to get strong and well only that I may fight with all the power and resource which God has given me. Thank goodness I fear nothing and I only want to save our people . . .

Bad Homburg. August 21 . . . We have had very bad weather nearly all the time but I just laze about and do nothing and it agrees with me . . .

I don't think there is anyone here who would be of interest to you. The place becomes more German and less English every year. The King came and the Emperor to unveil a monument just opposite my rooms here, so I had a good view of him . . . It was a very funny performance.

I have not been following the papers much so I have not seen anything but passing references to Lloyd George and Winston, but I expect they are working together. It makes me very sick that our destinies should be in the hands of such profligate politicians and that Sir E. Grey and Asquith should allow these things to go on . . .

Although there was no one in Homburg whom Carson thought was likely to interest Lady Londonderry, there was someone there whose acquaintance he made at this time and who was in the course of time to interest him very deeply. This was a charming young Englishwoman, Miss Ruby Frewen, daughter of Colonel Stephen Frewen of Charlton Musgrove, Somerset. She was staying in a villa which had been taken for the season by Mrs. Sophie Hall-Walker, later Lady Wavertree. They were never formally introduced to each other, but met casually whilst watching a game of tennis at the Tennis Club. Carson thought little of the meeting at the time, as he had much else on his mind.

It was while he was in Homburg that Carson received from James Craig the completed draft of the Covenant, together with the relevant Resolution of the Ulster Unionist Council. This document read as follows:

Ulster's Solemn League and Covenant

Being convinced in our consciences that Home Rule would be disastrous to the material well-being of Ulster as well as the whole of Ireland, subversive of our civil and religious freedom, destructive of our citizenship, and perilous to the unity of the Empire, we, whose names are underwritten, men of Ulster, loyal subjects of His Gracious Majesty, King George V, humbly relying on the God whom our fathers in days of stress and trial confidently trusted, do hereby pledge ourselves in solemn Covenant throughout this our time of threatened calamity to stand by one another in defending for ourselves and our children our cherished position of equal citizenship in the United Kingdom, and in using all means which may be found necessary to defeat the present conspiracy to set up a Home Rule Parliament in Ireland. And in the event of such a Parliament being forced upon us we further solemnly and mutually pledge ourselves to refuse to recognise its authority. In sure confidence that God will defend the right we hereto subscribe our names. And further, we individually declare that we have not already signed this Covenant. God Save the King.

It was arranged that the Covenant should be signed by all Ulster Unionists, as the climax to series of mass meetings throughout the province, on Saturday, September 28, the date to be designated 'Ulster Day'. Carson welcomed the declaration, not only for its contents, but also it would serve to relieve popular feelings, which desired some medium of expression. There had already been trouble in the shipyards, where Protestant workers, acting under great provocation, had attacked some of their Catholic workmates.

To James Craig

Bad Homburg. August 21. I would not alter a word in the declaration which I consider excellent. I also agree with what the Council have resolved about Northern Ireland. I do not know whether it is feasible, but I think if 'Ulster Day' could wind up with bonfires all through the country it would be impressive and create enthusiasm.

I am very much distressed about the men who are being prosecuted for the rows in the shipyards. Do you think they or their families ought to be assisted in any way? You know how much I feel about others suffering when I don't, and they received great provocation. Please think about this.

I don't know what we would do without you.

Your platform for Belfast is splendid. I hope as many as possible of the working men's representatives will get admission . . .

Carson returned to England at the end of August, feeling depressed, as he so often did, and perturbed by the prospect of the exhausting programme in front of him. Nor were his spirits improved by a harrowing session with the dentist, which obliged him to postpone his visit to Durham.

To Lady Londonderry

Northgate House, Rottingdean. September 7 . . . I am sorry I cannot manage a visit to Wynyard at present. I have been all the week with the dentist and suffering a lot!

On Friday I go to Ireland to stay with Ronald McNeill before commencing the campaign. I wish it was over as I find it so difficult to make speeches night after night . . .

I stayed a night with Bonar Law on my way home. He is full of fight and pluck. I think he is the most modest man I have ever met.

All here is depressing, though my wife progresses slowly, I think. But I find it hard to realize and get accustomed to her being an invalid . . .

CRAIGAVON, SEPTEMBER 23, 1911.

Back row, left to right: Earl of Leitrim; Mr. C. Scott Dickson, K.C., M.P.; Viscount Templetown, President of the Unionist Clubs of Ireland; Sir John Lonsdale, Bt., M.P., Hon. Secretary of the Irish Unionist Parliamentary Party.

Sitting, left to right: Lady Carson; Captain James Craig, M.P.; Sir Edward Carson, K.C., M.P.; Mrs. Craig.

From a photograph in the possession of the Hon. Mrs. Walter Carson.

SIR EDWARD CARSON SIGNING THE ULSTER COVENANT IN THE CITY HALL, BELFAST, SEPTEMBER 28, 1912.

Lord Londonderry is standing on the left of the picture.

Ronald McNeill, later Lord Cushendun, was an Ulster Unionist, and the future historian of the movement.* His home was in County Antrim, but he represented an English constituency in the House of Commons, where he was shortly to create a sensation by hurling a book during one of the Home Rule debates at the head of Mr. Winston Churchill. Carson's visit to him came none too soon. On the same day as he landed in Belfast a serious riot occurred at a football match which was being played between two teams of rival religious creeds at the Celtic ground, the scene of Mr. Churchill's ill-fated meeting in the previous February. This unfortunate incident, although he saw nothing of it himself, convinced Carson that a diversion was more than ever necessary.

3

The campaign which was designed to culminate in the signing of the Covenant opened in Enniskillen, the county town of Fermanagh, on September 18. The resolution put to the meeting there, and in every other district which the Unionist Leader visited, was a reaffirmation of the old battle-cry: 'We will not have Home Rule'. As Carson and his party were leaving by train from Belfast, the ticket collector who punched the Leader's ticket whispered to him: "Tell the stationmaster at Clones, Sir Edward, that we won't have it." Clones was a town of Nationalist complexion in County Monaghan, through which the train was due to pass and where it appears that this misguided official was of the prevailing political colour. At a huge open-air meeting held on Portrea Hill outside the town on the banks of Lough Erne, 40,000 people turned out to hear Carson and approve the anti-Home Rule resolution. "I declare here before you in the most solemn way that if this unprovoked and wicked attack is allowed to go on and this Bill to become law," he told them, "it is not only the right but a duty to prepare to resist it."

Back at Craigavon next day, which he made his headquarters for this momentous visit, Carson attended a meeting of the Ulster Unionist Council's Standing Committee, specially convened there for the purpose of ratifying the Covenant. The Committee, standing in a group outside the door leading from the arcade at Craigavon to

* His book, *Ulster's Stand for Union* (1922), contains an admirable account of the struggle against Home Rule.

the tennis-lawn, listened while their leader read the Covenant aloud from a stone step.* A few days later, on September 23, being the first anniversary of the original Craigavon demonstration, the Covenant was approved at a mass gathering of the Council delegates in the Old Town Hall in Belfast. "How often have I thought over this Covenant," he told the assembled delegates. "How many hours have I spent before it was published in counting the cost that may result! How many times have I thought of what it may mean to all we care about here! Does any man believe that I lightly took this matter in hand without considering with my colleagues all that it may mean either in the distant or the not too distant future? No, it is the gravest matter in all the grave matters in the various offices I have held that I have ever had to consider. But the more I consider it, the more I believe it to be right. I at all events am prepared to go to the end." Upon these words the whole company rose to its feet and with one voice shouted: "We will back you." Undeterred by this ovation Carson went on to give the delegates, "responsible men from every district in Ulster," an important piece of advice. "It is your duty, when you go back to your various districts," he told them, "to warn your people who trust you that, in entering into this solemn obligation, they are entering into a matter which, whatever may happen in the future, is the most serious matter that has ever confronted them in the course of their lives."

The speaking tour, on which Carson was accompanied by several House of Commons colleagues, including Admiral Lord Charles Beresford, Lord Castlereagh, Lord Hugh Cecil, Mr. Ronald McNeill and Mr. F. E. Smith, reached its climax at a huge meeting held in Belfast's historic Ulster Hall on the eve of the signing of the Covenant. McNeill subsequently expressed the opinion that Carson never spoke better than on this tour of the province, and this was borne out by other observers. He was fresh, vigorous and picturesque, and never a phrase passed his lips which did not tell. At the Ulster Hall meeting, though feeling much fatigued, he was particularly effective. "We will take deliberately a step forward, not in defiance but in defence," he declared, "and the Covenant which we will most willingly sign tomorrow will be a great step forward, in no spirit of aggression, in no spirit of ascendancy, but with a full knowledge that, if necessary, you and I—you trusting me, and I trusting you—will follow out everything that this Covenant means to the very end, whatever the consequences." At a final demon-

* This now bears an inscription recording the event.

stration which took place in the streets outside the Hall, now filled with cheering crowds, Carson received from Colonel Wallace, head of the Belfast Orangemen, a faded yellow silk banner, with the cross of St. George in the corner, which had been carried before King William III at the Battle of the Boyne. Holding it aloft in view of all, the Unionist Leader exclaimed: "May this flag ever float over a people that can boast of civil and religious liberty."

Next day—Saturday, September 28—was Ulster Day. It was regarded throughout the province as a day of solemn observance. The proceedings in Belfast began with a religious service in the Ulster Hall, outside which the onlookers, who had cheered Carson so enthusiastically the night before, now stood with heads bared in respectful silence as he passed within. The service, conducted jointly by Church of Ireland, Methodist and Presbyterian Ministers and thus reflecting complete harmony between the three Protestant denominations, ended about noon. From the Ulster Hall Carson then proceeded with his colleagues on foot to the City Hall near-by, where the ceremonial signing was to take place. The Leader was escorted by a guard of honour consisting of representatives of the Belfast Unionist Clubs and Orange Lodges, carrying the Boyne banner.

Arrived at the City Hall, generally regarded as Belfast's most imposing building, Carson was received by the Lord Mayor, Sir William McMordie, M.P., and members of the corporation wearing their scarlet robes of office, and by the various other civic bodies. Spread out on a large table, draped with a Union Jack in the middle of the entrance hall, was the first sheet of the Covenant ready for the Leader and others to sign. Then, as the sun streamed through the stained-glass window on the stairway, Carson picked up the silver pen which had been presented to him for the occasion. Behind him and around him stood many men of local mark and substance, industrialists, politicians, ministers of religion, professional men, merchants, shopkeepers and many humbler folk, stretching along the corridors and spilling into the gardens and streets outside. Through the open door could be seen a vast forest of heads, of seemingly endless length, each of whom was waiting to play his part in the historic ceremony which, for good or evil, must influence their lives and destinies.

As the Press cameras clicked to record the scene, Carson bent forward and wrote his signature on the sheet before him. When he had done so, he handed the silver pen to Lord Londonderry, who did likewise. His action was followed by the Moderator of the General Assembly, the Bishop of Down, the Dean of Belfast, the General Secretary of the Presbyterian Church, the ex-Chairman of the Congregational Union, the President of the Methodist Conference, Lord Castlereagh and James Chambers, M.P. for South Belfast. This completed the first sheet. When the rest of the company present had attached their signature to other sheets, the general public was admitted to the building.

Arrangements had been made, by placing lines of desks in all the corridors, for over 500 persons to sign the Covenant simultaneously. This process went on for the remainder of the day, concluding at 11 o'clock that night, by which time over 80,000 people had subscribed their names to the Covenant. A number did so with their own blood. The women signed a similar declaration of support. Meanwhile in other parts of Ireland and also in Great Britain similar scenes were enacted, so that in the result upwards of half a million Ulster men and women gave their adherence to the policy of which the Solemn League and Covenant was the pledge.* To every signatory at the same time was given a copy of the document printed on parchment, to be kept in memory of the occasion. This was destined to hang in an honoured place in many an Ulster home and to become its owner's most treasured possession.

The people were still streaming into the City Hall when Carson and the other visitors made their way through further dense and wildly cheering crowds to the quayside, there to embark for Liverpool. For Carson it meant more speeches, from the window of the Ulster Club, outside the dock gates and on the deck of the steamer, appropriately named *The Patriotic*, where his familiar features were illumined by a powerful searchlight. His send-off was tremendous. Nothing like it had ever been known before. "Don't leave us," they shouted. "You mustn't leave us." Carson promised that he would come back, "whether the occasion be for peace—I prefer it—or to fight, and if it be to fight, I shall not shrink." He added characteristically: "One thing I feel perfectly confident is that today we have taken a step which has put our enemies into such a state of difficulty that they are wondering what on earth they are going to do." As the ship moved away from the moorings into the channel, the crowd on shore sang 'Rule Britannia' and 'Auld Lang Syne', and

* In Ulster 218,206 men and 228,991 women signed; in the rest of Ireland and Great Britain 19,162 and 5,055 women. Total: 471,414 men and women. See *Annual Register*, 1911, at p. 211.

finally as the vessel disappeared into the night, 'God Save the King'. In the distance the bonfires could be seen blazing from the surrounding hills, and the firing of rockets. It was an impressive sight, and one which its central figure could never forget as long as he lived.

At the Prince's Landing Stage in Liverpool, Carson was greeted by another crowd singing 'Oh, God our Help in Ages Past'—for it was Sunday morning—as the steamer made fast in the Mersey. "I shake hands with you across the sea," he said to Alderman Salvidge, the Lord Mayor, as he stepped ashore with F. E. Smith. "I bring a message from the democracy of Belfast to the democracy of Liverpool. All that they ask is to be allowed to stay with you, and I do not think you will permit them to be driven out." Next day there were more meetings, including a monster demonstration in Shiel Park, attended by many thousands of working men from the city and its neighbourhood. It was on this occasion that F. E. Smith, who was of course on his home ground, publicly assured Carson that if it came to a fight between Ulster and the Irish Nationalists, "we will undertake to give you three ships that will take over 10,000 young men of Liverpool."

From Liverpool Carson went on to Glasgow, where he ended his campaign amid similar scenes of enthusiasm. He addressed a crowd of over 6,000 in an indoor meeting, where his reception was unprecedented. Time and again he was interrupted by cheering and waving of Union Jacks. Time and again he motioned the enthusiasts to sit down. At last came his peroration. In a few brief sentences he reminded those present that the men and women of Ulster were of the same flesh and blood as themselves, that they had always been loyal and faithful subjects of his Majesty the King, and that he would never believe that the men of Glasgow would allow their own kith and kin to be driven out of the Union. His voice, always sympathetic, seemed richer and deeper, no doubt owing to the strain of continual speaking, and its effect was to move many in the audience to tears. When he sat down, the entire assembly rose and cheered him for fully five minutes. Many of the audience were, of course, of Ulster stock or descent, which accounts for this amazing scene. Afterwards Carson told Lady Londonderry that it was the most magnificent and enthusiastic demonstration he had ever seen.

Two nights later he was back for a short rest in Rottingdean, and he found the whole village turned out to welcome him home. The villagers marched in a torchlight procession to Northgate House, where he was presented with an illuminated address on behalf of the local Conservative and Unionist Association. His wife and younger daughter Gladys were well enough to get up and attend this ceremony, which took place at the entrance to the house and was also witnessed by his other daughter Aileen and his sailor son Walter. He then said a few words, thanking the Rottingdean people for their many kindnesses to him during the twelve years he had been living there. "As you know, I came to Rottingdean not for politics," he said. "I came to it as a place I have learned to love, and where I might rest."

On October 5 he wrote to Lady Londonderry: "My wife is decidedly better and I hope may be strong enough to enjoy her life. She seems happier and less depressed. Gladys gives me great anxiety, but I am always hoping." In the same letter he reviewed the political campaign, which had just ended. "I think everything passed off without a hitch. I am especially pleased with the great good order and sobriety of the people. They are the finest I have ever seen. I never imagined the Covenant would be such a success both in Ireland and Great Britain."

On the same date he wrote to Dawson Bates, the Secretary of the Ulster Unionist Council, thanking him "and all our friends who helped to make the demonstration preceding Ulster Day and Ulster Day itself such a huge and magnificent success." At the same time he urged continued self-control and repeated his warning of the danger of isolated and unauthorised action. "We are now bound in solemn covenant each to the other," he wrote. "Let us each prove a worthy covenantor."

4

When Parliament reassembled for the autumn session a few days later, a shock awaited the Irish Unionist Party. The Prime Minister moved to apply a fixed time-table, under a 'guillotine' resolution, to the Home Rule Bill, within which its remaining stages had to be completed. The Government scheme was a mixture of the so-called 'compartment' and 'kangaroo' closure. For the Committee stage twenty-five days were allotted; for the Report, five; for the third reading, two. On any day in Committee the Chairman might arbitrarily select and pass over amendments. As Mr. Winston Churchill put it, "Those who talk of revolution ought to be prepared for the guillotine."

In the ensuing debate Mr. Bonar Law reasserted the proposition which he had previously argued on many occasions—that Home Rule in its present guise had never been submitted to the British electorate, and that that fact alone was full justification for Ulster's resolve to resist it. Carson, who also spoke, denounced the Government's subservience to the Nationalists, and declared that the whole object of the Bill was to get hold of Belfast and the northern counties to tax them. He also declared that the Government dared not prosecute him because they were afraid there might be riots. "I can only say this," he added, "I hate referring to a personal matter, and I only say it to leave it once and for ever—let no man suppose I am claiming immunity from anything to which the humblest man in the country is subject."

The 'guillotine' resolution was carried by the usual Government majority, and the procedure immediately came into operation. Carson had already described it as 'sheer tyranny', but he was determined to lose neither his head nor his temper and to stay in the House and fight the Bill to the last. "I fear we are in for a hard and stormy time," he told his faithful henchman Craig, "and the drastic closure of the Government shows how wise we are in Ulster to put no faith in them." His forebodings were only too true. During the next two months, when the Bill was in Committee, and during the later stages which concluded with the passing of the third reading on January 16, 1913, the 'guillotine' was applied with the result that, out of fifty-one clauses of the Bill, only six were fully and twenty-seven partly discussed. Not a single amendment put down by the Opposition was accepted by the Government. Thus, great sections of the Bill, involving important constitutional issues, were passed through the House of Commons without a word of discussion, though not without protest from Carson and others.

Parliament adjourned for an unusually short Christmas recess, only ten days, which Carson spent at Rottingdean. He found little change in Annette's condition. She had suffered a slight stroke earlier in the year, and though she had made some recovery at the time of Carson's return from Ulster after the signing of the Covenant, she was gradually losing ground again. In this time of domestic trouble Carson had the help and sympathy of two good friends, Lady Londonderry and Tommy Comyn-Platt. The latter was also assiduous in helping to raise funds for the Ulster Unionists in Great Britain and generally organising a panel of speakers.

To Lady Londonderry

Rottingdean, Xmas, 1912 . . . How kind and dear a friend you have been to me for so long I dare not say, but you know how I have always valued it . . .

We have such an overwhelming amount of work before us that I sometimes feel it will be impossible to cope with it, but that always adds to my determination which is some recompense. How I loathe and hate the apathy of the vast majority who shut their eyes and think everything is all right and no doubt often imagine they are the saviours of the community!

I am glad you saw B[onar] L[aw]. I think he understands all the difficulties, but he must be allowed to lead as he alone has all the strings in his hands. It would indeed be a disaster if he had to refuse to lead a divided party at this crisis. It is a great thing that he is animated only by his love of the country and is not 'on the make'.

We are quiet here as can be under the circumstances, but it is sad, sorrowful and heartbreaking, and no one knows what I suffer . . .

To T. Comyn-Platt

Rottingdean, Friday 27th [*December*]. Just a line to thank you for the souvenir which you so kindly sent me and especially for your affectionate letter. One wants good friends and true in these days and no one appreciates friendship more than I do. Thank you so much for all you say.

It is a trying time for me but we have been happy and quiet here for Xmas and I try to keep my mind off the distressing side of life . . .

I do not look forward to commencing work so soon again but it cannot be helped.

I hope we may bridge over all our difficulties. Patience is the essential. I am glad to see that all acknowledge the great worth of Bonar Law, even when they differ in methods . . .

The Commons met again three days later, and on New Year's Day Carson moved an amendment, in the Report stage of the Home Rule Bill, excluding 'the Province of Ulster' from the operation of the measure, in a speech which was described by Mr. Asquith as "very powerful and moving" and by Mr. Redmond as "serious and solemn." Carson had already given the Prime Minister public notice of his intention, which had the support of the Ulster Unionist Council's Standing Committee. He now made it clear that the Bill would be opposed as much as ever, even were it thus amended, but, this being probably the last occasion for considering the position of Ulster under its terms, he wanted to know if the Government were really bent on coercion. He warned Asquith that the Covenant would not be abandoned without force—but why should Ulster be forced out of the United Kingdom, of which she wished to remain a part, with full representation at Westminster and nowhere else? If there was to be exclusion from the Bill, it was better that the whole of Ulster should be excluded, and not selected portions of it as Mr. Agar-Robartes had proposed, and the Ulster Members by remaining in the Imperial Parliament would be better able to protect the Loyalists of the South and West. Moreover, he said: "They would have in Ireland itself an Imperial power and an Imperial force which could not be disregarded by the rest of Ireland."

But the amendment was a forlorn hope. Redmond and his followers would never agree to it. "Ireland for us is one entity," he said. Asquith was equally emphatic in rejecting it. "No Government," he said, "could allow so undemocratic a claim as that put forward by Ulster to veto Home Rule." Carson's motion was defeated by ninety-seven votes.

A fortnight later the Bill came up for the passage of its third reading. But Carson was not in his place on the Opposition Front Bench. He was at Rottingdean by his wife's bedside. "I grieve to say she seems to have lost much ground since last week," he told Lady Londonderry. "I do not think I can leave her any more unless she gets a change for the better. Oh, how I suffer with it all! But you are the kindest of friends and understand so well." He wrote to Bonar Law in a similar strain. "If it was possible I would have come up for a few hours," he assured the Conservative Leader on the eve of the third reading debate. "I am having a doctor from London this afternoon, but it is only to make me certain I have done all that is possible."

For several weeks poor Annette lay motionless from the effects of the stroke and, as Carson's sister Bella put it, "unable to raise her hand to brush a fly away." Carson cancelled all his engagements, never leaving the house for more than a few hours. On February 21 he wrote to Lady Londonderry: "I feel so miserable in having to tell you that my poor wife is growing weaker and with her high temperature the doctor thinks she can only live a few days more. It is difficult to dissolve partnership after thirty-four years and I feel utterly hopeless." She lingered on for another fortnight, the end coming at last on April 6. The grief-stricken husband telegraphed to Lady Londonderry: "My beloved is at rest in our little churchyard covered with flowers."

Many of Carson's Irish Unionist colleagues came down to Rottingdean for the funeral, and he received messages of sympathy from all parts of the United Kingdom, including one from the King.

Among the mourners at the grave was the faithful James Craig, whose guest Annette had been in happier times at Craigavon. "We lament her death," he said, "not only because she was the wife of our Leader, but for her own gifts. Her kindness and generosity and the great interest which she evinced in everything affecting the Loyalists of Ulster are gratefully remembered, and intensify the personal note of sorrow felt by those who had the privilege of her friendship."

When it was all over, Carson wrote to his three closest political and personal friends.

To James Craig

Northgate House,
Rottingdean.
April 10, 1913.

My dear James,

I must write my first letter to you to say how much I have been strengthened in my sorrow by the love and affection shown me by yourself and all my Irish colleagues. I feel deeply touched by the kindness of those who came to pay a last visit to my wife whom I shall so sadly miss.

I hope to resume all my work at once, and I promise that so long as I have strength no effort will be spared in the serious and responsible task we are all engaged in. It is the privilege of sorrow to try and abate its ravages by engaging in zealous work for others.

With love to you both,

Your affectionate friend,
Edward Carson.

To Bonar Law

Northgate House,
Rottingdean.
April 10, 1913.

My dear Bonar Law,

For all your many acts of kindness during my long sorrow I only want to say 'Thank you'. *You* understand.

I hope to return to work at once—it is best—and I must try and adequately discharge the sacred and serious duty I have undertaken to those who trust me.

Your affectionate friend,
Edward Carson.

To Lady Londonderry

5 *Eaton Place,*
S.W.
April 14, 1913.

My dear and good Friend,

Thank you for your letter and all your genuine sympathy. You were both always so kind to my poor wife that I know you understand everything . . .

I felt it so horrible to see my wife die in a few minutes, even though I had really gone through it all nearly every night for some months. I was so glad I was at home, as a few hours before she died the last thing she said was 'I want to see my old man'. Although she did not speak, she put her face up to be kissed and put her arm round my neck. But all this is only harrowing—she is at rest. She was with me through all my career and I did the best I could for her and her happiness.

I came here last night and did a case today in the Courts, and I intend to get immersed in work as far as possible. Aileen is with me here and I will go home with her for the week-end. She is a great treasure . . .

Everyone has been *so* kind to me I can never forget it. I wonder how one is to stop missing—it seems so impossible.

I hope to see B[onar] L[aw] tomorrow and have a talk.

My love to His Lordship and yourself.

Yours very affectionately,
EDWARD CARSON.

A few weeks afterwards he crossed over to Ulster for the opening of a new drill hall for the Ulster Volunteers in Belfast, a ceremony which had been postponed on account of his domestic trouble. "I am glad to be here tonight," he said in a voice full of emotion. "Heaven knows my one affection left me is my love of Ireland. When I undertook the Leadership of the Irish Unionist Parliamentary Party I said 'I dedicate myself to your service, whatever may happen.' No one ever foresees what can or will happen, but, through whatever trials we may go, a man must have fortitude to carry through his promise, and I am here once more to dedicate myself to your service. . . . Remember you have no quarrel with individuals. We welcome, aye, and we love, every individual Irishman, even though opposed to us. Our quarrel is with the Government. If they wish to test the legality of anything we are doing, or have done, do not let them take humble men. I am responsible for everything. They know where to find me, for I never ask any man to do what I am not myself ready to do."

5

At the time of his wife's illness and death Carson was concerned with two interesting libel cases arising out of the same matter—what was popularly known as 'The Marconi Scandal'. This affair created a good deal of political heat at the time, as several Liberal Ministers were involved in it, though, as Carson put it, "it all amounts to at most an indiscretion." Carson, since he appeared professionally for the Ministers, was severely criticised for his action by Members of his own party who had attacked the Ministers in the House of Commons for their part in the affair. However, Carson had as good a defence for his own conduct as he had for that of his clients.

The possibilities of transmitting messages outside the medium of wires or cables were appreciated by scientists by the middle of the nineteenth century. But it was not until 1901 that the first long-distance signals were sent across the Atlantic. The author of this original wireless communication was the Italian Guglielmo Marconi, who had established a company in England for the development of his process. The importance of wireless telegraphy, which enabled messages to be sent through the air without risk of interference by the enemy in time of war, was realised by Conservatives and Liberals alike, and as the Germans were experimenting with a similar process it seemed a wise move on the part of the British Government to encourage Signor Marconi. Consequently in 1912 the British Government, in accord with the Governments of various Dominions, entered into an agreement with the Marconi Company to establish a chain of wireless stations throughout the Commonwealth. Since the Marconi Company was the only one in England having experience of long-distance wireless telegraphy, competitive tenders were not asked for. The agreement was negotiated on behalf of the Government by the Postmaster-General, Mr. Herbert Samuel (later Lord Samuel), and on behalf of the company by its managing director, Mr. Godfrey Isaacs, who was a brother of the Liberal Attorney-General, Sir Rufus Isaacs. Godfrey Isaacs had a number of company directorships in the City and he had succeeded Signor Marconi as managing director of the Marconi Company in 1910, when the Italian inventor resigned owing to pressure of scientific research.

The news of the acceptance by the Post Office of the Marconi tender caused a boom in the company's shares, which, stimulated by the wreck of the *Titanic*, rose from about 14s. to £9 15s. Meanwhile, rumours began to circulate that Ministers and their relatives had bought Marconi shares with the knowledge that a contract was pending. The deal with the Government was also attacked by the Opposition as being too favourable to the Marconi Company. Meanwhile the rumours found expression in Parliament, where the Postmaster-General moved to appoint a Select Committee of Enquiry. During the ensuing debate Rufus Isaacs and Lloyd George, whose name had also been mentioned, stated that they had had nothing to do with the agreement nor had they had any dealings in the shares of the English Marconi Company. Unfortunately for them, they did not consider it worth while to inform the House that they had dealt in shares of the American Marconi Company, which, although it had played no part in the agreement, was a subsidiary of the English company and controlled by it.

The Select Committee began its sittings early in 1913 and heard evidence from numerous persons. Among these witnesses was Mr. Leo Maxse, editor of the *National Review*, who in this journal had attacked both the agreement and the circumstances in which it had been made public, and referred to persistent rumours then current in the City. "The rumours about particular Ministers are circumstantial and persistent," he told the Committee. But he was careful to confine his remarks to what he knew and he made a particular point of exempting the Postmaster-General from the subjects of censure. Two days later the London correspondent of the Paris newspaper *Le Matin* published a travesty of Maxse's evidence, which constituted a gross libel upon the Postmaster-General and Attorney-General. Mr. Maxse, wrote the correspondent, had intimated that Mr. Herbert Samuel had entered into an arrangement with Mr. Rufus Isaacs and Mr. Godfrey Isaacs, and that all three had bought shares in the Marconi company before the announcement of the acceptance of the tender, subsequently selling them at an immense profit.

The two Ministers whose honour had been thus impugned promptly sued *Le Matin* for libel. The offending newspaper apologised and did not attempt to defend the action, which came on before Mr. Justice Darling in the King's Bench Division on March 19, 1913. Carson and F. E. Smith led for the plaintiffs, while *Le Matin* was represented by J. H. Campbell.

In opening the case Carson said that, had the charges been made in an English newspaper, the plaintiffs would have pressed for damages, but as it was a foreign newspaper which was concerned, and the allegations were printed merely as gossip and were not prompted by political or personal malice, they were not doing so. The plaintiffs then went into the witness box and denied the allegations on oath. It was in the course of these statements that the public learned for the first time that Rufus Isaacs had bought 10,000 shares in the American Marconi Company and had subsequently sold a thousand of these shares to Lloyd George and another thousand to the Master of Elibank, the Liberal Chief Whip. On behalf of *Le Matin*, J. H. Campbell offered an unqualified withdrawal of, and apology for, the libel, and there the matter rested, so far as this case was concerned. But the new facts disclosed, though they had no bearing on the libel, came as an unpleasant surprise and led to serious repercussions in Parliament.

At the same time the unfounded charges were repeated in a more aggravated form by another journalist, Mr. Cecil Chesterton, in his journal *The Eye Witness* (later called *The New Witness*) where Godfrey Isaacs was branded as a vile conspirator, a corrupt man, a thief and a knave, who attempted to enrich himself by public plunder, with the help of his brother, the Attorney-General. Unfortunately Chesterton really believed in the truth of his accusations, and in discharging what he considered to be his duty of exposing a public scandal he went so far as to employ sandwichmen with offensive placards parading up and down outside Godfrey Isaacs's offices. At first Isaacs treated the attacks with contempt, but as they increased in strength he was driven to take action, and accordingly started proceedings for criminal libel. The case came on at the Old Bailey before Mr. Justice Phillimore and lasted for ten days. For the prosecution Carson and F. E. Smith led Richard Muir; Mr. Rigby Swift, K.C. (later Mr. Justice Swift), and Mr. Ernest Wild (later Sir Ernest Wild, Recorder of London) were the leading counsel for the defence.

The two brothers Isaacs and Mr. Samuel substantially repeated the evidence they had given at the previous trial, and completely vindicated their characters in the eyes of the jury. The defendant, on the other hand, made great play with the fact that some of Mr. Godfrey Isaacs's commercial ventures in the City had not been successful. But he failed to justify the libel in any particular, though he did his best to impart an atmosphere of political prejudice into the case. In his closing speech Carson begged the jury to remember that they were not there to sit in judgment on the conduct of Ministers dealing in Marconi shares. "There is another place for the consideration of those charges," he told them. "You have nothing to do with political rumours, which are often circulated in the interest of political bias. Let us in this Court keep ourselves aloof from politics and remember that anything which tends to impair the efficiency of a Court of Justice for the vindication of character will be detrimental to the whole body politic."

The jury convicted the defendant of criminal libel and found that it was unjustified. The judge thereupon sentenced Chesterton to a fine of £100 and ordered him to pay the costs of the prosecution; he would have sent him to prison but for the fact that Chesterton apparently believed in the truth of what he had written.

The political issues were raised a few days later in the House of Commons, when a Conservative back-bencher, Mr. George Cave, K.C. (afterwards Lord Chancellor), moved a resolution condemning the Ministers in question for their share dealings and 'the want of frankness' displayed by them in their communications on the subject to the House. Rufus Isaacs and Lloyd George each expressed their regret for what had happened, admitting that it was a mistake to have bought the shares. In these circumstances the House refused to censure them and rejected Cave's resolution by a majority of 346 votes to 268.

Neither Carson nor Smith intervened in the debate nor did they go into the division lobby, in view of their professional appearance in the two trials, which, though it earned for them the deep gratitude of Rufus Isaacs, exposed them to severe criticism from many of their political friends. Had they voted, on the other hand, no doubt criticism would have been equally hostile.* "The Bar will ever remember the part Carson and you played in this matter," the Attorney-General wrote to F. E. Smith. "You have both behaved so generously and indeed magnificently." On the other hand, the Conservative-minded Leo Maxse deplored the fact that "our Front-Bench lawyers should have been enticed into a trap" and described their action as "professionally correct but a public disaster," the suggestion being that they were retained as counsel in Court in order to silence them as politicians in the House of Commons. Even Lady Londonderry, who was the friend and patroness of both men, was quick to chide them on this account.

Although F. E. Smith wrote a characteristic letter to *The Times* defending his conduct, Carson thought it best to ignore the critics in public. He had always taken the view that a barrister is like a cab-driver 'on the rank' and that so long as he continues to ply for hire he must take the fares as they are offered to him. Since he had been associated with Rufus Isaacs so frequently in the Courts, it was natural that the Attorney-General should turn to him as his principal

* Carson wrote on the day after the division: 'I consulted Lord Halsbury about voting and he advised me not to do so, as it would be open to hostile criticism, and so I thought it best to go the straight line, having regard to my appearance in the Marconi case.' Carson to Bonar Law, June 20, 1913: Bonar Law Papers.

defender, and in the circumstances he could not refuse. Isaacs had also developed a strong friendship for Smith both in the Courts and in Parliament, and he was the obvious choice to second Carson's efforts. Nevertheless, many Conservatives, who saw in the Marconi affair an opportunity for discrediting the Government, were angry and unconvinced by these arguments. As Carson wrote to Lady Londonderry: "It is no use my explaining again the position I am in as a barrister. You would not listen! However, as I *know* I was right in my action, I am unrepentant."

Shortly afterwards Carson figured in another case of great public interest. This was 'The Million Pound Lawsuit', as the case of *Capron* v. *Scott and Others* was described in the newspapers. It arose out of the will of Sir John Scott, a wealthy bachelor, who left a number of substantial legacies to Lady Sackville, chatelaine of historic Knole in Kent. The will was disputed by Sir John's family on the grounds that undue influence had been brought to bear on the testator by Lady Sackville and her husband.

Sir John Scott was the son of Dr. John Scott, an English doctor practising in France, who was the close friend of Sir Richard Wallace, the heir and reputed natural son of the last Marquess of Hertford. When Lord Hertford died in 1870, he bequeathed his vast fortune and famous art collections to Wallace. These in turn passed to the latter's widow, Lady Wallace, who left the Wallace Collection to the nation at her death, and most of the residue of her estate to Sir John Scott, who had been her late husband's secretary. Soon after this, Scott made the acquaintance of Mrs. Sackville-West, as Lady Sackville then was, in a party which he took round the Wallace Collection in Hertford House. A friendship sprang up between them, based on a mutual love of 'fine things', as he called his art treasures, and Sir John became a frequent visitor to Knole. He was fascinated by his new friend, whose Spanish blood, tempestuous character and autocratic ways continued for a number of years to appeal to him strongly, even if he sometimes found her rather frightening. During this period he made a will and two codicils in her favour and gave her many handsome presents, though there was no question of anything immoral in their relations. Eventually they quarrelled and Sir John drafted a codicil revoking most of her legacies, but no completed codicil was ever found. They subsequently composed their differences and had an amicable talk. Next day Sir John suddenly collapsed and died in a chair at Hertford House. When his will was opened, it was found to contain legacies to Lady Sackville consisting of £150,000 in cash and art treasures worth an additional half million.*

Mr. F. W. Capron, one of the executors, propounded the will and codicils. The testator's brother, Mr. Donald Maxwell Scott, and other members of the family entered a defence and counter-claim, alleging undue influence on the part of the Sackvilles, who, it was stated, had established so complete an ascendancy over Sir John that "his mind had ceased to be his own." As evidence of the testator's intentions the defendants relied on the missing codicil, revoking the previous bequests to Lady Sackville and giving her greatly reduced benefits. The action began before Sir Samuel Evans, President of the Probate Division, on June 25, 1913, and occupied eight days. Mr. W. T. Barnard, K.C., led for the plaintiffs, Mr. F. E. Smith, K.C., and Mr. E. G. Hemmerde appeared for the defendants, while Lord and Lady Sackville were represented by Sir Edward Carson and Mr. Norman Craig.

In opening the case for his clients Carson referred to the "vitriolic blackwashing of Lord and Lady Sackville and to trivialities magnified by counsel which afford so splendid an example of Mr. Smith's great powers of mesmerism and fascination." Carson proceeded to argue that Lady Sackville and Sir John Scott were 'kindred spirits', united by their love of 'fine things' and in particular by the great and historic house of Knole, which had become encumbered by mortgages. To save Knole and its precious contents and preserve it intact for the Sackville family was a worthy and legitimate object, which became an absorbing interest with the testator. The latter was described as a "a huge old gentleman of twenty-five stone, dividing his attention between a *pâté* and a picture, and pathetically grateful for the platonic affections of a high-born lady." Carson also showed that he had treated his family well, giving them and leaving them handsome allowances in houses and money.

In the witness box Lady Sackville proved herself, in the words of the judge while summing up, "a lady of high mettle, very high mettle indeed." She stood up brilliantly to cross-examination by F. E. Smith, which lasted the best part of two days and which subsequently caused that great advocate to regard her as one of the most troublesome witnesses with whom he ever had to deal. Her

* The interesting background of the case has been well described by Lady Sackville's daughter, Miss V. Sackville-West (Mrs. Harold Nicolson), in her biography of her grandmother, *Pepita*, which was published in 1937.

answers also brought him into conflict with Carson, who accused Smith of misinterpreting what she said. For instance, on being questioned about the Hertford House jewels to be worn by the Misses Scott at Buckingham Palace, Lady Sackville said that the matter had not been discussed with her.

F. E. SMITH: I thought you said it was.

WITNESS: I did not.

SIR EDWARD CARSON: You really misinterpret every answer she gives.

F. E. SMITH (*to* CARSON): That is a statement without warrant of any kind. If you think so, you can object before my Lord.

SIR EDWARD CARSON: My Lord, I do object. Over and over again my friend, when she says one thing, pretends to think she said another.

F. E. SMITH: That is a grossly improper statement without warrant.

SIR EDWARD CARSON: I will not take any notice of ill-temper, I have been too long at the Bar to do so. But, my Lord, I do object to such inaccuracy.

THE JUDGE: Mr. Smith does not mean to be inaccurate, but he is sometimes so, in fact.

F. E. SMITH: What I resent is the suggestion that I am intentionally misrepresenting the witness. My friend ought not to have said what he said. He ought to know me too well for that.

THE JUDGE: It is much more agreeable to go on to the next question.

SIR EDWARD CARSON: I am not in the least inclined to be bullied.

THE JUDGE: Now the next question?

Soon the opposing advocates were sparring again, and the judge grew testy.

SIR EDWARD CARSON: I think everybody will agree.

F. E. SMITH: I would rather you spoke for yourself.

THE JUDGE: I wish you would neither speak for yourselves nor to one another, but would ask a question of the witness.

At the end of this sensational trial the judge summed up strongly in Lady Sackville's favour, observing that undue influence was much nearer to coercion than anything that had been proved. After an absence of twelve minutes the jury returned a verdict in which the disputed will was upheld. Costs were awarded against the defendants.

Carson collapsed at the end of the case and had to go to bed for several days. He consequently missed the third reading of the

Home Rule Bill on its introduction for the second time in the House of Commons. Feeling far from well he dragged himself from bed to keep a round of political engagements in Ulster, which foreshadowed the setting up of an Ulster Provisional Government. "Thank God," he told Lady Londonderry, "the time for speaking is nearly over."

6

When the House rose for the summer recess, Carson went off as usual to Homburg. His doctor found him very run down and insisted on his spending several weeks there. "I was overworked in Ulster and my doctor thinks I want a long rest to set me up," the invalid wrote. "I am trying hard to recuperate . . . but I feel out of my element as I feel too unhappy for any social distractions." However, he was far from lonely, as his younger son Walter joined him for part of the time, and there was also Miss Ruby Frewen to talk to. Their friendship was now ripening into affection, notwithstanding the considerable difference in their ages.

It was during this visit that Carson had a talk with the German Emperor William II, who spent a few days in Homburg in August. They met at a luncheon party, which included Lord Acton and other English visitors, and their conversation subsequently set tongues wagging that there was some deep-laid scheme afoot between the Kaiser and the Ulster Volunteers. In fact, their conversation was purely social, and any attempt by the Kaiser to bring it into political channels was deftly turned by Carson. "He takes an extraordinary interest in everything and loves a joke and a story," noted Carson afterwards, "and I was much fascinated by his great personality."

They chatted together on many subjects, particularly on gardens. The Emperor, who had received a picture of Lady Londonderry's, said they must be very beautiful, and Carson was able to inform him on that point. This topic led to the management of States, and the Kaiser remarked that he thought England did too little to consolidate her Empire. "We have our own ideas," Carson replied, "and we give them self-government."

The Kaiser said he would have liked to go to Ireland, but that his grandmother, Queen Victoria, would not let him, adding with a smile in a half-aside: "Perhaps she thought I wanted to take the little place."

"I think, sir," said Carson, "you are well out of it," at which there was general laughter.

However, when the Emperor began to talk about Ulster, Carson refused to be drawn. He cleverly steered the conversation on to the subject of town-planning in Berlin, on which subject the Emperor, who claimed the credit for the recent suburban extension there, was equally ready to converse.

Carson returned to London early in September for a few days, before going on to Belfast, where the Ulster Unionist Council was meeting to make public the scheme of a Provisional Government. While he was in London, a significant event occurred. Lord Loreburn, a Liberal ex-Lord Chancellor, who carried considerable weight with his party, wrote a letter to *The Times* pointing out that, through the working of the Parliament Act, the Home Rule Bill would become law in the following June, and if it did so in its present form there would be very serious riots in the North of Ireland, if not actual civil war, on such a scale that the bitterness of party strife could never be forgotten. Apparently on his own initiative, he now urged Ministers, "who assuredly have not taken leave of their senses . . . to consider proposals for accommodation," and he therefore suggested that a conference should be held behind closed doors with a view to effecting a settlement by consent.

To the extent that it alarmed Redmond as indicating a weakening of the Liberal position, Carson welcomed Lord Loreburn's intervention, since the ex-Lord Chancellor had been one of the strongest Home Rulers in the Cabinet and here surely was a sign that "serious and thinking men are beginning to realise the gravity of the situation." On the other hand, he distrusted any suggestion of compromise, for nothing would shake Ulster's determination not to be expelled from the Union and placed under a Dublin Parliament. "If that were attempted," said Carson, "then we are going to make Home Rule impossible by steady and persistent opposition." In that frame of mind Carson crossed over to Belfast to attend an important series of meetings, at which he was joined by Mr. F. E. Smith.

Meanwhile Bonar Law went off to Scotland to see the King, who was receiving the leading politicians at Balmoral, his aim being to bring the contending parties together in a friendly atmosphere. Mr. Churchill was the Minister in attendance on the King, and the Conservative Leader made it clear to him that the moment Home Rule was passed not only would Carson set up the Ulster Provisional Government but would allow no force to be used in that area except the force appointed by it. Suppose it comes to this, argued Bonar Law. The whole of the Unionist Party say that Ulster is right, that they are ready to support him, that if necessary all the Unionist Members are turned out of the House of Commons. Did Mr. Churchill suppose that the Army would obey orders to exercise force in Ulster? Bonar Law told him that "In that case undoubtedly we should regard it as civil war, and should urge the officers of the Army not to regard them as a real Government but to ignore their orders." He also said that the Conservatives and Unionists realised as clearly as Mr. Churchill did himself not only the seriousness but the actual calamity of allowing things to come to such a point.

"As you know, "wrote Bonar Law to Carson, informing him of this conversation, "I have long thought that, if it were possible to leave Ulster as she is, and have some form of Home Rule for the rest of Ireland, that is on the whole the only way out, because a discussion of the larger question of general devolution, even if the Government were ready to consider it, would involve a discussion, for instance, of the House of Lords, and probably other questions, and would really be impossible, I think, unless there were something in the nature of a coalition. . . . The whole question as to the exclusion of Ulster really turns upon this—whether or not it would be regarded as a betrayal by the solid body of Unionists in the south and west."

That Carson was in complete accord with the Conservative Leader appears from his reply to this letter.

To Bonar Law

Craigavon, Strandtown, Co.Down. September 23, 1913 . . . As regards the position here I am of opinion that on the whole things.are shaping towards a desire to settle on the terms of leaving 'Ulster' out. A difficulty arises as to defining Ulster. My own view is that the whole of Ulster should be excluded but the minimum would be the six plantation counties, and for that a good case could be made.

The South and West would present a difficulty, and it might be that *I* could not agree to their abandonment, though I feel certain it would be the best settlement if Home Rule is inevitable. Probably some more generous treatment could be dealt out to safeguard their interests, but with British rule in Ulster I don't think there would be so much to fear. Of course the ideal thing would be that this should be part of a general scheme for the U.K. and, even if that question is not practical to settle at the moment, it could be drafted in such a way as to make it fit in afterwards.

As regards myself you need not consider me at all except so far as I am of any use in helping a settlement. I have such a horror of what

> may happen if the Bill is passed as it stands and the mischief it will do to the whole Empire that I am fully conscious of the duty there is to try and come to some terms. I believe, however, that the Nationalist party will not consider the question of excluding Ulster. They would probably prefer a General Election as, even if it went against them, they would have their power and what is of great importance their 83 salaries in the House . . .
>
> Everything here is going on splendidly and I think enthusiasm grows instead of decreasing. The business men are coming out in the open and will hold a great meeting of their own in October.
>
> I have shown your letter to 'F.E.' and we have talked it over. I also showed it to James Craig. I could not very well avoid doing so as he so well understands the people here and he is always absolutely in my confidence . . .

Like Carson, F. E. Smith received the idea of a conference with reluctance, because he felt it would be unpopular with the Conservatives, who remembered the last conference with mixed feelings, and also with the Ulster Unionists, whose increasingly strong position would be bound to be weakened by negotiations. As he put it in a memorandum of his conversations with Carson at Craigavon: "Sir Edward pointed out the absurdity of inviting him or his friends into a conference on the condition of accepting a principle which they were pledged to resist, if necessary by arms." On the other hand, both Conservatives and Ulster Unionists could not very well reject an invitation to confer, particularly if it came from Buckingham Palace, and Home Rule for all Ireland except Ulster might form a basis of negotiation. If such a scheme were ultimately adopted, F. E. Smith told his own political friends that he felt Carson would do his best to make it workable, although it would involve very real sacrifices on his part. "He is a South of Ireland man," noted Smith. "He has spent his life in resisting Home Rule, not merely in Ulster, but in Ireland as a whole."

Carson's immediate task lay with Ulster. On September 23, 500 delegates of the Ulster Unionist Council met in the Ulster Hall in Belfast to approve the setting up of a Provisional Government, should the Home Rule Bill become law. Before the meeting began Carson implored his old friend Lord Londonderry, who was to preside, not to involve himself in an undertaking fraught with such danger to himself and his family. "They can do little to me," he told Londonderry, "therefore I have little to fear. But you have great possessions, a great title, friendships at Court, a seat in the House of Lords. You have to consider also the future of your son Charley.

The Government, when they grow vindictive, as they will, may strike at you—and him. For these good reasons keep out of it! Let me do it by myself. It matters little to me, but I do not want you to be involved in this last and ultimate matter." But Londonderry, to his everlasting credit, refused to hear of such a thing. With tears streaming down his face, he clasped Carson's hands and said he must never be asked to stand aside when his friends and when Ulster were going into danger. "My dear Edward," he said, "if I was to lose everything in the world, I will go with you to the end."

The Council, with Londonderry in the chair, proceeded to delegate its powers to a Provisional Government consisting of seventy-seven members, with a 'Commission of Five', of whom Carson was Chairman, as its Executive. Departmental matters, such as finance, military affairs, education, law, customs and post office were delegated to special committees. At the same time an indemnity guarantee fund was opened to compensate members of the Ulster Volunteer Force for any loss or disability they might suffer as a result of their service, and the widows and any dependents of any who might lose their lives. Londonderry, Carson and Craig headed the subscription list with £10,000 each, and a quarter of a million sterling was guaranteed on the spot. "Our duty," Carson told the assembled delegates, "is to guide and direct into the proper channels the methods of resisting the Home Rule Bill if the Government persist in forcing it upon us, and that is exactly what we are trying to do by setting up a Provisional Government . . . We may be coerced in the long run into submission, because of course they have got the Army and Navy . . . but if we are, we will be governed as a conquered community and nothing else."

Three days later a grand review of Volunteers, 15,000 men in all, took place at the Balmoral grounds outside Belfast, the scene of the great parade of eighteen months before. The men were reviewed by Lieutenant-General Sir George Richardson, a retired Indian Army officer who, at the suggestion of Lord Roberts, had assumed command of the Volunteer Force. As a body the men were magnificent, hardy toilers from shipyard and factory marching shoulder to shoulder with clergy, doctors, lawyers, business men and clerks. Carson, Londonderry and Craig stood near the saluting base and watched the march past, while F. E. Smith was particularly noticeable on this occasion in his role of 'galloper' to the General. The climax was reached when the Commanding Officer called for three cheers for the Union, followed by the unfurling of a huge Union

Jack in the centre of the ground and the singing of 'Rule Britannia' and the National Anthem.

The Government was now coming to realise that the Ulster folk were a distinct community, conditioned by special circumstances entitling them to special treatment. "Their claim for special consideration, if put forward with sincerity, cannot be ignored by a Government depending on the existing House," declared Mr. Churchill in a speech at Dundee on October 9. "There is no advance that they can make which will not be more than matched by their Irish fellow countrymen and the Liberal Party." But, however the Liberals might feel about advances on the basis of the exclusion of Ulster, there was no doubt about the feelings of the majority in the rest of Ireland on the subject of the proposed partition of their country. Speaking at Limerick three days later, Mr. Redmond said: "Irish Nationalists can never be assenting parties to the mutilation of the Irish nation; Ireland is a unit. . . . The two-nation theory is to us an abomination and a blasphemy."

On October 14 Bonar Law had the first of a series of secret meetings with Asquith at Cherkley, Sir Max Aitken's house near Leatherhead. Their talk proved inconclusive, since the Prime Minister, who was already in touch with Redmond, could not agree even to the exclusion of what Carson called "the six plantation counties" of Ulster. Nevertheless, Carson was hopeful that the Government would eventually give way as regards Ulster. "Although it would appear that Redmond has for the moment closed the matter," he wrote to Lady Londonderry on October 21, "I doubt if, after Lord Loreburn's letter and Churchill's statement, the Cabinet can really intend to go on to the bitter end."

There was also the position of the Irish Unionists outside Ulster to be considered. They felt that their case was different from that of the Northerners, because they were in a minority, and they had doubts whether it would be politic for Carson to continue to lead them in view of developments in Ulster. However, their doubts were resolved at a meeting in Carson's house, at which the Northern representatives were also present, when they saw the Leader, and James Craig had told them that "Carson, like a good doctor, will give to different patients different prescriptions."

As he used to do in Court before cross-examining a key witness, Carson had jotted down a few questions on the back of an envelope.

"Is it your decision that I am to go on fighting for Ulster?"

The Southern Unionists answered "Yes." Carson made a note and went on:

"Will my fight in Ulster interfere in any way with your fight in the South?"

"No."

Carson made another note. He then pointed out that, if the Southerners lost and the Ulstermen were now asked to fight, only to surrender in the end with them, it would take the heart out of the Ulster movement. "If I win in Ulster," he continued, "am I to refuse the fruits of victory because you have lost?"

The logic of Carson's case was clear. "No," they answered emphatically.

From then on the paths of the two sections of the Irish Unionists tended to become more and more divergent.*

Meanwhile, as Bonar Law and Carson made it clear in speeches up and down the country that Ulster demanded to be excluded completely from the Home Rule scheme, the attitude of the Government showed signs of stiffening. Speaking at Leeds on November 27, Asquith said: "We are not dissatisfied with the Government of Ireland Bill as it stands. We are not going to be frightened or deflected by menaces of civil war. We are not going to make any surrender of principle. We mean to see the thing through."

Carson and the Ulster Unionists were equally determined to resist. Indeed their minds had long been made up. If anything was needed to confirm them in their determination, it was a moving incident which occurred when Carson went to address a mass meeting in Birmingham that same month. Carson was accompanied by Austen Chamberlain, and they both spent the night as guests of Austen's father at Highbury.

'Joe' Chamberlain had been paralysed for the past seven years, and he was now nearing his end. But there was still some spark left in the old man.

"You—know—what—I—would—do?" he asked.

"I do not, sir," replied Carson.

The old man could only articulate with difficulty as he sat in his chair. But he thumped with his stick on the floor to help his words out. The other listened, as the words came slow and laboured.

* Cp. Carson to Lady Londonderry, Nov. 26, 1913: 'It will be exceedingly difficult to speak in Dublin and say anything which is of use. They are so different from the North of Ireland and do so little to help themselves'.

"If—I—were—you—I—would—fight—it—out—to—the—end."

Carson related this incident on his next visit to Belfast, when he again addressed the delegates of the Ulster Unionist Council. "We will take his advice. We will fight it out," he told them amid tremendous cheering. "God give us men—a time like this demands great hearts, strong minds, true faith and willing hands——

"Men whom the lusts of office do not kill,
Men whom the spoils of office do not buy,
Men who possess opinions and a will
Men who love honour, men who cannot lie."

7

Carson was invited to join the later conversations which took place between Asquith and Bonar Law. He met the Prime Minister at Cherkley and later at the house of Mr. Edwin Montagu, Asquith's parliamentary private secretary, in London. Somewhat to his surprise Asquith found the Irish Unionist Leader less pessimistic than his Conservative chief, but Carson also proved equally unyielding. He told Asquith very bluntly where persistence in the Home Rule policy would lead him.

"I have no doubt, Mr. Prime Minister," said Carson, "you have thought out very carefully what you intend to do when they resist your Bill in Ulster and when the first five hundred Ulstermen are shot down in Belfast."

Asquith looked alarmed. "My God," he exclaimed, jumping to his feet. "Five hundred! I tell you that if one Ulsterman were shot in such a quarrel it would be a disaster of the first magnitude."

In vain the Prime Minister sought to discover a legislative formula which, as he told Carson, would give "to the Ulster majority the substance of what they claim, while doing as little violence as possible to Nationalist sentiment." He suggested a form of what, with characteristic sophistry, he called "veiled exclusion", which gave Ulster a measure of local self-government and referred other matters to the jurisdiction of Westminster but at the same time implied Ulster's representation in an all-Ireland Parliament. This prompted Carson to make abundantly clear what he and his friends understood by 'exclusion'. On January 10, 1914, he wrote to Asquith: "I thought that it was always apparent that, when the exclusion of Ulster was discussed, I meant that Ulster should remain as at present under the Imperial Parliament and that a Dublin Parliament should have no legislative powers within the excluded area. Ulster would therefore send no members to the Dublin Parliament, but would continue as at present to send members of the Imperial Parliament. This would of course involve that the administration of Ulster should be under the control of the Imperial Parliament. I do not think I can say anything more specific."

A few days later Asquith reported to the Cabinet that he had received a letter from Carson "flatly refusing anything short of the exclusion of Ulster." For the time being, at least, the idea of a conference between the Conservative, Unionist and Nationalist leaders was at an end.

With the prospect of civil war in Ulster coming nearer, Bonar Law and Carson had to consider the position of the Army. They were in touch with the veteran Field-Marshal Lord Roberts, among other opponents of Home Rule in the armed forces, and the question of a letter from him in the Press was discussed, setting out his views as to the course the soldiers should take in the event of the Government ordering them to march on Ulster. There exists in the Bonar Law Papers a draft of such a letter, corrected by Bonar Law and Carson, of which the following is an extract:

> Every day I receive letters from soldiers asking my advice, and in my heart and conscience I believe it to be my duty to utter this word of warning. It is a soldier's duty to obey, but if and when Civil War breaks out no ordinary rules will apply. In that case a soldier will reflect that by joining the Army he has not ceased to be a citizen, and if he fights in such a quarrel he will fight on the side he believes to be right.
>
> If the attempt be made to coerce Ulster, Civil War, and nothing else, will inevitably follow. *Ulster will not be fighting against the Crown and the Flag and it will be idle to describe such men as 'The King's Enemies'.*

It is significant that the last sentence is in Carson's handwriting.

At the same time the Conservative 'shadow' Cabinet considered a proposal to introduce an amendment to the Army Act in the House of Lords. The Act was due to come up for annual renewal at the end of April, and the idea was that this should be done in such a way as to prevent the Government using the Army in Ireland until after a General Election. The 'shadow' Cabinet delegated the question to a committee consisting of Finlay, Carson, Lord Robert Cecil, Lord Salisbury and Mr. George Cave. Finlay eventually drafted an amendment which proposed to forbid the use of troops in aid of the civil power in Ulster. This was later altered, at Austen Chamberlain's suggestion, to forbid the retention of any troops in Ulster except to act against a foreign enemy.

The question then arose: supposing the Army Act was so amended, could the Government concentrate members of the Royal Irish Constabulary in Ulster and use them? Carson's reply when this question was put to him by Austen Chamberlain was threefold: first, there were not enough of them; secondly, they wouldn't do it; and thirdly, the Ulstermen would love to fight them for they were all Catholics! In answer to another observation of Chamberlain's that the Government were, at times at any rate, calculating on an explosion in Ulster taking the form of a riot instead of a revolution, Carson said he could guarantee that they would be disappointed in that expectation; the discipline of the Ulster Volunteers was admirable, he went on, and the need for it completely understood.

The letter designed to appear over Lord Roberts's name in the newspapers was never published. Nor was the proposed amendment to the Army Act introduced in the House of Lords in the form agreed by Carson and the other leading Unionists. Some time before the end of April, as we shall see, sensational and dramatic events occurred in Ireland to render both these moves unnecessary.

Carson now turned his attention to the business of arming the Ulster Volunteers. By this time the force was approximately 100,000 strong, but only a small proportion had weapons. Several consignments of rifles had been seized by the Customs and police, and, to make matters worse, the Government had recently issued proclamations completely banning the importation of arms and ammunition into Ireland. On his first visit to Belfast after the coming into operation of the ban, Carson, who had just been depicted with Redmond in an amusing cartoon on the subject in *Punch*, was asked by a Customs officer on the quayside whether he had any arms with him. "No," he answered, smiling, "only three blackthorn sticks." It may be added that these were gifts from Ulster admirers. But if the Leader had no arms on his journey, there were many others who smuggled them into the country, some of them by ingenious devices. There was, for instance, the heroic matron from the town of Dungannon in County Tyrone, whose story was related to Carson by one of the quayside porters in the Ulster vernacular. "She came off this boat not a fortnight ago," declared the porter in a voice which could be heard by most of the other passengers, "an' she came down this gangway, I declare to God you'd ha' swore she was within a week of her time—and divil a ha'porth the matter with her, only cartridges! An' the fun was that the Custom House boys knowed rightly what it was, but they dursn't lay a hand on her nor search her, for fear they were wrong."

When General Sir George Richardson took command of the Ulster Volunteers, they had only a few thousand rifles and most of their military training was being carried out with the aid of dummy weapons. The General proceeded to appoint an energetic young staff officer, Captain W. B. Spender (afterwards Sir Wilfrid Spender) as A.Q.M.G. charged with the supply of equipment, arms and ammunition, organisation of transport and supervision of communications. As regards arms and ammunition, Spender was instructed to confer with Major Fred Crawford, an enthusiastic Ulsterman who had signed the Covenant in his blood and who had been responsible for procuring many of the rifles and cartridges which were already in the hands of the Volunteers. Crawford was a remarkable character. As a young man in 1894 he had conceived a daring scheme to kidnap Gladstone on the sea-front at Brighton, convey him by a fast steam yacht to a Pacific island and there provide him with a copy of Homer and a Bible, paper for writing and an axe for felling palm trees, until a change of Government should avert the danger of Home Rule. He was very disappointed when a friend of his, Lord Ranfurly, whose assistance he sought to secure, refused to risk £10,000 on the venture.

Crawford, who was a Belfast business man, with twenty years' service in the militia artillery, possessed an expert knowledge of all kinds of firearms. As the individual responsible for procuring most of the weapons which had already been clandestinely imported, Crawford was in touch with various armament dealers on the continent. His principal intermediary was a little Hamburg Jew named Schmidt, whom he had good reason to trust. With the approval of the military committee of the embryo Ulster Provisional Government, Crawford proposed to purchase between 20,000 and 30,000 modern rifles and several million rounds of ammunition, also a suitable small steamer to convey such an important cargo to Ulster. However, although James Craig had given the project his blessing, there were others on the committee whom Crawford considered less than wholehearted in their support. Hence, on his next visit to

Hamburg, where he hoped to conclude the deal, Crawford called to see Carson on his way through London. They met at Carson's house in Eaton Place. Crawford pointed out that some of the committee had no idea of the seriousness of the undertaking, and, when they did realise what they were in for, might want to back out of it. "Once I cross this time to Hamburg," he went on, "there is no turning back for me, no matter what the circumstances are so far as my personal safety is concerned; and no contrary orders to cancel what they have agreed to with me will I obey. Now, Sir Edward, you know what I am about to undertake, and the risks those who back me up must run. Are you willing to back me to the finish in this undertaking? If you are not, I don't go. But if you are, I would go, even if I knew I should not return. It is for Ulster and her freedom I am working, and this alone."

Crawford could never forget the scene. They were alone, and Carson was sitting opposite to him. When Crawford had finished, his Leader's face was stern and grim, and there was a glint in his eye. He rose to his full height, advanced to Crawford's chair and staring down at him, shook his clenched fist in his face. Then he spoke in a steady, determined voice, which thrilled the other man. "Crawford," he said, "I'll see you through this business, if I should have to go to prison for it."

Crawford rose from his chair. He held out his hand and said: "Sir Edward, that is all I want. I leave tonight. Good-bye."

The two men shook hands and parted, Crawford for Hamburg and Carson for the House of Commons, where a new session of Parliament was beginning. It was February, 1914, and, if the Government adhered to its intention, the Home Rule Bill must reach the statute book within the next few months.

About this time the King authorised his Private Secretary, Lord Stamfordham, to visit Carson at his private house in the hope of persuading him not to make a violent speech when the Home Rule Bill was again introduced into Parliament. According to Lord Stamfordham, Carson informed him that he certainly intended to press the Prime Minister to say whether or no his Government were in favour of the exclusion of Ulster. All this delay, he said, was becoming intolerable and he did not know for how much longer he would be able to control his followers, who were becoming more and more indifferent to personal risk, and who were confident to a man that 'the King would not desert them'. At the same time Carson expressed his personal regard for Asquith and his trust in his sincerity. All that he himself desired was "a settlement which would satisfy the people of Ulster."*

This acutely controversial measure was accordingly introduced for the third time in the Commons, and on March 8 the Prime Minister moved its second reading. The only new feature about it, which embodied the utmost length to which the Government was prepared to go to conciliate Ulster, was what came to be known as 'county option with a time limit'. Any Ulster county, including the county boroughs of Belfast and Londonderry, was to be able to vote itself out of the jurisdiction of the proposed Dublin Parliament—but only for a period of six years. At the end of that time they must come in under Home Rule, unless the Imperial Parliament decided otherwise. It was obviously unacceptable to the Ulster Unionists. What it amounted to was that after six years Ulster would be forced to accept what she refused to submit to now, and in the meantime her preparations for resistance would probably have fallen away, since it would be impossible to keep the Volunteers on a virtual war footing for so long. This was not good enough for Carson. "So far as Ulster is concerned," he told the Commons in the course of the second reading debate, "be exclusion good or bad, Ulster wants the question settled now and for ever. We do not want sentence of death with a stay of execution for six years." On the other hand, if the time limit were dropped, Carson declared he would submit the amended Bill to a convention in Belfast. Meanwhile he warned the Government that Ulster was "ready for any exigency." On this tense note the debate was adjourned.

Thereafter events moved rapidly. On March 14 Colonel Seely, the War Minister, instructed Sir Arthur Paget, the Commander-in-Chief in Ireland, to take special precautions to safeguard certain military depots in Ulster in view of current reports that attempts might be made by 'evilly disposed persons' to raid Government stores for arms and ammunition. Speaking at Bradford on the same day, Mr. Churchill hinted that, if Ulster persisted in refusing the Prime Minister's offer, which was the Government's last word, the forces of the Crown would have to be employed against her. There were, said the First Lord, "worse things than bloodshed even on an extended scale." He described the Ulster Provisional Government as "a self-elected body, composed of persons who, to put it plainly, are engaged in a treasonable conspiracy." He spoke about the existence

* Quoted from the Royal Archives at Windsor by Harold Nicolson in his *King George V*, at p. 235.

of "a sinister and revolutionary purpose" in Ulster, and ended with these ominous words: "Let us go forward together and put these grave matters to the proof."*

Sir Arthur Paget was promptly summoned to London and given oral instructions, which would seem to have gone considerably beyond what was necessary for the protection of military stores in Ulster. He met Colonel Seely, Mr. Churchill and Mr. Birrell. On March 18 he saw Sir John French, the Chief of the Imperial General Staff, and Sir Spencer Ewart, the Adjutant-General. Immediately afterwards French gave an account of their discussion to Sir Henry Wilson, the Director of Military Operations and a Southern Irish Unionist, who passed it on to his Ulster friends. In fact, the same night Wilson met Carson, Lord Milner and Sir Leander Jameson ('Dr. Jim' of the Raid) at dinner and told them that the politicians wanted to scatter troops all over Ulster "as though it was a Pontypool coal strike." To Sir John French's objection that "this was opposed to all true strategy," apparently he had been told that "the political situation necessitated this dispersion." In other words, the secret and rapid garrisoning of strategic points on all the railways leading to Belfast and the disposition of the fleet, who were told to support the troops "by guns and searchlights from the ships," pointed strongly to the preparation of an offensive campaign against the capital city. As evidence of the precipitate haste with which the Government was acting, the Dorset Regiment, then quartered in Belfast's Victoria Barracks, was ordered to march several miles outside the city to Holywood, on the north shore of Belfast Lough, near Craigavon, and, incredible as it may seem, the men were told if necessary to leave their rifles behind, having first rendered them useless by removing the bolts. "If the Government want to crush the North," Wilson told Carson, repeating what he had already said to French, "they will have to mobilise the whole Army. Even so, I have great doubts whether they can do it. There will be a large proportion of officers and men who will refuse to coerce Ulster."

Rumours were circulating wildly that the Government was about to arrest Carson, Craig and other prominent Unionists, an eventuality

* Mr. Churchill subsequently asserted that he was opposed to the coercion of Ulster. 'My own personal view had always been that I would never coerce Ulster to make her come under a Dublin Parliament,' he wrote in *The World Crisis*, 'but I would do all that was necessary to prevent her stopping the rest of Ireland having the Parliament they desired. I believe this was sound and right, and in support of it I was certainly prepared to maintain the authority of the Crown and Parliament under the Constitution by whatever means was necessary. I spoke in this sense at Bradford on March 14.' See *The World Crisis*, 1911–1914, Vol. I, at p. 182.

CARSON FAMILY GROUP AT ROTTINGDEAN.

Back row, left to right: Walter, Father, Harry.
Sitting, left to right: Gladys, Mother, Aileen.

From a photograph in the possession of the
Hon. Mrs. G. Chesterman.

FORE-ARMED.

Sir Edward Carson (*in course of promenade on the quay, to Customs Officer Birrell*). "CAPITAL IDEA THIS OF STOPPING IMPORTATION OF ARMS. NOW THERE'S A DANGEROUS CHARACTER; YOU SHOULD SEARCH HIM. THAT'S JUST THE SORT OF BAG HE'D HAVE A COUPLE OF HOWITZERS CONCEALED IN."

Cartoon by Sir Bernard Partridge.

which the Leader and his lieutenant realised must be the signal for the outbreak of serious rioting and disorder in Ulster. Craig had already left for Craigavon, and Carson only stayed in London for a further twenty-four hours so as to take part in a vote of censure on the Government, which Bonar Law was moving in the House of Commons on the following afternoon. He was called early in the debate as he intended to cross to Belfast that night. "I hate all this talk about the Army being sent to Ulster," he declared before a crowded and excited House, pointing to the Front Government Bench. "Ulster people have always been, and are at the present moment, on the best of terms with your Army, and it is the only part of Ireland where that can be said. Your Army is welcome there as is your Fleet . . . as much as in any part of the United Kingdom, so much so that you think, before you commence your operations, of removing the regiments which are there at the present moment."

There were some angry exchanges with Mr. Churchill, whom Carson accused of being anxious to provoke the Ulster people to make an attack on the soldiers, and later with Joseph Devlin, the eloquent Nationalist M.P. for West Belfast, who taunted Carson with his former Liberal allegiance.* Finally, as it was getting near the hour of the boat-train's departure from Euston, Carson rose to leave the House. He was followed by several Ulster Members to the accompaniment of ringing cheers from the Opposition Benches. When he reached the Speaker's Chair, the Unionist Leader turned and looked down the Chamber, waving his hand. "I am off to Belfast," he said, and then immediately disappeared from view.

8

When Carson disembarked early next morning in Belfast harbour, he found James Craig and a full guard of honour, led by General Sir George Richardson and two companies of Volunteers, waiting to greet him on the quayside. With this impressive escort Carson was conveyed through the streets of the city, followed by cheering and excited crowds, to Craigavon, where he was to stay as Craig's guest. The excitement was natural, since the most alarming rumours were in circulation that Ulster was to be overrun by troops within a few hours. That there was some substance in these rumours has already been seen by the orders to the fleet. These were now

* See above p. 61–62.

reinforced by specific directions that two cruisers should take on board troops at Kingstown and proceed overnight to Carrickfergus, opposite Craigavon in Belfast Lough, the commanders being instructed to support the soldiers and to hold themselves in readiness to co-operate with the military. The cruisers were due to arrive at daybreak on the following day. At the same time Mr. Churchill, without apparently consulting the Board of the Admiralty, also ordered the Third Battle Squadron, then in Spanish waters, to steam to Lamlash, in the Isle of Arran, only a few miles from the coast of Ulster. It looked as if the purpose of these operations was to blockade the province by land and sea, at the same time exciting the Ulster people to such resistance as would justify an attack on the Volunteers.

To Bonar Law

Craigavon, Strandtown, Co. Down. Friday [*March* 20, 1914] I found Belfast and surroundings very excited. The Government have been moving troops and police all day through the province and from the south. I imagine it is a scare on their part and that they were under the impression our people were going to take action—or it may be they desire to provoke an outbreak . . .

This place is an armed camp with the General and officers here. It is all a strange 'message of peace' and really one would have thought it impossible in a country like ours . . .

I had a splendid crossing and slept well and think the change may take away my cold which bothers me.

I shall stay here a few days as it is just as well I should be here, and it will rest me from all the interviews in London . . .

That night the Volunteers kept guard at Craigavon and patrolled the shores of Belfast Lough; the police were also on duty, each force eyeing the other warily but not unfriendly. Some time after midnight the Assistant Commissioner of Police was inspecting his posts in the neighbourhood of the city and chanced to meet Colonel Spencer Chichester, who commanded the local Volunteers.

"Don't you think that we might all go to bed?" asked the police officer, who was tired.

"No," replied the Colonel. "I don't think we can, because we happen to know that you have a certain telegram, and it is upon that information we are out."

Friends of the Volunteers in the G.P.O. in Belfast had supplied Chichester with a copy of the telegram, which was addressed to the Police Commandant from Dublin Castle, but, since it was in code, he could make nothing of it.

Not appreciating this, the police officer remarked: "Oh, if it's only that, you need not be making all this trouble." He thereupon took the decoded version of the telegram out of his pocket. "Here it is," he went on, "read it for yourself. There's nothing in it."

Chichester took the piece of paper which the other handed him and read: "Expect important document tomorrow morning." On the face of it the message appeared harmless enough, but it conveyed much more than it seemed to do. It enabled the Government code to be broken, as a result of which Carson and the other Ulster leaders were able to read all the secret messages which passed between the authorities in London, Dublin and Belfast.

Next morning Volunteer dispatch riders reported to Carson that two cruisers had arrived in Belfast Lough in the dawn, and after disembarking troops at Carrickfergus, one of them, H.M.S. *Attentive*, had crossed the channel to Bangor, where she landed a man in plain clothes. It was, in fact, her commander, who had been instructed to proceed to Holywood Barracks and there interview General Sir Nevil Macready 'as to co-operation with military in certain eventualities.' Macready, who held a high staff post at the War Office under Sir John French, had just been appointed G.O.C. Belfast District with the unusual powers of a Resident Magistrate in order to control the local police within the limits of his command, since the R.I.C. were an armed force.

The morning's mail and newspapers carried bigger news than this—stories of mutiny and wholesale resignations from the Army. On his return to Dublin on the previous day Sir Arthur Paget sent for his general officers and told them, on War Office authority, that officers with homes in Ulster would be exempted from any operations that might take place against the North. They would be 'allowed to disappear'—this was the phrase in the official directive—and they would subsequently be reinstated in their positions, but they must give their word of honour that they would not fight for Ulster. Officers who were not prepared to undertake active operations against Ulster, by reason of conscientious or other scruples, were to send in their papers and would be dismissed the Service. Nor did Paget mince his words. "We are going to take immediate active military operations against Ulster," he told his generals. "By Saturday Ulster will be in a blaze."

It had been taken for granted in the War Office that all the officers to whom this choice was put, with the exception of a few Ulster natives, would take no action calculated to wreck their careers. Great was the surprise, therefore, in Whitehall when telegrams came in from Paget that the Commanding Officer and most of the other officers in the 3rd Cavalry Brigade, the 5th and 16th Lancers and the 4th Hussars, stationed at the Curragh, preferred to accept dismissal if ordered North. There was a quick reaction on the part of Colonel Seely, the War Minister. Instructions were immediately sent to Paget in Dublin to suspend any senior officers who had tendered their resignations, to refuse to accept the resignations of the junior officers, and to send General Hubert Gough, the Brigadier in command of the 3rd Cavalry Brigade, together with the Commanding Officers of the two Lancer regiments and the 4th Hussars, to report themselves immediately at the War Office after relieving them of their commands.

To Bonar Law

Craigavon, Saturday [*March* 21] . . . I have come to the conclusion that the present action of the Government is a demonstration of intimidation of our people here, but for that purpose it is quite useless.

We are quieting down and going ahead with preparations. I have just addressed here all the commanding officers and given the best direction I could on questions of policy. We have many offers of men of high standing to come over. Our fund here is going ahead and we are happy and calm.

. . . I will be a soldier by the time I return.

Meanwhile Paget, in carrying out his instructions, went down to the Curragh and delivered an extraordinary address to the officers there, appealing to those who were resigning to reconsider their decisions. They need not take part in any serious fighting, he said; they could hoist the white flag if it came to the pinch, and in the event of a big battle they would be placed on the flank and need not take part. "Cannot you trust me and do as I do and march up North?" he asked them. "And when the time comes you can put up the white flag or show the white feather. I assure you you won't be asked to do more than you like." In any event, he went on, though Ulster seemed quiet, the Ulstermen would be forced to fire the first shot, since the Government had made a move, which he did not disclose, but which might cause an immediate rising in the North. As for Gough and his colonels, they would be tried by general court-martial, and Gough himself might expect no mercy. Gough replied that he asked for none. Later in the day he left with the others for London.

To Bonar Law

Craigavon, March 23 . . . I expect you know everything that I do, but still it may interest you to know that a very large number of officers all over Ireland resigned. In fact it appears to me, from all I hear, the majority of them. It seems then that after this was effected, by reason of the extraordinary action of the Government in calling up the Regiments and in calling upon the officers that had conscientious objection, as I wrote you before, the Government then got in a panic, and Sir Arthur Paget appealed to most of them with the usual arguments of the Government about strikes, etc., and of course dragging in the King's name. I understand that a large body of them have consented to remain on, on condition that they are not expected to act in Ulster, otherwise than in guarding Government property and stores. No doubt, great pressure has been put, and is being put. I hear now that a large number of non-commissioned officers and men are saying that nothing will induce them to take sides against Ulster, and indeed many have said that they will join us in the event of an outbreak. . . .

This place is still a Barracks with a guard of 200. I have not yet been in Belfast, but I think I ought to stay here as long as I can. Everything is quiet, but I think that determination here has greatly increased by the action of the Government. My view of the situation is that the Government had at first intended and made up their minds to put themselves in a position to take such action as would be necessary to destroy our movement, and, as Winston's speech was made after the reported conferences, or some of them, between the Law Officers and the War Office, I have no doubt it was sent down to set the ball rolling. It is ridiculous to suppose that all these troops are being sent to guard buildings and stores, and I am told by military men that the idea of sending cavalry for that purpose is quite absurd . . .

Hundreds of letters and telegrams poured into Craigavon from all over the world. By the safe hand of the same messenger as took his letter to Bonar Law, Carson wrote to reassure his friend Comyn-Platt and his daughter Aileen. "If you are a good dear friend," he told the former, "you can tell everyone how I value the support and affection they have shown." To Aileen he wrote: "We are all peaceful here and it is the Government who have the jumps. Of course, if the Government had attempted to interfere with us it would have been the beginning of the end. They seem to have climbed down and have made a mess of everything, and now they are begging the men to come back. . . . Have no anxiety—all will be well somehow and in any event we are all prepared to suffer and of that you may be proud!"

When it was discovered that sympathy with Gough and the

colonels was widespread in the Army, the temperature at the War Office underwent a rapid change. When they arrived there on Sunday, Gough and the others were received coldly and told to return on the following day. Next morning they were informed by Colonel Seely that it was all a 'misunderstanding' and that they were in error in supposing that the Government had ever intended warlike operations against Ulster. It was explained that the measures taken had been purely 'precautionary' and, as a matter of fact, now that the transfer of troops to Carrickfergus had taken place safely, it had been considered unnecessary for the Third Battle Squadron to proceed to Lamlash. In other words, that Asquith's official biographer, J. A. Spender, described as "Mr. Churchill's slightly flamboyant orders for the movement of battleships" had been "countermanded" by the Prime Minister "as soon as he heard of them."* Gough asked for the assurance given by the Secretary of State to be put in black and white to prevent any further 'misunderstandings'. Seely had to go to a Cabinet meeting and he left the task of drafting the document to Sir Spencer Ewart, the Adjutant-General. From the Cabinet Seely went on to see the King at Buckingham Palace. When he returned to the War Office, he found that the document had already been approved by the Cabinet, but that it did not accurately reflect his verbal assurance to Gough. "Sir, we are plain soldiers," said Gough to the Minister. "We want plain words and no legal terms." Accordingly, with the help of Lord Morley, the Minister added two paragraphs to the effect that the Army would not be called upon "to crush political opposition to the policy or principles of the Home Rule Bill." The Government retained the right to use the armed forces of the Crown to maintain law and order and to support the civil power in the ordinary execution of its duty. The additions were initialled by French and Ewart.

But Gough wanted to be absolutely sure where he stood. "We understand by this last paragraph that we are not to be asked to take up arms against Ulster to enforce the present Home Rule Bill," he declared. "Can we return to tell our officers so?" "That is how I read the paragraph," replied Sir John French. Thus reassured and with the memorandum in his pocket, Gough returned to his command at the Curragh with the other officers, all of whom were reinstated.

When Asquith saw the additions—the "peccant paragraphs" as

* J. A. Spender and Cyril Asquith, *Life of Lord Oxford and Asquith*, II, 47.

Bonar Law called them—he disowned them on the ground that, "if it was not right to ask an officer what he would do in a hypothetical contingency, still less would it be right for an officer to ask the Government to give him any such assurance." Gough was thereupon informed that the added paragraphs were not to be considered as operative. In these circumstances Seely resigned, followed by French and Ewart, while the Prime Minister himself took over the portfolio for War.

Thus ended the so-called 'Curragh Mutiny', which was in fact no mutiny at all, since none of the officers involved had been guilty of any disobedience—they had simply been offered the choice between the possibility of having to carry out certain orders or being dismissed the Service.* The result had been to immobilise a considerable portion of the Army and to put an end to any likelihood of the armed forces of the Crown being employed against loyal Ulster.

Indeed the forces, both naval and military, in the neighbourhood of Belfast were already fraternising with the Volunteers. The officers and petty officers of H.M.S. *Pathfinder* visited Craigavon, and both they and the Volunteers engaged in signal practice together. As to the attitude of local population to the Army, Sir Nevil Macready was reassured on this point when he paid Carson a state visit in his stronghold and the guard was turned out to salute him at the entrance to Craigavon. Macready asked Carson why the Ulstermen should object to the presence of His Majesty's troops in their principal city. "So far from objecting," replied Carson, "we are delighted to see His Majesty's uniform at all times. There is nowhere in the King's dominions where the British soldier is assured of a more cordial welcome than in Belfast."

There is one important question to be answered. What was the precise nature of the operations, if any, which were planned against Ulster? The Government loudly denied the existence of any 'plot' or plan for the immediate coercion of the Northern Loyalists, and this denial has been endorsed by subsequent Liberal apologists like Asquith's biographers, who have asserted that it was a myth totally

* In replying to the toast of his health, which I proposed at a public dinner in London in 1938, General Sir Hubert Gough said: 'In referring to my lurid past Dr. Hyde went back to what was known as the Curragh incident. It was called a mutiny, but as a matter of fact I think you all know that was entirely a misnomer. The only question asked and the only point we had to decide was whether we would march against Ulster or would rather not do so. If I had been ordered to go, I think I would have gone, but, as I was given a free judgment on the matter and free right of expression of opinion, I said I would rather not fight against my fellow-countrymen, so I sent in my papers': see *Northern Whig and Belfast Post*, May 6, 1938.

without foundation.* On the other hand, the Unionists, both in Parliament and in the country, were convinced that there was a deliberate plan to attack Ulster on Saturday, March 21, and to arrest the Ulster leaders, and that this project, to use Sir Henry Wilson's words, was "frustrated by our action in the army." On the evidence available there is no doubt that the Unionists were right. In fact the strategy of their enemies was fully revealed through the contents of certain confidential documents which fell into the hands of Carson and the Ulster Unionist Council. From these it appeared that the general purpose of the operations was to blockade Ulster by land and sea, and to provoke the Ulstermen to shed the first blood.

Briefly the plan was to invade Ulster with about 25,000 troops operating in conjunction with naval units. Of these troops 10,000 were to be moved from Lichfield and Aldershot into Ireland. The feeling at the Curragh has already been described: it was equally strong in the other two camps, the officers and men at Aldershot being particularly resentful. In fact, Lord Lansdowne did not exaggerate when he said that a *coup d'état* had been planned against Ulster. It appears that the prime movers in this business were Mr. Churchill, Lloyd George, Birrell, Seely and French, who won over Paget in the hope of invading and disarming Ulster before the Volunteers were ready. As Colonel Repington, *The Times* military correspondent, put it in a letter which he wrote at the time to James Craig, "The plan was for Paget to sweep north with all the troops at his disposal, and for the ships at Lamlash to sweep down the coast from the north . . . a coup against Craigavon from Holywood may have formed part of the plan. The General Staff at the War Office are contemptuous of the plan, declaring that Paget would now be languishing in a Belfast gaol had he set out. It reads more like fiction concocted in a madhouse than fact, but Winston is capable of anything, Seely is a perfect ass, Birrell only a makeweight, and French a mere tool. A pretty junta for making war on peaceable inhabitants of the still United Kingdom! Paget accidentally let the cat out of the bag . . . and then providence sent us Hubert Gough." Furthermore, as Carson and Londonderry pointed out in a statement

* Mr. Churchill has written that the idea of ordering the battle squadron and flotilla to Lamlash was because it was thought that the popularity and the influence of the Royal Navy might produce a peaceable solution, even if the Army had failed. 'Beyond this nothing was authorised; but the Military Commanders, seeing themselves confronted with what well might be the opening movements in a civil war, began to study plans of a much more serious character on what was the inherently improbable assumption that the British troops would be forcibly resisted and fired upon by the Orange army'. *The World Crisis*, I (1911–1914), 184.

issued by them on behalf of the Ulster Unionist Council which was never officially contradicted, the gravity of the situation was emphasised by Paget's use of the words 'battle' and 'the enemy' and his statement to his officers that he would himself be 'in the firing line' at the first 'battle'. Nevertheless the Government refused to grant a judicial inquiry, for which Carson and his parliamentary colleagues pressed in the House of Commons.

One further matter requires a few words of explanation since it puzzled many people at the time. Why did not the Government arrest Carson and the other Ulster leaders and prosecute them? At one period indeed warrants were actually made out, but they were never executed.

The answer to this question is quite clear. For one thing, the Government fully realised that Carson and his principal supporters were a restraining influence, which would be removed with possibly terrible consequences should the Ulster Leader be put under lock and key. As Asquith told the King, it would be like throwing a lighted match into a powder barrel. Also, Redmond and the Nationalists were against such a move, pointing out that "it would inevitably secure for the victims an invaluable and much coveted place in the annals of Irish martyrology." Finally, there was considerable doubt whether an Ulster jury would convict. This last reason was advanced by Asquith when, reconciled with Carson with the passing of the years, he was talking over the problem with his old political opponent.

"You need have had no fear," said Carson, "for I should have pleaded guilty."

"Guilty!" Asquith gasped in astonishment.

"Yes. I should have pleaded guilty," Carson replied, "and I should have said: 'My Lord Judge and gentlemen of the jury: I was born under the British flag, a loyal subject of His Majesty the King. So much do I value this birthright that I was even prepared to rebel in order to defend it. If to fight, so as to remain, like yourselves, a loyal subject of His Majesty, be a crime, my Lord and gentlemen of the jury, I plead guilty.' " Carson paused a moment, then he added with a twinkle in his eye: "And where would you have been then?"

"That only shows," was Asquith's comment, "that I was even wiser in not prosecuting you than I thought I was."

CHAPTER TEN

Ireland and the War

I

WHILE public attention was focused on the Curragh and Craigavon, Major Crawford was working quietly in Hamburg on the task of procuring arms for the Volunteers. To pack 30,000 rifles and three million rounds of ammunition was no small undertaking, particularly as Crawford insisted that this should be done in small parcels each containing five rifles, bayonets and 500 rounds, so as to simplify the task of landing the whole cargo by night in Ulster. At the same time he was able to purchase a small tramp steamer of under 500 tons, named the *Fanny*, which seemed a suitable vessel for conveying the cargo to its intended destination. The *Fanny* had a Norwegian skipper and was manned by a Norwegian crew, who agreed to navigate the vessel under the directions of a seafaring Ulster friend of Crawford's, Captain Andrew Agnew. It was arranged that she should proceed to a rendezvous in the Kattegat, between the Danish islands of Langeland and Funen, and there wait for Crawford who would bring the precious packages by lighter down the Elbe and through the Kiel Canal. To throw the inquisitive off the scent, Crawford and his Hamburg friends spread the rumour around that the arms were destined for ex-President Castro of Mexico, who required them for a revolutionary *coup* he was planning in that country.

The rendezvous in the Kattegat was duly kept and the cargo transhipped to the *Fanny*. Unfortunately the local Danish harbourmaster was not satisfied that the German lighter carried only general cargo, and on opening one of the packages he found it contained rifles. It was unfortunate too that the *Fanny*'s papers showed she was bound for Iceland, a country then under Danish rule but anxious to gain its independence. The harbourmaster declared he must refer the matter to Copenhagen, since he knew of no lawful reason why the Icelanders should be importing rifles. He accordingly impounded the ship's papers.

Crawford felt he was caught like a rat in a trap. But he decided to make a dash for it to the open sea and, with the aid of a squall and a heavy mist, the *Fanny* succeeded in getting away unhindered. But the news soon leaked out. On April 1 the English newspapers carried the headline 'Guns Transhipped in the Baltic. Carson or Castro?'

In view of this report Captain Spender was instructed by his executive committee to order Crawford not to attempt to land the cargo in Ulster for the present but either to cruise in Baltic waters for three months until the scare had died down or else to store the arms in Hamburg until further instructions. Spender accordingly despatched a telegram which he hoped would reach Crawford. But Spender was filled with misgivings, and, as he left the post office, his worst fears were confirmed. His eyes fell on a news poster which read: 'Ulster's Mystery Arms-Ship Captured'. This news came as a staggering blow, as £70,000 had been invested in the venture.

"See what your mad plans have brought us to," said one of the committee to Spender as he sorrowfully returned to Craigavon. But Craig and Carson took him by the arm and Craig invited him to dinner. "Now we must begin all over again like a general after a defeat," said Carson, as they sat down at table. "We must have a new plan."

There was also a telegram waiting for Spender. When he opened it, he found it was from London to the effect that someone had arrived from Germany and wanted to see him as soon as possible. This pointed to definite and authentic news of Crawford, and Spender accordingly caught the next boat for England. On arrival in London he found Schmidt, the Hamburg arms dealer, who gave him some comforting news. The *Fanny* had not been captured, said Schmidt. She was somewhere in the North Sea, and would doubtless keep the rendezvous which Crawford had made with Spender, in Loch Laxford, off the coast of Sutherland. Spender and Schmidt hastened to Scotland, ostensibly on a fishing expedition, although they had no rods and Schmidt's frock-coat, cashmere trousers and patent-leather boots seemed hardly appropriate clothes for a sportsman. However, this expedition proved a wild goose chase, since the *Fanny*'s escape from the Kattegat necessitated a change of plan and Crawford was now heading for Great Yarmouth, where he put Agnew ashore with instructions to proceed to Belfast, there procure another ship and return to meet him off Lundy Island in the Bristol Channel. The object was again to tranship the arms to a less suspicious-looking vessel, as, in spite of repainting and changing her name to *Doreen*, the *Fanny* looked much too foreign to reach the North Irish coast unchallenged.

The *Fanny* now steamed up into the English Channel in the teeth of a terrific gale, keeping as near as possible to the French coast so as to avoid suspicion. To add to his troubles Crawford had an attack of malaria and appeared so ill that the Norwegian skipper, fearing for his life, headed towards Dunkirk for a doctor. But Crawford, staggering from his cabin, put a pistol to the captain's head and threatened to shoot him if he did not immediately put out to sea again. The captain obeyed and, surprising as it may seem, became the best of friends with the ailing gun-runner. He even tried his hand at cooking, to tempt Crawford to eat, declaring that in forty years' seafaring experience he had never sailed with such men as Crawford and Agnew.

Samuel Kelly, the owner of a fleet of colliery vessels in Belfast, sent Agnew in one of them to meet Crawford at Lundy Island, with instructions from the committee at Craigavon not to tranship the cargo but to act in accordance with the terms of Spender's telegram. Agnew was late at the rendezvous and the *Fanny* had to cruise about for two days and two nights expecting every moment to be intercepted by a gunboat of the Royal Navy. However, contact was safely made, and Agnew came on board with the change of plan, which infuriated Crawford, who said he would rather run the *Fanny* ashore at high water on the County Down coast and let his fellow countrymen salve the cargo. Leaving Agnew on board the *Fanny*, Crawford went ashore at Tenby and made as fast as he could for Belfast. He promised to meet Agnew several days later at the Tuskar Light, outside Rosslare harbour.

Crawford was still fuming with indignation when he arrived at Craigavon. "I will shake hands with no member of the committee," he said, "until I know what they propose to do with the *Fanny*'s cargo." "It's all right," replied Craig, taking him by the arm, "the Chief's here." A moment later Carson appeared. "Well done, Crawford," he said, "I'm proud of you." When the committee had assembled, Carson asked Crawford what were his immediate plans.

"The *Fanny* with a changed name is to meet me off the Tuskar Light on Friday night next. This is Tuesday. I want to purchase a British steamer into which I can tranship the cargo from the *Fanny* and then bring the guns to Larne."

General Richardson objected that it was impossible to tranship in open water, and several others supported this view. Crawford answered that he had gone into this with Agnew and that it was possible provided the weather was fine. "Gentlemen," he appealed, "I have promised nothing so far that I have not carried out. I promise you that I can do this, and it will be done."

Carson then intervened. "Crawford is right. We had better leave the details to him. I feel sure he will see his way to carry out his plan." He added that Crawford had brought the arms almost to their door, and, having done so much, surely he could be trusted to do the rest.

That settled the matter. Authority was given to purchase a vessel, the *Clydevalley*, then in Glasgow and due in Belfast to unload coal. This was done. The *Clydevalley* picked up Crawford on Llandudno sands two nights later, and after an anxious search for the *Fanny* and several further misunderstandings, the two vessels came together in a bay on the Welsh coast, and the arms were successfully transhipped to the *Clydevalley*'s hold. This vessel, which Crawford re-christened *Mountjoy II* after the famous ship which broke the boom which ended the siege of Londonderry in 1690, now sailed boldly for Belfast Lough. On the night of April 24 she came alongside the landing-stage at Larne, and the work of unloading the arms began.

This operation was carried through without a hitch. The whole Ulster Volunteer Force had been warned for a trial mobilisation on that night, and the owners of motor-cars and lorries had been asked to co-operate. The organisation was excellent and everyone worked with a will. Smaller consignments of arms were also landed at Donaghadee and Bangor, on the County Down coast, those for Bangor being unloaded in broad daylight next morning. Meanwhile all official telephone and telegraph wires had been 'earthed' by the Volunteers, and the police and coastguards surrounded and guarded in their barracks until the last gun and cartridge was safely ashore. The only casualty of any kind was the death of one coastguardsman from heart failure at Donaghadee. "The coup was really successful in every way," wrote Richardson to Carson after it was all over. "Nothing went wrong. Not a rifle or one round of ammunition astray. . . . Belfast is very steady and very pleased with itself."

The news was telegraphed to Carson and Londonderry in London by the pre-arranged code-word 'Lion'. Soon the newspapers and Press all over the world were full of the exploit. Craig crossed to London to give Carson a first-hand account and on his arrival at Carson's house in Eaton Place found the octogenarian Field-Marshal, Lord Roberts, closeted with Sir Edward. "Magnificent, magnificent," said the Field-Marshal. "Nothing could have been better done. It was a piece of organisation that any army in Europe might be proud of." Although he too was not informed of the operation until after the event, Bonar Law immediately associated himself with Carson and took full responsibility for what had happened. He subsequently told Ronald McNeill that Carson had deliberately kept him in the dark on the ground that it might be embarrassing for the Leader of the Opposition to know that a serious breach of the law was imminent.

That afternoon the House of Commons met in a buzz of excitement to hear what the Prime Minister had to say. In answer to a parliamentary question Mr. Asquith described the gun-running as "a grave and unprecedented outrage," and assured the House that "His Majesty's Government will take, without delay, appropriate steps to vindicate the authority of the law." The Irish Attorney-General was accordingly instructed by the Cabinet to prepare information against Carson and the other leaders with a view to the institution of criminal proceedings under the Treason-Felony Act.

The idea of criminal proceedings was speedily dropped. For one thing, the Cabinet was up against the old difficulty that no jury in the north of Ireland would be likely to convict the accused under ordinary legal process. On the other hand, any arbitrary action on the part of the Government would be calculated to precipitate a conflict which they were anxious to avoid.* All that happened, therefore, was the dispatch of a few destroyers to patrol the east coast of Ulster for a short time. The vessels were saluted by the

* There was a picturesque legend current at the time that the arrest of Carson and the other Ulster leaders had been stopped at the personal intervention of the King, following on a visit of Carson to Buckingham Palace, where he saw the King's private secretary, Lord Stamfordham, and told him that the arrests had been decided on and that Carson had arranged to send a coded telegram to Belfast which was to be the signal for the seizure of the Customs throughout Ulster. This story, which was propagated by Col. Repington, *The Times* military correspondent, in his diary (see *The First World War*, I, 69), was subsequently denied by Carson. It is true that he did call and see Stamfordham, but it was simply to give an account of what had happened in Ulster, in answer to Stamfordham's request: 'The King is much concerned at the fact of this large importation of arms into Ulster and at the circumstances under which the landing was carried out. His Majesty desires me to ask whether you are able to throw any light upon what has occurred. Were there special reasons for mobilising a certain number of Volunteers or was it done merely to ensure sufficient men to land the arms as quickly as possible?' Stamfordham to Carson, April 25, 1914: Carson MSS. Repington agreed to delete the offending passage from subsequent editions of his book. See Nicolson, *King George V*, 238 *note*.

Volunteer signalling stations and their officers were regaled on shore with typical Ulster hospitality by the local Loyalist residents.

The matter was raised again a few days later in the House of Commons, when the Conservative and Unionist Opposition pressed for a full inquiry into the "naval and military movements . . . contemplated by the Government against Ulster" in the previous month. Mr. Churchill, who replied for the Government, described the resolution in characteristic language as resembling "a vote of censure by the criminal classes on the police" and scornfully declined to give details of the precise measures to be taken against potential insurgents. He claimed that the Government had a perfect right to put 40,000 or 50,000 men into Ulster, to use the Fleet in support of the Army, to make arrests, seize arms, and prevent drilling. "If rebellion comes, we shall put it down," he declared, looking grimly in the direction of Carson, "and if it comes to civil war, we shall do our best to conquer in the civil war. But there will be neither rebellion nor civil war unless it is of your making."

The First Lord of the Admiralty concluded by making a direct appeal to the Ulster Leader in a carefully prepared peroration. Carson, he said, was running great risks—none could deny it—in strife. Why would he not run some risks for peace? The key was in his hands. "Why cannot the right hon. and learned gentleman say boldly '*Give me the Amendments to this Home Rule Bill which I ask for, to safeguard the dignity and the interests of Protestant Ulster, and I in return will use all my influence and goodwill to make Ireland an integral unit in a federal system*'? "

These words, as Mr. Churchill was quick to appreciate, gave the debate an entirely new turn, for it held out an olive branch, albeit a tiny one. Only the Radicals and Nationalists were disturbed by it, and that night Redmond wrote Asquith an indignant letter of protest. But the Nationalist Leader no longer possessed the authority with the Government that he once had. Next day the Prime Minister informed the House that he was heartily in sympathy with Mr. Churchill's proposal, although it had been made on his own account. Carson's reply, while admitting full responsibility for what had happened in Ulster, was unexpectedly conciliatory. After laying stress on the gravity of the crisis and the weakening it entailed in the position of Great Britain abroad, he said he would not quarrel with the matter or the manner of Mr. Churchill's proposal and that he was "not very far from the First Lord."

"If Home Rule is to pass," he went on, "much as I detest it, and little as I will take the responsibility for the passing of it, my earnest hope, and indeed I would say my earnest prayer would be that the Government of Ireland for the South and West would prove and might prove such a success in the future, notwithstanding all our anticipations, that it might be even for the interests of Ulster itself to move toward that Government, and come in under it and form one unit in relation to Ireland. May I say something more than that? I would be glad to see such a state of things arising in Ireland in which you would find that mutual confidence and goodwill between all classes in Ireland as would lead to a stronger Ireland as an integral unit in a federal scheme." For himself, all he wanted was "loyally to carry out the promises I have made to those who trust me, and to get for them such terms as will preserve for them their dignity and their civil and religious freedom."

It was a courageous and magnanimous gesture on Carson's part. Yet it evoked no echoing chord from the Nationalist benches. Many eyes turned expectantly towards Redmond. But Redmond made no move to rise from his seat.

2

Mr. Churchill's declared support of the federal principle as a solution of the Home Rule impasse had been prompted by an able group of young men led by Mr. Lionel Curtis and Mr. Edward Grigg (later Lord Altrincham), who had been assisting Lord Milner in formulating his schemes of imperial development. They shared the views of Carson's friend, F. S. Oliver, on federalism, and had advocated the idea strongly, in response to a challenge from Mr. Churchill, while they were recently cruising with him in the Admiralty yacht *Enchantress*, to suggest an alternative to bringing Ulster under a Dublin Parliament. In other words, their scheme was to confer on England, Scotland and Wales the same measure of Home Rule as on Ireland outside Ulster. Ulster would be left exactly as she was as a part of the United Kingdom unless—or until —she chose of her own accord to go in with the three other Irish provinces under an all-Ireland Home Rule arrangement.

Curtis and Grigg were authorised to sound Carson on the scheme, which appealed to both Mr. Churchill and Lloyd George. Carson agreed to accept it as a basis of discussion; indeed, as his speech in the House of Commons indicated, he was prepared to go further and commend it, provided that the six counties of North-East Ulster were firmly excluded from the Irish element. Bonar Law was also consulted and a secret meeting with the Liberal Premier was arranged at Edwin Montagu's house in London, the scene of similar gatherings in the past. The meeting took place, though not in the conditions of secrecy which had been planned, since F. E. Smith, who was anxious to ingratiate himself at the time with Lord Northcliffe, gave the *Daily Mail* advance news of it. "This will ruin Carson in Ulster," said Grigg, as he and Curtis hurried over to Eaton Place. But Carson appeared quite composed when they told him what had happened. "I don't care a damn," he said. "Only a fool would fight if there is a hope of accommodation. And what a great thing it would be if this long-standing controversy could be settled once and for all!"

In spite of this premature disclosure, the meeting took place as arranged. Unfortunately it achieved nothing, since Asquith could not be persuaded to give any decision. The reason was that Redmond, threatened by his own people at home, was now violently opposed to any further concessions. In fact he had made it clear to the Prime Minister that the Liberals must stick to their bargain with the Nationalists, otherwise he would force a political crisis which would make the Government's continuance in office impossible.

From the notes made at the time by Bonar Law, it appears that Asquith gave it as his opinion that the best course would be to have the third reading of the Home Rule Bill in the House of Commons, and then, when it was rejected in the House of Lords, negotiations could be seriously begun again. If they were successful, as he hoped, an Amending Bill would at once be introduced. Carson and Bonar Law both opposed this course as dangerous and unwise. When the Bill was read a third time in the Commons, Carson pointed out with emphasis, "there would be great rejoicings among the Nationalists in Belfast and it would be difficult, if not impossible, to prevent a serious collision between the two sections there." Asquith seemed impressed by this argument, and agreed that the Amending Bill should be introduced and put on the statute book at the same time as the original measure.

A week later, on May 12, Asquith announced the third reading of the Home Rule Bill for the third successive time, as required by the Parliament Act. At the same time he stated that the Amending Bill, which he had promised the Unionist leaders, would be introduced in the Lords "in the hope that a settlement might be arrived at." But the Prime Minister declined to state what the terms of the Amending Bill were to be, though Bonar Law pointed out that the House had a right to know this before it gave the original Bill a third reading. Notwithstanding the Opposition's demand, the Home Rule Bill passed through the House of Commons for the last time a fortnight later.

As Carson correctly guessed, the 'Bill to amend a Bill that is still a Bill' merely repeated Asquith's offer of county option and a time limit. "We are to be sentenced to death, but they are not to pull the rope round our necks till six years are expired," he said. "I would rather be hanged today." In Ulster the reaction to the final passage of the original Bill was Nationalist jubilation and a series of reviews and parades of the Volunteers, attended by Carson, Craig, Londonderry and the other leaders. These demonstrations excited intense enthusiasm throughout the Province, since for the first time the majority of the Volunteers no longer had dummy weapons in their hands. Here again Carson uttered a warning note. "I recognise some of the cargo of the *Mountjoy*," he told one regiment during an inspection. "I rely on you to keep your arms with a view to keeping the peace."

The vexed question of Home Rule for Ireland was not the only problem which troubled Asquith in domestic politics at this time. There was another which was a constant source of worry and which also had its impact on the Ulster Leader. This was the demand for female enfranchisement—as yet women were denied the vote in parliamentary and local government elections—and it found militant expression in the activities of the suffragettes which had been disturbing politicians of all parties in various ways for several years. One of these ladies had transferred her attentions to Carson and would waylay him as he entered and left his London house in Eaton Place. On several occasions she was removed by the police. Being of a persevering disposition, she then proceeded to chain herself to the railings outside the house. When the butler reported to his master what had happened, Carson conceived an ingenious and amusing device for ridding himself of this embarrassing manifestation. Anticipating the demands of nature, Carson told the butler to take a jug of water and distribute its contents so as to form a thin trail from the enchained lady along the pavement to the road. There is nothing which kills like ridicule, and having heard the pointed and irreverent comments of the crowd which soon collected on the spot, the suffragette soon unchained herself and shamefacedly made off.

On June 23 the Bill to amend the Home Rule Bill was introduced in the House of Lords by the Marquess of Crewe. To the Unionists it proved a sad disappointment, since it merely repeated the scheme of county option offered by Asquith when he moved the second reading of the original Bill on March 9. However, Lord Crewe did invite amendments to it, and in response to this invitation the Opposition, led by Lords Lansdowne, Londonderry, Milner and Roberts, proposed to substitute for county option with a time limit the permanent exclusion of the whole province of Ulster. The Amending Bill as thus amended passed its third reading on July 14 and was sent down to the Commons. It was due to be introduced there a week later, where it was a foregone conclusion the major Opposition amendment would be deleted at the behest of the Nationalists.

Meanwhile in Ulster the Boyne anniversary had passed off quietly, without any outbreak of disturbance which Carson had feared. For this satisfactory state of affairs the country had to thank the Ulster Leader. In the words of a native of Belfast, "Sir Edward was worth twenty battalions in keeping order." Nevertheless, it was becoming abundantly clear to everyone that Ireland was rapidly drifting toward civil war. Encouraged by the success of the Ulster Volunteer Force, the more radical elements in the South, subscribing to the gospel of Sinn Fein, preached by an able young journalist named Arthur Griffith, which advocated a complete break with Britain, enrolled their own Volunteers in defiance of John Redmond and the more moderate Nationalists. Although they were composed for the most part of farm labourers in the country districts and 'corner boys' in the towns and their discipline was not to be compared with that prevailing in the U.V.F., the Southern Volunteers were being drilled by old soldiers in the Irish regiments and, what is more, had acquired arms and ammunition. By midsummer they were said to number over 100,000, of which a third were mustered in Ulster. No wonder the immediate outlook appeared grave to Carson. "I see no hopes of peace. I see nothing at present but darkness and shadows," he declared during the 12th of July celebrations in Ulster. "We must be ready. In my own opinion the great climax and the great crisis of our fate, and the fate of our country, cannot be delayed for many weeks . . . unless something happens—when we shall have once more to assert the manhood of our race."

"Unless something happens——" Something, indeed, had happened, but its effect had not as yet been perceptible to many in either England or Ireland. At the end of the previous month the Austrian Archduke Franz Ferdinand and his wife had been murdered at Serajevo by Serbian fanatics. At the very moment Carson was speaking in Ulster the Austrian Foreign Minister was engaged in drafting an ultimatum to the Government of Serbia.

Before leaving Belfast Carson presided over a meeting of the Ulster Provisional Government and concerted with its members plans to take over 'in trust for His Majesty the King in every Court and office of the Crown in Northern Ireland.' This meant control of the postal services, customs and other sources of internal revenue. Carson then arranged with James Craig that he should send a code-word telegram from London as the signal for action. "You may take it," Craig told him, "that immediately you signify by the pre-arranged code that we are to go ahead, everything prepared will be carried out to the letter unless in the meantime you suggest any modification. All difficulties have been overcome and we are in a very strong position."

Instead of introducing the Amending Bill in the Commons on July 20, as he had previously announced, the Prime Minister informed the House that the King had called an all-party conference at Buckingham Palace for the following day in the hope of resolving the deadlock. Those nominated by their parties to attend were the Prime Minister and Mr. Lloyd George for the Government, Lord Lansdowne and Mr. Bonar Law for the Opposition, Sir Edward Carson and Captain James Craig for the Ulster Unionists and Mr. John Redmond and Mr. John Dillon for the Irish Nationalist Party. At the King's suggestion, the Speaker of the House of Commons, Mr. James Lowther, agreed to preside.

The delegates duly assembled in a room on the right of the Grand Hall of the Palace and adjoining the Ball Room. Here they were joined by His Majesty, who in a few simple sentences wished Godspeed to their deliberations, and then withdrew. "My intervention at this moment may be regarded as a new departure," he said. "But the exceptional circumstances in which you are brought together justify my action. For months we have watched with deep misgiving the course of events in Ireland. The trend has been surely and steadily toward an appeal to force, and today the cry of Civil War is on the lips of the most responsible and sober-minded of my people. We have in the past endeavoured to act as a civilising example to the world, and to me it is unthinkable, as it must be to you, that we should be brought to the brink of fratricidal strife upon issues apparently so capable of adjustment as those you are now asked to consider, if handled in a spirit of generous compromise."

Since the conference took place in secret, no accounts of its proceedings was published, except the King's opening remarks, which it was agreed should be given to the Press. However, some notes were made at the time by Bonar Law and Redmond, and from these it has been possible to reconstruct what took place.

The discussion centred round the question of area, specifically the counties of Fermanagh and Tyrone, in which part of Ulster the Catholic population was numerically strongest. On Carson urging that it was quite impossible for him to discuss any question of area if the time limit, as proposed by the Government, were to be still in force, Redmond and Dillon after a good deal of argument eventually intimated that they would give way on the time limit if agreement was reached on the main point. The conference then proceeded on this assumption.

Various maps and statistics were handed round and examined. Redmond then read a long statement of his case, the substance of which was that, assuming any part of Ireland was to be excluded, which he and his party were loath to agree to, areas predominantly Nationalist should be under the Home Rule Parliament and areas predominantly Unionist should be excluded.* His statement was intended to prove that, to reach this result, county option was the only possible plan. To this Carson objected that it would be unfair to take any district out of the existing arrangement on the ground of anything approaching a bare majority, contending that to compel people to change their government was only justifiable where the difference of population was, not merely predominant, but 'absolutely preponderating'.

Carson also observed that in his view the only statesmanlike solution of the problem, on the assumption that Home Rule was to be granted at all, was that the whole of Ulster should be excluded. "He gave it as his opinion," noted Bonar Law, "that, if this were done generously, then there would be a likelihood within a reasonable time of Ulster being willing to come into a united Ireland, whereas if any attempt to coerce any part of Ulster were made, a united Ireland within the lifetime of anyone now living would be out of the question."

Both Redmond and Dillon admitted that, if they were free

* The text of this statement will be found in Denis Gwynn, *The Life of John Redmond*, at pp. 338–340.

agents, this was a plan they would adopt. However, they were not free agents, and in the circumstances such a plan was absolutely out of the question. If they were to propose it, they said, it would mean they would be "without a party either in Ireland or anywhere else."

For the next three days both the conference and the Cabinet, in Mr. Churchill's words, "toiled around the muddy byways of Fermanagh and Tyrone." Lloyd George suggested a division of the latter county in accordance with Poor Law Union districts, but this was ruled out by both Carson and Redmond as impracticable since it involved 'swapping' districts in Ulster. Meanwhile, with the public outside the idea was growing that, if the principal protagonists should fail to agree, a decision should be imposed upon them from without, and this view was reflected in Government circles by Mr. Churchill. "Failing an Irish agreement there ought to be a British decision," he wrote to his Cabinet colleague, Sir Edward Grey, when the conference was in its most crucial stage. "Carson and Redmond, whatever their wishes, may be unable to agree about Tyrone; they may think it worth a war, and from their point of view it may be worth a war. But that is hardly the position of the forty million who dwell in Great Britain; and their interests must, when all is said and done, be our chief and final care. . . . I want peace by splitting the outstanding differences, if possible with Irish acquiescence, but if necessary over the heads of both Irish parties."*

But this was not to be. Asquith made a final effort to bring the parties together by proposing a definite area for exclusion, namely the six north-eastern counties which now constitute Northern Ireland, and letting them vote as such for or against Home Rule. But Redmond declared that he could no more consent to this than the exclusion of the whole province. On his part Carson pointed out that, if he was to accept this proposal, he would have to begin by announcing that he had thrown over something like two million male 'covenanters' in the three remaining counties of Cavan, Monaghan and Donegal, whom he had pledged himself not to desert. Thus the conference broke down. On the morning of July 24 Mr. Speaker Lowther accordingly issued a brief announcement to the effect that it had been unable to agree, either on principle or in detail, to the area to be excluded from the operations of the Home Rule Bill. At the same time Asquith told the House of Commons that the Amending Bill would be introduced on July 30.

The same afternoon the Cabinet met in Downing Street to

* Winston Churchill, *The World Crisis*, 1911–1914, I, 187.

receive the Prime Minister's report of the conference. What happened there, the shock which suddenly galvanised its members and directed their attentions and energies to another channel, is best described by one who was present at that memorable meeting. "The discussion had reached its inconclusive end," Mr. Churchill wrote afterwards in *The World Crisis*, "when the quiet grave tones of Sir Edward Grey's voice were heard reading a document which had just been brought to him from the Foreign Office. It was the Austrian note to Serbia. He had been reading or speaking for several minutes before I could disengage my mind from the tedious and bewildering debate which had just closed. We were all very tired, but gradually as the phrases and sentences followed one another, impressions of a wholly different character began to form in my mind. This note was clearly an ultimatum; but it was an ultimatum which had seldom been penned in modern times. As the reading proceeded it seemed absolutely impossible that any State in the world could accept it, or that any acceptance, however abject, would satisfy the aggressor. The parishes of Fermanagh and Tyrone faded back into the mists and squalls of Ireland, and a strange light began immediately, but by perceptible gradations, to fall and grow upon the map of Europe."*

In spite of the imminence of a European war, which the succeeding few days made plain, Asquith adhered to his plan of bringing in the Amending Bill on the day he had announced. In fact, he was sitting in the Cabinet room in Downing Street on the morning of July 30, with a map of Ulster and a mass of statistics about populations and religions, endeavouring to get something into shape for his speech, when a telephone message came from Bonar Law asking him to go and see him and Carson at his house in Kensington. Bonar Law had sent his motor, and the Prime Minister immediately got into it and drove off. Asquith told the two men that war between Great Britain and Germany was merely a matter of hours. Bonar Law thereupon suggested that the Amending Bill should be postponed, so as not to advertise Britain's domestic dissensions at such a time. Asquith naturally welcomed this attitude, and Carson concurred. In his pocket was the code telegram which he had intended to send to Craig in Belfast giving the Ulster Provisional Government the 'go ahead' signal. There was now no need to send it. According to Asquith, Carson observed that at first he had thought it impossible to agree to the postponement, as it would

* Winston Churchill, *The World Crisis*, 1911–1914, I, 193.

strain still further the well-known and much tried patience of the Ulster people. "But," he added, "I have come to see that it is now a patriotic duty." As he stepped into his motor outside Bonar Law's house, he turned to his chauffeur: "Brookes," he said, "there will be no more of Ireland until we have done with this job."

Asquith departed to consult his colleagues and Mr. Redmond. They agreed that it was right to close with the offer. Thus, during the period of the emergency, it was understood that Home Rule was to go into cold storage.

3

For the August Bank Holiday week-end, an Irish friend, Sir Edward Goulding,* had invited Carson to his pleasant country house at Wargrave, overlooking the Thames. Bonar Law had also been invited, and the two men motored down together to Wargrave Hall, where they were joined by two more guests, F. E. Smith and Sir Max Aitken. To Aitken, who was the last to arrive, the composition of the party suggested that it had been summoned to discuss Ulster. Actually the guests and their host discussed the attitude the Opposition should adopt towards the imminent war. Even as they talked news reached them of acute dissensions in the Cabinet on the subject of British intervention.

The recipient of this information was F. E. Smith, and the member of the Cabinet with whom he was in touch was Mr. Churchill. The gist of the news was that, while most of the leading Liberals were determined to stand by France, the Liberal newspapers were strongly opposed to Britain's participation in any continental conflict, and that at least half a dozen resignations might be expected. If these resignations took place, would the Opposition be prepared to come to the rescue of the Government, not merely with parliamentary support, but by forming a coalition to fill up the vacant offices?

All were in favour of giving the Government parliamentary support, but on the policy of going further the views were divided. The only strong advocate of coalition was F. E. Smith, and in the face of Bonar Law's expressed opposition neither he nor the others could have done anything effective, even had they wished to. The Conservative Leader objected to Mr. Churchill as a medium and the

* Afterwards Lord Wargrave.

negotiation savoured too much of an intrigue to suit him. Anyhow Bonar Law would have none of it, although the general idea was conceded that, should the Government declare war, the Tories would back it. Late that night F. E. Smith sat down and penned a note to Mr. Churchill. "I have spoken to my friends of whom you know," he wrote, "and I have no doubt on the facts as we understand them—and more particularly on the assumption (which we understand to be certain) that Germany contemplates a violation of Belgian neutrality—the Government can rely upon the support of the Unionist Party in whatever manner that support can be most effectively given."

Next morning the feeling of the house-party was that they should all return to London at once. But at Bonar Law's suggestion they agreed to wait for further news and go up to Town later in the day. No further news having been received by lunch-time, Carson went on the river, while the others played tennis. When Carson got back to the house, he discovered that Bonar Law had gone, while Mr. George Lloyd, M.P.*, and Lord Charles Beresford had come down to bring him back to a meeting urgently summoned, in view of the increasing gravity of the international situation, by Lord Lansdowne, the Conservative Leader in the Lords. Meanwhile Mr. Churchill had replied to F. E. Smith thanking him for his letter "with its generous and patriotic offer," which he had read to the Cabinet, where it produced a profound impression. "I cannot think war will be averted now," added the First Lord of the Admiralty. "Germany *must* march through Belgium, and I believe that the bulk of both parties will stand firm against that."

Another visitor had come to Wargrave in search of Carson. This was Captain Wilfrid Spender of the Ulster Volunteer Force. He was under orders by the War Office to join the Staff of the Eastern Coast Defence, and at the instigation of some other military friends in the Committee of Imperial Defence he had offered to go down to Wargrave and get a decision from the Ulster Leader on the future of the Volunteers. Carson promptly gave it and it was immediately published in the Press. "If required by them he declared, "a large body of Ulster Volunteers will be willing and ready to give their services for Home Defence and many will be willing to serve anywhere they are required."

Carson motored back to London that evening and, though he was not present at the meeting of the Conservatives at Lansdowne

* Later Lord Lloyd.

House, he met most of them at Bonar Law's house on Sunday morning, when the decision was endorsed urging the Government to stand true to its obligations toward France and Russia and pledging the party's support to the Government in any measures they might consider necessary for that object. Throughout the morning the Cabinet was also sitting in Downing Street, and Bonar Law sent Asquith a letter by hand setting forth his views in language similar to that which F. E. Smith had employed in writing to Mr. Churchill.

Germany was already at war with Russia, her troops had violated the territory of Luxembourg and she was preparing to invade Belgium. On that Sunday it looked as if the majority of the Cabinet would resign. Eventually next day, when the King of the Belgians appealed to the Powers who had guaranteed his country's neutrality and the decision was taken to send Germany the ultimatum which meant war, only two Ministers, Lord Morley and Mr. John Burns, left the Government. For a long time Mr. Lloyd George, who was naturally reluctant to face the possibility of his social welfare schemes being cast into the shadows, sided with the dissentient Radicals, but at the eleventh hour, realising that Great Britain was opposed by a Power which sought world domination and the destruction of the British Empire, he came out boldly in support of the policy of armed intervention in Europe. Chief protagonist of this policy in the Cabinet was Mr. Churchill, and throughout these critical days he played a truly national role, putting aside all party jealousies and prejudices.

We have seen how Carson had already put the Ulster Volunteers at the disposal of the Government. A similar gesture came from John Redmond. "If the dire necessity is forced upon this country," the Nationalist Leader told the House of Commons on the fateful Bank Holiday Monday, "we offer to the Government of the day that they may take their troops away, and that, if it is allowed to us, in comradeship with our brethren in the north, we will ourselves defend the coasts of our country." Thus Sir Edward Grey, in the grave speech which he made in the House that same afternoon, was able to describe Ireland as "the one bright spot" in the terrible situation. "The position of Ireland," he said, "—and I should like this to be clearly understood abroad—is not a consideration we have to take into account now."

As the Foreign Secretary was speaking, Carson looked at Mr. Churchill. Tears were running down the First Lord's face as he sat in his customary place on the Treasury Bench. Afterwards they left the Chamber together and, as they passed behind the Speaker's chair, Carson gripped Churchill warmly by the hand. Later he sent his old antagonist a note congratulating him on his patriotic conduct, to which Mr. Churchill responded gratefully. "The good wishes of my father's friends are dear to me, and yours I value especially," Mr. Churchill wrote. "I hope we shall sometimes in the future be able to act together."

In the hope of effecting a complete political reconciliation between Carson and Redmond, Mr. Speaker Lowther invited the two protagonists to meet privately in the Speaker's library in the House of Commons. The meeting took place during the afternoon of August 5, but the outcome was negative. Redmond had already asked Asquith to lose no time in placing the Home Rule Bill on the statute book and he now made it clear to Carson that he expected the Prime Minister to do this. Carson, who had already heard rumours to this effect, likewise made it clear that, if this happened, Asquith could not expect him and his followers to co-operate on other parliamentary business. That night he wrote in a despondent mood to Miss Ruby Frewen, to whom he had recently become engaged to be married: "I am very much depressed as I fear the Government mean, if they can, to betray us, and pass the Home Rule Bill over our heads and whilst it is impossible to resist in Ulster owing to the difficulties caused by the present situation. They are such a lot of scoundrels I believe they are quite capable of anything."

The same day as this discouraging meeting in the Speaker's library took place, Asquith, who had held the portfolio of War since Seely's resignation after the Curragh incident, divested himself of this additional burden. Field-Marshal Lord Kitchener was on the point of returning to his post as British Agent in Cairo when he was snatched off the Dover boat and informed that he had been appointed Secretary of State for War.

At this date Horatio Herbert Kitchener, first Earl Kitchener of Khartoum, was in his sixty-fifth year. No man then alive commanded such public confidence, and there was no one who had such intimate knowledge of the military resources of the British Empire as a whole. His weakness was that he had little experience of the Army at home and knew even less of the inner workings of the War Office. He had too a profound distrust of politicians. But he was a great national and imperial figure, and his immense prestige made his employment inevitable, the first high-ranking soldier to hold a Cabinet post since the days of the Duke of

Wellington. Also, when all the other statesmen and soldiers of Europe spoke of the war being over by Christmas, he was the only one to realise that it would last for at least three years. The impact of his personality immediately made itself felt in the recruiting drive to expand the British Army on the vast scale which he planned. Soon his familiar features gazed down from nearly every hoarding in the country, beckoning them to join the colours in increasing numbers. Said a wit to Lloyd George: "Lord Kitchener may or may not be a great General, but he is certainly a great Poster."

A day or so after the appointment was announced, Carson and Craig were shown into the new Secretary of State's spacious room in the War Office, overlooking the Horse Guards. They had come to offer the flower of the Ulster Volunteers, at least a division of trained men, provided that Home Rule was to be put into cold storage. Kitchener had already seen Redmond, who had intimated that he could do nothing with the Nationalist Volunteers until the Home Rule Bill had become law, and he was incensed at what he took to be an absurd wrangle at such a time between two tiresome politicians.

"Surely you're not going to hold out for Tyrone and Fermanagh?" the War Minister asked.

"You're a damned clever fellow telling me what I ought to be doing," answered Carson.

"If I'd been on the platform with you and Redmond," Kitchener observed, "I should have knocked your heads together!"

"Oi'd loike to see ye try," said Carson in his richest brogue.

In other respects the interview was not very encouraging. Carson and Craig both emphasised that if the men were forthcoming, they should be kept together as far as possible as a fighting unit. Up till then the name of Ulster had not appeared in the Army List, although regiments like the Royal Irish Rifles and the North Irish Horse were recruited in the province. Carson particularly asked that the word 'Ulster' should succeed the number of the Division which it was proposed to raise. But to this request Kitchener demurred. And so the first meeting with the War Minister and the two Ulster leaders terminated inconclusively.

Torn between the remonstrances of Carson and Redmond, Asquith's Cabinet could not immediately decide what to do. Meanwhile the rumour that the hated Bill was to become law had reached Belfast. "Now that it is believed that the Home Rule controversy is to be revived, the indignation in Ulster is extreme,"

Carson wrote to Asquith from Bonar Law's house on August 10. "They think they have been betrayed, and I am placed in the position that I must either resign the leadership of Ulster or go over to Belfast and throw in my lot with my people there in any action they may feel bound to take, however distasteful it might be to me and however much it might be disliked in England."

4

Playing for time, Asquith adjourned the House of Commons for a fortnight, during which interval he hoped to make proposals which might meet with 'something like general acquiescence'. Carson, who knew that no real acquiescence was possible, resented this policy of procrastination ("Asquithian delay", he called it), which was naturally reflected in the attitude of the War Office to the question of recruiting in Ireland.

To Lady Londonderry

Saturday [*August* 22, 1914] . . . The W.O. are great funkers in relation to Ireland. I believe they would let everything go to H[ell] rather than offend Redmond. They will not employ our people who are loyal because they cannot employ the others who are not. Politics! Politics! Always politics! We are rewarded not according to our merits but according to the demerits of others! Oh for a man!

I shudder to think what will happen if we have a defeat. Probably an ignominious outcry for 'peace' in the Radical press and resignation of the rotters. Poor Belgium has been ruined by procrastination and manœuvering to keep the Cabinet together . . .

Almost immediately after the reassembly of the Commons, Asquith obtained a further adjournment for ten days. "The Irish on both sides are giving me a lot of trouble just at a difficult moment," the harassed Prime Minister recorded in his diary on August 31. "I sometimes wish we could submerge the whole lot of them and their island for, say, ten years under the waves of the Atlantic. I have had an interview today, in the intervals of more urgent things, with Redmond and with Bonar Law, inspired by Carson, and they almost fill me with despair."

From Craigavon Carson's principal lieutenant clearly saw the course which they both must take. "However much we curse and damn the P.M. in the House," he wrote to his chief, "we must say all the same that we will do our best under the circumstances for the army and the country; then come over here and face the music and do our best.' Carson cordially agreed. Before leaving for Belfast at the beginning of September to launch the recruiting drive, he again saw Kitchener and offered unconditionally to put all the Ulster Volunteers at his disposal, assuring him that 35,000 of them were willing, if accepted, to enlist and go abroad. The War Minister gratefully accepted this offer, and waived his previous doubts and objections to the formation of exclusively Ulster units to be so described.

At the beginning of September Carson crossed over to Belfast to 'face the music'. He presided at a meeting of the Ulster Unionist Council in the Ulster Hall, at which his arrangements with the War Office were enthusiastically approved and at which he urged all Loyalists to come forward for the defence of the Empire, the honour of Ulster and of Ireland. "England's difficulty is not Ulster's opportunity," he declared amid frantic cheering, "England's difficulty is our difficulty, and England's sorrows have always been and will always be our sorrows . . . However we are treated, and however others act, let us act rightly. We do not seek to purchase terms by selling our patriotism . . . On the question of Home Rule we stand where we always have been. It will never be law in our country. We will postpone active measures in the interests of the country and the Empire, but when the country is more safe we will assert our powers as before . . . I never had any doubt from the first moment that Ulster would most willingly come to the front in giving all the assistance that was possible to the United Kingdom in the waging of this war . . . If we get enough men from the Ulster Volunteer Force they will go under the War Office as a Division of their own, and if we get enough they can go as two or more Divisions. I am very anxious that they should not separate. The good comradeship and the good fellowship that have grown up amongst our men in the face of the common danger for which they were formed will give them courage if they wanted it, and will give them confidence in their new venture . . . For my own part I have only one regret in the whole matter and it is that I am not young enough to enlist in the ranks and go with them."

To Miss Ruby Frewen

Ulster Club, Belfast. September 3, 1914. I sent you a wire today, after our meeting. It was a wonderful success and now I am in great hopes we will get our men in large numbers. The promise of making them into a division has been a great help . . .

I feel a great emotion at the way the people have trusted me and looked to me for advice . . .

Carson was back in London for the resumption of the parliamentary sittings on September 9. At that time the Opposition 'shadow' Cabinet was in the habit of meeting daily in Bonar Law's room in the House of Commons to see the latest War Office telegrams from the front, which by reason of the party truce the Opposition Leader received from the Prime Minister. These messages under seal would usually be brought into the room by Lord Beaverbrook, then Sir Max Aitken, who acted as Bonar Law's private secretary. Lord Beaverbrook was most anxious to know the contents of one of these messages, which he suspected contained news of other reverses in France. In fact it was a definitive statement of Asquith's intentions regarding the Home Rule Bill.

The secretary hung about outside the room so as to waylay the first person to come out. This happened to be Carson, and the secretary was immediately struck by his gloomy expression.

"For heaven's sake," Aitken exclaimed in alarm, "what is the news?"

"The very worst, my dear fellow, the very worst," replied Carson.

"But what has happened? Is the news very bad?"

"Bad, very bad," said Carson in a tone of tragic solemnity. "Asquith has decided to put the Bill on the statute book."

In recording this incident, Lord Beaverbrook has made it clear that he does not impute any blame to Carson. "The Home Rule struggle had been his life issue," writes Lord Beaverbrook in his valuable and engaging study of those times, "and if he took a little time to adjust his viewpoint to new conditions he was not the only public man by any manner of means who suffered from this defect. Soon he was to take the war very seriously indeed."* Indeed Carson had already begun to take the war very seriously, as must be apparent from his unconditional offer of the Ulster Volunteers to Lord Kitchener and his implementation of this offer in Belfast.

Asquith's action was capable of producing a most serious effect in Ulster, and no wonder Carson also took it seriously. But it had an important qualification, which the Prime Minister hoped would go far to satisfy both parties in Ireland. The Home Rule Bill was to become law, but its operation was to be suspended until the end of the war. The Amending Bill would be introduced in the next session. This news was publicly announced by Asquith in the House of Commons on September 15. At the same time Asquith paid a

* Lord Beaverbrook, *Politicians and the War*, I, 52.

tribute to the patriotic and public spirit shown by the Ulster Volunteers, whose conduct had made the employment of any kind of force for the coercion of Ulster "an absolutely unthinkable thing."

Carson left it to Bonar Law to reply on behalf of the whole Conservative and Unionist Party. In a strong speech Bonar Law declared regretfully that the Government had taken advantage of the Unionists to betray them. He reminded Asquith of his meetings with Carson and himself on the eve of the war when the Prime Minister had made it clear that the Home Rule Bill and the Amending Bill hung together and had promised that until the discussion of the Amending Bill no controversial legislation would be introduced, nor would the Home Rule Bill be presented for the King's assent till the Amending Bill had been disposed of in the Commons. That promise would not now be kept. Would Asquith's new pledge be any stronger? (It was indeed destined to be equally violated.) However, Ulster and the Unionists, said Bonar Law, in spite of all would help the Government to preserve the country till the war was over.

In protest at the Prime Minister's conduct, Bonar Law, at the conclusion of his speech, ostentatiously walked out of the Chamber. He was followed by Carson and the rest of his supporters on the Opposition benches.

5

Carson was not present to see the Home Rule Bill receive the Royal Assent in the House of Lords on September 18. Nor was he in his place in the Commons when the Nationalists streamed back to the Lower House flourishing an Irish flag with its golden harp. He was enjoying a brief honeymoon with his new bride in the country.

On the previous day Edward Carson and Ruby Frewen were quietly married in the parish church of Charlton Musgrove in Somerset, where the bride had been living with her mother. "We had a very quiet little wedding," he told Mrs. Craig, "and, as we only told the clergyman in the morning, not even a villager was there! I should have hated publicity in all the circumstances and I am so glad to defeat the camera." But a few close friends did travel down from London for the ceremony, including James Craig and Lord Londonderry. The latter, with characteristic generosity, gave the new Lady

THE ULSTER PROVISIONAL GOVERNMENT AT CRAIGAVON.

Back row, left to right: Mr. W. J. M. McCaw, M.P.; Mr. A. L. Horner, K.C., M.P.; Mr. George Sclater; Mr. John Gordon, K.C., M.P.; Mr. Ronald McNeill, M.P.; Capt. James Craig, M.P.; Mr. James Chambers, K.C., M.P.; Mr. C. C. Craig, M.P.; Capt. the Hon. Arthur O'Neill, M.P.; Mr. H. T. Barrie, M.P.; Mr. Peter Kerr-Smiley, M.P.; Mr. R. Dawson Bates, Secretary of the Ulster Unionist Council.

Sitting, left to right: Col. R. G. Sharman-Crawford, M.P.; Rt. Hon. Thomas Sinclair, P.C.; Col. J. M. McCalmont, M.P.; Duke of Abercorn; Sir Edward Carson, K.C., M.P.; Sir John Lonsdale, Bt., M.P.; Mr. R. J. McMordie, M.P., Lord Mayor of Belfast; Col. Robert Wallace, Grand Master of the Orange Order; Mr. William Moore, M.P.

From a photograph in the possession of the Ulster Unionist Council.

SIR EDWARD CARSON AND
MR. F. E. SMITH.

Outside Carson's house at Rottingdean.

ANDREW BONAR LAW.

From a photograph.

Carson a cheque for £1,000 as a wedding present, because, as he said, her husband "has done so much for Ulster."

The few days' honeymoon was spent in a hotel in Minehead. "It is quite nice here with miles of seashore and a good hotel," wrote the bridegroom to Lady Londonderry. "Ruby sends her love and many thanks for all your kindness—she seems to be very happy." They were indeed most happy together, in spite of the differences in their ages—Carson was sixty, his bride barely thirty. A new light had come into Carson's life which was to illumine all his remaining days and to give him the fullest domestic comfort.

A week later Carson took his bride to Ulster to introduce her to the Ulster people. Her welcome, as the wife of their beloved leader, was genuine and sincere. Like 'Sir Edward', the new Lady Carson was immediately taken to their hearts, but with that outspokenness which is a marked Ulster characteristic. A typical incident may be recalled here. Lady Carson was waiting outside the Ulster Club in her car, which had one window down. She was recognised by a woman millworker in a black shawl. The woman, known locally as a 'shawlie', got on the step of the car, looked inside and examined its occupant closely. "It's his wife," she said loudly. Then a second 'shawlie' got up, poked her head in, and shouted as she got down: "She's verra young." A third thereupon followed suit, and had a good look, got down and informed her friends in rather contemptuous tones: "She's no so young as a' that!"

On September 28—the second anniversary of the signing of the Covenant—Carson and Bonar Law addressed enthusiastic meetings in the Ulster Hall, and in the following days the two men visited the camps where the 1st Brigade of the Ulster Division was undergoing training. They were delighted at the response to the appeal for recruits. Indeed the flow outran the provision made for them by the War Office. Within the next fortnight the Protestant districts of Ulster had furnished some 21,000, of which Belfast alone had contributed over 7,500, the highest proportion of all the towns in the United Kingdom. Owing to his seniority in rank, Sir George Richardson was unable to command the Division: his place was taken by Major-General C. H. Powell, an ex-Indian Army officer with a fine record, while James Craig became A.A. and Q.M.G. and Captain Spender was appointed G.S.O.2.

Needless to say, both Carson's sons were already in the forces, Harry having joined up again in the Army and Walter, now a lieutenant, carrying on in the Navy.

To Lady Londonderry

5 *Eaton Place, S.W.* [*December*, 1914] . . . Walter came into Chatham and so we went down to see him and his ship at the Dockyard. It was all very full of interest . . .

There appears to be great wear and tear in the ships and constant refitting of the smaller craft seems to be very necessary. Apparently it is a very strenuous job for the destroyers and the Germans are full of resource and craftiness, *e.g.* they put mines on to a mock periscope in the hope that our boats may try to ram them, and they imitate our lights and signals. The larger vessels seem quite useless for the kind of work that has to be done. I believe there has been a shortage of mines and many other things and no great residuum of torpedoes . . .

He [Walter] is coming to dine with another Lieutenant tonight. They are always very interesting and their spirits are quite wonderful.

I am to see Lord Kitchener at the War Office with reference to the Ulster Regiments. I imagine they are afraid of the Nationalists . . .

Unfortunately a certain amount of political jealousy of the Ulster Division had developed, which showed itself in a tendency to belittle the recruiting figures in Ulster, which were a tremendous credit to the Province. The men themselves were desperately anxious to get to France, and they believed that sinister political influences were responsible for keeping them at home, while other formations were getting priority in the matter of equipment. As Carson put it, speaking at Maralin, County Down, on January 6, 1915, "There seems to be more joy in political circles of a particular character over one Nationalist that enlisted than over a whole Ulster Division." Their leader told the Ulster patriots not to be put out by any Nationalist sneers. "I never yet knew when I was beaten—even when it was in the Law Courts—and I never yet knew an Ulsterman who admitted he was beaten . . . I know that I was told over and over again that I had started regiments of rebels. Yes, and I always boasted that I was the chief rebel myself. If it was to be a rebel to love my country and to be determined that I should maintain what I inherited of freedom, I was always proud to be called a rebel. Yes, we have got 17,000 rebels in camp now. God bless the rebels! They are as loyal to their King as any that ever breathed the free air of heaven, men who will fight for their King with all the vigour and determination and courage of the great race that they are proud to belong to; men who will bring glory to you and glory to the province to which they belong. God bless them I say again!"

A few weeks later Ulster lost a great public figure, and Carson a close personal friend, in the sudden death of Lord Londonderry at the age of sixty-two. Although his passing, which took place at

Wynyard Park, his Durham estate, came as a surprise to the general public, things had been far from well with him for some months. He had grown very despondent both by reason of the war and the turn of events in Ulster. The fact that his son and heir, Lord Castlereagh, had gone out to the front preyed on his mind and he grew convinced that he would not return. He lost his former zest for living, so that when an attack of influenza turned to pneumonia, he made little or no attempt to survive it. Carson, who went to Wynyard for the funeral, subsequently described him as "a great leader, a great and devoted public servant, a great patriot, a great gentleman, and above all the greatest of great friends." These words were echoed by his widow. "I don't think there was anyone who was more beloved or thought more of in the two counties in which he lived," she wrote afterwards. "Apart from his having served his Government and his country in the Cabinet, he lived absolutely the life of a country gentleman and was identified with every political movement, every philanthropic institution, and every sport in both counties. I don't think anybody in this world had more friends than he had."

To Lady Londonderry

5 Eaton Place, S.W. March 13, 1915 . . . Everyone here was so genuinely sorry for Lord L. that I can only truly describe him as being universally missed, and I feel such a gap that I hardly realise that I have lost such a true and consistent friend. However, everything has to 'go on' no matter what happens and we all have to make the best of it.

Charley* came to see me before he left. He was most sensitive to his loss. I feel I liked him more than ever and I was so sorry for his great grief.

I work away daily in the Courts as it is a waste of time to go to the House or try any politics. It is no use being half hot and half cold, and pin pricks only give an idea of a desire to oppose without having any courage to do so!

. . . I hear that Winston went to [the] Dardanelles last night. It is great folly as his place is at the Admiralty and he can only be an amateur interfering out there . . .

As a matter of fact, Mr. Churchill had not gone to the Dardanelles. He had merely left London to visit the troops in the trenches in Flanders. However, the First Lord of the Admiralty was deeply committed to the Near East venture, which was designed to strike a blow at the heart of Germany's Turkish ally by capturing Con-

* Viscount Castlereagh, who succeeded his father as 7th Marquess of Londonderry.

stantinople. Instead of the rapid achievement of this objective, the expeditionary force which was despatched under Sir Ian Hamilton faced a long-drawn-out struggle with the Turks in Gallipoli. It was the plight of the Dardanelles Expedition which eventually led to the fall of the Government and incidentally to the end of Mr. Churchill's tenure of the Admiralty. The crisis came in May with the resignation from the Admiralty Board of Lord Fisher, the First Sea Lord, who objected to the continued drain of naval reinforcements for the Dardanelles.

Bonar Law took advantage of this development to send the Prime Minister an ultimatum. Either the Government must be reconstituted on a broader basis or else the Opposition would force a debate in Parliament which could bring it down. Asquith bowed to the inevitable and there followed what he described as "the most hellish fortnight" of his life, during which the First Coalition Government came into being. The portfolios were fairly evenly distributed between the parties, although the Liberals retained most of the key offices. Asquith remained at No. 10 Downing Street, Sir Edward Grey at the Foreign Office and Mr. Birrell in Dublin Castle; Lloyd George became Minister of Munitions; Sir John Simon, Home Secretary; and Reginald McKenna, Chancellor of the Exchequer. Bonar Law, who might have had the latter post had he insisted, contented himself with the Colonial Office, but he pressed for the inclusion of Carson as senior Law Officer with a seat in the Cabinet. Churchill fought hard to stay at the Admiralty, but the Conservatives would not hear of it, and he had to hand over the seals to Balfour. In the reshuffle he was relegated to the sinecure office of Chancellor of the Duchy of Lancaster. For the first time Labour was represented in the Administration. Mr. Arthur Henderson took the portfolio of Education.

So that the Nationalists might also be represented, Asquith was anxious that Redmond should join and he offered him a post. But acceptance was out of the question for the Nationalist Leader. His career was already in jeopardy with many of his followers, and this would have finished it. Not only did he refuse, however, but he did his best to prevent Carson's inclusion. "In view of the fact that it is impossible for me to join," he telegraphed Asquith on May 19, "I think most strongly Carson should not be included. From the Irish point of view inclusion would do infinite harm and make our efforts to help far more difficult." A few days later, on May 24, Redmond repeated his objections in a letter. "For the Irish people," he told the

Prime Minister, "it will mean installed in power the leader of the Ulster revolters, who, the other day, was threatening hostilities to the forces of the Crown and the decision of Parliament. It will arouse grave suspicion, and will most certainly enormously increase the difficulties of my friends and myself."

These remonstrances proved unavailing. Although Carson himself was reluctant to come in, Bonar Law and his colleagues were insistent and he eventually agreed. After all, as Birrell pointed out to Redmond, he was "the Opposition's best man". At the same time F. E. Smith became Solicitor-General, but remained outside the Cabinet.

The composition of the Coalition Government was announced in the newspapers on May 26, 1915. Next day the new Attorney-General attended his first Cabinet meeting in Downing Street. He kept the written summons, which all Cabinet Ministers receive, as a souvenir of the occasion.

6

Carson immediately found that the work of a Law Officer in war-time was much more burdensome than what he had to face as Solicitor-General in the previous decade. From the day he took office, when he received a note from Asquith asking for his opinion as to whether the newly-created Ministry of Munitions which Lloyd George was to fill required legislative authority, he was immersed in a mass of detailed work, concerning the Defence of the Realm regulations and other statutory rules and orders as well as enemy property, espionage and Prize Court cases. There was also his work in the Cabinet.

To Lady Londonderry

5 *Eaton Place, S.W. Sunday* [*June* 28, 1915] . . . The taking over of my office in the midst of all the work caused by the war has been no easy matter and I have found myself occupied from morning to night. Indeed I sometimes despair of being strong enough to 'carry on'.

There is little news to tell and certainly very little to cheer one as it is quite evident we have to settle down for another winter's war with all the gloom it involves. The difficulty is to find out where we can hope eventually to break the power of our enemies. It is no use, however, weeping over time gone by. The only question is, can we get the nation to undertake the necessary organisation and work? We are all doing our best now at any rate . . .

At the outset of his tenure of office Carson was obliged to prosecute two German agents named Hahn and Muller at the Old Bailey. The trial took place on June 4, 1915, before a special Court consisting of the Lord Chief Justice (Lord Reading), Mr. Justice Avory and Mr. Justice Lush. It was Carson's only important criminal prosecution as Attorney-General, and it was a task which he greatly disliked. For obvious security reasons the case was not reported at the time, but the facts have subsequently become known.

The clue which set the authorities in New Scotland Yard on the trail of the agents was provided by an intelligent postal censorship officer, who was examining parcels and newspapers in the mails. He picked out a newspaper going to an address in Amsterdam which was on the Watch List of suspects. The newspaper was not marked in any way which might suggest the use of an enemy code or cipher, but the examiner thought it might contain secret writing and he sent it to the censorship laboratory to undergo the usual chemical tests. These revealed a message written in invisible ink to the effect that 'C' had gone 'into the north' and that he was 'sending from 201.' The newspaper bore the postmark of Deptford.

Inquiries revealed that there was only one street in Deptford with such a number—High Street—and that the house in question was occupied by a baker and confectioner named Peter Hahn, who was a naturalised British subject. A search of these premises further revealed a phial of invisible ink concealed in an old shoe box. Hahn was thereupon arrested, but he refused to disclose the identity of his associate, who was in fact also his employer. However, it was not long before the neighbours were telling the police about a tall, well-dressed man, who often called at the baker's shop and was thought to be a Russian. His description was circulated to various boarding-houses, and eventually one landlady in Bloomsbury was able to identify him as Muller and to say that he had recently gone away on private business to Newcastle-on-Tyne. The business consisted in collecting information on naval matters and transmitting it to the German Admiralty.

Muller was arrested as he was boarding a train and taken to London to stand his trial with Hahn. Both men were prosecuted to conviction by Carson. However, the Attorney-General made it clear that Hahn was largely the other man's dupe and had lent his services because he was in need of money. Hahn accordingly got seven years' penal servitude, while Muller received the death sentence. In due course Muller was executed by a firing squad in the Tower of London.

Soon after joining the Coalition Government, Carson told Lady Londonderry: "We are a strange lot of bedfellows in the Cabinet, but I hope we think only of the country." Such indeed was the Attorney-General's overriding pre-occupation at this time. Unfortunately his methods of outspoken criticism did not endear him to his Cabinet colleagues, whom he once in a moment of despair collectively described to their faces as "twenty-three blind mice". The difficulties in directing the policy of the war through such a large and unwieldy body was obvious to him from the outset, and he was also made rapidly aware of the cardinal weaknesses of the two personalities upon whom the potency of direction mainly depended. Indeed Kitchener's secretiveness and absorption in comparatively unimportant details disturbed him as much as Asquith's lack of initiative and drive. "Cabinets, like Boards of Directors, are mostly composed of those who wish to believe that all is going well with a concern as long as they are responsible for the direction of its affairs," so Lloyd George wrote in his *War Memoirs*. "Carson's questions cut through complacency and irritated his colleagues of both parties. He exasperated the Prime Minister, whose almost morbid shrinking from unpleasantness was placed in constant jeopardy by the flourish of his deadly scalpel at every meeting of the Cabinet."*

Much time was taken up in discussion of the Dardanelles adventure. To deal specifically with it there was a Cabinet Committee, of which Carson became a member after the disastrous landings at Suvla Bay in the summer of 1915. Carson had been strongly opposed to the expedition before he entered the Cabinet. The line he took now was that either it should be carried through with all the forces and reinforcements at the disposal of the Allies or else there should be a total evacuation of the Gallipoli Peninsula. On this issue, it may be added, the Tory Party was split. Balfour, Curzon, Lansdowne and F. E. Smith, who realised like Carson that failure would have a calamitous effect on British prestige in the East, were for going on till the end; Bonar Law, Walter Long and Austen

* D. Lloyd George, *War Memoirs*, II, 1019. Cp. Lloyd George, in conversation with his friend, Lord Riddell: 'In the Cabinet no important questions were decided by vote. The P.M. usually declared that the general opinion seemed to be so and so. The deliberations of the Cabinet are conducted in an orderly way. Balfour, Curzon and Carson put their points very well. Bonar Law is not bad. Winston is very unequal.' See *Lord Riddell's War Diary*, at p. 118.

Chamberlain were for withdrawal, though Bonar Law seems eventually to have adopted Carson's view. In effect, however, Carson's advocacy favoured evacuation, since there were no great reinforcements available, and he deprecated the terrible sacrifices which were being made in fighting the Turks in that theatre. His views were strengthened by the letters he received from one of the divisional commanders in Gallipoli, General Sir Bryan Mahon, with whom he had been at school in Portarlington. "The truth is that we have neither the munitions nor the organisation to carry on two big campaigns at the same time," wrote Mahon on July 30, 1915, "and this has grown into a big campaign."

During this harassing summer Carson necessarily saw a good deal of Kitchener, particularly in connexion with the Ulster Division, and he did his best to penetrate the Minister's reserve and the atmosphere of lonely grandeur in which he lived and worked. "They expect too much of me, these fellows," Kitchener whispered to Carson one day at the Cabinet table. "I don't know Europe, I don't know England, and I don't know the British Army."

One night Kitchener invited Carson to dinner and further unburdened himself about the war. Like Carson, Kitchener had originally been opposed to the Dardanelles expedition, but, unlike him, he was now extremely unwilling to withdraw British forces. They discussed the subject of compulsory military service. He doubted whether the French armies could be kept at full strength beyond the end of October at the present rate of wastage.

"We shall only be able to persuade England to accept conscription when the French are beaten," the War Minister remarked.

"Better do it now," Carson advised.

"The Trade Unions will never consent."

"Leave that to us," said Carson. "It's no business of yours. I know this nation. Whatever you say you want, it will give."

They spoke of the Ulster Division, which was now completing its training at Seaford in Sussex before going to France. Kitchener had already inspected the troops, and he told Carson it was the finest Division in the New Armies he had yet seen. Their testing-time was to come in the great Somme offensive of the following year, when they fought with outstanding gallantry, suffering 5,000 casualties and winning three awards of the Victoria Cross in one day.

Otherwise Kitchener was despondent and complained of the attacks made on him by some Irish Nationalists. After all, he said, although he was not an Irishman by descent, he had been born and bred in the country.

"Ah," commented Carson, "but, as they say over there, to be born on a housetop does not make you a sparrow."

To James Craig

> *Charlton Musgrove, Somerset. August* 9, 1915 . . . I am staying down here with Ruby for a few days to 'rest', if such a word is applicable at the present time to anyone in the Government. I feel more exhausted than I dare say and wonder how I can carry on—tired, tired and always tired makes everything irksome . . .
>
> We went to see the Ulster Division on Thursday . . . and on Friday the whole Division went out on the Downs and I went round the ranks. The men seemed very pleased and I felt sad to think of all they have before them. They have won golden opinions for their conduct at Seaford, which is a bright spot in all the clouds. I dined with Lord K[itchener] one evening and he was for him quite expressful of his appreciation of the Division, and especially of the younger officers . . .
>
> I find the Cabinet work not at all satisfactory. It is hard to do anything that one would like to do, and the numbers are far too great. I should like to see a Cabinet of about 7 with power by Order in Council to pass such ordinances as are necessary. We won't win this war under existing methods of organisation and that is what makes me ill . . .

As every day which passed brought the news of terrible losses in the Dardanelles, Carson felt less and less happy in the Cabinet and talked to Bonar Law of resigning. He was only persuaded to hold his hand by the Conservative Leader, who pointed out that the French had now promised support at Gallipoli. "It would be a tremendous blow if you left the Government and I had to remain in it," Bonar Law wrote to him on September 6, 1915; "and especially on this subject in regard to which, up till now, I have been against every step we have taken. . . . To withdraw now [from the Dardanelles] would be really one of the greatest disasters which have ever happened to Britain. I think, therefore, we ought to take advantage of French approval and support to make a certainty of success at the Dardanelles, and at some risk in the French front [in the west] if the French are willing to run the risk."

Meanwhile at Cabinet meetings Carson continued to protest against the needless throwing away of further lives in Gallipoli, and to denounce the general lack of knowledge and method in the Eastern campaign.

To Lady Londonderry

> *Sunday* [*September* 18, 1915] . . . I am sorry to say I feel the strain of the present situation very much. Our machine is not suitable for war work and unless it is altered vitally we will drift on to the rocks.
>
> Oh, how I want to smash those Germans at any sacrifice!

He also brooded over the situation in the Balkans, which he felt to be singularly ominous. The Austrians were known to be massing troops in the villages near the Danube, they were being reinforced by German divisions, and Carson felt sure that a German-Austrian attack on Serbia was in contemplation. Bulgaria was also believed to be about to throw in her lot with the Central Powers and to join them in attacking her neighbour.

On September 25 Bulgaria declared war on the Allies. Sir Edward Grey, speaking in the House of Commons, immediately promised the Serbians "all the support in our power, in the manner that would be most welcome to them, in concert with our Allies, without reserve or qualification," should their country be attacked. A few days later the blow fell. On October 7, Germans and Austrians began to invade Serbia. Almost simultaneously the Bulgarians struck from the south-west. Unless something drastic were done quickly, it was clearly apparent that Serbia would be finished and Germany's lines of communication in the East would stretch from Berlin to Constantinople.

For some days indeed the news of the German advance into Serbia had been expected, and when the Cabinet met on October 9 Lloyd George asked Kitchener whether he had heard anything. Kitchener replied that up to the time he came to the Cabinet he had received no news. Lloyd George thought the news might have come in since then, and he asked the Prime Minister's secretary to telephone the War Office and find out. The secretary did so and returned with the news that a telegram had come in the day before. It was to the effect that late in the afternoon of October 7 the Germans had crossed the Danube with one battalion, and Austrian troops were also across the Slava at five different places. According to Lloyd George, the War Minister did not express the least surprise that he had not seen this telegram.

When the text of the telegram had been read to the Cabinet, Carson picked up a sheet of notepaper from the table and wrote a few words on it, which he passed to Lloyd George.

10, Downing Street,
Whitehall. S.W.

K does not read the
telegrams – & we don't
see them – it is intolerable
E. C

Carson then went for Kitchener about the position in Gallipoli and treated him as if he were a hostile witness in Court. Lady Londonderry, to whom the incident was reported, probably by Balfour, noted in her diary: "I hear his cross-examination of K. was the most marvellous thing that ever was as to places, times, ships and everything else."

After the Cabinet meeting was over—it was a Saturday—Kitchener invited Carson to come back with him to the War Office. When he entered his room, the Secretary of State pointed to a box in the corner. "There you will find Johnny Hamilton's dispatches, which you so much want to see," he observed gloomily. "You can spend the week-end over them, and damned unpleasant reading you will find them."

On Monday, October 11, there was a full meeting of the Dardanelles Committee of the Cabinet. General Joffre, the French Commander-in-Chief, had been urging on Kitchener the need to send both British and French forces to the aid of the hard-pressed Serbs in the Balkans. Carson, Bonar Law and Lloyd George all spoke strongly in favour of landing troops at Salonika and pushing along immediately to the help of Serbia. Sir William Robertson, the Chief of the Staff, who was present, objected that the Salonika railway was not equipped with the necessary means of transport to enable the Allies to carry a considerable body of troops even as far as Uskub, which was necessary to ensure communication with the Serbian Army. This revealed the fact that, although the Cabinet had instructed the War Minister as far back as the previous January to double the line, construct sidings and increase the rolling stock, nothing had been done to carry out that order. Other Ministers were for further reinforcing Gallipoli. Eventually, by way of compromise, it was decided to send a substantial force to Egypt, 'without prejudice to its ultimate destination, together with a general who should report as to which particular sphere, and with what particular objective, we should direct our attention.'

This decision, tantamount to leaving Serbia to her fate, was more than Carson could stomach. Next morning he wrote a short note to Asquith tendering his resignation from the Government. He followed it up the same day with a letter in which he explained his reasons. "I cannot understand how England can now abandon Serbia to her fate without national dishonour," he wrote; "even if we were not so bound in honour, such a course is in my judgment a policy of despair and an admission of failure, which could only be justified after every other alternative had been exhausted. . . . The loss to our prestige will be incalculable and a very grave menace will threaten our Eastern Empire. . . . I could understand a policy of limiting all our actions to the Western theatre and using all our resources there (which is I think in reality what the War Staff suggests) and that way to relieve the situation in the East. But to send an army to Egypt to await action which may or may not be possible on the report of a General to be sent to Gallipoli seems the most futile and hesitating decision that could be come to and one calculated merely to lead to a further dissipation of our forces. I do not believe that, once Germany has gained access to the lines of communication with Constantinople, it will be possible to maintain our efforts in Gallipoli—indeed I doubt very much if our troops can stay there until that event happens."

The prospect of the loss of his Attorney-General greatly perturbed Asquith, and he did his best to persuade Carson to withdraw his resignation. It was no use. Carson's mind was made up, though he agreed to delay the announcement for a few days to oblige the Prime Minister. But he ceased to attend Cabinet meetings, and his absence naturally started rumours in the Press that he had left the Government. Eventually the announcement was made on the following Monday night, October 19.

In a valedictory letter the Prime Minister wrote: "I have valued your services very highly, and I part from you in hearty sorrow and with real friendship." In reality Asquith was extremely relieved to be rid of such an embarrassing Minister.

7

The news of Carson's resignation produced a considerable impression in the country. People felt vaguely that something must be wrong in the highest counsels. Sir Edward was known to be a man of courage and ability, and, indeed, a certain greatness of character, and it seemed to many that the Government had lost the one civilian who was equal to the situation. Although the Prime Minister made haste to repair the dam by promoting the brilliant 'F.E.' in his place, what Carson did was the first herald of the downfall of Asquith's Coalition Government, which was to be completed a year later.

By some the wisdom of Carson's resignation was called in question. "Resignations in echelon, like attacks, are always a mistake," wrote Lord Beaverbrook of the event. Bonar Law's secretary and confidant took the view, for which there is much to be said, that Carson's single-handed action was insufficient to produce the only means of helping Serbia—namely, to clear the army out of Gallipoli and land it in Salonika. On the other hand, if he had remained in the Government, he would have been of the greatest assistance to Bonar Law in fighting for evacuation. But it is also permissible to take the view that Bonar Law and Lloyd George, both of whom had supported Carson in the Cabinet and denounced the abandonment of Serbia, should have resigned with him. Writing some years later in his *War Memoirs*, Mr. Lloyd George observed: "Mr. Bonar Law and I shared his opinion about the whole transaction, but on the whole decided that we could not withdraw from the Ministry at this critical juncture. I am not sure that we were right." Had they done so they would certainly have hastened the end of the disastrous Coalition.

To his friend Sir Henry Wilson, Carson gave the background of the events which had caused him to take such a momentous step. The same day Wilson made a characteristic entry in his diary: "Kitchener is frightened of Egypt, of India, of Mesopotamia, of going on with the Dardanelles, of coming away, of going to Salonika, of not going. He has no plan of any sort . . . Absolute indecision and chaos reign in the Cabinet, all due to Asquith who has now gone to bed to gain some more time." Carson also wrote to another friend, but in more guarded terms:

To Lady Londonderry

House of Commons. October 27, 1915 . . . I have never known exactly what I could *write.* Of course I have felt acutely having to leave the Cabinet, and one is always perplexed as to the best course in a grave situation. However, I dare say my temperament is not suited to dilatory tactics and anyway I feel I would have broken down if I did not act on my own opinions.

I suppose I will at once commence Bar work again, tho' it is not very agreeable to interest oneself again in the personal affairs of strangers.

A few days later Carson, speaking from his old place below the gangway in the House of Commons, made the customary personal statement by a Minister who has resigned. He read the letter of resignation which he had sent to Asquith, whose permission he had to do so, and he recapitulated all the arguments he had previously advanced against abandonment of Serbia, the disastrous Gallipoli campaign and the dilatory methods employed by a large and unwieldy Cabinet. "What is wanted is a small body of competent men—the smaller the better," he said, "sitting not once a week, but from day to day, with the best expert advisers you can get, working out the problems that arise." There was a similar need for the military staff. "So far as I could see, when I went to the Cabinet and until very recently," he went on, "there was no staff at all—or at least I never saw their productions."

There was one member of the Cabinet who fully shared Carson's misgivings and was not slow to act upon them. This was Mr. Churchill, who had resigned in mid-November and had immediately gone off to command a battalion in the trenches of France. Meanwhile, after Bonar Law had threatened to leave the Government as well, the Prime Minister promised to support his demand in the Cabinet that the troops should be withdrawn from Gallipoli. Kitchener, who had gone out to the Dardanelles to see things for himself and report to his colleagues, also counselled evacuation, and in the face of these moves the Cabinet took a decision long overdue. The evacuation was successfully carried out toward the end of December, after inexcusable dilatoriness on the part of Asquith and his Government.

To Lady Londonderry

Royal Victoria Hotel, Swanage, Dorset. December 31, 1915 . . . The delays about everything are most disastrous. The Dardanelles expedition should have been abandoned long ago and thousands of lives would have been saved and Serbia might have been helped—but

> the Government could not make up their minds and now they pretend the abandonment was a great victory!
>
> Months ago it was apparent that there would be no drafts for the dwindling regiments and yet we went on appointing committees and imagining we were gaining time. The result is (I am told) that nothing will be ready until midsummer.
>
> I believe any 22 men would do just as well [as the present Cabinet]. The whole machine is as rotten as possible and I cannot see how we are to begin to win until both sides are exhausted. I don't think the country will ever again trust what is euphemistically called 'The Governing Classes' with their everlasting playing for office and votes!

The dilatory conduct of the war formed a major preoccupation with Carson, and he determined that a concerted effort should be made "to improve the machine", as he put it. "It is quite evident we must either oppose the Government outright and get rid of them or do nothing," he told Lady Londonderry at this time. "A policy of pin-pricks is only weakening." With the object of more vigorous action a committee of Conservative and Unionist back-benchers of the House of Commons was formed, which came to be known as the Conservative 'Ginger' Group, in January, 1916, and Carson became the Chairman. It was soon co-operating with a similar Liberal committee, and together they were destined to exercise a decisive influence on the history of the ill-fated Coalition Government. Their activities were stimulated by an unofficial group of friends, also led by Carson, who used to dine together every Monday night in the house of one of them, Mr. L. S. Amery, M.P. The other members of this group were Lord Milner; F. S. Oliver; Geoffrey Dawson, editor of *The Times*; Dr. Jameson, of Raid fame; and sometimes Sir Henry Wilson, when he was on leave from G.H.Q.

Meanwhile Carson had resumed his Bar practice and at this time he appeared in a sensational matter, which occupied the Court of Appeal for sixteen days. This was known as the Slingsby case and concerned the legitimacy of the alleged heir to an old family estate in Yorkshire. The appeal was against the judgment of Mr. Justice Bargrave Deane, who had found in favour of the alleged heir, a boy of four whose reputed father was Charles Slingsby of Scriven Park, near Knaresborough. Mr. and Mrs. Slingsby had made their home in British Columbia, Mrs. Slingsby being an American widow and a Roman Catholic, who does not appear to have got on particularly well with her husband's Protestant relatives in Yorkshire. The child, who was alleged to have been born in San Francisco, was declared legitimate by Mr. Justice Bargrave Deane, who was impressed by what he considered "the extraordinary likeness of the little boy to Mr. Slingsby," and his opinion was reinforced by his friend, Sir George Frampton, the sculptor, who pointed out "a most remarkable resemblance between the boy's left ear and that of his mother." Her story, as set out by Carson in his opening on behalf of the relatives, was that on September 1, 1910, she went to the house of a certain Mrs. Hattie Blair, who was an intimate friend, at McAllister Street, San Francisco, and that the child was born there. A Doctor Fraser was in attendance and she stated that nobody else was in the house. But both Mrs. Blair and Dr. Fraser denied that such an incident ever took place.

The appeal opened before Lord Justice Cozens-Hardy, Master of the Rolls, Lord Justice Warrington and Mr. Justice Bray on January 17, 1916. Carson led for the appellants, Messrs. T. W. and A. P. Slingsby, uncles of Charles Slingsby, and he had with him as junior counsel Mr. T. R. D. Wright and Mr. J. M. Gorer. Mr. Tindal Atkinson, K.C., led for the infant Charles Eugene Edward Slingsby, who petitioned through his father.

The appellants' case, according to Carson, was that Mrs. Slingsby's story was a tissue of lies. They alleged that the child was the illegitimate offspring of a girl named Lillian Anderson and was born at Dr. Fraser's surgery at Grant Street, San Francisco, and was handed over by him to Mrs. Slingsby, who had inserted in the *San Francisco Examiner* an advertisement for a male child for adoption. Mrs. Slingsby had at first denied all knowledge of the advertisement, but she later admitted the authorship in case she might lose the child she was expecting. Also, the birth certificate originally gave the place of birth as Grant Street, but this had been erased and altered by Mrs. Slingsby to McAllister Street.

A mass of evidence had been taken on commission in America, and Carson's opening speech, in which he went through a huge bundle of affidavits and other documents, occupied several days. When he had first been consulted by the Slingsby relatives he had stated he was unable to understand how Mr. Justice Bargrave Deane's judgment could have been based on the evidence available and that he thought there had been a miscarriage of justice. Its cumulative effect as presented and analysed by Carson in this appeal was to demonstrate beyond all doubt that the child was not the Slingsbys'.

Commenting on the reliance on facial resemblance shown by Mr. Justice Deane and Sir George Frampton, Carson quoted a story which William Ballantine, the well-known nineteenth-century Serjeant-at-Law, was in the habit of telling. The Serjeant was engaged in a similar case and thought he was going to win it, when the judge suddenly gave judgment against him. "You were nearly misleading me," remarked the judge afterwards to him, "but I happened to catch sight of your client in Court, and the resemblance between him and the child was enough for me."

"Good heavens," replied Serjeant Ballantine. "My client was not in Court. It was the solicitor's clerk."

The Court took nearly six weeks to consider its judgment in this appeal. It was eventually delivered on March 14, by the Master of the Rolls, in favour of the appellants. The judge refused to believe Mrs. Slingsby, nor could he believe that an expectant mother would advertise for a child. "This is so repugnant to all that one knows of maternal instincts," he said, "that I cannot bring myself to doubt that her story ought to be rejected."

While this interesting case was being heard, Carson became seriously ill, and his place was taken in Court by one of his junior counsel. The doctor diagnosed a 'tired heart', and recommended a month's rest, preferably by the sea. A daughter of Carson's old friend, Charles Gill, had a house at Birchington in the Isle of Thanet, which she lent the invalid, and here in the cold bright spring of 1916 he was nursed back to health by his devoted wife.

The Radicals took advantage of his absence from the House of Commons by spreading the rumour that Carson had suffered a stroke. It had looked as if he had been cast in the role of Leader of the Opposition, but that he would be unable to fill it. Even some of his political friends believed this story. "He's done for, broken down completely," said Balfour, discussing the situation with H. A. Gwynne, editor of the *Morning Post* and a staunch Carsonite. "Not at all," said Gwynne, "he's taking a rest by his doctor's orders, and will emerge fitter than ever." Carson was naturally annoyed when he heard the stories which were in circulation about his health, and he promised his wife to stay in bed for an extra week to complete the cure. "*Then* I'll show them if I'm done for," he remarked grimly.

That Carson was coming to be regarded as the parliamentary Opposition Leader, and even as a possible future Prime Minister is evident from the testimony of a number of independent witnesses. On March 15, when Carson was still recuperating at Birchington, Bonar Law confided to Redmond his belief that the Government might be beaten at any time in the House of Commons and that, "if Sir Edward Carson had the health and the desire to take up such a position, he was quite sure he could drive the Government from office in no time." Mrs. Spender, Captain Wilfrid Spender's wife, who was helping Lady Carson to organise gift parcels for the Ulster Division and consequently saw a good deal of Carson at this time, wrote in a similar strain to her husband:

> *London. Thursday, March* 23, 1916. You ask me my views about Sir Edward . . . I think he is beginning to realise that he really is needed, and once he grasps that *fully*, I think his body will obey his mind, and all will be well. But he *must* give up the Law, and that is a terrible wrench, as he hates Politics and loves Law. He hasn't a spark of political ambition, and is incurably modest, astonishingly so.
>
> On Saturday he had a long letter from the *Morning Post* editor, imploring him to give up Law and devote himself to the nation, and emphasising our need of him as a Leader; and on Sunday Mr. Gill had a long talk with him on the same subject. But he *is* nervous about his health, and his heart bothers him still, which he thinks more serious than it is. But I really think he will be all right, if he doesn't try and run Law and Politics together.

By the end of March Carson was back in his old place in the House of Commons. The Unionist War Committee now numbered 150, and with the Liberal Committee urged that some form of military conscription must be introduced if the war was to be fought to a successful conclusion. 'Equal sacrifices from all men of military age' was the principle mutually agreed upon. Asquith once more temporised, and Bonar Law, who seems to have fallen under the Prime Minister's spell for a time, felt that the Unionist Committee was being too precipitate and became temporarily estranged from Carson in consequence. Early in April there was a political crisis. Lloyd George threatened resignation and Asquith agreed to a modified form of conscription extending by a year the service of time-expired men, after a debate in secret session. This was not good enough for Carson. He and his friends on the Unionist Committee forced the Government to withdraw this half-hearted measure and consent to introduce a measure of universal conscription.

This episode, which exposed the Prime Minister in such a humiliating light, had the effect of drawing Carson and Lloyd George closer together. "Carson is improving daily," noted the shrewd Munitions Minister. "He is managing his little group with great skill. He is a fine fellow."

8

At Easter, 1916, while England was deeply preoccupied by the war, rebellion broke out in Southern Ireland. It had been planned by the extreme Sinn Fein element in the country, and although Mr. Birrell and the authorities in Dublin Castle had been repeatedly warned of what was afoot, the outbreak found them off their guard. The insurrection was principally confined to Dublin, where the rebels took possession of the General Post Office and various other buildings in the city and declared the establishment of an Irish Republic, with Patrick Pearse as President. Carson immediately offered the services of such of the Ulster Volunteers as had not previously enlisted in the Army, for the purpose of keeping order, but the offer proved unnecessary, as the North remained quiet. In Dublin, however, there was serious street fighting, in which 300 people were killed and 1,000 wounded, £2 millions of property were destroyed and many fine buildings were laid in ruins before the rising was quelled. In the result fourteen of the leading rebels were executed, while Mr. Eamon De Valera, one of the principal ring-leaders, only escaped the firing party on the grounds of his American citizenship.

The Easter Week rising in Dublin had the immediate effect of reviving interest in the Home Rule question, which most people had hoped would remain in a state of suspended animation for the period of the War.

Incidentally Carson was blamed in many quarters for having given a lead in the matter of rebellion with the Ulster Volunteers. Mrs. Spender wrote about him to her husband:

> *May* 13, 1916 . . . He is simply deluged with threatening letters every day, and the most scurrilous abuse, and so is she [Lady Carson]. He doesn't mind them a bit, and she laughs at them too, but I think she feels it a bit, though unconsciously. . . . Yesterday a man tried to force his way into their house, and the butler had a tussle with him in the hall, and managed to put him out. He had been walking up and down outside the house for ages. Probably he is crazy, but I've no doubt there are plenty who would like to murder him.

Mr. Birrell, the incompetent Chief Secretary for Ireland, resigned, and on May 22 the Prime Minister asked Lloyd George to make Ireland his immediate interest and try to negotiate a settlement with the rival party leaders. "It is a unique opportunity," wrote Asquith to his Minister of Munitions, "and there is no one else who could do so much to bring about a permanent solution." Lloyd George agreed, and an announcement to this effect was immediately made by the Prime Minister in the House of Commons.

The executions in Dublin had made a profound impression in the United States, where a requiem mass was said in every Catholic church by order of the bishops in memory of the rebels. It was absolutely necessary to placate American opinion and make a real effort to reach a settlement with Ireland. Otherwise Britain would be defeated in the war. Lloyd George pressed this view at a meeting with Carson in the Hotel Metropole on May 30, 1916, at which a fragment of the conversation was recorded by the veteran Nationalist William O'Brien, who was also present.

O'Brien began the discussion by saying that "if Ulster would only join us in Dublin, she could practically name her own terms." The Irish Unionists, he went on, would become the biggest individual party in an Irish Parliament and might even be its rulers "if they threw themselves into a patriotic and sensible programme."

CARSON: You cannot expect Ulster to come in just now.

O'BRIEN: No, nor anybody else. That is why I urge there should be nothing precipitate. Spend the next six months in mollifying the present bitterness—take your military precautions by all means, but don't be afraid to own there were faults on both sides. Trust to leniency rather than to force, and we will then be all in a better humour to come together in a United Ireland.

LLOYD GEORGE (*with sudden energy*): In six months the war will be lost.

CARSON (*throwing up his arms*): If the war is lost, we are all lost.

LLOYD GEORGE: The Irish-American vote will go over to the German side. They will break our blockade and force an ignominious peace on us, unless something is done, even provisionally, to satisfy America.

O'BRIEN: That is to say, of course, that whatever is to be done shall be done for war purposes. Take care, I beg of you, in the interests of war as well as of Ireland, that you will not infuriate Irish-American feeling rather than appease us. I most solemnly believe that will be the result if you attempt anything on the basis of splitting up Ireland . . . All honest Irish feeling will be so fiercely against you, you will have to send an army corps to open your mutilated Dublin Parliament and in spite of them the people will bundle the whole crew of them into the Liffey.*

Lloyd George set to work with a will and invited the political leaders to consult with him at the Ministry of Munitions. Ulster was represented by Carson and Craig, and the Nationalists by Redmond, Dillon, T. P. O'Connor and Devlin. In a few days the Minister had drawn up certain 'Headings of Agreement', which Carson and Redmond agreed to take to Ireland and lay before their followers.

Briefly, the proposals were that the Home Rule Act should come into operation forthwith, an Amending Bill should be introduced providing for the retention of the whole Irish parliamentary representation and the exclusion of Ulster for the duration of the war emergency, and that immediately at the conclusion of the provisional war period an Imperial Conference should be held to consider the future Government of the Empire, including the Government of Ireland. '*We must make it clear*,' Lloyd George wrote to Carson enclosing these draft proposals, '*that at the end of the provisional period Ulster does not*, *whether she wills it or not*, *merge in the rest of Ireland*.' Carson also made this clear in a memorandum which he prepared at the time and sent to Lloyd George: "The six counties are to be excluded from the Government of Ireland Act and are not to be included unless at some future time the Imperial Parliament pass an Act for that purpose."†

Carson met the Ulster Unionist Council on two days in June, and though the task was far from his liking, he advised the delegates to accept the 'clean cut' for the six north-eastern counties. After all, he argued, the Home Rule Act was on the statute book, and the only hope Ulster had of escaping from it lay in the Amending Bill. He pointed out that after the war they could never expect to get any more by forcible resistance than what was offered by legislation.

Sorrowfully the delegates agreed, since this meant letting the

* William O'Brien, *The Irish Revolution and How it Came About* (1923), p. 271 *et seq.* The following exchange also took place. Lloyd George (*to* O'Brien): "Did not Sir Edward once prosecute you?" O'Brien (*laughingly*): "Have you already forgotten your old leader's injunction to 'Remember Mitchelstown'?" Carson (*with marked cordiality*): "I think Mr. O'Brien is the most forgiving Irishman I have ever met." O'Brien: "Oh, all these things were the fortunes of war, and we had the comfort of giving as good as we got." O'Brien subsequently admitted that he thought Lloyd George winced perceptibly at Carson's reference to O'Brien's readiness to forgive.

† Lloyd George subsequently forgot this correspondence when the question of appointing a Commission to rectify the boundary between Northern Ireland and the Irish Free State was before Parliament in 1924, and had to be sharply reminded of it by Carson: see *Morning Post*, Oct. 3, 1924.

three remaining Ulster counties go in with the south. They therefore agreed that they could not turn down such a solution at a time of national emergency, but they were careful to reserve their right to resume their opposition to the whole policy of Home Rule, should the negotiations break down.

To Bonar Law

5 *Eaton Place, S.W. June* 14, 1916 . . . The condition of Ireland at the present time is, in my opinion, a matter of very grave anxiety . . .

It is surely the duty of the Government, especially if they are going to bring in Home Rule in the South and West, to provide for the primary elements of government in assuring to the people there that Imperial Power will be exercised to preserve them their lives and property. There are daily outrages going on, and only the night before I left Belfast a British officer, who strayed into the Nationalist quarter in Belfast, was set upon by three men, who fortunately were unarmed, and as he was a robust and brave man he very nearly did for one of them. I myself had to drive about protected from morning to night by detectives, and yet every day the so-called Martial Law is being relaxed and men who have been in the Rebellion are being daily sent back to Ireland in the uniform in which they were arrested. There will be nothing but disaster and chaos and ignominy if the Government's proposals are carried out without any regard for Imperial obligations . . .

I shall also be glad if you would consider who is to look after Imperial matters in the event of a settlement maturing, and a new Bill being introduced. There is the whole western coast to be thought of and especially the coast of Donegal, with its large bay leading into Lough Swilly, where the *Audacious* was mined, and where at any time, in the event of the German fleet getting round, our fleet may have to find a base of operations.

For my own part I have had a very painful and difficult task in trying to induce the Six Counties to accept the terms the Government have offered. I think it is due, not only to these people, but also to the whole of the loyal population of Ireland, which includes at all events some Nationalists, that the Imperial Government should take some responsibility in protecting them . . . Of course, as the Home Rule Act was on the Statute Book, all I could do was to try and save something out of the wreckage, once you had all agreed that a settlement must be come to.

I feel very lonely in the whole matter, but I have found confidence reposed in me in the North of Ireland which was, to say the least of it, refreshing. I have heard some rumour today that the Cabinet have known nothing about the negotiations or the terms, but that I do not credit, as I do not suppose I should have been asked to go to Ireland and carry out a most distasteful mission in such circumstances, more especially as the papers have given daily accounts of the negotiations which were going on. I have been told that the London *Daily Express* voices your views. Of course I do not know whether that is true, but it certainly has done its best to put us in grave difficulties.

The Ulster Unionists' sacrifice was in vain. The settlement was opposed by some of the English Unionists, notably Lord Lansdowne and Walter Long, more out of pique than anything else at not having been consulted before Carson went to Belfast with the scheme. Also, Redmond in his meetings with his Nationalist followers explained that the exclusion of Ulster was only to be temporary. Thus the negotiations fell to the ground in the face of these differences and the Government abandoned Lloyd George's scheme. But there was one satisfactory outcome of the business. Feelings against Britain were to some extent mollified in America, when it was realised that the Government had made an effort to reach a solution of this age-old problem.

Carson and Redmond were both disheartened by this result. Carson was indeed sorry that the settlement had been 'smashed', as he dreaded the thought of fighting 'all over again' for the exclusion of Ulster. "The people who oppose this settlement don't realise how we fought to get Ulster excluded," he told his wife, "and what an achievement it is to have got that." In the Commons debate on the breakdown of the negotiations, which was initiated by Redmond, Carson paid a tribute to his old opponent, adding that it would not be a bad thing for either country—"nor a bad day's work in the war"—if they were to shake hands on the floor of the House. But Redmond sat in his place without moving a muscle, as he had done once before when Carson held out the hand of friendship. Poor Redmond! He saw little or no hope in the future. "Some tragic fatality," he said, "seems to dog the footsteps of this Government in all their dealings with Ireland." Thereafter the Irish Nationalists practically dropped all pretence of helping to carry on the war and in Parliament they tended to become more and more obstructive. Their day was nearly done. In Ireland power was rapidly passing into the hands of Sinn Fein.

Meanwhile a significant change had taken place in the composition of the Coalition Government. It was heralded by a telegram which Carson received when he was addressing the Ulster Unionist Council in Belfast on June 6, 1916, and which he read out to the assembled delegates. The telegram contained the sad news that the cruiser in which Lord Kitchener was sailing on a mission to Russia had struck a mine off the Orkneys and that the War Minister and his staff had all been drowned. Asquith took over the vacant portfolio pending the appointment of a successor. His difficulty was increased by Lloyd George choosing this moment to threaten resignation. The Minister of Munitions told his chief that for a long time he had been profoundly dissatisfied with the progress and conduct of the war. "Had it not been for the fact that I had undertaken a task the carrying out of which was vital to the success of our Army," he informed Asquith, "I should long ago have joined Carson in his criticisms of the conduct of the war."

Bonar Law, who was acquainted with Lloyd George's intention, begged him not to resign and join Carson, which would make his own position in the Government "quite intolerable". On Bonar Law promising to back his claim for the War Secretaryship if he would stay in, Lloyd George agreed. Meanwhile Asquith, who did not really want his brilliant subordinate in this key post, offered it to the Conservative Leader. "Too late," said Bonar Law. Last week, he told Asquith, he would have taken it, if pressed. Now he was pledged to support Lloyd George. Thus the Prime Minister had no alternative but to appoint the only other big man in his Cabinet. In doing so he must have known he was signing his political death warrant. "We are out," noted Mrs. Asquith in her diary on the day on which Lloyd George was gazetted War Minister. "It is only a question of time when we shall have to leave Downing Street."

Meanwhile, as the leader of the so-called Conservative 'Ginger Group' in Opposition, Carson continued to harass the Government. He became chairman of an 'Enemy Influence' Committee, which investigated the business activities and connections of naturalised Germans such as Sir Ernest Cassel and Sir Edgar Speyer. He demanded a new electoral register to include the soldiers and sailors on active service and the Government reluctantly agreed to bring in a Bill to this effect. He pressed for inquiries into the campaigns in the Dardanelles and Mesopotamia. He urged the application of compulsory military service to Ireland. In all these activities he was regarded with approval by Lloyd George, to whom he was drawn ever more closely. Indeed the War Minister was heard discussing with his friend Lord Riddell the advantage of a General Election and 'a new party' headed by Carson whom he described as "a man of resolution, good judgment and inspiring personality." Riddell, who felt that Lloyd George should be the alternative to Asquith, asked him whether he would be prepared to serve under Carson. "I should be glad and proud to serve under him," replied Lloyd George. "My only purpose is to get on with the war."

Carson's attacks, though directed at the Liberal Prime Minister, necessarily implicated Bonar Law, who remained loyal to Asquith in the Cabinet. The estrangement between the two old political friends, which began soon after Carson left the Government in the autumn of 1915, became more pronounced, although the two men continued to meet privately from time to time.* Sooner or later it was bound to lead to an open clash. The clash came in the House of Commons on November 8, 1916, and it heralded a political crisis of the first magnitude.

On that day the Carsonites initiated a debate on a subject which to the uninformed observer appeared trivial and remote, the sale by auction of certain enemy properties in Nigeria. In fact, the debate was cleverly designed to attract the maximum number of Conservatives and Unionists into the division lobby against the Government. Bonar Law, as Colonial Secretary, had proposed to allow neutrals to bid for these properties. Carson and his friends, who had information that some at least of the neutrals interested were really acting on behalf of the enemy, moved that the purchasers be confined to British natural-born subjects or companies wholly British. The debate was marked by a good deal of hostility directed against the Government by Conservative back-benchers, while Carson plainly accused Bonar Law of 'misrepresenting facts' and playing the enemy's game. Stung by these reproaches the Colonial Secretary declared that the issue was one of confidence in the Government and that he was sorry to be at such variance with his "right honourable friend opposite," whom he described as being "not very polite." "I am sure he realises the seriousness of the course he is taking," added Bonar Law, "and is prepared to take the consequences if the division is successful."

When the division bells rang, only seventy-three out of a total of

* After one of these meetings, at which Mrs. Spender was present, she wrote (September 10, 1916): 'There is something very attractive about Bonar Law, very simple and sincere. He evidently feels Sir Edward having left the Government very deeply, and was a little reproachful. Says if Sir Edward hadn't listened to somebody—I think Lloyd George—he would have been in the Government yet, which Sir Edward stoutly denied. We were talking of Asquith, and all agreeing in denouncing him when Bonar Law said: "There's one man I distrust more" (*i.e.* Lloyd George). But Sir Edward said: "No, that one is a plain man of the people and shows his hand, and, though you mayn't trust him, his crookednesses are all plain to see. But the other is clever and polished and knows how to conceal his crookedness." And Bonar Law said: "Well, perhaps you're right!" '

286 Conservative and Unionist Members went into the Government lobby. The Government carried the day by a majority of 114, but it was largely through Liberal, Labour and Irish Nationalist votes. After the division Sir Max Aitken (Lord Beaverbrook) went into the Colonial Secretary's room, where he found Bonar Law surrounded by supporters who were congratulating him on his triumph and quite unaware of the real significance of the division. Aitken was quick to see that further attacks of this sort must eventually result in a defeat of the Government in the division lobby; apart from that, they must render Bonar Law's claim to the confidence of the Conservative Party 'nugatory' and his position in the Government 'consequently impossible'. Aitken thereupon tried to persuade Bonar Law to resign, but Bonar Law refused, since he knew that this might well result in the withdrawal of Conservative support for the Government and the return to party warfare, to neither of which developments at that time he could reconcile himself.

A few days later, on November 13, Aitken called at the War Office to see Lloyd George at the Minister's request. Lloyd George expressed the opinion that the Government was ineffective for waging war and that some drastic reorganisation was essential. Aitken said he was prepared to work with him to this end, provided he was not called upon to sacrifice his confidence in and loyalty to Bonar Law. According to Aitken, Lloyd George then pointed out from his own political experience that "Carson would smash Bonar Law immediately, and that the best way out was for the two men to join hands." The War Minister added 'quite frankly' that Carson was working with him to bring into being a War Council with plenary powers. At this point Carson himself was announced and Aitken left.

The ensuing three weeks witnessed a series of meetings and discussions of this 'potential Triumvirate', as Mr. Churchill has described Lloyd George, Carson and Bonar Law at this time, designed eventually to end the life of Asquith's Coalition Government. The course of their deliberations, which has been traced in a full and frank narrative by Lord Beaverbrook in his *Politicians and the War*, need only be briefly summarised here. On November 24 Bonar Law was persuaded to give some measure of support for a War Council of four, consisting of Asquith as President, Lloyd George as chairman, with the real power, and Carson and himself as members. However, out of loyalty to the Prime Minister, he immediately revealed the scheme to Asquith, who promptly vetoed it.

Asquith told Bonar Law he saw in this proposed arrangement a pretext for Lloyd George ("he does not inspire trust") to displace him in the Premiership. "As regards Carson, for whom, as you know, I have the greatest personal regard," Asquith continued, "I do not see how it would be possible, in order to secure his services, to pass over Balfour, or Curzon or McKenna, all of whom have the advantage of intimate knowledge of the secret history of the past twelve months. That he should be admitted over their heads at this stage to the inner circle of the Government is a step which, I believe, would be deeply resented, not only by them and by my political friends, but by almost all your Unionist colleagues. It would be universally believed to be the price for shutting the mouth of our most formidable parliamentary critic—manifest sign of weakness and cowardice."

Carson and Lloyd George did not care who had the nominal post of head of the Government, provided that the War Council was not run by Asquith. In Lord Beaverbrook's words: "If Asquith would accept the titular role, well and good; if not, he must go." At first Bonar Law would not go as far as this. He was anxious "to run Lloyd George and Asquith in harness together." He discussed the situation with his Conservative colleagues in the Government, particularly Lord Lansdowne and Walter Long, and they declared their opposition to the scheme, in which they only saw the 'further aggrandisement' of Lloyd George. But Lord Lansdowne was known to be in favour of a negotiated peace and he actually submitted a memorandum in this sense to the Cabinet which had greatly impressed Asquith. The other two members of the triumvirate put it to Bonar Law that "the world was menaced with the prospect of a peace which would have left a militant Prussia still unchained," whereas "the triumph of Lloyd George and Bonar Law spelt Peace with Victory." On December 2 Lloyd George wrote to the Colonial Secretary: "The life of the country depends on resolute action by you now." This determined Bonar Law to insist on the supersession of Asquith in the conduct of the war, which he did at a party meeting next day, which was a Sunday. Asquith had seen Lloyd George two days previously and agreed to his scheme for a small executive body to run the war with Lloyd George as Chairman, subsequently modified at a second meeting on Sunday in the sense that the chairman was to report to him daily, that the Prime Minister could veto the Committee's conclusions and could, of course, attend meetings whenever he chose. The same night it was announced from

Downing Street that the Prime Minister had advised the King to consent to a reconstruction of the Government.

In Carson's mind it was clear that such an arrangement would prove futile, and he told the Colonial Secretary so in characteristic language.

To Bonar Law

Confidential. 5 *Eaton Place, S.W. December* 4, 1916. I am convinced after our talk last evening that no patchwork is possible. It would be unreal and couldn't last. A system founded on mistrust and jealousy and dislike is doomed to failure and in a crisis like the present it would really be disastrous on this account to the country.

The only solution I can see is for the P.M. to resign and for L.G. to form a Government—a very small one. If the House won't support it, he should go to the country and we would know where we are.

I quite admit that the want of patriotism of many Liberals may raise a good deal of opposition, but it will either be overcome or it will lead to peace, and in this latter case we will not be worse off than in the gulf to which we are now heading. If the country is sound, everything will come right. If not (and I think every day under the present regime is producing pacifists), we will save further sacrifice.

I am breakfasting with Derby and L.G. tomorrow and will state my view.*

The day which began with the breakfast party at Derby House, also attended by Bonar Law, was a fateful one for all in Government circles. When Lloyd George returned to the War Office, he found a letter from Asquith, reiterating his determination to retain supreme control of war policy. "Unless the impression is at once corrected that I am being relegated to the position of an irresponsible spectator of the war," the Prime Minister wrote, "I cannot possibly go on." The Prime Minister had been annoyed by a hostile leading article in *The Times* on Monday (December 4), which indicated knowledge of the negotiations of the preceding days and which the Prime Minister erroneously attributed to Lord Northcliffe by Lloyd George's inspiration, since it stressed the fact that Asquith was not to be a member of the new War Committee. (Actually the article had been written by the editor, Geoffrey Dawson, in consultation with Carson, whom he had seen on the Sunday night.) Meanwhile Asquith saw Reginald McKenna and other Liberal colleagues, who advised him to have nothing to do with Lloyd George's scheme. "You are indispensable," said McKenna to him. Lord Milner, an

* 'In this statement [as made at the breakfast party] Carson got nearer to the root of the matter than most of his colleagues and contemporaries were aware': Lord Beaverbrook, *Politicians and the War*, II, 258.

acute observer, summed up the position well: "L. G. is really making a gigantic effort to get rid of H. H. A., bring Carson back and form a real War Government," he wrote on the same day. "All the perfectly useless members of the Government—some 16 or perhaps 18 out of 23—are clinging round H. H. A.'s knees and beseeching him not to give in. No thought of what is happening to the country—you may observe. It is just their positions."

Consequently Asquith now went back on the original proposition. "I have come decidedly to the conclusion," he wrote to Lloyd George in a second letter which he received on the same day, "that it is not possible for such a Committee to be made workable and effective without the Prime Minister as its Chairman." This was a fatal move and it led to his immediate downfall.*

Lloyd George felt he could not continue to be a member of Asquith's Government in these circumstances and he wrote out a letter of resignation, which he immediately sent over to Downing Street. Bonar Law and the leading Conservatives had made up their minds to follow suit, when news was received that Asquith had tendered his own resignation to the King. That evening the King sent for Bonar Law and asked him to form a Government. Afterwards Bonar Law and Lloyd George both called to see Carson at his house. "He and I are going to see this thing through," Lloyd George told Lady Carson, indicating her husband. Lloyd George was quite prepared to serve under Bonar Law, just as he was under Carson.

Next day there were considerable comings and goings at Buckingham Palace. At first Bonar Law was inclined to think that, if he failed to form a Government, Balfour should be invited to try. But Balfour, like Bonar Law, said he could head no Government in which Asquith was not included—and Asquith refused to join either. Lloyd George, however, had no such scruples, and in the end Bonar Law advised the King to send for him as "the man whose leadership was most likely to win the war."

On the morning of December 7, 1916, Carson was standing with Lloyd George by the window of his room in the War Office. Outside in Whitehall there was an immense throng of people waiting to see the future Prime Minister. Presently the summons arrived from Buckingham Palace.

"Go," said Carson grimly, "and take what is coming to you."

* Carson used to say afterwards that Asquith had got all he required by Lloyd George's scheme, 'that if the Prime Minister cared to attend and preside over every sitting no one could have prevented him and he made a mistake in going back on this settlement': see Marjoribanks and Colvin, *Life of Lord Carson*, III, 209.

CHAPTER ELEVEN

Cabinet Minister

I

THOUGH he momentarily described himself as "the most miserable man on earth", Lloyd George in reality responded to the royal summons with a will. According to the new Prime Minister, the King was 'amazed' at his being able to make a Cabinet so swiftly. That he was able to do this was due to his seemingly boundless energy and the powers of persuasion which he exerted in his dealings with the various party groups. All the Tory leaders who had been members of the Asquith Coalition Government agreed to serve in the reconstructed Ministry. Similarly satisfactory negotiations took place with the Labour leaders, while the Premier was able to count on the support of at least half of the Liberals in the House of Commons. A conspicuous omission from the new Ministry was Mr. Churchill, to whose inclusion the Tories, except for Carson and F. E. Smith, were resolutely opposed. Lloyd George promised to try and find a place for him later. Among the recipients of minor posts was Carson's faithful Ulster henchman, James Craig, who became Treasurer of the Household with the duties of a Government Whip.

*Viscount Milner to Lady Edward Cecil**

London. 8.12.16. About the situation one thing is clear . . . I was absolutely right in insisting, as I did ceaselessly and almost with too much vehemence, that a Clean Cut was essential, and I rejoiced at the prospect of L.G. and Carson being left almost alone, with a hostile House of Commons, then appealing to the country and getting rid of the whole truck-load of Mandarins.

At the moment of crisis we were really divided into Men and Mandarins and the former won. Unfortunately, as I think, the *unexpected firmness* of B.L., while it certainly gave the *coup de grâce* to Squiff,† has resulted in the return of the old Unionist tail—A.J.B.‡ and all the rest of them—so that the new Government is really old Unionist hands, L.G. and some new men. So we have not, after all, sloughed off the old party skin.

* Milner MSS. Lady Edward Cecil, who was a sister of Leo Maxse, editor of the *National Review*, later married Lord Milner.

† Nickname for Asquith.

‡ Balfour became Foreign Secretary.

As for Carson, according to Lord Beaverbrook, "The moment that Asquith's fall was accomplished a kind of incuriousness seemed to descend upon him. He was like a man whose task is accomplished. He made no claim for himself."* Nevertheless, as one of the original 'triumvirate' in the crisis, Carson was much in Lloyd George's confidence, and virtually any office he wished was open to him. He refused the greatest prize of all for a man in his profession.

As Lloyd George was going over the list of top posts with him, the Prime Minister remarked: "There's the Lord Chancellor. That will be for you, Carson."

"No, that will not be for me," replied Carson firmly. He explained that in the circumstances of the war he did not think there would be enough for him to do in this office. According to Geoffrey Dawson, the editor of *The Times*, to whom Carson related the incident on the same day, "He did not want to have any cares of any sort or kind outside the prosecution of the war, and, if he must take office at all, would take it without portfolio." Also, there might be difficulty over Ireland and he might find himself at variance with the Government, which would oblige him to resign. In that event, he added, he would not have it said that a resignation which carried with it a pension of £6,000 a year was no sacrifice. As might be expected, this completely selfless view did not altogether find favour in Lady Carson's eyes. "Ruby can't help looking a little rueful over the £10,000 a year and the fat pension!" wrote Mrs. Spender to her husband. "She, very rightly, wants everyone to know he refused the Woolsack, so you can publish it freely."† As a result, Finlay, Carson's old colleague as Law Officer, filled the vacancy.‡

Lloyd George had planned a small War Council, soon to be known as the War Cabinet, the members of which should, with one exception, be free from departmental duties. He wished that Carson, who had consistently advocated the creation of this body for the conduct of the war, should be one of the members without portfolio. The others were to be Bonar Law, Chancellor of the Exchequer and Leader of the House of Commons; Lord Curzon, Lord President of the Council and Leader of the House of Lords; Arthur Henderson, the Labour Leader; and Lloyd George himself as chairman. For the

* Lord Beaverbrook, *Politicians and the War*, II, 335.

† See *The History of the Times* (1952), IV, 246, where some fresh material on the history of the formation of Lloyd George's Coalition will be found.

‡ Lady Londonderry wrote in her diary (December 13, 1916): 'Sir Robert Finlay is Chancellor, I do regret that Carson is not. Of course, if he had done as I wanted him to when Bonar Law undertook the leadership, he would now be Prime Minister, I expect.'

role of First Lord of the Admiralty, vacated by Balfour, the Premier originally cast Carson's friend Lord Milner, who was a Liberal imperialist with Radical views on domestic issues. However, at the last moment, Lloyd George decided that Carson should go to the Admiralty and that Milner should be taken into the War Cabinet instead. To this proposal Carson demurred somewhat, but he eventually agreed when Lloyd George promised that he should have an able administrator to assist him at the Admiralty and that he should always have the right to attend meetings of the War Cabinet when naval matters were on the agenda. He did indeed attend its first meeting on the morning of December 9 in this capacity and he came away from Downing Street very hopefully. Later that day Lady Carson noted in her diary: "Edward attended the War Council. He says more was done in a few hours than used to be done in a year."

Lloyd George's decision about the War Cabinet and the Admiralty was made with characteristic suddenness, so that Milner in fact received notice to attend the first meeting of the War Cabinet before he had been officially informed he was to be a member of it. Lloyd George later referred to the matter in his *War Memoirs*, in which he assigned an interesting reason for the last-moment change. "When my Administration was formed," he wrote, "I was convinced that Sir Edward Carson's great gifts would be better employed by giving him a seat in the War Cabinet. I had designated Lord Milner for the Admiralty. In that choice I was overridden by the personal prejudices of the majority of the Conservative leaders against Carson. They all admired but disapproved of him." Prominent among these Tories apparently were Curzon and Walter Long. The latter, who magnified his own position and influence in the Conservative Party, according to Lloyd George, was jealous of the idea of including Carson in a War Cabinet from which he was excluded. "So Carson was kept out of a place for which he was qualified and fitted to a post for which he was unsuited." Or, as Lord Beaverbrook put it, "He gave up the War Council readily and took the Admiralty which he really did not want."

Carson continued to live in Eaton Place, and would walk from his house to the Admiralty every morning. He and his wife were unable to move into the attractive living quarters in the Admiralty, traditionally occupied by the First Lord, since these were being used by other members of the staff. He would, of course, have preferred the War Cabinet post, but, as we have seen, he always had a great

DAVID LLOYD GEORGE

From the portrait by Sir William Orpen in the National Portrait Gallery.

SCENE IN THE HOUSE OF LORDS DURING THE DEBATE ON THE IRISH TREATY, DECEMBER 14, 1921.

Lord Morley is addressing the House. Carson is sitting behind him, fourth from the near end of the second row on the right. Lord Birkenhead is on the Woolsack.

From the painting by Sir John Lavery in the Corporation Picture Gallery, Glasgow.

liking for the sea, and of all the departmental offices the Admiralty was unquestionably that which most appealed to him. At the same time he admitted to having no technical knowledge and he strongly resisted the temptation, to which Lloyd George yielded, among others, to become an amateur naval strategist. And for this reason, he said: "Amateur strategists are always impatient, and are always ready for a gamble. We cannot afford to gamble with our fleet. If the gamble fails, it would be the end of the Empire, whereas if the Germans like to gamble with their fleet, it would not even be the end of the war." His idea was that the Navy should be put to the best use in the conduct of the war, and he was content to give the Board of Admiralty and the naval staff a free hand in achieving this object. "So long as I am at the Admiralty," he declared, "the sailors will have full scope. They will not be interfered with by me, and I will allow no one else to interfere with them." On his first day in office he introduced himself to his principal officers in a humorous manner, reminiscent of H.M.S. *Pinafore*, which put him on easy and friendly terms with all of them. "Gentlemen, I think we should know one another," he said to the assembled members of the Senior Admiralty Staff. "Some of you may possibly have heard of me as a lawyer of some eminence, but that is not why I am here. I am here because I know nothing about the job. My only great qualification for being put at the head of the Navy is that I am very much at sea."

A few days before Carson took over his new duties a most important staff change took place at the Admiralty. This was the transfer of Admiral Sir John Jellicoe from the command of the Grand Fleet, in which he was succeeded by Admiral Sir David Beatty,* to the key post of First Sea Lord. It was one of Balfour's last administrative acts and was brought about by the imperative need of having the best man available to deal with the growing menace of the enemy submarines which was playing havoc with Allied merchant shipping. Himself the son of a merchant sea captain, Jellicoe, at the age of fifty-nine, had risen virtually to the head of his profession through sheer merit unaided by social or political influence. His decisive engagement of the German battle fleet off the coast of Jutland earlier in the year had resulted in the infliction of

* Beatty wrote to Lady Londonderry on December 11, 1916: 'What manner of man is this Carson to be at the head of our great Navy, is he man enough, is he sound, do you approve will you tell me? It is a matter of the utmost national importance, and yet I notice it is referred to in the papers among the unimportant offices like Board of Agriculture, etc. And the country is at War fighting for its existence'.

such losses on the enemy that it was now reasonably certain that the Germans would not again risk their capital ships in a similar encounter. Carson was immediately attracted by the Admiral's congenial personality, his shrewd twinkling eyes and his sympathetic manner. Many years later when Lloyd George's *War Memoirs* were published, with their disparaging references to Jellicoe, Carson expressed a different view from that of the ex-Premier. "He was in my opinion," he recalled, "the best man at his job that I met with in the whole course of the war for knowledge, calmness, straightness and the confidence he inspired in his officers."

Jellicoe warmly reciprocated Carson's feelings toward himself. "I cannot forbear to mention the extreme cordiality of Sir Edward Carson's relations with the Board in general and myself in particular," Jellicoe wrote in his book, *The Crisis of the Naval War*. "His devotion to the naval service was obvious to all, and in him the Navy possessed indeed a true and powerful friend."

Their first official conversations were naturally directed toward the submarine menace. Jellicoe has recorded how Carson threw himself wholeheartedly into the work. These were the days before the unrestricted U-boat campaign and, although ships were frequently torpedoed, very large numbers were still being sunk by gunfire. One of the most pressing needs was consequently for a great increase in the guns for the defensive armament of merchant vessels. Carson, according to Jellicoe, fully realised the urgent necessity of the situation and was constant in his efforts to procure the necessary guns. He immediately raised the matter with the War Cabinet, and arrangements were made for obtaining supplies from France and Japan as well as the War Office and other sources. During the first six months of 1917, which approximated to Carson's tenure of the Admiralty, nearly 1,600 British merchant ships were thus defensively armed, a figure in excess of the aggregate number of those armed during the first two years of the war. The great majority of the new guns were twenty-pounders or larger guns, since experience had shown that smaller weapons were usually outranged by those carried by the U-boats.

During the first two-and-a-half years of the war the German submarines played a relatively minor part in the war, largely by reason of the restrictions imposed by the German Government on their operations against the mercantile marine. But at the beginning of 1917 it was decided in Berlin to remove these restrictions in order to blockade the British Isles effectively, and a campaign of unrestricted U-boat warfare thereupon began in which all ships, Allied and neutral, were to be attacked and sunk on sight. One of the Admiralty Board's first actions was the formation of an Anti-Submarine Division composed, as the First Lord put it, "of the best and most experienced men we could draw for that purpose of men serving at sea." A Board of Invention and Research was likewise brought into being, presided over by Admiral Lord Fisher and "associated with him are the greatest scientists the country possesses." Between them they developed and exploited such counter-measures as the hydrophone and depth charge, decoy vessels (the so-called 'Q-ships') and, above all, the convoy system.

The dangers of the new form of submarine warfare and the steps which the Admiralty was taking to meet them were described by Carson when he introduced the Navy Estimates in the House of Commons in the spring of 1917. "My duty is to tell the House and the country the whole extent of the menace," he declared. "It is grave. It is serious. It has not yet been solved. I can honestly say that we have never for a moment ceased to work at it in the Admiralty. But no single magic remedy exists, or probably will exist. Nevertheless, I am confident that in the development of measures which have been and are being devised its seriousness will by degrees be greatly mitigated." For obvious security reasons Carson did not divulge what these measures were, beyond a general allusion to patrols, destroyers and convoys.

Among those who heard the First Lord's speech on this occasion from the Ladies' Gallery was Carson's old friend, Lady Londonderry. She found it "excellent", though she did not think he put quite "enough fire" into his references to Jellicoe and Beatty.* "But," she added in her diary, "it was a great triumph to me to see the horse I have backed for thirty years—Carson—standing up in his place as a

* 'I cannot help saying that I think the country in the present crisis is extremely fortunate in having at the Admiralty Sir John Jellicoe. His knowledge of the Service is unparalleled. There is no important post in the Admiralty which he has not, between his services, filled. As one of the Sea Lords on two occasions, as the Director of the Naval Ordnance, and as an expert in gunnery, he is unique as an officer at the Admiralty. But in addition to that, what I value most is that with that experience he has held in his hands the destinies of this country for two and a half long years with faithful, able and watching service, preserving our shores from the assaults and attacks of the enemy.

'The other greatest change is the change of the Commander-in-Chief, who is now Admiral Sir David Beatty. He has had a unique career. At a very early age he is now commanding the greatest fleet that ever sailed the seas, and I believe that he has the confidence of every man who is serving under him. I believe he always had that confidence, but from what I have seen in my visits to the Fleet, I believe it is a daily growing confidence, founded upon the connexion of the officers and men with the distinguished Admiral.' Sir Edward Carson in the House of Commons, Feb. 21, 1917. (Parl. Deb. XC. cc. 1359–1360.)

Minister of the Crown and bringing in the Navy Estimates." She told her son, the new Lord Londonderry: "Of course I feel very triumphant over him as, having said he would get to the top for thirty years, it is extremely pleasing to know that he is there. He has speeded up the machine here to some tune."

The unrestricted U-boat campaign made the entry of the United States of America into the war only a matter of time. But it also caused a sharp increase in mercantile marine losses. In the first month of the campaign British merchant shipping sunk represented approximately 500,000 tons. Carson emphasised the effect on the country's food supplies if losses continued at this rate, in conversations with the newspaper owner, Lord Riddell, whose aid he enlisted in acquainting the Press with the seriousness of the situation. He told Riddell that the stock of grain in the country was equivalent to about three months' consumption, and he confessed he found his colleagues too optimistic. "He says the Germans are putting out more submarines than we are destroying and that if the war continues the result must be very serious," noted Lord Riddell in his diary on April 5, 1917. "He referred to the strain of his work due to the frequent losses of our ships and said that he often left the office absolutely worn out.' Incidentally Carson commented on what he considered Lloyd George's wonderful energy and spirits, and asked to what Lord Riddell attributed them. "Temperament and the ability to take short snatches of sleep when exhausted," was the reply. Unfortunately for Carson, he did not share these qualities with the Prime Minister.

The most effective answer to the submarine menace, though not a complete one, was the convoy system. The policy of convoying merchant ships through dangerous waters was pressed on the Admiralty by Lloyd George from the moment he entered Downing Street. Both Carson and Jellicoe were sympathetic to the idea, but there were difficulties in the way of its general introduction which had to be overcome. Many of the senior officers in the Service were opposed to it, as well as the masters of the vessels themselves. There were insufficient escort ships to carry out the system adequately and there was the problem, partiuclarly in the Atlantic, of 'keeping station' properly at night. However, Carson was anxious that the experiment should be tried. A week before he introduced the Navy Estimates in the House of Commons, Carson brought Jellicoe and Admiral Duff, head of the Anti-Submarine Division in the Admiralty, to breakfast with Lloyd George. It was agreed that the ships carrying coal to France should travel in convoy and that the system should also be tried out on the Scandinavian route. The immediate general operation of the system, which Lloyd George demanded with all the amateur strategist's inexpert knowledge, was impracticable, and Jellicoe had no hesitation in saying so.

When he came to write the chapter on the peril of the submarines in his *War Memoirs*, Lloyd George stated in the strongest language that Jellicoe was always opposed to the convoy system. The volume in question appeared in 1934, and Carson was asked by a leading morning newspaper what he thought of this statement. His answer was characteristically forthright.

"It is the biggest lie ever was told!" he said. "Why, I myself took the First Sea Lord to have breakfast with the Prime Minister in order to explain the position to him. Jellicoe did not oppose the convoy system, but he required time to organise it; he told Lloyd George that the time was not ripe. At first there were not enough suitable ships available for that work, and it was thought that to have a bad convoy was worse than to have no convoy at all. You can imagine what havoc might have been wrought if one or two submarines had found a rich concentration of merchantmen under the guard of ships unequal to the defence. It was not easy to provide the cruisers and destroyers, and the merchant skippers themselves said they would rather trust to their own heels, and their own judgment, in getting through than be packed together under the convoy of some old cruiser slower than themselves."

The situation was fundamentally altered by the entry of the United States into the war on the side of the Allies. This took place in April, on the very day after Carson's despondent interview with Lord Riddell. Thus, when Lloyd George visited the Admiralty a week or two later, he found that the official attitude to the convoy system had completely changed. America was now able to supply the necessary escort vessels. The system was rapidly organised with such efficiency that, though the losses in shipping remained heavy until the autumn, the disastrous effect of the German submarine campaign upon the conduct of the war was finally arrested.*

* It is significant that, unlike Lloyd George, Mr. Churchill in his history, *The World Crisis*, gives Carson credit for the measures which were taken in this connexion during his tenure of the Admiralty. See below, p. 489 and *note*.

2

While the new anti-submarine measures were being worked out, the Admiralty was subjected, quite unjustly, to continued criticism in the Press and elsewhere. As a result Carson felt that his authority was being undermined, and his thoughts turned once more to resignation. On top of this hostile campaign, Lloyd George was constantly pressing him to make sweeping changes in his department. "Sack the lot!" was the Prime Minister's favourite expression at this time, according to Carson. He also kept saying to his First Lord: "Why don't you get fresh men with sea experience?" Exasperated by the repetition of this advice, Carson replied to Lloyd George one day: "I must be under a strange hallucination, Mr. Prime Minister, for I thought that Admiral Jellicoe had just come from the sea!"

Carson had a list made out of all the naval officers at the Admiralty with a record of their services, which he had great pleasure in showing to the Prime Minister, since it proved how very many of them had seen active service. But this did not convince him a bit. He would meet some imaginative midshipman, or sub-lieutenant, from the fleet, who would 'set him going all over again'. On one occasion, at Lloyd George's request the First Lord consented to see a junior officer who, the Premier thought, was going to save the situation. The young gentleman came to Carson's room and the First Lord told him that he could speak with complete freedom. "Thank you, sir," said the officer. "Since you ask me to speak freely, let me say that I have no confidence in Admiral Jellicoe."

Carson then took the officer over the First Sea Lord's record, and the young man was compelled to admit that he could find no fault with it. "Beyond that," observed Carson, recalling the incident afterwards, "he had no practical suggestion to offer at all."

A day or two after this interview the Prime Minister saw Carson and asked him what he thought of the young officer. "I thought him rather a fool," said Carson.

"Well," Lloyd George replied, not in the least abashed, "I did not think so much of him in a second talk I had with him as I did in the first."

The Prime Minister liked to boast that he had his own private sources of information in the Admiralty. It turned out that some of his secretaries used to pick up gossip at lunch-time in the basement canteen there, mostly from Second Division clerks, which they duly retailed to their chief. This tittle-tattle grew to be such a plague that Carson was obliged to issue an order that if officers were found gossiping about the affairs of the Admiralty at people's luncheon tables, he would take a serious view of their conduct. "But I suppose Mr. Lloyd George must have listened to it," remarked Carson, when he had read the notorious chapter in that politician's *War Memoirs*.

Lloyd George now treated Jellicoe with such studied rudeness that the First Sea Lord came to Carson several times and urged him to accept his resignation, stating that, as the Prime Minister obviously had no confidence in him, it would be better if the Government got someone in whom they trusted.

"My dear Admiral," said Carson, "who is your Ministerial Chief?"

"Why, you, sir."

"Have you ever found that I lacked confidence in you?" Carson continued.

Jellicoe replied that the happiest relations existed between them.

"Then, my dear Admiral," said Carson, "let me say to you what I should say to the youngest officer in the Service—carry on."

As a result of the critical Press campaign coupled with renewed pressure from Lloyd George and the War Cabinet, Carson agreed to a reorganisation of the Board of Admiralty. In announcing it in the House of Commons in mid-May, the First Lord explained that its object was two-fold—to free the First Sea Lord and the heads of the Naval Staff as far as possible from administrative work in order that they might concentrate on the naval conduct of the war, and to strengthen the ship-building and production departments of the Admiralty. In this connexion a new civil office was created, that of 'Controller'. Its occupant was to be an additional Member of the Board and to carry the temporary rank of Vice-Admiral. The disclosure of his identity occasioned some surprise. He was Sir Eric Geddes, an energetic, hustling Scottish business man after Lloyd George's heart, whom the outbreak of the war had found in the post of deputy general manager of the London and North Eastern Railway. He had worked with Lloyd George in the Ministry of Munitions and latterly had been sent by the Prime Minister to re-organise transport and communications for the British Army in France. His age, at the time of this appointment, was forty-one. The other administrative chnages included the appointment of a Deputy First Sea Lord, Admiral Webster Wemyss, a Deputy Chief of the Naval Staff, Sir Henry Oliver, and various assistants.

These changes looked well on paper and no doubt gave the impression that the Admiralty would now show striking results, but in fact they meant little beyond presaging the eventual removal of the First Lord himself and the First Sea Lord. They left the material strength of the fleet and the anti-submarine precautions unaffected. Carson was quite prepared to work with Geddes, but he had little opportunity of doing so. Barely two months after the arrival of Sir Eric Geddes in the Admiralty, Geddes was occupying the room of the First Lord. Jellicoe's supersession was decided upon at the same time, but was postponed for a few months at Geddes's express request.

According to Lloyd George, it was a conversation he had with Sir Douglas Haig, the British Commander-in-Chief in France "in the early summer of 1917" which finally decided the Prime Minister on these changes. Haig, who was alarmed at the submarine ravages, is stated by Lloyd George to have been "apprehensive that the war might be lost at sea before he had a chance of winning it on land," while he thought that Jellicoe, despite his technical abilities, was much too rigid, narrow and conservative in his ideas. "As to Sir Edward Carson," Lloyd George continued in this passage in his *War Memoirs*, "I am afraid Sir Douglas Haig had no opinion of his qualities as an administrator. He thought he was distinctly out of place. He strongly urged upon me the appointment of Sir Eric Geddes to that post. The power, and especially the punch, which Sir Eric had displayed in the reorganisation of transport to and in France had made a considerable impression on the Commander-in-Chief's mind."*

Lloyd George had been seeing a good deal of various junior officers at the Admiralty, particularly Commander J. M. Kenworthy† and Captain Herbert Richmond.‡ The Prime Minister has

* Lloyd George, *War Memoirs*, III, 1176–77. To some extent this is borne out by Haig's correspondence and diaries at the time, although in his suggestions he seems to have been considerably influenced by Geddes. For instance, on May 7, 1917, Haig wrote to his wife: 'I met Jellicoe in Paris—and as you know, I met him in London two or three times—I am afraid he does not impress me. Indeed he strikes me as being an old woman. In fact the Admiralty is in such need that my Director-General of Transportation is going there! I think he ought to be put in Carson's place as the latter is worn out.' Six weeks later (June 20, 1917) Haig wrote in his diary: 'In the afternoon I visited the War Office, and also saw "Admiral" Sir Eric Geddes at the Admiralty. The latter is most anxious about the state of affairs at the Admiralty. The First Lord (Carson) has recently married, is very tired, and leaves everything to a number of incompetent sailors! . . . We agreed that I should do my best to arrange that Lloyd George should see Geddes when the latter would put the whole position of affairs before him. . . .'

† Now Lord Strabolgi.

‡ Later Admiral Sir Herbert Richmond.

stated that he passed on such information as he obtained from these officers to the First Lord, who, he added, "found it impossible to overcome the solid and stolid resistance of his Board of Admiralty." The Prime Minister decided, therefore, according to his own account, "to put someone in charge who was accustomed to force his will on his subordinates." In this intention, it may be added, the Prime Minister betrayed marked ignorance of the constitution of the Board of Admiralty. The Sea Lords are, of course, the equals and not the subordinates of the First Lord, although the latter remains the responsible Minister. One morning toward the end of June, the Prime Minister invited Haig and Geddes to breakfast in Downing Street. The result of this meeting, at which no one else was present, was that Lloyd George, in Haig's words, "decided to take immediate action to improve matters."

So far as Carson was concerned, Lloyd George hoped to soften the blow which he knew the First Lord must feel in his removal from the Admiralty by reverting to the idea which he had when forming his Government. A few days later—it was July 5, 1917—the Prime Minister said to him: "I think you'd much better come into the War Cabinet. We want you." Next day was a Friday, and Carson went off to spend the week-end with his wife at their small bungalow in Birchington. They were asleep that night, after 11 p.m., when a messenger arrived from Downing Street bearing an urgent letter from the Prime Minister. It was to say that he wished Carson to leave the Admiralty and join the War Cabinet, and would he let him know at once. (This was, of course, quite an unnecessary disturbance, since the messenger could not get back to London before noon next day and food and bed had consequently to be found for him.) Carson replied that he fully realised how the Admiralty was being criticised and that he would gladly resign, but that as to joining the War Cabinet, he could not possibly decide in such a hurry.

Next day brought another messenger from Downing Street with a further note to the effect that Carson had entirely misunderstood the previous letter. They did not really want him to leave the Admiralty at all, the Prime Minister told him in terms designed to be deceptively persuasive. But they *must* have him in the War Cabinet, so there was no alternative. Lloyd George added: "I always wanted you in the War Cabinet from the beginning but somebody thwarted me." The Prime Minister was also willing, so he said, that Carson should represent the Admiralty in the Cabinet and be the Navy's spokesman there. So to this appeal to patriotism and duty, which Lloyd George knew so well how to make, Carson succumbed. "Nevertheless," as Lloyd George was later to observe, "although membership of the War Directorate was a more exalted and powerful position, I am afraid he felt wounded by the change. To him it was an unpalatable proposal however we might wrap it up. But his intense patriotic sense prevailed over any personal feeling."

A day or two later one of the Sea Lords—a bluff, honest sailor—came to Carson and said: "Sir, you have let us down badly."

"I had nothing to do with it," replied Carson. "I never wanted to leave the Admiralty. I am sorry to leave the Admiralty." He added that he had been told that he would be more useful to the State elsewhere. "This is a time of war and every man must go where duty calls him."

To the dismay of all the senior officers at the Admiralty Carson's place as First Lord was taken by Sir Eric Geddes, who lost no time in displaying what Lady Londonderry called "all the attributes of a beggar on horseback" in his new office. He immediately ordered an enormous closed Rolls-Royce motor for town work "with Government petrol to match" and a huge open car for country work. "Sir Edward only had his one old car and *paid* for his petrol." When taking over from him Geddes asked Carson how many secretaries he had at the Admiralty. "Five," said Carson. "Oh," said Sir Eric, "I shall want at least fifteen more." "Well," said Carson, "I can't think what you will do with so many, I found five plenty." According to Mrs. Spender, Geddes also told Carson that he "loved 'honours' and letters after his name." "How could you in these days," retorted Carson in tones of contempt, "when they are so cheap?"

To Lady Londonderry

Offices of the War Cabinet, 2 *Whitehall Gardens*, *S.W. September* 11, 1917 . . . I have more or less got over my soreness at leaving the Admiralty. I think it was a pity just as I began to know something of the job and I am sure Geddes would have been a great help as Controller. However, I feel conscious that I did everything possible to push on while I was there, and I shall always think with pleasure of my short time as 1st Lord . . .

I go over this week-end to GHQ to see Field-Marshal Haig and Ronald [McNeill] is coming with me. The soldiers want all possible support and sympathy in their anxious job and ought to have more of it.

I am now liaison Minister for Propaganda, so I have plenty to do. Russia is the great fiasco of the war. However great democracy

> may be, it cannot carry on internal and external war at the same time. The lesson of order is writ plainly in everything that is taking place . . .

Sir Douglas Haig's comment on the visit which Carson paid him at his Headquarters is worth quoting. "It is quite a rest to deal with him after Winston," noted the Commander-in-Chief in his diary. "He is so straightforward and singleminded. He is convinced that the military experts must be given full power, not only to advise but to carry out their plans. He is all opposed to the meddling now practised by the Prime Minister and other politicians."

Two further extracts from Haig's diary may be given here. They show that, however Haig may have been prejudiced against Carson as an administrator at the Admiralty, no doubt through Geddes's influence, the Commander-in-Chief was attracted by his personality and thought highly of him as a political counsellor.

> *September* 15 [1917] I had a talk with Sir E. Carson before he went out this morning. He considers that Lloyd George has considerable driving powers, but recognises his danger. He [Lloyd George] has no knowledge of strategy or military operations, yet he thinks he is well qualified to direct his Military Advisers! Carson wished me to talk freely with Mr. Asquith because the latter, though in opposition, has great power.

> *September* 16. Sir E. Carson left at 9.30. He said he was delighted with his visit, and he assured me that the War Cabinet would not be allowed to interfere with me or my arrangements. I took quite a liking to Carson and think it is fortunate for the Empire that he is in the War Cabinet.

The Geddes axe now fell on Jellicoe, who was summarily dismissed on Christmas Eve, being replaced as First Sea Lord by Admiral Wemyss. Jellicoe and the other Sea Lords understood Geddes to have stated that Carson and Balfour had both agreed to the change at a meeting in the Prime Minister's room at which Lloyd George and Geddes were both present. The Sea Lords asked Carson for an explanation. He replied that he had never agreed to anything of the sort, and he wrote to Geddes a sharp letter to this effect. "The only conversation I had with you as to Admiral Jellicoe," wrote Carson, "was when I saw you at the Admiralty with reference to certain articles in the *Daily Mail* and when you expressed certain grounds of dissatisfaction with Jellicoe. I then stated that I knew of no one to replace him and that in my opinion Admiral Wemyss whom you mentioned was not at all to be compared with Admiral Jellicoe and was not qualified for the office of First Sea Lord, an opinion which I still hold." Geddes replied that he had been misreported, but his explanations were unconvincing and the incident left a nasty taste in Carson's mouth, more especially since Balfour, to whom Carson also appealed, entered a similar denial. "It is certainly quite untrue to suggest that I advised or suggested," he wrote, "either that the late First Sea Lord should go or that the present First Sea Lord should be appointed."

To A. J. Balfour

Offices of the War Cabinet, 2 Whitehall Gardens, S.W. January 5, 1918

> . . . The Sea Lords were very much upset at what they understood was the contention of the First Lord that both you and I had agreed that Admiral Jellicoe ought to cease to be First Lord. Whether they were right or wrong in their understanding of what Geddes said to them I cannot say, but they asked me whether I had ever made such a statement and of course I felt bound to say I had not.
>
> I feel very strongly that my name should not have been introduced into the matter at all, more especially as I had left the Admiralty because I refused to yield to Press and other pressure to make changes which in my judgment were not to the benefit of the Service and the Country . . .

The Sea Lords were indeed so upset that they threatened to resign in a body, but after Carson had seen one of them (Admiral Sir Lionel Halsey) on their joint behalf and poured oil on the troubled waters, they agreed to put duty before inclination and to remain at their posts. Jellicoe's wounded feelings were slightly solaced by the grant of a peerage.

3

When the United States entered the war, Lloyd George was strongly pressed through Mr. Walter Hines Page, the American Ambassador in London, to make another attempt to settle the question of Ireland. Accordingly the Prime Minister offered either the immediate application of the Home Rule Act to twenty-six of the thirty-two Irish counties, *i.e.* excluding North-East Ulster, for five years, or else a convention of Irishmen of all parties who should be asked to hammer out an instrument of their own Government. Let them reach what he called 'substantial agreement' and he would give legislative effect to it. This offer was contained in letters to the ageing and ailing Nationalist Leader, John Redmond, and to Sir John Lonsdale, who had temporarily taken Carson's place as Chairman of the Ulster Unionists while Carson was a member of the Government.

The first alternative was unacceptable to the Nationalists as involving partition and to the Unionists as involving only temporary exclusion. They both agreed to the proposal for a convention, but the Nationalists insisted that the membership should include representatives of the Roman Catholic hierarchy and chairmen of county councils and other public bodies. This had the effect of making the convention unwieldy as well as unrepresentative, since the increasingly powerful Sinn Fein element in the country ostentatiously boycotted the proceedings. "I think it pretty clear that if elections took place now," Carson wrote to Lloyd George at the time (May 22, 1917), "the Sinn Feiners would have a much increased representation on the County Councils." He afterwards went over to Ulster and advised his followers to come into the convention lest it might later be said that their refusal to participate was deliberately designed to wreck any settlement. Carson also told the Ulster Unionist Council that he had Lloyd George's assurance that their position would not be prejudiced by their action and he repeated the Prime Minister's pledge that Ulster was not to be coerced.

Carson suggested a total delegation of fifty or sixty. "I should think that anything else will be unworkable," he told Lloyd George. But in all about a hundred delegates attended the opening meeting of the Convention in Trinity College. The Ulster Group was led by Mr. H. T. Barrie, Unionist M.P. for North Derry, and included Mr. H. M. Pollock, Chairman of the Belfast Chamber of Commerce, and Sir George Clark, Chairman of the great Belfast shipbuilding concern of Workman and Clark, as well as the heads of the Protestant Churches. Lord Londonderry, son of Carson's old friend, acted as secretary of the Ulster delegation. The Southern Irish Unionists were headed by Lord Midleton. But it was noticed that the delegation as a whole was composed of elderly men. Nor were any women included. As chairman, after Redmond had declined the position, the delegates elected Sir Horace Plunkett, son of Lord Dunsany and a well-intentioned idealist who had formerly sat as a Unionist M.P. for South Dublin but had devoted most of his sixty-three years to experiments in co-operative agriculture in Ireland.

This is not the place to record in detail the history of the ill-starred Irish Convention. It sat in secret throughout the summer, autumn and winter in Dublin, and it also held meetings in Belfast and Cork. Its most significant development was a proposal by Lord Midleton agreeing to an Irish Parliament with much more considerable powers than the 1914 Act, virtually dominion status, including the transfer of Excise to the local Government and the collection, though not the imposition, of Customs. This attracted Redmond but not the Ulstermen, who saw the commercial prosperity of the province being placed in jeopardy. Redmond appealed to Lloyd George. "I am glad to hear you have sent for Barrie and his friends," he wrote on November 26, 1917, "and I can only repeat that I feel convinced it rests with you and Carson to make or mar the Convention. Everyone in Ireland believes that it is in your power to bring these men to reason, and if the Convention breaks down I can only repeat the most serious consequences will ensue immediately."

Eventually Lloyd George agreed that if Lord Midleton's scheme was generally acceptable to the Convention, exclusive of the Ulster Unionist delegates, he would use his influence with the Cabinet and in Parliament to bring the scheme into law. Thus it looked to Carson as if the Prime Minister was going back on his pledge that Ulster should not be coerced. In any event, the fact that the Irish question had come very much to the fore again embarrassed him in the Cabinet and he made up his mind to resign early in the New Year. "Ireland is such a worry," he told Lady Londonderry at this time, "and I am being constantly reminded of my *duty*, which is apparently to desert my friends and my convictions, which of course I will never do."

Meanwhile in Dublin the compact entered into between Redmond and Lord Midleton proved to be the undoing of these two politicians, who were each in turn disowned by their parties. On January 14, 1918, Redmond came into the conference hall and announced that he was not going to move the amendment implementing his understanding with Midleton, since "Devlin and the Bishops" had intimated their intention of voting against it. "The others will give their advice," he said in tragic tones. "I feel that I can be of no further service to the Convention." He accordingly withdrew from the hall and was seen no more in the Convention. To one of the Ulster delegates who asked him to put his cards on the table, he replied sadly: "I have no cards. I am a leader without a party." Less than two months later he was dead.

Speaking some months later of the events of this period, Carson declared: "The Irish Convention gave me more trouble than almost anything I ever had to do with in relation to Home Rule. In point of fact it eventually drove me out of the Cabinet in the middle of the war. And why? Never was Ulster in a more dangerous position than it was when the Convention was drawing to a close—for this reason. The Southern Unionists lost their courage. They gave their case away. I do not believe they represented anybody but themselves. They said we were traitors whereas as a matter of fact it was they under the leadership of Lord Midleton who were prepared to say: 'If we go down, Ulster must come down too.' "

Carson's decision to resign was made public on January 22, 1918. "When I joined your Cabinet," he wrote to Lloyd George in his letter of resignation, "I had no consideration in my mind but the prosecution of the war, and I did not anticipate that the question of Irish Government would be reopened during the war. Subsequently, when the Convention was proposed, I thought it right to use any influence I had in inducing my Ulster friends to take part in the effort to come to some settlement. But on account of the dual position as Member of the Government and as Leader of the Ulster Unionist Party, I have felt it incumbent on me to stand aloof from the proceedings of the Convention. It is, however, apparent that whatever the result of the Convention may be, its proceedings may lead to a situation demanding a decision by the Government of grave matters of policy in Ireland. After anxious consideration, I feel certain that it will be to the advantage of the War Cabinet to discuss this policy without my presence, having regard to the very prominent part which I have taken in the past in relation to the Home Rule controversy and to the pledges by which I am bound to my friends in Ulster."

Carson's action in leaving the Government was followed by his faithful henchman James Craig, who likewise resigned his post of Treasurer of the Household and Government Whip. "I appreciate greatly your confidence and affection," Carson wrote to him. "It cuts short for the moment the carrying on of the good work which you did so well—but I feel convinced my own action was inevitable."

Lloyd George told Carson he had received his letter to him "with the deepest and most unfeigned regret because of the value I attach to the unvarying courage and sagacity which you have brought to the nation at this juncture." Lord Finlay, the Lord Chancellor, said to him: "Why didn't you wait until Ulster *is* coerced, or some definite step of that kind taken? I should have left the Government myself then." According to Mrs. Spender, Carson replied that "if he had waited till then, others would have come too, and people would have said he did it to wreck the Government. By going now, he avoids that, and stands or falls by himself."

Immediately after the announcement of his resignation Carson went over to Belfast, where he was received with all the enthusiasm of the old volunteer days. Sir John Lonsdale had been raised to the peerage in the New Year honours, so that the Ulster Unionist leadership was vacant for Carson to resume. Carson was formally re-elected to the position on January 28.

To Lady Londonderry

Beach Hotel, Littlehampton. February 12, 1918. We have come here for a holiday . . . It is so long since I had a rest that I am not sorry to have this opportunity.

Belfast was very enthusiastic but we had such a crowded programme I nearly despaired of getting thro'. Of course the situation is a very difficult one as every effort will be made to make it appear that we are obstructing the war! As for Midleton, his scheme is the most illusory and ridiculous I have ever heard of and I am sure Ulster would have none of it . . .

To D. Lloyd George

Beach Hotel, Littlehampton. February 14, 1918. . . . Since I have returned from Ireland, I have been thinking a good deal of the possibilities of a settlement during the war. It is clear to my mind that no settlement consistent with the interests of Great Britain can be devised which will satisfy the Sinn Fein or the extreme Nationalist Party who sympathise with Sinn Fein.

If therefore attempt is made to bring Ulster into an Irish Parliament, to which they are averse, you will have both Sinn Fein and Ulster in opposition to the new Government, and I do not believe that any Government started under such circumstances would have the least chance of success. The promises made to Ulster when the war broke out were very distinct and were frequently repeated by me when I was asking people to join the Army, *viz.* that no attempt would be made to set up a Home Rule Parliament in Ireland during the continuance of the war, and indeed this was provided by legislation.

I can assure you that the Ulster people, who have suffered severely in the loss of their men at the Front, will regard it as an act of treachery if the promises are broken and Ulster is put under a Home Rule Parliament. Personally, I do not see how under the circumstances I could be expected to advise them to accept such a Parliament, nor do I believe I would have the least chance of persuading them to do so.

I have already, as you know, under great difficulty induced Ulster in the interest of the prosecution of the war to accept a solution on the basis of the exclusion of the six counties, which

> meant that the rest of Ireland could have Home Rule. Such a solution preserved the Union for the vast majority of those who desired it.
>
> The only other possible solution seems to me to lie in a system of Federation for the whole of the United Kingdom . . .

It will be remembered that the federal solution had been put forward by Mr. F. S. Oliver in 1910 and that Carson and the Ulster Unionists had objected to it at that time.* Now that the Home Rule Act was on the statute book and that some form of Home Rule for all Ireland outside Ulster was inevitable, Carson was now prepared to accept Oliver's scheme in the hope that the Union, which he still regarded as 'the keystone of the British Commonwealth' might nevertheless be preserved "on the principles of true federation." He put this alternative forward, he told the Prime Minister, "to show how untrue it is that Ulster presents a *non possumus* attitude."

While the Convention was debating such questions as whether or not proportional representation should form part of the hypothetical constitution of Ireland and thus bringing to a close its inconclusive and futile discussions, the great German offensive was launched on the Western Front and every day brought fresh tidings of reverses inflicted by the enemy on British arms. The Cabinet decided that conscription must be introduced in Ireland, and Lloyd George's idea was that Home Rule for the whole country should be the bait for the South to come in. Legislation was carried through Parliament in April in the teeth of Nationalist opposition, led by Dillon, since Redmond had died in the previous month. During the debate T. M. Healy spoke derisively of 'Carson's Army', and his reference roused the Unionist Leader to anger. "You may, if you like, call it with contempt Carson's Army," said its creator, "but it has just gone into action for the fourth time, and many of them have paid the supreme sacrifice. They have covered themselves with glory, and, what is more, they have covered Ireland with glory, and they have left behind sad homes throughout the small hamlets of Ulster, as I well know, losing three or four sons in many a home." On the other hand, most of the young men in the South had been disporting themselves at race-courses and playing football and hockey up and down the country for the greater part of the war.

At the end of May Mrs. Spender wrote: "Sir Edward is very depressed and unhappy. He feels it dreadfully being back in Town and yet absolutely out of things. Lloyd George has turned against

* See above pp. 278, 281.

him completely and is doing his best, very successfully, to turn everyone else in the Government against him too. If Sir Edward writes to him now on any Irish question, he doesn't even answer. Sir Edward is convinced the Government has no intention of bringing in either Home Rule or Conscription, as he has always said from the beginning."

About this time Lloyd George reproached Carson for speaking against him in the House.

"Yes," said Carson, "I did, and I shall do it again. But I didn't vote against you, though I shall do that too some day, no doubt!"

"Well," observed the Prime Minister, "I'd rather you voted against me than spoke against me!"

4

As Carson had foretold, no attempt was made to enforce military conscription in Southern Ireland—it was, of course, unnecessary in the North—and the Act in the South became a dead letter. The Nationalists joined with Sinn Fein in opposing it, with the backing of the Catholic Church in Ireland, and the Government gave way. The official excuse for dropping Home Rule for the time being was the discovery that the Sinn Fein leaders were in treasonable correspondence with Germany. Extensive arrests were made in Dublin and throughout the country on the orders of the Lord Lieutenant, Lord French, those caught in the police net including Arthur Griffith and Mr. De Valera.

That summer Carson was once more in Ulster, exhorting his followers to vigilance. On July 12 he addressed a concourse of 80,000 Orangemen outside Belfast. "Nothing has more disgusted me with the filth of politics," he told them, "than to find men going back on their word to those who have given their lives for the British cause." Shortly after this, Mr. Edward Shortt, the Chief Secretary to the Lord Lieutenant, on the pretext of disarming Ireland, came to Belfast and demanded that the rifles of the Ulster Volunteer Force be handed over to Government custody. This produced a delicate situation in the city, and Carson was asked to intervene with the authorities. He did so promptly and effectively. "Since the war began, these arms have been held at the disposal of the Government," he wrote to Bonar Law. "They have been used for quelling the Sinn Fein Rebellion. Whatever may be thought of the policy which brought them to Ireland before the war, no one has ever suggested that they have been used at any time to aid the enemy. These rifles have been stored in places well known to the police, there has been no secrecy about their location, and for the last four years the Government has been well content to leave them, being well assured that there was no danger of their falling into dangerous hands."

To Lady Londonderry

Orion Bungalow, Birchington, Kent. September 4, 1918 . . . Well, I am idle and doing nothing with the exception of attending to my correspondence with the help of a typist aged 14!

Ulster and the arms question is the most anxious one with which I have been concerned. Shortly I think the Chief Secretary wants a row to please and placate Dillon, but Lord French I am sure does not and, if he holds firm, he will be backed by the Cabinet . . .

I hope you will bear in mind how necessary it is that the women should have their full share in the organization in Ulster. I did my best when I was over to lay the foundations of this policy.

Now don't you think something ought to be done to get the King to visit Ulster? He has been to every shipyard and munition factory in England and Scotland, encouraging the workers, and yet Ulster has the biggest shipyards and has turned out all the aeroplane cloth which has been used. They get no royal smile simply because the rest of Ireland is disloyal! . . .

I hear Charley is going to present a copy of [the late] Lord L[ondonderry]'s portrait to the Carlton Club. I am so glad. The Club has never been the same since he died and the great centre of sincere friendship seems to have vanished. Ichabod!

On the arms question the Lord Lieutenant did 'hold firm', although his Chief Secretary threatened resignation, and the Ulstermen were allowed to keep their rifles in their own armouries, subject to military supervision. As for the King, he was unable to visit Ulster before the Armistice, but he sent Carson and the Ulster Unionist Council a telegram with a message for "my loyal Ulster subjects," recalling the heroic deeds of the Ulster Division at the Front. "Throughout the long years of struggle which have now so gloriously ended," said His Majesty, "the men of Ulster have proved how nobly they fight and die."

Armistice Day found Carson the luncheon guest of the British Empire Producers' Association in London. "My heart is very full," he told them. "It is very hard to find words to talk of what has happened." Having paid his tribute to those who had served, he touched on the problems of peace. "How are we to reward the men who have preserved for us everything we possess?" he asked.

"There must be no return to the old standards of living or low wages for the working class. You must let the men who have fought feel at the earliest possible moment the gratitude of the nation by giving them their share in the nation's wealth. We are not going to play these men to their homes on their return and march away and care no more about them."

Parliament, which had been elected in 1910, was dissolved a few days after the signing of the Armistice, and immediate preparations were made for a General Election under a new franchise. This practically amounted to universal suffrage and admitted women both as voters and candidates for the first time. Lloyd George and Bonar Law issued a joint manifesto appealing for support of the Coalition. Candidates—there were about 500 of them—who supported the Government were given a certificate or 'coupon' as a badge of their loyalty. The Opposition was provided by the Asquithian Liberals, Labour, Nationalists and Sinn Fein. In their election manifesto Lloyd George and Bonar Law could not, of course, escape the Irish question. "We regard it as a first object in British statemanship to explore all practical paths toward the settlement of this grave question, on the basis of self-government," they declared. Two paths were closed, they added—the one involving a complete break between Ireland and the British Empire and the other "the forcible submission of the six counties of Ulster to a Home Rule Parliament against their will."

With the elections coming on, Carson had to think about his constituency. He had represented Dublin University for twenty-six years, but now that a considerable degree of Home Rule for Southern Ireland was inevitable, it seemed to him more appropriate to find a seat, if he could, in that part of the country with which he had been especially closely associated in the political struggle and which wished to preserve the Union with Great Britain on a more intimate basis. Under the recent redistribution of seats the representation of Belfast in the House of Commons had been doubled and it was for one of these new divisions, Duncairn, that Carson was now invited to come forward as a Unionist candidate. Duncairn comprised the greater part of the old North Belfast Division and was largely a working-class constituency, with mill hands and shipyard workers preponderating, very different from the comparative academic calm of Trinity College, Dublin. The chairman of the Duncairn Unionist Association, who extended the invitation to the Ulster Leader, was Sir George Clark, a former M.P. for North Belfast and head of the great shipbuilding firm of Workman and Clark; he will be remembered as one of the Ulster delegates to the Irish Convention. "I feel that under existing circumstances," Carson wrote to Sir George Clark, "and as Leader since 1911 of the Ulster Unionist Party, as a Covenanter, and as one so closely connected in recent years with the political life of Belfast, it is my duty to accept the honour which has been offered to me by your association." Meanwhile the dons and Professors of Trinity wrote expressing their gratitude to Carson for the way in which he had so faithfully served the University's interests at Westminster for more than a quarter of a century.

To Lady Londonderry

5 *Eaton Place, S.W.*1. *November* 24, 1918 . . . As I have consented to contest one of the Belfast seats, I suppose I will have to stay there during the election period . . . James Craig and I have taken a house there for the election.

It looks as if we will have several contests and of course, as you say, no one knows much about the new electorate . . . I think we ought to be *independent* supporters of the Coalition. Whether it will last I do not know.

The South of Ireland people are very angry with us, but I do not think they know what else we could do.

Would you not have liked to see the surrender of the German fleet?

Craigavon, within whose friendly walls Carson had spent so many exciting hours, was now a hospital for shell-shocked soldiers. It was later to become a sanatorium for ex-servicemen and the Craigs were never to live there again. As a temporary home along with the Carsons they took a house, Mount Vernon, on the opposite side of Belfast Lough, in what was to be Carson's new constituency. From here Carson conducted a strenuous election campaign, since in addition to his own contest he had to appear on most of the other Unionist platforms. His adoption meeting took place, amid enthusiastic scenes, in the Unionist Club in Brougham Street on November 26, with his friend Sir George Clark in the chair.

There was already a Nationalist candidate in the field in Duncairn, and also a Sinn Feiner. Undismayed, Carson declared himself "ready to face all comers" and "ready to beat all comers." For the rest, he said "Keep your eyes, men of Ulster, on the main question, and the main question is that you should take your place in the march of the new era which arises after the war . . . There is a great deal to be done in the present crisis and a great deal for Belfast. Belfast seems to be like a big boy who has grown out of his clothes. We must make the clothes fit him. His clothes must go on growing with him. If they do not then we are not doing our duty to the rising generation." Finally, he begged his audience "just once more" to get rid of all parochialism and all merely local questions from their minds. "Remember that a people becomes great not merely by local politics or local questions," he said, "but by taking a broad survey in which each part of the city, as it may be, or the country, as it may be, or the Empire, as it may be, is a help one to the other in making mutual greatness for all."

Two days later he opened his campaign in the Clifton Street Orange Hall and explained why he was backing Lloyd George and the Coalition.

> The first question that really arises is, who is the Government that is going to represent us at the Peace Conference? No Government can represent us which has not behind it a united nation. No Government can possibly enter the Councils of Europe and win for this country all that it desires unless it has behind it a united people, and I say without fear of contradiction that it is not a Government of any party that can take upon itself to settle these great questions. These are not party questions. These are national questions and it is only a national Government that can attempt to solve them. Therefore it is that I strongly support the idea of a Coalition.
>
> I do not believe that the country has yet realised what it owes to Mr. Lloyd George. I have differed with him profoundly in the past, and I daresay I differ profoundly with him in the present. I left this Government over this very Ulster question. But for all that I recall to myself the days when I was a member of the War Cabinet, and I shall never forget the courage, the energy, the foresight, the character and the growth of the man who was acting as Prime Minister . . . For my own part, I feel certain that the man and those under him who were able to organise the country to carry on the war to a successful issue are the men to help us to organise the country to carry it to the fullest fruits of victory.

Polling took place on December 14 and the votes were counted a fortnight later. During this interval of waiting Carson and his wife were the guests of Sir Thomas and Lady Dixon at Cairndhu, a house with a magnificent sea view near Larne. Here Carson recovered from the strain of the campaign and heard the results of this remarkable election.

To Bonar Law

Cairndhu, Larne, Co. Antrim. December 21, 1918. I am glad the prospects of the Coalition are good. I think we have carried 9 out of the 10 seats in Belfast.

I have found the work very heavy and am suffering from a bad cold and insomnia. I imagine it is likely to be my last election.

I shall be glad if you see a chance in the reconstruction for James Craig. I know you like him—but I think I know his value more than anyone. He has great gifts of organisation and hard work and he would really do an office well as he has very broad views.

I hear great complaints of the Pensions Office, and I am sure it ought to be more up to date than any other, if we are to avoid chaos and dissatisfaction . . .

In Duncairn Carson's return was a foregone conclusion. The actual figures were:

Sir Edward Carson (Unionist)	11,637
Major W. H. Davey (Nationalist)	2,449
Dr. H. M. MacNabb (Sinn Fein)	249
Unionist Majority	9,188

As Carson had predicted, all the Unionist candidates in Belfast were returned, except in the Falls Division, being that part of West Belfast which had previously elected Devlin and which did so again. Under the redistribution arrangements the Irish Unionists improved their position, having twenty-six members compared with eighteen in the old Parliament. Except for a few Dublin seats, these were confined to the North. However, the most remarkable feature of the election in Ireland was the almost total annihilation of the Nationalist Party. The Nationalists managed to hold only six seats out of sixty-eight, their leader John Dillon being among the rejected, while Sinn Fein captured no less than seventy-three. It is certain that personation was rife at this election and that the dead voted in large numbers; there were many abstentions, and known opponents of Sinn Fein received warning that if they voted it would be at the risk of their lives. But notwithstanding these features, the election clearly proved that the South was overwhelmingly in favour of a Republic.

In Britain the Coalition candidates scored a striking success, and the Liberals a crushing defeat. "The Coalitionists are sweeping the country," noted Lady Carson in her diary. (It was still in the days before wireless and one of the Belfast newspapers kept telephoning the news.) "Asquith out, McKenna out, Simon out, Runciman out, in fact nearly all the old gang." The final results showed the Coalition Unionists and Liberals with a total strength of 478. Only twenty-seven of Asquith's followers managed to secure their return to the House of Commons. The residue of Opposition included fifty-nine Labour Members. The only woman candidate to be returned was a Sinn Feiner, Countess Markiewicz.

The victorious Sinn Fein group in Ireland had no intention of taking their seats at Westminster, since this would require them to take the oath of allegiance to the British Crown. Having assumed the title of the Irish Republican Party, they met in the Mansion House in Dublin and convened a legislative assembly for Ireland which was styled Dail Eireann. The first formal meeting of this body took place there on January 21, 1919. All Irish M.P.s were invited to be present irrespective of party. In due course Carson received a summons in Gaelic to attend this curious assembly. He kept the document as a souvenir.

5

Lloyd George was occupied for over a month in the formation of his Government. It was not until January 10, 1919, that the composition of the new Ministry was announced in the Press, and there was some disappointment that there were virtually no newcomers in the list. Of the seventy-seven names all but ten had been members of the old Government and most of the ten had held office before. Bonar Law and Curzon were Leaders respectively of the Commons and Lords, Balfour returned to the Foreign Office, Austen Chamberlain became Chancellor of the Exchequer and Mr. Winston Churchill combined the portfolios of War and Air under his direction. Carson was pressed by Lloyd George to come into the Cabinet, but he declined, saying that he preferred to go back to the Bar. "I long for a whiff of the Law Courts," he told his old friend and professional antagonist, Lord Reading. The office of Lord Chancellor, which he again declined, was given to F. E. Smith, who thus became the youngest occupant of the Woolsack in modern times. 'F. E.' was also raised to the peerage, taking the title of Lord Birkenhead.*

* Lady Londonderry wrote in her diary (January 16, 1919): 'Sir Edward Carson has not been made Lord Chancellor. It shows that if one ever has any political principles, as he had about Ulster, he is robbed of his right. F. E. is brilliant, and self-made . . . so he really deserves success, though he has no character.' And again, (February 22): 'I was amused at F. E. taking "Birkenhead" as his title. Curiously enough, his father was agent to my grandfather for his Birkenhead estate.' Lady Londonderry's grandfather was Henry John (Chetwynd-Talbot) 18th Earl of Shrewsbury.

In the distribution of junior posts, Bonar Law conveyed Carson's hint to Lloyd George and James Craig was not overlooked: he was appointed Parliamentary Secretary to the Ministry of Pensions. "I am so glad you like the new office and I know you will work at it with a will," Carson wrote to him a few days later. "It is one of the most important problems to solve and it has been allowed to drift into chaos. You might have had instead Parliamentary Secretary to the Board of Agriculture, but that is a purely *English* office and I am sure Pensions is far better. The P.M. and B[onar] L[aw] offered me a seat in the Cabinet but I refused and I am satisfied I am right."

Carson's friend Lady Londonderry, who had lately been suffering from heart trouble, resigned her office as President of the Ulster Women's Unionist Association, which she had held for some years. This set Carson thinking that perhaps the time was coming when he should likewise relinquish his own political leadership. The letter which he wrote to her on the subject was the last which she received from him, as she died suddenly a few weeks later. She lived, however, to see her son appointed Under-Secretary for Air, a recognition which also gave Carson great satisfaction.

To Lady Londonderry

5 *Eaton Place, S.W. January* 22, 1919. . . . Of course I feel very much your resignation. All such incidents are clothed with many sacred memories. I suppose the time must shortly come when I will be asking that a younger man should be 'The Ulster Leader', and in truth I felt the strain of the election and was in bed for 10 days after it. But Ulster is in a strong position now.

I was offered a seat in the Cabinet, but what is the use of going into a Government when you have a cause still unsettled which may necessitate your resignation any day? As you say, I have made great sacrifices for Ulster—everything in fact so far as personal ambition is concerned. However I had a cause in which I believed and the example of sincerity must do some good. Anyhow I am quite happy about it all which is something.

. . . I am very busy as I cannot afford to idle. My children and the Exchequer have ordained that.

I wish I could have gone to Mount Stewart but I was too ill.

Lady Londonderry's death came as a great shock to Carson, preoccupied with his own health as he so frequently was. She was two years younger than Carson, and they had been the closest of friends for more than thirty years. Her passing removed the only correspondent outside his family to whom Carson wrote regularly. At times she must have been sorely tried by his allusions to his illnesses and by the strain of fatalism which runs through all his letters to her. But she made no secret of her admiration for his talents and of her belief in his destiny, and Carson could never forget what her encouragement and friendship, as well as her husband's, had been to him throughout so much of his professional and political career. "She had the warmest of hearts," as Balfour's secretary, Jack Sandars, said of her at this time. "As a friend there was no better and her loyalty stood every test—as an adviser on a social problem, none wiser or shrewder. With an equal radiance she shone in the world of London and in her country homes. As a hostess her position was supreme; and this title, which was never challenged, is now extinct. There was hardly a branch of national sport in which she did not take part and that too with a knowledge of exceptional extent. Political associations and charitable movements she directed with the same energy and determination as she showed in the affairs of her household. In fact to all her interests she brought a boundless and ebullient spirit."

Carson's decision after the 'Coupon Election' to abandon politics and go back to the law was quickly rewarded. Briefs began to pile up again in Dr. Johnson's Buildings. One of them which he accepted early in the New Year and was marked with a four-figure fee was an interesting action for libel, where he was instructed to appear for the defendant, the well-known Oriental traveller and writer, Sir Valentine Chirol. The plaintiff was an elderly Hindu from the Bombay Presidency named Bal Gangadhur Tilak and he complained of certain statements about him contained in Sir Valentine's book, *Indian Unrest*, which was a revised reprint of articles which the defendant had contributed to *The Times*. Chirol had visited India on several occasions as a special correspondent for this newspaper, and in the course of his travels had paid particular attention to the Deccan District, because it had been the centre for many years of violent propaganda against British rule culminating in the murder of a civil servant named Jackson. Tilak, who was a violent anti-British political agitator, had been active in this part of India. The defendant had collected considerable evidence on the Jackson murder, among other things which he had incorporated in his book, showing that Tilak had sought to justify this assassination. Tilak alleged that Chirol had charged him in his book with provoking the Mohammedans to riot by the foundation of 'cow protection societies', with urging the Hindus to the use of violence by organising gymnastic exercises, with levying blackmail for the purpose of political propaganda and with having been associated with the murder of Indian Government officials.

The trial opened before Mr. Justice Darling and a special jury in the King's Bench Division on January 29, 1919. Sir John Simon and Mr. E. F. Spence were counsel for the plaintiff. Carson appeared for the defendant and he had with him Sir Ellis Hume-Williams as second 'leader' and Mr. Eustace Hills as junior counsel.

The hearing, which occupied ten days, and once again brought Carson and his old pupil into friendly conflict, was enlivened by plenty of witty and vigorous argument on both sides. Simon, for instance, frequently objected to some of the evidence which Carson sought to introduce in this case, such as statements by Indian judges on the prevalence of political crime in India. Darling, who sided with Carson on this point, observed that "on that argument one would not be allowed to quote the opinions of eminent judges because they happened to be dead."

> SIR EDWARD CARSON: Or imitate the patience of Job because he is dead.
>
> MR. JUSTICE Darling: Patience is the first of judicial qualities.
>
> SIR EDWARD CARSON: The first of an advocate's qualities, too, when he is against Sir John Simon, and of the jury's most of all, for they are the only people who aren't paid.

Sir John Simon represented his client as an idealist who had taken a great interest for many years in Indian public affairs and public work; he had been a member of the Indian National Congress and was thus "what unkind people called an agitator." When Mr. Tilak went into the witness box, however, he had to admit that he had served several prison sentences for sedition, although he denied that he had instigated murder. Yet one of the articles for which he had been prosecuted in India seemed to justify the death of Afizuhl Khan by the 'national hero' Shivaji. "What date was it?" asked the judge. "About 1688," replied Tilak. Here Sir John Simon could not resist the temptation to interject: "About the date of the Battle of the Boyne." This reference to the famous engagement held in especial reverence by the Ulster Orangemen raised a loud laugh in Court at Carson's expense. But quick as a flash came the retort from Carson: "which was not so recent as the battle of Walthamstow."

This time the laugh was against Simon, who had lost his seat as M.P. for Walthamstow in the recent General Election.

On the whole Tilak made a good impression in the witness box during his examination-in-chief. He appeared suave and subtle, pleading as he did that, although he had been punished for them, his so-called seditious articles were legitimate political criticism. When Carson rose to cross-examine the plaintiff, he exhibited all his old skill in the first few questions he put to Tilak.

CARSON: When did you last get out of prison?

WITNESS: June, 1914.

CARSON: Have you taken any proceedings in India to vindicate your character?

WITNESS: No.

CARSON: Why did you come all the way to England to vindicate your character?

WITNESS: The book is read all over the Empire, and a decision of an English court would have greater weight and be more effective in stopping the circulation of the book.

CARSON: Do you remember being sentenced to six years' transportation?

WITNESS: Yes.

CARSON: Was the judge a native of India?

WITNESS: Yes.

CARSON: Do you remember what the judge said in summing up?

WITNESS: Yes.

CARSON (*reading from the* JUDGE'S *summing up on the articles in question*): 'They were seething with sedition; they preach violence; they speak of murders with approval: and the cowardly and atrocious act of committing murders with bombs not only meets with your approval, but you hail the advent of the bomb into India as if something had to come to India for its good'. (*To* WITNESS) Did the judge say that?

WITNESS: Yes.

CARSON: Was that the reason why you took no proceedings in India to vindicate your character?

WITNESS: No.

CARSON: Can you point to any passage in Sir Valentine Chirol's book which is more severe than that?

WITNESS: I complain of being associated with murder.

For nearly three days Carson took the plaintiff through his writings and questioned him on the convictions which he had in respect of numbers of them. As he traced the connexion between these writings and the murders of English officials of the Indian Civil Service which followed their publication, the witness gradually lost all his suavity and self-confidence. He was seen to lean across the witness box, with an almost terrifying expression on his face, while he clutched the rail of the box convulsively. Carson afterwards admitted he thought Tilak at times was about to jump out of the witness box and hurl himself at his throat. Fortunately nothing of this kind happened.

In presenting the defendant's case Carson had no difficulty in showing that nothing Sir Valentine Chirol had written in his book was so severe as the remarks of the native Indian judges who dealt with Tilak in his various trials for sedition. Chirol proved a good witness, and his evidence was reinforced by various Indian civil servants who testified as to the effect of the plaintiff's political agitation in India. In his concluding speech to the jury Carson contrasted Tilak's seditious activities with recent professions of loyalty he had made to the British Raj. "That is all hypocrisy," he observed, "for in the critical days of the war he branded as thieves and robbers the brave men who enlisted." Carson also stressed the great public importance of the case, a view echoed by the judge in his summing up, when he said he did not think he had ever tried a more serious case having regard to its possible public consequences.

After an absence of twenty-five minutes the jury returned a verdict for Carson's client. It was indeed the only possible verdict on the evidence.

6

In Ulster there were misgivings that, as soon as the Peace Treaty was signed with Germany, the Home Rule Act, which had been passed in 1914 and was on the statute book, might automatically come into operation without anything having been done to bring in an Amending Bill, in accordance with the promise given by Asquith and reiterated by Lloyd George. The two Coalition leaders had referred to the necessity of a final settlement of the Irish question in their election programme, but Lloyd George had intimated that this would have to wait until the condition of Ireland warranted it. The state of that country was indeed such that the Government might well pause before deciding to hand over control to the Sinn Feiners there, who were daily instigating outrages against the forces of law and order and the lives and properties of those still loyal to the Crown. The Sinn Fein organisation was declared illegal by a Royal

Proclamation, but this made no difference to the mounting toll of violent crime, culminating toward the end of the year in a carefully planned but unsuccessful attempt to murder Lord French, the Lord Lieutenant, whose motor was made a target by bomb-throwers.

Meanwhile Carson watched the situation closely in the interests of Ulster. A fortnight after the signing of the Peace Treaty, he spoke grave words of warning to the Government at the 12th of July Orange Demonstration in Belfast. "If there is any attempt to take away one jot or tittle of your rights as British citizens and the advantages which have been won in this war of freedom," he told his audience on this occasion, "I will call out the Ulster Volunteers . . . We are loyal men, the Government and the Constitution and the British Empire are good enough for us, and the man who tries to knock bricks out of the sound and solid foundation, if he comes to Ulster, will know the real feelings of Ulstermen and Ulsterwomen."

This speech shocked many people in England, and an attempt was made by the Labour and a few remaining Nationalist M.P.s in the House of Commons to censure Carson for having made it. However, the Government came to his assistance, albeit somewhat uneasily, and the motion, moved by Mr. J. R. Clynes, was defeated. At the same time, it did stimulate the Prime Minister to action. He appointed a Cabinet Committee, with Walter Long as Chairman, to consider the future Government of Ireland, or, as Bonar Law put it in a letter to Carson at this time, to implement the view that "something must be done about the Home Rule Act this session."

At the Prime Minister's direction, the Committee accepted three 'basic facts', which became in effect the Committee's terms of reference. First, three-fourths of the Irish people were bitterly hostile and were at heart rebels against the Crown and the Government; secondly, Ulster was a complete contrast, which would make it an outrage to place her people under the rest of Ireland; and thirdly, no separation from the Empire could be tolerated, and any attempt to force it would be fought as the United States had fought against secession. One thing was clear both to the Committee and to everyone else who had studied the matter. The Act of 1914 was dead and must be scrapped completely. Commented Carson with characteristic common sense: "The Home Rule Act is not a settlement. . . . Can you have a settlement which disregards the views of seventy-five per cent of the representatives of the country you are going to settle and will not be accepted by the other twenty-five per cent?"

The Cabinet Committee's recommendations resulted in the formulation of the fourth Home Rule Bill, a measure which was to become known as the Government of Ireland Act. Whilst the finishing touches were being put to it by the parliamentary draftsmen, an event occurred in Carson's private life which gave him an immense sense of pride and satisfaction. Ever since his marriage five years previously he had longed for a child by his second wife. He had been struck by the way his wife took to his son Harry's children, when they stayed with them at Birchington in the summer of 1916. "My grandchildren are here bathing and wading all day on the strand and Ruby makes an excellent grandmother," he had written at that time to Lady Londonderry. "It is a pity she has no children. She seems to get on so well with them and has improved them a lot." His fondest domestic desire was fulfilled on the morning of February 17, 1920, when Lady Carson presented him with a son, whom they called after his father, "exactly like Edward", as the mother afterwards noted in her diary. The following day, after the news had become known, an extraordinary scene took place in the House of Commons. As soon as Carson had appeared through the swing doors at the entrance to the Chamber, he was greeted on both sides by friendly cheers which grew in volume as he walked to his customary place below the gangway in the Government side. As he took his seat, *The Times* lobby correspondent noted that "he acknowledged the greeting with a bashful smile."

Just over a week later, on February 26, 1920, the Government of Ireland Bill, which repealed Mr. Asquith's Home Rule Act of 1914, was formally introduced in the Commons. It was a long and complicated measure of seventy clauses and six schedules, and it provided for the partition of Ireland on approximately the lines which exist today. In principle it embodied the 'clean cut' of the six north-eastern counties, except that instead of retaining Ulster in full legislative union with Great Britain, as Carson and the majority of the Ulster people desired ("We want to remain with you," Carson told the House of Commons at the time. "Do not turn us out"), she was to have a separate Parliament of her own to deal with local affairs, with powers similar to those given to the proposed Dublin Parliament over the rest of Ireland. In view of the 'services' which were expressly 'reserved' to the Imperial Parliament, 'Northern Ireland' was also to return thirteen representatives to Westminster. These 'reserved' matters included foreign affairs, defence, external trade, postal and telegraph services and the principal sources of revenue, such as income tax and Customs and Excise. The Parliament in the South, on the other hand, was to consist of 128 members and, in addition, the South was to send thirty-three members to the Imperial Parliament. Furthermore, a Council of Ireland was to be created, which was to have power over minor matters affecting both parts of the island but which might eventually, by agreement of the two Parliaments, gradually establish a single self-governing constitution for the whole of the country.

The Bill found little immediate favour in any quarter of Ireland. The Sinn Feiners naturally refused to give any support to a measure which fell so far short of their own ideas of national independence. Unionists outside the specified 'six counties', particularly those in the three Ulster counties outside this area, denounced the scheme as a betrayal of their interests, since it left the Protestants there virtually unprotected. The Roman Catholic hierarchy loudly objected to a proposal which would put a substantial minority of their flock under a Protestant Parliament and Government in Belfast. At first in the six counties the Bill met with a frigid reception and Carson in his usual forthright language gave the English people the reason. "In the whole conduct of the war you can find no difference between the North-East of Ulster and any part of Great Britain," he declared. "They fought as you did, they sympathised as you did, they grieved with you, they rejoiced with you. . . . Believe me, they have proved a great asset for you in the late war, in their shipyards and in their factories and in their volunteers at the Front. Why now you should ask them to accept a Parliament if they do not want it, I cannot understand."

As was his wont when grave constitutional matters affecting Ulster were at stake, Carson consulted with the Ulster Unionist Council. His own feeling and that of the majority of the delegates was that, while taking no responsibility for a Bill which Ulster disliked on principle, they would not oppose its progress to the statute book, since at least it admitted Ulster's right to separate treatment in preference to the idea of an all-Ireland Parliament, which was embodied in the discarded Act of 1914. All they would do would be to instruct the Ulster Unionist M.P.s to press for such amendments as would make the measure less irksome in effect. A long discussion took place as to whether or not an amendment should be tabled so as to include the counties of Monaghan, Cavan and Donegal in the area to be subject to the 'Parliament of Northern Ireland', in other words to bring in all the nine counties of geo-

ARTICLES OF AGREEMENT

FOR A

TREATY BETWEEN GREAT BRITAIN AND IRELAND.

NOTES MADE BY LORD CARSON ON THE PRINTED TEXT OF THE IRISH TREATY FOR HIS MAIDEN SPEECH IN THE HOUSE OF LORDS.

From the original in the possession of Lady Carson.

LADY CARSON.

Carson's second wife.

From the drawing by T. Perceval Anderson in the possession of Lady Carson.

graphical Ulster, and Lord Farnham made a strong appeal on behalf of the Unionists in the three counties not to be left out. It was reckoned that this would still have given the Unionists a majority in the Ulster Parliament—but only a bare one, thirty-three Unionists to thirty-one Nationalists or Sinn Feiners—whereas the administration of the Nationalist areas from Belfast would have been bound to lead to endless friction. It was, therefore, decided that no proposal for extending the area should be made by the Ulster Members at Westminster. As one of their number, Mr. Thomas Moles, put it, in a sinking ship, with lifeboats sufficient for only two-thirds of the ship's company, were all to condemn themselves to death because all could not be saved?

The Bill was given its second reading in the Commons by a large majority. Only the Labour Members, Asquithian Liberals and the handful of Nationalists remaining in the House voted against it. Carson and the other Ulster M.P.s abstained. The Ulster Leader spoke with sadness of the passing of the Union and he expressed the thought that the process would be "fraught with disaster" for both countries. "Ireland is mad to give up her representation in this House," he declared. "Every injustice and every harm committed on Ireland . . . was inflicted before the Union and not since the Union, and none of them would be possible with the present representation of Ireland in the Imperial Parliament." As for himself, his duty was clear. "I cannot vote for Home Rule and I will not vote for Home Rule. At the same time I shall do nothing to prevent this Bill from becoming law." One sentence of his speech was curiously prophetic. "It may well turn out that the only part of Ireland which will have a Parliament is the part which never asked for it." This was but too true. Not only that, but the three-fourths of the island which had previously demanded Home Rule were to refuse to accept it when it was granted to them. The attitude of Ulster was made clear in an important letter which Carson wrote to the Lord Birkenhead at this time and which the Lord Chancellor read to the House of Lords a few days later.

To Lord Birkenhead

5 *Eaton Place, S.W.* *November* 26, 1920. With reference to the Government of Ireland Bill which will be before the House of Lords next week, I observe that it is frequently stated that no one in Ireland wants the Bill passed into law. May I say, with the full consent of all my colleagues in Ulster, that this is a fallacy.

It is quite true that we are all of opinion that to maintain the Union is the soundest policy, but we recognise that under the

> existing circumstances, and especially having regard to the fact that the Act of 1914 is upon the Statute Book, it is not possible to secure that position as it at present stands. Ulster wants peace, and above all things to be removed from the arena of party politics in the Imperial Parliament, and we have therefore made up our minds that in the interests of Ireland, Great Britain, and the Empire, the best and only solution of the question is to accept the present Bill and endeavour to work it loyally.

The Government of Ireland Bill duly passed through both Houses at Westminster and received the Royal Assent shortly before Christmas. Carson repeated publicly the assurance he had given Lord Birkenhead that in Ulster they would do their best to make the new legislature a success. "Let us stop talking about it as Home Rule," said Carson. "It is not what we ever meant by Home Rule when we were opposing Home Rule. We are not going to be children, and we are not going to say we are not going to work it. We are going to work it, and we are going to work it successfully." In compliance with this undertaking preparations were immediately put in hand to hold elections in Ulster as a preliminary to the setting up of the Parliament of Northern Ireland. The consequent formation of a Unionist Government in Belfast was a foregone conclusion and Carson was strongly pressed to take the leadership of the new Administration. He refused the invitation on the ground that the task of opening a new chapter in Ulster's history under new institutions created there was one for younger men. In Sir James Craig they had at hand the ideal leader for this purpose. As Carson told the Ulster Unionist Council, "he was my First Lieutenant in all the dangerous times we went through in the past and a dearer or more lovable friend I have never met." At Carson's prompting the Council invited Craig to accept the Premiership of Northern Ireland. Craig did so and thus assumed the mantle of the Leader. For the time being Carson promised to stay and 'hold the fort at Westminster.'

Carson formally relinquished the Ulster leadership on February 4, 1921, a few days before his sixty-seventh birthday. On that day he took leave of his friends on the Ulster Unionist Council. "I have been your Leader for some eleven years," he told them. "In that time I have never had a single quarrel, or if I have, I have forgotten it. I don't believe any leader has ever had such confidence reposed in him for so long a time, so much love and so much affection."

Thus, although they never desired it, the Unionists of Ulster were soon to enjoy a considerable measure of self-government.

Carson's advice to them as to how they should best use this unwanted liberty was characteristically statesmanlike and broad-minded. "From the outset," he said, "let us see that the Catholic minority have nothing to fear from the Protestant majority. Let us take care to win all that is best among those who have been opposed to us in the past. While maintaining intact our own religion let us give the same rights to the religion of our neighbours."

7

Throughout this time Carson was carrying on with his work at the Bar. His clerk could not complain of any shortage of briefs, and to the onlooker in Court his powers seemed as striking as ever. But the truth was he could no longer make the exertions that he used to. He showed a friend a brief marked 4,000 guineas which he was sending back to the instructing solicitors. The reason was that he had only been given ten days in which to prepare the case. "I could have done it once," he said, "but not now."

In a sensational trial in which he appeared in the spring of 1921, and which was destined to be his last big case, he put up a remarkable performance. This was the case of Archdeacon Wakeford. It was an appeal from a judgment of the Consistory Court of the Diocese of Lincoln, holding as proved on the prosecution of the Bishop of Lincoln charges against the Archdeacon that he committed adultery with an unknown woman at the Bull Hotel in Peterborough on two occasions in March and April, 1920, or alternatively that he occupied a bedroom at the hotel on those dates with a woman who was not his wife. It will be appreciated that this offence was one with which only an individual subject to ecclesiastical law could be charged, and not a layman. The appeal took the form of a retrial with some additional evidence not given in the Court below, began on April 8, 1921, and evoked widespread interest throughout the country.

The Court consisted of the Lord Chancellor, Lord Birkenhead, and Lords Buckmaster, Dunedin and Shaw, together with the Bishops of London, Gloucester, Rochester and Ely, who sat as assessors. The Archdeacon's counsel were Sir Edward Carson, K.C., M.P., Sir E. Marlay Sampson, K.C.,* Mr. Wilfrid Lewis† and

* Later stipendiary magistrate.
† Later Lord Justice Lewis.

Mr. J. A. Stainton. For the respondent, the Bishop of Lincoln, there appeared Mr. Douglas Hogg, K.C., M.P.,* Mr. E. W. Hansell† and Mr. W. N. Stable.‡ The appellant, the Venerable John Wakeford, Canon and Precentor of Lincoln Cathedral, Archdeacon of Stow and Vicar of Kirkstead, was sixty-two at the date of this trial. He was a distinguished lecturer on theological subjects at three universities and he had written twenty-four books on theology and devotion. According to his leading counsel, "no one was better known throughout the land as a preacher."

In opening the case for the Bishop of Lincoln, Mr. Hogg explained that it was not disputed that Archdeacon Wakeford had stayed at the Bull Hotel in Peterborough on the two occasions alleged. The question was whether on these two occasions he was accompanied by a woman.

Mr. Pugh, the manager of the Bull Hotel, was the first witness. He swore that he remembered the Archdeacon's arrival on the evening of Sunday, March 14, 1920. The Archdeacon had a woman with him. He signed the visitors' book 'J. Wakeford' and was given a double-bedded room. At first the Archdeacon gave no address, but on being asked by the manager to do so, subsequently wrote 'The Precincts, Lincoln' opposite his name in the book. Later the manager added the words 'and wife' in pencil after 'J. Wakeford'. The Archdeacon and the woman both left after lunch on the following Tuesday, and the bill for the two of them came to £4 2s. 6d. On the subject of the Archdeacon's second visit, this witness said that he received a postcard, which must have been destroyed, asking that a double bedroom be reserved. The Archdeacon arrived on April 12, which was Good Friday, about 6 o'clock. He had the same woman with him. This time, according to the manager, the Archdeacon wrote in the visitors' book 'J. Wakeford and wife, 8 Precincts, Lincoln' and immediately below the woman wrote 'M. Wakeford' with the same address. Later that night they had dinner together in the hotel and breakfast next morning.

Under cross-examination by Carson this witness stated that the police were on the look-out at the time for a clergyman suspected of passing false cheques, and after the local Chief Constable had warned him to be on the look-out, he and his wife went into the Archdeacon's room on the occasion of his first visit, while he was

* Later Viscount Hailsham, Lord Chancellor.
† Later Sir William Hansell, K.C., Official Referee.
‡ Later Mr. Justice Stable.

out, and looked at his linen "because we could not decipher his name in the visitors' book." There was a nightdress and a pair of pyjamas on the bed. On a tab on the pyjamas he swore he saw the name 'J. Wakeford'.

The manager's wife corroborated this evidence. "Instead of peering into an old clergyman's nightclothes," Carson asked her, "why did you not ask him what his name was?" "I don't know," was the reply. She also stated that in the course of the first evening her husband asked her to take the visitors' book to the bedroom for the lady's signature. Both the Archdeacon and the woman were in the room at the time, and the Archdeacon asked why this was necessary. Mrs. Pugh said it was "the usual thing," but as the Archdeacon still protested, the manager's wife, according to her story, left the room without the signature.

Various hotel servants and guests testified to the fact that the Archdeacon was accompanied by a woman on his visits. Although there were minor discrepancies in their evidence, as in that of the Pughs, Carson was unable in cross-examination to shake this evidence in any substantial degree. The Dean of Peterborough stated that on the first of the dates in question he saw the Archdeacon and a lady in Peterborough Cathedral. However, as will be seen later, there was a perfectly innocent explanation of this.

The Rev. Herbert Worthington, who was Mrs. Wakeford's brother, then stepped into the witness box. It was he who had first communicated with the Bishop. Because of what he had heard, he said, he went to the Bull Hotel and examined the register. He then went to see a fellow clergyman, the Rev. C. T. Moore, who had the right to the benefice of Kirkstead held by the Archdeacon but was on unfriendly terms with him. It appeared that seventeen years previously Moore had been charged with staying in an immoral house kept by a certain Mrs. Ellis, but had been exonerated on the ground that he did not know the nature of the house. The papers in this matter had been sent to the Bishop by Archdeacon Wakeford.

CARSON: Having gone to Moore, did you then go to your sister?

WITNESS: I arranged to see her as soon as I could.

CARSON: It was a serious matter for her. You have a brotherly affection for her and a Christian spirit toward her husband, and would help her in trouble?

WITNESS: I saw her on July 5.

CARSON: Why did you wait until then?

WITNESS: Because I wanted to be sure of certain facts.

CARSON: You had heard of this. As a clergyman and a brother, why did you not go and see your sister before?

WITNESS: I was in correspondence with the Bishop and he told me to be very careful.

It appeared that Moore had later employed a detective to watch Wakeford. Mr. Worthington further stated that his sister and brother-in-law were unhappily married. He said he suspected the woman in the case to be a certain Mrs. Evelyn Porter, who had been the Archdeacon's secretary and had later become a police court missionary at Marlborough Street Police Court. However, it transpired that the Pughs had made a journey to London in an attempt to identify this woman as the one who had stayed with the Archdeacon in the hotel, but they had been unable to do so satisfactorily and Mrs. Porter's reputation was in consequence completely cleared.

Finally, a handwriting expert was called by the prosecution. He said he had compared the words 'and wife' in the second entry with similar words written down by the Archdeacon on a piece of paper in Court at Lord Birkenhead's request, and he stated that in his opinion they were either written by Wakeford or else were a very skilful forgery.

Carson's defence was a categorical denial of the charges against his client. "The allegation of the prosecution," he said in his opening speech, "is not that this Archdeacon in some underhand and illicit manner, concealing his identity and leading a double life, was guilty of adultery, but that in broad daylight, without concealment, in the neighbouring diocese to his own he went in clerical garb with a young woman who was not his wife and openly stayed with her at an hotel on two occasions. If the case for the prosecution is true, there can be no explanation except that the Archdeacon was mad, and no one has ever made that suggestion." Carson then went on to submit that there was a conspiracy between Worthington, Moore and the Pughs to ruin his client's character.

The Archdeacon then told his story from the witness box. He gave his evidence confidently and precisely. He described how he had been exceptionally busy at the time with the preparation of sermons and other clerical work. He had gone to Peterborough with the full knowledge and approval of his wife and put up at the Bull Hotel, as he wanted to be quiet and "had no desire to be dragged into conversation with other clergymen." He had signed the visitors' book—rather illegibly, he admitted, as the light was bad, and he had to raise the book on his arm as he wrote. The book was not brought to his room at any time. He never wore pyjamas, except once when he went to France, and certainly not on the occasion of his visit to Peterborough. Neither was his name on any of his underclothes. There was no woman with him at the hotel on either occasion, and he denied that he ever wrote the words 'and wife' after his name in the register.

On the morning of March 15, continued the Archdeacon, he had gone to Peterborough Cathedral and had meditated in the nave, preparing his sermons. As he was leaving, he saw a girl of seventeen or eighteen looking at the well-known inscription to a sexton on the west wall: 'He buried here two Queens'. She seemed puzzled, so he explained to her that the Queens were Catherine of Aragon and Mary Queen of Scots. He then went to see the Dean and verger. Some time later he left the Cathedral. It was raining and the girl whom he had previously seen was sheltering in the porch. He told her she could get a postcard with the inscription to the sexton on it in the shop opposite. He accompanied her to the shop, where she bought the card, and they then parted. He did not see her again. She was the only woman he spoke to while he was in Peterborough. The reason for his second visit was that he had been conducting a series of services in London and was on his way to a conference of Archdeacons at Lincoln. On reaching Peterborough he discovered that the train went no further and he consequently stayed there for the night, again in the Bull, where he was given a double-bedded room.

Mrs. Wakeford supported her husband in the witness-box and said they were happily married. She had never complained to her brother of lightness of conduct on the part of her husband with any woman. On the contrary, the confidence which existed between them was 'absolute'. She had, however, been with her husband when the Rev. Mr. Moore had tried to block their way to Kirkstead Church, and she had heard Moore say: "All right, Wakeford, I'll get you yet."

The defence also called hotel guests to prove that they had seen the Archdeacon alone in the hotel. A remark attributed by a witness, who was a witness for the prosecution, to the Archdeacon that he told the lady with him at a meal to keep her hands under the table, as she was not wearing a wedding ring, was admitted as having been made by way of a joke by one of the other guests to his wife.

The judgment of the Court was given by Lord Birkenhead. Said to be the ablest that he ever delivered, it took him an hour-and-a-half to read, and it was unanimous against the Archdeacon. The Lord Chancellor dismissed as impossible the theory of conspiracy put forward by the defence, on the ground that any such conspiracy must have been framed at a date before the Archdeacon's first visit to Peterborough, at a time when no one could have anticipated that he was going there or that he would stay at the Bull. "By what amazing coincidence," said Lord Birkenhead, "did it come about that the appellant should have selected on this occasion the one hotel in Peterborough whose landlord was ready to be corrupted, able to carry with him into this maze of slander and perjury his wife and servants, and zealous to commence a systematic course of forgery in support of the plan?" The Court refused to accept the view that the disputed entries in the hotel register were forged, holding on the contrary that the writing furnished "an almost overwhelmng corroboration of the other evidence." The Archdeacon's appeal was accordingly dismissed, and thus Carson found himself on the losing side in what turned out to be his last great case.

Forty-eight hours later Carson made another valedictory speech, although no one recognised it as such at the time. He went down to the House of Commons, where he intervened briefly in a discussion on Ireland. The Government had been urged by previous speakers to postpone the elections for the Parliament of Southern Ireland as provided by the recently passed Home Rule Act. If they did so, Carson argued, what a victory it would be for the army of assassination in Ireland! "It would mean the triumph of the assassination campaign," he declared, "and therefore I heartily support what the Government have done, believing it to be only a right and honourable course to adopt, having regard to the policy which they announced last year."

These were the last words which Carson uttered in the House of Commons, where he had sat for close on thirty years. It so happened that Lord Moulton, who was a Lord of Appeal, had recently died, and Lloyd George now offered Carson the position which had thus become vacant in the House of Lords. On reflection, Carson felt that perhaps the time had come for him to leave the House of Commons and the Temple and lay aside his barrister's wig and gown. He accepted the Prime Minister's offer.

CHAPTER TWELVE

Lord of Appeal

I

CARSON'S appointment to the highest judicial court in the land was officially announced on May 24, 1921. Gossip, however, had been busy with his name in this connexion for some weeks, since Lord Moulton, whose place he was to fill, had died more than two months previously. Thus, when the general expectation was confirmed, congratulations flowed in on him from every quarter. The letters which he received from those who had been his colleagues at the Bar, both in Ireland and in England, gave him particular pleasure. "Nobody has followed your splendid career with greater pride and pleasure than I have," wrote his old friend John Ross, then a Chancery Judge in Dublin and soon to become the last Lord Chancellor of Ireland. "Your crowning glory is that success has never changed you and that you still continue just the same as when we were in college."

In the mass of congratulatory correspondence, which reached his house in Eaton Place, Carson was especially touched by a letter from a retired solicitor who had instructed him in his earliest days at the Irish Bar. This correspondent wrote: "In the eighties of the last century I often handed to your Lordship briefs marked £1 1s. 0d. I was then an apprentice in the office of the late Mr. William G. Toomey of Dublin. Very often the fee did not accompany the brief. I also have delivered similar briefs at your then house in Dublin which to the best of my memory was in a street called Herbert Place. I have been present at consultation of counsel when the late Dr. Houston, K.C. and the late Mr. David Lynch, Q.C., were your leaders. I have heard from you great speeches to juries on briefs marked £2 2s. 0d., and the late Mr. Toomey once remarked to me, 'He is killing at the money!' . . . Your Lordship can quite understand the satisfaction I feel when I contemplate the great position in Irish and English history your Lordship's name will forever occupy."

Others who wrote to Carson on this occasion included three leading members of the English Bar and two of his future judicial colleagues in the House of Lords. "I congratulate you with all my heart upon reaching the pleasantest of judicial positions," wrote Sir Edward Clarke, who had recently passed his eightieth birthday. "It is one that I coveted in former years, because, as I told Lord Salisbury, it would not cut me off from work in political affairs, of the larger and non-party kind." Sir Edward Marshall-Hall recalled their association in Carson's early days in London in cases where the great criminal advocate had 'led' him. "But then, as now," added Marshall-Hall, "I recognised that you were the leader and that no accident of professional etiquette could alter the reality of the position." From the Temple also wrote Carson's one-time pupil, Sir John Simon: "You must let me send you every good wish for your new work. I think you'll like it and I know those who appear before you will like it. And I shall never forget how much I owe, amid storm and stress, to the kindness of a real friend."

"Will you allow an old friend to say how glad he is?" wrote the former Liberal Lord Chancellor, Lord Loreburn. "We have often differed, but I know that we have honestly differed, and I have never had any share in the vulgar abuse which has been showered on you and which must have made your work difficult. You will find the House of Lords is the best audience in the country, or was, attentive and free from unworthy passions." Lord Sumner, one of the greatest judges of his time, wrote in a somewhat lighter vein of the prospect of Carson's joining their select circle. "You will be most welcome, though I am afraid you will find us stodgy, but the work is—well! not what some people would call work—and the job is respectable, and the hours and the honours are easy. If now and then you spoil for a fight, you can stay till after four and lay out Buckmaster or Parmoor: you can remember the Battle of the Boyne now and then with the L[ord] C[hancellor]; lament the decline of advocacy in the persons of the Law Officers; and sleep the sleep of the just when you feel inclined to."

Carson's own views on this milestone in his career he expressed to his closest political friends, Bonar Law and James Craig. "I feel as if I was leaving everything in public life I cared about," he told the Conservative Leader. "But I know it is provident and I am not ungrateful. As you say, I can take an interest in having an audience for a change!" To his successor in the Ulster leadership he wrote: "It is depressing to leave the fight and wear the stern calm of judicial office. Ulster will always be my first love and my greatest memory."

A week later he was introduced in the House of Lords and took his seat 'by the style and title of Baron Carson of Duncairn in the county of Antrim.' His old political ally Lord Birkenhead was on the Woolsack to welcome him. Like 'F. E.', Carson might have had a hereditary title on the strength of his political services—indeed he was offered and refused a viscounty—but he considered the life peerage which is usually conferred on a 'Law Lord' preferable in the circumstances of his family. This meant that Harry, his eldest son and heir, would not succeed to his peerage, which would die with him.

For the time being Carson postponed making his maiden speech in the Upper House and took no part in the debates there until Ireland gave him an excuse for a dramatic eruption at the end of the year. For the next few months he concentrated his energies on his new judicial work, which is considered as a whole later in this chapter. But he also kept a watchful eye on what was going on across the Irish Sea.

The elections for the new Parliament in the North were a remarkable triumph for Unionism. Out of fifty-two seats, Sir James Craig had expected to win thirty-two; actually he won forty. The remaining twelve seats were equally divided between the Nationalists, led by Devlin, and the Sinn Feiners, led by De Valera. "Bravo!" wrote Carson to Craig when he learned the news. "I am more than delighted with the result of the Ulster Elections and I need not say I rejoice in your success just as much as if I was the Leader myself. You were splendid all through and I followed the campaign daily with anxious interest. Of course, I feel lonely and depressed at being out of it all but, as you know, nothing matters to me so long as the cause for which we struggle is safe. It would take a very bold statesman after this demonstration to suggest putting the six counties under Home Rule in Dublin!"

In the previous autumn Carson had bought an old rambling house called Cleve Court in the Isle of Thanet which he and his wife had discovered by chance during one of their visits to Birchington. Inside, the house, most of which belonged to the early Georgian period, was finely panelled. Outside, there was a spacious lawn and kitchen garden. In these lovely surroundings Carson planned to spend the week-ends and vacations and eventually his retirement. He was delighted with the purchase, which included twenty acres of land and only cost him altogether £2,500. He wrote enthusiastically to Bonar Law: "I hope you will come to Kent. Our new house is near Minster and 5 miles from Margate and the air is splendid."

At considerable personal risk—for the whole of Ireland was in a seriously disturbed condition—King George V consented to open the new Ulster Parliament. This news delighted the loyal citizens of the Province, and patriotic feelings were further stirred when it was learned that Queen Mary was to accompany her husband. Among the invitations, which were sent to distinguished people to attend the ceremony, pride of place was naturally given to Lord Carson. But on consideration Carson decided that his new judicial duties in the House of Lords would not permit him to leave London. Possibly considerations of delicacy in regard to James Craig's position, not difficult to understand, determined him against arranging for his absence. Consequently he wrote to Craig that Lady Carson would represent him on this occasion.

House of Lords,
16 *June*, 1921.

MY DEAR JAMES,

I have come to the conclusion that it is better for me not to leave my work. It would involve my being away all the week and the Tribunal might get into a long case during my absence which would leave me out of work for several days more. This would be open to criticism and no doubt there are those who would be only too glad to raise it.

Ruby will be with you on Tuesday morning. I need hardly say how anxiously I will watch the launching of the ship and how earnestly I will pray that all will be well.

Love to you all,
Ever,
E.

The royal visit, fraught though it was with danger for its central figures, proved a striking success. Their Majesties arrived in Belfast on the morning of June 22, and after driving through the principal streets the King opened the first session of the Parliament of Northern Ireland in the City Hall, the same building which had witnessed the signing of the Ulster Covenant. The King's words, which are now known to have been inspired by the South African Prime Minister, General Smuts, moved everyone who heard them as a most human and statesmanlike utterance, and they created a great impression all over the world. "I speak from a full heart," declared His Majesty, "when I pray that my coming to Ireland today may prove to be the first step towards an end of strife among her people, whatever their race or creed. In that hope, I appeal to all Irishmen to pause, to stretch out the hand of forbearance and conciliation, to forgive and forget, and to join in making for the land they love a new era of peace, contentment and goodwill."

The King also expressed the hope that a similar ceremony might soon be performed in Southern Ireland, as provided for by the Act of 1920. Unfortunately, when the Lord Lieutenant opened the Dublin Parliament a week later, the occasion was a fiasco. Out of the 128 Members of the Southern Irish House of Commons only the four representatives of Trinity College turned up. After electing a Speaker, the House adjourned, never to meet again. As for the royal injunction 'to forgive and forget', Sinn Fein's reply was to blow up the train carrying the Hussar regiment which had formed part of the King's escort in Belfast. Three soldiers and a guard were killed, and a large number of horses were killed or mutilated.

For the past two years the history of Ireland had been largely one of murders, ambushes, burnings, torturings and other outrages. In the summer of 1920 the Sinn Fein terror had begun to be matched by the counter-terror of 'Black-and-Tans', auxiliary police mainly recruited from British ex-servicemen and so called because owing to a shortage of police uniforms they were clothed temporarily in military khaki with a black hat and arm-band. Profiting from the good impression created by the royal visit to Belfast, Lloyd George chose this moment to address a letter to De Valera, as 'the chosen leader of the great majority of Southern Ireland,' inviting him to attend a conference in London 'to explore to the utmost the possibility of a settlement' and bring with him for the purpose any colleagues whom he might select. After some delay the invitation was accepted and a truce agreed to by both sides.

Carson was greatly disturbed by this news, and his anxiety was increased when Lloyd George told him privately that "the game is up" and "we shall have to give in." Apparently the Government could not get the troops to 'go in' in Ireland and the Prime Minister intended to resign in consequence.

"Well, then, there is one thing I hope you won't do," said Carson, "and that is to involve the Conservative Members of your Government, Austen Chamberlain and Lord Birkenhead, in the discredit of such a surrender."

"Of course not," replied the Prime Minister. "Have I not said that I intend to resign?"

The next time Carson met Lloyd George, he found the Premier

had changed his mind about resigning. Lloyd George had discussed the matter with Austen Chamberlain, who had recently succeeded Bonar Law as Conservative Party Leader, since Law had been obliged to resign from the Government on account of his health and had temporarily withdrawn from politics. Far from seeing the necessity to resign, Chamberlain had said that he did not see why the Government should not conduct the negotiations. In fact, according to Lloyd George, Chamberlain had actually suggested their initiation.* Carson gasped in amazement. He could hardly believe his ears after all the talk there had previously been in Government circles about not giving in to any murder gang.

A particularly unfortunate result of the truce was that the gunmen in the South thereupon transferred their attentions to Ulster, and a terrible campaign of violence was inaugurated there which greatly added to the troubles of Craig and his Cabinet.

The view of most Irish Unionists, with which Carson identified himself, was expressed by Sir Henry Wilson, now Chief of the Imperial General Staff. Lloyd George had met him in Downing Street and told him that De Valera was coming over and that he would "have a chance of talking to him." "I do not speak to murderers," replied Wilson. "Oh, nonsense," said the Prime Minister, who was put out by this remark; "in public life we must do these things." He thereupon left the room, Wilson shouting after him that if he met De Valera he would hand him over to the police.

De Valera and his colleagues reached London in the middle of July, and there began the parleys which resulted six months later in the signing of the 'Treaty', as the agreement between the two sets of negotiators was called. That Lloyd George and other British political leaders should consent to negotiate at all with 'rebels' whose hands were stained with the blood of their fellow citizens was a novel constitutional departure which dismayed and disgusted Carson. Here it is necessary to touch only briefly on the course of these dealings. After considerable comings and goings between London and Dublin on the part of De Valera and his henchmen, the

* This is confirmed by Lord Pakenham in his valuable account of the negotiation of the Anglo-Irish Treaty, *Peace by Ordeal* (1935), at pp. 77–78, where he describes how Lloyd George and Chamberlain met on the terraces at the back of their respective houses in Downing Street on the day after the King had opened the Northern Ireland Parliament. Chamberlain argued strongly that 'the spirit of the King's message was incompatible with the whole idea of renewed coercion without one culminating effort for peace.' They were then joined by Birkenhead, who 'had reached exactly the same conclusion'.

negotiations proper began in Downing Street on October 10. The Sinn Fein delegation was led by Arthur Griffith, veteran pioneer of the movement, whom Mr. Churchill described as 'that unique figure, a silent Irishman'. His principal lieutenant was Michael Collins, the romantic gunman whom Lloyd George was to call 'one of the most courageous leaders ever produced by a valiant race,' but whom Carson, like the Irish Chief Secretary, Sir Hamar Greenwood, regarded as 'the head of the murder gang' in Ireland. This ill-assorted group also included two lawyers, Eamon Duggan and Charles Gavan Duffy; an economic expert, Robert Barton, who incidentally was the only Protestant; and finally the secretary, Erskine Childers, an Englishman recently converted to the Sinn Fein cause and well-known as the author of a thrilling adventure story, *The Riddle of the Sands*. De Valera remained in Dublin, considering it beneath his dignity to attend as head of an independent State. The British negotiators consisted of three representatives from each of the two major political parties: Mr. Churchill and Sir Hamar Greenwood represented the Liberals, in addition to the Prime Minister; the Tories were Lord Chancellor Birkenhead, Austen Chamberlain, Leader of the House of Commons, and Sir Laming Worthington-Evans, Secretary of State for War. Mr. Lionel Curtis acted as secretary on the British side.

Lloyd George managed to secure from Arthur Griffith a personal pledge of participation in the Commonwealth and allegiance to the Crown in return for the recognition of 'the essential unity of Ireland'. Ulster, which had not been consulted, was thus to be given the choice of coming into an all-Ireland Parliament, with certain safeguards, or of retaining her present Parliament, sharing all imperial burdens and submitting to a Boundary Commission which would redraw her boundaries as nearly as possible on sectarian lines. Southern Ireland was henceforth to be known as the 'Irish Free State' and to enjoy the status and rights of a self-governing Dominion. She was to have control of her finances and defence arrangements. Finally, the members of her legislature were to swear to be 'faithful' to King George V 'in virtue of the common citizenship of Ireland with Great Britain and her adherence to and membership of the group of nations forming the British Commonwealth of Nations.'

The Prime Minister had originally proposed an oath of explicit loyalty to the King. The form finally adopted and set out above had been drafted by Lord Birkenhead to meet the objections of Griffith and Collins to Lloyd George's version. "What hypocrisy!" was Carson's comment on this compromise. The oath could, of course, be abrogated, as indeed it subsequently was, whenever the 'Free State' exercised the right, which she claimed by virtue of her Dominion status, to recede from the Commonwealth.

The 'Treaty' was eventually signed in the early hours of the morning of December 6, 1921. Its terms were immediately published to the world. When he read them, Carson remarked: "I never thought I should live to see the day of such abject humiliation for Great Britain."

2

Whether or not the 'treaty' was a humiliation for Great Britain is a matter of opinion depending upon one's conception of national honour. Its signatories on the British side certainly did not regard it in this light. Indeed the Prime Minister openly boasted that in achieving it Britain had gained a reputation for generosity without sacrificing one of her essential interests—except, he might have added, the interests of those in Ireland who had trusted her. On the other hand, that it was a humiliation for the Imperial Parliament, which duly approved the agreement, is beyond question. The majority in both Houses consisted of 'Unionist' members of the party which for the past thirty-four years had opposed the comparatively mild form of Home Rule proposed by Gladstone and later by Asquith. The electorate had believed in their sincerity and had twice endorsed their policy in clear terms at the polls. Now the English Unionist leaders, with the notable exception of Bonar Law, had combined with the leading Liberals to smash the Union, which they had previously pledged themselves to uphold. What is more, they had in their action yielded not to arguments so much as to force. The measure of this betrayal and its consequences impressed themselves so deeply in Carson's mind that he made them the occasion of his maiden speech in the House of Lords. It remains perhaps the most brutally frank oration ever delivered in that assembly as well as a masterpiece of concentrated invective.

The debate was on a motion for an Address of thanks in reply to the King's Speech, which had intimated that the 'Articles of Agreement' of the treaty would shortly be submitted for their Lordships' approval. It was moved on December 14, 1921, by the veteran Liberal, the last of the original Home Rulers, John Morley, now

Viscount Morley, and the memorable scene was sketched from the gallery by the Irish painter, Sir John Lavery. The octogenarian Morley's appearance in front of the dispatch box gave Carson, as he confessed at the outset of his own remarks, the only pleasure he found in addressing the Upper House for the first time. Carson recalled that when he himself first spoke in the Commons in 1892, it was Morley's speech, as Liberal Chief Secretary for Ireland, which he had to answer. "I think it is befitting that he should attend here at these splendid obsequies of the 'Unionist Party'," he went on. "I think he is a very proper person to pronounce the funeral oration over that that has been said and done by that misguided Party for the last thirty-five years, dead and buried from today, with all this engineered splendour to cover up the defeat and humiliation you have had in Ireland—dead and buried, strangled, without consultation with their followers, by the leaders and trustees who were sent into the Government to protect them."

Carson had scribbled a few notes in pencil on the first page of the text of the 'Treaty' which he held in his hand and waved from time to time, proclaiming it to be England's shame. Soon his deep rich voice began to vibrate with passion, as he denounced former political friends and allies with an unexpected bitterness. "I speak for a good many," he exclaimed. "I speak—I can hardly speak—for all those who, relying on British honour and British justice, have in giving their best to the service of the State seen themselves now deserted and cast aside without one single line of recollection or recognition in the whole of what you call peace terms in Ireland."

It was unfortunate that the Government spokesman, who was put up to defend the treaty, was the Foreign Secretary and Leader of the House of Lords, Lord Curzon, who, although he held an Irish peerage, had never once in the course of his many travels set foot in Ireland. Carson had never forgiven him for his conduct in ratting over the Parliament Bill in 1911, and his feelings were in no way mollified by Curzon reminding him pompously that he had now become a judge of the highest Court in the realm and expressing the hope that "the equipoise of his judgment will soon be more solidly fixed." Carson's retort was scathing. He wished he had something of the eloquence of the noble Marquess of Curzon in advocating his new-found faith. For Curzon had "gone the whole hog," said Carson adopting a piece of boy's slang. "It is always the same with a man who has a newly-found faith. I believe in religion they call him a pervert, but I should be sorry to apply an epithet of that kind to so great, so eloquent and so superior a man as the noble Marquess." He recalled that when the "milk and watery" Home Rule Act was put on the statute book in 1914, he had been ordered by the Leader of the Unionist Party to walk out of the House of Commons, which he did. "And now not only am I to have no indignation at the grant of what they are pleased to call Dominion Home Rule for Ireland," he went on, "but I get a long lecture from the noble Marquess which, may I say, I hope in the future he will spare me, because the man—let me speak plainly—who, in my opinion at all events, has betrayed me has no right afterwards to lecture me."

And how beautifully the whole business of the Treaty had been stage-managed! "The stage-management is one of the most perfect things I ever recollect," Carson declared. He referred to the chorus of approval in the Press, particularly from *The Times* and the Liberal *Daily Chronicle* and *Daily News*. He continued:

> And do you think either we or the country are going to be taken in by this manufactured glorification of what you are pleased to call the Treaty between Great Britain and Ireland? No, we are not. We tell you, if you want to pass it, go and ask the country, but you will not dare. That is the last thing you will do, or the last thing you care about. And all this comes from the long continuance in office of a Coalition Government which was formed for entirely different objects and entirely different purposes.
>
> One thing the noble Marquess entirely forgot to tell us was how the Government came to the conclusion that these Articles of Treaty were so much for the benefit of the country. The difficulty I have in commenting upon them at all is that, unless as a matter of mere pretence, when we are seeming to be very dignified and concerned, there is not a noble Lord in this House who believes for a moment that these terms were passed upon their merits. Not at all. *They were passed with a revolver pointed at your head. And you know it. You know you passed them because you were beaten. You know you passed them because Sinn Fein with the army in Ireland has beaten you.* Why do you not say so? Your Press says so, and you may as well confess it. There may be nothing dishonourable in it.
>
> But when we are told that the reason why they had to pass the terms of the Treaty, and the reason why they could not put down crime in Ireland, was because they had neither the men nor the money, nor the backing, let me say that that is an awful confession to make to the British Empire. If you tell your Empire in India, in Egypt, and all over the world that you have not got the men, the money, the pluck, the inclination, and the backing to restore order in a country within twenty miles of your own shore, you may as well begin to abandon the attempt to make British rule prevail throughout the Empire at all . . .

> I ask your Lordships, ought Unionist leaders to have been a party to that—Unionist leaders who had undertaken to defend Unionist policy? . . . The truth of the matter is that if you go on like this, if you have men in high positions stating today that A is white, and tomorrow arguing that it is certainly black, you will destroy the confidence of the democracy of this country in its rulers and its institutions. I believe that is what has happened in this case, and it will make public life and politics stink in the nostrils of the country for the next twenty years.

Carson went on to quote, with deadly effect, from Lloyd George's speeches over the past few months, in which the Prime Minister had expressed himself as resolutely opposed to Southern Ireland having control of her ports, defence and foreign affairs and other rights subsequently accorded by the Treaty. "At that time," exclaimed Carson bitterly, "I did not know, as I know now, that I was a mere puppet in a political game. I was in earnest, I was not playing politics. I believed all this. I thought of the last thirty years, during which I was fighting with others whose friendship and comradeship I hope I will lose from tonight, because I do not value any friendship that is not founded upon confidence and trust. I was in earnest. What a fool I was! I was only a puppet, and so was Ulster, and so was Ireland, in the political game that was to get the Conservative Party into power."

He then turned savagely upon the foremost noble Lord to forfeit his friendship, the 'galloper' of the old Volunteer days, who as Viscount Birkenhead now sat a few paces away on the Woolsack. 'F. E.' had signed the Covenant; he had also signed the Treaty. No one could foretell in the event of war between the North and South, as Lord Farnham was to put it later in the debate, whether the Lord Chancellor would not end up as 'canterer' to Michael Collins. Carson put it like this:

> Of all the men in my experience that I think are the most loathsome it is those who will sell their friends for the purpose of conciliating their enemies, and, perhaps, still worse, the men who climb up a ladder into power of which even I may have been part of a humble rung, and then, when they have got into power, kick the ladder away without any concern for the pain, or injury, or mischief, or damage that they do to those who have helped them to gain power.

Another signatory of the Treaty who experienced the lash of Carson's terrible tongue was the Leader of the House of Commons.

> The other evening I saw with disgust that Mr. Austen Chamberlain, the son of Mr. Joseph Chamberlain, having agreed to put Ulster into these terms, then said he made an appeal to the comradeship of his old friend Sir James Craig to come in and submit to the domination of Sinn Fein. I could not help thinking that it was very like, after having shot a man in the back, going over to him and patting him on the shoulder and saying: 'Old man, die as quickly as you can, and do not make any noise'.

He went on to condemn the pressure being put upon Ulster to join with the South and the Press campaign directed against her. "Why is all this attack made upon Ulster? What has Ulster done?" he asked. "I will tell you. She has stuck too well to you, and you believe because she is loyal you can kick her as you like." As an inducement to Ulster to come in under an all-Ireland Parliament, it had been represented to her that she would probably only pay about 1s. 6d. income tax, whereas, if she remained as part of the United Kingdom she would have to pay 6s. "Ulster is not for sale," he said contemptuously. "Her loyalty does not depend upon taxes. Ulster values her heritage as citizens of the United Kingdom, and neither you, nor the Press, nor your friends in the South of Ireland need try to terrorise her by the bogey of having to pay more." Finally, he uttered some grave words of warning. "Do not do anything which, throughout the length and breadth of the Empire, will turn Ulster against the British connexion." He reminded his listeners that it was through the operation of English laws that Ulstermen were driven out of Ireland in the eighteenth century and went to America and that it was thirty-six Ulstermen who, smarting under a grievance, signed the Declaration of Independence.

> Loyalty is a strange thing. It is something which you cannot get by merely sitting round a table and trying to find a formula for an Oath of Allegiance which means nothing. It is something born and bred in you. I have often—I admit it—when we were threatened because we were loyal in Ulster in times past, threatened day after day and night after night, for no crime except that we were loyal—said to myself: 'Well, why don't you give it up and join the others?' And I never did, because I know I could not, because I know it is something that is born in you, inherited in you, and that is the safety of the State. But do not try us too high. Do recognise that we have tried to help you, as you have helped us, and do not, when we want to stay with you, do anything to turn us out.

This controversial speech alternately shocked and angered many who heard it, though it pleased some others. For instance, Lord

Salisbury described it as "great—one of the greatest that has been heard within the walls of Parliament." On the other hand, Lord Curzon, under a sense of injured pride, wrote to Lord Birkenhead protesting that it was "an outrage on every convention of the House and on decency, the speech of a prosecuting counsel at the Old Bailey." The Lord Chancellor himself was equally scathing. "As a constructive effort of statecraft," he remarked when the time came for him to reply, "it would have been immature upon the lips of a hysterical schoolgirl." When Birkenhead went on to say that Carson had not thought it necessary to make any single suggestion for dealing with the actualities of the situation, Carson jumped to his feet and declared that at Birkenhead's suggestion and that of his colleagues he had accepted the Act of 1920. An ugly altercation followed between the two men on the floor of the House. The Lord Chancellor said the Government had to consider certain courses. "Certain corpses, not courses," interjected Carson. Birkenhead affected not to follow the interruption, but sternly reminded Carson that "it is the custom in this House to allow speakers to proceed."

There is no doubt that the Lord Chancellor felt very keenly what he described as "the most wounding imputation upon my personal honour," when Carson spoke of the use he had made of the Ulster issue. "The noble and learned Lord," said Birkenhead, "has publicly repelled me from a friendship which had many memories for me, and which I deeply value. The noble and learned Lord can do that—no one can prevent him—but he cannot deprive me of memories indissolubly bound up with the past, when we ran common risks and in speech and act I matched and was glad to match the risks that he ran . . . I justify myself, even in my present position, for every irregularity I committed, and for all the steps I took when I stood side by side with Lord Carson at grave and critical moments, and neither he nor I knew what advice would be given to His Majesty's Government by those who were then the Law Officers of the Crown."

Simultaneously with Lord Birkenhead, the Leader of the House was speaking on the same subject in the Commons. But Members flocked to the Lords, leaving Austen Chamberlain to address half-empty benches. During the Lord Chancellor's speech almost the entire Cabinet was gathered round the steps of the Throne, while Carson sat gloomily in his place with his arms folded across his chest and his formidable chin tucked into the pit of his neck.

Lord Birkenhead's speech was the climax to the debate which had lasted for three days. A division followed on an amendment moved by the Duke of Northumberland regretting that the settlement "would involve the surrender of the rights of the Crown in Ireland, give power to establish an independent Irish Army and Navy, would require further sacrifices from Ulster, and would not safeguard the rights of the loyalist population in Southern Ireland." It attracted the support of only forty-seven out of a total of 213 peers. The minority of 'diehards', led by Carson, included two of Carson's judicial colleagues, Lord Sumner, who had recently welcomed him to the Bench, and Lord Atkinson, with whom Carson had once served as a Law Officer in Dublin. Lord Midleton, self-styled leader of the Southern Irish Unionists, went into the Government lobby with the majority.

The result of the vote was received in complete silence. Thus, in both Houses of Parliament, the seal was set on a revolution of far-reaching import for the United Kingdom and the Empire.

3

While the 'Treaty' was generally hailed outside Ireland with a great sigh of relief, feelings toward it in that island were very different. The majority in Ulster, who had accepted the Act of 1920 as a final settlement of their status, were alarmed at the prospect of her border with the South being altered by a Boundary Commission, the sole alternative to joining an all-Ireland Parliament, which the Ulster Cabinet flatly rejected. In the South the Unionists not unnaturally complained they had been betrayed. As for the victors in the surrender, they soon began to quarrel among themselves. In the Dail the decision to approve the 'Treaty' and the setting up of the 'Free State' was only carried by a narrow margin, after Mr. De Valera, who still wanted a Republic, had done his best to wreck the new arrangements. The motion to re-elect Mr. De Valera President was defeated by two votes, and he thereupon yielded his place to Arthur Griffith, who had led the 'Treaty' delegation to London. In the South a period of uneasy peace followed between the 'treatyites' and the 'anti-treatyites', as the British authorities handed over to the new Government. In the North outrages continued despite meetings between Craig and Collins. The I.R.A. carried out a number of raids against the North and made off with a number of hostages; they then proceeded to occupy a corner of the six counties, from which they were eventually driven out by British troops. Sir Henry Wilson, whose term as C.I.G.S. had come to an end and who had entered the Imperial Parliament as M.P. for an Ulster constituency, now undertook to reorganise the Ulster police force, which, like the old R.I.C., many of whose members joined the new force, was an armed constabulary.

In London, Carson, who saw no hope for any improvement in the Irish situation so long as the present Government was in power, openly proclaimed himself an opponent of the Coalition. Headquarters of the movement to return to the old party system and form 'a real Conservative Party' was Londonderry House, traditional centre of the Unionist 'diehards'. On January 14, 1922, Sir Henry Wilson, who was in the confidence of the Londonderrys, noted in his diary that "the new Lady Londonderry is working hard to this end with Salisbury, Northumberland, Carson, Ronald McNeill," adding, "I am sure this is a right thing to aim for." Some weeks later Carson addressed a public meeting at Burton-on-Trent in which he strongly attacked the Coalition, saying it was time to return to "the more honest party system" before Mr. Lloyd George completely destroyed the Conservative Party. In particular, he singled out Austen Chamberlain as a deserter of his friends and his principles and he made a jest about 'diehards' and 'livehards' which was obviously directed towards Birkenhead. This called forth an unprecedented rebuke in the House of Lords from the Lord Chancellor, who laid it down firmly that no judge had the slightest right to appear on a platform in the country and make political speeches. His arguments were reinforced by Lord Curzon, who agreed with the Lord Chancellor that Carson's best course would be to resign his judicial office. The ponderous Leader of the House made it clear that, if Carson continued to break this rule, the Government would be driven to lay down that when a Law Lord accepts his appointment he accepts 'certain obligations' at the same time.

Carson had no intention of allowing his activities to be circumscribed in this way. In a robust reply to Birkenhead, which he delivered in the Upper House, he said he was ready to resign if their Lordships thought he had done anything wrong. "What do you think I care for my office or salary compared with my honour?" he asked. "It is as nothing to me, much as I value being in your Lordships' House. If the time comes when there arises a controversy as to whether my honour or my salary can be kept, I need not tell your Lordships that I prefer my honour to the salary. . . . Believe me that so long as I hold my present office . . . you may remain perfectly sure that the honour of justice will remain untarnished." Anyhow, as he pointed out, there had been Law Lords in the past, notably Lord Cairns and Lord Macnaghten, as well as many ex-Lord Chancellors, who had also been prominent politically, while in the present House Lord Sumner and Lord Atkinson had both delivered political speeches from time to time on subjects which had interested them. Also, what about Recorders, Chairmen of Quarter Sessions and Justices of the Peace? Were they to take no part in politics? And what of the Lord Chancellor himself? Was he not the greatest politician of them all?

In his rejoinder Birkenhead dealt with his own position. He admitted that for centuries our constitutional law had tolerated an anomaly in the office of Lord Chancellor. The accepted view was that, in the interests both of the Executive and the Judiciary, it was convenient and desirable that there should be a connecting link. To reason that they were, therefore, to release the whole Bench to undertake partisan activity was "indeed an amazing doctrine", and he pictured every judge going to Burton, and delivering a platform speech "scathing and vehement in conception and expression, as Lord Carson thought proper to do." Was the Lord Chief Justice, for example, to intervene in by-elections? Were they to have the "cheerful judicial hurly-burly" suggested by Lord Carson's contention? The claim that every judge in the country was to be entitled to fling himself into party strife was ludicrous. While he did not suggest that Carson's procedure would impair his judicial independence, the Chancellor emphasised that the public should not be able to think that there was any ground for suspicion of the motives of a judge.

It is unnecessary to follow these exchanges further. So far as the rule proposed by Curzon went, Carson knew that the Government was bluffing, and that any attempt to introduce legislation to this effect in the Commons might well result in its application to the Lord Chancellor and to ex-Lord Chancellors. On the other hand, Carson seems to have realised that platform speeches such as he had made at Burton were liable to cause trouble, and during the remainder of the Coalition's life he delivered no further public attacks on it. He did, however, continue to speak his mind on Ireland, though his interventions here became less frequent with the creation and infant growth of the Irish Free State side by side with the Government of

Northern Ireland and the gradual return to fairly settled conditions throughout the country.

Before this object was achieved, there was to be much further loss of life and destruction of property. As the 'Free Staters' and 'Republicans' in the South were preparing for open warfare, their gunmen continued to harry the North and even carried the war into England in pursuit of their enemies. On May 22 Sir Henry Wilson was murdered on the steps of his house in Eaton Place, a few doors from Carson's. It was a crime which sent a thrill of horror through the civilised world. Happily for Ulster, though not for the rest of Ireland, the fight for 'freedom' was transferred to the South. There civil war broke out and was conducted on a wider and more bloodthirsty scale than anything against the hated British. Many beautiful houses which Carson had known well in his younger days were burnt by Mr. De Valera's Republican followers—'Irregulars', as they came to be known. Michael Collins and others prominent in the earlier struggle were killed by their former comrades, while Arthur Griffith also died, worn out by his exertions. Griffith's place as President was taken by William Cosgrave, a quiet Alderman in the Dublin Corporation, who was determined to restore law and order, and eventually succeeded in doing so, though his methods were necessarily ruthless.

Meanwhile, discontent with the Coalition was growing with the rank-and-file of the Conservative Party, and, as we have seen, Carson had not been idle in encouraging it. The principal Coalition Conservative was Austen Chamberlain, who had superseded Bonar Law as his party's Leader, and he wanted the next General Election, which would soon be due, to be fought by the party in conjunction with the Lloyd Georgian Liberals as in 1918. Chamberlain hoped to impose this view on the party and, rather than wait for the Conservative and Unionist Annual Conference in November, he summoned a meeting of the parliamentary party at the Carlton Club on October 19. On the eve of this historic meeting Carson, still fairly active behind the scenes, addressed a significant letter to Bonar Law, whose health had by this time considerably recovered.

Confidential. *Cleve Court,*
Minster-in-Thanet.
18.10.22

My dear Bonar Law,

I suppose you will take part in the proceedings at the C[arlton] C[lub] tomorrow. I only want to suggest to you that such a meeting is not the proper way to ascertain the view of the Unionist Party. It looks very much as if it was being held to 'blanket' the meeting of delegates at the National Union on 16th November.

The result therefore of any attempt to forestall that meeting would be disastrous to our whole system of organization and would make unity impossible. I would suggest Chamberlain's meeting or at all events any resolution should stand over till after the National Union.

I need hardly say this is only an individual opinion and I write only for myself. I hope you are well. I wish you were well enough to handle the whole situation.

Yours ever,

EDWARD.

To Carson's surprise and gratification Bonar Law proved himself fully equal to the occasion. Since the Carlton Club meeting was restricted to Unionist Members of the House of Commons, Carson could not attend, but he naturally received a first-hand account of what happened from Bonar Law and others. Chamberlain recommended that the existing Government as then constituted under Lloyd George should go to the country; it would be time to talk of changes when the victory had been won. A motion was at once proposed by a Conservative back-bencher, Mr. E. G. Pretyman, M.P., to the effect that the party "should fight the election as an independent party with its own leader and its own programme". After this resolution had been duly seconded by another back-bencher, Mr. George Lane-Fox, M.P., Bonar Law appealed to his audience not to disunite the party but to uphold it as a great instrument for the maintenance of Conservative principles. "I think that the time has now come to break up the Coalition," he added. The meeting applauded him rapturously and carried Mr. Pretyman's resolution by a majority of more than two to one. Later the same day Mr. Lloyd George resigned and advised the King to send for Bonar Law. "It has been a wonderful time," he said to his friend, Lord Riddell, as he prepared to leave Downing Street. "Yes, it has been a wonderful time."

"Well," wrote Bonar Law to Carson, as he was about to set out for Buckingham Palace, "I took the plunge and I believe it was the right thing to do—but I shall have a bad time. I am sure you will try to make things easy so far as it is possible for you to do so." Carson's view as to why the Coalition fell was expressed in the House of Lords shortly afterwards: "Mr. Austen Chamberlain, then supposed to be a Unionist Leader, has said that it was from the moment of the signing of this Treaty that the Coalition began to topple down. Of course it was, and I am glad of it. It is the just reward of the treachery of which he was at the head, and so may it always be."

Bonar Law became Prime Minister on October 23, having for a second time been elected Leader of the Conservative Party. In this transaction Carson played his part behind the scenes, and thus the hand which had raised Lloyd George to supreme power in the State six years previously had more than a little to do with his downfall. The change-over to an exclusively 'Unionist' Government was endorsed a few weeks later at the polls. However, there was not and could not be any question of reversing the Irish policy to which the nation was pledged in the 'Treaty', whatever might be thought of the nature of the agreement and the methods by which it had been reached. A fortnight after the new Parliament had assembled the Irish Free State Constitution Bill, implementing the 'Treaty' on the British side, was introduced in the House of Commons and rapidly passed through all its stages in both Houses. In view of everything that had happened, Carson naturally felt obliged to utter grave words of warning at the possible consequences of what he considered the abandonment of British interests. "You have agreed to a revolution in Ireland," he told the Government in the House of Lords. "Do not do it on the cheap." Bonar Law appreciated his position. "You may be sure that everything you feel compelled to do will not be regarded by me as unfriendly," the Prime Minister said to him, "for I know how friendly you are."

With the formal creation of the Irish Free State, the remaining organs of British Government in Dublin were handed over to Cosgrave and his Cabinet, and the British forces completely withdrew from the country. Lord Fitzalan, the last Lord Lieutenant, quitted the Viceregal Lodge in the Phœnix Park, and his place was taken by Carson's old antagonist in the Courts and in Parliament, Tim Healy, who thus became, under the new constitution first Governor-General of the Irish Free State. The war between the 'Free Staters' and the 'Republicans' continued for some months longer, with repercussions in the North, but toward the middle of 1923 the rival factions came to terms, hostilities were terminated and gradually the people in both parts of the country turned to the tasks of peaceful reconstruction.

Thus, when Carson went over to Belfast later in the year, he found a calmer atmosphere prevailing everywhere. True, the question of the boundary was still outstanding, but this was eventually to be settled without the loss of an inch of Ulster territory ("Not an inch," said Craig, and he showed that he meant it.*) The main purpose of Carson's visit was to cut the first sod in the building of a thirty-million-gallon reservoir in the Mourne Mountains so as to give the city of Belfast an adequate water supply. Advantage was taken of his presence to make him a presentation of a casket containing a beautifully decorated album inscribed with the names of many thousands of Ulster Loyalists, "as an expression of their love and admiration and to mark their appreciation of the invaluable services rendered by him to the Imperial Province and Empire." The immense gathering in the Ulster Hall when the presentation took place was like old times, and tears filled his eyes as the audience sang 'For he's a jolly good fellow' and the Ulster Premier, Sir James Craig, handed over the casket. "Thank you, thank you, thank you," he repeated, his voice choking. "Never forget me, for I never forget you."

4

Carson had some interest in painting, and he sat for his portrait on a number of occasions. He had been painted as a young man in Dublin in the 'eighties, and after he came to London, he was the subject of a striking work by an American woman artist, Miss Julia Folkard, which secured a place in the Royal Academy's Summer Exhibition in 1896. He later sat twice to Sir John Lavery and also to Philip de Laszlo, as well as to Sir Philip Burne-Jones, who had been his neighbour at Rottingdean. The first time he sat to Lavery it was at the invitation of the artist, who was also painting John Redmond and wished the two portraits to be hung side by side in the National Gallery of Ireland. Lavery was a Belfast Catholic and Carson, after seeing the two portraits together, remarked jokingly: "Ah, it's easy to see which side you're on!" Redmond, on the other hand, commented plaintively: "I have always had an idea that Carson and I might some day be hanged side by side in Dublin, and now it has come to pass." The second Lavery portrait, really a copy of the earlier one, was painted in 1922 for the Municipal Art Gallery in

* A new agreement between Great Britain and the Irish Free State was concluded in 1925, by which the Free State retained the existing boundary and in return was released from the obligations of the 1921 'Treaty' under which they had agreed to assume an 'equitable' share of the British National Debt. Carson had previously refused to serve on the Boundary Commission and the Northern Ireland Government had also declined to appoint a Commissioner.

Belfast. "Well now," said Carson to the artist when he had surveyed it carefully, "you can call that 'Edward Carson after the Surrender'." Lavery asked Lord D'Abernon for his opinion. "My dear John," said D'Abernon jokingly, "you have quite missed the character. It's not like him, you haven't caught the criminal look." "Well," remarked the artist, "his wife thinks it's the best portrait that has been done of him." "Yes, of course," retorted D'Abernon. "That damns it."

In the field of Irish art Carson associated himself at this time with an acutely controversial matter which exercised the minds of many people on both sides of the Irish Sea and remains unsettled to this day. This was the fate of the valuable collection of modern pictures known as the 'Lane Bequest'. The question had no party political significance, which, as Carson put it in explaining the matter to the House of Lords in 1924, "is not always the case in business relating to Ireland." The owner of the collection, Sir Hugh Lane, lost his life when the *Lusitania* was torpedoed and sunk by a German submarine in 1915. The dispute turned upon a codicil to his will, which revoked a previous disposition of the pictures. Unfortunately the codicil was not witnessed.

Hugh Lane, the son of a Church of Ireland clergyman in County Cork and nephew of the Irish playwright and poet, Lady Gregory, began life as a clerk in a London art dealer's. Developing a remarkable flair for the business, he set up for himself and rapidly acquired a fortune. Largely through his efforts and endowed with his gifts, a municipal gallery of modern art was founded in Dublin shortly after the turn of the century, and for this and his services to art generally Lane was knighted in 1909. The pictures, the work of Irish artists like J. B. Yeats and Sir William Orpen, were temporarily housed in a house in Harcourt Street, a few doors from Carson's birthplace, which had been provided by the Dublin Corporation. In order to make the collection more representative, Lane decided to lend the gallery thirty-nine pictures, mostly by French artists, such as Corot, Degas, Manet, Monet and Renoir, which he had recently bought, and in doing so he intimated that the loan would become a gift if a suitable permanent gallery were provided within the next few years. But a dispute over the site followed. Sir Edwin Lutyens, at Lane's request, submitted a plan for a most attractive building on either side of the River Liffey to be connected by a bridge, but this project was rejected by the Corporation, "whose hearts," in Carson's words, "were not altogether set upon art." Lane thereupon withdrew the thirty-nine pictures and sent them on loan to the National Gallery in London. At the same time he made a will leaving them to this gallery. This will was properly executed, although Lane, who was careless about legal formalities, at first proposed to sign it without witnesses and had to be reminded of their necessity.

Early in 1915 Lane made arrangements to pay a short business visit to America. Before leaving he drew up and signed a codicil to the will, in which he bequeathed the collection to the city of Dublin, but his signature was unattested. The codicil was discovered in a drawer of his desk a few days after it became known that he had lost his life in the sinking of the *Lusitania*. The unusual care with which he drew up the codicil, and the precautions he took to ensure its falling into proper hands in the event of his death, left little or no room for doubt that it was no mere draft, but a document to which at the time of its composition he attached the greatest importance. His omission to secure witnesses on this occasion was in no way inconsistent with his general habits and temperament. Furthermore, just before he sailed for America, he told several relatives and friends, including his aunt Lady Gregory and Sir Alec Martin of Christie's, that he had arranged to leave the pictures back to Dublin.

Lady Gregory immediately requested the return of the pictures from the British Government, and her claim was supported by all shades of Irish political opinion, including those represented by Carson and Redmond. The trouble was that the pictures were legally the property of the National Gallery in London and that institution had no right to part with them. The Government was pressed to introduce the requisite legislation, but in the circumstances of the times—the war was still on and after the 'Easter Week' rebellion the Government had plenty of other matters on its hands in Ireland—the question was repeatedly postponed. Michael Collins raised it without success during the 'Treaty' negotiations, and soon after the Irish Free State came into being it was the subject of motions in the Southern Parliament. Eventually, on July 14, 1924, Carson initiated a debate in the House of Lords and said he would welcome any inquiry which might lead to justice being done to Lane's wishes and memory in the matter.

Lord Arnold, the Under-Secretary of State for the Colonies, who replied for the Government, announced the setting up of a committee "consisting of three competent and impartial persons" to report (1) whether in their opinion Sir Hugh Lane, when he signed the codicil, thought he was making a legal disposition and, (2) if so, whether it was proper that, "in view of the international character of the matter at issue" the legal defect in the codicil should be remedied by legislation. Three M.P.s, one from each major political party, were appointed to constitute the committee. Their report was completed at the beginning of 1925, but was not published in the form of a Parliamentary White Paper until the middle of 1926. The report took the form of a most unsatisfactory compromise, since it found that Lane *did* think he was making a legal disposition when he signed the codicil, but, on the other hand, it went on to recommend that it would *not* be proper to modify the will by Act of Parliament since "to do so would, in addition to constituting a legal precedent of the utmost gravity, not justified by the facts, have the effect of bringing about a result contrary to the real spirit of Sir Hugh Lane's intentions."

Meanwhile, Carson, in consultation with Lady Gregory and Tim Healy, the Governor-General of the Irish Free State, had drafted a Bill to enable the trustees of the National Gallery, London, to transfer or lend the Lane collection to the trustees of the National Gallery of Ireland. On April 28, 1926, Carson introduced this Bill in the House of Lords. But an unhappy fate seemed to dog the pictures. Carson made a technical slip, which was odd for a lawyer. He omitted to communicate notices of the Bill to the *London Gazette* and to the London Press as he was formally required to do, so that two months later the Examiners of Bills in the House of Lords announced that the measure had been disqualified on the ground of this legal technicality. By this time the committee's report had been published, and, in view of its finding that it would not be proper to modify Lane's will by legislation, Carson did not consider it worthwhile reintroducing his Bill. Mr. Stanley Baldwin, who was then Prime Minister, stated that the Government must accept the conclusion reached by the committee and this view has prevailed with subsequent Governments.*

The outcome of the matter was a great disappointment to Carson, who felt, and continued to feel for the remainder of his life, that Lane's undoubted intentions as to the ultimate destination of the

* The collection is now in the Tate Gallery. The most recent request for its return was refused by the Government in 1948. The question was raised in that year in a motion on the adjournment in the House of Commons which was supported by the Hon. Edward Carson, M.P., Lord Carson's son. See *Parliamentary Debates*, Vol. 448, cols. 3426–3430 (March 25, 1948) and also statement by Mr. Herbert Morrison, M.P., in answer to a parliamentary question, *Parliamentary Debates*, Vol. 456, cols. 876–877 (Sept. 22, 1948). See also J. J. Reynolds, *Statement of the Claim for the Return to Dublin of the 39 Lane Bequest Pictures now at the Tate Gallery, London* (Dublin, 1932.)

pictures should be carried out and that the pictures should be given back to Dublin where, in Carson's words in the House of Lords, they "would be a valuable memorial to a great Irishman."

Carson had better success with another legislative project which he introduced in the House of Lords during this period and which reached the statute book. This was the Moneylenders Act of 1927, a measure imposing very stringent restrictions on moneylenders. These restrictions provided for the annual licensing of moneylenders, the forfeiting of moneylenders' licences for betting and other offences, the regulation of the enforcement of contracts of repayment, the limitation of interest to forty-eight per cent and the prohibition of compound interest and charges of expenses on loans; they also provided against the circulation of moneylenders' advertisements to individual members of the public except in response to written requests for them. The onus was put upon the moneylender to justify any rate of interest in excess of fifteen per cent if the borrower took him to the County Court, and no borrower was to be made bankrupt unless the case had first gone through the County Court. The object of Carson's Act was not to suppress moneylending—this would have been impossible in practice—but to regulate it strictly. "We have two things in view," said Carson in moving the second reading of this "far overdue" measure in the Upper House. "One is to make the moneylender hesitate more, and the other is to make the borrower less likely to please the moneylender by getting a loan. It is far better on the whole that people in straits—and God knows that I know well what they are, and the difficulties about money—should face the circumstances then and there. Once they get into the moneylender's clutches, within a year things will be ten times or a hundred times worse than they were before."

Carson also explained how he came to interest himself in the subject. "I was led into that inquiry," he said, "by having to go into a number of dealings with moneylenders with reference to one of my own family, though I am thankful to say that from the early stage of my own career, when I commenced without a shilling in the world, I never had personal dealing with a moneylender. . . . In the particular case which led me on the inquiry what happened was this. My young relative began to back horses of which he knew nothing. He got into difficulties and at once the bookmaker said to him: 'Oh, that need not stop you; I know a jolly good moneylender.' He went on and carried on the transactions for some four years, until, as a result, he had paid back the whole sum he borrowed *plus* fifty per cent at compound interest and still owed £600." It only remains to add that the relative in question was one of his own sons.

In the same year as the Moneylenders' Act passed into law, another question came before Parliament which prompted Carson to intervene vigorously. This was the proposal to approve the so-called Alternative Prayer Book for use in Church of England services. A few days before the question was debated in the House of Lords, Carson expressed his concern in a letter to a clergyman of the Church of Ireland who had written to him.

To The Rev. Canon H. O'Connor

5 *Eaton Place, London, S.W.* 9.12.27 . . . I need hardly say with what anxiety and misgiving I am watching the controversy over the Deposited Prayer Book and the struggle under very difficult circumstances to maintain the principles of the primitive Faith involved in the successful issue of the Reformation. The gradual abandonment without check or hindrance in many dioceses of these principles is now to be rewarded by their legislation and those who maintained them are to be driven elsewhere, I fear, to find a pure form of worship in accordance with the Faith and the doctrines in which they were content to abide.

I pray that the Church of Ireland (my own Church) may, as I am sure it will be under God's guidance, brought to sound decisions as to its future communion with the Church of England in the event of the new doctrines being sanctioned by law. Over here it will rest with every true Protestant to consider his own position in such a vital matter and I am grateful to know that we still have such truly Protestant Churches as the Presbyterian, Wesleyan Methodist and other Free Churches . . .

The motion to approve the new Prayer Book attracted as many spectators in the House of Lords as the debate on the Irish 'Treaty'. Carson's speech was one of the most moving and eloquent delivered on this occasion; it was also his last speech of any considerable length in the Upper House. "Let me make this one confession at the outset," he began. "It is the first time in my life—and I am a very old man—that I have ever felt grateful to Mr. Gladstone for disestablishing the Irish Church, and for this reason—whatever your Parliament may do here in relation to the Prayer Book, it will not bind the Irish Church, which can still go on cherishing the precious heritage of the Reformation." We need not follow in detail the arguments against the proposal which he developed for upwards of an hour. "We are here to legalise illegalities," was how he summarised them. "We are here to admit the triumph of those who for the past thirty years have refused to obey the rubrics of the Church." Nor did his speech, passionately sincere as it was, lack a characteristic touch of humour when he told them of a gentleman, "known to some of your Lordships," who was asked what he thought of the Alternative Prayer Book. He replied: "I suppose the next thing is that we shall have an alternative Bradshaw." Carson also attacked the alternative Communion Service with its provisions for the reservation of the Sacrament under conditions which lead to its adoration. "Do not let us have this chaos in the Church not only of two Prayer Books, which is bad enough, but of two Communion Services, in one of which something is declared to be absolute idolatry, while it is legalised in the other. How can a Church stand in these circumstances?"

So far as the Upper House was concerned, Carson was pleading a lost cause. The Lords carried the Prayer Book Measure by a large majority. But the Commons subsequently rejected it after an equally stirring debate, which gave Carson great satisfaction.

Among those who voted with Carson against the measure in the Lords was Ulster's Prime Minister, Sir James Craig, recently raised to the peerage with the title of Viscount Craigavon. It was the first time that he had been able to take part in the proceedings of the Upper House and he received a warm welcome from his old chief, who had been extremely gratified by the news of his honour. "No one perhaps knows better than I do all that the country and of course Ulster especially owes to you," Carson wrote to him at the time. "Your judgment, courage, tact and wisdom have been the guiding star throughout all these years of stress and anxiety, and no reward could be too great."

5

We may now consider Carson's judicial work in the House of Lords and the Privy Council. He was a Law Lord for a little over eight years, and during this period he had as his colleagues some of the greatest legal brains of the century in men like Birkenhead, Buckmaster, Dunedin and Sumner. For the most part, he was content to defer to their intellects. However, when he did deliver a separate judgment in a particular case, it was almost invariably a dissenting one. In his practising days at the Bar he always had a great belief in the innate common sense and spirit of fair play shown by juries. Consequently, any attempt made in an appeal to disturb a jury's verdict on the ground of the inadmissibility of evidence tended to be regarded by him with suspicion. If he was not especially distinguished on the Bench, he was certainly a competent and industrious judge, and equally liked by his judicial colleagues and those members of the Bar who appeared before him. In 1922 the fellow Benchers of his old Inn of Court, the Middle Temple, paid him the compliment of electing him its Treasurer.

But it cannot be said that he found his judicial duties altogether congenial. No outstanding advocate is ever really at home on the Bench. He missed the rough-and-tumble of the lower Courts, and there is no doubt he would have been happier as a trial judge with a jury, where in a summing up he would have been concerned largely with the facts of the case. "He rarely if ever really spread himself in judgment," wrote his Scottish colleague Lord Blanesburgh after his death. "The juristic side of the work—and most of it can be so described—did not appeal to him. He should have been Chief Justice. In that office, presiding over a jury at some great trial, he would have been as supreme as in similar circumstances he was at the Bar. But, unfortunately for us all, that office never came his way, and the judicial office which did was not really according to his humour."

Two appeals in which he participated call for detailed comment, since they both immediately became leading cases in English law. The first of these was the celebrated Russell divorce case, in which the majority of the Court held that the rule of law, that neither a husband nor wife is permitted to give evidence of non-intercourse after marriage so as to bastardise a child born in wedlock, applies to proceedings instituted in consequence of adultery and is not affected by the Act of Parliament passed in 1869 which makes the parties to such proceedings, and the husbands and wives of such parties, competent witnesses.* Carson followed Lord Sumner in dissenting from the majority judgment.

The facts were briefly as follows. In 1921 the Hon. John Russell, afterwards Lord Ampthill, petitioned for a divorce from his wife, Mrs. Christabel Russell, on the ground among others of her adultery with an unknown man, in consequence of which she had given birth to a male child of which Mr. Russell was not the father. It was admitted that husband and wife occupied the same bed on two nights in December, 1920, and medical evidence was called with

* *Russell v. Russell.* Law Reports [1924], A. C., 687.

the object of proving that the child might have been conceived on one of those two nights. However, thé husband swore that he had had no connexion with his wife on either of the two nights or indeed at any time when the child could have been conceived. In the result the jury found that the wife had committed adultery with the unknown man, and Mr. Russell was granted a decree *nisi*. This judgment was upheld in the Court of Appeal.

The only material ground of appeal to the House of Lords which could upset the decree *nisi* was whether or not the husband's evidence of non-access or non-connexion was admissible. In holding that it was not Lord Chancellor Birkenhead and Lords Finlay and Dunedin followed the rule laid down in the eighteenth century by Lord Mansfield and 'founded on decency, morality and policy', to the effect that husband and wife should not be permitted to say after marriage that they had no connexion and 'therefore that the offspring is spurious.'

Carson, in his dissenting judgment, suggested that this rule was intended to apply only to cases where the legitimacy of a child was directly in issue, and not to such issues as adultery and condonation. "If you take the rule as founded on decency and morality," he went on, "the very nature of the issues to be decided from day to day in the Divorce Court shows how consistently such decency and morality has to be outraged, and the books are full of cases where, to use the words of Lord Dunedin, the most secret and at the same time the most sacred of the legitimate relations of man and woman as husband and wife are laid bare to the world."

Carson referred to the fact that he had practised "to a considerable extent for some years" in the Divorce Courts and he thought that the prevailing view then of judges was that such evidence could be given on questions of adultery. Finally, in his customary forthright language he described the effect of the judgment of the majority of his colleagues in this case.

"My Lords," he said, "to what an extraordinary state would the objection of the evidence in the present case reduce the law of England! Here is a husband who knows, and who has proved to the satisfaction of the jury, that he has not had access or connexion with his wife, and that his wife must therefore be guilty of adultery, and he is to be informed that the law of England gives him no relief and binds him to his adulterous wife, because he is not allowed to give evidence which he alone is capable of giving!"

In the result the appeal succeeded and the decree *nisi* was rescinded.

At the time Divorce Court practitioners complained that the result would prove highly inconvenient, since this kind of evidence had been commonly admitted in the past, at least since the passing of the Act of 1869. The remedy lay with the legislature and it has since been adopted. The rule in *Russell* v. *Russell* is no longer the law of the land. It has recently been reversed by Parliament, thus confirming the views expressed by Lord Carson in his dissenting judgment."*

The other prominent leading case in which Carson figured as a Law Lord concerned what is known as the 'rolled-up plea' as a defence in actions for libel. This plea, that in so far as the words complained of consist of allegations of fact they are true in substance and in fact and in so far as they consist of expressions of opinion they are fair comments made in good faith and without malice on a matter of public interest, was held by the House of Lords in this case to amount to a plea of fair comment only. "It is not partly justification and partly fair comment," said Carson, "but fair comment pure and simple."†

Dr. Marie Stopes, the plaintiff in the original action, had published several books advocating the artificial prevention of conception and had established a birth-control clinic in one of the poorer districts of London, where mothers could obtain free advice on the subject. The defendants were Dr. Halliday Sutherland, a well-known Roman Catholic medical practitioner, and his publishers. Dr. Sutherland attacked Dr. Stopes and her methods in a controversial work designed to expose the alleged dangers of birth control. He stated, in effect, that Dr. Stopes was taking advantage of the ignorance of the poor to subject them to experiments, and that at her clinic working women were instructed in a mode of contraception stated by an eminent professor of gynæcology to be the most harmful of which she had experience. "It is truly amazing that this monstrous campaign of birth control should be tolerated by the Home Secretary," declared Dr. Sutherland. "Charles Bradlaugh was condemned to gaol for a less serious crime."

At the trial, which took place before the Lord Chief Justice, Lord Hewart and a special jury, the jury found that the words complained of were true in substance and in fact, but that they were not fair comment and awarded the plaintiff £100 damages and half the costs of the action. On these findings the Lord Chief Justice entered

* Law Reform (Matrimonial Causes) Act, 1949, re-enacted by the Matrimonial Causes Act, 1950.

† *Sutherland v. Stopes*. Law Reports [1925], A. C., 47.

judgment for the defendants. This judgment was reversed on appeal. In the House of Lords the original judgment was restored and Dr. Stopes was ordered to repay the sums by way of damages and costs which she had received. With one dissentient, Lord Wrenbury, the Court held that there was no evidence to support the jury's finding that the comment was unfair. Carson further held, along with Lord Shaw of Dunfermline, that the jury's finding on the plea of justification afforded a complete answer to the action.

A noteworthy feature of this case in the House of Lords was the judgment of the octogenarian Lord Wrenbury*, which, besides holding that the order of the Court of Appeal upholding the verdict of the jury on fair comment should be upheld, or alternatively that there should be a new trial, seemed to look with favour upon the works of Dr. Marie Stopes. This prompted Carson, who gave his judgment immediately afterwards, to make his own position clear. "But for the statements made by my noble and learned friend who has just addressed the House," said Carson, "I should not have thought it necessary or opportune, in considering the legal problems which arise for decision in this case, to have said anything whatever on the subject of the policy of birth control, or the merits or demerits of the plaintiff in the part she plays in furtherance of that object. I feel bound, however, after listening to the speech of my noble friend, to say that the recital of alleged facts and views he has expressed, which seem to me and will be read by others as being in sympathy with the actions of the plaintiff or her writings or of certain evidence produced on her behalf, must not be taken as in any way representing my own views if I had thought it necessary or relevant to discuss them."

Early in 1929 Carson's health began noticeably to fail. He had a long succession of sleepless nights and suffered from recurrent attacks of lumbago. A visit to Harrogate in the summer vacation failed to give him much relief. In these circumstances he decided that he could not carry on his work, as he told his old friend and colleague Lord Atkinson, "with any comfort to myself, or with such service to the public as one owes in the position of a Law Lord." To another friend and former comrade, Major Fred Crawford, organiser of the Ulster gun-running, he confessed that he found the work in the House of Lords very heavy and, "as I have been fifty-two years practising at the law, I thought the time had come when a

* Formerly Mr. Justice Buckley. He was the author of the legal classic, *Buckley on Companies*.

younger man might take it on." His decision was publicly announced on November 1, and it was received with regret by the Prime Minister, Mr. Ramsay MacDonald, as well as by a host of other friends and colleagues. "It saddens me to think how the years go," wrote Mr. MacDonald in replying to the official letter of resignation, "and that men, who were fresh and vigorous when I met them apparently only yesterday, retire one after another."

Of the tributes he received from the Bench two are typical. One of them came from a well-known King's Bench Judge. "I shall miss so much seeing your name in the Law Reports," wrote Mr. Justice McCardie. "It seems so long now since we were together at the Bar. *What a generous and kindly leader you were!* I always rejoiced to be with you, and you have given me many happy memories. I expect that you are tired and look forward to rest. You are entitled fully to it after so wonderful a life of effort and work."

The other was from a colleague in the House of Lords. "I had always looked forward specially to sitting with you," wrote Lord Atkin. "I only wish the occasions had been more frequent, but I enjoyed every one, and found to the full extent the patience, insight and independence that one expected. I have always been one of the innumerable members of the Bar who from below have watched your great career with admiration but also with affection. I doubt whether you realise with what warm hearts your brother barristers have regarded you: because, greatest advocate of the lot, you have always been so sincerely the brother barrister."

6

One subject in particular occupied Carson's mind in this later period, and even after his retirement as a Law Lord he continued to give it as much attention as his health and strength allowed. This was the position of the Southern Irish Loyalists, whom he considered had been grossly betrayed by the British Government. Many of those who had not been murdered had had their houses burnt and their family possessions destroyed. Every week, so he said, he received sixty or seventy complaints. A typical example was Sir Henry Wilson's brother, whose beautiful home in County Longford had suffered in this way. Carson told the House of Lords: "The brother of the gallant soldier is now living in humble lodgings in an English village, shattered in health and broken in spirit. I saw him lately, and I assure you it was hard to bear—the wreckage which all this had brought about."

Carson was especially indignant at the shabby treatment accorded to those who put in claims for compensation, and the way in which the Commission appointed by the British Government to investigate these claims whittled them down to a mere fraction of the original awards. For instance, in a case where the Recorder of Cork awarded £2,000 in respect of stock-in-trade valued at £3,500 which had been stolen or destroyed, the Commission reduced it to £77. "Fortunately in anything connected with my country there is always some slight cause for amusement," commented Carson sardonically. "They had the grace to allow nine shillings by way of interest and deducted income tax to the amount of seven shillings and eight pence."

In his heart he found it difficult to forgive those whom he regarded as responsible for the betrayal, notably the members of the Conservative and Unionist Party. Nor did he repose much faith in the dominion status enjoyed by the newly-created Irish Free State, feeling that the constitutional safeguards in the interests of the Crown contained in the arrangements between the two countries would soon be undermined and removed altogether. Events were to prove him abundantly right.

Carson's private views were forcefully expressed in the course of a conversation, hitherto unpublished, which he had at this time with Balfour's niece, Mrs. Blanche Dugdale. In the summer of 1928 Mrs. Dugdale was engaged in writing a biography of her uncle, and she asked Carson for his recollections. Carson related his impressions of Balfour's term of office as Chief Secretary forty years before, as well as his own work as Crown Prosecutor in those exciting days, and he described Mitchelstown as he 'remembered' it.* Later he got on to the topic of the Irish Free State.

> CARSON: If you got the letters I get every day, and knew how wretched it all is . . . Cosgrave has established order, I'll say that for him, and he has shot some dozens of his own friends, the men whose opinions he really shared in his heart, like Erskine Childers. And that's a vile thing he did. But, apart from that, it's all poverty and misery.
>
> MRS. DUGDALE: Their income tax is lower than ours though.
>
> CARSON: Because they borrowed to make up the deficit. No, I think there'd be more decency in a Republic than in this humbug. In fact I'd rather see a Republic.

* The conversation, which took place at Carson's London house on July 12, 1928, was recorded at the time by Mrs. Dugdale. The text is preserved in the Balfour Papers.

MRS. DUGDALE: What was your plan? You had a plan in the war, didn't you?

CARSON: Yes. I should have left Ulster out of it and given Southern Ireland something like Gladstone's Home Rule Bill. But, mind you, it wasn't *this* settlement I mind so much as the filthy way it was done, that midnight meeting, and no provisions for the men who had stuck to us. Surely we could at least have stipulated that we would keep order until they had got going? Was there any reason why we should walk off the battlefield and leave our wounded behind?

MRS. DUGDALE: You really don't think it was a losing battle all the time?

CARSON: Losing battle? Never. Why, at the very end, when Austen [Chamberlain] said to me that the thing was inevitable, I said, 'Rot. Joe would *never* have acquiesced.' Some of us went to stay with Joe when the last Home Rule fight was on, before the War. He was dying then, and he could hardly get out his words, but he sat in his chair and thumped with his stick to help his words out, and we listened while he said slowly like this, 'If—I—were—you—I—would—fight—it—out—to—the—end.' That was pretty well the last thing I ever did hear him say. And to think it was his own degenerate son——!

MRS. DUGDALE: You were very fond of Joe.

CARSON: I *revered* Joe. He was a very great man. Listen—two years ago I met Austen by chance, dining with [Lord] Revelstoke. I don't know if Revelstoke knew I don't meet Austen now. But of course at a friend's dinner table one can't——. Anyhow Austen came up to me after the ladies had gone, and he said: 'Carson, will you shake hands?' I said: 'Yes—on condition you don't mention Ireland to me, and because of the reverence I bore your father.' But that's enough about Austen.

MRS. DUGDALE: Do you hate him worse than Lloyd George?

CARSON: Austen's a coward. Lloyd George is a mass of corruption.

To the former Coalition Premier, indeed, Carson could not bring himself to speak. "The Little Man has betrayed Ulster," he said to one of Lloyd George's confidants on hearing the news of the conclusion of the 'Treaty' in 1921, "and I'll have nothing more to do with him." As we have seen, he was hurt even more by the defection of old party friends and colleagues—men like Birkenhead and Walter Long, as well as Austen Chamberlain—who had signed the Covenant and pledged themselves to stand by the Union. Between Carson and Bonar Law also a certain coolness sprang up by reason of the Conservative Leader's support of the settlement after his emergence from political retirement in 1922 to lead the party again. But this was eventually removed, largely through the skilful handling of

Bonar Law's sister, and the two men resumed their old friendly relations. These lasted throughout Bonar Law's short Premiership and until his death, which took place a few weeks after his departure from Downing Street. Carson acted as one of the pall-bearers at the funeral.

Birkenhead too he eventually forgave. "How could you keep up a quarrel with a man like that?" he said, describing the incident which brought them together again. Birkenhead was waiting for his car one rainy night at the entrance to the House of Lords. Carson saw him and shouted: "Jump in, F. E., and I'll drive you home." Birkenhead did so.

For some minutes the two men sat in silence. It was eventually broken by Birkenhead. "You know, Carson," he said, "some of the things you have said hit me pretty hard."

"You surprise me," said Carson.

"Yes, and perhaps you don't know why they hit me so hard," Birkenhead went on.

Carson shook his head.

"It was because they were so damnably true."

To this fortunate reconciliation may be attributed the sympathy with which Birkenhead wrote of Carson in the character sketch published in his *Contemporary Personalities* in 1924. "Decisions for which I was largely responsible, but which I knew and know to be disputable, had produced a revival of the old medieval antagonism. I thought then, and I think now, that Lord Carson, in the perspective of the whole tangled situation, was wrong. But I have read Irish history too closely to be certain that he was entirely wrong. Whether the truth in this controversy may ultimately be found or no, this at least is certain, that no man has ever in the history of Irish politics flung all his powers, all his eloquence, and all his health more recklessly into the Cause in which he passionately believed than Lord Carson."

It grieved Carson that another old friend and contemporary at Trinity College and the Irish Bar, Lord Glenavy, formerly J. H. Campbell, should have thrown in his lot with the new regime in Southern Ireland, and that a former Unionist Lord Chancellor of Ireland should have accepted office as President of the Irish Free State Senate. Yet their friendship survived this strain which Glenavy put upon it. As Carson wrote to him some years later, "it is one of those memories that give me great pleasure in considering how long it has lasted."

Nor could Carson bear any malice toward another signatory of the Irish Treaty, with whom he had worked closely at various stages of the war—Mr. Winston Churchill. In the summer of 1924 Mr. and Mrs. Churchill stayed as the guests of Carson and his wife at Cleve Court. During this period Mr. Churchill was engaged in writing his history of the war, and he sent Carson each volume of *The World Crisis*, as it appeared, with a friendly letter inscribed. "What days we have lived through?" he wrote in the first volume. "I am more interested in the past than in the present." In the next volume, which covered the year 1915, he wrote: "This will recall terrible days now surmounted." With the volumes dealing with the remainder of the war he sent a characteristic letter. By this time he had become Chancellor of the Exchequer in Mr. Baldwin's Conservative Government. In his official position he had recently visited Belfast—for the first time since his sensational appearance there in 1912—and he had been warmly welcomed and entertained in the Ulster Hall, from which building, it will be remembered, he had been excluded by the threatened action of the Ulster Volunteers on the occasion of his former visit.

Treasury Chambers,
Whitehall,

Private. *Feb.* 28, 1927.

MY DEAR CARSON,

I hope you will accept a copy of my new book about the War. We lived through a good deal of it together—hoped the same, suffered the same—and did not always think differently. You will find a few words, very inadequate, of reference to your work at the Admiralty, where you actually had to live through the worst period during which the great remedial decisions were taken.*

It is very strange how kind Ulstermen have been to me. I think they have treated me better than I have been treated by anybody else in public life, and I might also say better than they have treated anyone else who is not one of themselves. You, in particular, have always been a good friend to me, both in the War and afterwards, as much as you probably could. I take this opportunity, which affords itself to authors, of making a very small acknowledgement.

Believe me,
Yours very sincerely,
WINSTON S. CHURCHILL.

* 'It fell to Sir Edward Carson's lot during his tenure as First Lord to face the most anxious and trying time of the naval war. During those eight months the U-boat sinkings of merchantmen reached their terrible climax. It was under his administration that the peak was surmounted and most of the important decisions of principle were taken by which the peril was ultimately overcome.' Winston S. Churchill, *The World Crisis*, 1916–1918, II, 367.

One of the safeguards in the Treaty, by which great store was set at the time by the British negotiators, was the right of Southern Ireland to appeal to the Judicial Committee of the Privy Council. Yet, when some former British civil servants in Ireland successfully appealed to that Tribunal, the Free State Government denied them justice. When the British Government agreed to make up the difference between the Privy Council award and what had been allowed by the Free State Government, Carson protested in the House of Lords against this easy method of compromise. Shortly after this, Mr. Ernest Blythe, the Free State Finance Minister, publicly declared that his Government would take measures to render ineffective any appeal from Southern Ireland to the Privy Council. This provoked Carson to a further protest. "I want to know," he asked the House of Lords, "when this country hands over a large number of her subjects to those who have been her opponents—I won't say her enemies—all their lives, on special conditions, and when the sole protection, as far as I know, is an appeal to the Court of Privy Council, I want to know, is this Court to be laughed at as Mr. Blythe laughs at it?" Carson maintained that the Free State Minister had delivered the British Government up to ridicule, and had been guilty of a form of blackmail. "I am proud to be a part of the British Empire," he went on, "but why should you always be going about patting them on the back and yielding to them and almost licking the boots of people who are always insulting you and your King and the very treaties under which they exist?" As for the Free State Government and its members, he was careful to add that he was no longer animated by any feelings of hostility against them. "All that is buried: all that is gone. Hundreds of my friends have been ruined. Well, let it be. It was the policy of the British Government."

When his friend and former House of Commons colleague, Sir John Marriott, the historian, asked him whether in his opinion a settlement of the Irish Question during the previous half-century was possible, he expressed himself in a strongly worded letter:

To Sir John Marriott

5 *Eaton Place, S.W. November* 6, 1933 . . . I have never had the slightest doubt that it would have been impossible to have made any lasting settlement in Ireland after the G.O.M. had adopted the Home Rule policy, and everything that happens from day to day convinces me more and more that all the elements that had the real power were not only anti-English but are really far from being civilised. In my

long experience of the government of the country, I have always felt certain that the parties of disorder would in the long run come to the top.

I quite agree that in the end it is a question of nationhood. The Celts have done nothing in Ireland but create trouble and disorder. Irishmen who have turned out successful are not in any case that I know of true Celtic origin . . .

In 1931 was passed the Statute of Westminster which gave the Dominions far-reaching powers in the matter of self-government. In vain did Carson press for the reservation of the Treaty rights to the Crown. The Statute conferred upon the Irish Free State explicit powers to amend or abrogate the Treaty, and in the succeeding years they were exercised to the full. The abolition of the right of appeal to the Privy Council in 1933 removed the final safeguard, and it was clearly now only a matter of time before the Irish Free State would leave the Commonwealth and declare herself a Republic. The occasion provided Carson with the opportunity of making his last major speech in the House of Lords. He spoke in a spirit of bitterness, sadness and disillusion.

I only came into public life because I cared for my fellow Loyalists in Ireland. I went all through my public life doing my best for them, and I saw them in the end betrayed; but at all events betrayed under the pretext that certain safeguards were provided. Now I have lived to see every one of these safeguards absolutely set at naught and made useless. That is not a pleasant political career. I belong, I believe, to what is called the Unionist Party. Why it is called the Unionist Party I fail to understand unless it is to remind people in this country that it was the Party that betrayed the Unionists.

. . . Now they propose to abolish what I think is the last of the safeguards. The Oath is gone, the Veto of the King is gone, the Representative of the King is appointed by an Executive to whom he is subordinate—he is gone. They are all gone, and now they are to abolish—it has in fact been abolished for a long time—the only remaining safeguard which was so flaunted in our faces . . . Every single promise we have made to the Loyalists in Ireland has been broken, every pledge of law and order destroyed, everything that makes life and property safe has gone, and now the last remnant is to be taken away.

Earlier in the same year Carson sounded another warning note when the future of India was discussed at a Conservative Party Conference in London. He told the delegates that there never was a safeguard invented which could restrain a Government "created by a franchise which you yourselves have given," and he used Ireland as an illustration of the eventualities attendant on measures of self-government that were not cautious and gradual. He begged the party not to betray loyal servants and officers. "Don't be trying to conciliate your enemies at the expense of your friends," he adjured the delegates. "Our friends first, our friends second our friends always." The sight of the frail old man, speaking in deeply-moving tones, made a great impression on the conference, though some of the younger delegates and M.P.s who had never seen Carson, had to ask who he was. In the event he was regarded by the majority as an incorrigible 'diehard' and little heed was paid to his words in the counsels of the Conservative Party.

A week or so later he attended a ceremony where there was no doubt among those present as to his identity. In the previous year he had seen the opening of the Northern Ireland's spacious Parliament Buildings at Stormont, on the outskirts of Belfast. He now appeared again at Stormont, to witness the solemn dedication of a memorial to himself and his life's work. His statue, cast in bronze by the English sculptor, Leonard Stanford Merrifield, had been erected in front of the Parliament Buildings, so read the inscription on its base: 'By the Loyalists of Ulster as an expression of their love and admiration for its subject.' It was unveiled at a touching ceremony on July 8, 1933, by Lord Craigavon, in the presence of 40,000 people, including his wife and young son. It showed their beloved old leader in a characteristic pose, striding forward with hand upraised.

When he came to reply, Carson almost broke down. "I know of no words," he said, speaking on the verge of tears, "to express my gratitude to a great people who all through these years never for one moment deceived or deserted me . . . I would not, if I were going through life again, ask God Almighty to give me any greater privilege than to lead people so true and so loyal."

7

"I am afraid old age is not all joy." Thus Carson wrote on the morrow of his retirement. His health continued to be his main preoccupation. "I am sorry to say I still suffer a lot and can do little or nothing," he wrote to his old friend Sir Thomas Comyn-Platt from his home in Kent, "so I just stay here and grouse about my ailments!" Other old friends visited him and he had the companionship and comfort of a devoted wife and young son Ned. His married daughter

Mrs. Chesterman and his sailor son Walter also came to Cleve Court to see him. But there were others he missed, others who had run their course in life. Harry, his eldest son, and Gladys, his younger daughter, who had caused him so much anxiety during their lifetime, were now dead. Then his contemporaries at the Bar were slipping away one by one. In spite of a happy domestic background, he often felt lonely and depressed. His visitors did their best to cheer him up. "You may be ill," the former Mrs. Asquith, then Lady Oxford, told him, "but you must *think* and *believe* that you are well, as you have many very loving friends, and my father married again when he was seventy-five and had four beautiful children."

Soon after he had retired to Cleve Court, the question of writing his biography arose. Some of his friends were anxious that this should be projected while he was still alive. Sir Thomas Comyn-Platt thought of trying his hand at it—he had once written a short sketch of Carson during the Home Rule crisis—but abandoned the idea, as there were so many legal matters connected with it with which he did not feel qualified to deal. Eventually the work was undertaken by a brilliant young barrister and Conservative M.P., Edward Marjoribanks. He had recently written an excellent life of Sir Edward Marshall-Hall, and he now became a frequent visitor to Cleve Court, where his subject would good-humouredly submit himself to be cross-examined on his past, particularly his professional career. Unhappily the biographer was struck down, in a tragic moment, by his own hand, leaving the work barely half finished. What he had written was published as it stood in 1932, the year of his untimely death. The remainder of the story was recorded by Mr. Ian Colvin, the biographer of Dr. Jameson, who was a leader-writer on the *Morning Post* and had been recommended by Carson's friend, H. A. Gwynne, the editor of that journal.

Carson was laid up by illness in London soon after the publication of the first volume of his biography. When he was up and about again, he happened to run into Geoffrey Dawson, *The Times* editor, whom he used to meet at Mr. Amery's house for their Monday night dinners. *The Times* had supported the far-reaching constitutional reforms for India programme and in consequence Carson had seen little of the editor since that time.

"My dear Carson," said Dawson breezily, "what a long time since we met!"

"Sure, it's not my fault," said Carson, "lying ill in Eaton Place most of the time."

Dawson looked somewhat embarrassed and tried to excuse himself. "The truth is I'm very busy. Why, I've not even had time to read Marjoribanks' *Life* of you."

"Indeed, and I can't blame you," Carson replied. "Sure, I haven't read *The Times* these two years."

Thereafter Carson's visits to London became less and less frequent. At Cleve Court, with its calm and peaceful surroundings, he heard the news from the outside world and from time to time he would issue a protest at some political development which disturbed him, be it in connexion with the Navy, India or Ireland. The one bright spot was the news from Ulster, when the General Election which took place there for the local Parliament toward the end of 1933 showed Craigavon and the Unionist Party to be stronger than they were at the beginning of his rule twelve years previously. On December 4, 1933, Carson wrote to his old lieutenant: "I must send you a line of hearty congratulation on the confidence that the Imperial Province has shown in you and your Government. I am sure that they are very proud of all you have done for them, and I think you may well be proud of being Prime Minister of the most splendid people I know."

He was pleased too to think that they did not forget him in Ulster, although he was now no longer strong enough to make the journey there. A Member of the Parliament at Stormont, Sir Robert Lynn, who had been prominent in the Ulster Volunteer Force, wrote to him at this time:

> *Belfast. November* 26, 1933. I went to see your statue yesterday: it is a fine piece of work. What a flood of memories it brought back—hard work, dangers, anxieties, but every task made light by the sympathy, guidance and courage of our Incomparable Chief. How we loved you: how we still love you.
>
> It was indeed a crowded hour of glorious life and I treasure it as one of the happiest in my own. Oh that we could put the hands of the clock back twenty years when men fought for principles. At any rate this statue will be a reminder to future generations in Ulster of the noble heights to which you led the people.

In March, 1934, a few weeks after his eightieth birthday, he appeared in the House of Lords and intervened for a few minutes in a debate on a legal measure designed to safeguard the position of the judiciary. It was to be the last time that he addressed that assembly. "I practised in His Majesty's Courts as an advocate in Ireland and here for some forty-six years," he said, "and, looking back upon that time, I think I can say, with the most absolute sincerity, that I never myself for one moment had reason to suspect that a judge was actuated by anything but an absolute desire to do justice between the Crown and the subject."

At the beginning of June, 1935, Carson caught bronchial pneumonia. To this attack it seemed that he must succumb, but he put up a vigorous fight, as ever, and eventually pulled through. Among those who visited his sick-room was Dr. Charles D'Arcy, the Protestant Archbishop of Armagh and Primate of All Ireland. "I have seen much to shake my faith," said the invalid to him, "and what remains with me is no more than I learned at my mother's knee: 'God so loved the world that He gave His only begotten Son. . . .' " "It is enough," said the Primate.

In July the doctor announced that Carson was out of danger. But the patient's strength had been seriously undermined, and he never fully recovered. One of his last letters to be preserved he wrote in a very shaky hand to his old friend Comyn-Platt.

Cleve Court,
Minster. Nr. Ramsgate.
August 21, 1935.

My dear Tommy,

I must even from my bed write you a line to say how pleased I am to get your most affectionate letter. Our friendship never grows pale, even tho' we meet so seldom.

I have had a real rotten time and indeed I grow in strength very slowly if at *all*. I have not been in London this year and only 2 or 3 times outside my 'demesne'. I have found the hot weather very exhausting but I must still hope.

I go out every day and sit in the garden and watch the birds!

With every affectionate greeting,
Your old comrade
Edward Carson.

He grew weaker as the summer wore on and the first tints of autumn coloured the foliage of the trees. By the middle of October he was no longer able to leave his room. The doctor diagnosed leucæmia, fatal disease of the blood corpuscles. His strength began to ebb swiftly. The two surviving children of his first marriage, Aileen and Walter, were summoned to his bedside. His wife and young son Ned were already there. The end came peacefully, shortly after eight o'clock in the morning. The date was October 22, 1935.

In his will, which had been executed four years previously, Carson had left no instructions as to where he was to be buried.* But in conversation with Lord Craigavon he had expressed the desire that, when he died, his remains might be laid to rest in the land for which, as the Ulster Prime Minister put it, "he fought so long, so valiantly and so successfully." Accordingly, in a tribute to the dead Leader, which was broadcast by wireless from Belfast later the same day, Craigavon announced that the Government of Northern Ireland would provide a state funeral and that the burial would take place in the city's Cathedral. He added that the remains would be conveyed to Belfast in one of His Majesty's ships, as befitted a former First Lord of the Admiralty. "Ulster will thus be able to care tenderly for the body of her old Leader," Craigavon continued. "She will, in any event, perpetuate from generation to generation the memory of him who came to her deliverance in her hour of peril."

In this broadcast, which by a fortunate accident was picked up in London and recorded there, Lord Craigavon recalled the intimacy which he had enjoyed with his former chief for the past thirty years. "Behind the scenes," said the Premier of Northern Ireland, "either in his own house or mine at Craigavon, the centre of unprecedented happenings, where he spent so much of his time and where I got to know him intimately, he was the most attractive and lovable man, charming to old and young alike. I could recount innumerable instances of his extraordinary generosity and touching kindliness toward the poor and distressed. It is not enough to say he was loved by the working classes of this province—he was adored—and the loss we have just sustained will be felt more keenly by the humble Ulster working man and working woman than any words of mine could possibly portray."

Craigavon immediately introduced the necessary legislation in the Northern Ireland House of Commons to enable the burial to take place in St. Anne's Cathedral, and this passed through all its stages there and in the Senate during the same sitting. Saturday, October 26, was the day arranged for the funeral. It was a sad but proud homecoming. Shops and factories were closed. The familiar sounds of the shipyards were stilled as H.M.S. *Broke* slowly steamed up Belfast Lough, with her ensign at half-mast, and tied up to the same quayside where the Leader had so often stepped ashore in life, swinging his blackthorn. On the warship's deck lay the coffin draped by a Union Jack. It was carried ashore by two petty officers

* Carson left estate of the gross value of £150,295, with net personality £143,966. *The Times*, Dec. 23, 1935.

and six seamen and placed on a gun-carriage, waiting to take it on the final stage of the journey.

Bluejackets drew the gun-carriage through the streets of Belfast, thronged with silent crowds, bareheaded, many weeping. At the sides and in the rear of the carriage walked the pall-bearers led by Lord Craigavon; there were Wilfrid Spender, Fred Crawford, Dawson Bates and Lord Londonderry, and other old comrades of the Volunteer days. Lady Carson led the family mourners; Walter and young Ned walked with her. The procession halted for a few minutes outside the old Town Hall, headquarters and mainspring of the Ulster Unionist Organisation. The strains of the funeral march broke off, as a sudden hush descended on the multitude. The meaning of the gesture was understood. Again the procession paused outside the City Hall, where the Leader had signed the Covenant followed by thousands of Ulster men and women who now mourned his loss and had come to pay their last respects to his memory. The carriage reached the Cathedral, and the coffin was carried through the open West Door. The intoning of familiar words could be heard within. "I am the Resurrection and the Life . . ."

Primate D'Arcy led the funeral service in the Cathedral. "Here in Belfast is most truly the place where his mortal remains should rest," he told the large representative congregation. "It was nobly and rightly done to bring them here. His tomb will remain an object of veneration, every sight of it will call up affection in the hearts of those who knew him and of all who followed him in his great struggle for Ulster, and for the generations to come who never looked upon his face, lighted up with the fire of patriotism, or heard the thrilling tone of his voice, as a witness for what the great Leader did for the land he loved so well." Then came the solemn moment of committal. The coffin was lowered into the tomb. Soil from each of Ulster's six counties and the historic city of Londonderry was scattered upon it. "Earth to earth, ashes to ashes, dust to dust . . ." The buglers sounded the Last Post and the Reveille. Then everyone sang the dead Leader's favourite hymn 'O God our Help in Ages Past', just as they had done at the anti-Home Rule meetings in the old days. The mourners took a last look at the open grave and turned away.

Ulster's 'Sir Edward' had come home to his people.

BIBLIOGRAPHY

I. Manuscript Sources

THE principal MS authority is the collection of Carson Papers in the possession of Lady Carson. The Balfour and Bonar Law Papers contain letters of considerable importance on the private as well as the public side of Carson's life; his letters to Lady Londonderry are also of much interest, as are those to Sir James Craig (Viscount Craigavon) and Sir Thomas Comyn-Platt.

BALFOUR PAPERS. MSS of Arthur James Balfour, first Earl of Balfour. In the British Museum.

BONAR LAW PAPERS. MSS of Andrew Bonar Law. In the possession of Lord Beaverbrook.

CARSON PAPERS. (1) MSS of Edward Henry Carson, Lord Carson of Duncairn. In the possession of Lady Carson.

(2) Diaries of Lady Carson. In the possession of Lady Carson.

(3) Letters of Lord Carson. In the possession of the Hon. Mrs. Gerald Chesterman; Cecile Viscountess Craigavon; Sir Thomas Comyn-Platt; Mrs. Anna Debenham; the Marquess of Londonderry; A. F. Rountree, Esq., and Trinity College, Dublin, Historical Society.

LONDONDERRY PAPERS. MSS of Theresa Marchioness of Londonderry. In the possession of the Marchioness Dowager of Londonderry and the Marquess of Londonderry.

MILNER PAPERS. MSS of Alfred Milner, first Viscount Milner. In New College, Oxford.

SPENDER PAPERS. Letters from Lady Spender to her husband. In the possession of Sir Wilfrid Spender, D.S.O.

ULSTER UNIONIST COUNCIL MINUTE BOOKS. In the possession of the Ulster Unionist Council, Belfast.

II. Printed Sources

THE most important published work is the three-volume biography begun by Edward Marjoribanks during Carson's lifetime and completed by Ian Colvin in 1936. The first volume, which is the work of Marjoribanks, brings the story down to the year 1910. It is particularly full on the legal side, although the author omits several important cases, such as the Kraus trial and the "Gaiety Girl" Divorce case, which have been described in the present book. Neither Marjoribanks nor Colvin had access to such important collections as the Balfour, Bonar Law and Londonderry Papers and other sources, which have since become available.

Biographical sketches have been written by J. V. Bates, the first Earl of Birkenhead, Sir Thomas Comyn-Platt, A. G. Gardiner, T. H. Moles and Sir Douglas Savory.

ABINGER, EDWARD. *Forty Years at the Bar*. London, 1930.

ADDISON, CHRISTOPHER. *Politics from Within*, 1911–1918. 2 vols. London, 1924.

ALEXANDER, GILCHRIST. *The Temple of the Nineties*. Edinburgh and London, 1938.

ANNUAL REGISTER.

BACON, ADMIRAL SIR R. H. *Life of John Rushworth Earl Jellicoe*. London, 1936.

BATES, J. V. *Sir Edward Carson*. With an Introduction by the Rt. Hon. A. J. Balfour and a Foreword by Sir James Craig. London, 1921.

BEAVERBROOK, LORD. *Politicians and the War*, 1914–1916. 2 vols. London, 1928–1932.

BELFAST NEWS LETTER.

BELFAST TELEGRAPH.

BIGGS-DAVISON, JOHN N. *George Wyndham*. London, 1951.

BIRKENHEAD, 1ST EARL OF. *Contemporary Personalities*. London, 1924.

BIRKENHEAD, 2ND EARL OF. *Frederick Edwin Earl of Birkenhead*. 2 vols. 1933–1935.

BIRON, SIR CHARTRES. *Without Prejudice*. London, 1936.

BLAKE, R. W. *Private Diaries of Sir Douglas Haig*. London, 1952.

BLUNT, WILFRID SCAWEN. *The Land War in Ireland.* London, 1912.

CALLWELL, MAJ.-GEN. SIR C. E. *Field-Marshal Sir Henry Wilson: His Life and Diaries.* 2 vols. London, 1927.

CAMPBELL, T. J. *Fifty Years of Ulster.* Belfast, 1941.

CHAMBERLAIN, SIR AUSTEN. *Politics from Inside.* London, 1936.

CHURCHILL, WINSTON. *Life of Lord Randolph Churchill.* 2 vols. London, 1906.

The World Crisis. 6 vols. London, 1923–1931.

COMYN-PLATT, SIR THOMAS. "The Ulster Leader" in the *National Review*, October, 1913.

CRAWFORD, FREDERICK H. *Guns for Ulster.* Belfast, 1947.

DUGDALE, B. E. C. *Arthur James Balfour, First Earl of Balfour.* 2 vols. London, 1936.

ERVINE, ST. JOHN. *Craigavon Ulsterman.* London, 1949.

GARDINER, A. G. *Pillars of Society.* London, 1913.

GWYNN, DENIS. *Life of John Redmond.* London, 1932.

The History of Partition, 1912–1925. London, 1949.

HASTINGS, SIR PATRICK. *Autobiography.* London, 1948.

HEALY, MAURICE. *The Old Munster Circuit.* London, 1939.

HEALY, T. M. *Letters and Leaders of My Day.* 2 vols. London, 1928.

HUMPHREYS, SIR TRAVERS. *Criminal Days.* London, 1946.

JELLICOE, JOHN EARL. *The Crisis of the Naval War.* London, 1920.

JONES, THOMAS. *Lloyd George.* London, 1951.

LAVERY, SIR JOHN. *The Life of a Painter.* London, 1940.

LAW REPORTS.

LLOYD GEORGE, DAVID. *War Memoirs.* 6 vols. London, 1933–1936.

LUCAS, REGINALD. *Colonel Saunderson, M.P.* London, 1908.

MACNEILL, J. G. SWIFT. *What I Have Seen and Heard.* London, 1925.

McNEILL, RONALD. *Ulster's Stand for Union.* London, 1922.

MACREADY, SIR C. F. NEVIL. *Annals of an Active Life.* 2 vols. London, 1924.

MARJORIBANKS, EDWARD AND COLVIN, IAN. *Life of Lord Carson.* 3 vols. London, 1932–1936.

MAXWELL, HENRY. *Ulster Was Right.* London, 1934.

MOLES, T. H. *Lord Carson of Duncairn.* With a Foreword by Sir James Craig. Belfast, 1925.

MORLEY, JOHN VISCOUNT. *Life of William Ewart Gladstone.* 3 vols. London, 1903.

Recollections. 2 vols. London, 1917.

NICOLSON, HAROLD. *King George V. His Life and Reign.* London, 1952.

O'BRIEN, PETER LORD. *Reminiscences.* Edited by the Hon. Georgina O'Brien. London, 1916.

O'BRIEN, WILLIAM. *The Irish Revolution and How it Came About.* London, 1923.

O'CONNOR, SIR JAMES. *History of Ireland,* 1798–1924. 2 vols. London, 1925.

OXFORD AND ASQUITH, HENRY EARL OF. *Fifty Years of Parliament.* 2 vols. London, 1926.

Memories and Reflections. 2 vols. 1928.

PARLIAMENTARY DEBATES.

PETRIE, SIR CHARLES. *Life and Letters of the Right Hon. Sir Austen Chamberlain.* 2 vols. London, 1939–1940.

PHILLIPS, W. ALISON. *The Revolution in Ireland,* 1906–1923. London, 1923.

READING, 2ND MARQUESS OF. *Rufus Isaacs First Marquess of Reading.* 2 vols. London, 1942–1945.

RENTOUL, SIR GERVAIS. *This Is My Case.* London, 1944.

REPINGTON, C. A COURT. *The First World War.* 2 vols. London, 1920.

RIDDELL, LORD. *Lord Riddell's War Diary.* 1914–1918. London, 1933.

ROBERTS, C. E. BECHHOFER. *Sir John Simon.* London, 1938.

ROSS, SIR JOHN. *The Years of My Pilgrimage.* London, 1924.

SAVORY, SIR DOUGLAS L. Article on Lord Carson in the *Dictionary of National Biography,* 1931–1941.

SIMON, VISCOUNT. *Retrospect.* London, 1952.

SPENDER, J. A. AND ASQUITH, C. *Life of Lord Oxford and Asquith.* 2 vols. London, 1932.

TAYLOR, H. A. *The Strange Case of Andrew Bonar Law.* London, 1934.

THE TIMES.

WALKER-SMITH, DEREK. *Lord Reading and his Cases.* London, 1934.

The Life of Lord Darling. London, 1938.

Index